W9-CMN-770

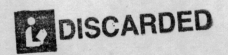
University of Winnipeg, 515 Portage Ave., Winnipeg, MB. R3B 2E9 Canada

WILLIAM PITT

AND

NATIONAL REVIVAL

Emery Walker Ph. sc.

William Pitt
as Chancellor of the Exchequer
from a painting by T. Gainsborough

WILLIAM PITT

AND

NATIONAL REVIVAL

BY

J. HOLLAND ROSE, Litt.D.

A rarer spirit never
Did steer humanity; but you, gods, will give us
Some faults to make us men.
SHAKESPEARE, *Antony and Cleopatra*.

LONDON
G. BELL AND SONS, LTD.
1911

CHISWICK PRESS: CHARLES WHITTINGHAM AND CO.
TOOKS COURT, CHANCERY LANE, LONDON.

PREFACE

IN this volume I seek to describe the work of national revival carried out by William Pitt the Younger up to the time of the commencement of friction with Revolutionary France, completing the story of his life in a volume entitled "William Pitt and the Great War." No apology is needed for an attempt to write a detailed description of his career. The task has not been essayed since the year 1862, when the fifth Earl Stanhope published his monumental work; and at that time the archives of the Foreign Office, War Office, Admiralty, and Home Office were not open for research in the period in question. Excellent monographs on Pitt were given to the world by Lord Rosebery and Mr. Charles Whibley in the years 1891 and 1906, but they were too brief to admit of an adequate treatment of the masses of new materials relating to that career. Of late these have been greatly augmented by the inclusion among the national archives of the Pitt Manuscripts, which comprise thousands of letters and memoranda hitherto little used. In recent years also the records of the Foreign Office and Home Office have become available for study, and at many points have yielded proofs of the influence which Pitt exerted on the foreign and domestic policy of Great Britain. Further, by the great kindness of the Countess Stanhope and Mr. E. G. Pretyman, M.P., I was enabled to utilize the Pitt Manuscripts preserved at Chevening and Orwell Park; and both His Grace the Duke of Portland and the Earl of Harrowby generously placed at my disposal unpublished correspondence of Pitt with their ancestors. These new sources render it necessary to reconstruct no small portion of his life.

Among recent publications bearing on this subject, the most important is that of " The Manuscripts of J. B. Fortescue, Esq.," preserved at Dropmore (Hist. MSS. Comm., 7 vols., 1892-1910), the seventh volume of which comprises details respecting the death of Pitt. This collection, containing many new letters of George III, Pitt, Lord Grenville, and British ambassadors, has proved of incalculable service. Many Memoirs, both English and foreign, have appeared of late. Among foreign historians who have dealt with this period, Sorel holds the first place; but his narrative is often defective on English affairs, to which he gave too little attention. The recent monograph of Dr. Felix Salomon on the early part of Pitt's career (Leipzig, 1901), and those of Herren Beer, Heidrich, Luckwaldt, Uhlmann, Vivenot, and Wittichen on German affairs, have been of service, as well as those of Ballot, Chassin, and Pallain on Anglo-French relations. The bias of Lecky against Pitt detracts somewhat from the value of the latter part of his work, " England in the Eighteenth Century "; and I have been able to throw new light on episodes which he treated inadequately.

Sometimes my narrative may seem to diverge far from the immediate incidents of the life of Pitt; but the enigmas in which it abounds can be solved only by a study of the policy of his rivals or allies at Paris, The Hague, Madrid, Vienna, Berlin, and St. Petersburg. These questions have not received due attention from English students; for Lecky did not treat the period 1793-1800 except in regard to Irish affairs. Accordingly, while by no means neglecting the private and social life of Pitt, I have sought in this volume to describe his achievements during the period dominated by Catharine of Russia, Joseph of Austria, and Mirabeau. That age is also memorable for political, fiscal, and social developments of high interest; and I have dealt with them as fully as possible, often with the aid of new materials drawn from Pitt's papers. It being impossible to extend the limits of this work, I ask the forbearance of specialists for not treating those problems more fully. It is a biography, not a series of monographs; and I have everywhere sought to keep the figure of Pitt in the foreground. New letters of George III, Pitt, Grenville, Windham, Burke, Canning, etc., which could only be referred to here, will be published in a volume entitled " Pitt and Napoleon Miscellanies," containing also essays and notes.

I wish to thank not only those whose generous assistance I have already acknowledged, but also Mr. Hubert Hall, of the Public Record Office, for advice given during my researches; the Rev. William Hunt, D.Litt., for a thorough recension of the proofs of this work; the Masters of Trinity College and Peterhouse, Cambridge; Professor Firth, and Mr. G. P. Gooch, M.A., for valued suggestions; the Ven. Archdeacon Cunningham and Mr. Hewins for assistance on economic subjects; M. Raymond Guyot and Herr Doctor Luckwaldt for information on French and German affairs; also Mr. E. G. Pretyman, M.P., for permission to reproduce the portrait of the first Countess of Chatham; Mr. R. A. Tatton, for similar permission to include Gainsborough's portrait of William Pitt; and last, but not least, Mr. A. M. Broadley for the communication of new letters relating to Pitt and his friends.

J. H. R.

FEBRUARY 1911.

CONTENTS

LIST OF ILLUSTRATIONS

ABBREVIATIONS OF THE TITLES OF THE CHIEF WORKS REFERRED TO IN THIS VOLUME

ANN. REG. = "Annual Register."

ASHBOURNE = "Pitt: some Chapters of his Life and Times," by the Rt. Hon. Lord Ashbourne. 1898.

AUCKLAND JOURNALS = "The Journal and Corresp. of William, Lord Auckland." 4 vols. 1861.

BUCKINGHAM P. = "Mems. of the Court and Cabinets of George III," by the Duke of Buckingham. 2 vols. 1853.

B.M. ADD. MSS. = Additional Manuscripts of the British Museum.

BEAUFORT P. = "MSS. of the Duke of Beaufort," etc. (Hist. MSS. Comm.). 1891.

CAMPBELL. = "Lives of the Lord Chancellors," by Lord Campbell. 8 vols. 1845-69.

CASTLEREAGH CORRESP. = "Mems. and Corresp. of Viscount Castlereagh." 8 vols. 1848- .

CHEVENING MSS. = Manuscripts of the Countess Stanhope, preserved at Chevening.

CUNNINGHAM = "Growth of Eng. Industry and Commerce (Modern Times)," by Dr. W. Cunningham. 1892.

DROPMORE P. = "The Manuscripts of J. B. Fortescue, Esq., preserved at Dropmore" (Hist. MSS. Comm.). 7 vols. 1892-1910.

FORTESCUE = "The History of the British Army," by the Hon. J. W. Fortescue. vol. iv.

HÄUSSER = "Deutsche Geschichte (1786-1804)," by L. Häusser. 4 vols. 1861-3.

HOLLAND = "Memoirs of the Whig Party," by Lord Holland. 2 vols. 1852.

JESSE = "Mems. of the Life and Reign of George III," by J. H. Jesse. 3 vols. 1867.

LECKY = "Hist. of England in the Eighteenth Century," by W. E. H. Lecky. 8 vols. Fifth edit. 1891-1904.

LUCKWALDT = "Die englisch-preussische Allianz von 1788," von F. Luckwaldt. 1902.

LEEDS MEM. = " Political Memoranda of Francis, Fifth Duke of Leeds," ed. by Mr. O. Browning. 1884.

MALMESBURY DIARIES = "Diaries and Corresp. of the First Earl of Malmesbury." 4 vols. 1844.

PARL. HIST. = "History of the Parliamentary Debates " (after 1804 continued in Hansard).

PELLEW = " Life and Corresp. of the first Viscount Sidmouth," by Rev. C. Pellew. 3 vols. 1847.

PITT MSS. = Pitt MSS., preserved at H.M. Public Record Office.

PITT-RUTLAND CORRESP. = "Corresp. between . . . W. Pitt and the Duke of Rutland." 1890.

ROSE G., " DIARIES " = " Diaries and Corresp. of Rt. Hon. G. Rose." 2 vols. 1860.

ROSE, "NAPOLEON" = "Life of Napoleon," by J. H. Rose. 2 vols. 1909.

RUTLAND P. = " MSS. of the Duke of Rutland " (Hist. MSS. Comm.). 3 vols. 1894.

RUVILLE = "William Pitt, Earl of Chatham," by A. von Ruville (Eng. transl.). 3 vols. 1907.

SOREL = " L'Europe et la Révolution française," par A. Sorel. Pts. II, III. 1889, 1897.

STANHOPE = " Life of . . . William Pitt," by Earl Stanhope. 4 vols. 3rd edition. 1867.

SYBEL = "Geschichte der Revolutionzeit" (1789-1800). Eng. translation. 4 vols. 1867-9.

VIVENOT = " Quellen zur Geschichte der deutschen Kaiserpolitik Œsterreichs . . ." von A. von Vivenot. 1873.

WITTICHEN = " Preussen und England in der europäischen Politik 1785-8," von F. K. Wittichen. 1902.

WRAXALL = " Memoirs of Sir N. W. Wraxall " (1772-84), edited by H. B. Wheatley. 5 vols. 1884.

ERRATA

On page 157, l. 23, *for* " Richard " *read* " Thomas."

    ,, 267, *ad fin., for* " Bob " *read* " Tom."

THE LIFE AND TIMES OF
WILLIAM PITT

INTRODUCTION

ENGLAND AT THE CLOSE OF THE AMERICAN
WAR (1780-3)

I think it proper before I commence my proposed work to pass under review the condition of the capital, the temper of the armies, the attitude of the provinces, and the elements of weakness and strength which existed throughout the whole Empire, so that we may become conversant, not only with the vicissitudes and issues of events, which are often matters of chance, but also with their relations and causes.—TACITUS, *The History*, bk. i, ch. iv.

IN the course of the session of 1782, when the American War was dragging to its disastrous close and a change of Ministers was imminent, one of the youngest members of the House of Commons declared that he would accept no subordinate office in a new administration. At the close of 1783, during a crisis of singular intensity, he became Chief Minister of the Crown, and thenceforth, with one short interval, controlled the destinies of Great Britain through twenty-two years marked by grave complications, both political and financial, social and diplomatic, ending in wars of unexampled magnitude. Early in the year 1806 he died of exhaustion, at the age of forty-seven. In these bald statements we may sum up the outstanding events of the life of William Pitt the Younger, which it is my aim to describe somewhat in detail.

Before reviewing his antecedents and the course of his early life, I propose to give some account of English affairs in the years when he entered on his career, so that we may picture him in his surroundings, realize the nature of the difficulties that

I   B

beset him, and, as it were, feel our way along some of the myriad
filaments which connect an individual with the collective activities
of his age.

William Pitt, Earl of Chatham, died in 1778. His second son,
named after him, began his political career at the close of the
year 1780, when he was elected Member of Parliament for
Appleby. The decade which then began marks a turning point
in British history. Then for the first time the old self-contained
life was shaken to its depths by forces of unsuspected power.
Democracy, Athene-like, sprang to maturity in the New World,
and threatened the stability of thrones in the Old World. For
while this militant creed won its first triumphs over the soldiery
of George III, it began also to colour the thoughts and wing
the aspirations of the masses, especially in France, so that, even
if the troops of Washington had been vanquished, the rising tide
of thought would none the less have swept away the outworn
barriers of class. The march of armies may be stayed; that of
thought never.

The speculations enshrined in the "Social Contract" of Rousseau
and the teachings of the Encyclopaedists contained much that
was crude, or even false. Nevertheless, they gave an impulse
such as no age ever had known, and none perhaps ever will know
again. The course of the American War of Independence
and the foundation of a State based on distinctly democratic
principles proved that the new doctrines might lead to very
practical results. The young giant now stood rooted in mother-
earth.

Side by side with this portent in the world of thought and
politics there came about another change. Other centuries
have witnessed experiments in the direction of democracy; but
in none have social speculations and their results been so
closely accompanied by mechanical inventions of wonder-working potency. Here we touch on the special characteristics of
the modern world. It is the product of two Revolutions, one
political, the other mechanical. The two movements began and
developed side by side. In 1762 Rousseau gave to the world
his "Contrat Social," the Bible of the French Revolutionists;
while only two years later Hargreaves, a weaver of Blackburn, produced his spinning-jenny. In 1769 Arkwright patented
his spinning-frame, and Watt patented his separate condenser.
The year 1776 is memorable alike for the American Declaration of

Independence, and for the publication of Adam Smith's "Wealth of Nations." In 1779 the Lancashire weaver, Crompton, produced his "mule-jenny," a vast improvement on the machines of Arkwright and Hargreaves. The year 1785 witnessed not only the Diamond-Necklace scandal, so fatal to the prestige of the French monarchy, but also the patenting of Watt's double-acting steam-engine and Cartwright's "power loom." In the year 1789, which sounded the knell of the old order of things on the Continent, there appeared the first example of the modern factory, spinning-machinery being then driven by steam power in Manchester. At the dawn of the nineteenth century, when the democratic movement had for the time gone astray and spent its force, the triumphs of science and industry continued peacefully to revolutionize human life. In 1803, the year of the renewal of war with France, William Radcliffe of Stockport greatly increased the efficiency of the power loom, and thereby cheapened the production of cloth. Finally, the year 1814 ought to be remembered, not only for the first abdication of Napoleon, but also for that peaceful and wholly beneficent triumph, George Stephenson's "No. 1," Killingworth locomotive.[1]

The list might be extended far beyond the limits of the period treated in this work, but enough has been said to show that the democratic and industrial forces closely synchronized at the outset, and that while the former waned the latter waxed more and more, proving in the years 1830-2 the most potent ally of English reformers in efforts which Pitt and his friends had failed to carry through in the years 1780-5. So intimate an interaction of new and potent forces had never been seen in the history of man. In truth no one but a sciolist will venture to ascribe the problems of the present age solely to the political movement which found its most powerful expression in the French Revolution. Only those can read aright the riddle of the modern sphinx who have ears for both her tones, who hearken not only to the shouts of leaders and the roar of mobs, but also listen for the multitudinous hum of the workshop, the factory, and the mine.

The lot of William Pitt the Younger was cast in the years when both these revolutions began their mighty work. The

---

[1] Baines, "Hist. of Cotton Manufacture," 226, 232-4. See Mr. G. P. Gooch's "Politics and Culture," for other coincidences.

active part of his father's career fell within the old order of things; the problems which confronted Chatham were merely political. They therefore presented none of that complexity which so often baffled the penetration and forethought of his son. It is true that, with a prophetic vision of the future, the old man foretold in thrilling words the invincibility of the American cause, but then his life-work was done; from his Pisgah-mount he could only warn, and vainly warn, the dwellers in the plain below. His son was destined to enter that unknown land; and he entered it when his people were burdened by debt, disaster, and disgrace.

What were the material resources of the nation? Were they equal to the strain imposed by a disastrous war? Could they resist the subtly warping influences of the coming age? The questions closely concern us in our present inquiry. For the greatness of a statesman is not to be assessed merely by an enumeration of his legislative, diplomatic, and warlike successes. There is a truer method of valuation than this haphazard avoir-dupois. It consists in weighing his achievements against his difficulties.

It is well, therefore, to remember that the British people of the year 1780 was a small and poor people, if we compare it not merely with modern standards (a method fallacious for the present inquiry), but with the burdens which it had to bear. The population of England and Wales at that time has been computed a little over 7,800,000; that of Scotland was perhaps about 1,400,000. That of Ireland is even less known. The increase of population in England and Wales during the years 1770-80 exceeded eight per cent., a rate less, indeed, than that of the previous decade, which had been one of abounding prosperity, but surpassing that of any previous period for which credible estimates can be framed.[1]

The wealth of the nation seems also to have suffered little decline; and after the conclusion of peace in 1783 it showed a surprising elasticity owing to causes which will soon be considered.

---

[1] The first trustworthy statistics of population were obtained in the census of 1801; but those given above are probably not very wide of the mark. The estimates are those of Rickman, quoted by Porter, "Progress of the Nation," 13. The estimate of the "Statistical Journal" (xliii, 462), quoted by Dr. Cunningham, "Eng. Industry and Commerce," 699, is 7,953,000 for the year 1780.

But in the years 1780-3 there was a universal conviction that the burden of debt and taxation was unendurable. Parliament in 1781 voted the enormous sum of £25,353,857 for Ways and Means, an increase of £814,060 on the previous year. As the finances and debt of Ireland were kept entirely separate up to the end of the century, this burden fell upon some 9,200,000 persons, and involved a payment of about £2 15s. per head, an amount then deemed absolutely crushing.

But two important facts should be remembered: firstly, that the investments of British capital in oversea undertakings, which are now enormous, were (apart from the British East and West Indies) practically non-existent in the year 1780, Great Britain being then an almost self-sufficing unit financially; secondly, that modern methods of taxation are less expensive in the collection and less burdensome to the taxpayer than those prevalent in that non-scientific era. The revenue of 1781 included the following items: £12,480,000 for "Annuities and Lottery," £2,788,000 for "Certain Surpluses of the Sinking Fund," £2,000,000 Bank Charter, and so on. Only about one fourth of the requisite amount was raised by means that would now be considered sound.[1]

The National Debt was then reckoned at £177,206,000; and the annual interest, amounting to £6,812,000, ate up considerably more than one fourth of the "bloated estimates" of that year. The burden of debt seemed appalling to that generation; and the Three per cent. Consols sank from 60¼ in January 1781 to 55 in November. But further blows were soon to be dealt by Ministers at the nation's credit; and the same stock ranged between 56 and 58 when William Pitt became Prime Minister in December 1783. Predictions of national bankruptcy were freely indulged in; and it should be remembered that Great Britain, vanquished by a mighty Coalition and bereft of her most valuable colonies, seemed far more likely to sink into the gulf of bankruptcy than triumphant France. The events of the next six years turned essentially on the management of the finances of the rival Powers by Pitt and by the Controllers-General of Versailles. Apart from the personal questions at issue, the history of that time affords the most instructive proof that victory may bear within itself the seeds of future disease and collapse;

[1] See Walter's "Origin of Commerce," iv, 401, for a full statement of this juggling with the nation's finance.

while a wise use of the lessons of adversity may lead the vanquished to a lease of healthier life.

If we turn our gaze away from the material resources of Great
Britain to the institutions and sentiments of our forefathers, there
will appear many bizarre contrasts and perplexing symptoms.
At first sight the self-contained, unreceptive, torpid society of
the Georgian era might appear to be wholly unfitted to bear
the triple strain of a serious national disaster, and of the warping influences of the new democracy and the new industrialism.
The situation was indeed most alarming: " What a dismal fragment of an Empire ! " wrote Horace Walpole in June 1780, " Yet
would that moment were come when we are to take a survey
of our ruins." In truth, had the majority of Britons been ad-
dicted to morbidly introspective broodings, they would have
been undone. There are times when a nation is saved by sheer
stolidity; and this characteristic alike in monarch and people,
which was responsible for the prolongation of the war, helped to
avert collapse at its close. The course of the narrative will show
that the brains of Englishmen were far from equal to the task of
facing the problems of the age then dawning; but Englishmen
were equal to the task of bearing the war-burdens manfully, and
thus were able to supply the material out of which Pitt, aided
by the new manufacturing forces, could work financial marvels.

Then again, British institutions offered that happy mixture of
firmness and adaptability which at many crises has been the
salvation of the race. Had they been as rigid as those of Sparta
they must have cracked and fallen asunder; had they been as
fluid as those of Athens they might have mouldered away. But,
like the structure of English society of which they form the
framework, they lend themselves to reverent restoration, and
thwart all efforts at reckless innovation. Sir Henry Maine happily assessed the worth of this truly national safeguard in the
statement that our institutions had, however undesignedly, arrived at a state in which satisfaction and impatience, the chief
sources of political conduct, were adequately called into play.
Of this self-adjusting process Pitt, at least during the best years
of his career, was to be the sage director.

There were many reasons why Englishmen should be a prey
alternately to feelings of satisfaction and discontent. Instinct and
tradition bade them be loyal to the throne and to the institutions

of their fathers. Reason and reflection bade them censure the war policy of George III and the means whereby he sought to carry it through to the bitter end. St. Stephen's, Westminster, had been the shrine of the nation's liberties; it now, so Burke declared, threatened them with a slow and inglorious extinction. Obedience to the laws had ever been the pride of the nation; but now that virtue might involve subservience to a corrupt and greedy faction.

Yet however great the provocations, Britons were minded to right these wrongs in their own way, and not after the fashions set at Geneva or Paris. In truth they had one great advantage denied to Continental reformers. At Paris reform almost necessarily implied innovation; for, despite the dictum of Burke to the contrary, it is safe to say that the relics of the old constitution of France offered no adequate basis on which to reconstruct her social and political fabric. In England the foundations and the walls were in good repair. The structure needed merely extension, not rebuilding. Moreover, British reformers were by nature and tradition inclined towards tentative methods and rejected wholesale schemes. Even in the dull years of George II the desire for a Reform of Parliament was not wholly without expression; and now, at the time of the American War, the desire became a demand, which nearly achieved success. In fact, the Reform programme of 1780 satisfied the aspirations of the more moderate men, even in the years 1791-4, when the excitements of the French Revolution, and the writings of Thomas Paine for a time popularized the levelling theories then in vogue at Paris.

Certainly, before the outbreak of the French Revolution, the writings of Continental thinkers had little vogue in Great Britain. The " Social Contract " of Rousseau was not widely known, and its most noteworthy theses, despite the fact that they were borrowed from Hobbes and Locke, aroused no thrill of sympathy. This curious fact may be explained by the innate repugnance of the islanders alike to the rigidly symmetrical form in which the Genevese prophet clothed his dogmas, and to the Jacobins' claim for them of universal applicability. The very qualities which carried conviction to the ardent and logic-loving French awakened doubts among the cooler northern folk.

Then again, however sharp might be the resentment against George III for this or that action, national sentiment ran strongly in the traditional channels. After the collapse of the Stuart cause loyalty to the throne and to the dynasty was the dominant feeling among all classes. As Burke finely said of the Tories after the accession of George III, "they changed their idol but they preserved their idolatry." The personality of George III was such as to help on this transformation. A certain *bonhomie*, as of an English squire, set off by charm of manner and graciousness of speech,[1] none too common in that class, went to the hearts of all who remembered the outlandish ways of the first two Georges. Furthermore, his morals were distinctly more reputable than theirs, as was seen at the time of his youth, when he withstood the wiles strewn in his path by several ladies of the Court with a frankness worthy of the Restoration times.[2] His good sense, straightforwardness, and his love of country life and of farming endeared him both to the masses of the people and to the more select circles which began to learn from Versailles the cult of Rousseau and the charms of butter making. Queen Charlotte, a princess of the House of Mecklenburg-Strelitz, also set her face against vice and extravagance, but in a primly austere manner which won few to the cause of virtue. Domesticity in her ceased to be alluring. Idle tongues wagged against her even when she sought to encourage the wearing of dresses woven in Spitalfields rather than those of ever-fashionable Paris; or again, when she prohibited the wearing of ostrich feathers at Court.[3]

The reader will fail to understand the political life of that time and the difficulties often besetting Pitt until he grasps the fact that George III not only reigned but governed. His long contest with the Whig factions left him victor; and it is singular that the shortsightedness of the elder Pitt signally aided the King in breaking up their power. Both of them aimed at overthrowing the supremacy of the old Whig families, but it was George III who profited by the efforts of the Earl of Chatham.[4] The result was seen in the twelve years of almost personal rule (1770-82), during which Lord North and the well-fed phalanx of the King's Friends

---

[1] "Diary of a Journey to England (1761-62)," by Count F. von Kielmansegge," 237.

[2] "The Coltness Collections," 116, quoted by J. H. Jesse; "Memoirs of the Reign of George III," i, 29.

[3] "Mems. of Queen Charlotte," by J. Watkins, 1819, pt. i, ch. x. The Duchess of Devonshire had flaunted a head-plume of an ell and three inches.

[4] See an excellent study, "Personal and Party Government (1760-1766)," by Mr. D. A. Winstanley, 1910.

bade fair to make the House of Commons the mere instrument
of the royal will. The King's influence, impaired for a time by
the disasters of the American War, asserted itself again at the
time of the Lord George Gordon Riots in June 1780. That outbreak of bigotry and rascality for a time paralyzed with fear
both Ministers and magistrates; but while all around him faltered,
George III held firm and compelled the authorities to act.[1]
The riots were quelled, but not before hundreds of drunken
desperadoes had perished in the flames which they had kindled.
Those who saw large parts of London ablaze long retained a
feeling of horror at all popular movements, and looked upon
George III as the saviour of society. This it was, in part, which
enabled him to retain his influence scarcely impaired even by the
disasters of the American War. The monarchy stood more
firmly rooted than at any time since the reign of Queen Anne.
Jacobitism survived among a few antiquated Tories, like Dr.
Johnson, as a pious belief or a fashionable affectation; but even
in the year 1763 the lexicographer, after receiving a pension from
George III, avowed to Boswell that the pleasure of cursing the
House of Hanover and of drinking King James's health was
amply overbalanced by an income of three hundred pounds.

As a sign of the reality of the royal power, we may note that
public affairs were nearly at a stand-still at the time of the lunacy
of George III (November 1788 to February 1789). The following
Foreign Office despatch, sent to the British Ambassador at
Berlin at a critical time in our diplomatic relations, shows that
Pitt and the Foreign Secretary, the Marquis of Carmarthen,
considered themselves the King's Secretaries of State, and
unable to move until the royal will was known:

Whitehall, January 6 1789.

To Mr. Ewart,
    Sir,
        I HAVE received your letters up to No. 93, but I have not any
commands to convey to you at present, the unhappy situation of His
Majesty's health making it impossible for me to lay them before him.
The present situation of this country renders it impossible for me to
send you any particular or precise instructions. I trust, however, that
the system for supplying the present unfortunate interruption in the
executive part of the Government will be speedily completed, at least
with as little delay as the importance of the object will admit of, and

----

[1] "Corresp. of George III with Lord North," ii, 323; Wraxall, i, 347.

which, being once more formed, will of course restore that part of the Constitution to its usual energy and effect.[1]

Ewart and our other ambassadors were therefore urged to mark time as energetically as might be; and no orders were sent to them until after 17th February 1789, when the King began to recover.

At ordinary times, then, the King's authority was looked upon as essential to the working of the Government, a fact which explains the eager interest, even of men not place-hunters, in the Regency disputes of 1788-9. In truth, the monarchy was the central fact of the nation's life; and, as it acquired stedfastness from the personal popularity of George III, the whole of the edifice had a solidity unknown in the years 1680-1760.[2]

Montesquieu praised the English constitution as providing without undue friction a balance of power between King, Lords, and Commons. This judgment (penned in 1748) still held good, though the royal authority had in the meantime certainly increased. But the power of the nobles was still very great. They largely controlled the House of Commons. The Lowthers secured the election of 11 Members in the Lake District; and through the whole country 71 Peers were able directly to nominate, and secure the election of, 88 commoners, while they powerfully influenced the return of 72 more. If we include all landowners, whether titled on untitled, it appears that they had the power to nominate 487 members out of the 658 who formed the House of Commons.

In these days, when the thought and activities of the towns overbear those of the country districts, we cry out against a system that designedly placed power in the hands of nobles and squires. But we must remember that the country then far outweighed the towns in importance; that the produce of the soil was far more valuable than all the manufactures; and that stability and stolidity are the characteristics of an ancient society, based on agriculture and reared in Feudalism. If we except that metropolitan orgy, the Wilkes' affair, London and Westminster were nearly as torpid politically as Dorset. Even in the year

---

[1] "F. O.," Prussia, 15, Carmarthen to Ewart, 6th January 1789.

[2] For the influence exerted by George III on elections see Porritt, "The Unreformed House of Commons," i, 409-15.

1791 the populace of Manchester and Birmingham blatantly
exulted in a constitution which left them without any direct voice
in Parliament. It was in the nature of things that Grampound,
Old Sarum, Gatton, and Castle Rising should return eight members; the choice of the Tudor Sovereigns had lit upon those
hamlets or villages as test-places for consulting the will of the
nation, and the nation acquiesced, because, even if Manchester,
Birmingham, Leeds, and Sheffield had enjoyed that privilege,
they would probably have sent up country gentlemen of the same
type, and after a far greater output of money and beer. Where
the will of the nation is almost entirely homogeneous there is no
injustice in selecting representatives by the haphazard methods
then in use.

Strong in their control of Parliament, the nobles sought to
hem in the throne by meshes of influence through which even
the masterful and pertinacious George III could with difficulty
break. Their circle was small. True, they had failed in their effort
of 1719 to limit the number of creations at any one time to six;
but jealousy had almost the force of law. Ultimately we find
George III declining to confer a dukedom on any but princes of
the blood, and Pitt incurred the displeasure of his cousin, Earl
Temple, because he failed to bend the royal will on that question.
The need of caution in respect to the granting of titles may be
inferred from the Pitt Papers, no small part of which refer to
requests for these honours. Pitt has been reproached with his
lavish use of this governmental device, for he created about 140
peerages in the years 1783-1801. I have, however, found proofs
that he used it reluctantly. In the Pitt Papers are several letters
which the statesman wrote refusing requests for peerages. On this
matter, as also with regard to places and appointments, he treated
any attempt at bargaining with cold disdain, witness this crushing reply to an Irish peer who, in September 1799, applied for a
British peerage: ". . . There is a passage in the conclusion of your
Lordship's letter on which it is impossible for me not to remark
that it appears to convey an intimation with respect to what
may be your political conduct, which would at all events induce
me to decline being the channel of bringing your application
before His Majesty." [1]

But rebukes and refusals seem to have made little impression on

---

[1] Pitt MSS., 195, pt. ii.

that generation, imbued as it was with a deep-seated belief that the victors had a right to the spoils and should apportion them among their followers according to rank and usefulness. The whole matter was spoken of under the convenient euphemism "influence," which, when used in a political sense, denoted the secret means for assuring the triumph of the Crown and the reward of the faithful. While not implying actual bribery, it signified persuasion exerted through peerages, places, and pensions. According to this scheme of things, strenuous support of "the King's cause" would earn a title, a bishopric, a judgeship, or a receivership in the customs or excise. These allurements offered irresistible attractions in an age which offered far fewer means of independent advancement than the present. With the exception of those strange persons who preferred to make their own way in life, men of all classes had their eyes fixed on some longed-for perch above them, and divided their attention between the symptoms of decay in its occupant and the signs of the favour of its patron. The expectant part of Society resembled a gigantic hen-roost at the approach of evening, except that the aspirations upward were not signs of quiescence but of ill-suppressed unrest. Those who delve among the confidential letters of that time must often picture the British nation as a mountain-climber. Perhaps one sixth part of Pitt's time was taken up in reading and answering requests of bewildering variety. College friends dunned him with requests for preferment, with or without cure of souls. Rectors longed to be canons; canons to be deans; deans to be bishops; and wealthy bishops coveted sinecure deaneries, among which, curiously enough, that of London was the greatest prize. The infection spread to all classes. Gaugers of beer longed to be collectors of His Majesty's revenue; faithful grooms confidently expected a gaugership; and elderly fishermen, who in their day had intercepted smugglers, demanded, as of right, the post of harbourmaster. A Frenchman once defended the old *régime* on the ground that it ranged all classes about the King in due gradations of privilege. Similarly Britons of their own free will grouped themselves around the throne on steps of expectancy.

A curious example of the motives which led to influential requests for preferment in the Church is to be found in the correspondence of the Marquis of Carmarthen (afterwards Duke of Leeds), who was at that time Foreign Secretary under Pitt. His letter to his chief may speak for itself:

Private.

Grosvenor Square, Nov. 13 1787.[1]

MY DEAR SIR,

I FEAR it will not be in my power to return to Hollwood to-day, by which I shall be prevented from so soon troubling you *viva voce* with the only subject I do not like to converse with you upon, viz., asking for Preferment. But my anxiety for my friend Jackson, and understanding that the Bishopric of Chester is not yet given away, will, I hope, plead my excuse to you for asking it for him, and perhaps you may forgive me adding that from local circumstances that preferment in his hands would be particularly agreeable to me, on account of a large part of my northern property being situated in the Diocese of Chester. I do assure you that a compliance with this request would make me truly happy.

Believe me, etc.
CARMARTHEN.

Reverting to matters which are purely secular, we may note that in the year 1783, at the time of Pitt's assumption of power, the number of English peers was comparatively small, namely about 240, and of these 15, being Roman Catholics, could not sit in Parliament.[2]

This select aristocracy was preserved from some of the worst evils incident to its station by healthful contact with men and affairs. The reversion of its younger sons to the rank of commoners prevented the formation of the huge caste of nobles, often very poor but always intensely proud, which crusted over the surface of society in Continental lands; and again, the infusion of commoners (generally the ablest governors, soldiers, and lawyers of the age) preserved the Order from intellectual stagnation such as had crept over the old *noblesse* of France. Both the downward and the upward streams kept the mass free from that decay which sooner or later besets every isolated body. Nor did the British aristocracy enjoy those flagrant immunities from taxation which were the curse of French social and political life.

But let us view this question in a more searching light. Montesquieu finely observes that an aristocracy may maintain its full vigour, if the laws be such as will habituate the nobles more to the perils and fatigues, than to the pleasures, of command.[3] In

---

[1] B. M. Add. MSS., 28062. Pitt's answer is not among these papers. But Dr. Jackson did not gain the bishopric.

[2] Lecky, v, 26.   [3] Montesquieu, "Esprit des Lois," bk. viii, ch. v.

this respect the British aristocracy ran some risk of degeneration. It is true that its members took an active part in public business. Their work in the House of Lords was praiseworthy. The debates there, if less exciting than those of the Commons, bear signs of experience, wisdom, dignity, and self-restraint, which were often lacking in the Lower House. The nobles also took a large share in the executive duties of the State. Not only did they and their younger sons fill most of the public offices, including the difficult, and often thankless, diplomatic posts, but they were active in their counties and on their estates, as lords-lieutenant, sheriffs, and magistrates. The days had not yet come when " Society " fled from the terrors of the English winter. For the most part nobles spent the parliamentary vacations at their country seats, sharing in the duties and sports which from immemorial times had knit our folk into a compact and sturdy whole. Yet we may question whether the pleasures of command did not then far exceed its perils and fatigues. Apart from the demoralizing struggle for higher honours, there were hosts of court and parliamentary sinecures to excite cupidity and encourage laziness. The rush after emoluments and pleasure became keener than ever after the glorious peace of 1763, and a perusal of the letters addressed to any statesman of the following age must awaken a doubt whether public life was less corrupt than at the time of Walpole.

Then, again, in the making and working of laws, the privileges of the nobles and gentry were dangerously large. Throughout the eighteenth century those classes strengthened their grip both on Parliament and on the counties and parishes. Up to the year 1711 no definite property qualification was required from members of Parliament; but in that year a law was passed limiting the right of representing counties to those who owned land worth £600 a year; and a rental of half that sum was expected from members of boroughs. This was equivalent to shutting out merchants and manufacturers, who were often Dissenters, from the county representation; and the system of pocket boroughs further enabled landowners to make a careful choice in the case of a large part of the members of towns. Again, the powers of the magistrates, or justices of the peace, in the affairs of the parish, were extraordinarily large. A French writer, M. Boutmy, computes them as equalling those of the the *préfet*, the *conseil d'arrondissement*, the *maire*, the *commissaire de police*, and the *juge de paix*, of the French local government of to-day. Of course the

Shallows of Pitt's time did not fulfil these manifold duties at all systematically; for that would be alien to the haphazard ways of the squires and far beyond their talents. Local despotism slumbered as much as it worked; and just as the Armenians prefer the fitful barbarities of the Turks to the ever-grinding pressure of the Russian bureaucracy, so the villagers of George III's reign may have have been no more oppressed than those of France and Italy are by a system fruitful in good works and jobs, in officials and taxes. On this point it is impossible to dogmatize; for the Georgian peasantry was dumb until the years after Waterloo, when Cobbett began to voice its feelings.

The use of the term " despotism " for the rule of the squires is no exaggeration. They were despots in their own domains. Appeals against the rulings of the local magistrates were always costly and generally futile. It was rare to find legal advisers at their side; and the unaided wits of local landowners decided on all the lesser crimes (many of them punishable with death at the assizes) and the varied needs of the district. With the justices of the peace it lay to nominate the guardians of the poor and " visitors," who supervised the relief of the poor in the new unions of parishes resulting from Gilbert's Act of 1782. The working of the Draconian game-laws was entirely in their hands, and that, too, in days when the right of sporting with firearms was limited to owners of land worth £100 a year. Finally, lest there should be any community of sentiment between the bench and the dock, at the oft-recurring trials for poaching, the same land and money test was applied to all applicants for the honoured post of magistrate. The country gentlemen ruled the parish and they virtually ruled the nation.[1] The fact was proclaimed with characteristic insolence by the Lord Justice Clerk, Macqueen of Braxfield, in his address to the jury at the close of the trial of Thomas Muir for sedition, at Edinburgh in August 1793: " A Government in every country should be just like a Corporation; and in this Country it is made up of the landed interest, which alone has a right to be represented. As for the rabble, who have nothing but personal property, what hold has the nation upon them? What security for the payment of their taxes? They may pack up all their property on their backs and leave

---

[1] See Sidney and Beatrice Webb, "The Parish and the County," bk. i, ch. iv; bk. ii, ch. ii; Boutmy, "The Eng. Constitution" (Eng. edit.), pt. iii, sect. 3.

the country in the twinkling of an eye. But landed property cannot be removed."[1] The Scottish nobles, especially in the Highlands, still claimed extensive rights over their vassals; and several of them made patriotic use of these powers in raising regiments during the great war with France. Thomas Graham, afterwards Lord Lynedoch, is the best known example of this feudal influence.[2]

In many districts the squires received unwelcome but powerful support from "nabobs." Those decades witnessed a steady flight homewards of Indian officials, for the most part gorged with plunder. They became an appreciable force in politics. Reckless of expense so long as they could enter the charmed circle of the higher gentry, they adopted the politics and aped the ways of their betters; so that many a countryside felt the influence of their greed and ostentation. The yeomen and villagers were the victims of their land-hunger; while the small squires (so says Grose in his Olio of the year 1792) often fell in the course of the feverish race for display. As the Roman moralist inveighed against the influx of Syrian ways into the life of his city, so too might Johnson have thundered at the blending of the barbaric profusion of the Orient with the primal simplicity of the old English life.

For the most part, however, that life still showed the tenacity that marks our race. Certainly in Court circles there were no signs of the advent of commercialism, still less of democracy. The distinctions of rank in England seemed very strict, even to a German, who was accustomed to the formalities of the Hanoverian and Rhenish Courts. Count von Kielmansegge in 1761 noted the precision of etiquette at the State balls: "Rank in England is decided exclusively according to class, and not according to service; consequently the duchesses dance first, then marchionesses, then dukes' daughters, then countesses. Foreigners had no rank at all in England, so they may not dance before the lords and barons. . . . For this reason foreigners seldom dance at Court." It was not etiquette for the King and Queen to dance at the state balls; but, even so, the formalism of those functions must have been pyramidal. The same spirit of formality, fortified by a nice sense of the gradations of rank, appears in the rules of a county club at Derby, where the proceedings seem to have

---

[1] Howell, State Trials, xxiii, 231.
[2] Delavoye, "Life of T. Graham," 87.

been modelled on the sun and planets, the latter being always accompanied by inferior satellites.[1]

The customs of the *beau monde* in London were regulated by one all-absorbing preoccupation, that of killing time in a gentlemanly and graceful manner. Fielding, in his " Joseph Andrews," thus maps out the day of a fop about the middle of the century:

> In the morning I rose, took my great stick, and walked out in my green frock, with my hair in papers, and sauntered about till ten. Went to the Auction; told Lady B. she had a dirty face, laughed heartily at something Captain G. said (I can't remember what, for I did not very well hear it), whispered to Lord ——, bowed to the Duke of ——, and was going to bid for a snuff-box, but did not, for fear I should have had it. From 2 to 4 dressed myself; 4 to 6 dined; 6 to 8 coffee-house; 8 to 9 Drury Lane Playhouse; 10 to 12 Drawing-room.

The sketch of West End life given by Moritz, a Prussian pastor who visited England in 1782, is very similar, but he enters into more detail. He describes fashionable people as walking about all the morning in a *négligé* attire, " your hair not dressed but merely rolled up in rollers, and in a frock and boots." The morning lasted till four or five o'clock, then the fashionable time for dinner. The most usual dress in that summer was a coat of very dark blue, a short white waistcoat, and white silk stockings. Black was worn for full dress, and Moritz noticed that the English seemed to prefer dark colours. Dress seemed to him to be one of the chief aims and occupations of our people; and he remarked on the extraordinary vogue which everything French then enjoyed.

One is tempted to pause here and dwell on the singular fact that, at the time when England and France were still engaged in deadly strife, each people should be intent on copying the customs and fashions of the other. The decade of the " eighties " witnessed the growth of " Anglomania " to ridiculous proportions in France; while here the governing class thought it an unfailing proof of good breeding to trick out every other sentence with a French phrase. Swift alone could have done justice to the irony of a situation wherein two great nations wasted their resources in encompassing one another's ruin, while every day their words and actions bore striking witness to their admiration of

[1] " Letters from Lady Jane Coke to her friend, Mrs. Eyre, at Derby (1747-58)."

the hereditary foe. Is it surprising that Pitt should have used all his efforts in 1786 to bring about an *entente cordiale* on the basis of the common interests of the two peoples?

To revert to our theme: the frivolities and absurdities of Mayfair, which figure so largely in the diaries and letters of the period, probably filled a smaller space in the life of the nation than we are apt to infer from those sources. Moritz, who had an eye for the homely as well as the courtly side of life, noticed the good qualities which kept the framework of society sound. He remarked that in London, outside the Court circles, the customs were plain and domestic, the people generally dined about three o'clock, and worked hard.[1] His tour on foot through the Midlands also gave him the impression that England enjoyed a well-balanced prosperity. He was everywhere pitied or despised, it being assumed that a pedestrian must be a tramp. There can be little doubt that even at the end of that disastrous war, our land was far more prosperous than any of the States of North Germany.

The wealth of the proud islanders was nowhere more obvious than at the chief pleasure resorts of Londoners, Vauxhall and Ranelagh. These gardens and promenades impressed Moritz greatly, and he pronounced the scene at the rotunda at Ranelagh the most brilliant which he had ever witnessed: "The incessant change of faces, the far greater number of which were strikingly beautiful, together with the illumination, the extent and majestic splendour of the place, with the continued sound of the music, makes an inconceivably delightful impression." Thanks to the curiosity of the Prussian pastor, we can look down with him on the gay throng, and discern the princes, lords, and knights, their stars far outshining all the commoners present; we see also a difference in the styles of wearing the hair, the French queues and bags contrasting markedly with plain English heads of hair or professional wigs. Most of the company moved in "an eternal circle, to see and to be seen"; others stood near to enjoy the music; others again regaled themselves at the tables with the excellent fare provided for the inclusive sum of half-a-crown; while a thoughtful minority gazed from the gallery and moralized on the scene. The display and extravagance evidently surprised

[1] C. P. Moritz, "Travels in England in 1782"; W. Wales, "Inquiry into the . . . Population of England" (1781), estimated the number of houses in London at 100,000, and the population at 650,000.

Moritz, as it surprises us when we remember that it was at the close of a ruinous war. In the third year of the struggle, the mercurial Horace Walpole deplored the universal distress, and declared that when he sat in his "blue window," he missed nine out of ten of the lordly chariots that used to roll before it. Yet, in the seventh year, when the half of Europe had entered the lists against the Island Power, the Prussian pastor saw nothing but affluence and heard nothing that did not savour of a determined and sometimes boastful patriotism. At Ranelagh he observed that everyone wore silk stockings, and he was informed that even poor people when they visited that abode of splendour, dressed so as to copy the great, and always hired a coach in order to draw up in state at the entrance.[1]

Ranelagh and Vauxhall, we may note in passing, were beyond the confines of the London of 1780. The city of Westminster was but slowly encroaching on Tothill Fields; and the Queen's House, standing on the site of the present Buckingham Palace, commanded an uninterrupted view westwards over the fields and market gardens spreading out towards the little village of Chelsea. On the south of the Thames there was a mere fringe of houses from the confines of Southwark to the Archbishop's palace at Lambeth; and revellers returning from Vauxhall, whether by river or road, were not seldom sobered by visits from footpads, or the even more dreaded Mohawks. Further afield everything was completely rural. Trotter, Fox's secretary, describes the statesman as living amidst bowers vocal with song-birds at St. Ann's Hill, Wandsworth; and Pitt, in his visits to Wilberforce or Dundas at Wimbledon, would probably pass not a score of houses between Chelsea and the little old wooden bridge at Putney. That village and Wimbledon stood in the same relation to London as Oxshott and Byfleet occupy to-day. North of Chelsea there was the hamlet of Knightsbridge, and beyond it the villages of Paddington and "Marybone."

As Hyde Park Corner marked the western limit of London, so Bedford House and its humbler neighbour, the British Museum, bounded it on the north. The Foundling Hospital stood in open fields. St. Pancras, Islington Spa, and Sadler's Wells were rivals of Epsom and Tunbridge Wells. Clerkenwell Church was the fashionable place for weddings for the richer citizens who dwelt

---

[1] See, too, Wroth's "London Pleasure Gardens of the Eighteenth Century."

in the northern suburbs opened up by the new City Road completed in 1761. On the east, London ended at White-chapel, though houses straggled on down the Mile End Road. The amount of the road-borne traffic is curiously illustrated by the fact that the Metropolis possessed only three bridges, London Bridge, Westminster Bridge, and Blackfriars Bridge; and not till the year 1763 did the City Fathers demolish the old houses standing on London Bridge which rendered it impossible for two carts to pass. Already, however, suburbs were spreading along the chief roads out of London. In the "Connoisseur" of September 1754 is a pleasingly ironical account of a week-end visit to the villa of a London tradesman, situated in the desolate fields near Kennington Common, from the windows of which one had a view of criminals hanging from gibbets and St. Paul's cupola enveloped in smoke.

Nevertheless, the Englishman's love of the country tended to drive Londoners out to the dull little suburbs around the Elephant and Castle, or beyond Tyburn or Clerkenwell; and thus, in the closing years of the century, there arose that dualism of interests (city versus suburbs) which weakens the civic and social life of the metropolis. A further consequence was the waning in popularity of Vauxhall and Ranelagh, as well as of social clubs in general. These last had furnished a very desir-able relief to the monotony of a stay-at-home existence. But the club became less necessary when the family lived beyond the river or at "Marybone," and when the merchant spent much time on horseback every day in passing from his office to his villa. Another cause for the decline of clubs of the old type is doubt-less to be found in the distress caused by the Revolutionary War, and in the increasing acerbity of political discussions after the year 1790. Hitherto clubs had been almost entirely devoted to relaxation or conviviality. A characteristic figure of Clubland up to the year 1784 had been Dr. Johnson, thundering forth his dicta and enforcing them with thumps on the table. The next generation cared little for conversation as a fine art; and men drifted off to clubs where either loyalty or freedom was the dominant idea. The political arena, which for two generations had been the scene of confused scrambles between greedy fac-tions, was soon to be cleared for that deadliest of all struggles, a war of principles. In that sterner age the butterfly life of Ranelagh became a meaningless anomaly.

For the present, however, no one in England dreamt of any such change. The spirit of the nation, far from sinking under the growing burdens of the American War, seemed buoyant. Sensitive *littérateurs* like Horace Walpole might moan over the ruin of the Empire; William Pitt might declaim against its wickedness with all his father's vehemence; but the nation for the most part plodded doggedly on in the old paths and recked little of reform, except in so far as it concerned the abolition of sinecures and pensions. In 1779-80 County Associations were founded in order to press on the cause of "œconomical reform"; but most of them expired by the year 1784. Alike in thought and in customs England seemed to be invincibly Conservative.

The reasons, other than racial and climatic, for the stolidity of Georgian England would seem to be these. Any approach to enthusiasm, whether in politics or religion, had been tabooed as dangerous ever since the vagaries of the High Church party in the reign of Anne had imperilled the Protestant Succession; and far into the century, especially after the adventure of "Bonnie Prince Charlie," all leanings towards romance were looked on as a reflection on the safe and solid House of Brunswick. Prudence was the first of political virtues, and common sense the supreme judge of creeds and conduct.

External events also favoured the triumph of the commonplace, which is so obvious in the Georgian literature and architecture. The call of the sea and the influence of the New World were no longer inspirations to mighty deeds. The age of adventure was past, and the day of company promoters and slave-raiders had fully dawned. Commerce of an almost Punic type ruled the world. Whereas the wars of the sixteenth and seventeenth centuries had turned mainly on questions of religion, those of the eighteenth centred more and more on the winning of colonial markets as close preserves for the mother-country. By the Peace of Utrecht (1713) England gained the first place in the race for Empire; and a clause of that treaty enabled her to participate in the most lucrative of trades, the kidnapping of negroes in Africa for the supply of Spanish-America. Never was there a more fateful gain. It built up the fortunes of many scores of merchants and shipowners, but it degraded the British marine and the populace of our ports, in some of which slaves were openly sold. The canker of its influence spread far beyond ships and harbours. Its results were seen in the seared conscience of the nation, and in the lowering of the sense of the sanctity of human life, which in its turn enabled the blind champions of law, especially after the scare of 1745, to multiply capital punishments until more than 160 crimes were punishable by death.

The barbarities of the law and the horrors of the slave-trade finally led to protests in the name of humanity and religion. These came in the first instance from the Society of Friends.[1] But the philanthropic movement did not gather volume until it was fed by the evangelical revival. Clarkson, Zachary Macaulay, Wilberforce (the ablest champion of the cause), and John Howard, the reformer of prisons, were living proofs of the connection which exists between spiritual fervour and love of man. With the foundation, in the year 1787, of the *Society for the Abolition of the Slave Trade*, the philanthropic movement began its career of self-denying effort, which for some five years received valuable support from Pitt. Other signs of a moral awakening were not wanting. In 1772 Lord Chief Justice Mansfield declared that all slaves brought to the United Kingdom became free—a judgement which dealt the death-blow to slave markets in this country. In 1773 John Howard began his crusade for the improvement of gaols; and seven years later Sunday Schools were started by Robert Raikes. The protests of Burke and Sir Charles Bunbury against the pillory, the efforts of the former in 1784-5 to prevent the disgraceful overcrowding of the prisons, and the crusade of Romilly against the barbarities of the penal code are also a tribute to the growth of enlightenment and kindliness.

These ennobling efforts, however, failed to make any impression on what is termed "Society." The highest and the lowest strata are, as a rule, the last to feel the thrill of new movements; for surfeit and starvation alike stunt the better instincts. Consequently, Georgian England became strangely differentiated. The new impulses were quickly permeating the middle classes; but there their influence ceased. The flinty hardness of the upper crust, and the clayey sediment at the bottom, defied all efforts of an ordinary kind. The old order of things was not to be changed save by the explosive forces let loose in France in 1789.

[1] See ch. xx of this volume for details; also T. Clarkson's "Hist. of the Abolition of the Slave Trade," especially chs. xvii, xviii; and Prof. Ramsay Muir's "Hist. of Liverpool," ch. xii.

That year forms a dividing line in European history, as it does in the career of William Pitt.

Though ominous signs of the approaching storm might already be seen, the noble and wealthy wasted their substance in the usual round of riotous living. It may be well to glance at two of the typical vices of the age, drinking and gambling, of course in those circles alone where they are deemed interesting, for thence only do records reach us.

Drinking did not count as a vice, it was a cherished custom. The depths of the potations after dinner, and on suitable occasions during the day, had always been a feature of English life. Shakespeare seems to aim these well-known lines at the English rather than the Danes:

> This heavy-headed revel east and west
> Makes us traduced and tax'd of other nations:
> They clepe us drunkards, and with swinish phrase
> Soil our addition.[1]

Certainly in the eighteenth century drinking came to be in a sense a flying buttress of the national fabric. The champions of our "mercantile system" brought about the signature of the Methuen Treaty of 1703 with Portugal, in order to favour trade with that harmless little land at the expense of that with our "natural enemy," France. Hostility to the French being the first of political maxims, good citizens thought it more patriotic to became intoxicated on port wine than to remain sober on French claret. Though we may not endorse Adam Smith's hopeful prediction that the abolition of all duties on wine would have furthered the cause of temperance, yet we may agree that the drunkenness of the age was partly due to "the sneaking arts of underling tradesmen"—when "erected into political maxims for the conduct of a great empire." Equally noteworthy is his verdict that drunkenness was not limited to people of fashion, and that "a gentleman drunk with ale has scarce ever been seen among us."[2]

The habit of tippling, which even the moralist Johnson (*aet.* 70) said might "be practised with great prudence," was everywhere dominant. The thinness and unpracticality of the studies at the old universities were relieved by the depth and seriousness

[1] "Hamlet," i, sc. 4.
[2] "Wealth of Nations," bk. iv, ch. iii, pt. 2.

of the potations. The phrase, "a port wine Fellow," lingered to the close of the nineteenth century as a reminiscence of the crusted veterans of a bygone age, whose talk mellowed at the second bottle, and became drivel only at the fourth. Lord Eldon relates how a reverend Silenus, a Doctor of Divinity of Oxford, was once discovered in the small hours feeling his way homewards by the delusive help of the railings encircling the Radcliffe Library, and making lay remarks as to the unwonted length of the journey.[1] Where doctors led the way, undergraduates bettered the example; and the customs of Cambridge, as well as the advice of physicians, served to ingrain in Pitt that love of port wine which helped to shorten his life.

But the Universities only reflected the customs of an age when "drunk as a lord" had become a phrase. In fashionable society it was usual to set about tippling in a methodical way. Sometimes, at the different stages of the progress, travellers' impressions were recorded in a quaintly introspective manner. Rigby, Master of the Rolls in Ireland, when jocularly asked at dinner by the Prince of Wales to advise him about his marriage, made the witty and wise reply: "Faith, your Royal Highness, I am not drunk enough yet to give advice to a Prince of Wales about marrying."[2] The saying recalls to mind the unofficial habit of training and selecting diplomatists and ambassadors, namely, to ply the aspirants hard and then notice who divulged fewest secrets when under the table.

Fortunately, amidst the Bacchic orgies of the time, the figure of George III stood steadfast for sobriety. His tastes and those of Queen Charlotte were simple and healthy. Further, he was deeply impressed by the miserable end of his uncle, the Duke of Cumberland, whose frame, always unwieldy, became a mass of gouty corpulence and staggered on to dissolution at the age of forty-four. The Duke, so it is said, had long before warned the King, if he wished to live to a healthy old age, to avoid all the pleasures of the table.[3] The life and death of the Duke—an example more potent than words—and the homely tastes of the royal pair themselves, served to keep the bill of fare at Windsor well within the compass of that of many a small squire. After hunting for a whole morning, the King was sometimes content to

[1] H. Twiss, "Life of Lord Eldon," vol. i, ch. ii.
[2] H. Walpole, "Letters," viii, 395.
[3] "Mems. of Queen Charlotte," 203.

lunch on a jug of barley-water. Stories to this effect endeared "farmer King George" to the plain, wholesome folk of the provinces in whom lay the strength of England; but they aroused no responsive feeling in courtiers and nobles, who looked on such lenten fare as scarcely human, certainly not regal.

The behaviour of the Prince of Wales, however, tended to bring matters back to the level beloved of the *Comus* rout. The orgies of Carlton House were not seldom bestial; and yet fashionable society seems to have suffered no qualms on hearing that the prince was more than once saved from suffocation by prompt removal of enswathing silks.[1] Dinners became later, longer, and more luxurious. Experienced diners were those who could reckon the banquet, not by the number of glasses, but of bottles. Instead of figuring as an incident in the course of the day, dinner became its climax. We find Horace Walpole in February 1777 complaining that it absorbed the whole of the evening: "Everything is changed; as always must happen when one grows old and is prejudiced to one's old ways. I do not like dining at nearly six, nor beginning the evening at ten at night. If one does not conform one must live alone."

Many letters of that amusing writer show how the latter part of the four hours was spent. Take this reference to the death of Lord Cholmondeley: "He was seventy and had a constitution to have carried him to a hundred, if he had not destroyed it by an intemperance that would have killed anybody else in half the time. As it was, he had outlived by fifteen years all his set, who have reeled into the ferry-boat so long before him." There Horace Walpole laid his finger on one of the sores of the age. Statesmen and generals, parsons and squires, were generally worn out at fifty-five; and if by reason of strength they reached three score years and ten, those years were indeed years of sorrow and gout. In the annals of that period it would be impossible to find a single man possessed of the vigour of Mr. Gladstone at eighty, or the subtlety and firmness displayed by Beaconsfield at Berlin at the age of seventy-four. A nonagenarian was never seen at St. Stephen's: at seventy statesmen were laid by in flannel and wheeled about in bath-chairs. The cause of it all may be summed up in one word—port wine.

---

[1] See the new letter of Hugh Elliot to Pitt from Brighthelmstone, 17th Oct. 1785, quoted in ch. xvii, as to the danger of the Prince losing his life if he did not amend his ways.

This chapter would extend to an unwieldy length if a full account were given of what was, perhaps, the most characteristic vice of the age. Gambling has always flourished in an uncultured, reckless and ostentatious society. Men who have no mental resources within themselves are all too apt to seek diversion in the vagaries of chance. Tacitus noted it as the worst vice of the savage Teutons whom in other respects he lauded; and certainly none of their descendants gamed more than the Englishmen of the Georgian era. In vain did the King set his face against the evil. The murmurs grew not loud but deep when he forbade gambling at Court on that much cherished occasion, "twelfth-night." The courtiers then substituted cards, and betted furiously on them, until they too were banished from the royal palaces, even on that merry festival.[1] But here again the Prince of Wales neutralized his father's example, and before long succeeded in contracting debts to a princely amount, whereupon they were considerately paid by Parliament. That sturdy opponent of George III, Charles James Fox, outran even the Prince of Wales in zeal. At an all night sitting he is known to have lost £12,000; and, putting fortune to the test, lost successively £12,000 and £11,000 more. His great rival, the younger Pitt, plunged into play for a brief space, but on finding it get too strong a hold over him, resolutely freed himself from its insidious meshes. Thereafter that genial wit, George Selwyn, pointed the moral of their early careers by comparing the rivals to the industrious and idle apprentices of Hogarth.

The mention of Hogarth awakens a train of thought alien to his self-satisfied age. One begins to inquire what was the manner of life of those coarse thickset figures who fill the background of his realistic canvases. Were Englishmen of the lower orders really given over to Bacchic orgies alternating with long spells of flesh-restoring torpor? What was their attitude towards public affairs? While Rousseau began to open out golden vistas of a social millennium, were the toilers really so indifferent to all save the grossest facts of existence? The question is difficult to answer. The Wilkes affair seemed for the time to arouse universal interest, but the low class Londoners who bawled themselves hoarse for "Wilkes and Liberty" probably cared for that demagogue mainly because he was a Londoner bent on defying

[1] "Mems. of Queen Charlotte," 187.

the House of Commons. Personal feelings rather than political convictions seem to have determined their conduct; for Wilkes was not reviled a few years later when he went over to the King's side. Meanwhile the Gordon Riots had shown the London populace in another light. As for the County Reform Associations of the years 1780-4, they had very little hold upon the large towns, except in Yorkshire; and there the movement was due to the exceptionally bad representation and to the support of the great Whig landlords. The experience of those decades proves that political action which arises out of temporary causes (especially of a material kind) will lead to little result.

That mercurial and ill-educated populace seems to have shaken off its political indifference only at the time of a general election. Moritz describes the tumultuous joy with which Londoners took part in the election of the year 1782. The sight of carters and draymen eagerly listening to the candidates at the hustings; their shouts for a speech from Fox; the close interest which even the poorest seemed to feel in their country's welfare, made a deep impression on Moritz, who found the sight far more exhilarating than that of reviews on the parade ground at Berlin. His mental comparison of Londoners with the Romans of the time of Coriolanus was, however, cut short when he saw " the rampant spirit of liberty and the wild impatience of a genuine English mob." At the end of the proceedings the assembly tore down the hustings, smashed the benches and chairs, and carried the fragments about with them as signs of triumph.[1] Rousseau and Marat, who saw something of English life during their stay in this country, declared that Britons were free only during an election; and the former averred that the use which they made of " the brief moments of freedom renders the loss of liberty well deserved." [2] Certainly their elections were times of wild licence; and the authorities seem to have acquiesced in the carnival as tending to promote a dull, if not penitential, obedience in the sequel. Not without reason, then, did Horace Walpole exclaim, at the close of the American War—" War is a tragedy; other politics but a farce."

The moralist who cons the stories of the frivolity and vice of that age is apt to wonder that any progress was made in a

---

[1] " Travels in England in 1782," by C. P. Moritz (Eng. trans., 1895), 53.
[2] Rousseau, " Social Contract," bk. iii, ch. xv.

society where war and waste seemed to be the dominant forces. Yet he should remember that it is the extravagant and exceptional which is chronicled, while the humdrum activities of life, being taken for granted, find no place either in newspapers, memoirs, or histories. We read that in the eight years of the American War the sum of £115,000,000 was added to the National Debt, the interest on which in the year 1784 amounted to £9,669,435.[1] But do we inquire how a country, which with great difficulty raised a revenue of £25,000,000 a year, could bear this load and the far heavier burdens of the Revolutionary and Napoleonic Wars? The problem seems insoluble until we remember that British industry was then entering on its most expansive phase. The condition of our land may be compared with that of a sturdy oak which has had one of its limbs torn away and its foliage blighted by a storm. Yet, if the roots grip the soil deep down, the sap of a single season will restore the verdure, and in a few years the dome of foliage will rise as shapely and imposing as ever. So was it to be with England. Her astonishingly quick recovery may be ascribed partly to the exertions of the great man whose public life will here be set forth. But one man can do little more than direct the toil of the many to fruitful issues; and the fruitfulness that marked the first decade of his supremacy resulted from the contact of the nation's roots with a new and fertile layer of soil.

Below the surface of the national life, with its wars and party intrigues, there lay another world, in which the thoughts of Watt and Trevithick, of Hargreaves, Arkwright and Cartwright, were slowly taking shape in actuality. There lay the England of the future. Already its strength, though but that of an embryo, sufficed to send up enough of vital sap quickly to repair the losses of war; and the first claim of the younger Pitt to the title of Statesman lay in his perception of the needs and claims of this hidden life.

The mechanical inventions which led up to the era of great production resulted indirectly from the outburst of industrial activity that followed the victorious issue of the Seven Years' War. " Necessity is the mother of Invention "; and the great need after 1763 was to quicken the spinning of yarn so that the spinsters of a household could keep the father supplied with

---

[1] Dr. Cunningham, " Eng. Industry and Commerce," pt. ii, 546, 698.

enough weft for his loom. This necessity quickened the wits of a Lancashire weaver, Hargreaves; and in 1764 he constructed his "jenny," to lighten the toil of his wife. In quick succession came the inventions of Arkwright and Crompton, as already noted. The results obtained by the latter were surprising, muslin and other delicate fabrics being wrought with success in Great Britain. In a special Report issued by the East India Company in 1793, the complaint was made that every shop in England offered for sale " British muslins equal in appearance and of more elegant patterns than those of India, for one fourth, or perhaps more than one third, less price." [1] Further improvements increased the efficiency of this machinery, which soon was used extensively in the north-west of England, and in Lanarkshire. The populations of Manchester, Leeds, Sheffield, and Birmingham, after 1780, began to increase amazingly.[2] Hitherto they had numbered between 30,000 and 60,000 souls. Now they began to outstrip Bristol and Norwich, the second and third of English cities.

It is noteworthy that the Industrial Revolution in this, its first phase, brought wealth and contentment to all members of the community. The quantities of thread, varying in fineness, but severally invariable in texture and strength, enabled the hand-loom weavers to push on with their work with none of the interruptions formerly caused by the inability of hard-pressed spinsters to supply the requisite amount of yarn. These last, it is true, lost somewhat in economic independence; for by degrees they sank to the position of wage-earners in mills, but they were on the whole less hard-worked than before, water furnishing the power previously applied by the spinster's foot; and the family retained its independence because the father and brothers continued to work up cloth on their own hand-looms and to sell the produce at the weekly markets of Manchester or Blackburn, Leeds or Halifax. In the case of the staple industry of Yorkshire, many men reared the sheep, dressed and dyed the fleeces, worked up the thread into cloth, and finally, with their sons, took it on a packhorse to the nearest cloth market. A more complete example of economic independence it would be difficult to find; and the prosperity of this class—at once farmers, and dyers, manufacturers, and cloth merchants—was enhanced by the new

---

[1] Quoted by Baines, "History of the Cotton Manufacture," 334.
[2] W. Wales, *op. cit.*, 5.

spinning machinery which came rapidly into use after the year 1770.

This fact is emphasized in a vivid sketch of life in a Lancashire village drawn by one who saw it at the time of these momentous developments. William Radcliffe describes the prosperity which they brought to the homes of the farmer-artisans who formed the bulk of the population of his native village of Mellor, about fourteen miles north of Manchester. He calls the years 1788 to 1803 the golden age of the cotton industry. Every outhouse in the village was fitted as a loom-shop; and the earnings of each family averaged from 80 to 100 or sometimes even 120 shillings a week.[1] This account, written by a man who rose to be a large manufacturer at Stockport is probably overdrawn; but there can be no doubt that the exuberant prosperity of the North of England provided the new vital force which enabled the country speedily to rise with strength renewed at the very time when friends and enemies looked to see her fall for ever. Some idea of the magnitude of this new source of wealth may be gained from the official returns of the value of the cotton goods exported from Great Britain at the following dates:

1710	.	.	.	.	£5,698
1751	.	.	.	.	45,986
1764	.	.	.	.	200,354
1780	.	.	.	.	355,060
1785	.	.	.	.	864,710
1790	.	.	.	.	1,662,369
1795	.	.	.	.	2,433,331
1800	.	.	.	.	3,572,217
1806	.	.	.	.	9,753,824

After 1803 Cartwright's power-loom came more and more into use, and that, too, at the time when Watt's steam-engine became available for general use. The pace of the Industrial Revolution was thus accelerated; and in this, its third phase, the far-reaching change brought distress to the homes of the weavers, as was to be seen in the Luddite riots of 1810-11. This, however, belongs to a period later than that dealt with in these pages. Very noteworthy is the fact that in the years 1785-1806, which nearly cover the official life of Pitt, the exports of cotton goods increased almost twelvefold in value; and that the changes in

[1] "Origin of Power-loom Weaving," by W. Radcliffe, 59 *et seq.*

the textile industries enhanced not only the wealth of the nation but also the prosperity of the working classes in districts which had been the poorest and most backward.

Limits of space preclude any reference to the revolution wrought in the iron industry when coal and coke began to take the place of wood in the smelting of that metal. It must suffice to say that, whereas the English iron industry had seemed in danger of extinction, it now made giant strides ahead. In 1777 the first iron bridge was erected at Coalbrookdale, over the Severn. Six years later Cort of Gosport obtained a patent for converting pig-iron into malleable-iron by a new and expeditious process;[1] and in 1790 the use of steam-engines at the blast furnaces trebled their efficiency. This and the former reference to the steam-engine will suffice to remind the reader of the enormous developments opened up in all manufactures when the skill and patience of Watt transformed a scientific toy into the most important generator of power hitherto used by man.

Thus, in the closing years of the eighteenth century—that much despised century, which really produced nearly all the great inventions that the over-praised nineteenth century was merely to develop—the Industrial Revolution entered on its second phase. The magnets which thenceforth irresistibly attracted industry, and therefore population, were coal and iron. Accordingly, as Great Britain had abundance of these minerals in close proximity, she was able in a very short space of time to become the workshop of the world. The Eldorado dreamt of by the followers of Columbus was at last found in the Midlands and moorlands of the north of England. For the present, the discovery brought no curse with it. While multiplying man's powers, it also stimulated his ingenuity in countless ways. Far from diverting his energies from work to what is, after all, only the token of work, it concentrated his thoughts upon productive activity, and thus helped not only to make work but to make man.

While the moors and vales of the North awakened to new and strange activities, the agricultural districts of the Midlands and

---

[1] In Pitt MSS., 221, is a petition signed by many persons connected with the navy in favour of granting a pension to Mr. Cort, who had made "malleable iron with raw pit-coal, and manufactured the same by means of grooved rollers, by a process of his own invention." The petitioners state that though the invention had brought no benefit to Cort, but rather the reverse, yet it had proved to be of national importance.

South also advanced in wealth and population. A scientific rotation of crops, deep ploughing, and thorough manuring of the soil altered the conditions of life. Here again England led the way. Arthur Young, in his "Travels in France" (1787-9) never tires of praising the intelligence and energy of our great land-owners, whereas in France his constant desire is to make the *seigneurs* " skip." In the main, no doubt, the verdict of Young was just. Landlords in England were the leaders of agricultural reform. In France they were clogs on progress. Yet, the changes here were not all for good. That is impossible. The semi-communal and almost torpid life of the village was unequal to the claims of the new age; and, amidst much of discomfort and injustice to the poor, individual tenures, enclosures, and high-farming became the order of the day.[1] New facilities for travel, especially in the form of mail-coaches, better newspapers (a result of the Wilkes affair)—these and other developments of the years 1770-84 heralded the dawn of an age which was to be more earnest, more enlightened, less restful, and far more complex. The times evidently called for a man who, while holding to all that was best in the old life, fully recognized the claims of the coming era. Such a man was William Pitt.

In many respects he summed up in his person the tendencies of the closing decades of the century, just as the supreme figure of his father reflected all that was most brilliant and chivalrous in the middle of the Georgian era. If the elder Pitt raised Eng-land to heights of splendour never reached before, the younger helped to retrieve the disasters brought on by those who blindly disregarded the warnings of his father. In the personality both of father and of son there was a stateliness that overawed ordinary mortals, but the younger man certainly came more closely into touch with the progressive tendencies of the age. A student of Adam Smith, he set himself to foster the industrial energies of the land. In order to further the cause of peace, he sought the friendship of the French nation, of which Chatham was the in-

[1] W. Wales, *op. cit.*, 44 *et seq.*, enumerates several cases where the rural population declined, but he attributed that fact not to the enclosures (for he states that the enclosures of wastes, which were more numerous than those of the open fields, increased employment), but rather to the refusal of landlords to build cottages, though they charged higher rents than before. For the question of enclosures, however, see Dr. Gilbert Slater's recent work on the subject (Constable and Co., 1907).

veterate enemy; and in the brightest years of his career he seemed about to inaugurate the golden age foretold by the Illuminati. As by contact with Adam Smith he marched at the head of the new and peaceful commercialism, so too through his friendship with Wilberforce he felt the throb of the philanthropic movements of his times.

For the new stirrings of life in the spheres of religion, art, and literature, Pitt felt no deep concern. Like his father, and like that great genius of the South who wrecked his career, he was "a political being." In truth, the circumstances of the time compelled him to concentrate all his energies on public affairs. It was his lot to steer the ship of state through twenty of the most critical years of its chequered voyage. Taking the tiller at a time of distress, he guided the bark into calmer waters; and if he himself did not live on to weather a storm more prolonged and awful than that from which he at first saved his people, yet even in the vortex of the Napoleonic cyclone he was to show the dauntless bearing, the firm faith in the cause of ordered freedom, the unshaken belief in the destinies of his race, which became the son of Chatham and the typical Englishman of the age.

CHAPTER I

EARLY YEARS

I am glad that I am not the eldest son, but that I can serve my country in the House of Commons like papa.—PITT, May 1766.

CHAMPIONS of the customs of primogeniture must have been disquieted by observing how frequently the mental endowments of the parents were withheld from their eldest son and showered upon his younger brother. The first Earl of Chatham was a second son, and found his doughtiest opponent in Henry Fox, Lord Holland, also a second son. By a singular coincidence the extraordinary talents of their second sons carried them in their turn to the head of their respective parties and engaged them in the longest duel which the annals of Parliament record. And when the ascendancy of William Pitt the Younger appeared to be unshakably established, it was shattered by the genius of the second surviving son of Charles Marie de Buonaparte.

The future defender of Great Britain was born on 28th May 1759, just ten years before the great Corsican. His ancestry, no less than the time of his birth, seemed to be propitious. The son of the Earl of Chatham, he saw the light in the year when the brilliant victories of Rodney, Boscawen, Hawke, and Wolfe lessened the French navy by sixty-four sail of the line, and secured Canada for Britain. The almost doting fondness which the father felt for the second son, "the hope and comfort of my life," may perhaps have been the outcome of the mental ecstasy of those glorious months.

If William Pitt was fortunate in the time of his birth, he was still more so in the character of his father. In the nature of "the Great Commoner," the strain of pride and vanity was commingled with feelings of burning patriotism, and with a fixed determination to use all honourable means for the exaltation of his country.

Never since the age of Elizabeth had Englishmen seen a man of personality so forceful, of self-confidence so indomitable, of patriotism so pure and intense. The effect produced by his hawk-like eye, his inspiring mien and oratory was heightened by the consciousness that here at last was an honest statesman. In an age when that great party manipulator, Walpole, had reduced politics to a game of give and take, the scrupulous probity of Chatham (who refused to touch a penny of the interest on the balance at the War Ministry which all his predecessors had appropriated) shone with redoubled lustre. His powers were such as to dazzle his contemporaries. The wide sweep of his aims in 1756-61, his superb confidence as to their realization, the power of his oratory, his magnetic influence, which made brave officers feel the braver after an interview with him—all this enabled him completely to dominate his contemporaries.

H. Pelham did not.

In truth his personality was so dazzling as to elude the art of portraiture. At ordinary times he might have been little more than a replica of that statesman of the reign of Charles II whom Dryden has immortalized:

> A man so various that he seemed to be
> Not one, but all mankind's epitome.

But Chatham was fortunate in his times. He certainly owed very much to the elevating force of a great idea. In the early part of his life, when no uplifting influence was at work, his actions were often grossly incongruous and at times petty and factious. Not until he felt the inspiration of the idea of Empire did his genius wing its way aloft. If it be true that the Great Commoner made the British Empire, it is also true that the Empire made him what he was, the inspirer of heroic deeds, the invigorator of his people.

In comparison with these qualities, which entitle him to figure in English annals as Aristotle's "magnificent man," his defects were venial. Nevertheless, as some of them lived on in a lesser degree in his son, we must remember his arrogance, his melodramatic airs, his over-weening self-will, and his strange inconsistencies. In no one else would these vices and defects have been tolerated; that they were overlooked in him is the highest tribute that can be paid to the splendour of his services and the sterling worth of his nature.

If we look further back into the antecedents of the Pitt family, we find it domiciled at or near Blandford in Dorset, where it had produced one poet of quite average abilities, Christopher Pitt (1699-1748), whose translation of Virgil had many admirers. The love of adventure and romance, so often found in West Country families, had already been seen in Thomas Pitt (1653-1726), who worked his way to the front in India despite the regulations of the Company, became Governor of Madras, and made his fortune by very questionable transactions.[1] His great stroke of good fortune was the purchase of the famous diamond, which he thereafter sold to the Regent of France for nearly six times the price of purchase. He married a lady who traced her descent to a natural son of James V of Scotland; and to this union of a daring adventurer with the scion of a chivalrous race we may perhaps refer the will-power and the mental endowments which shone so brightly in their grandson, the first Earl of Chatham.

On his mother's side the younger Pitt could claim a distinguished descent. Her maiden name was Hester Grenville, and she was the daughter of Richard Grenville and Hester, Countess Temple. The appended table will show the relation of the Pitt and Grenville families:

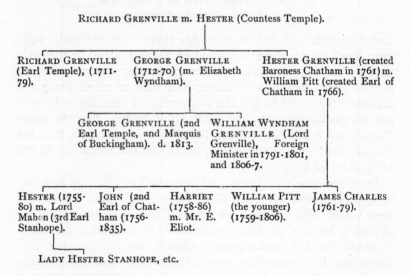

RICHARD GRENVILLE m. HESTER (Countess Temple).

RICHARD GRENVILLE (Earl Temple), (1711-79).	GEORGE GRENVILLE (1712-70) (m. Elizabeth Wyndham).	HESTER GRENVILLE (created Baroness Chatham in 1761) m. William Pitt (created Earl of Chatham in 1766).

GEORGE GRENVILLE (2nd Earl Temple, and Marquis of Buckingham). d. 1813.	WILLIAM WYNDHAM GRENVILLE (Lord Grenville), Foreign Minister in 1791-1801, and 1806-7.

HESTER (1755-80) m. Lord Mahon (3rd Earl Stanhope).	JOHN (2nd Earl of Chatham (1756-1835).	HARRIET (1758-86) m. Mr. E. Eliot.	WILLIAM PITT (the younger) (1759-1806).	JAMES CHARLES (1761-79).

LADY HESTER STANHOPE, etc.

The personality of Lady Chatham, if less remarkable, is more

---

[1] See Dr. von Ruville's work, "William Pitt, Earl of Chatham" (Eng. ed., 3 vols. 1907), for a full account of these forbears.

lovable than that of her husband. In contrast to his theatrical, lordly, and imperious ways, she shone by her simplicity and sweetness. His junior by many years, she accepted his devotion with something of awe, and probably felt his oft recurring attacks of gout, for which he magniloquently apologized, to be a link between them; for the Jove of the Senate became docile and human when he was racked with pain.[1] Her tender care at these times, and at others her tactful acquiescence in his moods and plans, ensured tranquillity and happiness in their household. Not that she lacked firmness of character, when occasion required; but we may ascribe her pliability to the personal ascendancy of her lord, to the customs of the times, and to her perception of the requisites for a peaceful existence. She carried her complaisance so far as to leave to her consort the choice of the residence at Hayes, near Bromley, in Kent, which he bought at the end of the year 1754. The following are the almost Griselda-like terms in which she defers to his opinion on the matter: " For the grand affair proposed by my dear love, I have only to reply that I wish him to follow what he judges best, for he can best judge what sort of economy suits with the different plans which he may choose to make hereafter. Whatever you decide upon will be secure of being approved by me."[2]

When a woman renounces all claim to a voice in the selection of her abode, we may be sure that she will neither interfere much in her husband's political career, nor seek to shine in a *salon* of blue-stockings. In fact, Lady Chatham's influence on her children was purely domestic. Her realm was the home. There is scarcely a trace of any intellectual impress consciously exerted upon her gifted son, William; but her loving care ensured his survival from the many illnesses of his early years; and she dowered him with the gentler traits for which we search in vain in the coldly glittering personality of Chatham. As examples of her loving care for her children, I may cite the following passages from her letters. In August 1794, when she felt old age coming on apace, she wrote in this tender strain:

I feel that I cannot support the idea of leaving you, my beloved sons, without saying unto ye how truly my fond affection has increasingly

---

[1] Ruville, i, 343-6.
[2] *Ibid.*, 345. Pitt finally bought about 100 acres, and further strained his resources by extensive building at Hayes.

ever attended ye both, and that my constant prayers have been daily
addresst to the Omnipotent Disposer of all events, that you might be
directed in all things by the blessing of heavenly wisdom . . .

Or take this gentle chiding to William (25th April 1796):

I do not [hear] from you, my dear son, but I hear often of you in a
way that makes up to me in the best manner possible for your silence.
I cannot, however, help wishing that my pleasure was increased by
receiving now and then a few words from you, and immediately comes
almost a reflection that obliges me to unwish it again, that I may not
take up any part of the small leisure you have to enjoy a little relaxation
from your various calls.

The old lady long retained her vigour; for in the autumn of
1795 she describes herself as " stout enough both in body and
mind to wish the wind to shift to the east so that the fleet
might not be detained." [1] Indeed, in the even strength of her
body, as in the constancy of her mind, she far excelled her
husband. We find Wilberforce, in the summer of 1791, entering
the following note in his diary: " Old Lady Chatham, a noble
antiquity—Lady Chatham asked about Fox's speaking—is much
interested about politics—seventy-five years old, and a very
active mind." [2]
Doubtless, her pride in the triumphs of her second son explains
the singular buoyancy of her nature almost up to the time of her
death. She must have recognized him as pre-eminently her child.
In appearance he certainly favoured her. A comparison of the
two noble Gainsboroughs of mother and son preserved at Orwell
Park shows William to have been more a Grenville than a Pitt.
His nose—that feature on which caricaturists eagerly fastened,
and on which he was said proudly to suspend the House of
Commons—had nothing in common with Chatham's aquiline
and terrifying prow. So, too, the whole bearing of the son was less
fiery and less formidable than that of the father. In Chatham
there lay the potentialities of a great warrior; but in the son's
nature these powers were wholly subordinate to the faculties that
make for supremacy in civil affairs, namely, patience, reasonableness, and aptitude for logic and finance. Above all, there shone

[1] " Pitt, some Chapters of his Life and Times," by Lord Ashbourne,
161-6.
[2] " The Life of William Wilberforce," by his Sons, i, 304.

Hester Grenville, Countess of Chatham
from a painting in the possession of E. G. Pretyman Esq.

in the younger Pitt a harmony of the faculties, in which the
father was lacking.

There is ample proof of the devotion with which Pitt regarded
his parents. His letters to them were long and loving; but
while he addressed Chatham in the stilted terms which the
Earl himself affected, he wrote to his mother in a simple and
direct style that tells of complete sympathy. In one of his
youthful letters to her he apologized humbly for some little
act of inattention; and in later years the busy Prime Minister often begged her forgiveness for his long silence. In all
363 letters to his mother have survived, and prove the tender-
ness of his love. Clearly also he valued her advice; for at the
crisis of the early part of 1783 he asked her opinion whether or
no he should take office as Prime Minister.[1] For the most part
the letters contain little more than references to private affairs,
which prove the warmth of his family feelings; but sometimes,
especially in the later years when the overworked Prime Minister could rarely visit his mother at her home, Burton Pynsent in
Somerset, he gives reasons for hoping that the progress of measures through Parliament, or the state of the negotiations with
France during the Revolutionary war, would permit him to pay
her a visit. The letters bear touching witness to the hopefulness
of spirit which buoyed him up; but sometimes they are overclouded by disappointments in the political sphere, which were
all the keener because they held him to his post and prevented
the longed-for stay at Burton Pynsent in August or at Christmas.
In such cases Lady Chatham's replies are restrained and dignified. I shall sometimes draw on this correspondence, especially
where it reveals Pitt's hopes for the work of the session or the
conclusion of peace.

Ingenious pleaders from the time of Macaulay onwards have
shown their skill in comparing the achievements of father and
son. The futility of all such tight-rope performances must be
obvious to those who remember the world-wide difference between the cataclysmic forces and novel problems of the revolutionary era and the comparatively simple tasks of the age of
Chatham. We shall have cause, later on, to insist on the difference in efficiency between Frederick the Great and Frederick
William II as an ally; and not even the most fervent panegyrists

---

[1] Pitt MSS., 11 and 13.

of Chatham will dare to assert that the ill-led and underfed armies of Louis XV were foes as redoubtable as the enthusiastic hosts called into being and marshalled by the French Revolution and Napoleon.

Nevertheless, there is one of these fallacious comparisons which deserves a brief notice. Lady Chatham, on being asked by one of her grandchildren which was the cleverer, the Earl of Chatham or Mr. Pitt, replied: " Your grandpapa without doubt."[1] The answer is remarkable. No woman in modern times has been blessed with such prodigality of power and talent both in husband and son; and we, with a knowledge of the inner forces of the two periods which she could not possess, may perhaps be inclined to ascribe her verdict to the triumph of the early memories of the wife even over the promptings of maternal pride. Explain it as we may, her judgement is certainly a signal instance of self-effacement; for the gifts of tact, prudence, and consistency whereby Pitt restored England to her rightful place in the years 1783-93 were precisely those which he derived from her.

It has often been remarked that great men have owed more to the mother's nature than to that of the father; and, while Chatham dowered his second son with the qualities that make for versatility, display, and domination, his mother certainly imparted to him forethought, steadiness of purpose, and the gentler gifts that endeared him to a select circle of friends. Here again, one might suggest a parallel between Pitt and his great opponent, Napoleon, who owed to his father characteristics not unlike those named above, but received from his mother the steel-like powers of mind and body which made him so terrible an opponent.

Enough has been said to indicate some of the influences of heredity which helped to shape the career of Pitt. It is a topic on which only sciolists would venture to dogmatize. Even in his early youth William began to outshine his elder brother. In their boyhood, mostly spent at Hayes, the difference of temperament between John and William made itself felt to the disadvantage of the former. He was reserved, not to say heavy and indolent, where William was bright and attractive. " Eager " is the epithet applied to him by Lady Chatham in 1766. The eldest son, having none of the intellectual gifts and

---

[1] Stanhope, ii, 125.

graces of Chatham, could not satisfy the imperious cravings of
the father, with the result that William received an undue share
of admiration. He was "the wonderful boy." John was designed
for the army, with results no less unfortunate for England than
a similar choice proved ultimately to be for France in the case
of Joseph Bonaparte. Well would it have been for the United
Kingdom had John Pitt allowed the glorious name of Chatham
to sink to comfortable mediocrity on the paternal estates of
Hayes or Burton Pynsent, and never to be associated with the
Isle of Walcheren. His colleagues in the Cabinet learnt to
respect his judgement as that of a safe man; but, as the sequel
will show, he was utterly lacking in energy and the power of
inspiring others.

William, having alertness of mind and brightness of speech,
was designed for Parliament. Or rather, this was his choice at
the age of seven. In May 1766, on hearing that his father was
raised to the Peerage, he told his tutor, the Rev. Edward Wilson, in all seriousness, that he was glad he was not the eldest
son, but that he could serve his country in the House of Commons like his papa.[1] The words have often been misquoted,
even by Earl Stanhope, the boy being reported as saying, " I
want to speak in the House of Commons like papa." The words,
when correctly cited, are remarkable, not for childish conceit,
but for a grave and premature sense of responsibility. They
show the strength of that patriotic instinct which inspired every
action of his career, spurring him on to his early studies, and to the
complex and crushing duties of his youth and manhood. They
sound the keynote of his character and enable us to form some
notion of the strength of that life-long desire to serve his native
land. This, his first recorded utterance, links itself in noble
unison with that last tragic gasp of 23rd January 1806—"My
country. How I leave my country!"

The health of the little William was so precarious that he and
his brothers and sisters spent much time at the seaside resorts,
Weymouth and Lyme Regis, which were not far from Burton
Pynsent, an estate bequeathed by an admirer to the Earl of
Chatham. Yet notwithstanding all the care bestowed on him,
the boy had but a frail hold on life. Illness beset him during
fully the half of his youth. At the age of fourteen he was still

[1] " Correspondence of the Earl of Chatham," iii, 27.

short and thin and weighed only six stone, two pounds.[1]
Observers, however, agree that his spirits always rose superior to
weakness; and to this characteristic, as also to his indomitable
will, we may attribute his struggling on through an exhausting
career to the age of forty-seven. The life of Pitt is a signal
proof of the victory which mind can, for a time, win over
matter.

Very naturally, his parents decided to have him trained at
home rather than at a public school. Chatham, while at Eton,
formed the most unfavourable impression of the public school
system and summed it up in his remark to Shelburne that he
had "scarce observed a boy who was not cowed for life at Eton;
that a public school might suit a boy of a turbulent, forward
disposition, but would not do where there was any gentleness."[2]

The tutor chosen for this purpose was the Rev. Edward Wilson,
of Pembroke Hall (now College), Cambridge, who had charge of
him from his sixth to his fourteenth year. The mutual affection
of tutor and pupil is seen in a letter which the tutor wrote at
Weymouth in September 1766, describing William as often
standing by him while he read, and making remarks that frequently lit up the subject and impressed it on the memory. His
ardour, he adds, could not be checked.[3] Wilson's training seems
to have been highly efficient, as will appear when we come to
consider the phenomenal attainments of his pupil at the time of
his admission to the University of Cambridge.

It is perhaps significant that that later prodigy of learning and
oratorical power, Macaulay, was also not brought into contact
with our public school system. Both of these remarkable men
may have owed some of their originality to the thoroughness of
the private tuition which they received before entering the
university. Had they passed through the mill of a public school
they would certainly have been less angular, and would have
gained in knowledge of men. Pitt especially might have cast off
that reserve and stiffness which often cost him so dear. But both
of them would assuredly have lost in individuality what they
might have gained in *bonhomie*. Still more certain is it that
those hotbeds of slang would have unfitted them for the free

---

[1] Notes by Bishop Tomline in the Pretyman MSS., Orwell Park.
[2] Lord Fitzmaurice, "Life of Shelburne," i, 72. See also two articles on
the early life of the elder Pitt in the "Edinburgh Review" for 1910.
[3] "Chatham Corresp.," iii, 65.

expression of their thoughts in dignified and classical English. The ease with which, from the time of his first entrance into Parliament, Pitt wielded the manifold resources of his mother tongue may be ascribed partly to hereditary genius but also to daily converse with one of the greatest of orators. It was Chatham's habit to read with his favourite son passages from the Bible or from some other great classic. We also know from one of the Earl's private memoranda that he made it a special study to clothe his thoughts in well-chosen words.[1] Indeed, he never talked but always conversed. We may be sure, then, that even the lighter efforts of the statesman must have been to the boy at once an inspiration to great deeds, a melodious delight, and a lesson in rhetoric. What youth possessed of genius would not have had his faculties braced by learning English from such a tongue, by viewing mankind through such a lens?

This education at home probably explains one of Pitt's marked characteristics, namely, his intense hopefulness. Brought up on the best authors, imbued with the highest principles, and lacking all knowledge of the seamy side of life, he cherished an invincible belief in the triumph of those aims which he felt to be good and true. This is an invaluable faculty; but it needs to be checked by acquaintance with the conduct of the average man; and that experience Pitt scarcely ever gained except by hearsay. Sir George Trevelyan has remarked that the comparative seclusion of Macaulay in youth led to his habitual over-estimate of the knowledge usually possessed by men. Certainly it led to the creation of that singular figment, "Macaulay's school-boy." A similar remark probably holds true of the quality of Pitt's nature noted above. Partly, no doubt, his hopefulness was the heritage bequeathed by Chatham; but it was strengthened by Pitt's bookish outlook on life.

The surroundings of his childhood and early youth must also have favoured the growth of that patrician virtue, confidence. Up to the year 1774 he lived on his father's estates at Hayes and Burton Pynsent, amidst some of the choicest scenery in the south of England. The land overflowed with prosperity, which was rightly ascribed in large measure to the genius of Chatham. Until the shadow of the American War of Independence fell on the youth, in his seventeenth year, he was the favourite son of a father

---

[1] "Chatham Corresp.," iv, 538.

whom all men revered; and his lot was cast in a land which seemed to be especially favoured. Thus pride of family and pride of race must have helped to stiffen the mental fibre of a youth on whom nature and art alike showered the gifts and graces of a chivalrous order. In a coarse nature the result would have been snobbishness. In William Pitt the outcome was devotion to the ideals of his father and buoyant confidence as to their ultimate triumph.

In some respects there is truth in the statement of Windham that Pitt never was young. Certainly for so delicate a plant the forcing process was perilously early and prolonged. In the Pitt Papers (No. XI) I have found a curious proof of the hold which the boy had over Latin at a very early age. It is a letter written to his father, the general correctness of which contrasts strangely with its large round letters enclosed within lines. It is not dated, but probably belongs to 1766, that is, to the seventh year of his age.

MI CHARISSIME PATER,

Gaudeo audire te rursum bene valere. Vidimus primates Mohecaunnuck et Wappinger, Tribuum Indicorum a septentrioli America, qui veniunt in Angliam supplicare regem ob quosdam agros. Gulielmus Johnson, eques auratus, desiderabat auxilium eorum in bello, et illi omnes abierunt ut pugnarent contra Gallos; sed, cum domum rediebant, sentiebant Batavos arripuisse omnes suos agros. Vulgus apud Portland illos parum commode tractabat.

Sum, mi charissime Pater,

tibi devinctissimus,

GULIELMUS PITT.

I have also found a curious proof of the stilted style in which the boy wrote to his father, while on the very same day he wrote to his brother almost in the terms which a boy of eleven would use. To the Earl of Chatham he thus begins a letter of 31st July 1770:

From the weather we have had here I flatter myself that the sun shone on your expedition, and that the views were enough enlivened thereby to prevent the drowsy Morpheus from taking the opportunity of the heat to diffuse his poppies upon the eyes of the travellers.[1]

This almost rises to the pomposity of style with which Chatham described to his son William the stinging of carriage-horses by

[1] Pitt MSS., II.

wasp. The insects figure as "an ambuscade of Pandours," and the horses as "these coursers of spirit not inferior to Xanthus and Podarges."[1]

Here on the other hand is the boy's letter to his brother:

Hayes, July 31 1770.

DEAR BROTHER,

I assure you that I am obliged to you beyond what is to be expressed for your epistle or journal. The dialogue between you and your host is very entertaining to those not interested in the want of provision in the inn. But I fancy it was not so to you, as it afforded little or no hope of dinner unless you could dine on the small tithes. The 2 Masons are incomparable. I think the intended candidate is to the full as likely as G. O. to succeed, and for what I know deserves it better. As I have seen neither the statue at Guilford nor that at South Carolina, I cannot judge which excels in point of workmanship, but I know which of the two noble Persons (in my opinion) is the superior. Your white mare I take to be more of the species of an elephant than any other; and can carry houses or castles on her back. Tho', great as She is, Long Sutton might perhaps keep her under her feet. These two mornings I have rode out before breakfast. Your Greek was excellent, and (I think) with practice you may become a Thucydides. Dapple is in good health; and we have taken the liberty to desire him to honour us with following the little chaise. I hope all stock is pure well.

I am, dear brother,
Affectionately yours,
WILLIAM PITT.[2]

The contrast between the two letters proves that Chatham's influence must have overwrought the boy's brain and inflated his style. The letter to John evinces a joy in life natural to a boy of eleven, together with a wide range of interests and accomplishments.

That the writers of the period also did much to form the boy's

---

[1] "Chatham Corresp.," iv, 363.

[2] Pitt MSS., 101. The disuse of past participles was a characteristic of that age. To write "rode" for "ridden" after the auxiliary verb was no more noticeable a defect than to walk unsteadily after dinner. One other early letter of Pitt's bears date 1772 at Lyme Regis, and refers to some fun which he and his brothers and sisters had had on a cutter yacht. Another letter undated, but in Pitt's round schoolboy hand, to a gentleman of Somerset, refers to sporting matters such as the lack of hares and the inability of his brother to catch those which he does start (Pitt MSS., 102).

style will appear from his first poem, "On the Genius of Poetry," which bears date May 1771.[1] It seems to be the joint product of Harriet and William Pitt:

Ye sacred Imps of thund'ring Jove descend,
Immortal Nine, to me propitious, bend
Inclining downward from Parnassus' brow;
To me, young Bard, some Heav'nly fire allow.
From Aganippe's murmur strait repair,
Assist my labours and attend my pray'r.
Inspire my verse. Of Poetry it sings.
Thro' *Her*, the deeds of Heroes and of Kings
Renown'd in arms, with fame immortal stand.
By *Her* no less, are spread thro' ev'ry land
Those patriot names, who in their country's cause
Triumphant fall, for Liberty and Laws.
Exalted high, the Spartan Hero stands,
Encircled with his far-renowned bands.
Whoe'er devoted for their country die,
Thro' *Her* their fame ascends the starry sky.
She too perpetuates each horrid deed;
When laws are trampled, when their guardians bleed,
That shall the Muse to infamy prolong
Example dread, and theme of tragic song.
Nor less immortal, than the Chiefs, resound
The Poets' names, who spread their deeds around.
Homer shall flourish first in rolls of fame;
And still shall leave the Roman Virgil's name;
With living bays is lofty Pindar crown'd;
In distant ages Horace stands renown'd.
These Bards, and more, fair Greece and Rome may boast,
And some may flourish on this British Coast.
Witness the man, on whom the Muse did smile,
Who sung our Parents' fall and Satan's guile,
A second Homer, favor'd by the Nine.
Sweet Spenser, Jonson, Shakspear the divine.
And He, fair Virtue's Bard, who rapt doth sing
The praise of Freedom and Laconia's King.
But high o'er Chiefs and Bards supremely great
Shall Publius shine, the Guardian of our state.
Him shall th' immortal Nine themselves record,
With deathless fame his gen'rous toil reward,
Shall tune the harp to loftier sounding lays
And thro' the world shall spread his ceaseless praise.
Their hands alone can match the Heav'nly strain
And with due fire his wond'rous glories sing.

---

[1] From Mr. A. M. Broadley's MSS.

The poem, which is in William's handwriting, shows that by
the age of twelve he had acquired the trick—it was no more—
of writing in the style of Pope and Johnson. The lines remind
us of the felicitous phrase in which Cowper characterized the
output of that school:

> The click-clock tintinnabulum of rhyme.

But they show neatness of thought and phrase. In a word, they
are good Johnsonese.

The same quality of sonorous ponderosity is observable in
Pitt's letters of 3rd June 1771 to his uncle the statesman, Earl
Temple, thanking him for a present, in which the names of
Lyttelton and Coke are invoked. In the following sentences the
trend of the boy's thoughts is very marked: " I revere this gift
the more, as I have heard Lyttelton and Coke were props of the
Constitution, which is a synonimous [*sic*] term for just Liberty."
The " marvellous boy " ends by quoting part of a line of Virgil,
which still more powerfully inspired him:

> avunculus excitat Hector.

The next year saw the production of a play, which he and his
brothers and sisters acted at Burton Pynsent on 30th May 1772.
Here again the motive is solely political: a King, Laurentius, on
his way homeward, after a successful war, suffers shipwreck, and
is mourned as dead. The news leads an ambitious counsellor,
Gordinus, to plot the overthrow of the regency of the Queen;
but his advances are repelled by a faithful minister, Pompilius
—the character played by William Pitt—in the following lines:

> Our honoured Master's steps may guide her on,
> Whose inmost soul she knew; and surely she
> Is fitted most to fill her husband's throne,
> She, whom maternal tenderness inspires,
> Will watch incessant o'er her lovely son
> And best pursue her dear Laurentius' plans.

Pompilius warns the Queen of the plot of Gordinus, and per-
suades her to entrust her son Florus to his care in a sylvan
retreat. Thither also Laurentius comes in disguise; for, after
landing as a forlorn survivor, he hears of dangerous novelties
that had poisoned men's minds and seduced the army from
allegiance to the Queen. Pompilius, while visiting the royal
heir, sees and recognizes Laurentius, brings him to Florus, and

prepares to overthrow the traitors. In due course the King's adherents defeat the forces of Gordinus, who is slain by Laurentius himself, while Pompilius, his standard bearer, kills another arch-conspirator. The King grants a general pardon in these lines:

> Us it behoves, to whom by gracious Heav'n
> The cares of nations and of States are giv'n—
> Us it behoves with clemency to sway
> That glorious sceptre which the gods bestow.
> We are the shepherds sent to tend the flock,
> Sent to protect from wrong, not to destroy.
> Oh! Florus! When thou govern'st our domains,
> Bear these thy father's precepts in thy mind.
> Thro' love control thy subjects, not thro' fear.
> The people's love the bulwark of thy throne.
> Give not thy mind to passion or revenge,
> But let fair Mercy ever sway thy soul.[1]

It is fairly certain that none of the children but William could have written these lines; and the fact that the mainspring of the action is political further stamps the play as his own. Some Spirit of the Future seems to have hovered over him, for the mental derangement of George III in 1788 brought to the front questions relating to a Regency not very unlike those sketched by the boy playwright. The sense of loyalty and devotion which informs the play was then also to guide Pitt's footsteps through a bewildering maze. Indeed this effusion seems almost like a marionette's version of the Regency affair: Laurentius is a more romantic George III, Pompilius quite startlingly foreshadows Pitt the Prime Minister, the Prince of Wales (an undutiful Florus) and Fox may pass for the conspirators; and the *motif* of the play twangs a mimic prelude to the intrigues of Carlton House. In the acting of the play the elder brother seems far to have surpassed William, who bore himself stiffly and awkwardly. Such was the testimony of young Addington, a lifelong friend, who saw the play acted on another occasion at Hayes.[2] The criticism is valuable as showing how ingrained in Pitt's nature was the shyness and *gaucherie* in public which were ever to hamper his progress.

Juvenile authorship has its dangers for a delicate child; and

---

[1] By the kindness of the Countess Stanhope I was allowed to peruse this most interesting MS., which is preserved, along with many other Pitt treasures, at Chevening.

[2] Pellew, "Sidmouth," i, 28.

we are not surprised to find from notes left by his first tutor to
Bishop Tomline that the half of Pitt's boyhood was beset by
illnesses which precluded all attempt at study. But nothing
stopped the growth of his mental powers, which Wilson summed
up in the Platonic phrase, " Pitt seemed never to learn but merely
to recollect." At the age of fourteen and a half, then, he was
ripe for Cambridge. It is true that youths then entered the
English Universities at an age fully as early as the Scottish lads
who went from the parish school, or manse, straight to Edinburgh
or Aberdeen. Charles James Fox, Gibbon, and the lad who
became Lord Eldon, entered Oxford at fifteen. Wilberforce,
who at seventeen went up from Hull to St. John's College, Cambridge, was probably the senior of most of the freshmen of his
year; but the case of Pitt was even then exceptional.

Cambridge on the whole enjoyed a better reputation than
Oxford for steady work; but this alone does not seem to have
turned the thoughts of the Earl of Chatham so far eastwards.
He himself was an Oxford man, and the distance of Cambridge
from Burton Pynsent, the usual abode of the family, would
naturally have told in favour of Oxford.

The determining facts seem to have been that Wilson's com-
panionship was deemed essential, and that he, as a graduate
of Pembroke Hall, Cambridge, turned the scale in favour of his
own college. This appears from Wilson's letter of 2nd December
1772 to his wife:

I could not have acted with more prudence than I have done in the
affair of Pembroke Hall. Mr. Pitt is not the child his years bespeak
him to be. He has now all the understanding of a man, and is, and
will be, my steady friend thro' life. . . . He will go to Pembroke, not a
weak boy to be made a property of, but to be admir'd as a prodigy;
not to hear lectures but to spread light. His parts are most astonishing
and universal. He will be fully qualified for a wrangler *before he goes*,
and be an accomplished classick, mathematician, historian and poet." [1]

How often have similar prophecies led to disappointment. In
the case of the " wonderful boy," they did but point the way to
a career whose meridian splendour has eclipsed the tender beauty
of its dawn.

[1] Ashbourne, *op. cit.*, 7-8.

CHAPTER II

AT CAMBRIDGE

A man that is young in yeares may be old in houres, if he have lost no time. But that happeneth rarely.—BACON.

ON 26th April 1773 Pitt's name was entered at Pembroke Hall, Cambridge; and he commenced residence there on 8th October 1772. His health being ever a matter of grave concern, Wilson stayed with him in order to prevent any boyish imprudences and accompany him in riding. But all precautions were in vain. Despite the invigorating influences of sea-air at Lyme Regis, where William and his brother had stayed from June up to 21st September, he soon fell ill at Cambridge, and remained in bed for several weeks. Thanks to the medical skill of Drs. Addington and Glynn (the former an old friend of Chatham), he gradually got the better of the hereditary foe, gout; but the letters which passed between Lady Chatham and Wilson attest the severity of the seizure.¹ The boy seems to have won the love of his medical attendants, as appears from this sentence in her letter of 22nd November. "What a gift William has to conciliate the love of those who are once acquainted with him."

There is a story told to Thomas Moore by the Bishop of Bath and Wells, that Pitt brought his nurse with him in the carriage to Cambridge, and that she stayed to look after him. This strange assertion is made in the poet's diary for 13th February 1826; and the distrust which that late date inspires is increased when we find that the Bishop had the anecdote from Paley, who "was very near being his [Pitt's] tutor, instead of Pretyman, but Paley did not like it."¹ As Paley was at Christ's, and there never was any question of Pitt entering at that college or receiving from the outset regular instruction outside the walls of Pembroke, the story lacks every element of credibility.

¹ "Diary of Thomas Moore," vol. v.

The facts are as follows: Mrs. Sparry, who was attendant or housekeeper at Burton Pynsent, went to Cambridge to nurse the boy through his long and serious illness, and finally brought him home. At last the invalid was strong enough to bear the journey. Four days were taken up in reaching London; and we find him writing thence to his mother on 6th December that he had not been fatigued and felt strong enough to walk all the way home; but, he added, Mrs. Sparry urged him not to write much.[1] He did not return to Cambridge ("the evacuated seat of the Muses" as Chatham styled it) until 13th July 1774. Then he informed Lady Chatham that Cambridge was empty, that Dr. Glynn had called on him and had inquired after Mrs. Sparry, who would be glad to hear that the bed at his rooms had been well aired. These trifles enable us to reduce the oft quoted nurse story to its proper insignificance.

Wilson seems to have done his best to amuse his charge in the dreary vacation time of July—September 1774; for on 24th August Pitt described to his mother a ride in which Wilson and he had lost their way among lanes and fields and regained the track with some damage to hedges, and after a chase of one of the steeds, but far too late to share in college dinner. Again, on 1st September, he wrote to the Earl of Chatham: "The ardour for celebrating this day is as great at Cambridge as anywhere; and Mr. Wilson himself, catching a spark of it, signalized himself by killing a crow on the wing after a walk of six hours."[2]

The natural vivacity of disposition, which charmed all his friends, must have played no small part in the recovery of his health. The medical authorities of to-day would also probably assign more importance to regular hours, exercise, and careful diet than to the use of port wine, adopted in compliance with his physicians' recommendation, on which some contemporary writers dwell with much gusto. Certain it is that from the year 1774 onwards "his health became progressively confirmed."

This phrase occurs in the biography of Pitt written by his college tutor, Dr. Pretyman, whose style it aptly characterizes. The book is indeed one of the most ponderous ever published. As tutor, friend, and adviser, the Rev. Dr. Pretyman had unique opportunities for giving to the world a complete and life-like portrait. Pitt was entrusted to his care and to that of his

---

[1] Pitt MSS., II.　　　　　　　　　　[2] *Ibid.*

colleague, Dr. Turner, in 1773-4, and thereafter to Pretyman
alone. The undergraduate soon conceived for him an affection
which was strong and lasting. Their intercourse suffered little
interruption, not even from the ecclesiastical honours which the
young Prime Minister so freely bestowed on his old tutor. The
bishop, who in 1803 took the name of Tomline, continued to be
the friend and adviser of the Statesman up to the dreary days
which succeeded the death-blow of Austerlitz. Pitt died in his
arms, and he was his literary executor. Yet, despite the mass of
materials put into his hands (or was it because of their mass?)[1]
he wrote one of the dullest biographies in the English language.

The solution of the riddle may perhaps be found in the cast
of his mind, which was that of a mathematician and divine, while
it lacked the gifts of interest in men and affairs, of insight into
character, of delicate and instinctive sympathy, and of historic
imagination, which enliven, reveal, interpret, and illuminate
personalities and situations. Talleyrand, with a flash of almost
diabolical wit, once described language as a means of *concealing*
thought. Tomline, with laboured conscientiousness, seems to
have looked on biography as a means of concealing character.
Certainly he portrayed only those features which are easily discernible in the tomes of the Parliamentary History. An almost
finnikin scrupulousness clogged him in the exercise of the scanty
powers of portraiture with which Nature had endowed him. The
biographer was continually being reined in by the literary
executor, the result being a progress, which, while meant to be
stately, succeeds only in being shambling. Here and there we
catch glimpses of Pitt under the senatorial robes with which his
friend adorned and concealed him, but they are tantalizingly
brief. The Bishop was beset by so many qualms concerning the
propriety of mentioning this or that incident as to " suppress
many circumstances and anecdotes of a more private nature,"
and to postpone the compilation of a volume on this more
frivolous subject. Death supervened while the Bishop was still
revolving the question of the proprieties; and we shall therefore
never fully know Pitt as he appeared to his life-long counsellor.[2]

[1] One remembers here the terrifying remark of Lord Acton that the mass
of documents which the modern historian must consult inevitably tells
against style.

[2] See an interesting fragment, " Bishop Tomline's Estimate of Pitt," by

There must have been sterling qualities in the man whom the statesman thus signally honoured. Dr. Pretyman's learning was vast. Senior Wrangler and Fellow of his College, he also became a Fellow of the Royal Society; and his attainments in the classics enabled him to command the respect of his pupil in a sphere where, according to Wilson, Pitt had the Platonic gift, not of learning, but of instinctive remembrance (ἀνάμνησις). Nevertheless, nearly all contemporaries seem to have found in the tutor and Bishop a primness and austerity which were far from attractive. Perhaps he lacked the vitality which might have energized that mass of learning. Or else the consciousness that he was a Senior Wrangler, together with the added load of tutorial and episcopal responsibility, may have been too much for him. To Pitt, nurtured amidst the magniloquence of Hayes and Burton Pynsent, the seriousness and pedantry of Pretyman doubtless appeared natural and pleasing. To outsiders they were tedious; and the general impression of half-amused, half-bored wonderment is cleverly, though spitefully, expressed in the lines of the *Rolliad*:

> Prim preacher, prince of priests and prince's priest,[1]
> Pembroke's pale pride, in Pitt's *praecordia* placed,
> Thy merits all shall future ages scan,
> And prince be lost in parson Pretyman.

Among the most interesting parts of the bishop's biography of Pitt are those in which he describes his attainments, and his studies at Pembroke Hall. The tutor found him, as Wilson expected, exceedingly well versed in the classics, so that he seldom met with any difficulties. Chatham had prescribed a careful study of Thucydides and Polybius; and the young undergraduate was often able, with little or no preparation, to translate six or seven pages of the former historian, without making more than one or two mistakes. This is very remarkable in a youth of fifteen; but his sense of the meaning and fitness of words seems to have been not less instinctive than his choice of language, which was soon to arouse the wonder and admiration of the most experienced debaters at Westminster.

the Earl of Rosebery (London, 1903), also in the "Monthly Review" for August 1903.

[1] Dr. Pretyman was chaplain to George III, and later on Bishop of Lincoln and Dean of St. Paul's.

As regards his mathematical attainments, Tomline states that he had already read the first six books of Euclid, and had mastered the elementary parts of Algebra, Trigonometry, and Natural Philosophy. The bent of his mind was towards the Humanities; but he had a good hold on mathematics, and became expert at the solution of problems. Newton's *Principia* aroused his deepest admiration. Various notes on mathematical and astronomical subjects extant in the Pitt Papers (too fragmentary for reproduction here) show that he retained his interest in the exact sciences.[1]

At Cambridge, above all, he deepened his knowledge of the classics. The ease with which he deciphered so obscure a work as Lycophron's " Cassandra " astonished even those who were familiar with his exceptional powers. Everything therefore conduced to give him an exceedingly wide and thorough knowledge of the literatures of Greece and Rome; for, fortunately for him, he had neither the need nor the inclination to bestow much time on the art of versifying in those languages, which absorbed, and still absorbs, so much of the energy of the dwellers by the Cam. Accordingly the life, thought, and statecraft of Athens and Rome became thoroughly familiar to him. His love for their masterpieces of art and imagination was profound; and the many comments in his handwriting on the margin of the chief authors suffice to refute the gibe of certain small-minded opponents, that he kept up his acquaintance with the classics in order to find tags for his speeches.[2] To some extent, it is true, his studies were directed towards his future vocation. At the wish of the Earl of Chatham, he bestowed great attention on the oratory of the ancients; and he seems to have bettered the precept by making critical notes on the speeches which he read, and remarking how the various arguments were, or might be, answered. Add to this a close and loving perusal of Shakespeare and Milton, and it will be seen that Pitt's studies at Cambridge were such as invigor-

---

[1] Pitt MSS., 196. The notes and diagrams refer to the movement of bodies considered dynamically: there are also some problems in algebra. More numerous are the notes on English History, especially on the parliamentary crises of the years 1603-27, where, unfortunately, they break off. I have also found notes on Plutarch, and translations of the speech of Germanicus in Tacitus ("Annals," Bk. I), and of parts of the Second Philippic.

[2] His books went in large measure to Bishop Pretyman (Tomline), and many of them are in the library of Orwell Park.

ated the mind, cultivated his oratorical gift, and thoroughly equipped him for the parliamentary arena.

From Tomline we glean a few details which enable us to picture the young undergraduate in his surroundings. He states that his manners even at that early age were formed and his behaviour manly, that he mixed in conversation with unaffected vivacity and perfect ease. His habits were most regular; he never failed to attend morning and evening chapel except when prevented by ill health. Owing to his father's habit of reading aloud a chapter of the Bible every day, his knowledge of the Holy Scripture was unusually good. Tomline mentions a circumstance which will serve also to illustrate Pitt's powers of memory and fine sense of sound. On hearing his former tutor read portions of Scripture in support of his "Exposition of the Thirty-nine Articles," the statesman (it was in that anxious year, 1797) stopped him at one text with the remark—"I do not recollect that passage in the Bible, and it does not sound like Scripture." He was right: the passage came from the Apocrypha, which he had not read.

The singular correctness of Pitt's life while at Cambridge exposed him to the risk of becoming a bookworm and a prig. From this he was saved by his good sense and his ill-health. "The wonderful boy" was begged by his parents not to court the Muses too assiduously. Chatham's fatherly anxiety and his love of classical allusions led him to run this metaphor to death; but the strained classicisms had the wished for effect. Pitt rode regularly and far. In the Pitt Papers (No. 221) I have found proof that, while at Cambridge, he was trained in the then essential art of fencing. At a later date his old fencing-master, Peter Renaud, sent to him a petition stating that he had "had the honour of teaching you when you was at Pembroke College," and that in consequence of the decline in the habit of fencing, he was now in poverty, and therefore begged for help from his illustrious pupil.

We clutch at these trifles which show the drift of Pitt's early habits; for the worthy Tomline, who had stacks, where we have only sheaves, does not condescend to notice them. From the Pitt Papers we can, however, in part reconstruct his Cambridge life. In his first term, Pitt described Pembroke as "a sober, staid college, and nothing but solid study there." Fortunately, too, no exceptional privileges were accorded to Chatham's favourite son. The father in his letter to the tutor had not claimed any, except those required on the score of health. Consequently though Pitt had the right to don the gorgeous gown of a "gentleman-commoner" (afterwards called "fellow commoner"), he did not do so. In his first letter to his father he stated that his cap was "to be stripped of its glories, in exchange for a plain loop and button."[1] It is further pleasing to know that his father wished him not to make use of that tattered mediaeval privilege which allowed sons of noblemen to receive the degree without sitting for examination; and that persistent ill-health alone led him to resort unwillingly to this miserable expedient.

We are here reminded of Wordsworth's reference to the sense of social equality to be found at Cambridge, even at a time when titled arrogance and old-world subservience ramped and cringed unchecked and unrelieved in most parts of the land. The lines are worthy of quotation because they show that the spirit prevalent at Cambridge, at least at St. John's College, prepared the poet to sympathize with the French democracy. He speaks of Cambridge as

> A Republic, where all stood thus far
> Upon equal ground, that we were brothers all
> In honour, as in one community,
> Scholars and gentlemen; where, furthermore,
> Distinction open lay to all that came,
> And wealth and titles were in less esteem
> Than talents, worth, and prosperous industry.

We do not know whether Pitt's feelings at this time were akin to those of Wordsworth, who entered St. John's in 1787. Pitt's surroundings were not such as to favour the infiltration of new ideas. In his first two years he mixed scarcely at all with undergraduates, and even after 1776 his circle seems to have been limited, doubtless owing to his intense shyness, ill-health, and constant association with Dr. Pretyman. On 4th November 1776 he writes home that he had been spending a few days at the house of Lord Granby (the future Duke of Rutland), and had returned to the "sober hours and studies" of college; but he rarely refers to pastimes and relaxations.

His letters also contain few references to study; but one of these is worthy of notice. On 10th November 1776 he asked per-

---

[1] "Chatham Corresp.," iv, 289.

mission to attend a month's course of lectures on Civil Law for
the fee of five guineas; and later on he stated that they were
"instructive and amusing," besides requiring little extra work.
In that term he took his degree in the manner aforesaid. Early
in 1777 he moved to other rooms which were small but perfectly
sheltered from wind and weather. About that time, too, he
launched out more freely into social life, so we may judge from
the not infrequent requests for increased supplies. On 30th June
1777 he writes that he has exceeded his allowance by £60, the
first sign of that heedlessness in money matters which was to
hamper him through life.

The chief feature of interest in these early letters is the frequent references to the politics of the time, which show that he
kept the service of his country steadily in view. Thus, on 23rd
March 1775 during vacation time at Hayes, he writes to his
brother, begging him, if he leaves his pillow before noon, to find
out the fate of Mr. Burke's motion on behalf of conciliation with
America. He signs the letters on behalf of "the Society at
Hayes," possibly a reference to a family debating club.[1] It is
noteworthy that the struggle of the American colonists with
George III was the first political event to arouse his interest,
which must have been heightened by the fervid speeches of
Chatham on the subject. A little later a side eddy must have
set in, for his elder brother, Lord Pitt, on receiving his commis-
sion in 1774, joined his regiment, which was quartered successively
at Quebec and Montreal. On 31st May 1775 William writes from
Cambridge that the papers are full of the bad news from Boston,
doubtless the fight at Lexington. Ten days later he requests Lady
Chatham to send, along with the "Ethics," Davenant on "Peace,
War, and Alliance," as it is not in any library in Cambridge.
Clearly, then, the youth was alive to the legal and international
questions then at stake.

Probably these wider interests carried him more into society.
His friendship with Lord Granby, then an undergraduate, is
more than once referred to; and thus was formed that connec-
tion which furthered Pitt's career, and led to the sending of Lord
Granby (after succeeding to the Dukedom of Rutland) to the
Viceregal Lodge at Dublin. The Duke, it may be mentioned,

---

[1] Chevening MSS.

bequeathed to Pitt the sum of £3,000.[1] Friendships formed at
the University counted for much in times when court and
governmental influence made or marred a man's career. We may
therefore note that as Pitt's health improved during the last
years at Cambridge, he also became friendly with the following:
Lord Westmorland, Lord Euston, Lowther (Lord Lonsdale),
Pratt (Lord Camden), Pepper Arden, Eliot, Bankes, Long, and
St. John.

The name of him who was perhaps Pitt's dearest friend is
here conspicuous by its absence. Wilberforce saw little of Pitt
at Cambridge, partly, perhaps, because he did not enter at
St. John's College until 1776 and then became associated with
a dissolute set; but he made Pitt's acquaintance towards the
end of their time there, and the youths were mutually attracted
by their brilliant conversational gifts and intellectual powers,
which were to be sharpened by delightful intercourse at London
and Wimbledon. In a passage penned in 1821, Wilberforce
contrasts the comparative ill fortune of Pitt with the good fortune of his rival, Charles James Fox, who at Oxford made the
acquaintance of a number of brilliant young men, Sheridan,
Windham, Erskine, Hare, General Fitzpatrick, and Lord John
Townshend. Nearly all of these, it is true, won distinction in public
life; but it is scarcely fair to say that Pitt's Cambridge friends
(to whose number Wilberforce adds Lords Abercorn and Spencer)
were deficient in parts. Their gifts, if less brilliant, were more
solid than those of Fox and Sheridan. Lords Camden and
Westmorland were to prove themselves able administrators, and
the future Duke of Rutland, though showy and dissolute, displayed much ability as Lord Lieutenant of Ireland. Bankes
"the precise" (as the *Rolliad* terms him) was a hard-hitter in
debate; while the gentler qualities of Eliot endeared him both
to Pitt and to his sister Harriet, whom he married in 1785.

Viewing the question more widely, we may surmise that Pitt's
career at Cambridge would have been more fruitful had he gone
up somewhat later and mixed more with undergraduates, especially with good talkers. In that case we can imagine that the
Grenville stiffness in him would almost have vanished. A *bon
vivant* like Fox or North he could never have been; but the
austerity of his life at Cambridge, save in its closing months,

---

[1] Pretyman MSS., quoted by Lord Ashbourne, *op. cit.*, 31, note.

did not tend to cure him of the awkward shyness which Wilberforce noted as so prominent a trait in his character;[1] and thus
he went forth into the life of Westminster weighted with that
serious defect, an incapacity for making a wide circle of friends
or winning over enemies. In a sense it may be said that Pitt
took political life too seriously. He prepared for it from boyhood so strenuously as partly to stunt his social faculties,
and thereby handicap himself for life. For in that age the
political arena was the close preserve of the nobles, gentry,
and nabobs, with whom a statesman could scarcely succeed
unless he had the manners of the clubs and the instincts of a
sportsman. A compromise between Lord Chatham and Tony
Lumpkin would have made the ideal leader. As it was, there
entered on the scene a compromise between Chatham and
Aristides.

Pitt's chief relaxation from the "sober studies" at Pembroke
Hall was found in visits to the great debates at Westminster.
The first of these visits belongs to the month of January 1775,
when his father was pleading passionately for conciliation with
America. Benjamin Franklin, the champion of the colonists,
was present; and the orator clearly aimed at persuading our
kinsmen beyond the seas that they had the sympathy of very
many British hearts. Those two orations echoed far and wide
amid the dales of New England and the rocks of the Alleghanies.
What, then, must have been the effect of the living voice and of
that superb presence, which trebled the power of every word, on
a sensitive youth whose being ever thrilled responsive to that of
his father? Language failed him to express his feelings. "Nothing prevented his speech," so he wrote to his mother, "from
being the most forcible that can be imagined, and [the] Administration fully felt it. The manner and matter both were striking;
far beyond what I can express. It was everything which was
superior; . . . his first speech lasted above an hour and the
second half an hour—surely the two finest speeches that ever
were made, unless by himself."[2] He heard also Chatham's great
effort of 30th May 1777, and describes it as marked by "a flow
of eloquence and beauty of expression, animated and striking
beyond expression."

For Pitt, indeed, the chief delights of the vacations centred in

[1] "Private Papers of W. Wilberforce," 65.
[2] "Chatham Corresp." iv, 376, 377.

St. Stephens. Never has there been a more eager listener to
the debates; and here his method of studying the orators of
Greece and Rome enabled him quickly to marshal the arguments of a speaker, assess them at their real worth, and fashion
a retort. During one of his visits to the House of Lords he was
introduced to Charles James Fox, already famous as the readiest
debater in the Lower House. The Whig leader afterwards described the rapt attention with which the youth at his side
listened to the speeches of the peers, and frequently turned to
him with the remark: "But surely, Mr. Fox, that might be met
thus," or "Yes; but he lays himself open to this retort." Little
can Fox have imagined that these gifts, when whetted by
maturity, were frequently to dash the hopes of the Whigs.[1]

The nice balancing of arguments, and the study of words,
together with the art of voice production, may make a clever
and persuasive speaker; but a great orator is he to whom such
things are but trifling adornments, needful, indeed, for a complete equipment, but lost amidst the grander endowments of
Nature, imagination and learning. Pitt excelled in the greater
gifts no less than in the smaller graces. He had the advantage of
a distinguished presence, a kindling eye, a sonorous voice; and to
these excellences were added those of the mind, which outshone
all adventitious aids. And these intellectual powers, which give
weight to attack and cover a retreat, were cultivated with a
wholeheartedness and persistence unparalleled in our annals. The
pompous greetings of the Earl of Chatham to "the civilians and
law of nations tribe" at Pembroke Hall show the thoroughness
of his son's application to law. It also seems probable that
during the latter part of his stay at Cambridge he widened his
outlook on public affairs by a study of Adam Smith's great
work, "The Wealth of Nations," which appeared in 1776. He
afterwards avowed himself a disciple of Adam Smith; and it is
questionable whether he would have had time after leaving
Cambridge thoroughly to master that work.

Books which bore upon the rise and fall of States seem to
have engaged his attention, as was also the case with the young
Napoleon—witness his copious notes on changes of dynasty
and revolutions. In truth, those questions were then "in the
air." In 1748 Montesquieu had published his "Spirit of Laws";

Macaulay, "Miscellaneous Writings" (Essay on William Pitt).

Rousseau had brought out in 1762 his "Social Contract," which Quinet has described as the seed of the French Revolution. Whether Pitt perused these works is doubtful; but it is clear that in his reading he had an eye for the causes that make or mar the fortunes of nations. Witness the remark in his letter of 19th March 1778, that nowhere in history could he find "any instance of a Nation so miserably sacrificed as this has been."[1] He shared the general conviction that none but Chatham could steer the ship of State into safe waters; and deep must have been his concern when the King refused to hear of Chatham forming a new Ministry for the purpose of conciliation. No consideration, not even the loss of his Crown (so he wrote to Lord North) would induce him to "stoop to the Opposition."[2]

Such conduct bordered on the insane now that France had made common cause with the United States; but there was no means of forcing the King's hand. The majority in Parliament supported his Minister, Lord North; and little could be expected from the Earl of Chatham in view of his growing infirmities of mind and body. His haughty and exacting ways no less than his inconsistencies of aim had scattered his following; and it was but a shadow of a name that appeared in the House of Lords on 7th April 1778. Encased in flannel, looking deadly pale, but with something of the old gleam in his eyes, he entered, staying his tottering frame on his sons, William and James. He spoke twice, urging the House not to debase the monarchy by conceding full independence to America, still less by giving way before France. "Shall this great kingdom now fall prostrate before the House of Bourbon? If we must fall, let us fall like men." Much of the speech was inconsistent with his former opinions; but the peers recked not of inconsistency; they listened with bated breath to words which recalled the glorious days of 1759—words which were to be prophetic both for himself and for his son. A second oratorical effort was too much for his overwrought frame. He pressed his hand to his heart and fell. The peers hard by caught him in their arms; his sons hurried up and helped to bear him to a house in Downing Street. Thence he was removed to Hayes, and there on 11th May 1778, in the midst of his family, he passed away.

[1] Macaulay, "Miscellaneous Writings" (Essay on William Pitt), iv, 510.
[2] "Corresp. of George III with Lord North," ii, 154 (17th March 1778).

For the greatest statesman and orator of his age there could
be but one place of sepulture. The House of Commons unanimously voted an address for a public funeral and a monument in
Westminster; and probably of all Englishmen there was only
one who regretted the decision. George III had revealed the
pettiness of his nature when, in a letter to Lord North, he referred to Chatham's breakdown in the House of Lords as his
"political exit." He now stated that, unless the inscription on
the monument dwelt only on Chatham's influence in "rouzing
the nation at the beginning of the last war," the compliment
paid to the deceased statesman would be "rather an offensive
measure" to him personally.[1] "The Court do everything with
an ill grace," is William's description of the preparations for the
funeral.[2] No one represented the King at the funeral on 9th
June, a fact which gave to the ceremony the appearance of a
great popular demonstration. It was the last of Chatham's
triumphs.

Owing to the absence of the eldest son with his regiment,
William was the chief mourner. Few of the beholders had
any knowledge of his manifold gifts; and the crowds which
gazed at the stately procession, as at the burial of England's
glories and hopes, could not surmise that the slim figure following the hearse was destined to retrieve the disasters of the
present and to link once more the name of Pitt with a great
work of national revival.

[1] "Corresp. of George III with Lord North," ii, 184.
[2] Pitt MSS., 12.

CHAPTER III

POLITICAL APPRENTICESHIP

I cannot approve of the requisition, in the studies of future statesmen, of so much theoretical knowledge, by which young people are often ruined before their time, both in mind and body. When they enter into practical life, they possess indeed an immense stock of philosophical and learned material; but in the narrow circle of their calling this cannot be practically applied, and will therefore be forgotten as useless. On the other hand what they most needed they have lost: they are deficient in the necessary mental and bodily energy, which is quite indispensable when one would enter efficiently into practical life.—GOETHE.

THE lives of English statesmen have very rarely, if ever, been enervated by that excessive zeal for education which the great German thinker discerned as a possible danger for his fellow countrymen. Certainly to those who had drunk deep of the learning of Leipzig, Heidelberg, or Göttingen, the transference to a Staats-secretariat at Weimar, Cassel, or even at Berlin, must have been a life of sheer drudgery. Doubtless, the *doctrinaire* policy of many a Continental State sprang from the persistent attempts of some Pegasus in harness to rise again to the serene heights of his youthful contemplations. In England our youths did not meditate on the science of politics. Both Oxford and Cambridge displayed a maternal care lest the brains of the rising generation should overtax the bodies; and never was the unsullied spring of Helicon ruffled by draughts taken under compulsion. Gibbon's experience at Magdalen College in 1752-3, of the genial indifference of his first tutor, and the unblushing neglect of his successor, seems to have been quite normal; and it is clear that the curriculum of that wealthy corporation had not the remotest connection with any known form of activity outside its walls.

Pitt's residence at Cambridge was more fruitful for the future. The dons of Pembroke Hall seem to have taken their duties less

lightly than was the rule elsewhere; and Pitt's lifelong gratitude
to Dr. Pretyman may have been partly due to the unusual
advancement in learning achieved under his watchful care. But
even so, the regular studies had no bearing on the life of a
statesman other than that which comes from an intelligent reading
of the philosophers and historians of Greece and Rome. Pitt's
choice of lectures on Civil Law was his own. And, after taking
his degree in the autumn of 1776, he seems largely to have
followed the bent of his mind, which, as we have seen, led
him to study the crises in national affairs, and the causes of
welfare or decay. It is significant that the young Napoleon
Bonaparte approached historical study in the same practical way.

Above all, Pitt haunted the precincts of Westminster, and
there learnt to view politics, not as a science, but a strife. For
him, therefore, there was little risk of being hampered by an ill-
digested mass of theoretical learning as he faced the ever
shifting problems of the Commonwealth; still less of undergoing
the transition from the breezy uplands of philosophy to the
political mill of some petty principality. It is the happy lot of
Britain's sons to come to ever widening spheres of activity; and
their minds, never " sicklied o'er " at the outset, should possess
the alertness and vigour which Goethe rightly praised as a
better equipment than the best elaborated theories and the
richest store of precedents. This natural course of development
ought to produce not *doctrinaires*, but statesmen.

The chief misfortunes of Pitt's early life were his appalling
precocity, which the Earl of Chatham in no wise checked, and
the sense of responsibility thrust upon him all too soon by the
terrible bereavement described above. As the eldest son was
then abroad with his regiment, William was at once involved in
a network of cares. The finances of the family were in an embarrassed state. Chatham's habits had been so lavish, and his
conduct in official life so honourably scrupulous, that the estate
was encumbered with debts. Parliament voted the sum of
£20,000 towards their payment; but, if we may judge from one
of the later letters of Lady Chatham, embarrassments at times
continued to beset her.[1] William also inherited property which
was to yield little more than an annual income of £250—a sum

---

[1] Ashbourne, *op. cit.*, 161, 162.

inadequate to meet the demands of an ambitious youth in an age when money no less than family standing served as the passport to a public career.

Nevertheless, the lack of resources seems to have stimulated energies that were ever braced by difficulty. About five months after the funeral of his father, we find him expressing to Lady Chatham his resolve to take rooms at Lincoln's Inn. In his view practice at the Bar was invaluable as a training for that wider and grander service to which he had early vowed himself.

In one important particular Pitt's conduct showed singular foresight. He did not, as might have been expected in days when travelling was slow and expensive, give up his rooms at Pembroke Hall, but for nearly two years he continued usually to reside there, even while keeping his terms at Lincoln's Inn. Extravagant though this arrangement seemed to be, it was based on prudential motives. In the miserable condition in which public affairs then were, he judged that a dissolution of Parliament could not be long deferred; and the chance of winning a seat at his University seemed to him, though still in his teens, greater than at an ordinary constituency, where the deep pockets of grandees or nabobs must mar his prospect.[1]

About Cambridge, then, his hopes fondly clustered, seeing that it was " a seat of all others the most desirable, as being free from expense, perfectly independent, and I think in every respect extremely honourable." [2] The words have the ring of manly determination which marks all his public utterances.

The following letter of his to Mr. John (afterwards Lord) Townshend, then one of the members for the University, marks the first official announcement of his intentions:

Pembroke Hall, July 15 1779.
DEAR TOWNSHEND,
  The very earnest and sincere wishes I expressed for your success in the late contest for the University of Cambridge, might perhaps lead you to imagine that I should take a similar part on every future occasion. I was therefore very sorry that it was not in my power to explain to you my situation when I had the pleasure of seeing you here. But, having since finally determined to offer myself a candidate for the

---

[1] See Porritt, "The Unreformed House of Commons," i, ch. ix, on the exclusion of poor men from Parliament.

[2] Letter of 3rd July 1779. Stanhope, i, 31.

I   F

University at the General Election, I am desirous of giving you immediate notice of a circumstance of which I imagine you will be glad to be apprised as soon as possible.

W. PITT.[1]

At the same time he informed his uncle, Earl Temple, of his resolve, and received the following reply. The italicizing of the Christian name speaks for itself:

Stowe, July 18 1779.

I cannot, my dear *William*, but interest myself most warmly in whatever relates to your honour or interest; I therefore learn with singular pleasure the hopes you conceive that the good old lady, the alma mater of Cambridge, may be inclined to treat you as her most favourite son. Such a testimony at your age from a learned body cannot but be very flattering. As to your prospect of success, I cannot form any opinion, being totally unacquainted with every circumstance but that of your merit. You must therefore be [*sic*] at present to receive from me nothing but sincere assurances of my best good wishes and readiness to serve you as may be in my power. How far it may be advisable for you before you have more ripened in your profession to launch out into the great ocean of politicks and expose yourself to the sweet music of those lovely syrens, which have already seduced your cousin Thomas from the destined and determined object of his life, is a matter of great doubt, and the reflection that it is so may prove some consolation to you should you not succeed. The memory of your father and the great character you have attained speak forcibly in your favour, but a dead minister, the most respectable that ever existed, weighs very light in the scale against any living one, at least if I may guess at your university by her good sister. All therefore I can say further is to recommend to you very thoroughly to examine the foundation of your hopes before you engage, not suffering your conduct to be warped by your wishes; because, if from the event this measure shall appear to be lightly taken up, such an outset in life will diminish much of those high expectations which you have so deservedly raised. Your young old friend and namesake salutes you very kindly and gratefully, Hester and Catherine very affectionately, without forgetting that antient spinster Mrs. Stapleton. We shall be happy to receive you here, candidate or no candidate. . . .[2]

TEMPLE.

Despite this response, Pitt resolved to persevere, and that too, though the political horizon had darkened owing to the

[1] Chevening MSS.   [2] Pitt MSS., 182.

declaration of war by Spain. At first he avowed his deep concern at this event; but the note of hopefulness, which is never long absent from his letters, soon begins to reassert itself in the expression of a belief that this new danger may " be productive of some good effects at home, and that there may still be spirit and resources in the country sufficient to preserve at least the remnant of a great empire." This forecast was justified. The struggle became one for national existence, waged against our hereditary rivals, the monarchs of the House of Bourbon; and the searchings of heart of England's sons, at warring against their own kith and kin, were in large measure stilled. The thrilling incidents that accompanied the three years' siege of Gibraltar by the Spaniards, our successes in India, and the naval triumphs of the closing years of the war showed the hardening of the nation's fibre under the strain of adversity and danger.

After residing at Burton Pynsent for some weeks in the autumn in order to reassure Lady Chatham while the invasion-scare was at its height, Pitt returned to Cambridge at the close of the year, and settled down at Lincoln's Inn in the early weeks of 1780. Thanks to the kindness of his uncle, Earl Temple, he had been able to procure a lease of rooms on the north side of the attic of staircase number 4 of Stone Buildings (those nearest to Holborn). The sum of £1,100, which in November 1778 he had pronounced " frightful," had been advanced on the property which Pitt was to inherit when he came of age.

Concerning Pitt's life at Lincoln's Inn we know next to nothing. The lack of official records of the Inns of Court, except unilluminating entries of dates, thwarts all efforts at reconstructing the early life of many famous men; and the denseness of the gloom which surrounds our institutions, academic and legal, is apt to provoke the investigator to unpatriotic reflections. Is there any French statesman of modern times about whose early career the records of the institutions with which he was associated are so scanty and uninteresting as are those of Cambridge and Lincoln's Inn concerning the life of the brilliant son of Chatham?

As it is, the investigator at Lincoln's Inn can discover little more than that Pitt was called to the Bar on 12th June 1780, and that on the next day a lease was taken out for his rooms for three " lives," namely, John, Earl of Chatham, aged 23, Wil-

liam Pitt, aged 21, and James Charles Pitt, aged 18. The rent
was £9 9s. 10d. per annum.[1]

The great preoccupation of Pitt, apart from the ever-pressing
topic of national danger, was the movement for Economic
Reform. Originating at York in December 1779, it gathered
volume until the petitioners in that county alone numbered
more than 8,000 freeholders. East Anglia responded to the
call of Yorkshire; and Pitt hoped to see London rally to the
cause of purity and political freedom. If ever there was a chance
of sweeping away the network of sinecures whereby the King
kept his hold on the House of Commons, it was now, when the
growth of debt and taxation rendered economy in non-essentials
the most urgent of public duties.

In February 1780 Burke introduced his proposals for Economic
Reform in a speech of great ability. He sought, firstly, to abolish
the special jurisdictions in Wales and Cheshire and in the
Duchies of Lancaster and Cornwall, which formed petty and
extravagant and corrupt governments. The great orator, like a
forensic *retiarius*, sought to enfold his great enemy, Corruption,
within the cloak of humour which he thus deftly threw in front.
Affecting the desire to free the royal prerogative from irritating
and absurd local restrictions, he proceeded thus: "Cross a brook,
and you lose the King of England, but you have some comfort
in coming again under His Majesty, though shorn of his beams,
and no more than Prince of Wales. Go to the north and you
find him dwindled to a Duke of Lancaster. Turn to the west
of that north, and he hops upon you in the humble character of
the Earl of Chester." Equally difficult and important was
Burke's attempt to reduce the Civil List and lessen the number
of sinecures attached to the King's household. He sought to
abolish the offices of Master of the Household, Treasurer,
Comptroller, Cofferer, Treasurer of the Chamber, the whole
Board of Green-Cloth, the Wardrobe and Jewel Offices, the
Board of Works, and the Keepers of stag-hounds, buck-hounds,
fox-hounds, and harriers, and other well-paid sinecures. With
playful irony he described the clatter of white-sticks and yellow-
sticks about the head of a reformer who would touch those
offices, or sought to exclude the King's turnspit from Parliament.
As regarded the Civil List, he proposed to fix its amount im-

---

[1] "The Black Book of Lincoln's Inn," iv, Preface.

mutably, to transfer to the general fund accounts which had ceased properly to belong to the King's private purse, and to regulate the whole on business-like principles. He also urged the suppression of useless offices in the general administration, especially the newly created Secretaryship for the Colonies and the Board of Trade, the latter of which then formed a desirable sinecure for eight members of Parliament.[1] Most important of all, perhaps, was the proposal, brought in by Sir Philip Clerk, to exclude from Parliament contractors—a class which had been proved to have battened on the funds, and to have urged the continuance of the war.

Had Burke's proposals stood in need of further vindication, it would have been supplied by the mysterious fate which befell them. Members of Parliament with scarcely an exception loudly commended the measure, and the eloquence and power with which Burke introduced it to the House. About the same time Lord Shelburne brought forward in the Upper House damning proofs of the greed of contractors and of the gross carelessness with which accounts were kept at the Admiralty and War Office.[2] The defence of ministers was strong only in personalities. Argument there was none; and it seemed that the whole festering sudd of corruption must be swept away by the flood of popular indignation.

From three of Pitt's letters, those of 9th and 26th February and 14th March 1780, we can imagine the high hopes of the young reformer as he listened to the scathing attack on Ministers by Lord Shelburne, and the comprehensive indictment framed by Burke. In the second letter he notes with joy the drop of the ministerial majority to two; and in the small hours of 14th March he was privileged to witness the stormy scene which occurred when Burke by a majority of eight carried his motion for abolishing the Board of Trade. And yet the sudd did not move. Despite the success of reformers in the House, and the growing excitement among their associations in the country, the clogging influences of the past prevailed. Members who praised Burke for his lofty and statesmanlike aims, voted in committee against the details of his scheme. Little by little it disappeared; and, in face of the greed, cowardice, or apathy of Parliament, Burke soon declared his indifference as to the fate of the few remaining

[1] " Life of Burke," by R. Bissett (1800), ii, 55-66.
[2] Fitzmaurice, " Shelburne," iii, 67-72.

clauses of his measure. The bill for the exclusion of contractors from Parliament passed the Commons, but was thrown out by the Lords.

Another surprise was in store for the House and the country. On 6th April Mr. Dunning brought forward a motion that "the influence of the Crown has increased, is increasing, and ought to be lessened." The motion was made suddenly and on the day when numerous petitions were laid on the table, signed by thousands of persons, on behalf of shorter parliaments and a larger addition to the representatives of counties who, as a rule, showed some independence. The proposal produced a great sensation. Ministers seemed to be "stunned." Pitt's relative, Thomas Pitt of Boccanoc, ably supported this daring motion. The Speaker himself left the chair and spoke in support of it, and the resolution, after a trifling change of form, was passed by a majority of eighteen. But again the forces of obscurantism triumphed. Apparently Dunning owed his success solely to the fear of the imminence of a general election, and as that fear lessened, so also did the numbers of the popular party in the House. North slowly but surely regained his hold on the waverers, and succeeded in defeating a motion begging the King not to dissolve or prorogue Parliament until steps had been taken to diminish the influence of the Crown at elections (24th April).

For the present Pitt stifled his disappointment at this fiasco by attendance at the opera and masquerades, so we may judge from his letters; but he probably hardened his resolve to effect the Reform of Parliament itself, which, as was now clear to all but Burke, must precede any attempt to cleanse the Augean stables of the Court and the Administration. That gifted thinker but somewhat erratic politician, whose character will concern us later, had gone so far as to defend the state of the representation and to urge reformers to concentrate their efforts on the task of freeing Parliament from the corrupt influences that were warping its character. To this belief he still clung, in spite of the recent damning proof that a Parliament of place-hunters and borough-mongers had refused to root out the canker of corruption, even at a time of great national danger. Pitt, for his part, looked for safety to that course of action which Chatham had so often taken; he turned away from Parliament and fixed his hopes in the nation. Even the oratory of Burke failed to satisfy him. He found in his great speech of 11th February not only "real beauties," but "ridiculous affectations." He added, however, in his letter of 14th March: "I have heard two less studied harangues from him since in reply that please me much more than this does now that it is upon paper." This criticism, coming from the son of Chatham, is a little surprising; but it may be considered symptomatic. As will appear later, there was something in Burke's temperament which jarred on the young statesman.

While disagreeing with Burke and the more academic wing of the reformers, Pitt did not consort with the men on the extreme left who now raised a great clamour through the country. He seems to have had no dealings at this time with the Reform or "Œconomic" Associations; and events now occurred which helped for a time to distract his attention from politics. While he was expecting to be called to the Bar, London fell a prey to the Lord George Gordon rioters (2nd to 9th June).

What must have been the disgust of the young patrician as he gazed at the scenes of rapine and drunkenness which went on under the name of Protestantism! The pretence of bigotry was soon flung aside, and then, when the thin crust of civilization was removed, men saw appalled the depths of villany that usually are hidden. For days the passions of the mob raged unchecked by timorous magistrates and ministers. The King alone was undismayed, and finally insisted on the use of vigorous measures. Thanks to his staunchness, the wheels of government began to move once more. Then the orgy quickly died down; but it left men with a dread of the newly-revealed Caliban, and a heightened respect for the one man whose firmness had ensured the vindication of law and order. How much the popular cause then suffered can never be known. When, in the course of the French Revolution, the Parisian mob carried the King and Queen from Versailles to Paris and completed its triumph at the harvest time of 1792, Englishmen viewed those events in the lurid light thrown by the flames of the Lord George Gordon riots; and it is probable that Pitt himself was no stranger to this feeling.

The cause of Parliamentary Reform in England also suffered untold harm. Why talk about manhood suffrage, vote by ballot and annual Parliaments, as the Westminster Committee had talked, when all around were proofs of the savagery of the many-headed monster? The Duke of Richmond, who then, along with

Fox, advocated a programme of reform which was to furnish the Chartists with their "six points," confessed in a letter to Shelburne that the riots "will tend to discredit any attempts of the people to do themselves justice on any future occasion when the cause may warrant it";[1] and though Charles James Fox retained his faith in the cause, yet he and all other democrats thenceforth found it a hopeless task to roll the stone up to the point to which the enthusiasm of the people carried it in the spring of 1780. After midsummer of that year the various committees and associations preached to deaf ears. The King had won.

To return to Pitt's fortunes, we may note that Lincoln's Inn had been in no immediate danger from the rioters, though surrounded with flames on all sides. In order to be ready for the worst, the benchers took arms and formed a corps, in which Pitt had his first experience of volunteering. The records of the Inn, however, show that it was also defended by 800 men of the Northumberland Militia, the sum of £364 12s. 0d. being paid for provisions to them for the ten days during which they were in garrison.[2]

The desire of the resident members of the Inn worthily to entertain the officers of that corps led to the appointment of a committee for that purpose, which included Pitt, Pepper Arden (afterwards Lord Alvanley), Mitford (afterwards Lord Redesdale), Bland Burges, and three others. The last named, in his reminiscences, tells how, when his turn came, he invited Gibbon and Lord Carmarthen to meet four officers and other company at dinner. The historian, as is well known, was a most entertaining talker, flitting easily from one topic to another, and lighting up all with sallies of wit which the listeners were expected to receive with deferential applause and unquestioning mirth. Judge then of his astonishment, when, after one of his best foreign anecdotes, which touched on "the fashionable levities of political doctrine then prevalent," a deep but clear voice was heard from the far end of the table calmly but civilly impugning the correctness of the story and the propriety of its political connexion. The applause ceased at once, and Gibbon turned his gaze petulantly on the slim youth who had dared to challenge his unquestioned supremacy, and sat there quietly eating grapes. As the interruption had been

---

[1] Fitzmaurice, "Shelburne," iii, 83.

[2] "Black Book of Lincoln's Inn," iv, Preface; "Bland Burges Papers," 58.

hailed with too much approval to be ignored or dismissed with a frown, he endeavoured to crush the youth by heavy artillery. A spirited fire came in return, and a sharp duel of wits began, which the company followed with the keenest interest. Finally the skill and vigour of the attack drove the historian from one position after another and left him defenceless; whereupon he left the room in high dudgeon. In vain did Bland Burges seek in the anteroom to calm his feelings and persuade him to return. "By no means," replied Gibbon; "that young gentleman is, I have no doubt, extremely ingenious and agreeable, but I must acknowledge that his style of conversation is not exactly what I am accustomed to, so you must positively excuse me." Meanwhile Pitt continued to hold forth on the topic in dispute, "which he discussed with such ability, strength of argument, and eloquence, that his hearers were filled with profound admiration."[1]

Such was the first recorded triumph of Pitt. Would that we knew more than the bare outlines of the discussion! But an unkind fate has vouchsafed here, as at so many points, enough of information to whet the appetite for more, enough to give us the merest glimpse of those surprising powers which easily discomfited Gibbon at his prime.

We know little about the extent of Pitt's legal attainments or his skill as a pleader. His practice was to last but a short time. Three days after the end of the riots he was called to the Bar and afterwards went on the Western Circuit, of which he was a member. As to the impression aroused by his pleading, I have found very few particulars except the statement in an almost contemporary biography that his first case, which must have been in London, was one concerning an East India trade dispute, and that he attracted the notice of Lord Mansfield on the Bench. He is said to have acted as junior counsel in several cases at Dorchester and Exeter, and to have commanded attention by the force of his reasoning rather than attracted it by playing upon the emotions. His style, in short, was clear and argumentative rather than "attractive and passionate."[2] From Exeter he was recalled in haste by news which was of far higher interest to him than the quarrels of Wessex squires and traders. The King had dissolved Parliament

---

[1] "Bland Burges Papers," 60, 61.
[2] "Life of William Pitt," by Henry Cleland (1807).

and had fixed 31st October for the date of assembly of its successor.

This action was what might have been expected from the most astute of electioneering agents. Disgust at the excesses of the Gordon rioters was still the dominant motive in the political world, and at such a time men looked askance at Reform. Further, in order to ensure the success of what he termed "my cause," George III condescended to the arts of the canvasser, entering the shop of a draper at Windsor, and saying in his quick peremptory way—"The queen wants a gown, wants a gown. No Keppel. No Keppel." Windsor rejected Keppel; Burke failed to keep his seat at Bristol; and Pitt made no impression whatever on the Toryism of the University of Cambridge. In any case his election was highly improbable. Dons and country clergymen are not wont to favour the claims of a young and unknown candidate; but the trend of thought at that time made his defeat certain.

He bore it with his usual serenity. "Mansfield and Townshend have run away with the prize," so he wrote on 16th September, "but my struggle has not been dishonourable." He now once more betook himself to legal affairs at Lincoln's Inn, but his thoughts still centred in Westminster. Despite the stagnation which marked our public life after the victory of the King and Lord North at the general election, the fate of the commonwealth drew Pitt to St. Stephen's for the earlier half of every day. His regular attendance at the House was perhaps instrumental in furthering his dearest hopes. The Duke of Rutland had been on cordial terms with Pitt at Cambridge; and he now mentioned the talents of his friend to Sir James Lowther. That magnate of Cumberland, who could secure the return of eleven candidates, welcomed the suggestion that Pitt should enter Parliament for one of his seats, and, with a generosity none too common among owners of "pocket boroughs," offered him a seat at Appleby unconditionally, save that he (Pitt) was to resign his seat if his political views should in the future become opposed to those of his patron.[1]

To this condition even the proud son of Chatham could not demur; and, though the connection with what was practically a pocket borough could not be quite palatable to a reformer, yet

[1] As a rule, Lowther exacted strict obedience from his nominees. In 1788 he compelled them to vote against Pitt on the Regency Question.

he doubtless remembered that his father first entered Parliament as member for Old Sarum.

While we smile at the vagaries of the old system, which enabled " the great commoner" to begin his public career as representative of an untenanted mound, and his son as member for a town which he did not even visit, let us remember that occasionally it opened a door easily for a man of genius. Gladstone, in his Tory years, eulogized the system on these grounds;[1] and it is certainly remarkable that, besides the two Pitts, many other famous men used these stepping-stones. Burke, through most of his public life, was member for a pocket borough, Wendover or Malton; and Canning entered Parliament as member for a scarcely discoverable village, Newtown, in the Isle of Wight. Fox and Peel also entered Parliament by similar means. However quaintly the old order of things misrepresented the British people, it did now and then help to bring brilliant men to the front with a speed that is no longer possible. But it is noteworthy that young men of spirit took care to be soon quit of pocket boroughs.[2]

Appleby having duly registered the decree of Sir James Lowther at the close of 1780, Pitt took his seat in the House of Commons on 23rd January 1781. From that time to the very same day in the year 1806 when he breathed his last, he was to expend his life in strenuous efforts throughout a quarter of a century which comprised such events as the close of the American War, the new grouping of the Powers of Europe, the French Revolution, and the rise of Napoleon.

[1] Hansard, cliii, 1056, 1057.   [2] Porritt, i, 315-7.

CHAPTER IV

AT WESTMINSTER AND GOOSTREE'S

A series of undesigned changes brought the English Constitution to such a condition that satisfaction and impatience, the two great sources of political conduct, were both reasonably gratified by it.—SIR HENRY MAINE.

IN the present age, marked by peaceful relations between the different parts of the Empire and by complete accord between the sovereign and his people, it is difficult to realize the condition of public affairs at the time when Pitt entered Parliament. The war with the United States, France, Spain and Holland, threatened the ruin of the nation, and it further brought to a climax a constitutional crisis of great importance. That struggle had resulted in no small measure from the personal methods of rule of George III; and, despite the disastrous influence of that policy on the Empire, there was still the chance of its winning at Westminster.

The reason for this paradox is to be found in the composition of the House of Commons and in the character of the King. Ten years had elapsed since the publication of Burke's indictment, that, whereas in the previous century the distempers of monarchy had been the chief cause for fear, now the main apprehension centred in the distempers of Parliament.[1] The facts given above, and those soon to be set forth, will show that the danger was still acute. The rallying of practically the whole of the Tory party to the King's side, the division of the Whigs into two chief groups, neither of which had any definite programme, the enormous power which the monarch wielded over the members of the Lower House by means of "influence," and, last but not least, the revival of his prestige owing to the Lord George Gordon crisis, all served to strengthen his hand even against

[1] Burke, "Thoughts on the present Discontents" (1770).

76

reformers who struggled for peace abroad and economy and purity in the administration.

In fact, the disintegration of the party system and the corruption of the House of Commons had provided George III with a most favourable opportunity for realizing the ideals set forth in Bolingbroke's " Patriot King." The old parties had for the time lost their *raison d'être*. All but a few fossilized Tory squires had given up the cause of the Stuarts. The Whigs could no longer claim to be defenders of the House of Brunswick and the liberties of England. For more than a century they had settled down comfortably on the spoils of office, until the sight of their magnates affecting to slay the slain and battening on the nation's spoils aroused general resentment. Of this feeling the King had made dexterous use. In the name of the nation he claimed to set aside the parties and govern in the interests of the whole. As generally happens in such cases, he called into being another party, the King's Friends, which, under the guise of acting for the nation, gradually ensured the subservience of Parliament to the royal will. By dint of honours, places, and money, the new policy won its way, until, as we have seen, it could defy the efforts for Reform. To the eye of alarmed patriots it seemed that the House of Commons would soon be little more than a tool of the King, and that George III would succeed in the enterprise which had cost Charles I his head.

There were some grounds for these fears. George III was on the whole a more formidable opponent than the first Charles. While lacking the personal charm of the Stuart sovereign and his power of calling forth enthusiastic service, he far excelled him in common sense and the power of adapting means to ends. Both men believed thoroughly in their cause, struggled with obstinate persistence towards the goal, and yet showed great finesse in the use to which they put men and events. Outwardly and mentally, they had nothing in common. Yet the parallel between them is closer than would at first sight appear. In a political sense George III is a rather gross replica of Charles I. Even the highest of Anglicans has never been tempted to canonize him; for, in truth, he lived in a material age, and had too great a belief in material interests ever to be in danger of " martyrdom."

Here, perhaps, lay the real danger to the liberties of England in the decade, 1770-80. They are more likely to be undermined by an appeal to material interests than by an open attack. Charles was foolish enough to assail both the consciences and the pockets of his subjects. George left consciences alone, and made use of the pockets of the governing classes to achieve his ends. This sapping process was more likely to succeed than a hasty attack above ground. The policy of Charles I braced men to resistance; that of George III drugged and enervated them.[1] Early in the seventeenth century Parliament was the champion of the nation's liberties; now there was some fear that it might degenerate into a King's Council. Parliament is but the register of the nation's will; and torpor at St. Stephen's bespoke political deadness throughout the land. Here, perhaps, was the most threatening symptom of all. The attempt to manipulate Parliament could come near to success only in an age of high living and plain thinking. Even the disasters of the American War did not awaken England at once. Her monitor was sleeping the sleep of surfeit. What were defeats on the other side of the Atlantic to the members for the pocket boroughs who virtually controlled the House for the King's cause? To what effect was it that London and Westminster now and again chafed at the losses of the war, when those cities returned only eight members, as against Cornwall's forty-four? Episodes like those connected with the names of Wilkes and Lord George Gordon roused for a time storms of tropical violence; but when they died down there ensued long and enervating lulls. All went on once more as in a land of lotus-eaters, who scarcely heeded the dim mutterings that came across the western ocean. Even the disaster at Yorktown, which virtually ended the American War, did not thoroughly arouse the nation. Two months after the receipt of that news, Romilly wrote to a friend, " The nation seems fallen into a deep sleep." [2]

The distributor of the soporific fruit seemed to be equal to every emergency. Lord North was a coarse and heavy man, with a wide mouth, thick lips, and puffy cheeks, which seemed typical of his policy. He resembled Walpole in his knowledge of men's foibles and contempt of humanity. True, he excelled him in affability; but he signally fell behind him in the sterner qualities which master men and beat down obstacles. For eleven years

[1] For details of bribery see May, "Constitutional History," i, 313-27; Porritt, i, 414-20.

[2] " Life of Romilly," i, 141.

he had been chief Minister of the Crown, latterly much against his will; and for fourteen months more the imperious monarch was to hold him to his post.

With Lord North were associated in the year 1781 men who were fully contented with the task of supervising their own departments and the patronage belonging to them. The most noteworthy of these Ministers were Lord Thurlow, a man of low tastes and violent temper, but considerable gifts for intrigue, who acted officially as Lord Chancellor and unofficially as chief of " the King's friends"; Earl Bathurst, Lord President; Germain (Viscount Sackville), Secretary of State for the Colonies; Lord Townshend, Master of the Ordnance; Mr. Jenkinson (afterwards the Earl of Liverpool), Secretary at War; the Earl of Sandwich, First Lord of the Admiralty; the Earl of Carlisle, Lord-Lieutenant of Ireland; and Mr. William Eden (afterwards Lord Auckland), Chief Secretary at Dublin Castle. The personality of some of these men will appear more fitly in the sequel. Here we may note that they resembled highly paid confidential clerks, working under the general direction of the King, rather than responsible Ministers. Of collective action and responsibility there was little under Lord North.[1] George III acted on the principle that had guided the Caesars, *Divide et impera.*

Such, in brief, was the system and such were the men who now had to confront a world in arms. Apart from the interminable conflict in America, the area of strife was spreading in Europe; for the Dutch, incensed by our maritime policy, were on the point of declaring war. In India Hyder Ali was ravaging the Carnatic; and Britons, looking forth in fear from Madras, could see the clouds of smoke that told of his devastations. In the Mediterranean Gibraltar still stoutly held out against the Franco-Spanish forces, but our possession, Minorca, was soon to fall. In the Baltic the League of the Armed Neutrality held the sword dangling over Briton's commerce, and was kept from striking only by the skill of Sir James Harris, our envoy at St. Petersburg, in playing on the foibles of Catharine II.

Yet against most of these difficulties British energy ultimately made headway; and they did not at present disturb the course of events in Parliament, with which we are here more especially concerned. The Opposition was divided into two chief groups,

---

[1] " Memorials of Fox," ii, 37, 38.

which had not yet begun to coalesce under the pressure of national calamity. The larger of these was the official Whig party under the nominal leadership of the Marquis of Rockingham, an affable and tactful man, with little strength of character, formidable only from his connections with the great Whig Houses. Among his followers two men stood forth, of powers so great and varied as to claim our attention at once. These were Fox and Burke.

Charles James Fox (1749-1806), the second son of Lord Holland, was now in the prime of his powers. Nature had dowered him with gifts so rich and varied as not to have been seriously marred even by the dissipations into which his father had encouraged him to plunge before he left Eton. While at Hertford College, Oxford, he gave proofs of his eager, vivacious, lovable temperament, and imbibed that passion for the classics and for all great literature which was to be his solace through life. Well would it have been for him had this been his only passion; unfortunately he never shook off the vices contracted in youth. His amour with Mrs. Armstead was notorious and avowed. Equally harmful was his mania for gambling. Many a time he ruined his speeches in the House by the fatigue or annoyance due to the losses of an all-night sitting at Brooks's. But whether he lost or won, whether caressed by Ministers in Parliament or turned out of his rooms in St. James's Street by Jews and bailiffs,[1] he was ever beloved, even by those whom he belaboured in the House.

His oratorical gifts were the outcome of a powerful mind, and they were enhanced by a melodious voice and forcible action. Perhaps the greatest charm of his speeches was their ease and naturalness. He spoke as if without premeditation, and at times he indulged in repetitions and digressions to an unpardonable extent. But all such faults and occasional carelessness in the choice of words scarcely lessened the effect of his efforts, which seemed to his hearers to be above all art. The unfailing vigour of thought, the power with which he could first recapitulate the arguments of his opponents and then tear them in pieces, and the good humour, which rarely left him even in his most scornful moods, served alike to convince and captivate the House. He was the prince of debaters, surpassing even Chatham himself in ease, wit, skill, and versatility, though lacking that awe-inspiring

---

[1] Selwyn, p. 140.

faculty that swayed Parliament as with a Jove-like frown. The years 1780-82 saw him at the height of his powers. Grattan afterwards remarked that no one could realize the force of Fox's oratory who had not heard him before his unnatural coalition with Lord North in 1783, after which event he always seemed on the defensive: "the mouth still spoke great things, but the swell of soul was no more."[1] How great must have been his blunders and indiscretions, both in public and private life, to have blighted a career of so transcendent a promise.

The figure of Edmund Burke belongs rather to the sphere of literature and political philosophy than to that of political action. Great in thought and great in his powers of oratory, he yet failed to impress the House of Commons, or the public at large; his speeches were too ornate, too overburdened with learning and reasoning, to please an audience that is plain, practical, and apt to be impressed more by the speaker himself than by the fullness of his arguments or the beauty of his style. In a word, Burke lacked the indefinable gift which Chatham, Fox, and Mirabeau so abundantly possessed—that of personality. His figure had not the forceful massiveness of that of Fox, and it wanted the dignity of the younger Pitt. Moreover his voice was harsh, and his action clumsy. His philosophic love of wedding facts to principles often led him to soar to heights where the question at issue appeared like a speck and votes a vulgar impertinence. Worst fault of all, his speeches were far too long. The fullness and richness which delights us to-day then had the effect of emptying the House. The result of it all was the decline of his influence and the increase of his irritability, Celtic vivacity leading him more than once shrilly to chide friends who sought to pull him back to his seat. These failings, together with the number of his impecunious relatives, probably explain why he never attained to Cabinet rank. In a subordinate office in the year 1783 he showed signal want of tact and discernment. Thus, in contrasting the effect produced by the perusal of his great orations with that which gained him the nickname of the dinner-bell of the House, one is reminded of the truth of the bitter line levelled at him by Goldsmith:

And to party gave up what was meant for mankind.

The other group, which rivalled the official Whigs in the zeal

---

[1] " Reminiscences of Charles Butler," i, 172.

of its opposition to Lord North, was that of the former followers of
Chatham. They had neither organization nor a programme; but
in general they inherited the imperial sentiments and non-parti-
san traditions of that great leader. They were less eager than the
Rockingham group for parliamentary reform and the limiting of
the royal prerogative; but, like the Girondins of the French
Revolution, the indefiniteness of their aims left much liberty of
action to their following; and Pitt, who naturally attached himself to this group, rivalled Fox in his zeal for Reform, both
economic and parliamentary.

The leader of the Chathamites was the Earl of Shelburne, who
had been driven into opposition by the arbitrary conduct of the
King at the time of the Wilkes affair. The estimates of his
character are very diverse. Burke wrote of him privately in 1783
as "this wicked man, and no less weak and stupid than false and
hypocritical," his chief crime being that of breaking in pieces the
Whig party. Few persons would have gone so far as the vehement
Irishman, who, on these lower levels, allowed party passion to
dull his eagle glance. Shelburne was one of the *grands seigneurs*
and political thinkers of the time. Polite and courtly, he dazzled
men by the splendour of his hospitality. In his library he shone
as a scholar and philosopher, and his conversation was the index
of his keen and supple intellect. In public life he showed that
he never lacked courage. Yet there was always something wanting about Shelburne. His speech and manner passed so quickly
and easily from the affable to the severe as to beget feelings of
distrust. His enemies accused him of duplicity and dubbed him
Malagrida, a well-known Portuguese Jesuit.[1]

We may note here that Pitt either shared or deferred to the
general feeling about Shelburne when he omitted him from his
Cabinet in December 1783.

Some of the specific charges against Shelburne (and most of
them are vague) have vanished now that the mists of passion,
amidst which he ever moved, have cleared away.[2] It is the lot of
some men to arouse undeserved dislike or distrust, owing to
unfortunate mannerisms. Yet it is certain that England owes

---

[1] Wraxall, "Memoirs," ii, 62; G. Rose, "Diaries," i, 28.

[2] Lecky, "Hist. of England in the XVIIIth Cent.," iv, 228-34, does not
absolve Shelburne of the charge of duplicity in the matter of the negotiations
for peace; but Sir G. C. Lewis, "Administrations of Great Britain," 31-48,
minimizes the importance of the point at issue.

much to the earl. He was one of the first to espouse the Free Trade principles of Adam Smith; he was chiefly responsible for the terms of peace of 1782-3; and the admiration of Benjamin Franklin for him largely conduced to the signature of the preliminaries with the United States. Posterity has therefore accorded to him a far higher place than was allowed by the jealousy or pettiness of his contemporaries. Such was the leader to whom Pitt attached himself.

On 25th January 1781 Shelburne protested manfully against the overbearing conduct of our Government in ordering the capture of Dutch merchantmen before the outbreak of war, and inveighed against the policy of the Ministry as fatal to liberty and to the welfare of the Empire. Finally he declared that the tactics of Government had proved that the conquest of the American colonies, if it could be accomplished, would entail fatal results at home; that he would be better pleased to see his country free, though curtailed in power and wealth, than acquiring greatness, if greatness were to be purchased at the expense of her constitution and liberty. The speech rang true to the traditions of Chatham; and it awoke responsive echoes in the breast of his son.[1]

Within the space of five weeks Pitt proved that his support was of the highest value. In a maiden speech, which perhaps bears away the palm from the first efforts of the greatest orators of all time, he gave proof of those astonishing powers which nature seemed to have implanted in a state of maturity. Practice and experience were to perfect them; but they then left on all his hearers an impression of wonder as at something almost supernatural in a youth of twenty-one years. This feeling was all the more natural as the speech dealt with economic subjects, which Wilberforce regarded as " of a low and vulgarizing quality." [2]

We must pause here to notice that the topic of economy was at that time of burning interest. On the whole it excited more general attention than the subject of parliamentary reform. In fact the latter was insisted on by practical men mainly with the view of stopping the frightful waste that resulted from sinecures, jobs, and other forms of corruption in the public service. Rigid doctrinaires like Major Cartwright might dilate on the heavenborn right of every man to have a vote, or depict the beauty of

---

[1] Fitzmaurice, " Shelburne," iii, 118-21.
[2] " Private Papers of W. Wilberforce," 79.

an electoral system which enlisted the virtuous energies of every citizen and called on him to renew Parliament every year, that being the natural time of renewal of all things.[1] A still stiffer theorist, Jebb, might go further and insist on the election of a new Parliament for each session. Together they might call for the ballot, equal electoral areas, and payment of members. Yet their arguments would have fallen on deaf ears but for the strain of war taxes, the dullness of trade, and the blunderings of placemen high in office. When London, Bristol, and Yorkshire felt the pinch of hard times, national expenditure became a matter of the most urgent concern.

It was in support of Burke's proposals for the better regulation of the King's Civil List and for abolishing several sinecures that Pitt made his maiden speech in the House (26th February 1781). At once he lifted the subject to a high level. The measure, he said, would have come with more grace, and with more benefit to the public service, had it sprung from the royal breast. Ministers ought themselves to have proposed it, thereby showing that His Majesty desired to participate in the suffering of the Empire.

They ought to consult the glory of their royal master, and seat him in the hearts of his people, by abating from magnificence what is due to necessity. . . . The abridgment of useless and unnecessary expense can be no abatement of royalty. Magnificence and grandeur are not inconsistent with retrenchment and economy, but, on the contrary, in a time of necessity and of common exertion, solid grandeur is dependent on the reduction of expense; and it is the general sentiment and observation of the House that economy is at this hour essentially necessary to national salvation.

He next ventured on an argument scarcely consistent with the assumption of the royal graciousness and generosity touched on in his first period by asserting that the most important object of the bill was

The reduction of the influence of the Crown—that influence which the last Parliament, by an express resolution, had declared to be increasing, and that it ought to be diminished—an influence which was more to be dreaded, because more secret in its attacks, and more concealed in its operations than the power of prerogative.

---

[1] Cartwright, "Take your Choice" (1776). In 1780 Cartwright founded "The Society for promoting Constitutional Information," the first of the modern clubs that was purely political.

After referring briefly to this delicate subject, he held up to scorn those who ridiculed the proposal on the ground that it would effect a saving of only £200,000 a year; as if the calamities of the present crisis were too great to be benefited by economy: as if, when millions were being spent, there was no need to think of thousands! Finally he declared that the Civil List had been granted by Parliament to His Majesty, not for his personal gratification, but in order

to support the power and the interests of the Empire, to maintain its grandeur, and pay the judges and the foreign ministers, and to maintain justice. . . . The people, who granted that revenue, under the circumstances of the occasion, were justified in resuming a part of it under the pressing demand of an altered situation. They clearly felt their right; but they exercised it with pain and regret. They approached the throne with hearts afflicted at the necessity of applying for retrenchment of the royal gratifications; but the request was at once loyal and submissive. It was justified by policy, and His Majesty's compliance with the request was inculcated by prudence as well as by affection.[1]

Admiration of the perfect manner in which the speech was delivered seems to have blinded contemporaries to its importance as a political pronouncement. Certainly in both respects it is remarkable. No speech ever won more general and more immediate praise. Burke declared the young orator to be not merely a chip of the old block but the old block itself. Charles James Fox hurried up to offer his congratulations on this oratorical triumph, and further showed his regard by proposing Pitt as a member of Brooks's club—a connection which he maintained unbroken through life. Lord North described the oration as the best first speech that he had ever heard; and another member of the House, Storer, commenting on the self-possession of the young speaker, which was far removed from "improper assurance," remarked that there was not a word or a look that one would have wished to correct.[2] In an age when dignity of diction and grace of deportment were deemed essential to the success of

---

[1] "The Speeches of William Pitt" (4 vols., 1806), i, 1-7.

[2] "George Selwyn: his Letters and his Life," p. 132 (Storer to Lord Carlisle, Feb. 28, 1781). He adds that Woodfall reportedt he debates "almost always faithfully." I therefore see no reason for refraining, as Earl Stanhope did, from citing many passages of his speeches, on the ground that they were very imperfectly reported.

a speech—that was the time when Windham used to spend hours beforehand in framing elegant *juncturae* for his periods—the verdicts quoted above imply in a young speaker the possession of a profusion of gifts and graces no less remarkable than the maturity of judgment which harmonized them.

Alas, the reader of to-day cannot fully realize the witchery of his diction, instinct with the fervour of youth, but balanced by the sagacity of manhood. The printed word can never reveal the nature of the spell cast on listeners by a noble countenance, harmonious gestures, musical cadences, and the free outpouring of inspiring thoughts. No great speeches, except those of a preeminently literary quality, such as shines in the stately rhetoric of Burke, can be appreciated apart from the speakers. It is the man who gives life to the words. A fervent admirer of Chatham's oratory summed up his chief impression in the suggestive remark that there was something in the speaker finer than his words; "that the man was infinitely greater than the orator." This must be so, if the speaker is to keep attention on tip-toe, ever on the look-out for new effects and charms. Hope is a necessary element in all admiration. The hearer, to be enthralled, must have been wafted up to that state of ecstasy wherein delight at present beauties is intensified by the expectation of other charms yet to come. Shakespeare has once for all time portrayed this mental bliss in the young and eager love of Florizel for Perdita:

> What you do
> Still betters what is done. When you speak, sweet,
> I'ld have you do it ever.

Some such wealth of gifts the Commons of Britain discerned in Pitt in that springtide of hope. Theirs was to be a rich harvest of joy. Ours is but a lean aftermath.

The reader, who naturally thinks more about the matter of this speech than the manner of its delivery, will be most impressed by the boldness of some of the arguments. That a new member should venture to remind Parliament and the nation of the King's control over the Civil List being that of a steward, not of a proprietor, was daring enough; but it is startling to find the future champion of the Crown asserting that the nation could *resume* at least a part of what it had granted. There is no essential difference between this plea and the dictum of Rousseau (used so effectively by the French Revolutionists against the

King and the Church) that the hypothetical contract once framed between prince and people empowered the latter at any time to enter into possession of property which was held merely in trust on their behalf. The sentiments expressed in Pitt's first speech enable us to gauge the astonishment of the world when the young orator at the close of 1783 became first Minister of the Crown.

His second speech, delivered on 31st May, was perhaps less effective than the first, though it marks an advance in argumentative power and the handling of details. Colonel Barré had proposed that the commissioners who supervised the public accounts should be chosen from the House of Commons. After a hostile speech from Lord North, Pitt rose to support the motion. He pointed out how essential this proposal was for the maintenance of the power of the Commons. He continued thus:

Every branch of the legislature has something peculiar to distinguish and to characterize it; and that which at once gives the character and elevation of the Commons House of Parliament is that they hold the strings of the national purse, and are entrusted with the great important power, first of granting the money, and then of correcting the expenditure. To delegate this right, then, is a violation of what gives them their chief consequence in the legislature, and what, above all other privileges, they cannot surrender or delegate without a violent breach of the constitution.

Tracking the Prime Minister into detail after detail, he finally begged the House to pass the motion as necessary for the prosperity of the land and as a pledge of further reforms.

But (said he) if the motion is rejected, and the old and vicious system of government is in every point tenaciously adhered to, the freedom of the people and the independence of this House must be buried in the same grave with the power, the opulence and the glory of the Empire.

Men so diverse in character as George Selwyn and the young reformer, Wilberforce, were loud in praise of the speech. The latter, though he regretfully voted against Pitt, declared him to be "a ready-made orator"; while the old place-hunter and *roué* found in it, "*du sel et du piquant à pleines mains. Charles* [Fox] *en fut enchanté.*"[1] Horace Walpole praised the speech in these terms:

[1] *Ibid.*, p. 143.

The young William Pitt has again displayed paternal oratory. The other day, on the commission of accounts, he answered Lord North, and tore him limb from limb. If Charles Fox could feel, one should think such a rival, with an unspotted character, would rouse him. What if a Pitt and Fox should again be rivals. . . . As young Pitt is modest too, one would hope some genuine English may revive.

So far as we know, not a single vote was gained by this oration, for the division list showed ninety-eight against Barré's motion and only forty-two for it. A Scottish member, Ferguson of Pitfour, a faithful supporter of Henry Dundas, on one occasion confessed that he had only once ventured to vote on his own conviction, and that was the worst vote he ever gave. Many members, while lacking the courage and wit to make the admission, acted with equal fidelity to their own interests; and hence even the best speeches rarely won over votes. In the present case no one answered, and no one could answer, Pitt's arguments; yet they had no effect on the docile flock which trooped into the lobby at the heels of Lord North. By a majority of forty-three the Commons decided that the King should not be requested to show his benevolence and disinterestedness.

The third effort of the young orator had no more effect. It came about, apparently without premeditation, in the course of a debate on the motion of Fox for the conclusion of an immediate peace with our American colonies (12th June). In the first part of his speech Pitt warmly controverted two members who claimed that Chatham had sympathized with the war; and, in his eagerness to clear his father's memory, he averred that his (Chatham's) conduct on this subject had been uniform and consistent. After this doubtful assertion he stated his own views in a most trenchant style. Falling upon Lord Westcote, who had declared the war to be a holy war, he uttered these remarkable words:

I am persuaded, and will affirm, that it is a most accursed, wicked, barbarous, cruel, unnatural, unjust, and diabolical war. It was conceived in injustice; it was nurtured and brought forth in folly;[1] its footsteps are marked with blood, slaughter, persecution and devastation; in truth everything which goes to constitute moral depravity and human turpitude are to be found in it. It is pregnant with misery of every

---

[1] These images are curiously like those used by Lord Shelburne on 25th January 1781. See Fitzmaurice, "Shelburne," iii, 120.

kind. The mischiefs, however, recoil on the unhappy people of this country, who are made the instruments by which the wicked purposes of its authors are effected.

He continued in the same vehement strain, and seems to have impressed the House less than before, Selwyn giving as his verdict that he was "a promising young man." The speech does, indeed, sound somewhat forced; and its declamation seems too turgid to be effective. On this occasion "the King's cause" once more triumphed, by 172 votes to 99.

In the middle of July, after the close of the session, Pitt went on the western circuit, but the notices of his speeches are very meagre. The only reference that I have found to this episode in his life is in a letter of 29th August 1781 to his Cambridge friend, Meeke:

I have this circuit amassed the immense sum of thirty guineas without the least expense either of sense or knowledge. . . . I shall return to town with the fullest intention of devoting myself to Westminster Hall and getting as much money as I can, notwithstanding such avocations as the House of Commons, and (which is a much more dangerous one) Goostree's itself. Adieu.

As a proof that Pitt did not merely play with the legal profession, I may quote this sentence from his letter of June 1782 to Meeke:

I have for many reasons chosen to be only a friend, without being a member, of Shelburne's Administration, and am at least as likely to continue a lawyer as you are to commence one.[1]

The second letter belongs to a time when the prospects of advancement were unpromising, and when, therefore, Pitt devoted much of his time to the select and charming club at Goostree's. As there is a widespread impression that he was a political automaton, who never unbent save under the spell of Bacchus, it will be well to turn our attention to his social life in London and at Wimbledon. It cannot be said that he ever felt the full charm of London—

The quick forge and working-house of thought.

Brought up in the aristocratic seclusion of Hayes and Burton

[1] Both letters are among the Chevening MSS.

Pynsent, and in Pretyman's prim coterie at Cambridge, he had no experience of the varied jostling life which the Londoner loves: and nature had not dowered him with the adaptability that makes up for the defects of training. Therefore he ever remained somewhat of a stranger in London. He was at home in Downing Street, and still more so in his own select club, or at Hayes, Wimbledon, or Holwood; but London never laid her spell on him, and his life was the poorer for it. He reminds us somewhat of that character in Dickens's " Great Expectations," who, though naive and jovial, when he entered his suburban retreat in Walworth Road and the mimic castle at the end of the garden, yet always fixed his features in chilling reserve when he went forth citywards. So, too, there were two Pitts, the austere man of affairs, and the lovable, delightful friend. London alone could have mixed up the two men and produced a sociable compound; but this was not to be.

Lincoln's Inn and the law did little towards unbending him; though the story, recounted in the previous chapter, of his intellectual duel with Gibbon at a dinner in Lincoln's Inn during the Gordon Riots shows that even then he had the power of keen and witty repartee which gained him the victory over an admitted autocrat of the table. Why these gifts did not draw him into general society is hard to say. Probably his shyness and awkwardness, on which Wilberforce lays so much stress, held him aloof.

Certainly the temptations of the West End had for him only a passing allurement. He felt no desire, besides having no means, to associate with the gambling *cohue* that played at Brooks's or Almack's. His preference for bright and entertaining talkers naturally linked him with those who had sufficient mental resources within themselves to scorn the usually dull cliques whose interest in life begins and ends with card tables. So far as opportunities had offered at Cambridge, he had cultivated conversation as a fine art; and now in the West End he found several of his University friends who welcomed him to a somewhat wider circle. It included about twenty-five young men, of whom the most noteworthy were Lords Althorpe, Apsley, G. Cavendish, Duncannon, Euston, Graham, and Lennox; as well as the following who were to become peers: Mr. Pratt (Marquis Camden), St. John (Lord St. John), Bridgeman (Lord Bradford), Morris Robinson (Lord Rokeby), W. Grenville (Lord

Grenville), Pepper Arden (Lord Alvanley), and R. Smith (Lord Carrington).

That was the age when the bestowal of titles was one of the means of influence used by the Crown for the defence of its prerogatives. Wilberforce late in life remarked that more than half of the Peers had received their titles during his lifetime, and certainly, if we look at the circle of Pitt's friends in 1781, we find that only he and seven others remained commoners. They were Bankes, Edwards (afterwards Sir Gerard Noel), Marsham, T. Steele, General Smith, Wilberforce and Windham, a friend of somewhat later date.

These and a few others, about thirty in all, formed what might be termed Pitt's Club. They met first at a house in Pall Mall, but afterwards occupied rooms in the premises of a man named Goostree, which later on were used as the Shakespeare Gallery.[1] Opposition to Lord North's Ministry was one of the shibboleths of this coterie; but in pre-revolutionary days, when the merely political club was almost unknown, conviviality held the first place at Goostree's. One who was in George Selwyn's set evid-ently thought the ideals aimed at in Pitt's little society too good for London; for he wrote, at the close of 1781: "Goostree's is a small society of young men in Opposition, and they are very nice in their admissions; as they discourage gaming as much as possible, their club will not do any harm to Brooks's, and probably not subsist a great while." In February 1782 Selwyn himself refers to Pitt as having formed a "society of young ministers who are to fight under his banner . . . and they assemble at Goostree's." Clearly, then, this club was political, at least in part. Pitt spent much of his time there, supping at the club every night during the winter of 1780-81; and there it was that he became intimate with William Wilberforce, the most fascinating of his friends.

The young and brilliant member for Hull was a living proof of the triumph which mind can win over physical disadvantages. In person he was slight and bent, and he early suffered from that weakness of the eyes which hampered him through life. Yet, "bodkin" though he was, his quickness of mind, the silvery tones of his voice, the wit that sparkled in his speech, and his uniform geniality and kindliness gained for him a continuous

[1] "Life of Wilberforce," i, 17.

round of social triumphs. His singing possessed a natural charm which drew from the Prince of Wales the statement that he would come at any time to hear Wilberforce sing. Equally attractive was his power of mimicking any public character; but what most of all endeared him to his friends was the genial raillery of his conversation, his power of lively repartee, and the chivalry which shone in all his words and deeds. Mme de Staël afterwards declared him to be the best talker among all the Englishmen she had known; and in that art of the *salons* the exuberant Genevese was an exacting connoisseur. She, however, could not know the warmth of feeling which animated that slight frame, or the sensitiveness of conscience which was to make him one of the chief uplifting forces of the age. Towards the close of his life he expressed regret that in his youth he had made intellectual conversation his all in all.[1] But regret was surely needless, when that gift attracted to him the young statesman whose life at some points he helped to inspire and elevate. Both of them, indeed, were artists in words; and the free play of mind on mind must have helped to strengthen those oratorical powers which were to be devoted to the service of their country and of mankind.

From the pages of Wilberforce's diary we catch a glimpse, tantalizingly brief, alas, of Pitt as a boon companion, losing among his intimates that shyness which outsiders mistook for pride.

He was the wittiest man I ever knew, and what was quite peculiar to himself, had at all times his wit under entire control. Others appeared struck by the unwonted association of brilliant images; but every possible combination of ideas seemed always present to his mind, and he could at once produce whatever he desired. I was one of those who met to spend an evening in memory of Shakespeare at the Boar's Head, East Cheap. Many professed wits were present, but Pitt was the most amusing of the party, and the readiest and most apt in the required allusions. He entered with the same energy into all our different amusements; we played a good deal at Goostree's, and I well remember the intense earnestness that he displayed when joining in these games of chance. He perceived their increasing fascination, and soon after suddenly abandoned them for ever.

This passage, together with its context, is interesting in more

[1] *Ibid.*, v, 292.

ways than one. Firstly it shows that the fashionable vice of the
age had crept into Goostree's more than was known by outsiders;
or else Selwyn's reference to the club belonged to a later period,
when Pitt's resolve to have done with gambling, and the remorse
of Wilberforce at having suddenly won a large sum from impecunious friends, had availed to curb the passion for it in their
society. The difference of the two friends in temperament is
equally noteworthy. In Wilberforce the resolve to break away
from gambling was the first sign of awakening of a sensitive conscience, which, though dulled by gaieties, was thenceforth to
assert itself more and more and finally to win over the whole of
his energies.

Pitt also felt the fascination of play in a manner which shows
the eagerness of his animal instincts; but the awakening in his
case seems to have been due to self-respect and also to a keen
sense of what he owed to the State. How could he, who had
early vowed himself to the service of his country, dull his powers
and tarnish his name by indulgence in an insidious and enslav-
ing vice? The career of Charles James Fox, we may believe, had
already been a warning to the young aspirant. In any case, by
an exercise of that imperious will, which controlled even his
vehement impulses, he crushed at once and for ever those
entangling desires, and came forth fancy-free from that Circean
domain, saved by his ennobling resolve to serve England.

In another sense—a less important one, it is true—Pitt was
the most unfortunate man of his age. All his friends agreed
that he was a delightful talker and the most charming of
companions. But there their information ends. Not one of them
had the Boswellian love of detail which enables us to peer right
into the heart of Johnson, and discern the loves and hates, the
prejudices and envyings, the whims and fancies which swayed it.
A man can never be known unless we have, not merely his great
speeches, but also his small talk. That of Pitt must have been of
singular charm, not only from the richness of his mental gifts,
but also from the width of the culture which informed them. In
learning he equalled the best of his compeers at Cambridge; and
we may imagine that his vivid knowledge of the life of Greece
and Rome lent to his comparisons and references a grace which
could be appreciated by few *raconteurs* of to-day. I have already
referred to the stories circulated by those who set themselves to
talk and write him down to their own level, that he studied the

classics merely in order to provide elegant tags to his speeches. The theme has been embroidered by certain admirers of Fox, who picture the Whig statesman as the disinterested lover of Greece and Rome, and Pitt as a kind of money-grubbing paramour. If these persons, instead of copying from the many malicious stories of that time, would investigate for themselves, they would see through the partisan spitefulness of all such tales. Fortunately, Pitt's copies of the classics preserved at Orwell Park reveal signs, not only of his frequent perusal of them, but of the pleasure which it brought, as evinced by marginal comments. Away, then, with the Foxite myth of the classical tags!

The passage from Wilberforce's Diary cited above also shows Pitt to have been well primed with Shakespearean lore, and to have had the mental agility and tact which could cull the right flower from that rich garner. Ill though we could spare any of Pitt's oratorical efforts, I doubt whether we would not give up any one of his speeches if we could have in return a full record of some of the evenings spent by him and his friends at Goostree's or the Boar's Head.

Concerning his ordinary talk we only know that he delighted his family by his gaiety, even amidst the heaviest cares of state. In that terrible year 1793, when England and France had closed in the death grapple, Lady Chatham refers to his " ease and gay spirits "; and she speaks of him as not looking like a man on whom rested the destinies of kingdoms. A further sentence explains the source of this buoyancy of spirits: " The uprightness of his intentions and the strength of his mind saved him from feeling any oppression from the weight upon him." [1]

Here we see the secret of that cheerfulness which charmed his friends. His high spirits were in part, no doubt, bequeathed to him by the ever confident Chatham; but their even flow was also the outcome of his own conscious rectitude. Hence also there came the brightness and sincerity which shone in Pitt's conversation as also in his life. Another characteristic on which Wilberforce insisted was his strict truthfulness, which his friend attributed to his self-respect and to the moral purity of his nature. Yet there was no taint of priggishness about it. Wilberforce describes him as "remarkably cheerful and pleasant, full of wit and playfulness, neither, like Mr. Fox, fond of arguing a

[1] Ashbourne, p. 159

question, nor yet holding forth like some others [Windham is here hinted at]. He was always ready to hear others as well as to talk himself." [1]

Obviously, then, Pitt's conversation was free from some of the defects which mar the efforts of professional talkers. He never used the sledge-hammer methods by which Dr. Johnson too often won an unfair advantage; he scorned to make use of feigned incidents or grossly exaggerated accounts whereby many small wits gain a passing repute. His speech, in private as in public, seems to have resembled a limpid stream, the natural overflow of a mind richly stocked and a nature at once lively and affectionate.

Sometimes the stream raced and danced along, as appears from an entry in the diary of George Selwyn, in March 1782:

When I left the House, I left in one room a party of young men, who made me, from their life and spirits, wish for one night to be twenty. There was a tablefull of them drinking—young Pitt, Lord Euston, Berkley, North, etc., singing and laughing à gorge déployée: some of them sang very good catches; one Wilberforce, a M. of P., sang the best.

This is only one of many signs that nature had bestowed on Pitt social gifts and graces which under more favourable conditions would have made him the centre of a devoted circle of friends. True, he was too shy and modest to figure as a political Dr. Johnson; too natural to pose as did the literary lion of Strawberry Hill; too prudent to vie with Fox as the chief wit and gamester of a great club. But in his own way and in his own sphere he might have carried on those honourable traditions which have invested the life of St. Stephen's with literary and social charm, had not Chatham's premature forcing of his powers devitalized him before the start of a singularly early and exacting career. Here was the ill fortune of Pitt. Like all precocious natures he needed times of rest and recuperation before he reached his prime. He sought them in vain either at Hayes, Cambridge, or Westminster. As we shall see, the very unusual state of English politics down to 1789 would have made the accession of Fox, the unofficial representative of the Prince of Wales, a public misfortune; and soon afterwards there occurred

---

[1] " Private Papers of Wilberforce," 68.

in quick succession the disputes with Spain, Russia, and France, which, after two false alarms, ended in a tremendous war. In such a period how could a delicate man rise to the height of his faculties, either political or social? On both sides of his nature Pitt showed signs of the most brilliant promise; but the premature and incessant strain of public duty robbed him and his country of the full fruition.

CHAPTER V

THE PEACE WITH AMERICA

Since the accession of our most gracious sovereign to the throne, we have seen a system of government, which may well be called a reign of experiments.—JUNIUS, Letter to the Duke of Grafton, 8th July 1769.

James I was contemptible, but he did not lose an America. His eldest grandson sold us, his younger lost us—but we kept ourselves. Now we have run to meet the ruin—and it is coming.—HORACE WALPOLE, 27th November 1781.

I N the autumn of the year 1781 occurred a series of events which brought Pitt for a time into open opposition to the King. As we have seen, he had not hesitated to invite George III to enter the path of Economical Reform which was peculiarly odious to him. But now the divergence of their convictions seemed hopeless. For if Pitt inherited the firmness of the Pitts and Grenvilles, George III summed up in his person the pertinacity characteristic of the Guelfs and the Stuarts. The gift of firmness, the blending of which with foresight and intelligence produces the greatest of characters, was united in George III with narrowness of vision, absorption in the claims of self, and a pedantic clinging to the old and traditional. Coming of a tough stock, and being admittedly slow and backward, he needed an exceptionally good education in order to give him width of outlook and some acquaintance with the lessons of history. But unfortunately his training was of the most superficial character. Lord Waldegrave, his governor, found him at the age of fourteen "uncommonly full of prejudices, contracted in the nursery, and improved by bedchamber women and pages of the back stairs."[1] From these cramping influences he was never to shake himself free. The death of his father, Frederick, Prince of Wales, in 1751, left him under the influence of his mother, an ambitious and

[1] Lord Waldegrave's "Memoirs," p. 63.

intriguing woman, who instilled into him the desire to govern as well as reign. That advice accorded with the leanings of his nature, which, though torpid, was yet masterful.

As will appear in the sequel, George III possessed characteristics which made him a formidable opponent. His lack of mental endowments was partly made up by his insight into character, and still more by his determined will. If he was dull, he was dogged—a quality dear to the Britons of that age. His private virtues, his homely good sense, a bearing that was generally genial, and a courage which never quailed, made him in many ways a pattern king for a plain people in ordinary times.

Unhappily for him and his people, the times were extraordinary. Like his contemporary, Louis XVI of France, he needed an intellectual equipment wider than that which goes to make a model country squire. In a period remarkable beyond all others for the infiltration of new ideas, neither of these unfortunate monarchs had the least skill in reading the signs of the times. But, while the royal hunter of Versailles was so conscious of his defects as frequently to lean too much on advisers and therefore waver, his equally Boeotian brother of Windsor had an absolute belief in his prognostications (save sometimes on foreign affairs) and scorned to change his mind. This last peculiarity appears in a letter which he wrote to Pitt on 2nd March 1797. After chiding his Prime Minister for complying too much with the Opposition, he continues:

My nature is quite different. I never assent till I am convinced what is proposed is right, and then I keep [sic]; then I never allow that to be destroyed by afterthoughts, which on all subjects tend to weaken, never to strengthen, the original proposal.[1]

This is doubtless sound advice, provided that the first decision emanates from a statesmanlike brain. How ruinous the results can be if that resolve be the outcome of a narrow, proud, and self-complacent understanding, the fortunes of the British Empire in the years 1774-83 may testify. Those who love to dwell on the "might-have-beens" of history, may imagine what would have happened if the mild and wavering King of France had ruled Great Britain, and if our pertinacious sovereign had

[1] Pitt MSS., 103.

been in the place of the hapless Bourbon whose vacillations marred everything in the memorable spring of 1789.

In certain matters George III showed great ability. If he was not a statesman, he was a skilled intriguer. Shelburne, himself no tyro in that art, rated the King's powers high, stating that "by the familiarity of his intercourse he obtained your confidence, procured from you your opinion of different public characters, and then availed himself of this knowledge to sow dissension."[1] Further, the skill and pertinacity with which he pulled the wires at elections is astonishing. No British monarch has equalled him in his knowledge of the means by which classes and individuals could be "got at." Some of his letters on these subjects, especially that on the need of making up for the "bad votes" cast for Fox in the famous Westminster Election of 1784, tempt one to think that George III missed his vocation, which should have been that of electioneering agent of the Tory party. In truth he almost succeeded in making Windsor and St. James's the headquarters of that faction.[2]

Despite his private virtues, he rarely attached men to him by the ties of affection and devotion—the mark of a narrow and selfish nature. His relations to his sons were of the coolest; and all his Ministers, except, perhaps, Addington, left him on terms that bordered on dislike if not hostility. The signs of the royal displeasure (as Junius justly observed to the Duke of Grafton) were generally in proportion to the abilities and integrity of the Minister. This singular conduct may be referred to the profound egotism of the King which led him to view politics solely from his own standpoint, to treat government as the art of manipulating men by means of titles, places, and money,[3] and to regard his Ministers as confidential clerks, trustworthy only when they distrusted one another. The union of the Machiavellian traits with signal virtue and piety in private life is a riddle that can be explained only by his narrow outlook, which regarded all means as justifiable for the "right cause," and believed all opponents to be wicked or contemptible. In fact, the narrowing lens of his vision alike stunted and distorted all opponents until they appeared an indistinguishable mass. A curious instance of facility in jumbling together even irreconcilable opposites

---

[1] Nicholl, "Recollections of George III," i, 389.   [2] Porritt, i, 409-15.

[3] See May's "Const. History," i, 315 et seq. for the increase of the Secret Service Fund under George III.

appeared in his remark to Lord Malmesbury in 1793 that the
Illuminés (the Jacobins of Germany) "were a sect invented by
the Jesuits to overthrow all governments and all order."[1] Such
was the mental equipment of the monarch on whom now rested
the fate of the Empire.

On Sunday, 25th November 1781, news arrived in London
which sealed the doom of Lord North's Ministry. Cornwallis,
with rather less than seven thousand men, had surrendered to
the Franco-American forces at Yorktown. The blow was
not heavy enough to daunt a really united kingdom. On the
Britain of that year, weary of the struggle, and doubtful alike
of its justice and its utility, the effect was decisive. Lord
North, on hearing the news from his colleague, Lord George
Germain, received it "as he would have taken a bullet through
his breast." He threw up his arms and paced up and down the
room, exclaimed wildly: "Oh, God! it is all over." This, if we
may believe Wraxall,[2] was the ejaculation of the man who latterly had been the unwilling tool of his sovereign in the coercion
of the American colonists.

While Lord North, the Parliament, and the nation were
desirous of ending the war, the King still held to his oft expressed opinion, that it would be total ruin for Great Britain to
give way in the struggle, seeing that a great Power which begins
to "moulder" must be annihilated.[3] He therefore kept North
to his post, and allowed the King's speech for the forthcoming
autumn session to be only slightly altered; the crucial sentence
ran as follows:

No endeavours have been wanting on my part to extinguish that
spirit of rebellion which our enemies have found means to foment and
maintain in the colonies, & to restore to my deluded subjects in
America that happy and prosperous condition which they formerly
derived from a due obedience to the laws; but the late misfortune in
that quarter calls loudly for your firm concurrence and assistance to
frustrate the designs of our enemies, equally prejudicial to the real interests of America and to those of Great Britain.

The gauntlet thus defiantly flung down was taken up with
spirit by Fox and Burke, who even ventured to threaten with
impeachment the Secretary for the Colonies, Germain, and the

---

[1] Malmesbury Diaries, iii, 8.   [2] Wraxall, ii, 434-5 (3rd edit.).
[3] "Letters of George III to Lord North," ii, 336.

First Lord of the Admiralty, the Earl of Sandwich. This was unfair. They were little more than puppets moved by the King; and he was responsible ultimately for the bad condition of the army and navy, and was sole cause for the continuance of the war. No one imagined (so Romilly wrote on 4th December 1781) that the war would go on after the disaster at Yorktown.[1]

In the ensuing debates on the King's speech, Pitt made an effective attack on Ministers, upbraiding them with the inconsistency of their statements and the obscurity in which they shrouded their plans. For himself, with his profound conviction as to the need of promptly terminating the war, he adjured them to state clearly what line of conduct they meant to pursue. This last challenge went home because the language of Ministers was openly inconsistent, that of the Lord Advocate, Dundas, being hardly different from the views held by the Opposition. In fact it was now said that there were three parties on the Government benches—the King's, Lord North's, and that of Dundas, shading off from war à outrance to something like conciliation with America.

Nevertheless, the House (as Fox wrote in his Journal) was "tenacious of places and pensions," and at first supported the Government by substantial majorities; but a typical placeman like Selwyn wrote early in December that if the measures and conduct of the Ministry were not changed, they were completely undone. Nervousness about his sinecure made the wit a true prophet. Not only was the majority breaking into groups, but the Opposition was acting well together. This again was a result of the Yorktown disaster. Only a few days previously, Shelburne, the leader of the Chathamites, had in vain proposed to the official chief of the Whigs, Rockingham, that they should unite their followers, so that there should be but two parties, ' that of the Crown and that of the people."

Now, however, as victory came in sight, the Opposition closed its ranks, while the once serried phalanx of placemen opposite began to split up from sheer panic. During this interesting time Pitt made another speech, which won high encomiums from Horace Walpole for its "amazing logical abilities." Equally notable was the alertness which fastened on a slight incident. In the midst of his tirade against the inconsistencies of Ministers,

[1] " Life of Romilly," i, 135.

North and Germain began to whisper together, while that wary
little placeman, Welbore Ellis, who was between them, bent
down his head to listen. At once Pitt exclaimed: " I will wait
until the unanimity is a little better restored. I will wait until
the Nestor of the Treasury has reconciled the difference between
the Agamemnon and the Achilles of the American War." [1]

Little by little Lord North's majority dwindled away. It sank
to a single vote on 22nd February 1782, when General Conway
brought forward a motion for the termination of the war. On
the renewal of the motion five days later, the House, amidst a
scene of great excitement, declared against North by 234 votes
to 215. The Ministry, under pressure from the King, held on
for a few days, and, on 8th March, even defeated a vote of
censure by a majority of ten.

Pitt, who was one of the tellers for the minority, had startled
the House, in the course of a fighting speech, by the following
notable words: " For myself, I could not expect to form part of
a new administration; but, were my doing so more within my
reach, I would never accept a subordinate situation." On the
authority of Admiral Keppel, his neighbour in the House, he is
said to have repented immediately of this declaration, and to
have wished to rise and explain or mitigate it. If so, the feeling
must surely have been only momentary. Pitt, as we have seen,
was essentially methodical. His feelings, his words, even his
lightest jests, were always completely under control. It is therefore impossible to regard so important a statement as due to the
whim of the moment, or to the exaggeration of which a nervous
or unskilful speaker is often guilty. Still less can we believe
that he seriously intended to explain away his words. So weak
an action would have been wholly repugnant to another of his
characteristics—pride. The declaration was probably the outcome of his unwavering self-confidence and of a belief that any
Ministry which could be formed must be short lived.

If so, his conduct was well suited to bring him to the front at
a time more opportune than the present. It was inconceivable
that a monarch so masterful and skilled in intrigue as George III
should long submit to be controlled by the now victorious Whig
families, whose overthrow had been his chief aim. To foment
the schisms in their ranks, and shelve them at the first possible

[1] Stanhope, i, 67.

time was an alternative far preferable to that of retiring to Hanover—a suggestion which he once more threw out to Lord North. When the struggle between Crown and Commons had come to its second phase, it would be time for a young member to take a leading place.

A crisis became imminent forthwith, on the House passing a declaration that it would "consider as enemies to His Majesty and to this country all who should advise or by any means attempt the further prosecution of offensive war on the continent of America." By this Act the Commons reasserted their undoubted right of controlling the prerogative of the Crown even in the question of peace or war.[1] The declaration was a preliminary to impeachment of Ministers in case they still persisted in defying the House.

It also led the King, on 11th March, to send his champion, the Chancellor, Lord Thurlow, to consult with Lord Rockingham. The leader of the official Whigs knew that he had the game in his hands, and sought to dictate the conditions on which alone he would form an administration. They were as follows: "American Independence; no Veto; Establishment Bill; great parts of Contractors Bill; Custom House and Excise, etc., Bill. Peace in general, if possible; Economy in every branch."[2] The King demurred to these terms, and after eight days the overture lapsed. Meanwhile Lord North's position in the House was becoming intolerable, and on 20th March he announced the resignation of his Ministry. On going to take leave of the King, he was greeted by the following characteristic words: "Remember, my Lord, that it is you who desert me, not I you."

Most sovereigns would now have accepted defeat. But George III was no less dogged of will than ingenious in finding a way of escape. He had one chance left. Beside the official Whig families, headed by Rockingham, there were the Chathamites, led by Shelburne, who occupied an intermediate position not easy to define. Like most political groups which profess to be above party, they had succeeded in forming another party. They differed from the Whigs in not desiring to see the royal prerogative shorn of power, as it had been under the first two Georges to the advantage of the old governing families. In foreign and colonial affairs they aimed at the triumph of a truly

[1] May, "Const. History," i, 458.
[2] Rockingham, "Memoirs," ii, 452-3.

national policy, which, while furthering the cause of freedom, also made for the greatness of the Empire. Even amidst his protests against the continuance of the war, Shelburne raised his voice, as Chatham had done, against a complete severance of the tie uniting the colonies to the motherland.[1] These opinions seem to us now unpractical in view of the existing state of things. Certainly, if we may judge by the speeches of William Pitt, he had overshot the limits of the Chathamite traditions which his chief still observed.

Nevertheless, the Chathamites, albeit a somewhat *doctrinaire* group, indeed scarcely a party, might now be utilized as a buffer between the throne and the Whig magnates. Accordingly, the King, during an interview with Shelburne, in which he expressed his dislike of Rockingham, proposed that Shelburne should form a Cabinet with Rockingham as head, Shelburne being the intermediary between the King and the Prime Minister. As Shelburne knew that he could not stand without the support of the Whigs, the latter had their way at nearly all points. The King most reluctantly consented not to veto American Independence —a matter on which Rockingham stood firm. In smaller and personal matters, on which George III set much store, he partly succeeded. He refused to see Rockingham until the latter was Prime Minister; he insisted on keeping his factotum, Lord Thurlow, as Chancellor, and he fought hard to keep the gentlemen of the royal household unchanged; but, as he wrote to Lord North, "the number I have saved is incredibly few." Among them was Lord Montagu, the governor of the King's son, whom Horace Walpole dubbed the King's spy on the Prince of Wales, and the only man in whom he (George III) had any confidence. The same sharp critic noted that the King now used, with some success, the only artifice in which he had ever succeeded, that of sowing discord. He had openly shown that Shelburne and Thurlow were his men in the Cabinet; and Fox, who became Secretary of State for Foreign Affairs, said that the new Cabinet belonged partly to the King and partly to the people. In the very limited sense in which the Whigs were a popular party (for the official Whigs sought the support of the people mainly in order to browbeat the King), the remark was correct.

However that may be, the King had certainly contrived

---

[1] Speech of 7th February 1782 ("Parl. Hist.," xxii, p. 987).

largely to nullify the victory of the Whigs by fomenting discords in the Cabinet. So astute an intriguer as Shelburne was certain to chafe at the ascendancy of Rockingham; and the King's tactics, while humiliating the Prime Minister, enabled Shelburne secretly to arrange matters according to the royal behests. Shelburne held the secretaryship for Home Affairs, which then carried with it a supervision of the executive at Dublin Castle. He also brought in Dunning (now created Lord Ashburton without the knowledge of Rockingham) as Chancellor of the Duchy of Lancaster; and it has been ascertained that he sought to include Pitt in the Cabinet with some high office. Which office he was to have is not clear; but Lady Chatham wrote to Shelburne on 28th March in terms which implied an office of Cabinet rank. Here, however, Rockingham protested with success; and as a result only the Vice-Treasurership of Ireland was offered him, an office which by his previous declaration he had bound himself to refuse.[1] His exclusion from the Cabinet by the influence of the official Whigs served to alienate him from that party, and brought him more in contact with men who were beginning to figure as supporters of the royal prerogative.

As a private member, Pitt gave his support to the new Ministry; and on 29th April he made a brief but telling appeal for unanimity, "from which the salvation of the nation could alone be hoped for." Certainly the Ministry needed the help of all patriots. The prestige of Britain was at the lowest ebb. Beaten alike in the New World and in the Mediterranean, where Minorca had recently been recovered by the Spaniards, she seemed at the end of her resources. Ireland was in a state of veiled rebellion. The Parliament at Dublin unanimously demanded the repeal of Poynings Act and that of the year 1720, which assured its dependence on the British Government; and some 100,000 Volunteers were ready to take the field to make good the claim. In vain did the new Lord Lieutenant, the Duke of Portland, seek to gain time. Grattan, whom the Earl of Mornington styled "the most upright and temperate demagogue that ever appeared in any country," had Ireland at his back. He refused to wait; and in the month of May the British Parliament gave effect to his demands by unanimously conceding legislative independence to the Dublin Parliament.[2] Pitt

---

[1] Fitzmaurice, "Shelburne," iii, 136.
[2] "Dropmore P.," i, 163; Lecky, iv *ad fin.*

did not speak on the subject, but he probably agreed with the change, which in the circumstances was inevitable. The news aroused in Ireland a storm of enthusiasm, and the Dublin Parliament voted the sum of £100,000 for raising 20,000 seamen. For the present, then, the Irish question was shelved, but at the cost of many difficulties in the future.

About the same time, the cloud which had hung so ominously over Britain's navy cleared away. News arrived of the victory which Rodney gained over the French fleet under Count de Grasse near Dominica on 12th April 1782,[1] which saved the West Indian colonies and restored Britain's supremacy on the ocean. Equally fortunate was Eliott's repulse of a determined attack on Gibraltar by the French and Spaniards, which brought about the relief of the garrison and ensured the total failure of the prolonged and desperate efforts of France and Spain to seize the key of the Mediterranean.

The spirit of the nation rose with these successes; and Shelburne brought forward a Bill for arming the people. The motion came to little, probably because of the fear which the Lord George Gordon riots had aroused;[2] but, as the sequel will show, it took effect in some quarters and provided the basis for the far more important Volunteer Movement of the Great French War.

It is remarkable, as showing the strong bent of Pitt's nature towards civil affairs, that he spoke, not on these topics, but solely on the cause of Parliamentary Reform. His insistence on this topic at a time of national peril can be paralleled by the action of another statesman a century later; and it is significant that, when Mr. Gladstone introduced his Franchise Bill in 1884, he was warmly reproached by Lord Randolph Churchill for bringing forward this topic amidst the conflicts or complications in which we were involved in Egypt, the Sudan, Afghanistan, and South Africa. But the Liberal leader claimed that by conferring the franchise on some two million of citizens, the people would be arrayed "in one solid compacted mass around the ancient throne which it has loved so well and round a constitution now to be more than ever powerful and more than ever

---

[1] Hood, Rodney's second in command, asserted that if Rodney had fought and pursued vigorously he would have taken not five but twenty French ships of the line. See "Rodney's Letters and Despatches," ed. by D. Hannay for the Navy Records Society, p. 103.

[2] "Parl. Hist.," xxiii, 1.

free." The plea has been justified by events; and we can now gauge at its true value the politic daring of the two statesmen who sought to meet dangers from without by strengthening the fabric of the Empire at its base.

In the year 1782 the gravity of the crisis was far greater than that of the year 1884; for the storms were beating on an edifice dangerously narrow at the ground. Realizing that the subject of the representation was too complicated to be handled except after an official investigation, Pitt for the present proposed merely the formation of a Committee of Inquiry which should report on the best means of carrying out "a moderate and substantial reform." His proposals, and still more the fame of his eloquence, aroused great interest; so that on the morning of 7th May a crowd endeavoured to gain access to Westminster Hall. Many of the "news-writers" were excluded, with results harmful to the printed reports of the speech.[1] Pitt prefaced his remarks by acknowledging most thankfully that they had now to do with a Ministry which desired such a measure, and not with one that "laboured to exert the corrupt influence of the Crown in support of an inadequate representation of the people." He assumed it as proven that the House of Commons had received an improper and dangerous bias, which impaired the constitution.

That beautiful frame of government which has made us the envy and admiration of mankind, in which the people are entitled to hold so distinguished a share, is so far dwindled, and has so far departed from its original purity, as that the representatives have ceased, in a great degree, to be connected with the people. It is of the essence of the constitution that the people should have a share in the government by the means of representation; and its excellence and permanency is calculated to consist in this representation, having been designed to be equal, easy, practicable, and complete. When it ceases to be so; when the representative ceases to have connection with the constituent, and is either dependent on the Crown or the aristocracy, there is a defect in the frame of representation, and it is not innovation but recovery of constitution, to repair it.

[1] "Life of Romilly," i, 162. Romilly, who was present, quotes a sentence of the speech, which did not appear in the official report: "This House is not the representative of the people of Great Britain; it is the representative of nominal boroughs, of ruined and exterminated towns, of noble families, of wealthy individuals, of foreign potentates."

He then pointed out some of the worst anomalies of the existing system. There were some boroughs wholly controlled, or absolutely possessed, by the Treasury. In others its influence was contested solely by a great landowner, but never by the inhabitants in their own right. Some few boroughs [Old Sarum is the classical instance] had only one or two voters. Other towns,

in the lofty possession of English freedom, claim to themselves the right to bring their votes to market. They have no other market, no other property, and no other stake in the country, than the property and price which they procure for their votes. Such boroughs are the most dangerous of all. So far from consulting the interests of their country in the choice which they make, they hold out their borough to the best purchaser. . . . It is a fact pretty well known that the Nabob of Arcot had no less than seven or eight members in that House. May not a foreign State in enmity with this country, by means of these boroughs, procure a party of men to act for them under the mask and character of members of that House?

Pitt then warned the Commons that the forces of corruption might soon be found to be as strong as ever. Though they had grown with our growth, they had not decayed with our decay. For years they had maintained in power a Ministry which had worked ruin to the Empire. Finally, he referred to the opinion of his father on this great subject and besought members to satisfy the longings now widely expressed throughout the kingdom, which must carry the matter to a triumphant issue. His speech was loudly cheered. The able orations of Fox and Sheridan also seemed to carry the House with them; but, as in former cases, the undercurrent of self-interest worked potently against Reform, and ensured the rejection of Pitt's proposal by 161 votes to 141. The country gentlemen were alarmed at his motion, the opposition of Pitt's relative, Thomas Pitt, being especially strong.

Probably it was a tactical mistake for Pitt, a private member, to bring forward such a motion. If he had waited until the Ministry had so far prevailed over its external difficulties and internal dissensions as to be able to take up the question, his support might have ensured the triumph of the Government proposals. As it was, the misgivings of the cautious, the vested interests of nominee members, the embarrassments of the

Ministry, and the opposition of the old Whig families, doomed to failure his second effort in this direction. Not for the space of forty-eight years was so favourable an opportunity to recur; and then it was a new Industrial England which burst through the trammels of an old-world representation.

Undaunted by this rebuff, he spoke on 17th May in favour of the motion of a veteran reformer, Alderman Sawbridge, for shortening the duration of Parliaments. Only one of his arguments has come down to us, namely his contention that the Septennial Act placed undue influence in the hands of Ministers, as appeared from the strenuous opposition which the enemies of political purity had always offered to the repeal of that measure. Fox spoke for the motion; but Burke, who had been persuaded to absent himself from the earlier debate, now let loose the vials of his wrath against a Reform of Parliament in whatever shape it came. Sheridan describes him as attacking Pitt " in a scream of passion," with the assertion that Parliament was just what it ought to be, and that all change would be fatal to the welfare of the nation.

Burke's diatribe prepares us for the part which he played during the French Revolution. The man who discerned perfection in a Parliamentary system, in which Scotland had only 4,000 voters and 45 members, while 19 Cornish villages returned 38 members; in which the Duke of Norfolk could put in 11 members, and the Nabob of Arcot 7 or 8, while Manchester, Leeds, Sheffield, and Birmingham remained politically dumb— such a man might well regard the French revolutionists as " the ablest architects of ruin " that the world had ever seen. His tirade against short Parliaments carried the House with him, the motion being rejected by a majority of 88.

It is interesting to find Pitt taking part at a meeting of friends of Reform at the Thatched House Tavern (18th May 1782), which seems to have been held under the auspices of Major Cartwright's " Society for Promoting Constitutional Information." The Duke of Richmond, Lord Mahon, Sir Cecil Wray, and the Lord Mayor were present. A motion was passed urging the need of petitioning Parliament for " a substantial reformation of the Commons House of Parliament "; and the minutes of the meeting were in Pitt's handwriting. He was then in correspondence with John Frost, an attorney of Percy Street, who was secretary for the Middlesex Reform Committee; and in the second letter the young statesman refers to some honour which that committee proposed to confer on him for his efforts on their behalf. These facts and Pitt's letters to Frost were produced by Erskine during his defence of Frost against a charge of sedition early in the Hilary Term 1793.[1] The episode was highly effective and probably ensured the mitigation of Frost's sentence. The whole incident is noteworthy, as it points the contrast between the earlier and later phases of Pitt's career which was to be produced by the French Revolution.

Pitt did not speak during the debates on two other measures which alone of all the reformers' programme passed through Parliament in 1782. They were the Contractors Bill, which, by excluding all contractors from Parliament and disfranchising all revenue officers, dealt a blow at some forms of political corruption.[2] By the other Act several sinecures, with salaries of about £70,000 a year, were swept away. The King exerted his influence against both measures, his man, Lord Thurlow, striving by every means to defeat the former of them in the Lords; while the Economy Bill was shorn of some of its more drastic clauses by the action of Shelburne and Thurlow in Cabinet Councils.

The difficulty of common action was seen during the discussion of a Bill for the repression of bribery at elections (19th June). Pitt spoke in favour of the motion, but, strange to say, Fox opposed it. This was the first occasion on which they voted in opposite lobbies, though there had been no friendship or close intercourse between them. The motion was of course lost.

Their relations were destined quickly to alter, owing to an event which opened another phase of the long struggle between the King and the hostile Whig " phalanx." On 1st July 1782 the Marquis of Rockingham died. Of small ability, he yet held a conspicuous place in the affairs of State, owing to his vast landed estates, the strength of his political and family connections, and to his high character. At once the King and the " phalanx " girded themselves for the conflict. On the very next day George III offered the Premiership to the Earl of Shelburne, now more than ever inclining to the King's side. With an openness which did not always characterize him, that Minister at

---

[1] "Speeches of Lord Erskine" (edit. of 1880), p. 293; "The Papers of Christopher Wyvil," i, 424-5; State Trials, xxii, 492-4.

[2] See Mahon, " Hist. of England," vii, 17; Porritt, i, 217.

once referred the proposal to his colleagues, only to have it
rejected by the official Whigs. Four of Rockingham's most
decided friends in the Cabinet—Fox, the Duke of Richmond,
Lord John Cavendish, and Admiral Keppel—demanded that
the Duke of Portland should be Prime Minister.[1] Such a
proposal was doubly objectionable; first, because the Duke, as
then appeared from his conduct at Dublin Castle, had little
insight and no strength of character; secondly, because the proposal itself was scarcely constitutional; for the King had, as he
still has, the right to select his Prime Minister. Nevertheless,
Shelburne consented to refer the proposal to George III, who
emphatically rejected it. Thereupon Fox and Lord John
Cavendish resigned; Shelburne undertook to form an Administration and offered the Chancellorship of the Exchequer,
vacated by Lord John Cavendish, to William Pitt. He at once
accepted it.

The other chief changes were that Thomas Townshend (soon
to become Lord Sydney) took the Secretaryship of State held
by Shelburne, while Fox was succeeded as Secretary for Foreign
Affairs by Lord Grantham, and the Duke of Portland, Lord
Lieutenant of Ireland, by Earl Temple. Burke and Sheridan
marked their attachment to the Whigs by resigning their subordinate offices. It was in face of able, eloquent, and exasperated
men like these that Pitt took up the burden of office, along
with the virtual leadership of the House of Commons, at the
age of twenty-three.

The conduct of Fox and his friends in resigning office was
hotly arraigned. A debate on their action in voting a pension of
£3,200 a year to Colonel Barré turned mainly on the larger
question (9th July). Fox, conscious that Barré's pension was
a blot on Ministers who had posed as champions of economy,
retorted fiercely on his critics, declaring Shelburne and his followers to be heedless alike " of promises which they had made,
of engagements into which they had entered, of principles which
they had maintained, of the system on which they had set out.
. . . They would abandon fifty principles for the sake of power,
and forget fifty promises when they were no longer requisite to
their ends; . . . and he expected to see that, in a very short
time, they would be joined by those men whom that House had
precipitated from their seats." [2]

---

[1] "Buckingham Papers," i, 50. [2] "Parl. Hist.," xxiii, 163.

Had Fox been satisfied with defending his own resignation on the ground of disagreement with Shelburne on details of policy, his relations to the Chathamites might have remained cordial. But the attack on Pitt's chief was so violent as to provoke sharp rejoinders. General Conway defended Shelburne from the charge of apostasy, and stated that it was he who had convinced George III of the need of recognizing the independence of the American colonies; also that the differences between Shelburne and Fox on that point were merely differing shades of opinion.[1] Pitt expressed his regret at the resignation of Fox, but attributed it in the main to a dislike of Shelburne rather than of his policy. For himself, he said, he completely trusted the noble earl, and if he were called upon to serve under him (his appointment was not yet confirmed) he would do so cheerfully in any capacity and to the utmost of his power. The strictures of Fox were further discounted by the fact that Richmond and Keppel did not resign their seats in the Cabinet.

On reviewing the action of Fox after this lapse of time it seems impossible to acquit him of the charge of acting with haste and bad temper. His charges against the sincerity of Shelburne respecting the details of the negotiation then begun with France and America have been refuted, or at least minimized, by an eminent authority.[2] Fox must have known as well as Conway that Shelburne had induced George III to recognize the independence of the American colonies—a political service of the highest order; and if on matters of detail he sharply differed from him, and thought him insincere, meddlesome, and too friendly to the King, it was his duty to remain in office with his Whig friends so as to curb those tendencies. It is by no means certain (as Mr. Lecky asserted) that he would have been always, or generally, outvoted;[3] and his presence in the Cabinet would have strengthened his party in the Commons. It may be granted that he believed he was taking the only straightforward course; but his vehement nature often led him to unwise conclusions. True, his colleagues nearly always forgave him; for it was a signal proof

---

[1] "Parl. Hist.," xxiii, 175; "Life of Romilly," i, 173. Fox had announced to the Cabinet his intention of resigning a few days before Rockingham's death. See the "Memorials of Fox," i, 435 et seq.

[2] Sir G. C. Lewis, "Administrations of Great Britain," pp. 31-48.

[3] Lecky, iv, 239. The original Cabinet numbered five Rockingham Whigs and five Shelburne Whigs.

of the warmth of his disposition that his friends loved him even when he offended them; but they came by degrees to distrust his judgement, and to see that other gifts than courage, eloquence, and personal charm were needed in a leader. Certain it is that public opinion condemned his resignation as hasty, ill-timed, and compromising to the cause of Reform.

His action was especially unfortunate in this last respect. In April he had written that, if the Rockingham Cabinet could stay in office long enough to deal "a good stout blow to the influence of the Crown," it would not matter if the Ministry broke up. But the blow had not been dealt; the passing of the Economy Bill and the exclusion of contractors from Parliament and revenue officers from the franchise had only scotched the snake of corruption, not killed it. Yet the party which alone could deal the final blow was now weakened by the action of the most ardent of reformers. The worst result of all, perhaps, remains to be noticed. When Fox maliciously taunted Shelburne with being about to unite with Lord North in order to keep in office, no one could have imagined that the speaker would soon have recourse to that despicable manœuvre; but the curse, flung out in heedless wrath, was destined to come home to roost.

Pitt now came to office by a path which necessitated a sharp divergence from Fox—a divergence, be it noted, due to party tactics and not to the inner convictions of the men themselves. After the foregoing account of the session of 1782—it ended on 11th July—the reader will be in a position to judge for himself whether up to that time Pitt or Fox was to blame for a split which seems unnatural and blameworthy.

In the month of August Pitt moved into the "vast awkward house" in Downing Street which was to be his official residence. Dissensions soon arose in the Cabinet; and in addition there were the dangers resulting from the war and the urgent need of concluding peace. Accordingly Pitt was able to spend but very few days out of town at his beloved Hayes, even in the heat of summer, still less to go on circuit as he had intended. The Shelburne Ministry contrived to simplify the diplomatic situation by offering to recognize the independence of the United States (27th September). The frankness with which this was done, at a time when Vergennes, the French Foreign Minister, showed a keen desire to shut those growing communities out from the valley of the Mississippi,[1] served somewhat to allay the anti-British fury kindled by the War. The Americans saw, what had long been discerned at Westminster, that the Bourbons were using them as pawns in their game for the overthrow of the British Empire; and their envoys resolved to break loose from their engagement not to treat separately for a peace with England. The preliminaries of peace, signed on 30th November, accorded to the young Commonwealth the Mississippi as its boundary on the west, and the larger part of the great lakes on the north, together with fishery rights off Newfoundland. All these terms, including that of the independence of the States, were provisional, taking effect whenever peace should be settled with France and Spain.

The negotiations with France and Spain were rendered easier by the ill-will now existing between the Bourbon Powers and the United States. The relief of the garrison of Gibraltar by Lord Howe further disposed them to abate their terms. On the other hand, they knew of the difficulties of the British Cabinet, and the general desire of the nation for peace. Matters were therefore in a complicated state at the end of the year 1782; and we learn from a statement of Shelburne that during November he refrained from summoning Cabinet Councils in order to preserve unanimity.[2] Ministers had indeed differed sharply, firstly, on the question whether Gibraltar should be handed back to Spain, and secondly, on that of the indemnity. The King and Shelburne wished to have Porto Rico and West Florida in exchange for Gibraltar; Grafton preferred Porto Rico and Trinidad; while Richmond, Keppel (probably also Pitt) objected to the cession of the great fortress which had been so stoutly held against a three years' siege.[3]

Such was the state of affairs when, on 5th December, Parliament reassembled. On the next day Pitt committed a mistake which exposed him to a reprimand from the King through Shelburne. Fox pressed Ministers to declare that the acknowledgement of American independence was unconditional. The senior Minister in the House, Townshend, replied that that condition of peace would take effect only on the conclusion of a general peace. Pitt, however, added that "the clear indisputable

---

[1] Fitzmaurice, "Shelburne," vol. iii, chs. iv-vi.
[2] "Buckingham Papers," i, 76.
[3] Fitzmaurice, "Shelburne," iii, 305; Stanhope, "Pitt," i, 86.

meaning of the provisional agreements made with the American commissioners was the unqualified recognition of their independence "; and it would form part of the treaty with the belligerent powers.[1] Here he overshot the mark. That recognition depended on the conclusion of treaties with France and Spain. The King, therefore, sent him a rebuke through Shelburne, adding, however, " It is no wonder that so young a man should have made a slip."—We cannot regret the occurrence, for it shows how anxious Pitt was to have that great question settled.

In the ensuing debates Pitt sharply retorted on Burke, who, quoting from " Hudibras," had accused Ministers of making the King speak—

> As if hypocrisy and nonsense
> Had got the advowson of his conscience.

The son of Chatham showed something of his father's fire, reprobating the unseemly jeer of the speaker and declaring that he repelled the further charge of hypocrisy "with scorn and contempt." A retort courteous, or humorous, would have been more in place after Burke's raillery; but Pitt, though witty in private, rarely used this gift in the House, probably because he wished to be taken seriously. In this he succeeded. In all but name he was leader of the House of Commons. The task of keeping together a majority was extremely difficult; for, according to Gibbon, the Ministry could command only 140 votes, while as many as 120 voted with Lord North, 90 with Fox, the rest drifted about as marketable flotsam. The situation became worse still late in the year, when rumours began to fly about that Fox and Lord North were about to join their discordant forces for the overthrow of the Ministry.

In these circumstances the Shelburne Cabinet rendered the greatest possible service by holding on to office, while they pressed through the negotiations with France, Spain, and Holland. Ultimately, the preliminaries of peace were signed on 20th January 1783. They brought no disgrace on a Power which had latterly been warring against half the world. The chief loss in the West Indies was Tobago, a small but wealthy island, in which British merchants had large interests. It was surrendered to the French, who recovered their former possession, St. Lucia.

---

[1] " Parl. Hist.," xxiii, 265.

On the other hand, they gave back to Britain Dominica, Grenada, St. Vincent, St. Kitts, Nevis, and Montserrat. The cession of the islands of Miquelon and St. Pierre enabled France to gain a firmer footing in the Newfoundland fisheries. In Africa we gave back Senegal and Goree to France; while her stations in India, conquered by us, were likewise restored. Spain gained more largely than France. She retained her recent conquests, West Florida and Minorca, and she acquired East Florida, while recognizing the reconquest of the Bahamas by England. The Dutch ceded Negapatam but recovered Trincomalee. These conditions were ultimately ratified by the Treaty of Versailles (3rd September 1783).

Terms so favourable could not have been secured had not the Court of Versailles felt the need of peace in order to repair its shattered finances. It was the shadow of the oncoming eclipse of 1789 which warned Louis XVI and Vergennes to agree with their adversary while they were in the way with him. Nevertheless, the Shelburne Ministry deserves the highest credit for making head against internal difficulties, and for gaining terms which were far less burdensome than those imposed on France by the Seven Years' War.

This is the light in which they are regarded now. In that age, when the spoils of office rather than patriotism prompted the words and votes of members, the details of the peace afforded a welcome opportunity for undermining the Ministry. Already it seemed to be in difficulties. The waverers inside the Cabinet, or those who were chafed by the overbearing ways and personal diplomacy of Shelburne, began to leave the labouring ship. Keppel threw up the Admiralty, the Duke of Richmond absented himself from the Cabinet Councils, and Grafton and Conway seemed on the point of retiring.[1] Pitt remained faithful, but urged the need of strengthening the Ministry by alliance with Fox and his followers. Shelburne at first inclined to a compact with Lord North's party; though both he and Pitt objected strongly to the inclusion of North himself in the Cabinet. As " the lord in the blue ribbon " had his party well in hand, it

---

[1] Keppel resigned on the question of the terms of peace; the Duke of Richmond disapproved them; Grafton was lukewarm. See their speeches, 17th February 1783 (" Parl. Hist.," xxiii, 392-6). W. W. Grenville refused to move the resolution in the Commons in favour of the peace, as Pitt urged him to do (" Dropmore P.," i, 194).

was impossible to bring them in without him. It remained, then, to seek help from the Foxites. Here the bitter personal feud between Shelburne and Fox complicated the situation fatally both for Shelburne, Fox, and Pitt. But before the fight began in Parliament on the burning topic of the hour, Pitt made an attempt to bring in Fox (11th February). He acted with the consent of Shelburne and with the knowledge, and probably the grudging permission, of the King.

Few private interviews have been more important. On it depended the fortunes of the Ministry, and to some extent, of the Empire. If it succeeded, the terms of peace were certain to pass through Parliament. An alliance would also be formed between two political groups which had almost the same aims and were held apart only by the personal pique of their leaders. A union of the best elements of the Whigs and the Chathamites would tend to curb the power of the King, maintain the honour of the flag, and secure the passage of much-needed reforms. The defeat, or at least the postponement, of these salutary aims must necessarily result from persistence in the miserable feud. For the two men themselves that interview was fraught with grave issues. The repulse of the natural affinities was certain to doom one of them to an unnatural alliance or to helpless opposition.

It must have been with a keen sense of the importance of the crisis that these able men faced one another. The interview was soon over. Pitt stated to Fox the object of his visit; whereupon the Whig leader asked whether it was proposed that Lord Shelburne should remain First Lord of the Treasury. On Pitt answering in the affirmative, Fox remarked that it was impossible for him to form part of any Administration of which Lord Shelburne was the head. Pitt at once drew himself up (so Dundas afterwards declared), and the proud movement of his head, the significance of which many an opponent was destined to feel, ended the interview. According to Bishop Tomline, he broke off the conversation with the words: " I did not come here to betray Lord Shelburne." The breach was irreparable.[1]

Three days later, Dundas (soon to be a firm supporter of Pitt) made a despairing effort to win over Lord North, who coolly repulsed him. On that same day Fox offered his alliance to

---

[1] " Memorials of Fox," ii, 33.

the man whom for thirteen years he had railed at as the instrument of corruption and tyranny. They agreed

that nothing more was required to be done in reducing the influence of the Crown by economical reform, and that on parliamentary reform every man should follow his own opinion. Mr. Fox having urged that the King should not be suffered to be his own Minister, Lord North replied: "If you mean there should not be a government by departments, I agree with you. I think it a very bad system. There should be one man, or a Cabinet, to govern the whole and direct every measure. Government by departments was not brought in by me. I found it so, and had not vigour and resolution to put an end to it. The King ought to be treated with all sort of respect and attention, but the appearance of power is all that a King of this country can have."[1]

They then began to consider the question of the distribution of offices, and finally decided to oppose the forthcoming address to the King expressing thankfulness at the peace.

Thus was formed the famous, or infamous, Coalition of 1783. With the policy of reducing the governing power of the King, it is impossible not to feel much sympathy. George III had hitherto governed England without much let or hindrance, except from Chatham and Rockingham. His narrowness and obstinacy were the chief causes of the American War; and we now know that during four years he had kept Lord North to that work, despite his remonstrances. But nothing could reconcile the new alliance to the public. A shiver of disgust ran through the nation when it transpired that Fox had plighted troth with the man whom he had threatened to impeach; and that impression was never to die away.

Further, it is doubtful whether enthusiasm for Reform was the chief motive that prompted Fox's action.[2] As we have seen, he gave up Economic Reform; and his stipulation respecting Parliamentary Reform was so half-hearted as to doom that question to failure. How could that cause thrive when it would have the effect of sending the chiefs of the future Ministry into opposite lobbies? Fox must have known enough of Parliament to see

---

[1] "Memorials of Fox," ii, 37, 38; "Auckland Journals," i, 40-5. Lord John Townshend, Adam, Eden, Lord Loughborough, and George North helped to bring about the Coalition. Burke favoured the plan, also Sheridan, though later on he vehemently declared the contrary (*ibid.*, pp. 21-4).

[2] Mr. Le B. Hammond, "Life of Fox," pp. 57, 58.

that his present conduct hopelessly impaired the strength of the reformers, in what was at all times an uphill fight. In truth, the whole incident brings into sharp relief the defects of his character, which, while rich in enthusiasms, ever lacked balance, and so frequently led him to a reckless use of most questionable means for the compassing of ends in themselves desirable.

In this instance his recklessness was to blast his whole career. He seems not to have considered the general impression certain to be created by his facile union with a long-loathed opponent. But the public, always prone to harsh judgements on political inconsistencies, at once inferred that he joined North, partly in order to be revenged on Shelburne for some personal slights, but mainly with the view of snatching at the sweets of office which he had of late so unaccountably cast aside. His conduct seemed oddly to blend all that was foolish in wayward boyhood with the cunning of an unscrupulous politician. The cynical majority argued that such extremes as Fox and North could meet only under the overmastering pressure of greed; and to idealists or patriots the Coalition of 1783 seemed to plunge England back into the old slough of selfishness from which the noble pride of Chatham had raised her.

The name of Chatham reminds us of the Coalition which in 1757 he framed with his former opponent, the Duke of Newcastle. The two cases have indeed been compared; but they have very little in common. Then the very existence of England was at stake. She was in the midst of a war which was being grossly mismanaged; and the union of the one able statesman of the age with the manipulator of patronage, was practically the only means of avoiding a national disaster. Now, in February 1783, hostilities were at an end; the terms of peace were arranged, and were certain to take effect, if the new Coalition allowed it. The action of the elder Pitt in 1757 was inspired by patriotism and crowned by deserved triumph. That of Fox and North rested, in part, on more sordid motives, jeopardized the conclusion of peace, threw the political world into utter confusion, and ended in disaster.

The fruits of the new Coalition were soon to appear. On Monday 17th February, the debates opened on the address to the King relative to the peace. In the Lords the opposition of Keppel and Richmond to their late colleagues was an ominous sign; but still more so was the combined attack of Foxites and

Northites in the Lower House. North spoke with something of the restraint which became a man so largely responsible for the present humiliations. He fastened on the worst parts of the treaty—the cession of Minorca and the Floridas to Spain, and the absence of any guarantees for the American Loyalists. Where he trod with measured steps, Sheridan and Fox rushed in with frothy violence. Sheridan declared that the treaty " relinquished completely everything that was glorious and great in the country "; and his chief branded it as " the most disastrous and disgraceful peace that ever this country had made." Then adverting to the understanding with North, which was generally known, Fox defended it by quoting the phrase, " Amicitiae sempiternae, inimicitiae placabiles." [1]

Pitt's speech, in reply to Fox, was not one of his happiest efforts, and Ministers were left in a minority of sixteen. He excelled himself, however, four days later during the debate on a vote of censure brought against the Administration by his former colleague, Lord John Cavendish. The attack was ingeniously made under cover of a series of resolutions, affirming that the House of Commons accepted the peace, while believing the concessions made to our enemies to be excessive, and demanding better terms for the American Loyalists. Fox spoke with his usual ardour in favour of these mutually destructive resolutions. After declaring that all who looked at the terms of peace must " blush for the ignominy of the national character," he proceeded to defend his alliance with Lord North. The times, he said, were now changed; they had to deal with a Prime Minister, Shelburne, who was " in his nature, habitudes, and principles, an enemy to the privileges of the people." They must therefore form " the strongest Coalition which may re-instate the people in their rights, privileges, and possessions." [2]

We do not know whether Pitt was aware that the orator had just bartered away the cause of Parliamentary Reform; but he certainly suspected it; and the surmise must have kindled a fire of indignation before which his bodily weakness vanished. During the long speech of his opponent he suffered from fits of vomiting which compelled him at times to hold open a small door behind him, called Solomon's porch. But when, at one o'clock in the morning, he rose to reply, all his weakness

[1] " My friendships are eternal, my hatreds can be appeased."
[2] " Parl. Hist.," xxiii, 541.

vanished. In a speech of three hours he traversed the whole ground of the treaty and reviewed the situation brought about by the recent monstrous Coalition. He fought hard for the Peace, which the present resolutions imperilled, and still more so for the maintenance of the honourable traditions of public life.

After briefly adverting to the strange part now played by Fox, he continued in terms which showed that he appealed more to the nation than to Parliament.

The triumphs of party, Sir, with which this self-appointed Minister seems so highly elate, shall never seduce me to any inconsistency which the busiest suspicion shall presume to glance at. I will never engage in political enmities without a public cause. I will never forego such enmities without the public approbation; nor will I be questioned and cast off in the face of this House by one virtuous and dissatisfied friend.[1] These, Sir, the sober and durable triumphs of reason over the weak and profligate inconsistencies of party violence; these, Sir, the steady triumphs of virtue over success itself, shall be mine, not only in my present situation but through every future condition of my life—triumphs which no length of time shall diminish, which no change of principle shall sully.

He then showed that a continuance of war would be full of peril and might lead to national bankruptcy; that Ministers were not, as at the end of the Seven Years' War, able to dictate terms of peace, and that those now proposed were as favourable as could be expected. If we had ceded Florida, we had regained the Bahamas and Providence. While losing Tobago and St. Lucia, we recovered Grenada, Dominica, St. Kitts, Nevis, and Montserrat. In Africa we should once more hold Senegambia, the best and healthiest settlement. The loss of Minorca was bearable, for the island was expensive in peace and never tenable in war. Then, adverting to the alleged betrayal of the American Loyalists, he appealed warmly for reconciliation with the United States, and still more warmly deprecated the suspicion that Congress would be guilty of the base injustice of doing nothing for those sufferers. His words have the ring of sincere conviction; but it is painful to have to add that these magnanimous hopes were doomed to disappointment.[2]

---

[1] Fox's friends, Mr. Powys and Sir Cecil Wray, had reprobated his present action.

[2] "Parl. Hist.," xxiii, 543-50. I may here note that after the resignation

Descending to the lower levels of party strife, he declared that his opponents were aiming their shafts, not at the Treaty, but at the Earl of Shelburne. Their unnatural coalition was brought about by personal spite; and, he added with thrilling emphasis : " If this ill-omened marriage is not already solemnized, I know a just and lawful impediment, and, in the name of the public safety, I here forbid the banns." Finally, in what seemed a farewell to the cares of office, he vindicated his conduct, as inspired by the traditions of Chatham, and he appealed to the House and to the nation at large in this noble peroration:

You may take from me, Sir, the privileges and emoluments of place, but you cannot, and you shall not, take from me those habitual and warm regards for the prosperity of Great Britain, which constitute the honour, the happiness, the pride of my life, and which I trust death alone can extinguish. And, with this consolation, the loss of power, Sir, and the loss of fortune, though I affect not to despise them, I hope I soon shall be able to forget:

> Laudo manentem. Si celeres quatit
> Pennas, resigno quae dedit
>   . . . probamque
> Pauperiem sine dote quaero.[1]

A member of the House relates that when he came to the words —" et mea virtute me involvo "—he paused for a moment, drew his handkerchief across his lips, and then, as if recovering from a slight embarrassment, gave the final words with thrilling effect.

The whole speech aroused an interest and emotion unequalled since the time of Chatham's mighty orations. North complimented the young Chancellor on his amazing eloquence, which had so deeply affected every member of the House, and stated that, though he himself was the object of his thunder, he

---

of Shelburne, Pitt framed a Bill for regulating in friendly terms commerce with the United States. It was sharply criticized and much altered in committee; but his Bill as well as the words quoted above prove the depth of his conviction as to the need of winning back if possible the good-will of those young communities.

[1] Horace, " Odes," bk. iii, 29. From modesty he omitted the words " et mea Virtute me involvo." (" If she [Fortune] abides, I commend her. If her fleet wings quiver for flight, I resign her gifts—and hail honest, dowerless poverty as mine.")

[2] Wraxall, iii, 15.

had listened to that thunder with astonishment and delight. He then asserted that better terms might have been gained, especially from the Americans, and declared his belief that the new Coalition would greatly benefit the country. The House by a majority of seventeen decided for North and against Pitt.

In the Lords, Shelburne had a majority of thirteen; but the victory of North and Fox in the Commons led him to offer to resign office on 24th February 1783. In this honourable manner ended Pitt's first tenure of office.

CHAPTER VI

THE COALITION

Of all the public characters of this devoted country (Mr. Pitt alone excepted) there is not a man who has, or who deserves, the nation's confidence.
—ROMILLY 21st March 1783.

IN politics, as in war, victories sometimes prove to be more disastrous than defeats. When triumph lures a leader on into ever increasing difficulties, he may well rue his seeming good fortune; while, on the other hand, the retreat of his opponents may lessen their responsibilities, and, by enabling them to concentrate, double the strength of their next blow.

Such was the case with Fox and Pitt. Fox's triumph over the former was seen by discerning friends to be of the Pyrrhic kind. He owed it to an unprincipled alliance, and for it he threw away the support of public opinion. Pitt, on the other hand, fell gloriously, fighting strenuously for terms of peace which, in the nature of things, his successors could not sensibly ameliorate. Accordingly, events worked for him and against the victors. Only a well organized party can resist the wear and tear of parliamentary strife; and it lay in the nature of things that greed of place and pension—to say nothing of political differences—should sunder these hungry and unprincipled groups.

But while the voice of prudence counselled delay, missives from Windsor urgently requested Pitt to assume the supreme command of the beaten host. Well might the King be insistent. In the young statesman, and in him alone, could he discern a possible saviour from the two-headed monster of the Coalition. As usual, he viewed the crisis from a purely personal point of view. In a characteristic letter to Shelburne he said nothing on the wider issues that were at stake, still less did he vouchsafe a word of thanks for his valuable services; but he deplored his own lot in having to reign in a most profligate age, and declared once more that he would never submit to the Coalition.

It seems probable that the credit of advising the choice of Pitt as the new Prime Minister rests with Shelburne. Certainly the idea did not originate with Henry Dundas, as he afterwards claimed; for on Monday morning, 24th February 1783, Dundas wrote to Shelburne as follows:

> MY DEAR LORD,
> I cannot refrain from troubling your Lordship with a few lines upon a subject of the most serious importance; and the particular ground of my addressing you arises from the words which dropped from you yesterday morning relative to Mr. Pitt. I did not pay much attention to them when you uttered them, but I have revolved them seriously and candidly in the course of the day yesterday, and I completely satisfied my own mind that, young as he is, the appointment of him to the Government of the country is the only step that can be taken in the present moment attended with the most distant chance of rearing up the Government of this country. . . . He is perfectly new ground, against whom no opposition can arise except what may be expected from the desperation of that lately allied faction, which I am satisfied will likewise gradually decline till at last it will consist only of that insolent aristocratical band who assume to themselves the prerogative of appointing the rulers of the kingdom. I repeat it again that I am certain the experiment will succeed if His Majesty will try it.[1]
>
> HENRY DUNDAS.

The King warmly welcomed Shelburne's suggestion, sent for Pitt, and urged him to form a Ministry on his own terms. The young statesman, far from succumbing to the glamour of the moment, at once foresaw the difficulties of the proposal, and requested time for reflection. Dundas sat up with him through that night, going through the names of members of the House, and calculating the chances of adequate support. In a letter which Pitt wrote to his mother on the 25th, he speaks of the question as turning on that of numbers in the House. On the next day and the morning of the 27th he seemed ready to accept the King's offer, on the strength of an assurance given by Dundas that Lord North would not actively oppose him. But on the afternoon of that day he laid before the King his reasons for declining the proposal.

The interview was long and earnest. It marked the beginning

---

[1] Chevening MSS. Yet on 25th February, Dundas wrote of the plan as "my project" (Stanhope, i, 105).

of that contest of wills which only ceased with life itself. The King strove hard to gain for his service the only man of note who stood between him and the new Coalition. He plied the young Minister with every possible argument.

Nothing [so the King wrote to Shelburne on that day] could get him to depart from the ground he took, that nothing less than a moral certainty of a majority in the House of Commons could make him undertake the task; for that it would be dishonourable not to succeed, if attempted; all I could obtain was that he should again try, but as fixed a declaration that, if he cannot meet with what he thinks certainty, he shall decline.[1]

We could wish to know more about this interview and to follow the mental wrestling of the Sovereign with the young barrister. Rarely, except perhaps from Chatham, had George III met with so firm a resolve not to accept office; and we may reasonably infer that the reluctance which baffled the arts of the King sprang from a deep fund of pride. Pitt scorned to be Minister by sufferance of North—a man whom he loathed. Further, why should he take up that burden at the bidding of the Sovereign whom he knew to be the chief cause of the present difficulties? Was it not better that George III and his former tool should unravel the tangle of their own making? As North and Fox for the present commanded the House of Commons, they must govern, as long as they could hold together. Reasons of varied kinds, therefore, must have led Pitt to hold back; and though he promised the King to consider the matter, we may be sure that his resolve was virtually formed.

Other names were then mooted, including those of Thomas Pitt and Earl Temple; but, as George III bitterly complained, not one of them had spirit enough to stand forth. All his efforts to escape the meshes of the Coalition were in vain. Meanwhile, public affairs went from bad to worse. "Our internal regulations (so William Grenville wrote to Temple), our loan, our commerce, our army, everything is at a stand . . . we have no money, and our troops and seamen are in mutiny."[2] But, for a

---

[1] Fitzmaurice, "Shelburne," iii, 369-70; Stanhope, i, 104-9; "Memorials of Fox," ii, 40-2. The King's letter to Shelburne refutes Horace Walpole's statement that the King made the offer very drily and ungraciously: also that Pitt's vanity was at first "staggered" by the offer.

[2] "Buckingham P.," i, 170.

whole month, nothing bent the King's purpose. It was clear that he was seeking to sow discord among his opponents.[1] In this he failed. Finally the Coalition succeeded in imposing its nominee, the Duke of Portland, on the King; but, as George insisted that his " friend," Lord Thurlow, should continue to be Lord Chancellor, the duke and his backers broke off the negotiations (18th to 20th March). At once the King sent for Pitt in the following curt note—the first in his long correspondence with him.[2]

Queen's House, March 20, 1783.

Mr. Pitt, I desire you will come here immediately.

G. R.

Once more, then, the King made his offer to the young statesman. For five days he sought to bend that stubborn will, urging the needs of the public service and his own resolve never to admit the Duke of Portland and North after their treatment of him. But on 25th March Pitt politely, but most firmly, declined, on the same grounds as before. The King thereupon declared himself much hurt at his refusal to stand forth against "the most daring and unprincipled faction that the annals of this kingdom ever produced."[3] Once more he talked of retiring to Hanover and leaving to the Coalition the task of governing Great Britain. But on mentioning this scheme to his hard-headed counsellor, Lord Thurlow, he is said to have received the illuminating advice that the journey to Hanover was easy enough; but the example of James II's travels abroad warranted the conclusion that the return journey was more difficult.[4] The story is *ben trovato*; but we may doubt whether even Thurlow's assurance was equal to this ironical dissuasiveness, and whether George III would ask advice on a step never meant to be taken, and threatened merely in petulance. Equally unconvincing is the story of the King bursting into tears in the presence of the hated Duke of Portland. If the age was lachrymose,[5] George III was not.

In any case, the Coalition had conquered. They dictated their terms. George bent before the parliamentary storm, perhaps taking heart from Thurlow's words, that time and patience

---

[1] " Buckingham P.," i, 194.

[3] Stanhope, i, App. III.

[5] Sichel, " Sheridan," i, 133.

[2] Pitt MSS., 103.

[4] Wraxall, iii, 36.

would cure the present evils. On the last day of March, Pitt, with the relic of Shelburne's Ministry, resigned office; and on the 2nd of April the new Ministers kissed hands. One who saw that function declared that he foresaw the fate of the Coalition Ministry; for when Fox came up for that ceremony, " George III turned back his ears and eyes just like the horse at Astley's when the tailor he had determined to throw was getting on him." [1]

The observer augured well. Fox's eagerness to mount the saddle, and Pitt's determination to stand aloof largely determined their future careers and the course of history. Success comes to the man who knows, not only when to strike swiftly and hard, but also how to bide his time. The examples of Pericles and Epaminondas; of Fabius Maximus, Caesar and Caesar Augustus in ancient history; of Louis XI, Elizabeth, Cromwell, William of Orange, Talleyrand, and even of Napoleon, might be cited as proofs of the power inherent in far-seeing patience. With Pitt's refusal of power in the spring of 1783 we may compare Napoleon's prudent reserve in the French political game of the years 1797-8, based as it was on his declaration to Talleyrand in October 1797: " It is only with prudence, wisdom and great dexterity that obstacles are surmounted and important ends attained. . . . I see no impossibility in attaining, in the course of a few years, those splendid results of which the heated and enthusiastic imagination catches a glimpse, but which the extremely cool, persevering and positive man alone can grasp." Pitt's great speech of 21st February 1783 showed him to possess imaginative gifts and ambition of a high order; his refusal of office, owing to the stubborn facts of arithmetic, was the outcome of those cool and calculating instincts without which aspiring genius is a balloon devoid of ballast.

The reception accorded by the public to the Coalition Ministry was far from flattering. No sooner were the names of Ministers known, on 2nd April 1783, than indignation ran high. The Duke of Portland, as First Lord of the Treasury, was seen to be an ornamental figure, easily controllable by Fox. The two Secretaries of State were North and Fox, the latter leading the House of Commons; and this close official union of two men who had spent their lives in vilifying each other was generally reprobated. [2] Fox, formerly the bitterest of North's revilers, was

---

[1] " Memorials of Fox," ii, 28.   [2] Wraxall, iii, 89, 143-5.

held to have betrayed his Whig principles; and his once enthusiastic constituents at Westminster, at his re-election refused him a hearing, shouting him down several times. The conduct of North, the reviled, seemed incredibly base and unmanly. For the rest, Lord John Cavendish (dubbed by Selwyn "the learned canary-bird") took Pitt's place at the Exchequer; Lord Stormont became President of the Council, the Earl of Carlisle, Lord Privy Seal; and Keppel returned to the Admiralty. The foregoing formed the Cabinet. As the King was forced to part with his man, Thurlow, the Lord Chancellor's seal was put in commission, Lord Loughborough (formerly Mr. Wedderburn, a man apt at betrayal) becoming first commissioner. Burke and Sheridan were rewarded with the subordinate posts of Paymaster of the Forces and Secretary to the Treasury. Thus the Whig members were in the ascendant, though North's party predominated in the House of Commons. Temple resigned the Lord-Lieutenancy of Ireland, which went, after an embarrassing delay, to one of Fox's boon companions at Brooks's, Lord Northington.[1]

Wilberforce, with his usual power of hitting off a situation, declared that the Fox-North Coalition inherited the defects of its progenitors, the violence of Fox and the corruption of North. This was the general opinion. As for George III, he raged against this unnatural union. He could not mention the subject without falling into the flurried incoherent kind of talk which afterwards marked the on-coming of attacks of lunacy. Private hatred of Fox, as the man who led astray the Prince of Wales into the equally odious paths of gambling and political opposition, fed the King's animosity against the Whig orator as the foe of the constitution. But the vials of his wrath were poured forth on North, for his betrayal of the royal confidence lavished on him for a decade. On 1st April, George III informed Temple that he hoped the nation's eyes would soon be opened, and that the Pitts and Grenvilles would deliver him from the thraldom of the Coalition. For the present, he would certainly refuse to grant any honours asked for by the new Ministry.[2] As

---

[1] "Dropmore P.," i, 197-212. Mr. Sichel ("Sheridan," ii, ch. ii), following the earlier biographer, Thomas Moore, proves that Sheridan sought to dissuade Fox from the coalition with North. This is doubtless true. But determined opposition should have led him to refuse office.

[2] "Buckingham P.," i, 189, 219.

the greed of the Coalition was notorious, the situation thus
became piquant in the extreme. Amusement at the irony of the
situation must have helped, in Pitt's case, to lighten the disappointment of retiring from office. Certainly he was never down-
cast. Wilberforce's journal shows him to have been a frequent
and a joyous visitor to Wimbledon. This was the time of the
spring-sowing of the flower-beds of Lauriston House with the
fragments of Ryder's opera hat. (See Chapter XII.)

Other and more practical fruits of his hopefulness were his
efforts for Parliamentary Reform, clouded over though that cause
was by the alliance of Whigs and the former " King's Friends."
Acting not as a partisan (for, just before resigning office, he informed the House that he belonged to no party), he introduced
a motion on 7th May for the Reform of Parliament. On this
occasion London and Kent seemed to take an interest in the
motion, and the approaches to St. Stephen's as well as the
galleries were thronged by petitioners in favour of Reform. The
freeholders of Kent, the householders of the Tower Hamlets, and
the electors of Westminster (the last headed by Fox!), came in
great numbers to give weight to their petitions. Horace Walpole
noted that Kent and Essex had joined the Quintuple Alliance
(*i.e.*, of counties) in favour of Reform.[1]

In due course Pitt rose to bring in his motion. He claimed
that the disasters of the past years had at length caused the
people " to turn their eyes inward on themselves " to find out the
cause of the evil. No one could now doubt that the radical fault
in the constitution was the secret influence of the Crown as
exerted on the House of Commons. For the redress of this evil
three plans had been proposed, first, the extension of the franchise to every man—a proposal which he scouted as both impracticable and even undesirable, seeing that the minority must
then hold themselves to be slaves to the majority. (It is difficult
to follow Pitt here; for every electoral system implies a majority
and minority; and hardship arises only when the majority is
subservient to the minority—as was the case in 1783.) Their
forefathers, he added, had never contemplated giving a vote

---

[1] Horace Walpole's Letters (8th May 1783). He thought Pitt's motion
"most dangerous. We know pretty well what good or evil the present state
of the House of Commons can do. What an enlargement might achieve no
man can tell." Later on he notes that Pitt was very little supported, but
shone marvellously in debate.

to every man, and the scheme was " a mere speculative proposition
that may be good in theory but which it would be absurd and
chimerical to endeavour to reduce to practice." These words
should be noted. For they refute the slander that Pitt "ratted"
from the cause of Reform in and after 1790, when it was based
on the Jacobin theory of universal suffrage, which he had always
repudiated.

Pitt's second proposal of Reform was to abolish the "rotten
boroughs." He confessed that they were "deformities" in our
system, but he felt that they could not be removed without en-
dangering the whole pile. The third proposal seemed to him far
better, namely, to add a number of members for the counties and
the metropolis. He summed up his contentions in three Resolutions: (1) for the prevention of bribery and undue expense at
elections; (2) the disfranchisement of boroughs where corruption
was proven ; (3) an addition to members of counties and of the
metropolis. The details of these proposals were to be specified
in a Bill, if the Resolutions were carried. They met with support
from Fox, while their very limited character, which Sheridan
ridiculed, commended them to Dundas and Thomas Pitt, who
previously had opposed Reform.[1] As a pledge of his sincerity,
Thomas Pitt offered to surrender his rights over the parliamentary borough of Old Sarum.

All was of no avail. North, Colonel Luttrell, Lord Mulgrave,
and others declaimed against any change in the glorious constitution. The House by a majority of one hundred and forty-
four reprobated the dangerous spirit of innovation which was
abroad. Doubtless the demoralization of the Whigs made defeat
inevitable. Pitt himself spoke with less than his usual effective-
ness ; and the absence of petitions from the new manufacturing
towns showed that the country at large cared little for the question. This apathy seems to us unaccountable until we remember
that Manchester, Leeds, and Halifax tamely suffered Richard
Cromwell to annul the act of enfranchisement which the great
Oliver had bestowed upon them. Evidently the age-long torpor
still lay upon the land.

In the rest of the session, Pitt brought in measures for effecting retrenchment in the public offices. He commented on
such abuses as the following: that the chief clerk of the navy

---

[1] Mr. Sichel ("Sheridan," ii, 36) admits the strong personal element in
Sheridan's opposition to Pitt.

office received a salary of £250 a year, but ten times that amount in gifts, and other clerks in the same proportion. The Secretary of the Post Office raised his salary of £500 to a total of £3,000 by a 2½ per cent. charge on all packets—a curiously cumbrous method of redress. The expense of stationery at the office of Lord North during his term at the Treasury was £1,300 a year, one item being £340 for whip-cord! By careful economies Pitt hoped to save the nation £40,000 a year. The debate was rendered remarkable by a speech from Burke. The great man was smarting under the censure of the House for reinstating two dishonest officials, and had betrayed the Celtic sensitiveness of his nature by drearily ranting until Fox and Sheridan fairly pulled him to his seat. He now rallied Pitt on " prying into the little perquisites of little men in little offices, while he suffered the greatest abuses to exist in the offices under his eye. He seemed to have that nice olfactory nerve which could smell a ball of horsedung a thousand miles off, but which was not affected by the stench of a dunghill under his very window." Burke, however, failed to substantiate the latter part of his mal-odorous simile. The measure passed the Commons, only to perish in the Lords. Keppel denied that there were any abuses at the Admiralty; the Duke of Portland opined that Pitt's reforms would cost as much as they saved; and Stormont declared that they would be highly inconvenient.[1] The same fate befell a measure, which Pitt warmly supported, for lessening expenses at elections.

In his speech on Lord John Cavendish's Budget, Pitt showed a practical knowledge of finance which enabled him trenchantly to expose the weak points of his successor's proposals; and he further pointed out the best means for launching a loan on the most favourable terms. His reputation gained in solidity during the session; and if his speeches, after the great effort of 21st February, lacked brilliance, they exhibited his capacity and his grasp of affairs.

Ministers, on the other hand, lost ground, owing to their own blunders and the widening of the gulf between their discordant sections. A case in point was their treatment of the question of the allowance for the Prince of Wales. As will appear later more in detail, the relations between the King and the Prince were

[1] " Parl. Hist.," xxiii, 926, 945, 1,114.

already so strained that the Ministry—"my son's Ministry," the King sometimes called it—must have known the question to be thorny. The tastes of George III being as frugal as those of his son were extravagant, a clear understanding with the King seemed the first essential to a settlement. Yet Fox and his supporters in the Cabinet prevailed on the other Ministers, rather reluctantly, to allot the sum of £100,000 a year to the Prince, and that, too, without consulting the King. According to Horace Walpole, the proposal came to light during a casual conversation between the King and the Duke of Portland on 11th June. The account given in the "Fox Memorials" seems, however, to convict George III of inconsistency.[1] In any case, he angrily declaimed against the proposal, as showing that Ministers, despite their professions of economy, "were ready to sacrifice the public interests to the wishes of *an ill-advised young man*"; he declared his readiness to allow the Prince £50,000 a year from the Civil List, so as not to burden the public. This was the sum which he himself had received as Prince of Wales; and he held strong ground in proposing to support his bachelor son on a similar allowance.

This was the mine sprung upon the Ministry on 16th June. It promised to end their existence; and Fox believed that the King would seize the opportunity to dismiss Ministers, dissolve Parliament, and appeal to the country on the cry of economy, paternal authority, and no mischief-making between father and son. Doubtless he would have done so but for the very speedy compliance of the Prince of Wales with his expressed wishes— an act of submission due less to the filial devotion of the Prince than to his desire to save his favourite from a crushing defeat at the polls. Ultimately, on 23rd June, the House agreed to vote the sum of £60,000 for the present needs of the Prince, as regards debts and the furnishing of Carlton House, and £50,000 a year out of the Civil List. The incident led to some regrettable complications. Fox seems to have attributed the King's sudden anger to an intrigue of Pitt, whom he dubbed "an unscrupulous opposer."[2] Further, the Prince thenceforth more than ever looked on his father and the opponents of Fox as his own personal enemies,

---

[1] "Memorials of Fox," ii, 113. Jesse, "Memoirs of George III," iii, 435, states that the Shelburne Ministry had named £100,000 as the allowance for the Prince. I find no proof of this.

[2] "Memorials of Fox," ii, 113, 119.

in that they bound him down to an insufficient allowance, which he felt no scruple in exceeding. The wretched business of the Prince of Wales's debts, and even that of the Regency, resulted in no small measure from the bad blood engendered in the strife of June 1783.

The King, also, as we can now see by the new light which the Dropmore Papers have thrown on events, watched the course of affairs more closely than ever in order to pave the way to office for the Pitts and Grenvilles. But his rancour did not blunt his prudence. He was resolved not to exchange one set of masters for another. If Pitt came in, it must be on terms favourable to the Crown. George saw Temple after his abandonment of the cares of State at Dublin Castle, and soon began to sound him and Pitt as to their ideas on a future Ministry.[1]

There was one grave objection to Pitt, namely, his zeal for Reform. Seeing that the Coalition Ministry was lukewarm on this subject, the King strove to ensure similar complaisance on the part of its successor. He therefore commissioned his secret bargainer, Thurlow, to see Pitt and clear up this question. The ex-Lord Chancellor invited his former colleague to dinner on 19th July, five days after the end of the session. He was very wary in his overtures, and Pitt complained to Grenville that he had a very good meal, but little information. Thurlow was profuse in hints and innuendos, which Pitt gauged at their real value. First he depicted the situation as by no means unfavourable to the King, who had gone through the worst when he admitted the Foxites to office. On Pitt suggesting that perhaps he would become reconciled to them, Thurlow hastened to add that that was impossible, especially after the affair of the Prince's allowance. The "King's friend" then turned the conversation to the subject of Parliamentary Reform and the influence of the Crown.

His object (so Pitt wrote to Earl Temple) was to insinuate that a change was not so necessary to the King; and to endeavour to make it (if it should take place) rather our act than his; and on that ground to try whether terms might not be imposed that could not otherwise. This is so totally contrary to every idea we both entertain that I thought it necessary to take full care to counteract it. I stated in general that if the King's feelings did not point strongly to a change, it was not what

[1] "Buckingham P.," i, 303-5.

we sought. But that if they did, and we could form a permanent system, consistent with our principles, and on public ground, we should not decline it. I reminded him how much I was personally pledged to Parliamentary Reform on the principles I had publicly explained, which I should support on every seasonable occasion. I treated as out of the question any idea of measures being taken to extend [Crown] influence, though such means as are fairly in the hands of Ministers would undoubtedly be to be exerted. And I said that I wished those with whom I might act, and the King (if he called upon me) to be fully apprized of the grounds on which I should necessarily proceed. . . .[1]

This is a declaration of the highest importance. If Thurlow was not very explicit, Pitt certainly was; and it is clear that he fathomed the intentions of George III. They were, in brief, to use the present unsatisfactory state of things as an inducement to a patriotic and ambitious young man to come forward as a " King's friend," taking up the place which North's defection had left vacant. Shelving the problem of Parliamentary Reform, Pitt was to govern for the King and by means of his influence. The young statesman saw the snare, skilfully evaded it, and let it be understood that, if he took office, he would come in on his own terms, not on those of the King. Firm in the alliance of the Grenvilles, and all who detested the Coalition Ministry, he needed not to supplicate the royal favour. Once more he would bide his time, until the King sued for his support. Temple in his reply warmly commended his sound sense and honourable conduct, acknowledging that Pitt was pledged to Reform, so long as there was any chance of success.

A time of skilful balancing now ensued. The King, disappointed at Pitt's independent attitude, took Temple's advice, and decided to leave to his Ministers the odium of concluding peace, and of bringing in proposals of Reform which would certainly disappoint some and exasperate others of their following. It is clear, however, that, after his annoyance at the question of the Prince of Wales's allowance, George resolved to dismiss his Ministers as soon as their popularity waned, and to recur to personal rule, if he could find a serviceable instrument. It was generally known by the end of the session that Pitt might play that part as soon as he chose. George hinted

---

[1] "Dropmore P.," i, 216; also Earl Stanhope's "Miscellanies," ii, 23-6, who rightly places the date as 20th July.

as much to Thurlow, who passed it on to the political world. The news was well known when Pitt went down to Brighthelmstone for sea-bathing in August.[1]

Other causes, however, besides the aloofness of Pitt, concurred to postpone the crisis. The Cabinet, feeling its position insecure, was in no haste to sign the definitive treaties of peace, feeling the interval of uncertainty to be some guarantee of continuance in office. There was also some hope that the Czarina, Catharine II, intent as she was on plans against Turkey, would court our alliance and thus end our isolation.[2] Thus the state of party affairs in England, as well as the changing ambitions of the Czarina, helped to postpone the final settlement; but ultimately the treaties were signed on 3rd September at Versailles. They varied very slightly from the preliminaries which Ministers, when in opposition, had so violently attacked. Apart from a stipulation for the safeguarding of British property in the ceded island of Tobago, and the better definition of our rights in the gum trade, there was no material change. The American Loyalists, for whom Fox and Burke had so passionately pleaded, were left in the same position as in the preliminary treaty. The Coalition Ministry in five months of bargaining secured no better terms from France and Spain than Shelburne had arranged. Fox and North, who had blamed their predecessors for failing to make a commercial agreement with the United States, now had to confess their own failure. Finally, the Preliminaries with Holland, signed on 2nd September, showed that Fox, who, with Sheridan, had declaimed against the expected retrocession of Trincomalee to the Dutch, now consented to it. Negapatam, a far less commanding post, was retained.

These actions exposed Ministers to the charge of gross inconsistency in ratifying conditions of peace against which they had inveighed in unmeasured terms. On 11th November Pitt rallied them on this topic, and then, soaring from the low levels of partisan warfare, to the heights of statesmanlike survey, he uttered these words:

The nation has a right to expect that, without delay, a complete commercial system, suited to the novelty of our situation, will be laid before

---

[1] " Buckingham P.," i, 304; " Rutland P.," iii, 70; Stanhope, " Misc.," ii, 32-5.

[2] *Ibid.*, i, 218; " Memorials of Fox," ii, 131-9.

Parliament. I am acquainted with the difficulty of the business and will not attribute the delay hitherto to any neglect on the part of Ministers. I am willing to ascribe it to the nature of the negotiation; but I expect that the business will soon be brought forward, not by piece-meal, but that one grand system of commerce, built upon the circumstances of the times, will be submitted to the House for their consideration.[1]

This is the first sign of Pitt's resolve to give effect to the teachings of Adam Smith, and to aid in founding on the ruins of our old colonial system a fabric far sounder and more beneficent. It is further significant, as showing the absence of factiousness in the Opposition, that the address to the King of thanks for the peace was carried unanimously.

We have looked ahead in order to glance at Pitt's conduct respecting the treaties of peace concluded on 3rd September; let us turn to his movements during the vacation. First he ran down to Brighthelmstone to take some dips in the sea; and then struck away westwards towards Somerset for a flying visit to Lady Chatham at Burton Pynsent. Next, after a short stay at Kingston Hall, Bankes's country house in Dorset, in company with Wilberforce and Eliot, he returned to town on 7th September in order to look into the political situation. He found that the Ministry was losing favour mainly because the King refused to grant any peerages at their request. Apart from this, however, there was no sign of a collapse. That stormy petrel of politics, Lord Thurlow, was abroad; and Pitt probably considered it tactful not to linger about town, but to visit the Continent. Before setting out, he attended the *levée* at St. James's on 10th September; and the King inquired the time of his return "in a rather significant manner."[2]

On the next day he met Wilberforce and Eliot at Canterbury, and on the 12th they crossed to Calais. He found the journey to Reims more comfortable, and the appearance of the people more prosperous, than he had expected; but "the face of the country the dullest I ever saw." The reception of the party at Reims, where they proposed to improve their French before proceeding to Paris, had a spice of novelty. Each of the three friends had trusted to the others to provide the needful introduc-

[1] "Parl. Hist.," xxiii, 1143.
[2] "Dropmore P.," i, 219, 220; Stanhope, "Misc.," ii, 35.

tions. As a result they were able only to obtain one introduction, through the London banker, Thellusson, and this proved to be to a grocer, whom they found behind his counter selling figs and raisins. Somewhat crestfallen, the three *milords anglais* returned to their inn. Not for ten days did they gain an *entrée* to the intendant of Reims, and through him to the Archbishop. His Grace was by no means an awe-inspiring personage; he figures in Wilberforce's letters as a jolly fellow, about forty years of age, who played billiards like other people. The three friends also met an Abbé de Lageard, "a fellow of infinite humour," who used to entertain them by visits of five or six hours at a stretch. To him, early in their acquaintance, Pitt mooted a grievance, that there, in the middle of Champagne, they could get no wine that was even tolerable. The abbé thereupon entertained them at his house with the best wine of the province, and with five hours of breezy talk.

Pitt, so we learn from Wilberforce, was the most fluent of the visitors on these occasions. His ear, "quick for every sound but music," readily caught the intonations of the language, and he soon conversed with ease and fair accuracy. Some few of his *mots* are preserved by Wilberforce. In answer to the abbé's inquiry about his opinion of French institutions, Pitt replied: " Sir, you have no political liberty, but as for liberty in civil affairs, you have more than you think." His opinion on the durability of the English constitution is even more surprising. " The part of our constitution which will first perish is the prerogative of the King and the authority of the House of Peers."[1] None of Pitt's sayings is more remarkable than this, uttered as it was long before the storms of the French Revolution, and after the British monarchy had easily weathered the Atlantic gale. Possibly the conviction here recorded helps to explain why, at the close of the year, Pitt undertook to support the monarchy, in order to maintain that balance of the English constitution which all thinkers (especially Montesquieu) had praised as its peculiar excellence.

The third of the *mots* mentioned by Wilberforce illustrates the generosity of Pitt's character, a trait in which his opponents, judging from his generally cold exterior, believed him to be deficient. On the abbé expressing surprise at so moral a country as

---

[1] " Life of Wilberforce," i, 38.

England allowing itself to be governed by Fox, a man signally deficient in private character, Pitt replied: "Ah! you have not been under the wand of the magician." Out of the varied scintillations of wit and gaiety with which Pitt brightened this five weeks' sojourn in France, we catch a glimpse of these three sparks alone. Doubtless the weakness of Wilberforce's eyes at that time accounts for the tantalizingly meagre entries in his diary; but, seeing how elusive a figure Pitt is, we must be thankful even for these slight jottings.

We are therefore left wondering about the intercourse between the three Englishmen and Talleyrand, who was then staying with his uncle, the Archbishop of Reims. Of their brilliant conversations—for where Talleyrand was dullness could not dwell—we know nothing. Talleyrand and Pitt, we are told, instructed one another in their mother tongues and exchanged ideas, especially on literature and the advantages of Free Trade.[1] What a subject for Landor, this interchange of thoughts between the ablest young men of the age, who agreed on all the essentials of politics and yet were soon to be forced by destiny into bitter conflict! How different the future might have been had Talleyrand had enough strength and straightforwardness to become chief of the French Republic!

The stay of the three friends at Reims ended on 9th October, owing to Pitt's desire to reach Paris in time to see George Rose, a Secretary of the Treasury, who had been travelling on the Continent with Lord Thurlow. There can be little doubt that Pitt hoped to hear from him news respecting the situation in London; for they had confidential converse, in which Pitt gained over Rose completely to his side.[2] At Paris he had intercourse with Lafayette, Benjamin Franklin, and many other celebrities. By special invitation they shared in the gala festivities of the Court at Fontainebleau, and there saw not only the French Ministers and chief nobles, but also the King and Queen (15th-19th October). That was the heyday of Louis XVI and Marie Antoinette. The conclusion of the Peace of Versailles with England seemed to place France without question at the head of the political world. She had sundered the Empire of her rival, and with ordinary wisdom she might hope to keep the lead as a com-

[1] Lady Blennerhassett, "Life of Talleyrand," i, 46. It is strange that the "Talleyrand Memoirs" do not mention the meeting.

[2] G. Rose, "Diaries," i, 32.

mercial and colonizing power. Strong in the alliance of Austria
and Spain, with her friendship courted by the United States,
Prussia, Sweden, and Holland—at times by the Czarina Catharine
—France seemed to be high above the reach of adverse fortune.
The prestige of the monarchy was as yet undimmed by the affair
of the Diamond Necklace. The factious opposition of the Parle-
ments had scarcely begun; and the days of hunting and festivity
at Fontainebleau must have realized those visions of charm and
beauty in which Burke has enshrined Marie Antoinette, "glittering like the morning star, full of life and splendour and joy."

By her side at Court and in the hunting field was that strange
opposite, her husband. What the friends thought of Louis XVI
in hunting attire is shown by Wilberforce's note—"clumsy
strange figure in immense boots." Whether the King spoke to
them is doubtful, for his words were ever few, and etiquette forbade his conversing much with foreigners.[1] But the Queen, with
her usual vivacity and wit, rallied them upon their friend, the
grocer, at Reims. The courtiers often crowded round Pitt (so
Wilberforce recalls), "and he behaved with great spirit, though
he was sometimes a little bored when they talked to him about
Parliamentary Reform." At Fontainebleau Pitt met Lafayette
at dinner in company with the American Minister, Franklin.
Again we long to know of the converse of these representative
men. Only one scrap survives, namely, that Pitt informed the
Frenchman, whom his admirers termed "the hero of both
worlds," that his principles were too democratic for him.[2] When
the tempest burst upon Western Europe, this soon became
apparent.

Necker, the Minister who in 1789 aspired to ride on the winds
and control the storm, was desirous of allying his family with
that of Pitt. The ex-Controller-General of French Finances and
his ambitious consort sought to strengthen their claims on the
Government for a return to office, by an alliance with a powerful family. What alliance could be so brilliant for these Genevese
Protestants as with the son of Chatham? We now know for
certain that Necker and his wife urgently wished for this union;
for a year later the mother, when seriously ill, wrote to her
daughter (the future Mme. de Staël) in these terms:

I did desire that you should marry Mr. Pitt. I wished to confide you

---

[1] Wraxall, iii, 122.   [2] "Early Life of Samuel Rogers," 134.

to the care of a husband who had made for himself a great name; I
also could have wished for a son-in-law to whose care I could commend
your poor father, and who would feel the full weight of his charge.
You were not disposed to give me this satisfaction. Well! All is now
forgiven.[1]

Clearly the match was to have been of an eleemosynary character; and all who rejoice in the eager exuberance of the life of
Mme. de Staël cannot be surprised at her refusal, even when a
young girl, to become a testamentary asset in the life of her
father. Whether her repugnance at the idea was further increased
by seeing Pitt in one of his "bored" moods, we do not know.
Indeed it is uncertain whether they ever met. If we may judge
from the sketch of Pitt written by Wilberforce in 1821, the affair
was mooted in the frigid bargaining manner usual with French
parents. Horace Walpole, a close friend of M. Necker, remarked
to Lord Camden, who thereupon passed it on to Pitt, that the
Neckers had so much respect for him that, if he claimed the
hand of their daughter, he would not be refused—by the parents.
What would have happened when Mlle. Necker came to be
asked must be left to the imagination.[2]

From the charms of the French Court and the meshes of
matrimonial schemes Pitt was suddenly called away. A special
messenger bade him return at once to London. What he had
all along hoped now came to pass. The King's dislike of his
Ministers had overcome all other feelings, and he now appealed
to Pitt to free him from the toils of the Coalition. The friends
spent twenty-four hours in a carriage, then suffered the usual
miseries of a Channel passage, and reached London on 24th
October.

The situation was serious. Though delivered from fear of war,
the country was beset by many perils. Consols were on the
decline. The state of Ireland was alarming. The Associations
of Volunteers overshadowed the Government at Dublin, and
seemed about to dictate terms to that at Westminster. Their
attitude aroused keen resentment, seeing that the legislative independence of Ireland had been proclaimed to be the cure for

---

[1] D'Haussonville, "The Salon of Mme. Necker," ii, 50 (Eng. ed.).
[2] "Private Papers of W. Wilberforce," 58. Strange to say, Horace
Walpole does not mention the affair in his letters.

all her evils. "What! (exclaimed Horace Walpole) Would they throw off our Parliament and yet amend it." Worst of all, perhaps, was the almost complete indifference of Britons to the political situation. The same rather cynical observer had already noted that no one, except interested politicians, really cared who was in, or out of, office. His words deserve quotation:

Our levity is unlike that' of the French. They turn everything into a jest, an epigram, or a ballad. We are not pleasant but violent, and yet remember nothing for a moment. This was not our character formerly. . . . Can the people be much attached to any man if they think well of none? Can they hate any man superlatively if they think ill of all? In my own opinion we have no positive character at present at all. We are not so bad as most great nations have been when sinking. We have no excessive vices, no raging animosities.[1]

The passage is interesting in more ways than one. Milton dubbed us fickle and alleged our insular situation as the cause.[2] Addison in one of his essays repeated the charge, which was perfectly natural early in the eighteenth century. Further, Horace Walpole's criticism is remarkable as that of a shrewd observer during what he termed a time of " comfortable calm." He saw the two leading nations, as it were, drifting sluggishly in a Sargasso Sea of politics after one storm; and they and he never suspected the approach of a far more terrible tempest. Neither in London nor Paris had any inspiring personality come to the front. Pitt had not fully emerged. Robespierre was intent on his briefs at Arras; the Corsican, who was to quicken the pulse of all peoples, still studied under the monks of Brienne; and Horace Walpole could therefore complain of the pettiness of politics, the aimless brawlings of Westminster, the lighter vagaries of Versailles, and the dullness of the world.

At London all was soon to change. Though Fox and North kept their majority solid on the question of the peace, yet they came to grief over a measure of almost equal importance. On 18th November, amidst scenes of unequalled excitement, Fox brought forward his India Bill; and on a question where vast patronage was at stake passions rose to fever heat. Indian affairs will be treated more fully in another chapter; and it must suffice to

---

[1] Horace Walpole (24th Feb. 1783).
[2] Milton, " A Free Commonwealth."

state here that the East India Company was in a deplorable condition, mainly owing to the war with Hyder Ali and the insubordination and rapacity of the Company's servants, which led to abuses degrading to Britain and oppressive to the natives of India. According to the terms of North's Regulating Act of 1773, Parliament had the right of intervention in all matters of high policy; but in one important question the Company had set its behests at naught. In April 1782 a vote of censure was passed on the Governor-General, Warren Hastings, and the Company was requested to recall him. The Court of Directors issued an order to this effect; but the Court of Proprietors reversed their decision, and Hastings was left in a position ambiguous and irritating to all parties. Consequently dictates of policy and the interests of the nation compelled Parliament to assert its paramount authority.

But the manner of the intervention and the act itself were alike extraordinary. The new India Bill was the joint work of Fox and Burke with some aid from the law-officers of the Crown. It has often been said, on the scantiest of evidence, to have been framed mainly by Burke; but the clauses which abrogated the Charter of the East India Company and vested the control of Indian affairs chiefly in Parliament, bear the imprint of the mind of Fox rather than of the more cautious and conservative statesman.[1] In strict propriety the measure ought to have originated with Lord North. He privately expressed his approval, and then, alleging indisposition, stayed away from Parliament on the day of its introduction.[2]

Fox opened his case in a speech of great power. He dilated on the ills resulting from the disorders in the Company's service, and, in particular, from the ambition of Warren Hastings. He then showed the tendency of the parliamentary reports on Indian affairs, and claimed that, in the virtual bankruptcy of the Company (which could not discharge its debts to the Crown), Parliament had the right to take the supreme control of its territories. We may pause here to notice that the Directors of the Company stoutly denied the assertion as to their bankruptcy, and claimed that, when its expenses were reduced to a peace footing, the Company's creditors would be in a better position than any

---

[1] See, too, "Memorials of Fox," ii, 98. Probably the second Bill contained more of the suggestions of Burke.

[2] Wraxall, iii, 146, 155.

creditors in Europe.[1] Their printed report of 23rd January 1784 laid stress on the heavy charge involved by conquests in India "which the wisdom of the nation has given up for equivalents in other parts of the world." It also claimed the payment of £260,687, the charge incurred by the Company for the maintenance of French prisoners in the Seven Years' War. The Directors further stated that, if Government would check the very extensive smuggling in tea (an article which formed the most valuable of the monopolies of the Company), more than double the amount would be sold by legitimate means. These facts should be borne in mind, as the Company succeeded in spreading a conviction that the attack of Fox was unjust.

In the rest of his speech Fox detailed his proposals for effecting drastic changes in India, and explained the reasons for separating administrative affairs from purely mercantile affairs. Many authorities claimed that the territories of the Company belonged in reality to the Crown; others denied this claim. On one point all must agree, that the Crown could not possibly deal with "a remote and difficult trade." Accordingly he sought to form "a mixed system of government, adapted to the mixed complexion of our interests in India." For administrative work he proposed to establish a Board of seven commissioners, nominated by Parliament, for three or five years—four years was the term finally suggested—having full power to appoint and dismiss officers in India, and complete control over its government. The Board was to sit in London, "under the very eye of Parliament," and the minutes of its meetings were to be open to inspection by Parliament. If this experiment succeeded, he proposed that in future the King should nominate the seven commissioners, and he was to fill up vacancies that might occur in the meantime. As for the mercantile interests of the Company, they were to be managed by a subordinate Board or Council, consisting of eight members chosen by Parliament from among the larger proprietors.

He further proposed to remedy the worst abuses in India in a second Bill which would abolish the holding of monopolies, such as that for opium, which had been jobbed away to the son of a former chairman of the Company. Security of tenure would be granted to the Zamindars, or native landlords, and the accept-

---

[1] Paper dated 4th Dec. 1783, in Pitt MSS., 354.

ance of presents by the Company's servants in India—a fertile source of corruption and oppression—would be strictly forbidden. Fox admitted that the private influence of the Crown, even in its worst days, was nothing compared with that of the East India Company, and wisely abstained for the present from naming the seven commissioners whom he proposed to appoint.[1]

Here was the weak point of an otherwise excellent measure; and Pitt, towards whom all eyes were directed, fastened upon it. While admitting the urgent need of reform, he deprecated the abrogation of all the charters and privileges of an ancient Company under the plea of necessity. " Is not necessity," he said, "the plea of every illegal exertion of power? Is not necessity the pretence of every usurpation? Necessity is the argument of tyrants: it is the creed of slaves." Further, what evils must result if that formidable political weapon, the patronage of the Company, were transferred to the Ministers then in power, and finally to the Crown? On the one side it would tend to the grossest corruption, on the other, to despotism.[2]

Pitt, it will be seen, opposed the measure owing to the indirect but inevitable consequences which it would entail in the vitiated state of affairs then existing in Parliament, where an unwholesome Coalition held together only with the aim of enjoying the spoils of office and even richer booty in the future.[3] The possession of the enormous patronage of the India Company opened up golden vistas that fired the imaginations even of the dull squires who trooped after Lord North. As for the far livelier followers of Fox, they were jubilant at prospects which promised not only places in the East, but a long lease of power at St. Stephen's. Their opponents were alike depressed and indignant. A former friend of Fox, Sir Nathaniel Wraxall, commented on the " spirit of ambition, rapacity and confiscation " that characterized his proposals; and the bad impression caused by the patronage section of his Bill was intensified when it appeared that four of the seven new commissioners were to be declared Foxites, better known at Brooks's Club than at the India House, namely, Lord Fitzwilliam, Frederick Montagu, Sir Henry

---

[1] " Parl. Hist.," xxiii, 1187-1208. [2] *Ibid.*, 1209-11.
[3] I cannot agree with Lecky's statement (iv, 293) that Pitt's charges were extravagant. Seven partisan commissioners, jobbing away vast patronage, would have been a canker in the State, whether they acted for their party or the Crown.

I L

Fletcher, and Robert Gregory. In Lord North's interest there were his son, Colonel North, Viscount Lewisham, and Sir Gilbert Elliot.

The appointment of seven pronounced partisans to these posts of almost unbounded responsibility wrecked the measure. In itself the Bill contained many excellent features. The transference of governing power from the Company to Parliament in conjunction with the Crown, on terms ultimately favourable to the latter, was a bold step; but much could be said for it, and Pitt certainly overshot the limits of fair criticism in his first speech. If Fox and North had chosen the seven commissioners fairly from among all three parties, the mouths of gainsayers would have been stopped. Now, however, the partisan corollary to the measure justified the most vehement strictures. A flood of satire was poured on the Bill. Two caricatures in particular had a very wide circulation, probably at the expense of the threatened Company. One represented Fox as Samson carrying off the ruins of the East India House; the second, by Sayer, who soon became Pitt's man and received a small post from him, showed Fox as Carlo Khan riding into Delhi on an elephant having the face of Lord North, and preceded by Burke as trumpeter.

Pitt wrote privately to the Governor of the Company suggesting that its prestige would be enhanced if a meeting of its creditors could be arranged and a declaration could be procured that they would allow ample time for the discharge of their claims.[1] But caricatures, suggestions, and petitions were needless. The same facts which discredited the Bill in the country whetted the eagerness of the ministerial majority in Parliament. At the second reading Pitt briskly renewed his attacks; and he now had the support of William Grenville in a statesmanlike speech, which lacked "the commanding tone, the majesty, and all the captivating rotundity and splendour of Pitt's eloquence," but equalled it in argumentative power.[2] Dundas, Jenkinson, and Scott (the future Lord Eldon), reinforced the assault: but all was in vain. Burke, in a majestic oration, proclaimed that the Bill would save India from manifold evils which he depicted with righteous indignation.[3] But material interests told more than eloquence and morality. The influence of Ministers and the hopes of their followers ensured the speedy passing of this com-

[1] Pitt MSS., 102. Letter of 25th Nov. 1783.
[2] Wraxall, iii, 161.   [3] "Parl. Hist.," xxiii, 1312-86.

plex and far-reaching measure through the Commons by a final majority of 208 votes to 102 (3rd December).

This was a heavy blow to the Opposition, especially to Pitt, who had said that he would fight the whole Bill, clause by clause. Horace Walpole wrote two days later that Pitt had slunk from the contest, but that the check would do him good, dazzled as he had been by his premature fame. Walpole also remarked that, while excelling Chatham in logical power, the son had much less firmness and perseverance. Readers of those charming letters will note with some amusement that in the middle of the next month, Walpole wrote that nothing but obstinacy prevented Pitt resigning his post as Prime Minister. After that Walpole gave up the rôle of political prophet.

For now there occurred a series of events which taught modesty to wiseacres. The King intervened in a surprising manner. In the House of Lords influence from above was suddenly pitted against the interests of the nether world. George III had long been awaiting a fit opportunity for tripping up the hated Ministry. A few weeks before, he had covered Fox and North with ridicule in front of the whole Court. Acting on the first rumour of the death of Sir Eyre Coote in India, they had proffered a request that his ribbon of the Order of the Bath should go to a friend, and believed that they had secured the granted assent of the Sovereign. The aspirant therefore appeared at the next levée at St. James's Palace with the officers of the Order; but the King, affecting great surprise at the unseemly haste of his ministers in acting on unofficial information, refused to confer the ribbon, repulsed their entreaties, and postponed the ceremony.[1]

George was now to taste the sweets of revenge in a matter more than ceremonial. His coadjutor was Earl Temple, who had advised him to wait until the times were ripe; and from a MS. preserved at Chevening we learn that the King hastily sent for the Earl on the night of 11th December. Thurlow also had an interview with him and pointed out in unmeasured terms the humiliations which he would suffer from Fox's India Bill, namely, that it would transfer to the present Ministers " more than half the royal power." Always jealous of his patronage, the King at once determined to ward off so insidious an attack. But he and his advisers acted with characteristic caution. They considered

[1] Wraxall, iii, 150.

—and this is an interesting point in our constitutional history— that the exercise of the royal veto on the Bill, if it should pass both Houses, would be a "violent" step.[1] They preferred to act secretly and indirectly through the Lords.

In order to exert pressure in the most drastic way possible, a card was written (probably in the King's hand) stating "That His Majesty allowed Earl Temple to say that whoever voted for the India Bill was not only not his friend, but would be considered by him as an enemy; and if these words were not strong enough, Earl Temple might use whatever words he might deem stronger and more to the purpose."[2] Armed with this card, Temple set to work to whittle down the Fox-North majority. His success was startling and complete. The golden glint of the spoils of the Indies paled under the thunder-cloud of the royal displeasure. The fear of losing all chance of advancement at home, whether titular or material, sent place-hunters and trimmers trooping over to the Opposition; and a measure, the success of which seemed assured, was thrown out on 17th December by a majority of nineteen. On the next day the King ordered Lord North and Fox to send in their Seals of office by their Under-Secretaries, "as a personal interview on the occasion would be disagreeable to him." He entrusted the Seals at once to Temple, who on the day following signified to the other Ministers their dismissal from office. On the same day, 19th December, the King sent for Pitt and appointed him First Lord of the Treasury and Chancellor of the Exchequer.

Thus it was that Pitt became Prime Minister before he attained his twenty-fifth year. His acceptance of office after the recent use of the royal prerogative is an action that stands in need of defence. There can be no doubt that George III abused his power by seeking in an underhand way to influence the votes of the Peers. The assertion of Earl Stanhope that his action did not involve the infraction of any specific rule of the constitution will not pass muster. As was ably pointed out in the debate in the Commons on 17th December, the three parts of the constitution, King, Lords, and Commons, exist independently; and, just as the interference of one branch of the Legislature in the debates and actions of the other is most properly resented,

---

[1] "Buckingham P.," i, 289.   [2] *Ibid.*, 285.

so too the intervention of the Crown during the debates is un-doubtedly an infraction of the liberties of Parliament. While not forbidden by any specific rule of the constitution, such action contravenes the spirit of the ninth clause of the Bill of Rights, which stipulates for complete freedom of debate and speech in Parliament.

The attitude of Pitt towards this question during the debate of 17th December in the Commons is noteworthy. He did not attempt to defend such a use of the royal prerogative as was then first reported: he asserted, no doubt with perfect sincerity, that the report was an idle rumour, of which the House could take no cognizance. The House did not share his opinion. Swayed by a vehement speech of Fox, who declaimed against the "infernal spirit of intrigue" ever present in the King's counsels, and charged Pitt with an underhand attempt to gain power, members decided by a majority of nearly two to one that to report the opinion, or pretended opinion, of the King on any Bill under discussion in Parliament, was a high crime and misdemeanour, subversive of the constitution.[1]

It was in face of these resolutions that Pitt, on 19th December, took office. If he looked solely to Parliament, his position was hopeless. Confronting him was a hostile majority, smarting under a great disappointment, and threatening him, and still more his relative, Earl Temple, with the penalties of the con-stitution. On hearing the news of his acceptance of office, the members of the Coalition burst into loud laughter, and gleefully trooped over to the Opposition benches. Scarcely could they conceal their mirth during the ensuing debates; and on 22nd December the House resolved itself into a Committee to con-sider the state of the nation. Certainly Pitt's position was trying enough; for his triumph seemed to be the result of a backstairs intrigue, unworthy of the son of Chatham, and fatal to the in-fluence of Parliament. He figured as the King's Minister, carried to office by the votes of nineteen Peers, against the will of the Commons. One can therefore understand the persistence of the Whig tradition, in which his action appeared the great betrayal of the liberties of Parliament.

Nevertheless, if we carry the question to the highest Court of Appeal, the action of Pitt is justifiable. The prerogatives of

[1] "Parl. Hist.," xxiv, 196-225.

Parliament are subservient to the interests of the nation. And when the majority of the House of Commons acts in a way strongly reprobated by public opinion, its authority undergoes an immediate eclipse. In a not dissimilar case, Chatham dared to appeal from a discredited House to the people at large; and his son was justified in taking a step which involved a reference to the people's will at the first favourable opportunity. Pitt always looked on the Coalition as an unprincipled intrigue, in which the forms of the constitution were used in order to violate its spirit. He knew that the country condemned what Romilly termed "that scandalous alliance." The original crime of the Coalition seemed more than ever heinous when Ministers appointed solely their own nominees to regulate Indian affairs. This very fact damned the India Bill in the eyes of the public, which cared not a jot for parliamentary majorities held together by hopes of booty. Men who had formerly inveighed against George III now began to revise their judgements and to pronounce even his last device justifiable when directed against Ministers who were about to perpetrate the most gigantic job of the century. In looking away from the votes of a corrupt Parliament to the will of the nation, Pitt was but following in the footsteps of his father, who had more than once made a similar appeal, and never in vain.

Finally we must remember that Pitt did not take office as a "King's Friend." He had consistently refused to bind himself down to the conditions which George III sought to impose. The King knew full well that he had to deal with a man of sternly independent nature. He had failed to bend Pitt's will in the summer, when conditions favoured his own "cause." Now, when he was accused of violating the constitution, and a hostile majority in the Commons held most threatening language, he could not but uphold a Minister who stood forth in his defence. If in July Pitt refused to bow before the royal behests, surely he might expect to dictate his own terms in December. The King's difficulty was Pitt's opportunity; and, as events were to prove, George III had, at least for a time, to give up his attempts at personal rule and to acquiesce in the rule of a Prime Minister who gave unity and strength to the administration. While freeing himself from the loathed yoke of the Whig oligarchy, the King unwittingly accepted the control of a man who personified the nation.

The importance of the events of 17th-22nd December 1783 can scarcely be overrated. In a personal sense they exerted an incalculable influence on the fortunes of George III, Pitt, Fox, Burke, and many lesser men. In constitutional history, as will afterwards appear, they brought about the development of the Cabinet and the reconstruction of the two chief political parties in their modern forms. The happy ending of the crisis enabled the ship of State to reach smoother waters and make harbour, though many of her crew and all foreign beholders looked on her as wellnigh a castaway. All this, and more, depended on Pitt's action in those days. He knew the serious nature of the emergency; and at such a time it behoves the one able steersman to take the helm, regardless of all cries as to his youth and his forwardness. Pitt had the proud confidence of Chatham, that he and he alone could save the kingdom, and the verdict of mankind has applauded the resolve of the father in the crisis of 1756, and the determination of his youthful son in the equally dark days at the close of 1783. Conduct, which in a weak and pliable man would have been a crime, is one of the many titles to fame of William Pitt the Younger.

CHAPTER VII

THE STRUGGLE WITH FOX

Let me lament,
With tears as sovereign as the blood of hearts,
That thou, my brother, my competitor
In top of all design, my mate in empire,
Friend and companion in the front of war,
The arm of mine own body, and the heart
Where mine his thoughts did kindle—that our stars,
Unreconciliable, should divide
Our equalness to this.

SHAKESPEARE, *Antony and Cleopatra.*

THE first difficulty which confronted the young Prime Minister was of a personal nature. On or about 23rd December, his cousin, Earl Temple, threw up the Seals and forthwith retired to his domain of Stowe in Buckinghamshire. This event seemed to presage the death of the infant administration, which the action of the Earl had largely helped to call to being. So assured was Fox of victory that he ascribed Temple's resignation to cowardice, and expressed regret at it because the inevitable fall of the new Ministry would be explained away by the action of the Earl.[1] Undoubtedly it was a severe blow to Pitt. Bishop Tomline states that, on visiting him early on the next morning, he found he had not had a moment's sleep, an occurrence without parallel in time of health.[2] For Pitt, like Napoleon, Wellington, and other hard workers, enjoyed the priceless boon of sound and restful slumber.

The reasons for Temple's retirement cannot fully be fathomed

---

[1] " Memorials of Fox," ii, 224.

[2] Tomline (i, 233) gives the date as 21st December. The date is doubtful, in view of the two perfectly friendly letters of Pitt to his uncle on 23rd December, quoted by Stanhope ("Miscellanies," ii, 36, 37). Wilberforce places the Earl's resignation on 22nd December. I incline to place it late on the 23rd.

owing to the loss of his letters in these important weeks; but we know from the Buckingham Papers that he was disgusted with political life and had claimed the award of some honour as a sign of the King's approval of his services in Ireland, after his abrupt dismissal by Fox and North. The proud and sensitive nobleman doubtless entered into the plan for the overthrow of those enemies, in the hope of benefiting the State and setting the crown on his own career. Rumour had already assigned to him the Dukedom of Buckingham, and in this case that lying jade truthfully voiced his desires.[1]

The prominent part which he had played in the late intrigue doubtless led him to insist on some high honour. As to the nature of the claim and its reception by Pitt we know nothing; for he loyally maintained silence as to the cause of the rupture; but the Earl's letter of 29th December to Pitt breathes suppressed resentment in every line. It is the peevish outpouring of a disappointed man, who saw his *protégés* in Ireland neglected, and his own wishes slighted.[2]

The question arises—why did not Pitt press the claims of his cousin? His services in Ireland had been valuable; and to him the Prime Minister very largely owed his present position. The answer would seem to be that Pitt soon found out the truth as to his objectionable use of the King's name. At first he rejected the rumour to that effect, and it is consonant with his character to suppose that, after probing the matter to the bottom, he declined to press on the King Earl Temple's claims. The rupture was sharp and sudden. It is even possible that high words passed between them. In any case, it is certain that Pitt did not raise the question of a reward for the Earl's services until ten months later. Good taste may also have determined his conduct in this matter. How could he at once confer a high dignity on the very man whose politic whisperings had helped to raise him to power? Time must elapse before Temple could gain the reward for his services in Ireland; and it was not until early in October 1784 that Pitt mooted the question of the Marquisate of Buckingham or the Order of the Garter.[3] The following new letter from Pitt to his cousin, preserved in the Chevening

---

[1] "Dropmore P.," i, 163, 526-9. The Earl did not gain his desire, and deeply resented the refusal of George III to make him a duke.

[2] Quoted in full in "Buckingham P.," i, 291-3.

[3] "Dropmore P.," i, 239, 240.

archives, contains the official notification of the former of these honours.

Downing St.
Nov. 23, 1784.

MY DEAR LORD,

Your Lordship will receive from Lord Sydney the official notification of His Majesty's having given orders for preparing a Patent giving your Lordship the rank of Marquis. In addition to this mark of His Majesty's favour, I have great satisfaction in being authorized to assure your Lordship that, if His Majesty should depart from His present determination, of not giving the rank of Duke out of His Royal Family, it is His gracious intention to include your Lordship in any such promotion. I need not add how happy I am in obeying H. M.'s commands on this occasion, nor how truly I am at all times,

My dear Lord,
Your most affectionate and faithful servant,
W. PITT.

Turning from this personal matter, which brought friction for a time between the Pitt and Grenville families, we notice other difficulties confronting the young Premier, which might have daunted an experienced statesman. The frivolous looked on with amusement at his efforts.—" Well, Mr. Pitt may do what he likes during the holidays; but it will only be a mince-pie administration, depend upon it." So spake that truest of true blues, Mrs. Crewe, to Wilberforce on 22nd December; and she voiced the general opinion. Yet Pitt never faltered. On the next day Wilberforce noted in his journal: " Pitt nobly firm. Evening [at] Pitt's. Cabinet formed." On one topic alone did the young chief show any anxiety. " What am I to do," he asked, " if they stop the supplies? " " They will not stop them," replied his brother-in-law, Lord Mahon, " it is the very thing they will not venture to do." [1] The surmise of this vivacious young nobleman (afterwards Earl Stanhope) was for a time correct; but Pitt had rightly foreseen the chief difficulty in his path. For the present, on the receipt of a message from the King that no dissolution or prorogation would take place, Parliament separated quietly for the vacation (26th December).

For Pitt that Christmastide brought little but disappointment and anxiety. His cares were not lessened by the conduct which

---

[1] " Life of Wilberforce," i, 48.

he found it desirable to pursue towards the Earl of Shelburne, long the official leader of the Chathamites. He did not include him in his Ministry, partly, perhaps, from a feeling of delicacy at asking his former chief to serve under him, but mainly from a conviction that his unpopularity would needlessly burden the labouring ship of State. To Orde he expressed his deep obligations to the Earl, but lamented his inability to leave out of count "the absolute influence of prejudice" against him. He did not even consult Shelburne as to the choice of coadjutors; and the Earl let it be known that he would have no connection with the new men, "lest he should injure them."[1] Pitt also sustained several direct rebuffs. Though, on 19th December, he sent an obsequious request to the Duke of Grafton to strengthen his hands by accepting the Privy Seal, that nobleman declined.[2] Camden was equally coy; and, strangest of all, his own brother-in-law, Mahon, would not come forward. We can detect a note of anxiety in the following letter of Pitt to Lord Sackville, formerly Germain, which I have discovered in the Pitt Papers (No. 102):

Dec. 29, 1783.

My Lord,

In the arduous situation in which His Majesty has condescended to command my services at this important juncture, I am necessarily anxious to obtain the honor of a support and assistance so important as your Lordship's. I flatter myself Mr. Herbert will have had the goodness to express my sense of the honor your Lordship did me by your obliging expressions towards me. Permit me to add how much mortification I received in being disappointed of his assistance at the Board of the Admiralty, which I took the liberty of proposing to him, in consequence of the conversation Lord Temple had had with your Lordship. I should sincerely lament if any change of arrangements produced by Lord Temple's resignation should deprive the King and country in any degree of a support which the present crisis renders so highly material to both. If your Lordship would still allow us to hope that you might be induced to mark by Mr. Herbert's acceptance your disposition in favour of the King's Government, the opening may be made with the greatest ease at any moment, and Your Lordship's commands on the subject would give me particular satisfaction.

[1] Fitzmaurice, "Shelburne," iii, 406-13. Pitt soothed the feelings of the Earl by persuading the King to create him Marquis of Lansdowne. (*Ibid.*, 419-25).

[2] Grafton MSS. in the Chevening Library.

From Wraxall's Memoirs [1] we learn that the writer undertook to pave the way for the receipt of Pitt's letter; but all was in vain. Lord Sackville refused to take office, though he promised a general support.

The most serious refusal was that of the Lord-Lieutenancy of Ireland by Earl Cornwallis. George III highly approved of Pitt's proposal of that nobleman, whose tact and forbearance would have proved of infinite service in so troublous a time.[2] Who knows whether the rebellion and savage reprisals of 1798 might not have been averted by the adoption of wiser methods at Dublin Castle in the eighties? As it was, the most difficult administrative duty in the Empire was soon to devolve upon a young nobleman, the Duke of Rutland, whose chief qualifications seem to have been his showy parts, his splendid hospitality, and his early patronage of Pitt.

The Cabinet as finally formed comprised the following seven members: Pitt, First Lord of the Treasury and Chancellor of the Exchequer; the Marquis of Carmarthen (son of the Duke of Leeds), an amiable but unenterprising Secretary for Foreign Affairs; Lord Sydney (T. Townshend), Home Secretary; Earl Gower, President of the Council (up to December 1784, when Earl Camden succeeded him); the Duke of Rutland, Lord Privy Seal (up to November 1784, when Earl Gower succeeded him, the Duke taking the Viceroyalty of Ireland); Lord Howe, First Lord of the Admiralty; Lord Thurlow, Lord Chancellor. In debating power this Cabinet was deficient. Apart from Pitt and Thurlow, not one of the Ministers could make a tolerable speech, or possessed the strength of character which makes up for oratorical deficiencies.

Thurlow might have been a tower of strength in the Lords, but for his duplicity, bad temper, and domineering ways. For the present, Pitt had to put up with him as a disagreeable necessity. There was something so threatening in his aspect as to elicit Thelwall's picturesque description of him as a man with

[1] Wraxall, iii, 252.

[2] The letter of George III to Pitt, quoted in "Pitt and Napoleon Miscellanies," rebuts the statement of the editor of "The Cornwallis Correspondence" (i, 162, *n.*) that there is no trace of any offer of an office to Cornwallis. The letters of the Earl at that time show that he declined office because he believed Pitt's administration must speedily fall, whereupon "the virtuous Coalition" would return in triumph.

the Norman Conquest in his eyebrow and the Feudal System in every feature of his face. Add to these formidable gifts a sonorous voice, his powers of crushing retort, above all, his secret connection with George III, and his influence in the Upper House can be imagined. Yet his reputation rested on a slight basis; his knowledge of law was narrow, his culture slight, and his private character contemptible. He was known to bully his mistress and his illegitimate daughters, just as he browbeat juries and Whigs.[1] On the whole his reputation is hard to explain save on the ground that the majority of mankind is apt to be imposed on by externals, and is too uncritical or too lazy to sound the depths of character.

For the present Pitt tolerated Thurlow just as the commander of an untried warship might tolerate the presence of an imposing gun of uncertain power, in the midst of light weapons. The boom of his voice was worth something to a Ministry in which the posts not of Cabinet rank were filled as follows: The Duke of Richmond, Master-General of the Ordnance;[2] Kenyon, Attorney-General; Pepper Arden, Solicitor-General; William Grenville (afterwards Lord Grenville) and Lord Mulgrave, joint Paymasters of the Forces; Henry Dundas (afterwards Lord Melville), Treasurer of the Navy; Sir George Yonge, Secretary at War; George Rose and Richard Steele, Secretaries of the Treasury; Thomas Orde, Secretary to the Lord-Lieutenant of Ireland. Of these the Duke of Richmond had great private influence, but was personally unpopular. Grenville and Rose were useful, hard-working men, but uninteresting in personality and speech. Their characters and that of Dundas will concern us in Chapter XII. Here we may note that the bold and jovial nature of Dundas made him popular as a man; but his defection from Lord North, and his capacity for intrigue impaired his influence in the House. Nevertheless his fighting powers, his legal training, his knowledge of men and affairs, and his skill in parrying the blows of the Opposition made him an effective lieutenant in the House. By degrees, as we shall see, he acquired great influence over Pitt; and after his entry to the Cabinet as Home Secretary in 1791, he, together with Grenville, came to form around Pitt what may almost be termed an inner Cabinet. For the present,

---

[1] "Mems. of the Whig Party," ii, 5-7.

[2] The Duke of Richmond did not join the Cabinet until 13th January. See Lord Carmarthen's Mem. ("Leeds Mem.," 94).

however, the distrust with which the "Caledonian thane" was regarded permitted him to be no more than the chief among Pitt's subordinates; and the ingenious poetaster of the "Rolliad" maliciously aimed these lines at his weakest point, his inconsistency:

> His ready tongue with sophistries at will
> Can say, unsay, and be consistent still;
> This day can censure, and the next retract,
> In speech extol, and stigmatize in act.

The other subordinates claim only the briefest notice. Sir George Yonge was a nonentity, under whom the British army sank to the nadir of efficiency. Kenyon and Pepper Arden were very young men; the latter was one of Pitt's Cambridge friends, lively and amiable, but having little influence in debate. The House could not take Pepper seriously. On the whole the Ministry aroused little confidence among friends and much derision among opponents. The general opinion was expressed by Sir Gilbert Elliot (first Earl of Minto) that Pitt's colleagues were "a set of children playing at Ministers, and must be sent back to school, and in a few days all will have returned to its former course."[1] On the other hand Daniel Pulteney, writing to the Duke of Rutland, said that people approved the appointments and were glad that Pitt, in showing attention to existing interests, proved himself to be not "too virtuous and speculative for a Minister."[2]

Such were the predictions concerning a premiership which was to last nearly eighteen years. In one respect the mediocrity of his colleagues made Pitt's task easier. His commanding temper would never have brooked the superior airs of the earls, Temple and Shelburne. From the outset he could carry out his plan of moulding the Cabinet to his will and enforcing its discipline, without hindrance except from Thurlow; and the final ejection of that cross-grained egoist marked not only the triumph of Pitt, but also the consolidation of the Cabinet in what seems to be its permanent form, a body moulded by, and largely responsible to, the Prime Minister.

All this was hidden from the gaze of the most discerning amidst the gloom and uncertainties of the first days of the year 1784. Shortly before Parliament re-assembled events occurred

---

[1] "Life and Letters of Sir G. Elliot," i, 91.   [2] "Rutland P.," iii, 73.

which helped to strengthen a confessedly weak administration.
At the request of Pitt, George III created four new peerages.
Thomas Pitt received the title of Lord Camelford; Edward Eliot
(father of Pitt's brother-in-law) became Lord Eliot; Henry
Thynne was created Lord Carteret; and a barony was conferred on the second son of the Duke of Northumberland. Thus
the sources of nobility, which had remained hermetically sealed
during the previous administration, were now opened with a
highly suggestive readiness.

Another incident, which it is more pleasing to relate, concerned Pitt alone. On 11th January the Clerkship of the Pells,
a sinecure worth £3,000 a year for life, fell vacant by the death
of Sir Edward Walpole, a younger son of the Whig statesman.
According to precedent, it would have been not only justifiable,
but usual for Pitt to take this post. Despite the advice of his
friends to this effect, Pitt refused to increase his very slender
private income at the public expense, and prevailed on Colonel
Barré to accept the sinecure in place of the pension of £3,200 a
year generously voted to him by the economical Rockingham.
This most unexpected conduct, which of course saved the public
funds the amount of that pension, was loudly praised by Barré
himself and by all who were not inveterate partisans. These last
decried Pitt's action as resulting either from love of applause or
from priggishness. The taunt has been echoed in later times,
even by those who laud to the skies Chatham's self-abnegation
in the matter of official perquisites. Nothing better illustrates
the malice which has dogged the footsteps of the son than that
sneers should be his reward for an action similar in all respects
to that which has elicited praise for his father. Both of them,
surely, desired at the outset to emphasize their resolve to put
down financial jobbery in the public service. Their actions
were prompted solely by patriotism.

On 12th January, when Parliament met, Pitt had to bear the
brunt of reiterated attacks from Fox, Erskine, and General
Conway, under cover of motions for resuming a Committee to
consider the state of the nation. The young Minister parried
their blows by stating his resolve to bring in very soon an India
Bill. Then, flinging back their taunts, that he had crept into
office by the backstairs, he uttered these memorable words:
" The integrity of my own heart and the probity of the public,
as well as my private principles, shall always be my sources of

action. I will never condescend to be the instrument of any secret advisers whatever; nor in any one instance, while I have the honour to act as Minister of the Crown in this House, will I be responsible for measures not my own, or at least in which my heart and judgement do not cordially acquiesce." The glance of contempt which he flung at Lord North (the unwilling tool of George III in the American War) gave point to this declaration. In truth, it sounded the keynote of Pitt's career. He came into office to save the country from the Coalition, but he came in untrammelled by royal control; and his action in resigning in 1801 evinced the proud consistency of his convictions.

Beaten in the first division in the House of Commons by a majority of thirty-nine, and on the next day by even larger numbers, he held on his way unmoved.[1] In consonance with the traditions of Chatham, he cared little for Parliament provided that the country was with him; and of this there were unmistakable proofs. The East India Company, acting through a sub-committee which sat permanently for the defence of its interests, was arousing all the chartered bodies of the land against a policy that seemed to threaten other vested interests. " Our property and charter are forcibly invaded: look to your own." This was the battle-cry, unscrupulous but effective, which made aldermen, freemen, wardens, and liverymen of venerable companies bestir themselves. A little later the City of London sent an address of thanks to the King for his action in saving the country from the evils of Fox's India Bill.

Thus Pitt, wafted onwards by the breath of popular favour, could confidently expose his India Bill to the contrary gusts that eddied in the House of Commons (14th January 1784). The methods used in its preparation were in signal contrast to those employed by Fox. The Whig leader, far from consulting the East India Company, had drawn up his Bill in concert with Burke and others hostile to its interests and ill-informed as to its working. Pitt, on the contrary, took care to find out the views entertained in Leadenhall Street. The Pitt Papers show that the

---

[1] Lord Carmarthen stated that in the Cabinet meeting of 13th January Pitt talked of giving up the struggle, but this is against all other contemporary evidence (" Leeds Mems.," 94). These notes on the Cabinet meetings show how long were the discussions there respecting a dissolution, and Pitt's anxiety to defer it to a favourable moment.

Company manifested a desire to meet him more than half way, and that their representative officials conferred with him on 5th January 1784. Indeed, his Bill was in large measure the outcome of resolutions which seem to have been framed at that conference and which gained the assent of five-sixths of those present at a General Court of the Company held on 10th January. The resolutions were to this effect:—That the Company, confiding in the justice of Government for the relief of some of its most pressing claims, consented that the following powers should be vested in the Crown: (1) All despatches to or from India to be communicated to one of the King's Ministers, and the Directors must conform to the King's pleasure. The controlling power to be vested in the Minister and other responsible persons delegated to attend to the affairs of the Company. (2) Despatches relating to commercial affairs must likewise be submitted to the Minister, who may negative them if they bear on civil or military Government, or on the revenues of the Company. In case of dispute, the decision of His Majesty in Council shall be final. (3) The General Court of the Company shall be restrained from rescinding any act of the Court of Directors only after the King's pleasure shall have been signified on the same. (4) The Government in India to be carried on in the name of the Company by a Governor and three councillors in each of the Presidencies, the Governor and the Commander-in-Chief (who shall be next in Council to the Governor) being appointed and recalled by the Crown, while the Company appointed the two other councillors, subject to His Majesty's approbation. They could be recalled either by the Crown or by the Company.[1]

When the Company agreed to sacrifice so much of its powers, the battle was half won; but, for the present, the chief difficulty lay in the House of Commons. In introducing his India Bill on 14th January, Pitt sought to forestall the criticisms of the hostile majority by reminding the House that the government of territories so remote and so different from our own must be in a sense irrational—"inconvenient to the mother and supreme power, oppressive and inadequate to the necessities of the governed." In such a case any scheme of government must be a choice between

---

[1] Pitt MSS., 353. I cannot accept Mr. Sichel's statement ("Sheridan," ii, 45), that Dundas prescribed Pitt's India Bill, and Burke helped in it. Dundas doubtless helped in its compilation, but Pitt must have conferred directly with the Company and found out how far it was inclined to meet his views.

I   M

inconveniences. He then stated the principles on which he based his proposals. Firstly, the Indian dominion must not be in the hands of the Company of merchants in Leadenhall Street. Nevertheless, any change should be made not violently, but with the concurrence of that Company, its commercial affairs being left as far as possible to its supervision, wherever they were not mixed up with questions of policy and revenue. Where these questions were involved, obviously Government must have a voice.

Having laid down these guiding principles, he proceeded to fill in details. He claimed that his proposals were such as not to interfere arbitrarily with the privileges of the Company; and that his new Board of Control would be found to be, not the organ of a party, but an adjunct of the governmental machinery. It was to consist of at least two of the Ministers of the Crown, namely, the Secretary for Home Affairs and the Chancellor of the Exchequer, along with a certain number of Privy Councillors named by the King. These last were to attend regularly, and were not to be paid. All the despatches of the Company, except those of a completely commercial nature, were to be submitted to the new India Board and countersigned by it. While not controlling the patronage of the Company, the Board would have the right to negative their chief appointments. The three Presidencies were henceforth to be administered, each by a Governor (a Governor-General in the case of Bengal), a Commander-in-Chief, and a Council. The Crown would appoint these three Commanders-in-Chief, and would have the right of recalling the Governors and their councillors—a clause calculated to prevent such a fiasco as that of the attempted recall of Warren Hastings. Finally, in order to curb the abuses in the Company's service, Pitt proposed to institute at Westminster a tribunal for the trial of offences committed in India, and he suggested that parts of the second India Bill of Fox might be adopted for the prevention of abuses in India.

There can be no doubt that this measure excelled that of Fox in many respects. It left the actual details of administration to Governors and councillors who were on the spot and could act therefore with promptitude; but, by subjecting them in all matters other than commercial to what was in effect a special committee of the Privy Council, it associated the Government of India with the British constitution in a way that answered the needs of the time and the developments of the future.

But the House of Commons was in no mood to gauge the excellences of the scheme. It was swayed rather by the vehement criticisms of Fox, who declared that the Bill gave far too much influence to the Crown, and that, if passed, it must inevitably lead to the loss of India. The Fox-North Coalition still voted solidly for their chiefs, and on 23rd January the measure was thrown out on the second reading by 222 votes to 214.

Scenes of great excitement ensued. Fox and his followers loudly called on the Ministry to resign. Pitt sat still, vouchsafing no reply to the clamour, except when General Conway accused him of sending agents over the land to corrupt the voters. Then he started to his feet, defying Conway to substantiate the charge, but, for the rest, declaring his indifference to the slanders of opponents, and his determination to work for the welfare of the State.

Three days later, when Fox charged him with acting as the unconstitutional Minister of the Crown and overriding the powers of Parliament, he replied that such was not his act and intention. His conduct was unusual because the occasion was unprecedented. To have resigned after the recent vote would have brought to power Ministers who, he believed, had not the confidence of the nation; and he further pointed to the recent diminution of the votes of the Opposition. The argument was telling, for the hostile majority had dwindled from one hundred and six on 3rd December, to thirty-nine on 12th January, and now to eight. These facts clinched his contention that the feeling of the House was inclining to the favourable verdict which the country had begun to declare. A shrewd observer like Wraxall came to see that Pitt was vindicating the constitution even in his seeming breach of it.[1]

Nevertheless, everything was at hazard. Though the majority against him lessened, it was still a clear majority; and to appeal from an indisputable fact to what was at most a surmise, seemed a defiance of the House. As such it met with severe handling at the hands of Fox and his sturdy henchman, Coke of Norfolk. They, however, finally agreed to adjourn the whole question for three days. Why Fox did not at once press his advantage to the utmost is hard to say. Perhaps he feared to let loose the passions of the House upon the country at large when Consols were

[1] Wraxall, iii, 85.

down at 54 and national ruin seemed imminent. He may have
desired to gain time in order to watch the trend of public
opinion, and to appear as a peace-restoring Neptune rather than
an inconsiderate Aeolus.

An influential minority of the House longed for calm. On
that very day fifty-three of its members met privately at the
St. Albans Tavern to urge a union of parties on a more natural
and less unpopular basis than the Fox-North Coalition. Ap-
pointing a committee of five, they besought the Duke of Portland to use his influence to bring about a connection between
Fox and Pitt. As we have seen, the hostility of these statesmen
had arisen, not from difference of principles, but from the
divergent interests of party groups. It had, however, been in-
flamed by Pitt's acceptance of office in circumstances that
were especially odious to Fox; and the Whig leader, in his
speech of 26th January, pointedly declared that, while admitting
the urgent need of union and conciliation, he must insist on the
vindication of the honour of the House by the resignation of the
present unconstitutional Ministry. A similar declaration was
sent on the same day by the Duke of Portland to the committee
of the St. Albans Tavern meeting.

Such a beginning was far from promising. Clearly an understanding existed between the nominal and real chiefs of the Whig
party with a view to forcing on a dissolution. This implied
that the conciliators were appealing to party-leaders to act as
arbiters, and that they at once passed judgement against the Pitt
Ministry. Matters were not improved during a debate in the
House on the need of forming an extended Administration (2nd
February). Fox, while disclaiming any personal hostility to Pitt,
insisted on the resignation of Ministers as the first step towards
the formation of a wider Administration. On his side Pitt once
more declared that any union between them must be formed in
an honourable way, and that it would be paltry for him to
resign merely in order to treat for re-admission to office. The
original motion having passed unanimously, a hostile resolution
was then brought forward substantiating Fox's declaration.
Whereupon Pitt, nettled by these insidious tactics, declared
that he would never change his armour and beg to be received
as a volunteer among the forces of the enemy. Never, he
exclaimed, would he consent to resign before the terms of such
a union were arranged. If the House desired to drive the Ministry

from office there were two ways open—either to petition the King for their removal, or to impeach them. At present their remaining in office was not unconstitutional. The hostile motion, however, passed by a majority of nineteen; and by a slightly larger majority the House resolved to lay its decision before the King.

That day was perhaps the most critical of Pitt's parliamentary career. The feeling of the House seemed to be turning against him; and the negotiations at the St. Albans Tavern (which went on intermittently until 1st March) were far from favourable to his interests. Both sides agreed as to the goal to be reached, but each threw on the other the responsibility of taking the first step, which that other declined on points of honour. At the outset the Duke of Portland declined to see Pitt with respect to a union until he had resigned. Then, on 31st January, he hinted, obscurely enough, that the Minister might find a middle way; and when Pitt requested an explanation, he referred him to recent precedents, which were in effect resignations.

The good sense which rarely deserts the House of Commons for long reappeared on 11th February. Fox then professed not only his readiness to serve with Pitt, when he had complied with the terms of the constitution, but also his desire to meet him half-way as to the details of a new India Bill of which he had given notice. Pitt replied in a similar spirit, but declared that there were some men with whom he could not serve. Thereupon Lord North, at whom this shaft was levelled, declared his willingness to stand aside if the voice of the country demanded it. No act in his career did him more credit, and the incident aroused a general hope that Pitt would now feel himself able with honour to resign.

He refused, however, to take that step, probably because of the continued obduracy of the Duke of Portland. The St. Albans Tavern Committee had besought the King to intervene in order to facilitate an interview between Pitt and the Duke. Accordingly on Sunday, 16th February, the King rather reluctantly urged the Duke to meet the Prime Minister, but signified privately to Pitt his resolve never to apply to His Grace again if he still declined.[1] Nevertheless the Duke refused to unbend.

The last stage of the negotiations illustrates the niggling

---

[1] Stanhope, i, App., p. viii.

methods of partisanship prevalent in those times. In answer to
a final appeal from the committee, Pitt and his colleagues urged
the King to make one more effort to bring the Duke of Portland
to an accommodation. The reply of the King on 26th February
shows that, in spite of his strong objections, he made that effort,
but with the stipulation that the Duke should have " no right to
anything above an equal share to others in the new administration, not to be the head of it, whatever employment he may
hold." Pitt amplified this statement by declaring that the new
Ministry would be formed " on a wide basis, and on fair and
equal terms." Obviously this implied the entry of the followers
of Portland and Fox on equal terms with those of Pitt; but the
Duke, while approving the word " fair," required to know the
meaning of the word " equal"; and when Pitt replied that this
could be best explained in their interview, the Duke refused to
come unless the meaning of the word were first made clear.[1]
This straining at gnats put an end to the negotiations. It is now
abundantly clear that Pitt went as far as could be expected, and
that the continuation of the deadlock resulted from the captious-
ness of the Duke of Portland.

Ten years were to elapse before the Portland Whigs came in
to strengthen Pitt's hands, and their accession amid the storms
of the French Revolution involved the break up of the Whig
party. In February 1784 there was a chance that the whole
party would form a working alliance with Pitt and the Chathamites. Such a union would have formed a phalanx strong enough
to renovate the life of Great Britain and to prepare her better to
stand the strain of the coming crises. It was not to be. Obviously
no union could be lasting where the party knocking for admission insisted on dictating its terms and gaining admission to the
citadel.

There is, indeed, an air of unreality about these negotiations,
probably due to the fact that each party was intent on the state
of public opinion and the chances of a dissolution. The same
fact probably explains the action of Fox in the House. Time
after time he carried motions of censure against Pitt, though by
wavering majorities. He and his followers hindered the appor-
tionment of the supplies, threatened to block the annual Mutiny
Bill, and went so far as to hold the menace of impeachment over

---

[1] " Ann. Reg." (1784-5), 271 ; " Memorials of Fox," ii, 238-41.

the heads of Ministers. When the Lords by a large majority reprobated the actions of the Commons and begged the King to continue his Ministers in office, the intervention of the Upper House was strongly resented by the Coalition majority.[1]

Yet Fox never pressed his attacks home. The threats of impeachment remained mere stage thunder, probably because he doubted his power to launch the bolt. There was, indeed, much truth in Pitt's description of him as "the champion of a small majority of this House against the loud and decided voice of this people." Hatred of the unnatural Coalition, far from declining, was intensified by Pitt's manly and consistent conduct. The popular imagination thrilled at the sight of the young Premier braving the clamour of Foxites and Northites in reliance upon the final verdict of the nation. According to all the constitutional text-books, the Whig leader spoke sound doctrine when he declaimed against Pitt's tenure of office in the teeth of the repeated censures of the House; but men discerned the weakness of the Opposition; they weighed it rather than counted heads; and in the balances of common sense the Fox-North majority kicked the beam. Westminster and Banbury, the very places which had returned Fox and North, now sent up addresses of thanks to the King for dismissing them from office. Middlesex, Edinburgh, York, Worcester, Exeter, and Southwark, besides many smaller places, sent in addresses to the same effect, thereby in some cases dishonouring the parliamentary drafts of their members. The City of London, the home of blatant Whiggism at the time of the Wilkes affair, now thanked Pitt for his services and voted him its freedom, with the accompaniment of a gold box. His ride into the city on 28th February to receive this honour resembled a royal progress, and Wilkes was the man who welcomed him to the Hall of the Grocers' Company, where he was entertained at a great banquet.

Nor was his popularity lessened by an incident that attended his return to his brother's residence in Berkeley Square. His carriage, drawn along by a cheering crowd, was passing the chief social centre of the Foxites, Brooks's Club, when a sudden rush was made at it by a body of stalwart ruffians armed with sticks and the broken poles of sedan-chairs. So fierce was the onset that the carriage doors crashed in, and Lord Chatham with

[1] Hearn, "The Government of England," 140-4, 147.

difficulty parried the blows aimed at his brother. For some moments they were in serious danger, but, aided by their partisans, they succeeded in escaping to White's Club, hard by. Fox was loudly accused of being the author of this outrage. But, of course, it would be foolish to lay this brutal attack to his charge. It seems probable, however, that hangers-on of the party paid some scoundrels to incapacitate Pitt for the rest of the parliamentary strifes. He, and he alone, could make headway against the storm; and his removal even for a week would have led to the triumph of Fox and North. We may note here that Pitt did not resign his membership of Brooks's Club on account of this outrage—a proof that he was far above all thoughts of revenge or rancour.

The prospects of the Opposition were somewhat marred by the events of 28th February. Everything tended to hamper the actions of that ill-assorted couple, North and Fox. True, on 1st March they carried by twelve votes an address to the King for the removal of Ministers; but George III acted not only with firmness but with dignity. He replied, as he had before replied to a similar address, that he deplored the failure of the efforts to form an extended Administration on *fair and equal terms*, but saw in that failure no reason for dismissing Ministers who appeared to have the confidence of the country, and against whom no specific charges were urged. These skilful retorts struck home; and a long and reproachful representation to the King, said to have been drawn up by Burke, was carried by a majority of only one. Pitt looked on this as tantamount to a triumph; for two days later he wrote to the Duke of Rutland that he was "tired to death even with victory; for I think our present state is entitled to that name." [1] His forecast was correct. In face of these dwindling numbers, Fox and North did not venture to oppose the passing of the Mutiny Bill, which, since the beginning of William III's reign, has year by year legalized the existence of a standing army. [2]

To allow this measure to pass, after threatening to obstruct the work of Government, was a virtual confession of failure; and not only the House but the country took it as such. The inner

---

[1] "Corresp. between Pitt and the Duke of Rutland," 9. Cornwallis ("Corresp.," i, 171) also prophesied after that vote that if Ministers acted wisely, they might hold office for many years.

[2] "Leeds Mems.," 99.

weakness of the Coalition now became daily more evident. Discontents that were hidden during the months of seeming triumph broke forth as the prospect of defeat loomed large ahead. The tension of the past two months now gave way to a strange slackness, resulting doubtless from the uncertainties of the situation. Fox relapsed into silence. Pitt rarely spoke and scarcely vouchsafed a reply to the smaller men who kept up the aimless strife. In truth, the heavy-laden air at St. Stephen's gave premonitory signs of that portent in nature when songsters become mute and animals creep about with anxious restlessness under the shadow of an oncoming eclipse.

The nation was now to give its verdict. On 24th March the King dissolved Parliament. The Great Seal disappeared from the house of the Lord Chancellor on that very morning; but by great efforts another was ready by noon of the 25th. For some weeks the land had simmered with suspense. "Even ladies," wrote Horace Walpole on 12th March, "talk of nothing but politics." In truth, a time of new political fashions was at hand. The old having been discarded, very much depended on a decided lead given by some of the leading constituencies.

For various reasons men looked eagerly to the example set by Yorkshire and Westminster. Both had recently led the way in the agitation for Economic and Parliamentary Reform and were strongholds of Whiggism; yet both the county and the city had recently acclaimed the conduct of Pitt. Canon Mason, a well-known poet of those days, who, with the reforming parson, Wyvill, had fathered the Yorkshire Reform Association, was now working hard on behalf of George III and Pitt—a fact which spoke volumes. Yet, despite the strength of the Association, and the ardent Toryism of most of the clothing towns of the West Riding, the influence of the great Whig Houses, especially the Cavendishes in Wharfedale, the Fitzwilliams at Wentworth, and the Earl of Carlisle at Castle Howard, was so strong as to make the issue doubtful.

The feeling of the county was tested first at a great meeting of its freeholders held in the yard of the Castle at York on Lady Day. Despite driving hail-storms and a bitter wind, thousands of sturdy yeomen, together with throngs of clothiers from the towns of the West Riding, poured into that historic space. Then came the magnates of the county, driving up in their coaches-

and-six. In good old English style the two sides of the case were set forth on the hustings in fair and open rivalry by the best speakers of both parties. The large towns and the yeomen evidently favoured the royal prerogative upheld by Pitt, while the claims of the Whigs and of North's followers were championed by the great lords and their tenantry, by sticklers for constitutional precedents, and all who hoped to benefit by a change of Ministry. The issues at stake being as obscure as the cleavage between parties was zigzag, the speeches for the most part fell ineffectively. What with the sleet and the confusion of parties the meeting seemed about to break up in disorder, when there appeared on the daïs a figure so slim and weak as to quail before the blasts. But the first few sentences of that silvery voice penetrated the storm and dominated the swaying crowd. It was the voice of Wilberforce, who once more showed the influence of clearness of thought and beauty of utterance over a confused throng. Boswell, describing the whole incident to Dundas, said: "I saw what seemed a mere shrimp mount upon the table; but, as I listened he grew and grew until the shrimp became a whale."

The victory of mind over matter was decisive. His arraignment of the Coalition and defence of Pitt carried the meeting with him; and a great shout arose: "We'll have this man as our county member." The instinct of the meeting was sound. The tact of Wilberforce in uniting all Whigs and Tories who were not committed to the Coalition or bound by the magnates greatly furthered his cause; so that finally an election which had of late always been decided by the three great Houses named above, resulted in the triumphant return of Wilberforce and Duncombe. The show of hands was so overwhelmingly in their favour that the Whigs accepted the verdict and did not demand a poll. The victory was not only a severe blow to the county families and an assertion of the growing independence of the middle classes and yeomen; it was also a gain for the cause of purity, the total expenses of the successful candidates being less than £5,000.

The example set in Yorkshire was followed in most parts of Great Britain. The supporters of the Coalition were smitten hip and thigh; as many as 160 members of the Opposition were thrown out, and by a very obvious joke they were termed Fox's Martyrs, the details of their deaths being recorded with

tragi-comic solemnity.[1] The strength and universality of the
popular impulse surprised even Pitt.[2] He was carried in
triumphantly by 334 votes for the University of Cambridge, his
friend, Lord Euston, gaining 288, while their opponents, Townshend and Mansfield, polled only 267 and 181 respectively.[3]
Wilkes swept Middlesex by a large majority—for the Crown.
Skilful speakers like Erskine, county magnates like Earl Verney
and Thomas Grenville, were thrust aside for the crime of supporting the Coalition; and in certain boroughs, where no one had
been sent down to oppose that hated union, travellers who declaimed against it were forcibly detained and returned as members of Parliament. Never, we are assured by Wraxall, was there
less bribery used in the interests of the Crown; for, as he naively
asserts, "corruption for once became almost unnecessary."[4]

The reasons of this extraordinary overthrow of the Coalition
are not far to seek. Tories felt far more regard for the royal
prerogative than for Lord North, now that he had gone over to
the King's enemies; and independent Whigs refused to follow
Fox in his ex-centric march towards the Northites. Thus the
Coalition was in reality defeated by—the Coalition. That jaundiced old Whig, Horace Walpole, might abjure his friendship
with Mason for heading "the pert and ignorant cabal at York";
he might declare that the nation must be intoxicated to applaud
the use of the royal prerogative against "the Palladium of the
people" (the House of Commons). "Junius" might raise his once
dreaded voice to assure his countrymen that the victory of Pitt
would put an end to their boasted liberties. It was useless. The

---

[1] "Fox's Martyrs: a new Book of the Sufferings of the Faithful" (London, 3rd edit., 1784).

[2] Letter to Wilberforce, 6th April 1784.

[3] I have found in the Pitt MSS. (No. 315) only two references to Pitt's
election for Cambridge. One is a letter of that year from "F. B." giving
numerous hints how this or that M.A. should be "got at" so as to secure his
vote, and ending: "Go on and prosper, thou godlike young man, worthy of
your immortal father." The other is a note, not dated, signed J. T[urner?]:

"DEAR PRETYMAN,

"Our canvas goes on very successfully, but we are yet very desirous
of your being here to-morrow night if possible, since Mr. Pitt cannot come
himself. His appearance on Thursday did immense service. . . . We depend
on seeing you to-morrow; next to Mr. Pitt's appearance yours will certainly
be of the utmost importance."

[4] Wraxall, iii, 338.

nation's instinct bade it break with the past and start afresh on
a path that promised steady progress. That instinct now swept
aside the old party lines and organizations in a way that had not
been seen since the advent of the Georges.

Only at one place was the rout of the Whigs stayed; and the
doubtful issue of the conflict at Westminster attested the won-
drous personal powers of Fox. A union of strength with geniality,
of eloquence with frankness, which appeals to Englishmen, was
seen in him in all its potency. The "magician" (to use Pitt's
phrase about his rival) waved his wand with startling effect. A
few days of platform speaking sufficed to restore his earlier
popularity. Despite the utmost efforts of the Court and Government on behalf of their candidates, Admiral Hood and Sir Cecil
Wray, the Whig totals crept up day by day, so as to threaten the
seat of the latter, which at one time seemed assured.[1] George III
followed the course of the Westminster election with an eager
interest that reveals his hatred of the Whig leader. This is seen
in his suggestion on 13th April to Pitt that bad votes should be
fabricated at Westminster to counterbalance those which must
have been trumped up for Fox; or again (1st May) that the
Quackers [*sic*] might perhaps be induced to come to the poll in
the interests of the Government.

All was of no avail. The arts of Windsor were foiled by the
charms of Devonshire House. Georgiana, the beauteous duchess,
used her allurements to rally voters to the Whig cause, and is
said to have carried her complaisance so far as to kiss a butcher
for a promise of his vote. Certain it is that she and her sister,
the Viscountess Duncannon, conveyed artisans from the out-
lying districts to the poll in their own chariots. The Countesses
of Carlisle and Derby, Lady Beauchamp, and Mrs. Crewe, also
used their charms on behalf of the Whig cause, so that a favouring rhymester could write:

> Sure Heaven approves of Fox's cause
> (Though slaves at Court abhor him),
> To vote for Fox, then, who can pause
> Since *Angels* canvass for him?[2]

In vain did the Court put forward the Countess of Salisbury
to keep waverers steadfast. The Countess possessed beauty, but

---

[1] For the daily figures see "Ann. Reg." (1784), 34.
[2] "Hist. of Westminster Election," 483.

tempered by age and discretion. Thanks to the exertions of Georgiana, and to the influence of the Prince of Wales and of the Dukes of Portland and Devonshire, Fox, at the end of an exciting contest of forty days, headed Sir Cecil Wray by 236 votes, though he still fell 460 votes below Lord Hood. The Prince of Wales celebrated this triumph by a great reception in the grounds of Carlton House at the very time when the King was passing outside to open Parliament.

But the local success of the Whigs was not yet complete. Many suspicious facts during the election seemed to discredit the result; and when Sir Cecil Wray demanded a scrutiny, the High Bailiff of Westminster not only granted the request, but refused to make any return for Westminster, thus invalidating the election of Fox and even of Hood until an inquiry was held.[1] Fox entered Parliament, but it was through the kindness and foresight of Sir Thomas Dundas, who had procured his election for the Orkney and Shetland Islands. At once he attacked the High Bailiff as well as the Government, which he accused of influencing the action of that official. The matter is too involved and technical to enter upon here. Its chief interest lies in the manly and massive oration which Fox flung against Pitt on 8th June. The Prime Minister evaded the missile with much dexterity; and a large majority insisted on the scrutiny. After nine months of inquiry the position of the candidates was virtually unchanged. The Government's following strongly desired to end this expensive and fruitless inquiry; but Pitt opposed the motions to this effect, and early in the session of 1785 found himself abandoned by his majority.

The motives which prompted his action on this affair will be considered in Chapter XII; but we may here note that it certainly lessened his personal influence in the critical session of 1785. His own position had hitherto been so well assured that generous behaviour towards one of the most affable and open-handed men of his time would have been both natural and becoming. As it was, many of his friends were disgusted, and some thought his conduct would fatally prejudice his future. Thus, on 10th February 1785 Daniel Pulteney wrote as follows: " Contrary to the wish of all his real friends, and only supported

---

[1] From the letter of George III to Pitt of 1st May it seems that the High Bailiff had previously decided to grant a scrutiny, if asked for, owing to the many doubtful votes that had been polled.

by Dundas, Lord Mulgrave, and Bearcroft, Pitt persevered in
this cursed business. . . . The consequence of this will be trifling
if Pitt will *now* recede and agree to order the return, but . . .
many will form a very different idea of the Administration if
such an odious business is forced down by a small majority."[1]
Fortunately Pitt's own friends abandoned him before matters
went too far. The affair unsteadied his followers for a time; and
the impression was spread abroad that he had all the qualifications for winning a decisive victory, but none of the graces that
add lustre to its laurels. Apart from this personal detail, which
influenced public opinion more than far wider questions, Pitt's
triumph in and after 1784 was so complete as to usher in a new
era in British politics. We may therefore pause to review both
its causes and its significance.

Besides the irremediable blunder committed by Fox in framing the Coalition with Lord North, he made several mistakes
during the early weeks of 1784. It was in the highest degree
unwise to stake everything on the cohesion of his majority in
the Commons, and to seek to avert a dissolution. Judging by
his motions in the House, it was the worst of crimes for Pitt to
advise the King to appeal to the nation. But surely that was the
natural and almost inevitable step, seeing that Parliament had
sat for four years, and the opponents were very nearly matched.
Yet, while hindering the course of public business by the postponement of votes for the public service, Fox claimed to be
acting with a single eye to the public welfare. Such conduct
evinced no insight into the essentials of the problem before
him. For surely, if Ministers were acting as illegally as he
averred, it was his duty to impeach them. If their offence was
more venial, the verdict of the people would suffice. The question
could be decided only in one of two ways—either by an impeachment or a dissolution. He decided in neither way, but allowed
the tangle to grow worse, until men came to believe that his
sole aims were to shirk any appeal, either to the laws of England
or to the hustings, and to force his way once more to power
along with Lord North by means of their large but unstable
majority. This was the suspicion which thinned their following
at St. Stephen's and ruined them at the polls.

---

[1] "Dropmore P.," i, 177.

Pitt, on the other hand, showed great tactical skill in working his way out from an apparently hopeless position. Admitting that his tenure of office was irregular, he justified it by the unanswerable retort that the Opposition could not govern. Accepting their decision, that supplies should be postponed so as to prevent a dissolution, he made it clear whose was the responsibility for the resulting disorganization. Finally, when the inability of his opponents to block the Mutiny Bill had set free the administrative machine, he appealed to the country. Men were quick to see which side had best consulted the interests of the State. Over against the impotently factious conduct of Fox stood the patriotic good sense of his rival in disregarding the wavering censures of a discredited House in order on the fitting occasion to consult the will of the nation.

So soon as the essential facts of that unparalleled situation are fully grasped, the diatribes against Pitt for making an illegal use of the royal prerogative for selfish purposes are seen to be mere verbiage. Equally futile is it to inquire, with Lord John Russell, why the constitution was not afterwards altered in favour of the Crown, and why the Court did not gain more advantage by its triumph in the General Election of 1784.[1] The fact is that Pitt had never intended to govern as a Court minion, or to subject the constitution to the royal will. It was not merely that his pride revolted against any such degradation; but his principles, no less than the tough consistency of his nature, forbade it. Because he insisted on maintaining the King's prerogative at one point, namely, that Ministers were dismissed by him and not by the House of Commons, he was far from supporting it at all points. Even in that particular, he admitted that Government could not be carried on by Ministers who had not the confidence of the House of Commons, but he asserted, and triumphantly proved, that that House had not the confidence of the nation. For the long delay in putting the matter to the test, Fox, not he, was responsible.

In reality, then, there was no violation of the constitution, and no change in Pitt's relations to the Crown. True, he had sought to reconcile its prerogatives with the functions of Parliament; but his attitude towards George III was still marked by a proud independence, which often caused annoyance.[2] He brought for-

---

[1] " Memorials of Fox," ii, 244-6.　　[2] " Malmesbury Diaries," iv, 22.

ward measures which the King disapproved; and in all important matters he had his way down to the spring of 1801, when George III demurred on conscientious grounds. The shelving of the cause of Parliamentary Reform by Pitt after the year 1785 resulted from the utter indifference of the nation, not from any bargain that he had corruptly struck with the King.

But if the memorable contest of 1784 has not the significance sometimes ascribed to it in partisan narratives, it is of great moment in regard to the monarchy, the Cabinet, and the course of events at St. Stephen's. George III came forth victorious from his long struggle with the Whig Houses; but the magnitude of the peril had taught him prudence and self-restraint; and, while keeping a tight hand on patronage, he was thenceforth content, in the more important sphere of legislation, to leave a free hand to the Minister who had saved him from the open conflict with the Commons which Fox had sought to precipitate. The relations between the King and Prime Minister therefore came to resemble those which had subsisted between the first two Georges and Walpole.

Consequently, the growth in the powers of the Cabinet, which had been interrupted since the fall of that Minister, now proceeded normally. During the seventeen years of Pitt's supremacy the principle became firmly established that the chief Minister of the Crown was the centre of authority, and that, while holding that authority nominally from the King, he exercised it by virtue of a mandate from the people. George, therefore, had escaped from the thraldom of the Coalition only in order to bow before an authority which was at once constitutional and irresistible. He no longer had to do with the nominee of a dozen great families, but with a man who had the clearly expressed confidence of the nation. The same fact tended to make the Cabinet of the future more and more a homogeneous and well disciplined Council, obeying the impulsion of the first Minister, and adding force to his declarations of policy. No longer was it possible, as in Lord North's decade of office, for the Ministers to act singly and at the behests of the sovereign. George III's policy of *divide et impera* might succeed with North; it could not but fail before the iron resolution of Pitt. The King's acquiescence in the new order of things enabled him to regain much of the ground which he had earlier lost by his masterful efforts to govern as well as reign. Well was it for the British monarchy that those disputes were settled before the storms of the French Revolution beat upon that ancient fabric.

Finally, we may note that Pitt was far more than a second Walpole. The sturdy Norfolk squire wielded power, as a nominee of the Whig Houses; but Pitt was established in office by a wider and grander mandate. The General Election of 1784 ended the existing party system and shattered the rule of the Whig families who had hitherto dominated the Georgian Era. The somnolent acquiescence of the populace in that headship now gave way to a more critical spirit, to a sense that the traditional parties must readjust themselves under a new leader. Chatham's conception of a union which should absorb the best elements of both Whigs and Tories received a startlingly complete fulfilment; for the greatest of the results of the election of 1784 was the emergence of a party which may be termed national.

CHAPTER VIII

RETRENCHMENT

In the arithmetic of the customs, two and two, instead of making four, make sometimes only one.—DEAN SWIFT.

WHEN the sixteenth Parliament of Great Britain met on 18th May 1784 the arrears of legislation and accumulation of debt were as serious as at any time in our history; for, owing to fierce party strifes and the distractions of war, very few remedial measures had been passed in recent years. The "Economic Reform" passed by Lord Rockingham's Government is the only oasis in an otherwise arid waste, strewn with the wrecks of partisan warfare. The condition of affairs was therefore becoming most serious; and a collapse could be averted only by the utmost skill and care. The three per cent. government stocks told a tale of waning confidence. Even after the peace they steadily declined, from an average of 65 in January 1783 to 56 at the close of that year. They were as low as 53⅞ in part of January 1784; and it is a striking tribute to the confidence which Pitt inspired that, on the results of the elections of the spring of 1784 being known, they rose to more than 58. That first essential to a revival of national credit, a firm Government, was now assured, and patriots looked anxiously for the measures whereby the young Minister might stave off disaster.

The King's Speech laid stress on two topics, finance and the East India Company. Within the limits of a short session Pitt could not possibly hope to pass other large measures; and he urged Alderman Sawbridge not to persevere with his annual motion in favour of Parliamentary Reform, promising to bring it forward himself in the session of 1785. When the Alderman pressed the matter to a division, he was defeated by a majority of seventy-four—a result damaging to the cause which he sought to serve.[1]

[1] "Parl. Hist.," xxiv, 1006.

The way being thus left clear for the two great questions that would admit of no delay, Pitt sought to lay the ghost of national bankruptcy. The imminence of the danger can scarcely be realized. In that decade we link together the thought of bankruptcy with that of France; but if those years closed with the Revolution in France and prosperity in England, the result may be ascribed very largely to the wasteful financial system pursued at Versailles and to the wise husbanding of Britain's resources by Pitt. According to the French statesman, Necker, the National Debts of the two countries were almost exactly equal.[1] The pamphlet literature of the years 1783-84 reveals a state of things wellnigh as serious in England as that which brought about the crash in France. One of the closest students of finance, Dr. Price, in a pamphlet of the early part of 1783, stated that the Fox-North Ministry openly avowed its inability to pay off any of the public debts; and he asserted that such helpless conduct must carry us fast to the brink of disaster. Another writer urged that, in order to abolish the National Debt, tithes must be swept away, the revenues of the Church reformed, and all citizens must submit to the payment of one-sixth part of their incomes. The National Debt, which amounted to £215,717,709 in January 1783, was denounced in language whose extravagance would cause a mild surprise to a generation that placidly bears a burden nearly four times as great; but, to a kingdom which with the utmost difficulty raised £25,000,000 in revenue, this burden seemed overwhelming. Dr. Price summed up a wide-spread conviction in his statement that the growth of debt brought about increased subservience to the Crown, prosperity to stock-jobbers, and depression to all honest traders.[2]

The war which ended in 1783 had been carried on in a singularly wasteful manner. Price computed that the increase to the National Debt owing to the war had been £115,654,000 up to January 1783, when all the accounts had not yet come in; he also reckoned that the last four years of that struggle had cost £80,016,000 as against £60,835,000 for the last four years of the Seven Years' War. This increase resulted largely from the

---

[1] Necker, "De l'Administration des Finances de la France," 3 vols. (1784).

[2] "Observations on Reversionary Payments," by R. Price, i, 206. When all the expenses of the war were added, by the year 1786, the National Debt amounted to £245,466,855. See Parl. Paper, No. 443, Sept. 1858.

reckless way in which North had issued loans, so that bankers and subscribers, and, it is said, the Ministers themselves, reaped large profits, while the nation suffered. According to Price, loans which cost the nation £85,857,691, actually brought to the exchequer only £57,500,000.[1] This resulted partly from corrupt practices, but also from North's endeavour to keep down the rate of interest to three or four per cent.; the outcome being that, in the impaired state of public credit of the year 1781 he had to allot £150 of stock in the three per cents and £25 in the four per cents for every £100 actually borrowed. Thus, the raising of a sum of £12,000,000 on these terms actually cost the nation £21,000,000; and interest had to be paid on £9,000,000 which never came into the exchequer. Obviously he would have done better to raise £100 for £100 stock, even had he given 6 or 7 per cent. interest; for the experience of the past showed that in time of peace and prosperity the rate of interest could be reduced without much difficulty. Nevertheless, the advisers of the Crown always preferred to keep to a low rate of interest, even at the cost of tempting lenders by allotting £175 of Government stock for every £100 of cash.

Such was the state of affairs when Pitt introduced his Budget (30th June 1784). It will be convenient to set forth and explain his proposals singly and in connection with the facts which he had to face. The first was the appallingly large deficit, constantly swollen by the coming in of bills for war expenses. The champion of peace and retrenchment had to confess that, despite all his efforts to balance income and expenditure, he must raise a loan of £6,000,000. Obviously, as Consols still stood as low as 58, he could borrow only on exorbitant terms; but it is regrettable that he now fell back on North's plan of borrowing at a low rate of interest and of burdening the funds with a vast amount of fictitious debt. He proposed to allot to every subscriber of £100 no less an amount of stock than £100 of three per cents, £50 of four per cents, and 5s. 6d. of long annuities, besides three fifths of a lottery ticket in a lottery of 36,000 tickets.[2] He computed that the terms and chances now offered were actually worth £103 14s. 4½d., and that lenders would therefore be tempted

[1] R. Price, "State of the Public Debts and Finances in January 1783," 5, 8, 19.
[2] Pitt reckoned a State lottery as yielding a profit of £140,000; but obviously he disliked this means of raising money ("Parl. Hist.," xxv, 1307).

to lend.[1] This was so. But, for the reasons stated above, the burdens bequeathed to posterity were crushing, though less than those entailed by North's loan of 1781.

As regards Pitt's personal dealings with financiers, his conduct shone radiantly clear when contrasted with those of Lord North. It had been the custom for that guardian of the public purse to arrange the price of the loan with a few favoured supporters in the City, and then allot scrip on scandalously low terms to his friends in Parliament, who could thereafter sell at a handsome profit. Pitt now threw open to public competition all tenders for his loan; and the proposals sent in were formally opened at the Bank in a way which precluded jobbery and safeguarded the nation's interests.

Scarcely less serious was the problem of the huge floating, or unfunded, debt, that is, that portion of the National Debt for which no provision whatever had been made by Parliament. In the main it consisted of unpaid bills, which had been increased by about one quarter or even one third of their original amount. It now stood at about £14,000,000. Pitt ardently desired to fund the whole of it, but he found that so great an effort would cause too much disturbance in the money market. He therefore proposed to fund at present only £6,600,000, forming it into stock bearing 5 per cent. interest and issued at 93. He defended this high rate of interest on the ground that such a stock could in the future be redeemed on more favourable terms than a three per cent. stock which might be worth a comparatively small sum when capitalized. The argument was surely just as applicable to the former loan of £6,000,000.[2]

It still remains to notice the worst ills that beset the fiscal and commercial life of our land. Indeed, we shall not understand the daring nature of Pitt's experiment of the year 1784 unless we take a comprehensive view of the losses, both material and moral, which resulted from the extraordinary prevalence of smuggling. Never had contraband trade been so active as of late. How should it be otherwise, when the customs dues were tangled and burdensome; when the Navigation Laws, especially respecting the coasting trade in Scotland, were so annoyingly complex that the papers which a vessel needed for crossing the Firth of Forth

---

[1] " Parl. Hist.," xxiv, 1021.   [2] Ibid., 1022-4.

involved nearly as much expense and delay as if she were bound
for Canada.¹ In such a state of things illicit trade was ever gaining recruits from the ranks of honest merchants and seamen.

For monopoly, too, depressed their calling and exalted that of
the smuggler. By far the most important article subject to
monopoly was tea. That expensive luxury of the days of
Queen Anne, a "dish of tea," was now fast becoming a comfort of the many. Indeed, Arthur Young found that the use of
tea had spread into the homes of cottagers; and he classed as
extravagant those villages which owed their refreshment to China,
and commended the frugality of those which adhered to home-
brewed ale.² The increased use of Bohea was certainly not due to
the East India Company or to the State; for the former sold the
"drug" at the high prices warranted by its monopoly of trade
with China; and on the arrival of the precious chests at our
shores, an *ad valorem* duty of 119 per cent. had to be met. The
increase of habits which Arthur Young deprecated and temperance reformers now applaud was due to smugglers. We learn from
Adam Smith that Dutch, French, and Swedish merchants imported tea largely;³ and from their ports enterprising skippers
conveyed it to our shores, there to be eagerly welcomed by a
populace which found the cheating of Government far more
attractive and gainful than agriculture. The annals of the time
show how deeply the coast population was infected. The large
barns which the tourist admires in many an East Anglian coast
village, more often held contraband than corn. Thomas Hardy
has shown how the dull life of a Wessex village kindled at the
news of a successful "run in," and how all classes helped to defeat the "King's men." The poet Crabbe, with his keen eye for
the stern realities of life in his parish of Aldborough, tells of his
grief at finding there, not the simple home-loving life of an old
English village,

> But a bold, artful, surly savage race.

Their sport was not cricket or wrestling on the village green,
but smuggling.

> Beneath yon cliff they stand
> To show the freighted pinnace where to land,

---

¹ "Parl. Hist.," xxiv, 1015.   ² A. Young, "Farmer's Letters," 197.
³ "Wealth of Nations," bk. i, ch. xi, pt. 3; "Parl. Hist.," xxiv, 1012.

> To load the ready steed with guilty haste,
> To fly with terror o'er the pathless waste,
> Or, when detected in their straggling course,
> To foil their foes by cunning or by force,
> Or yielding part (which equal knaves demand)
> To gain a lawless passport through the land.

These are the words of a moralist. To the easy-going many the smuggler was merely a plucky fellow who cheated the common foe of all, the Government, and helped poor folks to get spirits, tea, and tobacco at cheap prices. As for showing any reluctance to buy smuggled goods, this seemed "a pedantic piece of hypocrisy." [1] It must also be admitted that Government had sinned against light; for the great reduction of the tea duty by Pelham in 1745 had almost put an end to smuggling in that article; but unfortunately his successors, when confronted with the results of war, re-imposed the old duties and thereby gave new life to the smuggler's calling. [2]

The excess of an evil sometimes works its cure. It was the stupidity of the fiscal regulations in France which helped to turn the attention of her most original thinkers to the subject of national finance; whence it came about that Political Economy had its first beginnings in the land where waste and want were rampant. So, too, it was reserved for the son of a Kirkcaldy customs officer to note early in life the follies of our system; and, when further enlightened by contact with men and affairs, especially with the French *Economistes*, he was able to give to the world that illuminating survey of a subject where tradition and prejudice had previously reigned supreme. Finally, it was in the very darkest hour of Britain's commercial and financial annals that remedial measures were set on foot by the young statesman who had laid to heart the teachings of the "Wealth of Nations."

It is not easy to say whether Pitt owed more to Adam Smith or to Earl Shelburne. Probably the influence of the Scottish thinker on the young statesman at this time has been exaggerated; for it seems certain that the later editions of the "Wealth of Nations" were modified so as to bring them into line with some of Pitt's enactments. [3] Further, Pitt made no public ac-

---

[1] "Wealth of Nations," bk. v, ch. ii, § 4.

[2] Dowell, "Hist. of Taxation," ii, 183.

[3] I owe this interesting fact to the Rev. Dr. Cunningham.

knowledgement of his debt to Adam Smith until his Budget
speech of 1792, when he expressed the belief that the philosopher, then deceased, had given to the world the best solution
to all commercial and economic questions. It may be, then, that
Pitt in 1784 owed less to Adam Smith than to his first chief,
Shelburne, and to other men of affairs, including his own brother-
in-law, that able though eccentric nobleman, Lord Mahon.
Shelburne was the depository of the enlightened aims of that
age; and, as Price pointed out, he and Pitt in the year 1782 were
about to make reforms in the public service which would have
saved the revenue some half a million a year.[1]

Now, with a freer hand, he took up the task which the
Coalition of Fox and North had interrupted; and in a measure
which supplemented his Budget, he proposed to cut the ground
from under the smuggler by reducing the duty on tea from an
average of 119 per cent. to 12½ per cent. on the cheaper varieties,
though on the finer kinds of tea (Suchong, Singlo, and Hyson)
he imposed a higher scale of duties.[2] Even so, he expected that
the produce of the tea duty would sink at first from £800,000 to
£169,000, though he must have hoped soon to recoup a large
part of this sum. As there was a large deficit on the past year,
it was necessary to devise a tax which would help to make up
the temporary loss with no risk of leakage.

Such a source of revenue Pitt found in an increase of the
window-tax. Every house with seven windows was now to pay,
not four shillings, but seven shillings a year. On a house with
eight windows eight shillings were paid, and so on, except that
houses with more than ten windows paid half-a-crown per window. He reckoned the increase from this source at about
£700,000. Whatever objections might be urged against the tax
on the score of health, it certainly fell mainly on the middle and
wealthy classes; for as many as 300,000 of the poorest houses
went duty free. The impost may therefore be considered as a
first rough attempt at taxation according to income. The change
was beneficial in another way. The old customs duty on tea
violated the canon of taxation laid down by Adam Smith—that
a tax should take from the pockets of the people as little as possible over and above what it brings into the treasury of the State.
The 119 per cent. duty seemed to challenge evasion, and the

---

[1] R. Price, *op. cit.*, 18, 19 (note).   [2] "Parl. Hist.," xxiv, 1009.

attempt to enforce it probably cost the country more than the tax yielded. The window tax belonged to the class of excise duties the expenses of which amounted only to about $5\frac{1}{2}$ per cent. of the total yield; and the new impost could not possibly be evaded except by the heroic remedy of blocking up windows.

Thus, both in regard to economic doctrine and common sense (the former is but the latter systematized) Pitt's experiment ushered in a new era in British finance and therefore in British commerce. The City of London welcomed the change, which promised to lead to the employment of twenty more clipper ships for the China tea-trade and to the destruction of the contraband tea-trade to these shores carried on hitherto by the French and Dutch East India Companies. Indeed, no sooner did this Commutation Bill (as it was called) gain general assent than the Dutch Company offered to sell to us its cargoes of tea at a loss of 40 per cent. on prime cost and expenses. This fact alone ought to have stilled all opposition to the measure; but Fox continued to oppose it with a vehemence worthy of a better cause; he was ultimately beaten by 143 votes to 40 (10th August 1784).[1]

We may note here that by further regulations of the year 1784 and by what was called the "Manifest Act" of 1786, frauds on the revenue were made far more difficult. Thus to Pitt belongs the credit of having done more than any minister (for he succeeded where Walpole largely failed) to stop a material loss and a grave moral evil.

It would be incorrect to claim that Pitt was the first to light on the idea of substituting lower and effective duties for the exorbitant and ineffective duty on tea. William Eden (the future Lord Auckland) declared that very many persons had advocated some such change, and he attributed to Lord John Cavendish the formation of the revenue committee, the results of whose inquiries were now utilized by the Prime Minister. Pitt, on the other hand, gave the credit of the measure to his relative, Lord Mahon. The mention of that nobleman reminds us of an incident which enlivened the debate. While sawing the air in order to emphasize his hearty approval of the death blow now dealt to smuggling, he gave Pitt a smart knock on the head, to the unbounded amusement of the House.

---

[1] "Parl. Hist.," xxiv, 1354.

The details of the Budget itself do not imply a very firm belief in the principles of what is called Free Trade. As has been shown, the difficulties in Pitt's way were enormous. The new loan, the funding operation, and the interest on the unfunded debt altogether entailed an added charge of £910,000 a year. This sum he proposed to raise by means that may be termed old-fashioned. Looking round the domain of industry, he singled out for taxation the few articles that were duty-free or were only lightly burdened. Men's hats were now to pay a toll of two shillings a-piece (felt hats only sixpence), and thus bring £150,000 to the nation's purse; female finery (ribbons and gauzes) was mulcted to the extent of £120,000. He also estimated that a duty of three shillings on every chaldron of coals (not only in London as heretofore, but throughout Great Britain) would bring in about £150,000; but he proposed to free from its operations all manufacturers who met with sharp foreign competition. Further, he imposed a tax on all horses used for riding or for pleasure, which he estimated at £100,000; and he eked out the remainder of the sum by duties on printed linens and calicoes, candles, hackney coaches, bricks and tiles, paper, licences for shooting, and licences for traders in excisable goods.

Most of these proposals were received with resignation, but several members urgently protested against the impost on coals as likely to be ruinous to industry, and ultimately Pitt withdrew it. This, however, led him to impose a tax on race-horses (especially winners), to raise the licence for shooting from one guinea to two guineas, to increase the postage for letters, and to curtail the privileges of franking letters by Members of Parliament. This had been disgracefully abused. Every member of both Houses had the right both of sending and of receiving letters free. As if this were not sufficient, in days when a shilling was an ordinary charge for the receiver of a letter, several members were known to sell envelopes which they had franked; and a large firm is said to have paid a member £300 a year for franking their correspondence. Pitt struck at these abuses by requiring that franked letters must bear the name of the member, the date, and the post town from which the letter was to be sent. By this and other restrictions a leakage which had amounted to nearly £200,000 a year was stopped, at least in part. The notion that every Member of Parliament ought to enjoy privileges which were withheld from the many was so

deeply rooted that the abuses of "franking" persisted up to the
time of the complete abolition of the privilege in 1840, when
penny postage became the law of the land. Thus in January
1802 we find a distinguished diplomatist, Sir George Jackson,
commiserating his sister on the scarcity of noblemen in Bath,
which implied "a dearth of *frank-men* to fly to."

The effort to curb the abuses of that hateful class privilege
forms the best feature of Pitt's Budget of 1784. In other respects
it is not remarkable. The new imposts have none of the merits
attending his Commutation Act for the repression of smuggling.
What is surprising is that he did not try the experiment of
increasing the House Duty, an impost which fell mainly upon
the rich, was easy to collect, and could be made very remunera-
tive.[1] It was actually tried by North in 1778, apparently because
it had borne good results in Holland.[2] Thus, the machinery
was at hand, and only needed to be more strenuously worked.
I have failed to find in the Pitt Papers the reason why the
statesman did not try this expedient; still less why he imposed
the niggling and irritating little taxes named above. He estimated the yield of the duties on bricks, paper, and hackney
coaches at no more than £50,000, £18,000, and £12,000 respectively. Further, the tax on candles, though only of one halfpenny
the pound, was certainly burdensome to the poor. On the whole,
it is not surprising that a rhymester thus set forth the condition
of John Bull:

> One would think there's not room one new impost to put
> From the crown of the head to the sole of the foot.
> Like Job, thus John Bull his condition deplores,
> Very patient, indeed, and all covered with sores.

Other persons of a quasi-scientific turn sought comfort in the
reflection that taxation ought, like the air, to press on the individual at all points in order not to be felt.

In truth, Pitt's financial genius matured slowly. Possibly he
thought the situation too serious to admit of doubtful experiments. Certainly he went step by step, as is seen by reference
to his next Budget. Its most significant feature was the endeavour to simplify the collection of taxes. Hitherto there had
been much overlapping and consequent waste of effort, owing to
the existence of three Boards or Committees. The Excise

---

[1] "Wealth of Nations," bk. v, ch. ii, § 1.	[2] Cunningham, 548.

Department managed the taxes on carriages, wagons, carts, and male-servants; the new taxes on horses and race-horses were under the Commissioners of Stamps; while separate Commissioners administered the imposts on houses and windows. In place of this complex, expensive, and inefficient machinery, Pitt instituted a single "Board for Taxes," which supervised affairs more cheaply and left few loopholes for evasion. The imposts named above were thenceforth termed "the assessed taxes." [1] In that year he also imposed taxes on female servants, shops, and attorneys. Here again his fiscal policy distinctly belonged to the old order of things, when men, despairing of finding any widespread and very lucrative tax, grumblingly submitted to duties on every article of consumption and every important action of life. The days of a few simple and highly productive taxes had not fully dawned.[2] The sequel will show that, only under the intolerable pressure of the long war with France, did Pitt work his way to the Income Tax; and the terms in which he replied to the Lord Provost of Glasgow, who in March 1798 recommended that impost, show that, while always favouring it on theoretical grounds, he doubted the possibility of collecting it systematically.

In 1785 we are still in the age of youthful hopes and experiments. We find Pitt writing to Wilberforce on the last day of September: "The produce of our revenues is glorious, and I am half mad with a project which will give our supplies the effect almost of magic in the reduction of debt." [3] Equally hopeful is his letter to Lord Buckingham on 8th November, in which he speaks of the rise of stocks being fully justified by the splendid surplus of "£800,000 per annum at least. The little that is wanting to make good the complete million may be had with ease." [4] Both references are to the plan of a Sinking Fund which was to work wonders with the National Debt, blotting it out in two or three generations by the alchemy of compound interest.

The plan of a Sinking Fund was not wholly his, although it came to bear Pitt's name. Walpole, early in his career, had

---

[1] Dowell, ii, 187, 188.

[2] In Pitt MSS., 353, I have found a memoir of the East India Company containing this sentence: "Much will he deserve of his country who can devise a mode of anything like equal taxation by any single tax."

[3] "Corresp. of W. Wilberforce," i, 9.   [4] Chevening MSS.

started a scheme whereby a certain sum was annually set apart
for forming a fund which would accumulate by compound interest and finally be available for the extinction of the National
Debt. This plan came to grief, because in 1732 Walpole began
to draw on his own fund rather than increase the Land Tax and
annoy country gentlemen. This, we may note, is one of the
perils of a Sinking Fund that, guard it as its founder may, some
thriftless Chancellor of the Exchequer will insist on filching
from it. That was the fate of Walpole's fund. The scheme,
however, survived, and received a new impulse in 1772, when
Dr. Price, a Nonconformist minister, called public attention to
it by a pamphlet on the National Debt. In this he proved
by irrefutable arithmetic that a Sinking Fund, if honestly
worked, must ultimately wipe out the largest debt that can be
conceived. For, as he hopefully pointed out, a single seed,
if its produce could be entirely set apart for sowing, would in
course of time multiply so vastly as to fill all the lands where
it could grow. This is true; but the simile implies singular
powers of self-control in the sowers, especially if they are beset
by hunger before that glorious climax is attained. Descending
to the more practical domain of the money market, Price
proved that a sum of £200,000, set apart annually, together
with its compound interest, would in eighty-six years be worth
£258,000,000. Whether the nation were at peace or at war,
said Dr. Price, the stipulated sum must be set aside, even if it
were borrowed at a high rate of interest; for the nation borrowed
at simple interest in order to gain the advantages of compound
interest. While admitting the folly of such conduct for a private
individual, he maintained with equal *naïveté* that a State must
benefit by it, even if there were no surplus of revenue and if
money were dear.[1]

Such was the scheme which fired Pitt with hope; but it is very
questionable whether he accepted all its details. Certainly he
did not act precipitately. On 11th April 1785 he felt the pulse
of the House of Commons by stating his confident hope of
having a surplus of one million available for the present plan,
and his determination next year to found "a real Sinking Fund"
on a basis which would absolutely preclude pilfering in the
future. It is also noteworthy that he resolved to raise that

---

[1] R. Price, "Treatise on Reversionary Annuities" (1772).

million by taxation, not by borrowing. This is a fact which has been ignored by Hamilton, McCulloch, Lecky, and other critics of Pitt's experiment; but the debate just referred to and those soon to be considered place it beyond possibility of denial. Mr. Dempster urged him to begin at once, even if he had to borrow, seeing that France had started a Sinking Fund which "would enable her in a few years to get rid of the greatest part of her National Debt." But the Prime Minister declined to be hurried, especially if he had to borrow at a high rate of interest.[1] Clearly, then, Pitt did not share the extravagant hopes of Price.

His relations to Price cannot be wholly cleared up. Early in January 1786 he wrote to him in the following terms:

> The situation of the revenue certainly makes this the time to establish an effectual Sinking Fund. The general idea of converting the 3 per cents with a fund bearing a higher rate of interest, with a view to facilitate redemption, you have on many occasions suggested, and particularly in the papers you were so good as to send me last year. The rise of the stocks has made a material change since that period, and I am inclined to think something like the plan I now send you may be more adapted to the present circumstances.[2] There may be, I believe, some inaccuracies in the calculations, but not such as to be very material. Before I form any decisive opinion, I wish to learn your sentiments upon it, and shall think myself obliged to you for any improvement you can suggest if you think the principle a right one, or for any other proposal which from your knowledge of the subject you may think preferable.

With his reply Price sent the three alternative plans which the curious may peruse in his "Memoir and Works." Unfortunately the ten volumes consecrated to his fame by his nephew, William Morgan, are instinct with so bitter a prejudice against Pitt as to be worthless on all questions affecting him. Morgan does not print Pitt's proposal, but brushes it aside as puerile, and gives the impression that Price did so; he gives no account of the interview which Pitt had with Price in the middle of January, but asserts that the Minister threw aside his own proposals, adopted the third and least efficient of Price's plans, mangled it in the process, and never acknowledged his debt to

---

[1] "Parl. Hist.," xxv, 419-30.

[2] Consols which touched $54\frac{1}{4}$ in January 1785 rose to $69\frac{3}{4}$-$73\frac{1}{2}$ in December of that year.

his benefactor.[1] The first of these charges can be refuted by Price's reply to Pitt's letter given above. He pronounced the Prime Minister's proposals "very just," but pointed out some defects, especially the proviso which placed the Sinking Fund at the disposal of Parliament when the interest on it amounted to £4,000,000, as he expected it would by the year 1812.[2] Morgan's unfairness is further revealed by his statement that Pitt did not choose to increase the taxes in 1786 so as to provide the million surplus which ought to have been forthcoming. Whereas the fact is that in the Budget of 1785 the Minister imposed taxes for that very purpose; and when these proved scarcely sufficient, he imposed others on 29th March 1786.[3]

False and acrid charges such as these do not surprise us in the partisan biographies of that age. What is surprising is that McCulloch and Lecky should have endorsed some of Morgan's statements, especially respecting Pitt's omission of his acknowledgements to Price.[4] On this I must observe, firstly, that it is not proven that Pitt owed to Price everything that was good in his Sinking Fund, and spoiled the plan by his own alterations of it; for the omission of Pitt's proposal by Morgan leaves us without means of comparing the original proposals of the two men; secondly, that the official reports of the three debates of the spring of 1786 on this subject are so meagre as to furnish no decisive evidence on what was, after all, a minor detail. Further, it is probable that Price's influence on Pitt's proposal was less than has been supposed. In the Pitt Papers is a letter of Pulteney to Pitt dated 18th April 1786, in which he urges him carefully to reconsider Price's third plan before finally adopting it. He states that Sir John Sinclair, Sir Edward Ferguson, Mr. Beaufoy, and Mr. Dempster had yesterday met Dr. Price at Bath House in order to discuss the merits of Price's plan, and also one by Mr. Gale. The discussion left Pulteney with the conviction that Gale's plan was "infinitely preferable to any of the three produced by Dr. Price," and he begged Pitt to add it to his Bill as an alternative.[5] I have not found a copy of Gale's plan or any evidence as to its adoption in part by Pitt; but the statesman certainly repudiated the notion of borrowing

---

[1] "Memoir and Works of R. Price," by W. Morgan (1816), i, 120-5; "A Review of Dr. Price's Writings on Finance," by W. Morgan (1792).

[2] Pitt MSS., 169.   [3] "Parl. Hist.," xxv, 419-30, 1303.

[4] Lecky, v, 51.   [5] Pitt MSS., 169.

in order to pay off debt, on which Price had laid stress. And yet by a strange irony of fate, this expedient, to which the statesman had temporary recourse only under the strain of war, is that which has been pronounced by nearly all critics the characteristic part of his scheme.

The chief features of Pitt's proposals were his efforts to raise the whole of the annual million from revenue, and to safeguard this fund from the depredations of wasteful financiers in the future.[1] He therefore placed it under the control of six responsible persons, among whom were the Chancellor of the Exchequer and the Governor of the Bank of England. The disposal by Parliament of the fund when the yearly income arising from it should amount to four millions, may be termed a concession of the financier to the parliamentary spirit.

The scheme met merely with indirect criticism, the debates turning on general policy, or on the question whether there was a surplus of a million, or any surplus at all. These were the issues to which the eager partisanship of Fox and Sheridan sought to divert the attention of the House. Let them beware, exclaimed Fox, of tying up a sum of a million a year, when they might want all their available resources for a war. As for Sheridan, he sought to ridicule the experiment, not on financial grounds, but because it was the height of folly to add to the present enormous burdens when " we had but one foe, and that the whole world."

There seems to have been in these debates no reference to Dr. Price's schemes, though they then enjoyed considerable notoriety. Mention was made of the writings of Baron Maseres on the efficacy of Compound Interest; but the Opposition confined itself almost entirely to complaints about the taxes, and gloomy prophecies about the advent of another war. Surely some member of that angry and disappointed group would have accused Pitt of filching his scheme wholesale from that of Price, if the charge had been possible. We can imagine that Sheridan, instead of croaking over the impending coalition of Europe against England, would in that case have declaimed against Pitt as the thief of the magic wand of the real Prospero of finance. Would not Fox also have brought his sound and sturdy sense to the congenial task of exposing the fallacies of

---

[1] " Parl. Hist.," xxv, 1294-1312, 1367, 1368, 1416-30.

Price and the imposture of Pitt? The darling of Brooks's Club, who well knew the perils of borrowing in order to pay off old debts, would have fastened on the folly of borrowing at high rates in order to gain the advantage of Compound Interest. We can picture him asking how a plan, which was admittedly foolish for an individual, could be profitable for a nation, and where the taxes could be raised that would make good the interest on the sums set apart every year for the wonder-working fund. Surely the Opposition was not so ignorant of finance and of Price's proposals as not to detect the weakness of the Prime Minister's plan, had it been modelled solely on them.[1]

The debates in which the Commons dealt with this great and complex subject seem to have been fruitful only in personalities. At the final stage of the Bill, however, Fox moved an amendment with the aim of lightening the burdens on the nation in time of war. He proposed that, whenever a new loan should be raised, the Minister should be pledged to raise moneys sufficient to pay the interest on the loan, and also to make good to the Sinking Fund what might be taken from it. He stated as a concrete example that, if a new loan of £6,000,000 were required in time of war, and if £1,000,000 were in the hands of the Commissioners of the National Debt, that sum should be transferred to the account of the loan; for this, he claimed, would save the public the expense of raising that million through bankers and the Stock Exchange, and the Sinking Fund would not be injured if the million temporarily borrowed from it were made good by taxation. His speech contained one statement of personal interest, namely, that he had shown his proposal to the Chancellor of the Exchequer, who approved of it. This, then, was one of the few occasions on which Pitt conferred with Fox. He now accepted Fox's amendment, because (to take the supposed case), apart from the saving of commission on the million, Government would be able to raise the five millions on better terms than the six millions. Pitt also expressed the hope that the addition of the amendment to his Bill would do away with all temptation to a Minister to rob the Sinking Fund.[2]

This last argument cut both ways. As Earl Stanhope

---

[1] These formed the chief charges urged against the Sinking Fund by R. Hamilton, "An Inquiry concerning . . . the Management of the National Debt" (1813).

[2] "Parl. Hist.," xxv, 1430-32.

(formerly Lord Mahon) pointed out to the Lords, when he introduced a rival scheme a few days later, it would be absurd to lessen the temptation to commit an offence which he (Pitt) had declared to be thenceforth impossible. In fact, the permission to transfer the yearly million to another fund rather tended to strengthen the argument for alienation in any other case where expediency might be urged. Stanhope's plan for rendering the Sinking Fund permanent is too complex to be discussed here; the debates on it were closed by the royal assent being given to Pitt's measure on 26th May.[1]

If we examine carefully the many criticisms that have been levelled against Pitt's Sinking Fund, they apply only to his handling of the fund during the Great War with France. Every sciolist in finance can now see the folly of borrowing money at a high rate of interest in order to provide the fund with its quarterly supply.[2] It is clearly a case of feeding a dog on his own tail. But such a proceeding, though lauded by Price, was quite contrary to Pitt's original intention, which was the thoroughly sound one of paying off debt by a steady application of the annual surplus. He departed from this only under stress of circumstances which he looked on as exceptional and temporary.

Strange to say, even the officials of the Treasury seem to have overlooked the fact that the nation was thereby increasing its debt in a cumbrous attempt to lessen it. In 1799, when the pinch caused by the withdrawal of a million a year was severely felt, George Rose, the Secretary of the Treasury, praised the Sinking Fund as an example of integrity and economy which must in the highest degree promote the prosperity of the nation. And Lord Henry Petty, who succeeded Pitt as Chancellor of the Exchequer, stated in his first Budget Speech in March 1806 that " it was owing to the institution of the Sinking Fund that the country was not charged with a much larger amount of debt. It was an advantage gained by nothing." This extraordinary statement, coming from a political opponent, shows how that generation was mesmerized by the potency of Compound Interest.

---

[1] " Parl. Hist.," xxvi, 17-36. Earl Stanhope's measure will be described by Miss Ghita Stanhope in her monograph on the Earl.

[2] J. R. McCulloch, " Taxation and the Funding System," 3rd edit., 1883, 477-81.

Yet, delusive as the scheme came to be, it conferred two benefits on Great Britain. Firstly, it tended to the reduction of the National Debt during the time of peace. Nearly eleven millions were written off in the years 1784-1792;[1] and the country felt no inconvenience until the million had to be borrowed at ruinous rates. But, far more than this, faith in the Sinking Fund buoyed up British credit at a time when confidence was the first essential of the public safety. In the dark days of 1797 and 1805 Britons were nerved by the spirit of their leader, who never quailed even in face of mutiny, disaster, and the near approach of bankruptcy. There are times when unjustifiable trust is better than the most searching scrutiny. Finally, it is the barest justice to the memory of Pitt to remember that his whole financial policy in the early part of the Great War rested on the assumption that France would soon be overborne; and, as we shall see, that assumption was justified by the experience of the past and by every outward sign in her present life. It was the incalculable element in the French Revolution, from the *levée en masse* of 1793 down to Austerlitz in 1805, which baffled Pitt and metamorphosed his Sinking Fund into a load of lead.

[1] Hamilton, *op. cit.* McCulloch admits only half that amount. In the Pitt MSS. (No. 275) is an account of the stocks purchased for the Sinking Fund up to 5th January 1796. They amounted to £18,001,655 and Annuities equal to £89,675. See, too, Pitt's Memoranda on the Sinking Fund in "Pitt and Napoleon Miscellanies."

CHAPTER IX

REFORM

Unblest by Virtue, Government a league
Becomes, a circling junto of the great
To rob by law; Religion mild, a yoke
To tame the stooping soul, a trick of State
To mask their rapine, and to share their prey.
THOMSON, *Liberty.*

The distempers of monarchy were the great subjects of apprehension and redress in the last century; in this, the distempers of Parliament.—BURKE, *Thoughts on the present Discontents.*

THE experience of statesmen has generally led them to link together the question of retrenchment with that of Reform. The connection between these two topics indeed lies in the nature of things. The brunt of taxation has in the past fallen on the middle and artisan classes; and where they have only a small share in the government, the spending departments are apt to run riot. Under an oligarchy or plutocracy the Government is likely to become a close preserve for the benefit of landless younger sons, the preservation of great estates being thus assured by means which lower the public services to the level of eleemosynary institutions. Whenever the mass of taxpayers gains political power, it will insist on efficiency and economy; or, at the worst, it will claim that the unprivileged shall also have an entry into the domain of Government. In either case, the result will be not unlike that which happens in a household where the husband sleepily pays and the wife lavishly spends. When the rude awakening comes, the spending department will probably yield to the power that holds the purse. The *ultima ratio* of husbands and Parliaments is, after all, much the same. On the other hand, if the House of Commons represents little more than the rent-receiving classes, what hope is there that it will draw the purse strings? Whence it comes about that economists have for the most part pleaded for a truly representative system.

As we have seen, Pitt had twice brought forward the question of the Reform of Parliament, and had twice suffered defeat. The need of caution was obvious; and this explains his conduct in begging that veteran reformer, Alderman Sawbridge, not to press his motion on this subject in the short session of May— August 1784. The Prime Minister, however, promised to bring it before the House of Commons early in the following session.[1] Some surprise was therefore felt on the opening day, 25th January 1785, when the King's Speech contained no promise more definite than that he would concur in every measure which would "secure the true principles of the constitution."[2] Pitt himself, while admitting that the King's Speech might in that House be assumed to be the speech of the chief Minister, stated that it was impossible to include in it a reference to that topic. The inference was obvious, that the King objected to its inclusion in the speech.

For Pitt's interest in the subject certainly had not cooled. In the spring of 1784 he had assured the Rev. Christopher Wyvill and the Yorkshire Association of his devotion to the cause in the following as yet unpublished letter.

London, March 11, 1784.[3]

Gentlemen,

I consider myself greatly obliged to you for the favour of your letter, which I received upon the 6th instant. I beg leave to assure you that my zeal for Reform in Parliament is by no means abated, and that I will ever exert my best endeavours to accomplish that important object.

(Signed) W. Pitt.

Further, on 27th December 1784 he stated to Wyvill his intention to bring forward a Reform Bill as early as possible in the next session, and that he would "exert his whole power and credit *as a man, and as a minister, honestly and boldly*, to carry such a meliorated system of representation as may place the constitution on a footing of permanent security."[4] This at least was the version of his words which Wyvill at once circulated to Reform Committees throughout the country. With a be-

---

[1] "Parl. Hist.," xxiv, 998.   [2] *Ibid.*, 1383.
[3] From Mr. Broadley's MSS.   [4] "Parl. Hist.," xxiv, 1396.

lated access of prudence, he added a postscript, urging that
it must in no case be published; but some foolish friend or
wise opponent bruited it abroad, with the result that members
of the House now contrasted his eagerness for Reform with his
inability to secure any mention of it in the King's Speech. He
might declare that the subject was the nearest to his heart, and
that nothing but its complexity prevented him sketching an outline of his proposal; but members drew their own conclusions.
North made a skilful use of Wyvill's letter, but elicited from
Pitt no definite disclaimer of the words quoted from it. Indeed
Pitt afterwards assured Wyvill that those words well expressed
his thoughts.[1]

Pitt judged that it would be best to proceed circumspectly in
the matter of Reform, perhaps because he wished the affair of
Wyvill's letter to blow over, or because he had obstacles to face
in his Cabinet. Owing to these or other causes he decided to
give precedence to his resolutions for according greater freedom
of trade to Ireland, which will be dealt with in another chapter;
and not until 18 April 1785 did he bring before Parliament
the subject of parliamentary Reform. The delay was unfortunate, for the trading classes were by this time ruffled by proposals which promised to bring in the products of Irish cheap
labour.

Meanwhile Pitt drew up a draft scheme of Reform and sent it
to Wyvill for his perusal. He proposed to set aside a sum of
somewhat more than £1,000,000 in order to indemnify electors
in nomination boroughs, provided that two-thirds of their total
number should agree to forego their right of sending members
to Parliament. In that case the borough should be disfranchised,
the electors receiving compensation by a Parliamentary Committee after due examination of their claims. The seats thus
vacated were to be added to counties or to districts of the larger
counties. Pitt also hinted at the enfranchisement of certain
suburban areas of London, and suggested that notoriously corrupt boroughs (such as Shoreham and Cricklade) should be
disfranchised without compensation, their electoral powers being
transferred to counties. He further proposed to widen the
county franchise by admitting copyholders of 40 shillings a year
and leaseholders whose leases had a certain term yet to run.[2]

---

[1] "Corresp. of Wyvill with Pitt," pt. i, 1796, 13.
[2] "Corresp. of Pitt with Wyvill," pt. ii, 1797, 1-7.

These suggestions strike us as strangely cramped, except in the matter of copyholds, which were dealt with more generously than in Earl Grey's Bill of 1831. The proposals for disfranchising the pocket boroughs resemble a political auction, Pitt dangling a million before the potwallers of Gatton, Grampound, Castle Rising, etc., as the sole means of endowing the great counties with political power, and of enabling Manchester, Birmingham, Leeds, and Sheffield to find articulate utterance. Wyvill in 1797 noted that these towns formed a part of Pitt's scheme of enfranchisement; but the Prime Minister does not seem in 1785 to have ventured distinctly to formulate so revolutionary a proposal. In the draft of a preamble to his Bill he suggested the advisability of enlarging the electorate in the case of several towns such as Edinburgh, Glasgow, and Winchester, where the Corporation or the Guild Merchant alone returned the members of Parliament.

These draft proposals reveal the caution, not to say nervousness, with which Pitt approached this great subject; and the same characteristics appear in the speech of 18th April 1785 in which he introduced his measure. While lacking glow and enthusiasm, it was instinct with moderation and persuasiveness. He started with the assumption that the House of Commons ought to be " an Assembly freely elected, between whom and the mass of the people there was the closest union and most perfect sympathy"; but he proceeded to allay the fears of those who, like Burke, saw in any change a death-blow to the constitution, by disclaiming " vague and unlimited notions." He desired, he said, " a sober and practicable scheme which should have for its basis the original principle of representation." He then showed how that principle had been warped by time and Court intrigues. Sometimes method was discoverable, and he cited a case that occurred shortly after the Restoration when, after the disfranchisement of 72 boroughs, 36 of them regained their rights on petition, but the 36 others, having decreased in size, remained without representatives. Therefore, by the discretionary powers of the Crown to grant, or to withhold, representation, there was a clear recognition of the principle that the chief towns, not the decayed towns, should return members to Parliament. Who, he asked, was the truer supporter of the constitution? He who sought to preserve the mere form of it, or he who preferred its substance and essence to the empty shell? Coming next to the outlines of his scheme, he declared that he would change neither the proportion of Scottish to English members, as settled by the Act of Union of 1707, nor the numbers of the House. All that he aimed at for the present was to disenfranchise 36 decayed boroughs and to assign their 72 members to the counties which most needed a larger representation, as also to London and Westminster.

Moderation such as this implies timidity. Moreover this was not all. As we have seen, Pitt did not intend to carry out this reform by compulsion; and he now declared that, recognizing as he did the monetary value of the franchises of these decayed boroughs, he proposed to form a fund whence they might gain compensation for this undoubted loss. Very skilfully he introduced this novel proposal by deprecating the "squeamish and maiden coyness" which members affected in speaking there on a topic which they frankly discussed outside the House. For himself he faced the fact that the right of returning two members to Parliament had a certain monetary value, and he therefore offered a due indemnity. Further, if in the future any other decayed borough should wish to surrender its franchise "on an adequate consideration," he proposed to facilitate such a surrender, and to allot the two seats to any district or town that seemed most to need the franchise. Finally he desired to widen the electorate in the counties by including copyholders, whose property was as secure as, sometimes more secure than, that of the freeholders.[1]

Such were the proposals. They were brought forward at a time when Pitt had suffered in the opinion of the House, first by his obstinacy in persevering with the Westminster election scrutiny, and, secondly, by the Irish Commercial Resolutions. Members were therefore in an unsettled state of mind, and an eye-witness describes them as listening to the Prime Minister "with that sort of civil attention which people give to a person who has a good claim to be heard, but with whom the hearers are determined to disagree." The same witness, Daniel Pulteney, found that most of Pitt's friends "lamented that he would not

---

[1] In the "Pitt and Napoleon Miscellanies," I include a Memorandum —"Notes on Reform of Parliament"—from the Pretyman MSS. It is undated; but the notes form undoubtedly the rough draft of the speech outlined above, except that there is no mention of the buying out proposals at the end. May we infer that this was an afterthought, due to Dundas?

keep clear of this absurd business—this Yorkshire system of Reform." [1]

Despite this chilling reception, Pitt set forth his proposals " with the attractions of a most seductive eloquence." Such is the testimony of Wraxall, which by itself would tend to refute the venomous assertion that Pitt was not in earnest. The contrary is proved by his words and deeds. At Christmastide 1784 he begged Wilberforce to return from the south of France in order to work in the cause of Reform; and on 12th January 1785 he wrote to the Duke of Rutland in these terms: " I really think that I see more than ever the chance of effecting a safe and temperate plan [of Reform], and I think its success as essential to the credit, if not to the stability, of the present administration, as it is to the good government of the country hereafter." [2] Further, it is certain that those ardent reformers, Robert Smith (afterwards Lord Carrington) and Wyvill, had no doubt of his earnestness. The latter stated in his letters that Pitt was striving his hardest to arouse interest in the Reform of Parliament. [3]

There is also ground for thinking that the King had privately assured him that, though he regretted his advocacy of Reform, no word of his should influence any one against that measure. Wraxall, who voted against Pitt, admits that his plan of Reform was highly attractive in theory—a phrase which leaves us wondering what would have been the practical scheme of reform after which this earth-born soul was dimly groping. [4] Even Burke, who saw mortal danger to the body politic in the removal of the smallest rag of antiquity, complimented the Minister on the skill with which he had sought to make the change palateable to all parties. None the less did that fervid Celt consider the whole plan an *ignis fatuus*, calculated to mislead and bewilder. Herein Burke for once voiced the feelings of the country gentry who thought the fate of the constitution bound up with the maintenance of the rotten boroughs. The speeches of Duncombe and Wilberforce in support of the measure were poor and rambling. Dundas, an unwilling convert to Reform,

---

[1] " Rutland P.," iii, 202.

[2] " Corresp. of Pitt with the Duke of Rutland," 84.

[3] " Corresp. of Wilberforce," i, 4 ; " Life of Wilberforce," i, 77 ; " Corresp. of Wyvill with Pitt," pt. i, 15 *n.*

[4] Stanhope, i, xv ; Wraxall, iii, 116.

had nothing better to say than that he highly approved the principle of compensation.

The chief arguments against the measure were those of North, Fox, and Bankes. The first declared that the country cared not a jot for Reform. Birmingham had not petitioned for it. One of the members for Suffolk, who sought advice from his constituents, had received no instructions from them. The effort to get up a Reform meeting in London had resulted in the attendance of only three hundred persons; and the outcome of similar efforts in the provinces might be summed up in the line from "The Rehearsal":

What horrid sound of *silence* doth assail mine ear?

As for Fox, though he voted with Pitt, he did his best to defeat the measure. He wittily explained the silence of the people by their alarm at Pitt's Irish Resolutions; for when on the point of emigrating from a land on the brink of ruin, why should they trouble about its constitution? Further, he stoutly objected to the award of any indemnity to the owners of pocket boroughs. The same point was shrewdly pressed by Bankes. The measure, he said, was absurd on the face of it. For why declare against the whole principle of the traffic in such boroughs, and yet proceed to allow liberal compensation to the traffickers? The argument was more clever than sound, as appeared in 1834 when Parliament awarded £20,000,000 to slave-owners. The taunt also came with an ill grace from the owner and representative of Corfe Castle; but it cut Pitt to the quick. He immediately arose and avowed that the remark wounded him deeply on account of his long friendship with the speaker; the point touched was a tender one; but the evil was such that it must be cured, and it could be cured in no other way than the present. And so, in this mood of "Et tu, Brute," Pitt and his friends withdrew into the lobby, and soon learned that his third attempt to redress the glaring ills of the representation had been defeated by 248 votes to 174.

The blow was crushing and final as regards Parliamentary Reform in that age. The storms of the French Revolution and the mightier subterranean forces of the Industrial Revolution were to work upon the old order of things before the governing classes of England were brought to see the need of renovation; and when the change came in 1832, it was not until the nation

had drawn near to the verge of civil war. In 1785 the transition
would have been peaceful and progressive. Pitt was content
to work by permissive methods, and to leave open the decision
as to which of the rising industrial towns should gain the franchise as it was sold by the decaying boroughs. Such a mode of
advance seems to us that of a snail, and marked by a trail of
slime. But we must remember that the brains of that generation worked very slowly on political questions; for in truth
they had to do with a society which was to ours almost as a
lake is to a torrent. Further, it is noteworthy that the offer to
buy out the pocket boroughs was the chief recommendation of
Pitt's measure to the House of Commons. Burke praised him
for thus gilding his pill; and Dundas's chief plea for the
measure was that it did not outrage "the sacred inheritance of
property." Alone among Pitt's supporters Bankes reprobated
these bartering methods. The attitude of the House should be
remembered, as it bears on the question how far Pitt was
justified in buying off the opposition of the Irish borough-
holders and others who suffered by the Act of Union of 1800.

Could Pitt have taken any further steps to ensure the passing
of his Reform Bill? Mr. Lecky, followed in this by lesser
historians, has maintained the affirmative. He avers that, by
making it a ministerial measure, Pitt could have brought to bear
on it all the influence of party discipline.[1] To this it may be
replied that Pitt's majority, though large, was very independent.
As will appear in the next chapter, we find him writing that he
could not then count on the support of many of his followers
from one day to another. They had floated together from the
wreckage of the Fox and North parties, and had as yet gained
no distinct cohesion, except such as arose from admiration of
him. Further, he strained this feeling too severely in the session
of 1785 by his harsh treatment of Fox over the Westminster
election, and by pressing on three unpopular measures, namely,
the Irish Resolutions (22nd February), the fortification of Portsmouth and Plymouth (14th March), and Parliamentary Reform
(18th April). Sooner or later he suffered defeat on all these
proposals. Yet it is clear that his followers did not intend to
drive him from office, but merely to teach him caution. In this
they succeeded only too well. Thereafter he acted far more

---

[1] Lecky, v, 62, 63; Jephson, "The Platform," i, 166.

warily; and, except in the Warren Hastings' case, and in the French Commercial Treaty, he for some time showed little of that power of initiative which marked the early part of the session of 1785. The fact is to be regretted; but the need of caution is manifest when we remember that a single irretrievable blunder would have entailed a Fox-North Ministry with all the discords and confusion that must have come in its train. Even zealous reformers, while regretting that Pitt did not persevere with Reform, continued to prefer him to Fox and North. This appears in a letter written by Major Cartwright at the close of the year 1788. On the news of the mental derangement of George III, that veteran reformer wrote to Wilberforce: "I very much fear that the King's present derangement is likely to produce other derangements not for the public benefit. I hope we are not to be sold to the Coalition faction. Mr. Fox is, I see, arrived, and cabal, I doubt not, is labouring with redoubled zeal under his direction to overturn the present Government."[1] The distrust felt for Fox after his union with North survived in full force even in 1788. Their accession to power, and the triumph of the Prince of Wales, were looked on as the worst of all political evils. This, I repeat, explains and justifies the determination of Pitt to continue in office.

But other reasons must also have influenced his decision to shelve the question of Reform at least for the present. His Cabinet was too divided on it to warrant his risking its existence on a proposal which had always been rejected. The marvel was that a Prime Minister should bring it forward. Further, if we may judge from George III's letter of 20th March, the active though secret opposition of the King was averted only by Pitt giving an unmistakable hint that he would resign if it were used against the measure.[2] Having secured the King's neutrality, Pitt could hardly go further and leave his sovereign in the lurch by breaking up his Cabinet on a question on which he alone of the executive Government felt strongly.

Another possible alternative was that he himself should resign. But this again would almost certainly have involved the fall of an Administration of which he was the keystone. It is also noteworthy that the doctrine of ministerial responsibility,

---

[1] "Life of Wilberforce," i, 191.

[2] I agree with Dr. W. Hunt ("Political Hist. of England," x, 287) in his interpretation of the King's letter quoted by Stanhope, i, App., xv.

whether collective or personal, had not then been definitely established. Cabinets and individual Ministers resigned on points of honour, or when they held that the Government could no longer be satisfactorily carried on. But neither of these cases had arisen. The Government of the country obviously could go on as well as before. True, a legislative proposal of great importance had been rejected; but it cannot be too clearly stated that in that century the chief work of Government was to govern, not to pass new laws. Far on in the next century the main business of a Cabinet came to be the proposing and carrying through of new measures; but this idea was foreign to that more stationary age; and probably everyone would have accused Pitt of deserting his post had he resigned owing to his inability to carry a legislative enactment of a very debatable character. Walpole has not been blamed because he held to office despite his failure to carry his very important Excise Bill.

Again, why should Pitt have persevered with the cause of Reform? Despite all the efforts of Wyvill and the Associations, only eight petitions had been sent up to the House in favour of it. The taunts of North as to the apathy of the country were unanswerable. No voice was heard in protest against the rejection of the measure; and the judgement of Wilberforce was that of practically all reformers, that, after Pitt's failure, Reform was hopeless.[1] Wyvill himself, in a pamphlet written amidst the excitements of 1793, admitted that Pitt's measure received little attention in 1785, and soon fell into oblivion—a fact which he explained by the complete satisfaction which the nation then felt with its new Ministry. Here we have the true explanation, furnished by the man who had his hand on the nation's pulse. Wyvill saw that the practical character of the reforms already carried by Pitt had reconciled the people even to rotten boroughs. He also stated that the proposals of 1785 did not go far enough to satisfy many reformers, but that they aroused the bitter hostility of the boroughmongers. There, indeed, was the gist of the difficulty. The boroughmongers carried the House with them; and it was impossible at that period to stir up a national enthusiasm which would brush aside the fears of the timid and the sophistries of the corrupt. Only under the overpowering

---

[1] "Life of Wilberforce," i, 113.

impulse of 1832 could the House be brought to pass sentence against itself. Because Grey and Russell carried a Reform Bill nearly half a century later, is Pitt to be blamed for abandoning, after the third attempt, a measure which aroused invincible opposition in Parliament, and only the most languid interest in the nation at large?

Further, be it noted that the conduct of Fox had irretrievably damaged the cause of Reform. His union with Lord North had split in twain the party of progress; and we have the testimony of an ardent young reformer, Francis Place, that that unprincipled union dealt a death blow to the London Society for promoting Constitutional Information, the last expiring effort of which was to publish a volume of political tracts in the year 1784.[1] Not until the year 1791 was this useful society revived, and then owing to the impulses set in motion by French democracy.

Finally, it is noteworthy that Pitt gave his support to a smaller measure of Reform brought forward in the session of 1786 by Earl Stanhope. That nobleman had persuaded Wilberforce to widen the scope of a proposal which the member for Yorkshire had first designed for that county alone. It provided for the registration of all freeholders and the holding of the poll in several places at the same time. Pitt spoke warmly for the Bill as tending to remedy the chief defects in the county representation, and he expressed the hope that at some future time the whole of the representation would undergo the same improvements (15th May). Despite the opposition of Grenville and Powys, leave was granted to bring in the measure by 98 votes to 22. Though Stanhope emphatically declared in the Lords that the summary rejection of a Bill affecting the Commons would be an act of " unutterable indecency," the Peers rejected the measure by 38 votes to 15.[2]

This was the last effort made by Pitt's friends and supporters to improve the old system. For the present, Reform had come to an *impasse*. Even practical little proposals which passed the Commons were doomed to failure in the Lords; and it was clear that nothing short of a convulsion would open up a passage. The events that followed tended to discredit the cause of progress. As will appear in Chapter XIV, the violence of the

[1] B.M. Add. MSS., 27808.
[2] " Parl. Hist.," xxvi, 1-5, 178-86; " Life of Wilberforce," i, 114.

Dutch democrats threatened to wreck their constitution, to degrade the position of the Prince of Orange, and to make their country a footstool of the French monarchy. Pitt perforce took the side of the Prince; and this question, together with the torpor of the populace, served by degrees to detach the young statesman from uncompromising reformers like Stanhope and Wyvill.

The defection or apathy of many of his friends in the session of 1785 was undoubtedly a severe blow to Pitt. It sounded the death-knell of his earlier idealism, and led him on, somewhat dazed, to a time marked by compromise and a tendency to rely upon "influence." Daniel Pulteney noted, when he saw him in the park on the day following the rebuff, that he was in deep sorrow.[1] That was natural in a man who had hoped to arouse the nation to a vivid interest in good government, and suddenly found himself headed back to the old paths. The shock must have been the greater as he had been guided by what I have termed his bookish outlook on life.

Pulteney, as a man of the world, pointed out to his patron, the Duke of Rutland, this defect in the young Prime Minister: "This system of Pitt's, to act upon general ideas of the propriety or wisdom of a measure, without attending enough to the means by which it can be best and most happily introduced—I mean, knowing the general opinion of the House at the time—must, I foresee, involve him in time in one or other of these difficulties," namely, the rash introduction of a measure, or its abandonment through a sudden access of distrust. Again he says that Pitt is very much "fettered in his conduct on great affairs. From a very partial and confined knowledge of the world, he is too full of caution and suspicions where there does not exist the shadow of a pretext for them; and, from having no immediate inter-course with the generality of the House of Commons here, he is as ignorant of their opinions on particular questions as if he was Minister of another country." He then states that, when Pitt suddenly came to see the facts of the case, he was apt to be unduly despondent and to bring forward only those questions on which he was sure of a majority. He concludes that this habit of "acting only on abstract principles" would greatly

[1] "Rutland P.," iii, 202.

embarrass him; but that he might expect long to continue in power, because "whenever he was to quit, I think no Ministry, not founded on corruption, could stand against him."[1]

This estimate, by a practical politician, though marked by a desire to depreciate Pitt and exalt the Duke of Rutland, goes far towards explaining the symptoms of change which are thereafter noticeable in Pitt's career. It shows us Pitt, not a superb parliamentarian dominating men and affairs from the outset, but rather an idealist, almost a *doctrinaire*, who hoped to lead his majority at his will by the inspiring power of lofty principles, but now and again found that he had to do, not with Humanity, but with humdrum men. We see him in the midst of his upward gazings, disconcerted by the force of material interests, and driven thenceforth to pay more attention to the prejudices of his party.

First in importance among the expedients to which he was driven after the spring of 1785 was the use of "influence." As was shown in the Introduction, that word, when used in a political sense, denoted the system of rewards or coercion whereby the King and his Prime Minister assured the triumph of their policy. Peerages, bishoprics, judgeships, magistracies, sinecures and gaugerships, were the dainties held out by every Ministry in order to keep their sleek following close to heel and thin the ranks of the lean and hungry Opposition. Peerages alone counted for much; for we find Pitt writing, during the Fox-North Ministry of 1783, that the King's determination not to create a single peer during their term of office must sooner or later be fatal to them. Government by rewards and exclusions was looked upon as the natural order of things; but up to the session of 1785 Pitt used "influence" sparingly. At a later date Wilberforce ventured on the very questionable assertion that Pitt's command over Parliament after the General Election of 1784 was so great that he might have governed by "principle" and have dispensed with "influence." He expressed, however, his admiration of him for refusing to associate with trading politicians, a connection which, even in the hours of recreation, was certain to bring defilement.[2]

Pitt, as we have seen, never stooped to associate with jobbers, but he seems to have decided, after the severe rebuffs of Feb-

---

[1] "Rutland P.," iii, 198, 203; Letters of 11th and 23rd April 1785.
[2] "Private Papers of W. Wilberforce," 72.

ruary-April 1785, to use "influence" more and more. We notice
in his letters to the Duke of Rutland and Orde several injunc-
tions as to the management of members in the Irish Parliament;
and he sought to conciliate waverers by other means, such as
the abandonment of those clauses of the Irish Resolutions which
were most obnoxious to British traders, and an almost lavish
use of honours and places. This last expedient he adopted unwillingly; for on 19th July 1785 he wrote to the Duke of Rutland that circumstances compelled him to recommend a larger
addition to the British peerage than he liked, and that he was
very desirous not to increase it farther than was absolutely necessary.[1] This shows that his hand was forced either by his colleagues or by the exigencies of the time. Possibly the promises
of peerages had to be made in order to secure the passing of
the Irish Resolutions even in their modified form. It is humiliating to reflect that this descent from a higher to a lower level
of policy thenceforth secured him a majority which followed his
lead, except on the isolated questions of the fortification of
Portsmouth and Plymouth, and of the impeachment of Warren
Hastings, the latter of which he left entirely open.

It will be convenient to consider here the question of the
fortification of the chief national dockyards, as it shows the
determination of the Prime Minister to secure economy and
efficiency in the public services. As we have seen, his great aim
was to carry out a work of revival in every sphere of the nation's
life. When thwarted in one direction he did not relax his
energies, but turned them into new channels. On the rejection
of the Irish Resolutions, he urged the Duke of Rutland to seek
out the most practicable means of healing the discontent in that
island. Above all he suggested an alleviation in the matter of
tithe (then the most flagrant of all material grievances), if possible, with the assent of the (Protestant) Established Church.[2]
Similarly in the cause of Free Trade, when foiled by Anglo-
Irish jealousies, he turned towards France; and, after discovering
the impossibility of carrying out his aim for the regeneration of
Parliament, he vindicated the claims of morality in the administration of India. Finally, it is a crowning proof of the many-
sidedness and practical character of his efforts that, amidst all

[1] "Corresp. of Pitt with the Duke of Rutland," 150, 151.
[2] Ibid., 174, 175.

I   P

his strivings to reduce the National Debt, he sought to strengthen the nation's defences.

Despite the many distractions of the years 1785-1786, he devoted much care and thought to the navy. Already, in 1784, he had instituted a Parliamentary inquiry into the state of the fleet and the dockyards, which brought to light many defects and pointed the way to remedies. His anxiety respecting the first line of defence also led him to keep the number of seamen at 18,000, a higher total than ever was known in time of peace; and he allotted the large sum of £2,400,000 for the building of warships by contract. Further, he sought to stop the corruption which was rife in the dockyards and the naval service.

The letter which Sir Charles Middleton (afterwards Lord Barham) wrote to him on 24th August 1786 reveals an astounding state of affairs. From his official knowledge he declared—

> The principle of our dockyards at present is a total disregard to public œconomy in all its branches; and it is so rooted in the professional officers that they cannot divest themselves of it when brought into higher stations. They have so many relatives and dependants, too, in the dockyards, that can only be served by countenancing and promoting improper expences, that they never lose an opportunity of supporting them when in their power, and on this account ought to have as small a voice as possible in creating them.[1]

In this and other letters to Pitt, Middleton expressed his belief that much might be done to check these evils by the help of a firm and upright Minister. Probably this appeal from a patriotic and hard-working official sharpened the attention which Pitt bestowed on naval affairs. We know from the notes of Sir T. Byam Martin that Pitt frequently visited the Navy Office in order to discuss business details with the Comptroller, and by his commanding ability left the impression that he might have been all his life engaged on naval affairs. In particular he used to inspect the reports of the building and repairing of the ships-of-the-line.—" He also (wrote Martin) desired to have a periodical statement from the Comptroller of the state of the fleet, wisely holding that officer responsible personally to him without any regard to the Board." The results of this impulse given by one master mind were speedily seen. More work was got out of the

---

[1] Pitt MSS., 111. Printed in the "Barham Papers" (ii, 219), edited by Sir John Laughton for the Navy Records Society.

dockyards, and twenty-four new sail-of-the-line were forthcoming from private yards in the years 1783-1790. Thus, by the time of the Spanish war-scare in 1790, ninety-three line-of-battle ships were ready for commission.[1] The crises of the years 1786-1788. had also been so serious that they might speedily have led to war had not Britain's first line of defence been invincible.

In regard to the proposal to strengthen the defences of Portsmouth and Plymouth, Pitt was less fortunate. The proposal really came from the Duke of Richmond, Master of the Ordnance, who was far from popular—a fact which perhaps influenced the votes of members. Though Pitt and other Ministers adduced excellent reasons for not leaving those vital points in their present weak state, he did not carry the House of Commons with him. After an exciting debate, which lasted till 7 a.m. of 28th February 1786, the numbers on a division were found to be exactly equal. Then there arose a shout such as had not been heard since the memorable vote which wrecked Lord North's Ministry. At once all eyes turned to the Speaker, Cornwall. He declared that he was too exhausted to give his reasons for his vote, but he would merely declare that the "Noes" had it. Wraxall states that the sense of the House was against Pitt, the country gentlemen especially disliking the addition of £700,000 to the next year's expenses.[2] One of the arguments of the Opposition seems to us curious. It was urged that the fortification of the two towns in question might be the beginning of a despotic system which would undermine the liberties of Englishmen. While treating this argument with the contempt it deserved, Pitt declared that he bowed before the feeling of the House. The commencement of huge works at Cherbourg later in the year must have caused qualms even to the watch-dogs of the constitution.

Some of the more eager Whigs called out for him to resign, it being the third time in twenty-two months that he had failed to carry an important measure. We may, however, point out that the proposal emanated from the Duke of Richmond; and there is the curious fact that Courtenay during the debate of 20th March 1789 asserted that the plan was merely the Duke's, and

---

[1] "Journals and Letters of Sir T. Byam Martin," iii, 380-2 (Navy Records Society).

[2] Wraxall, iv, 268-70. For some details on the inquiries at Portsmouth and Plymouth see the "Cornwallis Corresp.," i, 195-8.

had not come from the Royal Engineers. He was also not contradicted.[1] Further, it should be noticed that though Pitt made the proposal his own, Dundas and others of his Cabinet were known to dislike it. There is the final consideration already dwelt on, that the custom which requires a Ministry to resign on the rejection of any important measure, had not yet crystallized into a rule.

This was the last severe check which Pitt sustained in Parliament for many years. The fact that he suffered as many as three in twenty-two months with little or no diminution of prestige shows that his majority really trusted him and had no desire to put Fox and North in power. That alternative was out of the question, as Fox knew, even when he twitted his rival with being kept in office solely by the royal favour.

Nevertheless in the years following 1785 we notice a distinct weakening in Pitt's progressive tendencies. Whig though he was in his inmost convictions, he drifted slowly but surely towards the Tory position. Fortunately for him, the folly of his rivals in the year 1784, and again in the Regency crisis of 1788-9, enabled him to link the cause of the King with that of the nation. But these occasions were exceptional. It is never safe to owe a triumph to the mistakes of opponents amidst unusual conditions. For mistakes will be made good; and in the whirl of life circumstances will arise which range men and parties according to elemental principles.

Even before the French Revolution tested the strength of Pitt's reforming convictions, there came a question which acted as a touchstone. This was the proposal to repeal the Corporation and Test Acts of the reign of Charles II. Those measures had excluded from office in Corporations, or under Government, all who would not receive the Sacrament according to the rites of the Church of England. By this ban a large body of intelligent and loyal citizens were thrust out of the pale of political and civic preferment; and though the Toleration Act and Annual Acts of Indemnity screened them from actual persecution, their

[1] Porter, "Hist. of the Royal Engineers," ii, 209-11. The Duke of Richmond was, however, able to fortify some points at Portsmouth before the war of 1793 with France. See "Professional Papers of the Corps of Royal Engineers," xii (1886), 83, 86. Fort Monckton and smaller forts on Stokes Bay were built.

position was yet one of hardship. Certain bodies had not scrupled to make money out of their conscientious objections. As is well known, the Corporation of the City of London hit upon the plan of augmenting the building fund of their new Mansion House by passing a by-law in 1748 fining any Londoner who refused to serve when presented for nomination as Sheriff, and then proposing rich Nonconformists for that office. Not until 1767 did the able pronouncement of Lord Mansfield in the Upper House secure the rejection of this odious device. Thenceforth Nonconformists secured immunity from fines for refusing to serve in offices that were barred by the test of the Sacrament.

Nevertheless their position was far from enviable. By the freaks of insular logic Protestant Dissenters were allowed to vote in parliamentary elections and even to sit in the House of Commons; but though they had a share in the making and amending of laws, they could hold no office in a Corporation, or any of the great London Companies; commissions in the army, navy, and offices in other public services were also legally closed to them. Severe penalties hung over the head of any one who, in reliance on the annual Act of Indemnity, ventured to infringe any of these singular enactments. Public opinion approved this exclusiveness; and an anecdote told of that humorous mass of intolerance, Dr. Johnson, shows that prejudice was still keen in the circles which he frequented. He, Sir Robert Chambers, and John Scott (the future Lord Eldon), were walking in the gardens of New Inn Hall at Oxford, when Chambers began picking up snails and throwing them into the next garden. Johnson sharply rebuked him for this boorish act, until there came the soothing explanation that the neighbour was a Dissenter.—" Oh," said the Doctor, " if so, Chambers, toss away, toss away as hard as you can." [1]

The choice blend of Anglicanism and culture discernible in Chambers and Johnson, might be seen elsewhere than in the seat of learning on the Isis. It was the rule in the rural districts, except among the sturdy yeomen of the Eastern Counties, where the spirit that fought at Naseby had so far survived as to render snail-throwing a pastime of doubtful expediency. The same remark applies to London, where the tactics of the city fathers had

---

[1] H. Twiss, " Life of Lord Eldon," i, ch. iv.

signally failed to suppress Dissent. Very many churchmen were
ashamed of these petty attempts at persecution, and the progress
of the Evangelical revival aroused a feeling of uneasiness at seeing
the most sacred rite of the Church degraded into a political shib-
boleth. Comprehension within the bosom of Mother Church was
highly desirable; but clearly it might be too dearly purchased
by Erastian laws which enabled a lax Nonconformist to buy his
way into the Customs or Excise by presenting himself at the
altar of the nearest church along with convinced communicants.

Accordingly Nonconformists had a strong body of opinion on
their side in the session of 1787, when they asked for the repeal
of those exclusive statutes. A staunch churchman, Mr. Beaufoy,
championed their cause in a very powerful and eloquent speech,
which won the admiration of Wraxall.[1] Beaufoy dwelt on the
anomaly of retaining this old-world exclusiveness, which would
expose to the penalties of the law the illustrious John Howard,
if ever he returned to this country. He showed that no danger
need be apprehended for the Established Church, especially as
the Act of Supremacy would continue to exclude from office
all Roman Catholics, as well as Quakers. Further, the loyalty
of the Protestant Dissenters had been sufficiently shown in the
election of 1784, when they voted with Pitt on behalf of the
prerogatives of the Crown. He then inveighed against the continuance of enactments which " degraded the altar into a quali-
fication-desk for tax-gatherers and public extortioners." Fox
followed with a strong plea for religious toleration, quoting
Locke and other writers who denounced the imposition of religious tests in political matters. The Church of England, said
the Whig leader, was disgraced by the present state of things;
and, seeing that it represented the majority of the English
people, it could not be endangered by the proposed change.

On the other hand North, now quite blind, came into the
House leaning on his son, Colonel North, in order to oppose the
motion. Speaking with much earnestness, he declared that the
Test and Corporation Acts were the bulwarks of our Constitution. Pitt must have felt some surprise at speaking on the
same side as North; but he now asserted that those Acts did not
impose any stigma or penalty on Nonconformists, for whom,
indeed, he had a great respect. There must be a Church Estab-

[1] Wraxall, iv, 436.

lishment, and it of necessity implied some restrictions on those outside its pale. The constitution of Society involved limitations of individual rights; and he averred that the laws in question were justified by that consideration. Further, there were no means whereby moderate Dissenters could be admitted to these privileges while the more violent were excluded. If all were admitted, they might overthrow the outworks of the Establishment. These arguments carried the day by one hundred and seventy-six votes to ninety-eight (28th March 1787).[1]

Bishop Watson, of Llandaff, in his " Reminiscences," explains Pitt's conduct on this occasion. He declares that the Chancellor of the Exchequer had no strong feelings of his own on the subject, and had therefore referred the matter to the Archbishop of Canterbury. The Primate had assembled his colleagues at Lambeth, and by ten votes to two they had decided to uphold the Caroline enactments. If this be correct, Pitt's action was weak. Certainly his speech was half-hearted, and utterly different in tone from his orations on Reform, the Regency, Slavery, and other topics which moved him deeply. Moreover, the referring a matter of this kind to the bench of bishops was about as reasonable as taking the opinion of country squires on a proposed mitigation of the Game Laws, or of college dons on a reform of their university. A Prime Minister abdicates his functions when he defers to the opinions of a class respecting a proposal which will trench on its prerogatives.

---

[1] "Parl. Hist.," xxvi, 780-832. On 8th May 1789, a similar motion by Beaufoy was defeated by 122 votes to 102 (*Ibid.*, xxviii, 1-41).

CHAPTER X

INDIA

" We hold ourselves bound to the natives of our Indian territory by the same obligations of duty which bind us to all our other subjects."—(Proclamation of Queen Victoria, 1st November 1858.)

MONTAIGNE once uttered a protest against those historians who "chew the mouthfuls for us," and spoil all in the process. He coupled with it, however, another vice which is really far more serious, namely, their habit of laying down rules for judging, and "for bending history to their fancy." As for the presenting history in mouthfuls, it is probably the only way of making it digestible except for those mighty intellects which seize facts and figures with avidity, and assimilate them as if by magic.

Further, the modern historian may urge in defence of the topical method that it is the only practicable way of dealing with the infinity of topics of the last two centuries, ranging over parliamentary debates and wars, finance and social gossip, mean intrigues and philanthropic movements, industrial changes and empire-building, the efforts of great men and the impersonal forces that mould and move great nations, together with the denuding agencies that weather away the old surface and the resistless powers that thrust up a new world. How shall a finite intellect grasp at once all the moving details of this varied life? The mind craves to consider at any one time only one part of the majestic procession, just as it demands that the facts of Nature shall be grasped under different sciences. Human life is one as Nature is one; but the division in each case is necessitated by the increasing width of man's outlook. All that is essential in the sorting-out process is that it shall honestly set forth all the important facts, and here and there open out vistas revealing the connection with other fields of human activity. In short, history can no longer be a detailed panorama of life, but it can and ought to be a series of companion pictures, informed by the personality of the artist and devoid of conscious prejudice.

Among the diverse subjects which confront us in the many-sided career of Pitt, none stands more apart than that of his relations to India. Of his Herculean labours we may, perhaps, term this one the cleansing of the Augean stables. The corruption that clung about the Indian Government, the baffling remoteness of its duties, the singular relations of the East India Company to the Crown, and of its own officials to it, above all, the storms of passion which had been aroused by the masterful dealings of Warren Hastings and the furious invectives of Burke, presented a problem which could not be solved save by the exercise of insight, patience, and wise forcefulness. It would greatly overburden this narrative to recount the signal services, albeit marred by deeds of severity and injustice, whereby Hastings grappled with the Mahratta War and the incursion of Hyder Ali into the Carnatic. All that need be remembered here is that Parliament had censured some of his actions and demanded his recall, that the Court of Directors of the Company had endorsed that demand, but that the Court of Proprietors had annulled it. Hastings therefore remained at his post, mainly, it would appear, from a conviction that he alone could safeguard British supremacy.

Accordingly, on this all-important question there was division in the executive powers at Calcutta, and in the East India Company itself; while the insubordination of very many of the Company's servants in India further revealed the insufficiency of Lord North's Regulating Act of 1773. Fortunately, however, the finances of the Company were in such disorder as to make it amenable to pressure from Westminster. It owed a very large sum to the Home Government for duties on its imports into Great Britain; and Parliament was thus the better able to assert the supremacy of the nation.

It was high time to make good this claim. The India Bills of Fox and of Pitt had been thrown out; and thus, despite an infinity of talk, the whole situation remained unchanged, except that nearly every one now agreed that it must be changed. On questions of detail opinions differed widely. Some of the proprietors and Directors of the Company protested against any interference whatsoever with chartered rights which they were perfectly able to uphold and vindicate. The opposite extreme was touched by Fox during a preliminary debate on the affairs of the Company, when he declared that body to be a sink of corruption and iniquity, a mere conduit for bringing home the wealth acquired by its servants in India. If, said he, the patronage of the India service must be vested either in the Directors or in the Crown, let the Crown take that influence from hands which had so shamefully abused it.

Pitt's position, it soon appeared, was intermediate between these extremes. Four days later, on 6th July 1784, he introduced his second India Bill in a speech marked by great circumspection. He started from the same principles which had fashioned the outlines of his former measure (see chapter vii), that, though a charter ought not to override the needs of the State, yet nothing but absolute necessity could justify its abrogation. The affairs of the Company, he claimed, did not warrant so extreme a measure. His aim would be, not to abolish, but improve on, the existing plan of government for India. There were two essentials to be aimed at, namely, a due share of activity and resourcefulness in the Indian Government and obedience to the measures dictated by Parliament. The former of these requisites could be attained only by according to the Indian Government a certain degree of power, and from the latter it resulted that that power must be subject to the control of a regulating Board at home.

Pitt therefore recurred to his former plan. He left to the Governments of the Presidencies, above all, to the Governor-General, enough authority to enable them to cope with emergencies; but he also proposed to subject them to a Board consisting of members chosen by the Crown from the Privy Council. To this special committee of the Privy Council would be entrusted the power of devising legislation for India, of controlling Indian policy, and of recalling any of the Company's officials. It was not, however, to have a voice in those questions of patronage which might deflect it from the path of duty and impartiality. The proceedings of the Board might be open to perusal by the Directors of the Company; but its behests would be final. In case of flagrant disobedience, or of other grave offences, the officials and servants of the Company were to be tried by a Commission consisting of members of the two Houses of Parliament chosen by ballot shortly before the trial.

Such were the chief proposals. As for the spirit which informed the measures, it may be divined from that part of the speech in which the Prime Minister set forth the fundamental principles of our Indian policy. They were in brief these, the avoidance of war and of alliances that might lead to war, and the use of such conciliatory methods as would further the aim which we had chiefly in view—pacific commerce.[1]

Neither the spirit of enlightened patriotism, which pervaded the speech, nor the practical nature of the proposals screened the measure from fierce opposition. That acrid opponent of Warren Hastings, Mr. Francis, taunted Pitt with leaving to the Directors of the Company the mere shadow of authority, but he prophesied that the large powers vested in the Governor-General and in the Governments of the Presidencies would be abused as flagrantly as ever they had been in the past. Fox expanded these objections with his usual force, asserting that far too large powers were given to the Crown, and that the proposed Board would be quite as partisan a body as the Commissioners to whom he in his India Bill had entrusted the regulating power. He further insisted that to leave appointments to the Company, while depriving it of authority, was a miserably weak expedient which must sap the base of government. On their side, the Directors of the Company complained that the present Bill at several points trenched on their trading rights, which they had always expressly reserved to themselves; and they urged that they must retain in their own hands the right of recalling their own servants. As for the proposed tribunal for the trial of disobedient officials, it seemed to them an unsatisfactory experiment, seeing that both trial by jury and impeachment were ill adapted to the complex questions of Indian administration.[2]

Nevertheless, the Company had to give way at nearly all points. The powers of the Court of Proprietors almost entirely lapsed (to the satisfaction of all but themselves); and a clause was passed, compelling the Company's officials to state on oath the amount of their fortunes at the end of their service, Pitt himself suggesting that private gains up to £2,000 a year after the first five years of service should not be deemed culpable. Though the Bill prohibited the receiving of "presents" from natives, it

---

[1] "Parl. Hist.," xxiv, 1086-99.   [2] Pitt MSS., 353.

was clear that officials would use other equally objectionable means in order to arrive at that unobjectionable sum.

On the whole, however, the principle of controlling Indian affairs from Westminster, which Lord North had rather haltingly asserted eleven years earlier, now became the dominant fact of the situation. This will be clear if we review the constitution and powers of the new Board of Control. It was to consist of six members of the Privy Council chosen by the King; the Chancellor of the Exchequer and one of the Secretaries of State being always included. In the absence of these two, the senior member of the remaining four was to preside; and finally the conduct of the Board's affairs came to rest virtually with him, so that he became, in all but name, Secretary of State for India. For the present, however, as appears from a letter of Dundas to Cornwallis of 29th July 1787, Pitt attended the Board regularly and thoroughly mastered its business.

To this Board were submitted all letters and despatches between the Company and its officials in India, except those which referred solely to trade. Every proceeding and resolution of the Court of Directors must come to it; and from it there issued orders which the Directors were bound to enforce. Further, at the second reading Pitt amended his Bill so as to allow the Board in urgent cases to frame and transmit their commands to India without communicating them to the Directors. Finally, if the Company appealed against the Board's decisions, the ultimate judgement lay with the King in Council, that is, with a body largely the same as that from which it appealed.[1] While, therefore, Pitt instituted what was called a system of dual control, that control, save in the lower sphere of commerce, was really exercised by the Home Government. In the long series of changes which transformed the venture of a company of London merchants into an Empire administered by the British people, no step is more important than that taken by him in this, his first great constructive effort.

But this was not all. Various circumstances in the next eighteen months showed the need of still further strengthening the Indian executive. Certain ominous moves of the French caused anxiety. In the spring of 1785 their East India Company

---

[1] Mill, " Hist. of British India," iv, 559 (4th edit.).

was revived on an imposing scale; and the close relations subsisting between France and the Dutch Republic augured ill for
the British dominions in the Orient. Everything, therefore,
tended to emphasize the need of strong Government at Calcutta;
and the attention directed to Indian affairs, consequent on the
charges brought against Warren Hastings early in the year
1786, further convinced many competent judges of the need of
strengthening the Indian executive. These considerations furnish
the reasons which led Pitt to bring in an Amending Act.

If we may judge from Pitt's speeches of 17th and 22nd March of
that year, he had been much impressed by the sagacity of the
Governor-General in seeking to frame an alliance with the Great
Mogul for the purpose of counterbalancing the offensive league of
Tippoo Sahib with the French. The action of Hastings' Council
in frustrating this statesmanlike plan, because it contravened the
instructions of the Company, showed the unwisdom of doubly
tying the hands of a competent governor, first by instructions
drawn up in Leadenhall Street, and secondly by a Council in
which pedantry or personal spite could paralyze great enterprises. Obviously what was required was to choose the right
man as Governor-General, then to grant him powers large
enough to meet serious crises, and to place him in such a relation to the Home Government that those powers would not be
abused. None of these conditions could be satisfied so long as
the Company appointed the supreme officials and prescribed
their functions.

But Pitt's Bill of 1784 had changed all this. As we have seen,
the British Government was now the driving force of the Indian
machinery, the Company acting merely as an intermediate wheel.
The responsibility of the Governor-General to the new India
Board and to Parliament having been decisively asserted, his
powers could now safely be increased.

This formed the *raison d'être* of Pitt's Amending Act of
March 1786. Though introduced by Dundas—a graceful compliment to his exertions in Indian matters in time past—it
emanated from the Prime Minister. It applied the principles of
the India Bill of 1784 to the servants of the Company in Great
Britain. But, what was far more important, it enabled the
Governor-General to override the opinions of his Council at
Calcutta, the members thenceforth merely recording in writing
their protests or the grounds of their opposition. The like

powers were also conferred on the Governors of Madras and Bombay. Finally, the Governor-General was empowered to fill up any vacancy in the Council occasioned by death, and was also to act as Commander-in-Chief.

These far-reaching proposals caused Burke's spleen to overflow. He burst forth into a violent diatribe against this "raw-head and bloody bones Bill." Pitt's first India Bill, he declared, was an abortion of tyranny, an imperfect foetus in a bottle, to be handed about as a show, but hypocrisy had nursed it till now the full-grown monster was before them.

> And at his heels,
> Leash'd in like hounds, shall famine, sword, and fire
> Crouch for employment.

It was absurd, he said, to expect energy and despatch from a despotism like that about to be set up in India. Democracy owed most of its triumphs to the openness and strength of its operations. The joint experience of many must prevail over the fallible judgements even of the best mind on earth. After this outburst, which Burke must have regretfully recalled when he undertook his crusade against French democracy, Fox emptied the vials of his wrath on the measure, especially taunting Pitt with robbing the Council at Calcutta of all administrative functions. This was not surprising, he said, as the Minister so obviously preferred speech to action. His speeches were splendid, his actions presented a long record of failure. " Let others act, the honourable gentleman desired only to argue." Pitt wisely declined to notice heated personalities, and limited his speech to the task of proving that the Bill cured several of the weaknesses of the Indian Government, and met the needs of the situation. This reply, quiet, dignified, and practical, carried the House with him by a majority of eighty-nine. The Bill passed the third reading without a division on 27th March. Such was Pitt's retort to the windy declamation of his opponents.

Thus was completed the fabric begun two years before. Thenceforth the Governor-General wielded a concentrated power such as India had not known since the decline of the Moguls. No longer could he be thwarted by the members of his own Council as Warren Hastings had often been by the intrigues of Monson and Francis. In truth the Viceroyalty was now an autocracy such as orientals could understand and respect. But this autocracy was, after all, local and conditional—a fact which Burke overlooked or ignored. While wielding despotic authority in India, the new Viceroy was but an adjunct of the British constitutional machine. It is perhaps the highest of Pitt's achievements that he saw how to combine two ideals of Government, the oriental and the occidental, in a way that conduced to vigour of action in Bengal, and did not impair popular progress at home. While investing the real ruler of India with powers far greater than those wielded by Warren Hastings, he subordinated them to the will of King and Parliament.

It has been asserted that Pitt was weak as a legislator.[1] It will be well to notice this charge at the close of these volumes. But surely, when judged by all conceivable standards, his India Bills must take rank amongst the greatest of legislative achievements. For by those measures, Pitt subordinated the most powerful of all Companies to the British Parliament. By it, as we have seen, he harmonized the claims of a viceregal autocracy in the Orient with those of popular government at home; and he thereby saved the British Empire from the fate which befell that of Rome. Historians of the Roman Republic agree that the favourites of the Senate of the type of Verres who were let loose on the provinces beyond the sea, not only proved the most frightful scourge to the subject peoples, but also undermined popular liberty at home by the unscrupulous use of their plundered hoards. The same system palsied the limbs of that Empire and drugged its brain. Whether the "nabobs" who rolled off from India and settled down in England would finally have exerted this doubly baleful influence, it is futile to inquire; but, had they gorged and bribed for several generations, the results must have been serious among a people that look on politics from a very practical standpoint.

On the other hand, to have run amok at that class, like Burke, might have yielded them the ultimate victory. Pitt observed the golden mean. For the present, the Company hailed him as its champion. But, while saving it from the Quixotic crusader, he bound it and its servants by strong ties, which it was found easy to tighten at every renewal of the Charter. Above all he strengthened the hands of the Viceroy even while binding him more closely to the Home Government. Has any other states-

---

[1] Lord Acton, "Letters to Mary Gladstone," 45.

man succeeded in the task of linking an oriental autocracy with the ancient parliamentary system of a Teutonic race?

The first of the parliamentary Governors-General was the man whom Pitt early in 1784 designed for the equally difficult post of Lord Lieutenant of Ireland. In the summer of that year, as also early in 1785, he urged Earl Cornwallis to combine the functions of Governor-General and Commander-in-Chief of India; but the earl at that time declined, partly because the powers of the Commander-in-Chief were unduly restricted.[1] The high hopes which Dundas had long entertained of the abilities of Cornwallis, shown by his desire to offer to him the Viceroyalty in 1782, now led the Ministry to meet his objections by introducing the Amending Act for extending the powers of the Governor-General in cases of emergency.[2] Cornwallis accordingly accepted office; and in the seven years of his Viceroyalty (1786-1793) British rule was so far strengthened as to withstand the attacks of the Mahrattas and the far-reaching combinations of Bonaparte.

The same year which saw the dawn of a new era for India, witnessed also the impeachment of Warren Hastings. We are not concerned here with the series of events which provided material for that longest and most famous of our State trials. What does concern us is the behaviour of Pitt in what was perhaps the most complex problem confronted in his early manhood. Seeing that he was chiefly responsible for the vote in the House of Commons which made impeachment inevitable, this part of the question cannot be passed by. Difficult though it is to separate one of the charges brought by Burke and Fox against Hastings from the others, yet limits of space compel us to restrict our survey to that one which induced Pitt to vote for the impeachment. It related to Hastings' treatment of Cheyt Singh, the Zamindar (not quite correctly termed the Rajah) of Benares.

The reader is doubtless aware that Hastings' tenure of the Governorship of Bengal in and after the year 1772 coincided with a period of exceptional difficulty, which was enhanced by the acrid and often underhand opposition of Francis, Clavering, and Monson in the Governing Council at Calcutta. Further, the

---

[1] "Cornwallis Correspondence," i, 180, 191.   [2] Ibid., 220, 221.

East India Company was often on the verge of bankruptcy. Undoubtedly the perpetual want of money led Hastings to the most questionable of his enterprises, the letting out of the Company's troops to the Rajah of Oude for the purpose of driving out or subjecting the Rohillas, a race of freebooters on his north-western borders. But difficulties thickened with the outbreak of the war with the Mahrattas and the French. The climax came in 1780 when Hyder Ali, the usurper of Mysore, let loose his hordes upon the Carnatic, and threatened to sweep the British into the sea. Then it was that the genius of Hastings awoke to full strength. He strained every nerve to send from the Hooghly a large force of troops to the relief of the despairing settlement at Madras; and, money being an essential, he cast about for all means of finding it without wholly depleting the exchequer of the embarrassed Company. Among other devices he pressed one of his feudatories, Cheyt Singh, Zamindar of Benares, for a sum of £50,000 in addition to the annual tribute. Seeing that the British held the paramountcy in India, and therefore enjoyed the right of calling on the vassal princes for help in time of emergency, the claim was reasonable, especially as Cheyt Singh's father owed his position to the East India Company. After giving extra assistance in each of the years 1778-80, Cheyt Singh began to grow restive in 1780 when the demand was renewed, and showed signs of disloyalty. Hastings thereupon imposed a fine of £500,000. More than this, he went to Benares in person, hoping to browbeat the Zamindar; but, his following being scanty, the troops of the latter rose against him, and cooped him up in his residence. With the splendid coolness which never deserted him, he manfully faced the danger. Secretly he sent warning to some of the Company's forces not far distant, and British valour rescued him from his desperate plight. An Englishman in resolution, Hastings was an oriental in his methods of punishment and revenge. Forthwith he deposed Cheyt Singh, and set in his place another Zamindar with a much enhanced tribute (September 1781).

The same plea of overmastering necessity impelled him to interfere in the affairs of Oude, an episode which, when tricked out in the gorgeous rhetoric of Burke and Sheridan, shocked the conscience of the British people. Sheridan's oration on "The Spoliation of the Begums of Oude" is perhaps the most thrilling Philippic of the modern world; but its force is sensibly lessened

I   Q

when we know that Burke derived his version of facts from a poisoned source. Francis, the bitter enemy of Warren Hastings, had been worsted by that master-mind in the Council-chamber at Calcutta; and, on challenging him to a duel, had been wounded in fair fight. It was this man, beaten twice over, who in 1781 returned to England to brood over means of revenge, and found them incarnate in Burke.

The genius which enabled that great Irishman to pour out serene and soul-satisfying judgements on the affairs of nations was allied with a more than feminine sensitiveness that often left him at the mercy of first impressions and Quixotic impulses. On all points of honour, whether personal or national, his chivalrous nature carried him to extremes bordering on the fantastic. The two incidents recounted above kindled in him a passion of indignation, which cooled but slowly, even when hatred of the French Revolution obsessed him. All attempts to ascribe Burke's crusade against Hastings to partisanship or personal spite have egregiously failed. As Macaulay has shown in his brilliant but untrustworthy essay on Warren Hastings, Burke's opposition to Hastings began in 1781, survived the kaleidoscopic changes of the next decade, and lived on into the new world of the Revolutionary Era. Clearly it resulted from a profound difference of view on Indian affairs. Even to-day, when the justificatory facts of Hastings' career are well known, his actions are wholly condemned by men of a similar bent of mind. On the other hand his policy appears statesmanlike to those who look first at the wealth of benefits conferred on India by the British Raj and pay little heed to miscarriages of justice which they regard as incidental to an alien administration. The Hastings episode will ever range in hostile groups men of strongly marked dispositions; while the judicial minority will feel themselves drawn perplexingly first to the sentimental side and then to the practical side as new facts and considerations emerge from the welter of evidence.

From midsummer 1785, when Hastings landed at Plymouth and repaired to the Court at Windsor, England was rent asunder by these prepossessions. The King, as might be expected, received him with marked favour; but it caused some surprise that Queen Charlotte, who was propriety personified, should affably receive his wife, the *divorcée* of a complaisant Baron Imhoff. For a time it seemed that Hastings could afford to scorn the efforts of his opponents. Burke had given notice of a hostile motion in the House of Commons; but, in the then discredited state of the Opposition, it was unlikely to pass. Ministers for the most part approved the conduct of Hastings. Pitt also is said to have been favourably impressed by an interview which they had towards the end of June. Unfortunately no account survives of what must have been a memorable meeting. Hastings was then fifty-two years of age, exactly double the span of life passed by the Prime Minister. But the young statesman had by instinct the same faculty of controlling his feelings under a calm exterior which the Governor-General had perfected during years of vindictive opposition at Calcutta. The countenance of each was thin and worn by the workings of a too active brain, reminding the beholder of the noble lines of Milton:

> Deep on his front engraven
> Deliberation sat and public care;
> And princely counsel in his face yet shone
> Majestic.

Undoubtedly they were then the ablest men of action of our race; and, despite envious surmises to the contrary, we may be sure that Pitt looked with admiration on the placid intellectual features of the man whose gigantic toil had saved British India. Both of them had the power of throwing off the cares of state and of indulging in playful intercourse with friends;[1] and charm of manner and conversation must have enlivened the interview.

Yet each was closely on his guard. The opposition of Dundas to Hastings (for he it was who moved the vote of censure on him in May 1782) must have coloured Pitt's feelings; and Hastings, as we know, believed that the India Bill of 1784 was a veiled attack upon himself. The interview certainly did not reassure him; for he thenceforth informed his friends that he could not depend on the support of Pitt.[2] The doubts were strengthened by the omission of the honours that so distinguished a man might have expected; but this fact was attributable to the motion of censure of which Burke had given notice in the House.

Thus Pitt maintained a cautious reserve. To say that he was waiting to see which way the wind would blow is manifestly un-

---

[1] Wraxall, iv, 142-4.
[2] Malleson, "Life of Warren Hastings" (1894), 456.

just. He was awaiting further information in what was a most complicated case. We know that he sent to Hastings for an explanation of the terms of a zamindar's tenure of office, evidently in order to clear up some of the questions respecting the Zamindar of Benares.[1] Thus, while Lansdowne, Mansfield, and Thurlow loudly proclaimed their confidence in Hastings; while the King continued to converse with him most affably at the *levées*, and Queen Charlotte accepted a splendid ivory bedstead presented by his wife, Pitt remained guardedly neutral.

Many members of the Opposition wished to let the motion of censure drop, and urged this at a private meeting held at the Duke of Portland's residence shortly before the meeting of Parliament in January 1786. But the zeal of Burke and Fox had not cooled with time. Further, on the first day of the session they were pointedly challenged by Major Scott, the accredited agent of Hastings in the House. At best Scott was a poor champion. Verbose, tedious, and ever harping on the same theme, he wearied the House with the wrongs of Hastings before they came officially before it; and on the first day of the great trial Fanny Burney remarked: "What a pity that Mr. Hastings should have trusted his cause to so frivolous an agent! I believe—and indeed it is the general belief, both of friends and foes—that to his officious and injudicious zeal the present prosecution is wholly owing."[2]

Yet Scott would scarcely have flung down the gauntlet without the knowledge and consent of his patron. Indeed on all grounds it is probable that Hastings, with his customary daring, preferred that the question should come to the clear light of a trial rather than swell with the accretions of gossip and dark innuendoes.[3] We must also remember that until the vote of censure of 28th May 1782 was removed from the journals of the House his name was under a cloud; and now that the accusations of Burke and Francis hurtled more thickly through the air, the whole matter was bound to come to the arbitrament of the law or of pistols.

On Hastings and Scott, then, rests the responsibility for renewing the strife. While they thus rashly opened the game, Burke replied on 17th February 1786 by a move of unusual skill. He

[1] Malleson, "Life of Warren Hastings" (1894), 455.
[2] Wraxall, iv, 250; "Diary of Mme. d'Arblay," iv, 60 (edit. 1854).
[3] Malleson, *op. cit.*, 449.

requested that the Clerk of the House should read Dundas's resolutions of censure of May 1782, and then ironically suggested that that gentleman, formerly the president of the special committee of the House, was the man who now ought to take action against the ex-Viceroy. He himself was but a humble member of that committee, and he now looked, but in vain, to those in power to give effect to the earlier resolutions. "But I perceive," he said, with his eyes on Pitt, "that any operations by which the three per cents may be raised in value affect Ministers more deeply than the violated rights of millions of the human race."[1] Dundas, never an effective speaker, failed to wriggle away from the charge of inconsistency thus pointedly driven home. The attitude of Pitt was calm and dignified. In the course of the adjourned debate he professed his neutrality on the question. While commending Burke for the moderation with which he then urged his demands, he admitted that the charges brought against Hastings ought to be investigated and his guilt or innocence proved by incontestable evidence. "I am," he said, "neither a determined friend nor foe of Mr. Hastings, but I will support the principles of justice and equity. I recommend a calm dispassionate investigation, leaving every man to follow the impulse of his own mind."[2]

This declaration of neutrality, the import of which will appear in the sequel, did not imply that there was to be no investigation. The challenge having been thrown down, the tournament was bound to proceed. Thenceforth Pitt confined himself to the functions of arbiter. Burke now enlarged his motion so as to include all the official correspondence respecting Oude, whereupon the Minister urged him always to state his reasons for the production of documents, and not to expect those which revealed any secret policy. Burke said he was ready to specify his charges, and he did so. He further said that he was in possession of abundant evidence to make good those charges. On his applying for certain confidential papers, Pitt opposed the motion; but he agreed to sixteen other motions for papers. In face of these facts, how can the panegyrists of Warren Hastings claim that Pitt objected to Burke's procedure and carried a motion against it?[3] Burke's motions were agreed to without a division, the Prime Minister having merely given

[1] Wraxall, iv, 260.   [2] Ibid., 261; "Parl. Hist.," xxv, 1094-5.
            [3] E.g., Malleson, op. cit., 450.

an obviously necessary veto in the case of confidential documents.

In view of the charges of gross inconsistency that have been brought against Pitt on the Hastings trial, it will be well to look into details somewhat closely. On 3rd March 1786 Burke returned to the charge by pressing for the communication of papers respecting the recent peace with the Mahrattas and cognate subjects. At once Dundas and Pitt objected, on the ground that very many of those documents were of the most confidential character, revealing, as they did, the secret means whereby the Mahratta confederacy was dissolved. In the course of his speech Pitt declared that Hastings had made that peace " with an address and ingenuity that did him immortal honour." But he added that other charges against him might be substantiated. In vain did Fox and Burke protest against the withholding of documents bearing on the present topic. The sense of the House was against them. Wilberforce applauded the caution of Ministers, as did eighty-seven members against forty-four on a division. A similar motion by the accusers for the production of papers relative to Delhi met with the same fate three days later.

On Fox renewing his demand for the Delhi papers (17th March), Pitt took occasion to state his views clearly. If State papers were called for in order to set on foot a criminal prosecution, he required the mover to "show a probable ground of guilt," and secondly, that the papers were necessary to substantiate that guilt; the third condition was that the public service would not suffer by publication.[1] He then proceeded to prove that the action of Hastings in seeking to form an alliance with the Great Mogul (despite the orders of the Company) was timely and statesmanlike, as it promised to thwart the alluring offers of Tippoo Sahib and the French to that potentate. Finally he asserted that, if he could reveal the Delhi correspondence to the House, all members would see how improper its publication would be. For his own ease and for the reputation of Hastings, which would be enhanced by such a step, he could wish to give it to the world, especially as all the documents hitherto granted were hostile to the ex-Viceroy; but in the interests of the country he must oppose the demand of the prosecutors for the

---

[1] "Parl. Hist.," xxv, 1256.

Delhi papers. In spite of the slap-dash assertions of Sheridan that the contents of those papers were perfectly well known, the House upheld Pitt's decision by 140 votes to 73.[1]

The next move of the prosecutors was to demand the presence of certain witnesses at the bar of the House. The Master of the Rolls objected on points of form, and also protested against the appearance of pamphlets hostile to Hastings which had been industriously circulated among the members of both Houses. Burke then admitted that most of the State Papers asked for had been granted, though some had been denied, but acridly complained that Ministers were now trying to quash the prosecution. Pitt did not speak.[2] On 26th April Burke brought forward two more charges, whereupon Pitt remarked that they contained much criminal matter, but he had formed no opinion as to their correctness; he hoped that it would appear otherwise, but the House must examine them with the utmost impartiality. Fox having taunted him with pretending to see no guilt where he saw too much, Pitt deprecated such outbursts. Later in the debate he demurred to the examination of witnesses called by the prosecutors before Hastings himself had been heard at the bar. Justice, he said, demanded that the accused should have a hearing before the accusers substantiated their case. He also declared that he would not consent to the examination of witnesses, still less to vote the impeachment of Hastings, on the vague and indefinite charges as yet before the House. Wilberforce expressed the hope that the Minister would persevere in the steady path he had pursued and would not be driven from it by the intemperate attacks of opponents. Burke inveighed against Pitt's decision; but the latter carried the day by 139 votes to 80.

It was therefore by Pitt's action that Hastings procured a hearing in the House—an opportunity which, if tactfully used, might have disconcerted his accusers. But the opportunity was lost. Instead of making a telling speech, Hastings proceeded to read a long and laboured reply, which occupied all the sittings of 1st and 2nd May, and emptied the House. Members accustomed to the faultless oratory of Pitt and the debating vigour of Fox, yawned at the dreary recital of remote events of which

---

[1] The debate of 26th April seems to show that Burke was acquainted with the substance of those papers.

[2] " Parl. Hist.," xxv, 1384-94.

they knew little and cared less. Accordingly, it was with enhanced hope of success that Burke, after a month of careful
preparation, brought forward his charges respecting the Rohilla
War. On 13th June he introduced them. On the former of
them Grenville defended the conduct of Hastings on the ground
that the Rohillas had by their raids provoked the war, and that it
was well to remove them. Dundas censured the Rohilla War, but
maintained that, while the Governor-General should have been recalled for it twelve years ago, there was no ground for impeaching
him for it now, especially as in the interval Parliament had three
times named him Governor-General. Wilberforce, whose opinion
weighed much with Pitt, took the same view. The most significant speech of the defence was that of Wilbraham who, on
behalf of Hastings' honour, urged the House to refer the charges
to the House of Lords, where alone a full acquittal could be
pronounced.[1] Pitt spoke only on a small technical point, but
voted with Grenville and Dundas. Despite a long and powerful
speech by Fox, the House sided with what seemed to be the
ministerial view, and at half-past seven in the morning of
3rd June rejected Burke's motion by 119 votes to 67.

Undaunted by this further rebuff, Fox, on 13th June, very
ably brought up the charge relating to the treatment of Cheyt
Singh, Zamindar of Benares.[2] He allowed that the continuance
of Hastings in power twelve years after the Rohilla War seemed
to imply that Parliament had condoned that offence; but this
plea could not be urged respecting the Benares affair of 1781.
He showed that the Company had agreed to respect the independence of the Zamindar of Benares, and that Hastings had
pressed on him remorselessly for aids in money and cavalry,
and had finally mulcted the exhausted prince of half a million
sterling. The fate of Bengal, he claimed, depended on their condemnation of so tyrannical a proceeding.

All eyes were turned on Pitt as he rose to state his views on
this question; and Wraxall avers that never did the range of his

---

[1] "Parl. Hist.," xxvi, 37-90.

[2] "Zamindar" means no more than landowner. Hastings had confirmed
Cheyt Singh in his powers. Sir Alfred Lyall and Mr. G. W. Hastings in their
works on Warren Hastings lay stress on the fact that Cheyt Singh was a
parvenu, not one of the old hereditary princes of India. I fail to see that
this has any bearing on the justice or injustice of Hastings' treatment of
him.

faculties appear greater, his marshalling of facts more lucid, or his elocution more easy and graceful. This is the more remarkable as the young Minister avowed his desire on personal grounds to absent himself from the discussion of so complex and remote a problem. We also know from his letter of 10th June to Eden, that he had "hardly hours enough to read all the papers on that voluminous article" (the Benares charge).[1] It is therefore clear that he formed his judgement within a very short time of his speech. In this, however, he soon showed that he had probed the intricacies of the question. Setting forth in detail the terms of a zamindar's tenure, he disproved Fox's contention that the Company had no right to exact an "aid" from an "independent rajah." He demurred to the epithet "independent," at least as regarded the supreme power in India. The suzerain power has as good a right in time of crisis to exact "aids" from its feudatories as any Suzerain in Europe from his feudal dependents. Next he crushed Francis by citing his own written opinion that extraordinary demands might be exacted from such feudatories. Having set forth the question in its true light, and exposed the inconsistency and malice of Francis, he approached the crux of the whole problem, whether the fine ultimately exacted from Cheyt Singh was not excessive. Here he objected to the drawing of precedents solely from the days of the Indian Emperors. It was the duty of every British administrator to behave according to the rules of justice and liberty; and, said he, "On this ground I feel it impossible to acquit Mr. Hastings of the whole of the charge brought against him; for I feel in my conscience that he has pushed the exercise of that arbitrary discretion which, from the nature of the Eastern Government, was intrusted to him to a greater length than he was warranted to do by the necessity of the service." While justified in imposing a penalty, he continued, Hastings had not proportioned the punishment to the guilt. In fining Cheyt Singh £500,000 for a mere delay to pay £50,000 (which £50,000 in the last instance was actually paid) Hastings had "proceeded in an arbitrary tyrannical manner." As to the restoration of Cheyt Singh to his possessions, it was beset by certain difficulties, and he preferred for the present to withhold his opinion.

That speech led to the impeachment of Warren Hastings;

---

[1] "Auckland Journals," i, 127.

for though Grenville, Lord Mulgrave, and the Attorney-General (Pepper Arden) spoke against the Prime Minister, the judgement of the last named prevailed; the House endorsed it by 119 votes to 79, or about the same numbers as had rejected the previous charge. The conduct of Pitt on this occasion has been vehemently assailed. Wraxall, writing many years later, maintained that it was a sudden and unaccountable change of front; and he further suggested that the jealousy which was said to be felt by Dundas for the superior abilities of Hastings might have influenced Pitt's action.

As the insinuation has been endlessly repeated, I may be pardoned for dwelling on it somewhat fully. The story has been tricked out with a wealth of details. It is asserted that Pitt issued a Treasury circular calling for the attendance of his supporters on the 13th of June, as if it were for the defence of Hastings. No proof of this statement has ever been given; and there are good grounds for disbelieving it. In the first place it should be remembered that attendance at the House had been greatly thinned by the Whitsuntide holidays. The vacation was just over; and, as everyone acquainted with Parliament ought to know, a full House was hardly to be expected at the first sitting afterwards. Pitt's letter of 10th June to Eden contains the following sentence. After stating that there had recently been a short and languid debate, and a division of seventy-one to thirty-three, he continues: " We shall probably have some attendance next Tuesday when Mr. Fox moves the charge respecting Benares; and after that our chief difficulty will be to get a House for the next fortnight. In the meantime I have hardly hours enough to read all the papers necessary on that voluminous article." [1]

These are not the words of a man who is about to perform an act of treachery. It is clear that Pitt found great difficulty in getting through the evidence on that charge before the debate came on; and further, that he was doing his duty as leader of the House in trying to assure as good an attendance as the holiday season permitted on a charge of this importance. Wraxall, who here opposed Pitt, makes no mention of any ministerial " whip " in favour of Hastings, as he would certainly have done if he could thereby have strengthened his case against him. The

---

[1] "Auckland Correspondence," i, 127; Wraxall, iv, 336.

fact that neither he nor Tomline refers to the calumny proves the lateness of its origin. Further, if a special "whip" had been sent out for the support of Hastings, would not some of the ex-Viceroy's friends, especially Major Scott, have exposed the fraud? But no reference to it is to be found in the report of that debate. Are we also to suppose that the forty or fifty members who changed sides with Pitt, would have gone over to the accusers if he had been guilty of such duplicity? Finally, it is clear from the remarks of Grenville, Mulgrave, and Pepper Arden, that even the colleagues of Pitt felt perfectly free to vote as they chose. Mulgrave declared that the Prime Minister would not be fit to remain in office a single day if he expected his friends and associates to give up their opinions on this subject. Pitt, as we have seen, had at the outset called on members to exercise their impartiality; and he now assented to Mulgrave's statement.[1] The story that Pitt sent round a "whip" for the support of Hastings, and then drove his followers like sheep into the opposite lobby, may therefore be dismissed as a malicious fiction, at variance with all the known facts of the case.

Then again it is stated by Lord Campbell in his sketch of the life of Lord Eldon,[2] that Pitt mysteriously abandoned Hastings, "and—contrary to the wish of Lord Thurlow who had a scheme for making Hastings a peer, perhaps a Minister—gave him up to impeachment." The charge is made in a very loose way; but on it the detractors of Pitt have built a theory that Dundas and he feared the advent of Hastings to the India Board, or to the Ministry, or to the House of Lords. This story has been varied and amplified, so that in one version George III appears as desirous of forcing him into the Cabinet, or granting him a peerage on the sole recommendation of Thurlow. But the letter which the King wrote to Pitt on 14th June shows that, while regretting his action concerning Hastings, he respected his conscientiousness, and harboured no thought of breaking with him.[3] That Thurlow had boasted of his power to further the interests of Hastings is

---

[1] "Parl. Hist.," xxvi, 115.

[2] "Lives of the Lord Chancellors," ix, 175 (4th edit.). The words quoted above furnish no ground for the assertion of Sir H. Lyall in his "Warren Hastings" that Pitt heard news of Thurlow's boast just before the debate of 13th June. Campbell's words are quite vague, and are entitled to little credence.

[3] Stanhope, i, App., xix.

likely enough; but it is certain that the King never thought of thrusting the ex-Viceroy into the Cabinet, or the India Board of Control, or of raising him to the House of Lords without the approval of his Prime Minister. The King's letters to Pitt [1] show that his chief desire then was to meet the large and growing expenses of his family; and Pitt's economic policy made his continuance in power at that time especially desirable. Royal condescension towards Hastings set all tongues wagging; and they have wagged ever since on the malignant jealousy of Dundas, and the gross inconsistency of Pitt; but the proofs adduced are of the flimsiest character. Wraxall and Bland Burges, who later on jotted down their impressions of parliamentary life, asserted that Dundas had somehow become convinced that the King intended to eject him from the India Board of Control and put Hastings in his place. But neither of them gave any proof. Wraxall merely stated that "the public believed" that Dundas feared such a change.[2] Bland Burges averred that Dundas had "by some means" come to know the secret intention of the King, and therefore "sedulously fanned Mr. Pitt's jealousy and uneasiness and so alarmed his mind that he hurried him on to a decision before he had time to satisfy himself as to its justice or expediency." [3]

Equally unconvincing is the story, which Hastings himself told some thirty years later, that on the morning of 13th June Dundas called on Pitt, remained closeted with him for some hours, and convinced him that they must abandon the ex-Viceroy. The insinuation conveyed in this belated anecdote is that Pitt was then and there won over by Dundas, and owing to the mean motives mentioned above. The ingrained tendency of men to seek for petty personal pretexts rather than larger, more generous, and more obvious causes, seems to be the *raison d'être* of the story and of its perpetuation. There are also some natures so warped by partisanship that they naturally refer actions of political opponents to discreditable motives; and it is a sign of the bias which detracts from the value of Macaulay's "Warren Hastings," that he did not mention the late date at which the story was started, while he gives it as an historic fact that Pitt's change of front was "the result of this conference."

No statement of what went on at this alleged interview has

---

[1] For new letters of George III see "Pitt and Napoleon Miscellanies."
[2] Wraxall, iv, 342.   [3] "Bland Burges P.," 89, 90.

ever been forthcoming; but, fortunately, on the all important
question of motive, we have the clear testimony of one who knew
Pitt most intimately, and whose political differences never distorted his imagination. Wilberforce, who had followed Pitt's
actions closely throughout the case, afterwards declared that
justice had not been done to Pitt:—

> People [he said] were asking what could make Pitt support him
> [Hastings] on this point and on that, as if he was acting from political
> motives; whereas he was always weighing in every particular whether
> Hastings had exceeded the discretionary power lodged in him. I well
> remember (I could swear to it now) Pitt listening most attentively to
> some facts which were coming out either in the first or second case. He
> beckoned me over, and went with me behind the chair, and said: "Does
> not this look very ill to you?" "Very bad indeed." He then returned
> to his place and made his speech, giving up Hastings' case. He paid as
> much impartial attention to it as if he were a juryman.[1]

Here we have evidence at first hand, though belonging to
Wilberforce's later years. Clearly it must refer to the events of
13th June; and it shows that if any one person was responsible
for Pitt's change of front that person was Wilberforce. Late in
life the philanthropist declared that Pitt's regard for truth was
exceptionally keen, springing as it did "from a moral purity
which appeared to be a part of his nature." He also added that
the want of simplicity and frankness sometimes observable in
his answers really sprang from this scrupulous veracity.[2]

To quote the opinion of another experienced politician.
William Pulteney wrote to Pitt the following hitherto unpublished
letter:

LONDON, 15th June 1786.

I cannot abstain from congratulating you on the line you took on
Tuesday. It will do you great credit everywhere, but, what you will
always think of more importance, I am convinced it will have the most
salutary effects in every part of this great Empire, and particularly in
India. Such is the powerful influence of strict honour and justice in
those who govern kingdoms that it pervades every mind and in a great
degree regulates the conduct of individuals. On the other hand, the
wilfully permitting persons in high and responsible situations to go

---

[1] "Life of Wilberforce," v, 340, 341.
[2] "Private Papers of Wilberforce," 69, 70. A similar remark may be
applied to Mr. Gladstone's replies, which often disgusted simple men.

unpunished and uncensured, when guilty of important offences, is sufficient to foster the bad and corrupt principles in all other minds and to lay a foundation for similar and greater offences. You have my hearty thanks, and I am sure will have the thanks of all who understand the importance of your conduct.

I am, etc.

W. PULTENEY.[1]

Few persons did understand his conduct, and sensitive pride kept his lips sealed. Nevertheless to all unprejudiced minds his conduct needed no defence. On that higher plane where truth and justice are alone considered (for justice is applied truth), Pitt did not swerve from the principles which he at first laid down. From the beginning of the Hastings case he had sought to hold the balances even. He left it open to his colleagues to differ from him. He refused the publication of papers favourable to Hastings where they compromised the welfare of the State or the characters of our Indian feudatories. He insisted that the charges against Hastings should be clearly drawn up, and that he should be allowed to answer those charges in person. On the topic of the Rohilla War he did not speak, doubtless because his mind was not made up. The fact that Parliament had three times re-appointed Hastings after that very censurable event, did in a technical sense screen him from prosecution now. But on the Benares affair, no such plea could be urged. It was a question on which the present Parliament alone had to decide.

The enormous vogue enjoyed by Macaulay's Essays compels me once more to notice his treatment of Pitt respecting the Benares charge. A man of philosophic temperament once expressed a wish that he was as sure about anything, as the great Whig historian was about everything. This assertiveness peeps through the veil of diffidence which Macaulay donned before delivering the verdict, that any man with a tenth part of Pitt's abilities ought to have convicted Hastings on the Rohilla charge and acquitted him on the Benares charge.[2] In order to establish this assertion Macaulay passed by the technical plea above named, which must have weighed with Pitt, and then used his powers of special pleading to whittle down Pitt's arguments on

[1] Pitt MSS., 169.

[2] This opinion is repeated by Mr. G. W. Hastings, "A Vindication of Warren Hastings," ch. vi.

the Benares case, so that they seem to turn ultimately on the
trumpery question whether the fine inflicted on the Zamindar
was rather too large or not. But we may ask, firstly, was it a
small affair to exact half a million sterling from a prince who
during three years had been hard pressed, and as a matter of
fact had paid up the arrears for which that fine was imposed?
Did it concern the Zamindar alone? Did it not concern all the
subjects from whom that half million must ultimately be
wrung?

Not only did the conduct of Hastings far exceed the limits
required by justice; it was also bound up with a question on
which the stability of our Indian Empire has ever rested. So
long as the feudatories of the British Raj feel confidence in his
sense of justice, India is safe. Whenever they have cause to
believe that injustice and oppression are the characteristics of
his rule, the foundations of the Indian Empire are shaken to
their base. Not without reason did Fox declare that the decision
on the Benares affair was vital to the preservation of our ascendancy in Bengal. The statesmanlike eye of Pitt, we may be sure,
discerned the same truth. Besides, there was an additional
reason why he should now more than ever resolve to engrave
the names of Justice and Mercy on the newly formed arch of the
Indian Government. As has been shown, the recent India Bill
placed greatly increased powers in the hands of the Governor-
General. Burke and Fox had taunted Pitt with setting up a
despotism from which endless suffering must flow. The charge
was hollow; but, adorned as it was by splendid rhetoric, it
created a deep impression. Was it not well, then, to show by a
concrete example that any Viceroy who violated the principles
of justice would meet with condign punishment at Westminster?
A statesman has to consider, not merely the principles of justice,
as applied to an individual; he must also think of the results of
his actions on the millions whom they will affect; and we may
reasonably infer that among the motives which led Pitt to break
with many of his friends not the least was a heartfelt desire to
safeguard the relations of the feudatories to the Suzerain Power,
and to protect the myriads of Hindoos who had no protection
save in the dimly known court of appeal at Westminster.

On the charge respecting the spoliation of the Begums of
Oude, Pitt also cast his vote against Hastings; and again a
majority followed him. It is questionable whether even the

sensationally brilliant oration of Sheridan on this affecting topic moved the House so much as the silent but scornful disapproval expressed in Pitt's vote.[1] The impeachment was thenceforth inevitable.

With the forensic pageant that ensued we are not here concerned. Thenceforth the case belonged strictly to the legal domain. Its duration throughout the years 1788-95 was certainly discreditable to British law. Hastings out of his never affluent fortunes spent some £71,000 in the vindication of his actions,[2] and at last secured an acquittal. But though men in Europe forgot the case amidst the potent distractions of the French Revolution, the effect of it was not lost upon the Orient. The comparative calm which settled benignly on India for twelve years may be attributed largely to a renewal of confidence in the sense of justice of our people. After the events of the year 1786 princes and peasants alike felt assured that the most transcendent services, if smirched with acts of injustice, would never screen a Viceroy from the censure of the British Parliament.

[1] For a hostile account of Pitt's conduct here, see the "Bland Burges P.," 81-9.

[2] "Hist. of the Trial of Warren Hastings," pt. v, 308, 309. His net fortune on 31st January 1786 was given as £65,313, exclusive of £12,000 made over to Mrs. Hastings.

CHAPTER XI

THE IRISH PROBLEM

(1785)

We have the satisfaction of having proposed a system which will not be discredited even by its failure, and we must wait times and seasons for carrying it into effect.—PITT TO THE DUKE OF RUTLAND, 17th August 1785.

THERE is a story, uncertain as to date and origin, which picturesquely describes Pitt's indebtedness to the author of "The Wealth of Nations."[1] Adam Smith had been invited to meet the young Prime Minister at dinner; but some mischance delayed his arrival. Nevertheless, the guests patiently waited for him, and on his entrance Pitt exclaimed, "Nay, we will stand until you are seated; for we are all your scholars." The compliment came with none the less graciousness because the father of Political Economy had in his work incautiously defined a statesman as "that insidious and crafty animal." Pitt was now to give a new connotation to the word. Almost alone among the politicians of the eighteenth century, he had set himself to gain a store of knowledge which would enable him to cope with the increasingly complex problems of his craft; and thus, in an age when a university degree, the grand tour, and London club-life were held to be a sufficient preparation for a political career, he came forth like a Minerva fully armed at all points.

Among the practical questions to which the Scottish thinker turned the attention of his age, none was more important than those dealing with the relations between England and her American colonies, the desirability of an unfettered trade with France, and the need of a close union with Ireland. The first of

---

[1] It may belong to the spring of 1787, when, as we learn from the "Corresp. of Wilberforce," i, 40, Dundas introduced Adam Smith to Pitt and Wilberforce; but the latter does not record the anecdote.

these questions had been disposed of by war, and the second will engage our attention in a later chapter. On the Irish question Adam Smith strongly advocated union with Great Britain as conferring on the smaller island the boons which had breathed new life into Scotland, namely, freedom of trade and deliverance from an oppressive dominant caste.

These contentions must have secured the approval of Pitt; for the outlines of his policy both towards Ireland and France bear a striking resemblance to those sketched in " The Wealth of Nations," with this important difference, that after the gain of independence by the Irish Legislature in 1782 the union of the two Parliaments was clearly impossible for the present. We therefore find Pitt turning his attention to the two topics which then chiefly agitated public opinion in Ireland, viz., the reform of Parliament and the fiscal relations to Great Britain. In order to understand Pitt's handling of these problems it is necessary briefly to review the course of Anglo-Irish affairs.

The story of the dealings of England with the sister isle in the years 1688-1778 is one that it is painful to contemplate. The efforts to dragoon the Catholic Irish out of their creed, or to grind them into the lowest stratum of society, produced a race hatred of which we are still reaping the dire harvest. The Celt broods over the past; and his memory clings round the days when Papists were excluded from Parliament, from the possession of freehold estates, from the professions and from juries; when they might not act as guardians or possess a horse worth more than £5; and when their Protestant neighbours on tendering £5 could take any horse that pleased them. All this and far more may be read in the pages of Lecky. As for the ruffianly enactments of the Irish penal code, many of them were so monstrous as to bring their own cure. In the latter half of the eighteenth century even the arrogant Protestant squirearchy of Ireland found it impossible or undesirable to enforce them.

The growth of principles of toleration and enlightenment which marked the years 1760-80 had some effect even on the nominees of Protestant landlords and borough-mongers who formed the bulk of the Irish Parliament. It is a curious fact that even the narrowest and most bigoted of governing castes cannot wholly resist the tendencies of the times; and the Dublin Parliament, representing only a part even of the Protestant minority of Irishmen, was no more able to keep out new ideas than the members of the pocket boroughs of Britain could withstand the Reform movement of 1830-32. The infiltration of novel principles into the Irish Legislature was slower and more partial, inasmuch as that body misrepresented even more ludicrously the opinions of the mass of Irishmen.[1] It had long been swayed by a clique of politicians who were termed "Undertakers," because they undertook its manipulation, ostensibly in the interests of the British Government, but really in their own. The traditions of the past and the determination of the members of the Protestant Established Church to keep the Government in their own hands, formed a massive barrier against change. Yet the dissolving touch of the Time-Spirit and the shocks of war were at work upon that barrier; and when the war with the American colonies and France strained the resources of Great Britain and Ireland past endurance, it showed signs of giving way on two questions, the one religious, the other fiscal. In the year 1778, Catholics who took the oath of allegiance were allowed to become in effect owners of land, that is, they might hold land on lease for 999 years. Further, the odious temptations formerly held out to sons of Catholics to abjure their creed were also abrogated. That year therefore seemed to be the beginning of an epoch of toleration, which it was the ardent desire of Pitt to crown with an act of justice too long delayed.

At present, however, we are concerned mainly with his attempt to reform the fiscal relations between the two islands. Until the year 1778 Irishmen were still in the state of economic vassalage to England which the Parliaments of William III had forcibly imposed. In some respects, especially in regard to the woollen industry, they were now worse off than in that time of humiliation. The enactment of 1699, which absolutely forbade the export of her woollen goods, hopelessly crippled an otherwise promising industry. Nor was this all. Her staple product, wool, might not be sent to foreign lands lest their manufacturers might benefit, and become rivals to ours. That fear was not wholly groundless in the case of France; for French weavers found that Irish wool supplied the qualities lacking in their own wool. The result was the rise of an extensive smuggling trade in that article from

---

[1] Of the 118 Parliamentary boroughs as many as 87 (including Belfast!) were "close," that is, were controlled by Government or by a local magnate or the Corporation. See a list in "Castlereagh P.," iv, 428-30; also Porritt, "Unreformed House of Commons," ii, pt. vi.

Ireland to France, which the Government utterly failed to stop.

The outbreak of war with the American colonies, as I have said, brought all these questions to an acute phase; and in 1776 the British Government so far relaxed the prohibitions on export as to allow Irish woollens to be exported for the clothing of the Irish troops serving away from their own country. At the same time Irish fishermen were admitted to a share in the Newfoundland and other fisheries from which they had been excluded.

Nothing, however, was done for the most important of Irish manufactures. The linen industry had not been severely hampered by the British Government. While prohibiting the export of fine linens, and of sail-cloth, in the supposed interests of British manufacturers, the British Government granted bounties on the coarse linens exported from Ireland; and up to the year 1771 that industry had greatly prospered. Thereafter it underwent a serious decline. So alarming was the shrinkage of trade and the rise of Ireland's debt, that in 1778 Lord North's Ministry was fain to propose the abolition of many of the fiscal disabilities which sapped her strength. She was to be allowed to send her products to the British colonies and to receive theirs directly in return; but, in order to allay the fears of British manufacturers, the old restrictions on the Irish woollen trade remained in force. Nothing, however, could allay those fears. At once loud complaints were raised from Aberdeen to Plymouth, so that North gave up nearly all his proposals; and Ireland gained little or nothing from his well meant efforts, except that ships built in Ireland thenceforth counted as British-built, and could receive bounties granted for the fisheries.[1]

Where reason and statesmanship had failed, force was to succeed. The utter inability of the British Government to defend Ireland against threatened French invasions furnished the pretext for the formation of powerful Volunteer corps, consisting solely of Protestants, and therefore especially strong in Ulster. The Presbyterians of that province, smarting under the civic disabilities imposed by the old Test Act, and under an equally archaic system of commerce, demanded redress of these grievances, in the latter of which the more lethargic

[1] Lecky, iv, 429, 440, 450.

Romanists gave them increasing support. Religious antipathies were forgotten in the face of Ireland's urgent needs. The governing coterie at Dublin Castle failed either to check the movement or to revive the old schisms. It seemed that the intolerable burdens of the British fiscal system were about to mould the jarring elements of Irish society into the unity that marks a nation.

Though they failed to reach that far-off goal, they for the present won a noteworthy success. By combining to refrain from the purchase of British goods they dealt a severe blow at the system thrust upon them. Nor did they abstain from threats of force. The Volunteers paraded the streets of Dublin with cannon bearing the motto, "Free Trade—or this." In face of an overwhelming opposition, the Lord-Lieutenant, the Earl of Carlisle, advised the British Government to give way; and at the close of the year 1779, and early in 1780, a series of enactments was passed at Westminster withdrawing the prohibitions on the export of woollen goods and glass from Ireland. Commerce with the British colonies was now also provisionally thrown open to Irish merchants, and they were admitted to a share in the Levant trade.

At the same time the cause of religious toleration gained an equally signal triumph. The strength of the Ulster Volunteers and the abatement of religious bigotry brought the Irish Parliament to pass a measure for relieving the Protestant Dissenters of that land from the sacramental test which had been looked on as one of the bulwarks of the Established Church; and in the spring of 1780 the British Parliament gave its grudging assent to that boon for Ireland which for nearly half a century longer it persisted in withholding from Nonconformists in England and Wales. As was stated in Chapter V of this work, the Irish Volunteers in the year 1782 gained another most important concession, namely, the recognition of the legislative independence of the Irish Parliament. Fortunately the British Government on this occasion acted with grace and dignity. The Rockingham Ministry advocated the change, which passed both Houses with but a single adverse vote, that of Lord Loughborough. The disagreeable fact, that this last boon, like the others, was extorted by force, was thus tactfully glozed over; and when the suspicions of the good faith of England aroused in Ireland by that restless demagogue, Flood, were laid to rest by the Renunciation Act of the year 1783, the relations of the two islands became almost cordial.

Causes of friction, however, remained. The royal veto might, and probably would, still tell against the Irish Legislature, even though the veto of the British Parliament and of the Privy Council had lapsed. The influence of the Lord Lieutenant and of his Chief Secretary on the Irish Ministers was also great; and his influence was distinctly British. Dublin Castle could also generally determine the votes of a majority in both Houses of Parliament. Further, it was quite possible that on commercial questions the Irish Parliament would differ sharply from that of Westminster. This seemed so in the early months of Pitt's Ministry. The beginning of the year 1784 found Ireland depressed by a very inclement winter; and the cry was raised that her Parliament should " protect " her industries, especially that of wool, from English competition. The exertions of the new Lord Lieutenant, the Duke of Rutland, aided perhaps by the reluctance of the more moderate members to enter on a commercial war with England, sufficed to defeat these proposals; but the Irish House of Commons, in May 1784, unanimously passed an address to the King, emphasizing the need of " a wise and well-digested plan for a liberal arrangement of a commercial intercourse between Great Britain and Ireland." This was the friendly challenge which Pitt determined to take up. From the outset he made the Irish commercial question peculiarly his own. More than once in his correspondence with the Duke of Rutland he describes it as the nearest to his heart.[1]

No problem could have been more tangled. Ireland was still in a very restless state. Despite the warnings of that uncrowned King of Ireland, Grattan, the Volunteers began to enroll Catholics and to threaten the coercion of the Dublin Parliament. But, as the Duke of Rutland wrote to Pitt, Parliament " does not bear the smallest resemblance to representation "; and a petition from a great meeting held at Belfast in July 1784 declared that " the [Irish] House of Commons has degenerated into a fixed body so little connected with the people that it ceases to be a guardian of their property, and hath become the representative of an over-bearing aristocracy." The petitioners asserted that the delegates of the Volunteers were a representative body, and urged the King

---

[1] " Pitt-Rutland Corresp.," 74, 96, 107, 119; " Rutland P.," iii, 193.

to dissolve the Irish House of Commons.[1] This demand was widely echoed. The Volunteers, having already through their delegates exerted on Parliament a pressure which was semi-national, refused either to let politics alone, or to disband. Ultimately their recklessness and the efforts of Grattan undermined their influence, and they gradually dwindled away; but, for the present, they seemed able to extort all their demands, prominent among which was that for the " protection " of Irish industries and products. In his first long communication to Pitt, the Duke of Rutland dwelt on the urgent need of investigating Irish claims, though he frankly declared that he could not understand the commercial question. Open-handed to ostentation, and devoted to the pleasures of the table, this affable young aristocrat occasionally showed signs of political foresight, as when he ventured to predict " that without *an union* Ireland will not be connected with Great Britain in twenty years longer." [2]

Far abler and more painstaking was his chief secretary, Orde, on whom was to fall the burden of work connected with the proposed Reform. The letters which passed between him and Pitt in the summer of 1784 show the care taken by both of them to master the facts of the situation. Orde (the future Lord Bolton) warned Pitt that a resolute effort would soon be made to effect the entire separation of the two Kingdoms, and urged him to " act towards Ireland with the utmost liberality consistent with your own safety: it must in the long run be the wisest policy." Above all he insisted, as the duke had also done, on the need of a firm decision, which even the malcontents must regard as final.[3]

Pitt on his side sought to procure the fullest information on all points. In regard to the Reform of the Irish Parliament he deprecated any extreme measure such as the admission of the Roman Catholics then appeared to be; but he advocated the extension of political rights to Protestant Dissenters; for, as he forcibly put it, " we may keep the Parliament, but lose the people." As for the fiscal question he required first of all a satisfactory knowledge of the facts, so that some general principles of action could be agreed on; and he urged that the financial relations of the Kingdoms should be regulated according as the prosperity of Ireland increased with her enlarged

---

[1] Pitt MSS., 324.   [2] " Pitt-Rutland Corresp.," 17, 19.
[3] Ashbourne, 84, 85.

commercial opportunities. Justice required that Ireland should then take her share of the imperial burdens, which at present rested almost entirely with Great Britain. Finally they must seek some means calculated to bestow on Ireland that permanent tranquillity which the late commercial concessions had failed to secure.[1]

In this letter, dated 19th September 1784, we see not only an outline of the scheme which took definite form in the Irish Propositions, or Resolutions, of the session of 1785, but also an instructive example of Pitt's methods of procedure. He began by collecting all the ascertainable facts, including the causes of previous failures, and, by sifting these data, he sought to arrive at general principles which would illuminate the whole question. In a word, his method was inductive. It begun with facts and ended with principles. Unlike the French legislators of 1789-93, who first enunciated principles and then sought to square the facts of life to them, he started with a solid basis and reared on it a structure from whose summit the toiler might take a wide survey. The Revolutionists built symmetrically and grandly, but without foundations.

In order thoroughly to master details, Pitt summoned from Ireland not only Orde but also Foster, Chancellor of the Exchequer, and Beresford, Chief Commissioner of the Revenue. Both were able and masterful men, the former the doughtiest opponent, the latter the staunchest champion, of Pitt's Act of Union. Beresford did much to beautify Dublin, and his name lives on in Beresford Place. With these experienced officials Pitt had many conferences at Downing Street, or at the house on the north side of Putney Heath, which he rented for the latter part of 1784. They confirmed Orde's advice as to the wisdom of granting to Ireland complete liberty and equality in matters of trade, but warned him as to the difficulty of drawing from Ireland any contribution to the imperial funds. Here it should be remembered that Ireland supported 15,000 regular troops, 3,000 of whom were at the disposal of the British Executive in Ireland, while the others could be moved from Ireland with the consent of her Parliament.

Converse with Foster must also have strengthened Pitt's resolve to press on the Reform of the Irish Parliament; for he

[1] Ashbourne, 85-91.

now warned the Duke of Rutland, who stoutly opposed Reform, not to confuse peaceable efforts in that direction with subversive or treasonable schemes; and in a notable phrase of his letter of 4th December, he declared that Parliamentary Reform must sooner or later be carried in both countries. As regards pro-cedure, he thought it best to postpone a change in the Irish franchise until a similar measure came forward at Westminster; for this, if successful, would impart to the movement in Ireland an irresistible force. In the meantime it would be well to take up the commercial problem.

Pitt's sanguine temperament here led him into a tactical mis-take. The Irish Resolutions were destined to arouse in Great Britain a storm of opposition which swept away the hopes of the Reform Associations; and the collapse of their efforts told un-favourably on the Irish political movement. Probably also he erred in bringing forward his proposals first in Dublin—a mat-ter on which Fox readily aroused resentment at Westminster. Yet, where the issues were so tangled, it is difficult to say whether success could have crowned Pitt's efforts had they been put forth in a different order.[1] From his letter of 7th October 1784 to the Lord Lieutenant we see that he looked on the Reform of the Irish Parliament as simpler, but yet "perhaps more difficult and hazardous," than the commercial questions then at stake.

Here again he calculated wrongly. Ireland's demand for equality of trading advantages with Great Britain was certain to meet with vehement opposition from our manufacturers, as the events of the year 1778 convincingly showed. His mistake is the more remarkable as he proposed "to give Ireland an almost unlimited communication of commercial advantage, if we can receive in return some security that her strength and riches will be our benefit, and that she will contribute from time to time in their increasing proportions to the common exigencies of the Empire."[2] How buoyant was Pitt's nature to cherish the hope that British merchants would concede commercial equality to Ireland, or that the factions at Dublin would take up the bur-dens of Empire!

No letter of Pitt's rings with more enthusiasm, though an

[1] Grenville, writing in November 1798, said that he considered the faulty procedure adopted in 1785 largely contributed to the failure. ("Bucking-ham P.," ii, 412.)

[2] "Pitt-Rutland Corresp.," 43.

undertone of anxiety can be detected, than the very long one of 6th-7th January 1785. Writing until far past midnight he explained to the Lord-Lieutenant in great detail the aim which he had in view, namely, the sweeping aside of all local prejudices, so that England and Ireland might become "one country in effect, though for local concerns under distinct Legislatures." The pupil of Adam Smith had caught a clear glimpse of the truth that States which throw down their customs' barriers become effectually parts of the same body. But he now saw that British manufacturers would probably resist so sweeping a change; and he pointed out to Rutland that the admission of Ireland to commercial equality, even in the case of the export trade from British Colonies, to which, he said, she had no claim of right, involved a solemn duty to respond to imperial duties. He then pointed out that Ireland would have more than mere equality; for Great Britain was burdened by taxes which were the outcome of those duties; and Irish shippers, with their lighter burdens, might find it possible to export the produce of those colonies to Great Britain to the detriment of British shippers. In many ways he sought to disprove the claims or excuses put forward by Irish patriots why they should receive much and give little in return. He showed the impossibility of conceding so much unless Ireland would irrevocably pledge herself to contribute, according to her ability, to the expenses of the Empire.[1]

The despatches sent by the Home Secretary, Lord Sydney, to the Lord Lieutenant, and the letters of Pitt to Orde, contained precise instructions on this last point. Pitt first desired that Ireland's contribution should go towards the navy.[2] Then for a time he harboured the notion that it should go towards his proposed Sinking Fund, because that money would not pass beyond England, and would return in the form of a trade the balance of which was known to be in favour of Ireland.[3] But the Cabinet adopted the earlier proposal, with the proviso that the contribution towards the naval expenses of the Empire should be made in such a way as the Irish Parliament might direct. The letter of George III to Pitt, of 28th January 1785, shows that the King insisted on a contribution from Ireland as essential.

---

[1] "Pitt-Rutland Corresp.," 55-75.   [2] *Ibid.*, 73.
[3] Ashbourne, 104 (Letter of Pitt to Orde, 1st February 1785). Irish exports to Great Britain for 1779 were £2,256,659, her imports thence only £1,644,770 (Pitt MSS., 322).

The ten Propositions, or Resolutions, embodying the aims of Pitt, were brought before the Irish Parliament on 7th February 1785. They embodied the information gleaned from Beresford, Foster, and Orde; and a report recently drawn up by a special committee of the British Privy Council also furnished useful information. Modified in some particulars, and, with the addition of a Proposition soon to be noticed, they passed the Dublin Parliament with little difficulty. In their modified form they may be summarized as follows. Foreign and colonial products were to pass between Great Britain and Ireland, in either direction, without any increase of duty. The goods and products of the sister islands were also to be imported either free or at identical rates; or again, where the duties were not equal, they were to be reduced to the lower of the two tariffs hitherto in operation. All prohibitions on inter-insular trade were to lapse without renewal, unless it should seem expedient in the case of corn, meal, malt, flour, and biscuits. The British Government required that, when the " hereditary revenue " exceeded a certain sum, Ireland should pay over the surplus as a contribution to the naval expenses of the Empire. As the " hereditary revenue " consisted mainly of custom and excise duties, its increase (which was generally steady) afforded the best index of the prosperity of Ireland. Moreover that branch of the revenue had hitherto been under the general direction of the Crown; and Pitt's proposal to transfer its surplus to the control of the Irish Parliament was both statesmanlike and conciliatory.[1]

Nevertheless, the letters of the Duke of Rutland to Pitt revealed the conviction even of the best friends of Government that the Propositions would fail if they were coupled with any demand for a money payment. The time, said the Duke, was very critical. They were seeking to organize a legal militia force in place of the self-constituted Volunteers; Grattan and Daly had spoken splendidly for the change; but the demand for a subsidy would jeopardize everything, even the connection with Great Britain.[2] A secret report which he sent to Pitt showed that of the members of the large towns of Ireland, only Londonderry was well disposed to the Resolutions. In the case of Waterford (" well governed, under Lord Tyrone's influence ") the freemen opposed

---

[1] " Parl. Hist.," xxv, 311-14. Lecky, vi, 390, 395, and his " Leaders of Public Opinion in Ireland," 114.

[2] " Rutland P." (Hist. MSS. Comm.), iii, 162-68.

them while the two members supported them. Belfast, a close borough, opposed them. In all, he reckoned forty-five members hostile, twelve friendly, and the others absent or not accounted for. A list followed of the " expectations " of members as regards judgeships, pensions and sinecures.[1]

As Rutland and Orde had foreseen, the assailants of the measure fastened on the question of the contribution. How could a country, whose annual expenditure at present exceeded income by £150,000, and whose absentee landlords drained her of a million a year, pay a large sum to the richer island? Did not Ireland contribute largely in men and money to the army? And was not a great part of her administration controlled by a Monarch and a Ministry in whose succession and appointment she had no voice? Such were the invectives of that most acrid and restless of demagogues, Flood. Far more statesmanlike was the conduct of Grattan. Equalling, nay excelling, Flood in his oratorical powers, he held them under the control of a masculine reason. As his energy and tact had gained for his land the boon of legislative independence, so now he sought to cement friendly relations with Great Britain, and therefore gave a general assent to the commercial proposals. The Irish Ministers also pointed out that Great Britain opened a far larger market than Ireland did; that the industries of the larger island, being handicapped by war taxes and high wages, could be exploited by Irishmen, whose national burdens were comparatively light, and that the colonial trade was now to be opened up in its entirety and for ever, not on terms that were revocable at the option of the British Government, as was the case in 1780.

All these arguments were of no avail to carry the proposal respecting Ireland's contribution to the navy. Though Pitt had carefully framed it so that Ireland would pay nothing until she was in a prosperous state, he failed to meet the rooted objections of the Dublin Parliament to money going out of the country. Grattan focused the opposition by demanding that Ireland should pay nothing until her Government had put an end to the long series of deficits. In private conversations with him Orde failed to weaken this decision, in which nearly all Irishmen concurred. A Resolution to that effect was therefore added. It was further arranged that when the annual hereditary revenue,

[1] Pitt MSS., 320.

which then stood at £652,000, should exceed £656,000 in time of peace, the surplus should go towards the support of the imperial navy in such a way as the Irish Parliament should direct. Additional taxes were then voted which were estimated to yield £140,000 a year.

No beginning could have been less auspicious. The arrangement was far less satisfactory than the worst of the alternative plans to which Pitt expressed the hope that Orde would never resort. The contribution, on the present terms, could be evaded by any juggling Chancellor of the Exchequer who should contrive a series of small and profitable deficits. Consequently Orde, who came to London to persuade Pitt of the need of the change, found him inexorable. Pitt was resolved "not to proceed until the condition should be taken away from the last Resolution." [1] This also appears in a part of his letter to the Marquis of Buckingham:

[*Secret.*]

Sunday, February 20, 1785.[2]

. . . I am able to tell you confidentially that we shall certainly *suspend* the final approbation of the commercial system, and declare the impossibility of completing it till more satisfaction and explicit provision is made in Ireland respecting the object of contribution.

Yours ever,

W. PITT.

In opening his case at Westminster on 22nd February, Pitt had to contend with the discouragement caused by this rebuff, and with a fit of hoarseness, which he informed Grenville he had been trying to sleep off without much success. Nevertheless his speech was allowed to be a fine effort. He besought members fairly to consider his proposals, which aimed at settling the relations of the two islands on a liberal and permanent basis. Glancing scornfully at the tactics of the Opposition and the campaign of malice and misrepresentation started by the "Gazetteer" and taken up by various trading bodies, he claimed that there should be fair play, at least until he had stated his case fully. It was complex, and his proposals might need modification in details. The old system of cruel and abominable restraint imposed on Irish trade had vanished. They now had

---

[1] "Rutland P.," iii, 191; "Parl. Hist.," xxv, 314; Ashbourne, 105, 108.
[2] Chevening MSS.

to complete a new system, and community of benefits was the only principle on which they could proceed. They proposed entirely and for ever to open to Ireland the trade of our colonies except that of India, which was a monopoly of the East India Company. There was no solid ground for the fear that so poor a country as Ireland would become the emporium of colonial goods, and would re-export them to our shores. Equally unlikely was the suggestion that Ireland would undersell us in manufactures; for British energy had secured for our goods a fairly large market in Ireland even against her import duties. He then referred guardedly to the subject of Ireland's contribution to the imperial navy. Finally, while deprecating any immediate decision, he declared that what England lost by the bargain she would more than recoup from the growing friendliness and prosperity of the sister island. He therefore proposed a general motion for the permanent and irrevocable admission of Ireland to all the advantages of British commerce when she irrevocably pledged herself to pay a sum towards the defence of commerce.[1]

The Opposition, exasperated by Pitt's ungenerous treatment of Fox concerning the Westminster election, at once opened a furious fire of criticisms. Fox, who held the old Whig views in favour of a "national commerce," that is, protection, urged that Ireland would probably smuggle into Great Britain the produce of foreign colonies, and would become the "grand arbitress of all the commercial interests of the Empire." The Resolutions ought, he claimed, first to have been moved at Westminster, in which he was probably right. If they were passed, he said, Great Britain would never have anything more to concede to Ireland. The Navigation Acts, the source of England's prosperity, would be a dead letter. As for Ireland's contribution to the navy, he would "trust everything to her generosity, but not much to her prudence." Eden, formerly Irish Secretary, then dwelt on the danger of allowing a lightly taxed country to compete with a heavily burdened country. The debt of Great Britain was a hundredfold that of Ireland; and, while a Briton paid on an average fifty shillings a year in taxes, an Irishman paid only eight shillings. The plan now proposed would be a revolution in British trade. These words are remarkable in view of Eden's desertion of North and his assistance to Pitt in carrying through

[1] "Parl. Hist.," xxv, 311-28.

a still greater "revolution," the commercial treaty with France of 1786. The speeches of Fox and Eden did some good; their attack on Pitt's measure convinced Irishmen that it must have many excellences. The Earl of Mornington (afterwards the Marquis Wellesley) declared that Ireland would warmly support Pitt. Beresford also stated that the Irish members now only wanted an excuse for siding with him; but England must beware of pressing Ireland too hard in this bargain. A rebuff would seriously jeopardize the cause of order.[1]

No sense of prudence or responsibility restrained the action of the British Opposition and their mercantile allies. A campaign had already begun. It bore signs of careful organization. The signal was given by the "Gazetteer" of 16th February, which pointed out that the Navigation Acts, the source of Britain's prosperity, would be virtually annulled by Pitt's proposals. On the next day it showed that Irish competition, based on low wages, must ruin our industries. On 18th February a meeting of silk manufacturers protested against the Resolutions. On the 24th the planters and merchants of the West Indies followed suit. On that day the "Gazetteer" stated that, if Pitt's measure became law, the Exchange would be transferred from Cornhill to Cork; later on it declared that Arkwright and Dempster would set up their factories in Ireland. On 3rd March the "Morning Chronicle," the organ of the middle classes, joined in the hue and cry, declaring that even as it was the balance of trade between Great Britain and Ireland was in favour of the latter, and that the larger island must be drained of money by the smaller if the old restrictions were not maintained.

Meetings of protest were now in full swing. Delegates of the West India merchants had an interview with Pitt and declared his answer to be unsatisfactory. The merchants themselves refused, by fifty-nine to forty, to petition against his proposals, but the minority published and circulated their opinions. The manufacturing towns, except those of the woollen districts, petitioned strongly against the Resolutions. Manchester, Lancaster, and Dudley each sent two petitions to that effect; while three apiece emanated from Glasgow, Paisley, and Bristol. So the game of misrepresentation went on. A petition from Lancashire contained 80,000 signatures; and a document purporting to come

---

[1] "Dropmore P.," i, 247, 248.

from 13,243 weavers of Glasgow and Rutherglen, shows that
artisans were as much alarmed as the merchants. The weavers
stated their conviction that if the Resolutions became law,
they would be undersold by the Irish in the home market
and reduced to beggary.[1] This solidarity of interest is noteworthy. In those days the "manufacturer" was actually, as well
as in name, the weaver; and tens of thousands of households,
where the hand-loom kept the wolf from the door through the
winter, saw pale Ruin stalking behind the figure of thrifty,
resourceful, energetic Paddy. The agitation therefore spread
through all classes with a unanimity that would scarcely be
possible now, when the term "manufacturer" has come to mean
a capitalist who owns a factory where nothing is done by hand.
Then the solidarity of interest between merchants and weavers
was obvious. In imagination both classes saw their industries
wafted by a cruel east wind to a land whose inhabitants they
disliked and despised.

Some of the petitions were based on false information. That
of the Glasgow cotton workers complained that the fourth Resolution, as it left the Irish Parliament, would place a heavy duty on
British cottons.[2] But Pitt had throughout insisted that there
must be an equalizing of duties on both sides of the Irish Sea,
the lower level being always taken. In truth, all reasoning was
in vain. The protectionist spirit was proof against all arguments.
Thus, the committee of the merchants and manufacturers of
Sheffield declared that their industry could not be carried on
without grave injury if the present duty on bar iron imported
into Great Britain, namely, 56 shillings per ton, were reduced to
the level then obtaining in Ireland, that is, 10 shillings a ton.

Still keener was the opposition in Bristol. The protectionist
feeling had lost none of the bitterness which mainly caused the
unseating of Burke in the election of 1774. The sugar refiners of
that town now declared that they had spent more than £150,000
in buildings and plant, all of which would go for naught, if the
Irish Parliament, "under the privilege of importing raw and
refined sugars through that country to this [should] lay a heavy
duty on loaf and lump sugar and a small duty on bastard and
ground sugars and molasses"; for the Irish merchants would

---

[1] Pitt MSS., 321.

[2] This is refuted by the official wording of that Resolution as passed at
Dublin, in "Parl. Hist.," xxv, 312.

then "effectually prevent our exporting the former to that kingdom and also to foreign markets, and enable them to send the latter into Great Britain at a less price than it can be manufactured here under the burthen of the high duties, the high price of labour, and heavy taxes, which would inevitably tend to the ruin of that valuable branch of trade in this kingdom."[1] The Bristol sugar-refiners can scarcely have read Pitt's proposals, which implied equal duties on all articles at British and Irish ports; and the Irish Parliament had agreed to this. The notion that Irish sugar-refiners, by complex duties of their own devising, would soon beat their British rivals out of foreign markets and ruin them in the home market, is a sign of the mad folly of the time. Against stupidity such as this even the gods fight in vain.

By no arguments could the hubbub be appeased. Pamphlets, especially one by Lord Sheffield, denounced the doom awaiting England should Pitt's Resolutions pass. In a short time sixty-four petitions poured in against them;[2] and the manufacturers of Great Britain, under the chairmanship of Wedgwood, formed a "Great Chamber" in order to stave off the catastrophe. Yet Pitt's energies and spirits seemed to rise with the rising opposition. In order to emphasize the importance of commerce, he had recently appointed a Committee of Council for Commerce, which promised to answer the purposes which that ornamental body, the Board of Trade (abolished in 1782), had signally failed to fulfil. The new Council was charged to examine manufacturers and others as to the relations of Anglo-Irish commerce and the probable effect of the Resolutions. Similar investigations were made at the bar of the House of Commons. Pitt cherished high hopes from these inquiries. "The more the subject is discussed," he wrote to Orde on 4th April, "the more our cause will be benefited in the end. . . . I do not myself entertain a doubt of complete success." To the Duke of Rutland he wrote on the 16th: "Though we may lose a little in popularity for the time,

---

[1] Pitt MSS., 321.

[2] Fifty-six petitions had been sent in against Lord North's proposals in 1778. Daniel Pulteney wrote on 22nd March: "The selfishness, ignorance, and credulity of many more commercial towns has been too successfully practised on by Opposition." He says Nottingham was worked on by "Portland's emissaries." The day before he expressed regret at Pitt's obstinacy over the "cursed" Westminster scrutiny ("Rutland P.," iii, 192, 193).

I   S

we shall ultimately gain—at least the country will, which is enough."[1]

The report of the committee is very curious, as showing the difficulty of obtaining trustworthy statistics even on the weightiest topics. The Irish accounts showed a far larger export of goods to Great Britain than of imports from Great Britain; while, on the contrary, the British Custom House returns gave the balance of trade as largely against Ireland. The committee could discover no means of accounting for this extraordinary discrepancy.[2] Thus, while protectionists on both sides of the Irish Sea were croaking over the decline of their trade and the growth of that of their rival, the official returns showed that (as they would have phrased it) the balance of trade was so largely in their favour as to warrant the hope of the speedy exhaustion of that rival.

In matters which were within the ken of the financiers of that age, the report was reassuring. The woollen manufacturers of Norwich declared that, though the wages of Irish spinners were less by one-half than those of English spinners, Irish competition was not to be feared under the conditions now proposed. Everett, a London merchant, maintained that the British manufacturers, owing to their skill, taste, and ingenuity, would always have a superiority over those of Ireland, provided that British sheep and wool were not exported thither. Nine woollen manufacturers of Yorkshire were decidedly of this opinion. The chief clothier of Devizes expected harm from Irish competition only in the cheaper stuffs.[3] For the cotton industry the evidence was less encouraging, the witnesses from Manchester claiming that Irish thread could be spun 20 per cent. cheaper than British thread, and that an import duty of $10\frac{1}{2}$ per cent. was needed to protect the home market.[4] Representative silk merchants of London and Scotland had little apprehension for the future, until the Irish workers developed skill and taste.[5] As for the iron trade, the evidence of eight iron-masters who were examined refuted the reasoning of the Sheffield petition. Provided that Ireland did not pay a smaller duty than Great Britain on imports

---

[1] Ashbourne, 121.

[2] "Report of the Lords of the Committee of Council" (1st March 1785). (J. Stockdale,) 4. Pitt stated in his letter of 6th January 1785 to Rutland, that Ireland bought far less from Great Britain than she sold to her.

[3] *Ibid.*, 8-30.   [4] *Ibid.*, 31-42.   [5] *Ibid.*, 43-49.

of bar iron, they asserted that they could hold their own against her small and struggling iron industry.[1]

In face of the alarmist statements of Wedgwood in public, his evidence before the committee is of some interest. When asked whether he feared Irish competition in pottery if the duties in both kingdoms were equalized, he replied that "there might be danger of a competition in time, in their own and every foreign market.[2] I should think we were safer if earthenware was allowed to be imported free of all duties into both countries." This was the man who headed the protectionist "Great Chamber of Manufacturers." Wedgwood's chief manager admitted that he had only the day before heard that any pottery at all was made in Ireland. Is it surprising that Pitt sharply criticized Wedgwood's tactics?

Other strange features of this report are, first, that the outcry in England against any relaxation of duties was greatest in the case of the very articles, calicoes and sugar, in which the Irish Parliament had recently imposed higher duties; secondly, that whereas much of the evidence told in favour of inter-insular Free Trade, the committee decided in favour of a system of moderate duties to be agreed on by the two Governments.[3] Some such conclusion was perhaps inevitable in view of the popular clamour; but the committee made no suggestion how the two Parliaments, now drifting into fiscal hostility, were to come to terms.

If the evidence contained in the report had been duly weighed, the scare among British traders must have passed away; but official reports are of little avail to thwart the efforts of panic-mongers. In vain did George Rose, in an unsigned pamphlet, point the moral of the case, and appeal to the common sense of his countrymen.[4] The Opposition had the ear of the public, and the fate of the Resolutions in their present form was evidently sealed. Probably Pulteney was right in stating that the report came out too late to influence public opinion, and that Pitt had unaccountably underrated the force of the prejudices contending against him. Now, when the vote on the Westminster Scrutiny alarmed him, he became perhaps unduly cautious.[5] This may

---

[1] "Report of the Lords of the Committee of Council," 50-55.
[2] Ibid., 68.   [3] Ibid., 78, 79.
[4] "The Proposed System of Trade with Ireland explained" (1785).
[5] Letter of 6th April to Duke of Rutland in "Rutland P.," iii, 197.

be the true explanation of his disposition to compromise. In his letter of 21st May, to the Duke of Rutland, he dwelt on the difficulties arising from the unscrupulous tactics of the enemy and the very marked independence of a large number of his supporters, so that "we are hardly sure from day to day what impression they may receive."

This avowal is of some interest. It shows how critical was Pitt's position in the spring of 1785. As has been seen in a former chapter, he had strained the allegiance of his motley following by taking up too many thorny questions at once. The composite elements—Foxite, Northite, and Chathamite—had not yet been fused into unity by the power of his genius and the threatening pressure of France. Only by the most careful leading could he keep his supporters together, and save the country from the turmoil which a Fox-North Ministry must have caused. There was the danger; and we may be sure that Pitt clung to office, not merely from love of power (though he did love power), but because, in the proud words of Chatham, he knew that he could guide his country aright, and that no one else could.

Viewing the question of the independence of members of Parliament in a more general way, we may hazard the conjecture that in the days of pocket boroughs and small electorates members probably acted more independently than in the present time, when their action is apt to be the resultant of two external forces, pressure from constituents and pressure from the party "whip." However we may explain the fact, it is certain that Pitt, despite his huge majority, failed to carry three important proposals in 1785-6; and in the case of the Irish Propositions he hesitated and lost the day.

In the second week of May, 1785, the Prime Minister bent before the storm, and on the 12th presented his modified measure in the form of twenty Propositions. The chief changes were those tending to safeguard our West India planters and merchant against the secret importation of the products of the French o Spanish colonies into this country on Irish ships. He main tained the monopoly of the East India Company in all the sea and lands between the Cape of Good Hope and the Straits o Magellan, but allowed the Company's ships to export good from Ireland to the East Indies. Further, he proposed that th Navigation Laws, whether present or future, and the enac

ments respecting colonial commerce, should be equally binding on both kingdoms. Respecting the reduction of duties
in either country, it was suggested that they should not fall
below 10½ per cent.; also that no new duties should be imposed
except such as would "balance duties on internal consumption."
He also added a Proposition concerning the copyright of books.
Respecting Ireland's contribution to the navy, Pitt annulled the
Irish proposal asserting the prior need of balancing income and
expenditure, and required that the proposed financial arrangement should be perpetual.

In his speeches of 12th May and succeeding days he showed
that most of the petitions against his plan were founded on error,
and he refuted the hackneyed assertion that, because Ireland
was lightly taxed and wages were low, she would therefore
undersell Britons in their own markets. Considering her extreme
poverty, he said, her burdens were in effect as great as those of
England; her backwardness in industry would long cripple her;
moreover, for skilled labour she had to pay as dearly as British
employers. He claimed that a liberal scheme of commercial
union would benefit both islands, just as the Union with Scotland
had immensely furthered the prosperity of Great Britain
despite the prophecies of ruin with which it was at the time
received.

His opponents now changed their tactics. Seeing that the
Propositions had been altered largely in deference to their fears,
they could scarcely meet them with a direct attack. They
therefore sought to procure their rejection, if not at Westminster,
then at Dublin. Congratulating themselves on having caused
the abandonment of the first proposals, as fraught with ruin to
Great Britain, they sought to set Ireland in a flame against the
amended measure. It is true that Fox deprecated the concession
of the proposed advantages to Ireland, on the ground that they
would subject our workers to the caprices of the Dublin Parliament. But he reserved his denunciations for the proposals
which treated Ireland as a subsidiary State, in the matter of
the Navigation Acts. Above all, he declared, he would trust
Ireland where the Prime Minister distrusted her, namely, in the
contribution to the navy. Put that to her as a debt of honour,
said he, and she would discharge it. Compel her, and she would
either refuse from injured pride or concede it grudgingly, while
perhaps equally withdrawing her support from the army. " I will

not," he exclaimed, "barter English commerce for Irish slavery: that is not the price I would pay, nor is this the thing I would purchase." Finally he declared that the House could not understand these matters so well as the traders and workers of Great Britain, who had overwhelmingly declared against the measure. Fox did well to disclaim any positive opinions on these subjects; for he took no interest in them, and is known never to have read Adam Smith's work, which he scoffed at as a collection of entertaining theories.[1] We can now understand his conduct in declaiming against the new safeguards for British industry, which he himself had demanded; and if we may judge from Wraxall, the most telling parts of his speech were the personal touches in which he reprobated Pitt's lofty dictatorial manner, and his novel connection with the "King's friend," Jenkinson. Formerly War Secretary under Lord North,[2] he had recently been appointed by Pitt head of the new "Committee of Council for the Superintendence of Commerce." Burke, who must have approved Pitt's proposals (except the contribution from Ireland, against which he hotly inveighed), made capital out of the new "Coalition," calling Jenkinson Pitt's pedestal, and wittily declaring that he envied not the statue its pedestal or the pedestal its statue.[3] Other members, including Fox and Pitt, skilfully played with the simile, and thus beguiled the hours of these otherwise exhausting debates, which, we may note, caused Wilberforce to faint in the midst of his efforts to defend his chief.

The most brilliant, though not the least mischievous, speech of these debates was that of Richard Brinsley Sheridan. It is needless to dilate on the Celtic charm and vivacity of this great *littérateur*. Descended from an old Irish family, which gave to Swift one of his dearest friends, and to Dublin one of its leading actors and authors, he was born in 1751, doomed to sparkle. Educated at Harrow, and called to the Bar, he soon attracted attention by his speeches and still more by his plays. His "Rivals" and "School for Scandal" attested the versatility of his wit and the cynical geniality of his nature. In 1780 he made what was perhaps the chief mistake of his life in entering Parliament as member for Stafford; for his character was too volatile

---

[1] T. Moore, "Life of Sheridan," i, 424.   [2] Wraxall, iv, 127-38.
[3] Lord Morley ("Burke," 125) allows that Burke was wrong in following Fox's factious opposition, and that he "allowed his political integrity to be bewildered."

his satire too caustic, to ensure success except as a *frondeur*.
Friendship with Fox condemned him almost entirely to this
rôle and exaggerated the recklessness of his utterances. He was
the Charles O'Malley of politics. When, therefore, that engaging
political satire, " The Rolliad," appeared, in castigation of Rolle,
the somewhat roisterous member for Devonshire, everyone attributed the poems to Sheridan; and his strenuous denial found
little credence.[1]

One of the " Probationary Odes " amusingly hit off the alliance
of Jenkinson with Pitt and the increase in the number of the
Irish Propositions:

> Lo! hand in hand advance th' enamour'd pair
> This Chatham's son and that the drudge of Bute.
> Proud of their mutual love
> Like Nisus and Euryalus they move
> To Glory's steepest heights together tend,
> Each careless for himself, each anxious for his friend.

> CHORUS
> Hail! most prudent Politicians!
> Hail! correct Arithmeticians!
> Hail! vast exhaustless source of Irish Propositions!

Elsewhere in dolorous strains the Muse

> Sees fair Ierne rise from England's flame,
> And build on British ruin Irish fame.[2]

In these witticisms we have the high-water mark of the
achievements of the Opposition. Sheridan inveighed against
the exaction of a contribution from Ireland towards the navy,
and the re-imposition of the Navigation Laws (certainly the
weakest part of Pitt's case) as implying a legislative inferiority
from which she had escaped in 1782. He scoffed at the commercial boons as a mean and worthless bribe, and the whole
scheme as " a fraud, cheat and robbery," fatal to the confidence
of the Irish in the good faith of Britain. The playwright further
exclaimed that it would be a misfortune if the Irish Parliament
dared to pass the Resolutions, and that, as it was not by Par-

---

[1] The actual authors of these amusing poems were Tickell, General Fitzpatrick, Lord John Townsend, Richardson, George Ellis, and Burke's friend
and literary executor, Dr. Lawrence, who contributed the prose parts.
(T. Moore, " Sheridan," i, 421.)

[2] " The Rolliad," 90, 370.

liament that the independence of Ireland had been obtained, so it was not by Parliament that it should be given up. This was tantamount to an invitation to the Irish Volunteers to renew their coercion of the Dublin Parliament; and it was now clear that Fox and his friends, in despair of defeating the proposals at Westminster, were seeking to wreck them at Dublin, if need be, at the cost of civil broils.

In this they succeeded. By substantial majorities Ministers carried the Irish Propositions at the end of May; and the Lords passed them on 18th July. But long before this the storm-centre had moved across St. George's Channel. Throughout the length and breadth of Ireland an outcry was raised against the state of ignominious dependence in which Ireland would be placed by the contribution now imposed on her for ever in return for greatly diminished advantages. Fox's telling phrase about the bartering of Irish liberty against British commerce was on every lip. The results were at once obvious. Though Pitt, with his usually sanguine forecast, had expressed the belief that the Dublin Parliament would be more manageable than that of Westminster, it set at naught all the Viceregal blandishments. Some of its members even taunted Pitt with acting treacherously towards Ireland throughout. Grattan, while refraining from this taunt, opposed the new scheme, especially clause iv and the perpetual contribution, in a speech which the Lord Lieutenant described to Pitt as "seditious and inflammatory to a degree scarcely credible." Flood excelled himself in recklessness; and in that body of usually subservient placemen, leave to bring in the Bill was granted only by a majority of nineteen (12th August).

In face of this storm-signal the Irish Government decided to furl their sails and come to anchor. The measure was deferred to another session; and of course was never heard of again. Considering the "very great clamour"[1] in the country, this was inevitable; and Dublin manifested its joy by a spontaneous and general illumination. Woodfall, an opponent of Pitt's policy, admitted to Eden that neither the populace nor the members could explain the cause of their recent fury or their present joy.[2]

[1] "Dropmore P.," i, 255. See ch. xii of this work for a new letter of Wilberforce to Pitt on the crisis.

[2] "Auckland Journals," i, 79.

The excitement soon abated; and it must be allowed that the popular party in Ireland did not adopt the hostile measures against British trade which might have been expected after the break-down of these enlightened proposals. Lord Westmorland, during his viceroyalty five years later, admitted that complete harmony existed in the commercial relations of the two kingdoms.

This may have salved the wound which the events of 1785 dealt to Pitt. Up to the very end he had hoped for success in what had been the dearest object of his life. After hearing of the ominous vote of 12th August in Dublin, he wrote to the Marquis of Buckingham in the following manly terms:

Putney Heath, Aug. 17, 1785.[1]

My Dear Lord,

I have many thanks to return you for your letter. Grenville will probably send you the account we received to-day from Ireland, after a long period of suspense. The motion for bringing in a Bill has been carried only by 127 against 108; and such a victory undoubtedly par-takes, for the present at least, of the nature of a defeat. A motion was announced for Monday last, declaratory against the 4th Resolution. The event of this motion seemed to be thought uncertain. The prob-able issue of all this seems to be that the settlement is put at some distance, but I still believe the principles of it too sound, not to find their way at last.

To the Duke of Rutland he also wrote in the same lofty spirit, using the words quoted at the head of this chapter, and adding that, when experience had brought more wisdom, " we shall see all our views realised in both countries and for the advantage of both."

Faith and courage such as this are never lost upon colleagues and subordinates, especially when they can rely on loyal support from their chief. Both to the Duke and to Orde Pitt now tendered his thanks for their tact and resolution in face of overwhelming difficulties, and thus manifested that kindliness and magnanimity which wins heartfelt devotion. For, as usually happens after defeat, envious surmises were rife. Some spiteful influence (probably that of the Marquis of Buckingham),[2] had sought to

---

[1] Chevening MSS. Pitt continued to reside at the house on the north side of Putney Heath, next to Lord Ashburton's, until October or November 1785, when he removed to Holwood Hill, Kent.

[2] " Dropmore P.," i, 254; " Pitt-Rutland Corresp.," 125-33.

poison Pitt's mind against Orde as the chief cause of the failure in Dublin. As for Beresford, he believed that some of Pitt's colleagues had turned traitors. Lesser men might pry into corners to find petty causes for that heart-breaking collapse; but no such suspicions mar the dignity of Pitt's voluminous correspondence, a perusal of which enables the reader to understand why Orde once exclaimed: " I am so sensible of the manly and noble part which Mr. Pitt has acted, that I will die by inches in the cause of his support." [1]

The real reason of failure, as Pitt clearly saw, was the determination of powerful factions in both kingdoms to wreck his proposals by representing each concession made to the sister-island as an injury or an insult, or both. At all times it is easier to fan to a flame the fears and jealousies of nations than to allay them; and in that age the susceptibilities both of Britons and Irishmen were highly inflammable. Twelve decades, marked by reforming efforts and closer intercourse, have softened the feelings then so easily aroused; and as we look back over efforts of conciliation, not yet crowned with complete success, we see no figure nobler and more pathetic than that of the statesman who struggled hard to bring together those hitherto alien peoples by the ties of interest and friendship; we see also few figures more sinister than those of his political opponents at Westminster who set themselves doggedly to the task of thwarting his efforts by means of slander and misrepresentation.

[1] Ashbourne, 146.

CHAPTER XII

PITT AND HIS FRIENDS

(1783-94)

Keep thy friend
Under thy own life's key.
SHAKESPEARE, *All's Well that Ends Well.*

A crowd is not company, and faces are but a gallery of pictures, and talk
but a tinkling cymball where there is no love.—BACON.

SOME statesmen merit notice solely from the magnitude of
their achievements; others attract attention by the charm
of their personality. Pitt claims homage on both accounts. Accordingly I propose to devote this chapter to his private life and
friendships during the early part of his career, beginning with
the time when he laid down the Chancellorship of the Exchequer
and fled to the house of his friend Wilberforce at Wimbledon.
In the Diary of the latter we read this brief but suggestive
entry: "April 3 [1783]. To Wimbledon, where Pitt, etc., dined
and slept. Evening walk—to bed a little past two. April 4.
Delicious day: lounged the morning at Wimbledon with friends:
foining at night, and run about the garden for an hour or two."

We can picture the scene. Lauriston House, Wilberforce's
abode on the south side of Wimbledon Common, is a spacious
villa, comfortable in its eighteenth-century solidity, and scarcely
changed since those days. One of the front bedrooms is known
as "Mr. Pitt's room." There he would look forth on the Common, which had for him a peculiar charm. At the back, the
south windows look upon an extensive lawn, bordered not too
thickly by trees, under one of which, a maple, tradition says
that he was wont to lounge away his Sunday mornings, to the
distress of his host. At other times the garden was the scene of
half riotous mirth. Pitt, Dudley Ryder, Pepper Arden, Bob

267

Steele, and Wilberforce there broke loose from the restraints of
Westminster, and indulged in *foyning*. That old-English word,
denoting thrusting or fencing, conjures up visions of quips and
pranks such as Horace loved. Would that Pitt had had more
time for these wholesome follies!

Imagine these youths, with the freshness of Cambridge still
upon them, cheating the hours with fun. Pitt, the stately,
austere leader of the House of Commons, who, on entering its
precincts, fixed his eyes straight on his seat, and tilted his nose
loftily in air during his State progress thither, with not so
much as a nod to his supporters[1]—yet here, on the lawn of
Lauriston House, is all fun and laughter, sharpening his wit
against the edge of Wilberforce's fancy, answering jest with jest,
quotation with quotation, in a fresh mingling of jollity and
culture. As yet all is joyous in the lives of the friends. Wilberforce has inherited from an uncle an ample fortune along with
Lauriston House, and adds rooms to it so as fitly to entertain
the friends who always cluster about him. The woes of the
slaves have not yet struck a chill to his life, and he lives amidst
a buzz of friends and admirers. He reminds us of that character
in Disraeli's "Lothair," who proved an irresistible magnet at
every party—no one quite knew why; but every one sought to be
next him. The magnetism of Wilberforce is easily intelligible;
it lay in his lovable and gifted nature, which welled forth freely
in genial anecdote, friendly parody, sparkling retort.

For Pitt, too, there were as yet no oppressive cares. True, at
that time, there loomed before him the toilsome career of an
impecunious barrister, but that did not daunt his serene and
self-reliant nature. Doubtless the troubles of England moved
him more, now that the prospect of peace with America and
the half of Europe was overclouded by the triumph of Fox and
North. But Pitt had that protective faculty, inherent in all great
natures, of laying aside personal and even national cares in the
company of his dearest friends, and it set him free for life-
restoring mirth. Then, too, his nature, shy and stiff to mere
acquaintances, blossomed forth radiantly to a chosen circle, such
as he found at Wimbledon. Here, then, was seen the real man.
Away went the mask of official reserve, which prudence compelled him to wear at Westminster as a defence against his

[1] Wraxall, iii, 217.

seniors. Here, among youths and friends, his pranks were startling. One of them must be told in the words of Wilberforce: "We found one morning the fruits of Pitt's earlier rising in the careful sowing of the garden beds with the fragments of a dress-hat in which Dudley Ryder had overnight come down from the opera."

Would that we knew more of those bright days! For Pitt the man, not Pitt the statesman, is seen at Wimbledon. The pillar of State, columnar in its Doric austerity, becomes a lithe facile form, twined about with social graces, gay with the flowers of friendship. The hours of recreation, rather than those spent in the office, reveal the inner life. Alas! the self-revealing episodes in the life of Pitt are hidden from us. None of his friends was a Boswell. Wilberforce, who might have been the enlightener, was troubled by defective eyesight, which curtailed his correspondence; and his Diary is a series of tantalizing jottings, a veritable Barmecide feast. As for Pitt's relatives, they never drew him out of himself. Lord Chatham, though a good talker in general company, seems to have exerted on his younger brother a slightly chilling influence; and their letters were fraternally business-like. We therefore search in vain for those lighter traits of character, those sparkles of wit, which enlivened the joyous years 1783-5. This side of Pitt's character is little more known to us than are the hidden regions of the moon. We wish to know it all the more because it is not the frozen but the sunny side of his being.

Failing to catch more than one sportive echo of those glad times, the chronicler falls back on mere externals, such as Pitt's occasional reluctance to attend the parish church at Wimbledon, or his fondness for fishing in Lord Spencer's lake on the lower land east of the Common. Clearly the neighbourhood must have attracted him; for in August 1784 he leased the house next to Lord Ashburton's, on the north side of Putney Heath, scarcely two miles distant from the abode of Wilberforce. He resided there up to the autumn of 1785, when the opportunity of buying the house at Holwood drew him to the scenes of his boyhood, near Hayes, in Kent. Nevertheless the Surrey Common was to win him back. For, during his last term of office, he purchased Bowling Green House, on the old Portsmouth road, near the middle of that beautiful space.

There it was that he fought his duel with Tierney on Whitsunday 1798. There, too, he breathed his last, on 23rd January 1806. In the dark days that followed on the news of Austerlitz, his thoughts turned with one final flicker of hope towards the news which he expected from his special envoy to Berlin, the Earl of Harrowby, formerly Dudley Ryder. The news proved to be heart-breaking. But fancy persists in wondering whether, perchance, during the time of waiting, the dauntless spirit did not for a brief space fling off the thraldom of the present and flit across the open to dwell with fond remembrance on that spring sowing of the flower-beds of his friend Wilberforce.[1]

After the severe disappointments of the session of 1785, the signs of friskiness vanish from the life of Pitt. Up to that time his hopefulness is of almost boyish intensity. Confidence in himself, and in the goodness of his cause, and determination to carry out a work of national revival, lead him to grapple with great enterprises in a way that astonishes friends and baffles opponents. The nation having given him a mandate in 1784, he hopes to solve the most urgent of existing problems. They are the restoration of public credit, the reduction of the National Debt, the reform of Parliament, the subordination of the East India Company to the control of Parliament, the opening up of freer trade not only with Ireland but also with France, and the preservation of peace, so that, as he phrased it—"Let peace continue for five years, and we shall again look any Power in Europe in the face."[2]

Here was a programme which transcended anything previously seen. But to it were added the many unforeseen events and problems that provide a full stock in trade for an ordinary parliamentary leader. The Warren Hastings affair alone would have occupied a whole session under a quiescent Minister; and we may here note that Pitt's conscientious treatment of it, as a matter on which Ministers and members must vote according to their convictions, tended to relax the bonds of party discipline to a dangerous extent.

Indeed, there is only one of his important actions during the

---

[1] Wilberforce gave up Lauriston House in 1786. A little later Dundas and Grenville came to reside at Wimbledon, on the east and west sides of the Green. Grenville's is now called Eagle House. Dundas's stood on the site of "Canizzaro."

[2] "Pitt-Rutland Corresp.," 111.

first years of power that needs apology. This is the persistence with which he pressed against Fox the demand for a complete scrutiny of the Westminster election. Despite the fact that that wearisome and very expensive inquiry brought to light few bad votes, and did not exclude Fox from Parliament (for as we saw, he sat as Member for Orkney), the Prime Minister refused to put an end to "this cursed business," as Pulteney termed it,[1] until his own supporters compelled him to desist. How are we to explain this conduct? It led to waste of time and temper in Parliament, besides annoying many of his friends, and straining to breaking-point the allegiance of his composite majority. There can be no doubt that he committed a blunder, and one which Englishmen detest; for his conduct seemed ungenerous to a beaten foe and a violation of the unwritten rules of fair-play.

Nevertheless, it is likely that he acted, not from rancour, not from a desire to ban his enemy, least of all under any dictation from Windsor (of this I have found no sign), but rather from the dictates of political morality. That there had been trumping up of false votes was notorious; for the votes polled exceeded the total number of voters; and Pitt, as the champion of purity at elections, may have deemed it his duty to probe the sore to the bottom. In these days an avowed champion of Reform would be praised for such conduct. In that age he was condemned; and it was certainly tactless to single out Fox from among the many candidates for whom corrupt practices had been used. Such an act appeared the outcome of personal pique, not of zeal for electoral purity. So at least men looked on it in the spring of 1785. Pulteney, Wraxall, and the ordinary ruck of members failed to see anything but personal motives in the whole affair.[2] Fox, who always gauged the temper of the House aright, carried it with him when he protested that he had little expected to find Pitt acting as the agent of the Crown in his persecution; that it was clearly the aim of the Ministry to ruin him, for he was a poor man. "Yet," he added, "in such a cause I will lay down my last shilling. If ultimately I lose my election, it will be for want of money, not from want of a legal majority of votes, while Westminster will be deprived of its franchise because I am unable to prosecute a pecuniary contest with the Treasury." This is the most effective type of parliamentary speech.

---

[1] "Rutland P.," iii, 177.   [2] Ibid., 178; Wraxall, iv, 72-9, 98.

It avoided all reference to the abstract principles which were at stake, and it appealed with telling force to the sporting instincts of squires. Little wonder is it that Pitt's followers went over to the side which seemed to stand for fair play to a poor man in his contest with a spiteful bureaucracy. A few days later Pitt could muster only a majority of nine (21st February 1785), and this clearly foreshadowed the end of the scrutiny, which came with a vote hostile to Ministers on 3rd March. On a subordinate motion, six days later, several malcontents returned to their allegiance, thus proving, in Wraxall's words, that "they wished to control and restrain, but had no desire to overturn, the Administration."[1]

This affair deserves mention here because it illustrates what was the chief weakness of Pitt. His secluded childhood, his education apart from other youths, even at Cambridge, his shyness in general company, and his decided preference for the society of a few friends, gave him very few opportunities for knowing ordinary men. He therefore was slow in understanding the temper of the House, and he never gained what we may call the Palmerston touch. Well would it have been for him if he had mixed more with men and shown towards members of the House the affability with which Fox and North charmed friends and foes alike. But, like Peel, Pitt had neither parliamentary graces nor small talk for the lobby. In truth he was too shy or too proud to unbend with ease. Or rather he did so only in a circle of friends or among his juniors. Then his sense of fun could go to surprising lengths, witness that historic romp when Lady Hester Stanhope, two of her younger brothers, and young William Napier (the future historian) managed to get him down and blacken his face. In the midst of their jubilant triumph there came a knock at the door. Two Ministers were announced as desirous of taking his commands on some question. For a few minutes State business stood still until the Prime Minister shook off his assailants and washed his face for the interview. Then the boys marvelled more at the change of manner than of colour. The Prime Minister threw up his chin, loftily inquired the cause of the visit, imparted his decision, stiffly dismissed the Ministers—and resumed the romp.[2] Clearly there were two Pitts.

---

[1] Wraxall, iv, 98.
[2] Bruce, "Life of Sir W. Napier," i, 28; quoted by Lecky, v, 16.

His rather stilted manners at Westminster were doubtless a reflection—a lunar reflection—of the melodramatic splendours of his father. Never was a colleague or a subordinate introduced to Chatham's presence until the effects of light were Rembrandt-esque, and the telling phrase had been coined. But where the father triumphed by the force of his personality, the son only half succeeded. For he was more a Grenville than a Pitt, and he inherited from that family some of its congenital stiffness. Hence the efforts which the son put forth, as if with the aim of fulfilling the precept of St. Paul to Timothy—" Let no man despise thy youth "—were calculated, not to impress beholders, but rather to freeze them.

Far different was the easy good nature of Fox, which often salved the wounds inflicted in the course of debate. It is said that Lord North, after one of the debates on the American War, in which Fox had mercilessly belaboured one of the Ministers, good-humouredly remarked to the orator, " You were in fine feather to-night, Charles; I am glad that it was not my turn to be fallen upon." Fox, we may add, reciprocated these senti-ments. However he might threaten North with impeachment, he was ready in private to shake him by the hand; and shortly before the fall of that Minister he publicly asked his pardon for offending him by his tremendous indictment, adding that he meant it not. To us this sounds unreal. Either the in-dictment against the author of the nation's ruin was not quite sincere, or the apology was hollow. Pitt, with his exceptionally high standard of truthfulness,[1] could not have tendered it. Fox did; and Wraxall praised his conduct, adding that Pitt was less placable, and was wanting in those frank, winning, open ways which made friends and retained them through adversity.[2]

This rather superficial verdict—for Wraxall knew Pitt only very slightly—summed up the views of the easy-going mass, which cares nothing for principles, little for measures, and very much for men, provided that they keep up the parliamentary game according to the old rules and in a sportsmanlike way. It must always be remembered that few members of Parliament took their duties seriously, and looked on the debates mainly as a change from the life of the other fashionable clubs. To such an assembly the political philosophy of Burke was foolishness,

[1] " Private Papers of Wilberforce," 69.　　　[2] Wraxall, ii, 234, 235.

I　　　　　　　　　　T

and the lofty principles of Pitt, mere Pharisaism. Its ideal would have been Esau, provided that he had held fast to the customs of primogeniture.

We have little or nothing that directly shows the impression produced on Pitt by his discovery of the shallowness and fickleness of his supporters. Perhaps it intensified his natural shyness and awkwardness of manner, which Wilberforce assures us were very great. Certainly he did not mix more with men. " Pitt does not make friends " is a significant entry in Wilberforce's Diary for March 1785.[1] This inability to make a wide circle of friends was not incompatible with those rarer gifts which link a man closely to those with whom he had real kinship of spirit. If we may read Shakespeare's thoughts into the well-known words of Polonius to Laertes, the poet supremely admired a man who inspired the few with ardent affection and held the many at arm's length. In regard to character, then, we may honour Pitt for the very characteristic which to men like Wraxall seemed a blemish.

Nevertheless, it was a serious failing in a parliamentary tactician. Onlookers, who saw only the cold and reserved exterior, described Pitt as the embodiment of egotism and pride. His friends knew full well that he was the soul of kindness. Dundas and Wilberforce testify to his affable behaviour to subordinates, his fund of good temper, which was proof even against contradiction and the advent of bad news. Wilberforce mentions a case in point. Pitt had long been ruminating on some revenue proposal, and at length mentioned it to the Attorney-General, only to learn that there would be grave legal objections to the scheme; far from showing annoyance, he received the announcement " with the most unruffled good-humour," and, giving up his plan, " pursued his other business as cheerfully and pleasantly as usual." [2]

It is not thus that a proud and egotistical nature sees his castle vanish into air. Anecdotes such as this have been known only since the year 1897. Now we know the real Pitt; the men of these times saw only the professional mask; and therefore we find exclamations like that of Sir Gilbert Elliot who, after hearing the almost inspired speech of Pitt on the abolition of

---

[1] " Private Papers of Wilberforce," 65; " Life of Wilberforce," i, 78.
[2] " Private Papers of Wilberforce," 66, 67.

the slave-trade, remarked: "One felt almost to like the man";[1] or again Lady Anne Hamilton in her "Memoirs of the Court of George III," asserted that Pitt was always cold and carried his frostiness even into his carouses.

This certainly was the general belief. In one particular Pitt's behaviour often gave colour to the charge of pride or egotism. His letters were as stiff as his parliamentary attitudes. Worst of all, he very often left letters unanswered; and this applied not merely to begging letters, against which silence is a Prime Minister's panoply, but even to important matters of State. We find Eden, in the midst of the commercial negotiations with France, writing from Paris in despairing terms about the Prime Minister's silence, and finally suggesting that all his letters of the last fortnight must have sunk in the Channel. Sir James Harris, too, when fighting an unequal battle against the French party in Holland, begged Pitt to send a few lines to encourage the hard pressed friends of England. For four months not a line came; and at last Harris begged Carmarthen to cajole a letter out of his chief: "Is it impossible to move him, *who speaks* so well, to write one poor line to these sound shillings and pence men?"[2] The excuse doubtless was, that Pitt was overworked in Parliament (as indeed he stated to Eden);[3] but, even with the then scanty facilities for dealing with a vast correspondence, he should certainly have handled it with more method and tact. Careless correspondents will readily conjecture how much a Prime Minister may harm his prospects by subjecting friends and foes alike to a peculiarly annoying slight.

Pitt, then, owed little or nothing to social graces; and Horace Walpole gave a very superficial judgement, when, in his companion sketches of Pitt and Fox, he stated that the former "cultivated friends to form a party." On the contrary, he harmed his party by cooling his friends.

The men who most helped Pitt to keep in touch with his following were Dundas, Grenville, and Jenkinson. They did not,

---

[1] "Life and Letters of the Earl of Minto," ii, 5.

[2] B.M. Add. MSS., 28061. This postscript to Harris's letter of 18th July 1786 to Carmarthen is omitted from "The Malmesbury Diaries"; so, too are most personal touches, often of great interest.

[3] "Auckland Journals," i, 117.

as Wraxall avers, hold the first place in his confidence. That was still held by Wilberforce; and to their friendship we may apply the apt remark of Montaigne, that the amity which possesses and sways the soul cannot be double. For political reasons Pitt after the year 1784 came into closer contact with his subalterns, among whom Dundas and Grenville claim notice.

Henry Dundas (1742-1811), a younger son of the Right Honourable Robert Dundas, Lord President of the Scottish Court of Session, and of Anne Gordon of Invergordon, was born at Edinburgh, where he was educated first at school, then in the University. The atmosphere in which he grew up was strictly legal; and his ancestry, no less than his upbringing, seemed to fit him for success at the Bar, at which he appeared in 1763. His rise was rapid, and in 1774 he entered Parliament as member for Midlothian. At Westminster he attached himself to North's party and became known as a hard worker and hard hitter. United as these powers were with a manly presence, genial gifts, and the full fund of Scottish shrewdness, he acquired favour and became Lord Advocate. Grace and persuasiveness of speech he lacked; a harsh voice, a still harsher accent, and awkward gestures told against him; but above these defects he rose triumphant, thanks to indomitable courage, which enabled him unabashed to bear the heaviest blows of debate. Napoleon once expressed his admiration of Blücher, because, however badly he was beaten, "the old devil" came up again as though nothing had happened. So it was with Dundas in his many encounters with Fox. He might be repulsed but never routed. His features were bold and handsome, and, if they were "tinged with convivial purple," that perhaps enhanced their charm. For the House loved a *bon vivant*, who entertained with lairdly lavishness and had good store, not only of wine, but of broad stories.

Wraxall, while admitting Dundas's appearance to be "manly and advantageous," avers that his conviviality was part of a deep-laid scheme for managing men and tightening his grip on the Administration; for "never did any man conceal deeper views of every kind under the appearance of careless inattention to self-interest." The same insinuation is wittily conveyed by the authors of "The Rolliad" in a skit on the Cabinet Meetings which Dundas was supposed to hold in his villa. "March 9th, 1787. Got Thurlow to dine with us at Wimbledon—gave him

my best Burgundy and blasphemy to put him into good
humour. After a brace of bottles ventured to drop a hint of
business. Thurlow cursed me, and asked Pitt for a sentiment.
Pitt looked foolish, Grenville wise. Mulgrave stared. Sydney's
chin lengthened. Tried the effect of another bottle. Pitt began
a long speech on the subject of our meeting. Sydney fell asleep
by the fire"—and so on.

In one respect Dundas was the great political agent of the
age. He managed Scotland, so thoroughly, indeed, that he has
been termed "the foremost Scotsman of the eighteenth century."[1]
No civilian since the time of John Knox has ever controlled the
energies of that people so thoroughly as Henry Dundas. What
the great Reformer achieved by an appeal to their highest
aspirations, the party manipulator achieved by an appeal to the
purse. Since the collapse of the Stuart cause material interests
had been paramount; and their deadening effect on national
character appears in the political torpor which lay upon Scotland until the strident call of the French Revolution awakened
her. The men north of the Tweed had even more reason than
Englishmen to desire Parliamentary Reform; for, as will be seen
in a later chapter, in all Scotland there were only 1303 electors;
and these returned 45 members as against 44 who misrepresented
Cornwall. But so long as the Scots slumbered, it mattered not
whether they had 45 members or 4; for the return of 45, and
their course of conduct at Westminster were alike prescribed by
Dundas. The soporific fruit which drugged the Scottish people
and kept their representatives close to his heel was "patronage."
Dundas it was who dispensed all important prizes both in Church
and State. Valuable livings at home, lucrative posts in India or
speedy advancement in the navy, these and many other rewards
were in his hands. His influence at the Admiralty and at the
India Board of Control was immense; he worked hard for his
men; and it may be admitted that his choice of officials, especially for India, was often sound. Certain it is that he opened up
golden avenues to hundreds of poor Scottish families, so that he
was often hailed as the benefactor of his people.

In one respect Dundas conferred a substantial boon. He
persuaded Pitt to extinguish the embers of hatred to the
reigning dynasty which still smouldered in the Highlands, by

[1] Omond, G. W. T., "The Lord Advocates of Scotland," ch. xiv.

restoring the estates that were confiscated after the " Forty-five."
By this act of clemency Pitt and Dundas linked their names to
the work of reconciliation so tactfully begun by Chatham,
and helped to foster the sentiment of British nationality, which
bore a rich harvest on the fields of Salamanca and Waterloo. It
is not surprising, then, that Dundas had the small governing
clique in Scotland entirely at his beck and call. One of his forty-
five henchmen at Westminster, Ferguson of Pitfour, frankly
stated that he had never heard a speech which had influenced his
vote, and that there was only one defect in Dundas's leadership,
namely, that he was not quite tall enough to enable his followers
readily to see into which lobby he was going at division-time.[1]

Even so, the magnetic influence of Dundas upon the obedient
Caledonian squad was a political asset of no small worth. Not
seldom could the laird of Melville decide the fate of Cabinets
by throwing his forty-five votes into this or that scale. He
himself was fully aware of his importance; for in a letter which
he wrote to Grenville early in 1789, he declined another official
post because in his present position (or positions) he was " a
cement of political strength to the present Administration," the
dissolution of which might be ruinous. The words are instinct,
not only with the Scottish canniness, but with Scottish loyalty.
In truth, the staunchness of Dundas's friendship to Pitt suffices
to refute those critics, both of his own and later times, who
speak of him as of a political Vicar of Bray. In his early days his
trimming propensities were often disagreeably prominent; and
the speech in which he hailed the rising sun of Pitt, and slighted
the waning orb of North, was quite characteristic of the earlier
half of his career.[2] But, for him as for some others, the splendour
of Pitt's genius, and the glow of his pure patriotism, inaugurated
a brighter future; and he might well say of his tergiversation
at that time what Talleyrand said of his still more numerous
changes of front: " I have never deserted a party before it
deserted itself." While recognizing in this new ally great powers
of work, and still greater powers of "influence," Pitt did not at
once give him his whole confidence; and we shall probably not
be far wrong in inferring that only after the disillusionment of
the spring of 1785, did " Henry VIIIth of Scotland " become his
counsellor on matters of the highest moment. Thenceforth his

[1] Porritt, "Unreformed House of Commons," ii, 8.
[2] Wraxall, ii, 123.

influence over Pitt steadily increased, while that of Wilberforce somewhat waned; and we find the latter declaring at a later time that Pitt's connection with Dundas was his "great misfortune," a remark which applied mainly to the slavery question.[1] It is, however, still more applicable to Dundas's conduct of the war, when, as we shall see, his absorption in other work, and his utter inexperience of military affairs, should have made him backward in giving advice. Far from that, he was for some time the guiding spirit; and from his seat at the Home Office or the India Board, or from his suburban villa, he dashed off orders of momentous import, which were to gladden the heart of Carnot.

Such, then, was the man at whose house, on the west side of Wimbledon Common, Pitt was a frequent visitor. There the conviviality was unrestrained by those scruples which more and more prevailed at Wilberforce's abode hard by; and after the latter gave up that villa, in the autumn of 1786, the associations of Pitt with Wimbledon are somewhat vinous. Both Pitt and Dundas were hard drinkers. The former frequently tossed off several tumblers of port wine before a great speech in the House of Commons; and it would seem, if rumour spoke truly, that at Dundas's the potations were long and deep. It must not, however, be supposed that Pitt performed no serious work there. The long and important despatches which he wrote at Wimbledon show the contrary; and their contents prove them to have been written before the Bacchic pleasures, which men of that age deemed the appropriate close of a busy day. Only once did the pleasures of dessert at Dundas's cause Pitt and his host to compromise themselves in public. But on one occasion they came to the House of Commons obviously the worse for liquor. The occasion was equally remarkable. It was on the acceptance of the French Declaration of War, in February 1793. Fox generously forebore from taking advantage of his rival's incapacity,[2] but the situation was hit off in the following lines:

> I cannot see the Speaker, Hal, can you?
> What! Cannot see the Speaker, I see two.

---

[1] "Life of Wilberforce," i, 179, 233, 350, 351; also iii, 212, for the decline of Dundas's influence on Pitt. Omond, "Lord Advocates of Scotland," vol. ii, ch. xiv.

[2] Lord Macaulay told this to Earl Stanhope (author of the "Life of Pitt") at the British Museum in December 1846 (Note of Earl Stanhope in the Chevening MSS.).

A man so frank and intriguing, so subtle and pugnacious as Dundas, is fair game for the satirist; and it is not surprising that the Whig rhymsters who compiled the " Rolliad " scourged the factotum of Caledonia:

> Whose exalted soul
> No bonds of vulgar prejudice control.
> Of shame unconscious in his bold career
> He spurns that honour which the weak revere;
> For, true to public Virtue's patriot plan,
> He loves the *Minister* and not the *Man.*
> Alike the advocate of North and Wit,
> The friend of Shelburne and the guide of Pitt,
> His ready tongue with sophistries at will
> Can say, unsay, and be consistent still.

This is, of course, the effusion of unscrupulous party hacks; but it shows the skill with which the enemies of Dundas seized on the weak points in his career. As a matter of fact, few men have worked harder than the future Viscount Melville, and on few men has fortune at the close pressed more unkindly.

William Wyndham Grenville (1759-1834) is a less interesting man than Dundas. First cousin to Pitt, and born in the same year, he seemed destined to advance hand in hand with him, just as his father had signally helped Chatham in certain parts of that meteoric career. Nature, however, had clearly designed the Grenvilles, both father and son, not to be comets, scarcely planets, but rather satellites. The traditional pride of the Grenvilles (in which Pitt was by no means lacking) appeared in William Grenville, blended with a freezing manner, the effect of which was enhanced by his heavy features and stiff carriage. To counterbalance these defects, he was dowered with an upright and virtuous disposition, great industry, a choice store of classical learning, good sense, though not illuminated by imagination, and oratorical gifts, which, if neither majestic nor pleasing, partook of his native solidity. As Paymaster of the Forces (conjointly with Lord Mulgrave) he did useful work, the higher branches of which involved questions of foreign policy.

Pitt's appreciation of his sound sense appeared in his choice of Grenville for very delicate diplomatic missions to The Hague and Paris in the crisis of 1787. The evenness of his judgement and temper procured him the Speakership of the House of

William Wyndham, Lord Grenville
from a painting by Hoppner

Commons in 1789, after the death of Cornwall. From this honourable post he was soon transferred to more congenial duties, as Secretary of State, and entered the Upper House as Lord Grenville. In 1791 he became Secretary for Foreign Affairs, his conduct of which will engage our attention later on. Here we may note that in all his undertakings he gained a reputation for soundness; and if the neutral tints of his character procured for him neither the enthusiastic love of friends nor the hatred of foes, he won the respect of all. The envious railers who penned the " Rolliad " could fasten on nothing worse than his solidity—

> A youth who boasts no common share of head.
> What plenteous stores of knowledge may contain
> The spacious tenement of Grenville's brain!
> Nature, in all her dispensations wise,
> Who formed his head-piece of so vast a size,
> Hath not, 'tis true, neglected to bestow
> Its due proportion to the part below.

Unfortunately, though Grenville could manage business, he could not manage men; and at this point he failed to make good a defect in the political panoply of Pitt. On neither of the cousins had nature bestowed the social tact which might have smoothed the rubs of diplomatic discussion, say, in those with the French envoy, Chauvelin, in 1792. That fervid royalist, Hyde de Neuville, complained bitterly of the freezing powers of Downing Street. The enthusiastic young Canning found it impossible to work with Grenville, who was also on strained terms with Dundas. The " inner Cabinet," composed of Pitt, Grenville, Dundas, must have been the scene of many triangular duels; and it needed all the mental and moral superiority of Pitt (as to which every one bears witness) to preserve even the appearance of harmony between seconds who were alike opinionated, obstinate, and covetous of patronage.[1] On the whole, the personality of Grenville must rank among the dullest of that age. I have found no striking phrase which glitters amidst the leaden mass of his speeches and correspondence. His life has never been written. He would be a very conscientious zealot who would undertake it.

Turning to the central figure of the group, we have once more

---

[1] " Malmesbury Diaries," iii, 292, 516, 590-2; " Dropmore P.," iii, 167.

to mourn the lack of information about those smaller details which light up traits of character. Few of Pitt's letters refer to his private affairs in the years 1784-86; and the knowledge which we have of them is largely inferential. Even the secondary sources fared badly; for it seems that Pitt's housemaid made a holocaust of the many letters which Wilberforce wrote to him during his foreign tour in 1785.[1] In the Pitt Papers there is only one letter of Wilberforce of this period; and as it throws light on their friendship and the anxiety felt by Pitt's friends at the time of the Irish Propositions, I print it here almost *in extenso*.[2]

Lausanne, 2nd Aug., 1785.

MY DEAR PITT,

. . . If I were to suffer myself to think on politics, I should be very unhappy at the accounts I hear from all quarters: nothing has come from any great authority; but all the reports, such as they are, are of one tendency. I repose myself with confidence on you, being sure that you have spirit enough not to be deterred by difficulties if you can carry your point thro'; and trusting that you will have that greater degree of spirit which is requisite to make a person give up at once when the bad consequences which would follow his going on are at a distance. Yet I cannot help being extremely anxious: your own character, as well as the welfare of the country are at stake; but we may congratulate ourselves that they are here inseparably connected. In the opinion of unprejudiced men I do not think you will suffer from adjourning the Irish propositions *ad calendas Graecas*, if the state of Ireland makes it dangerous to proceed and you can make it evident you had good reason to bring them on, which I think you can. At the worst, the consequences on this side are only that you suffer (the Country may suffer too, but I am taking for granted this is the lesser evil); but I tremble and look forward to what may happen if the Irish Parliament should pass the propositions, and the Irish nation refuse to accept them; nor would it be one struggle only; but as often as any Bill should come over from our House of Commons to be passed in theirs, which was obnoxious, there would be a fresh opportunity for reviving it, especially as you have an Opposition to deal with as unprincipled and mischievous as ever embroiled the affairs of any country. God bless you, my dear Pitt and carry you thro' all your difficulties! You may reckon yourself most fortunate in that chearfulness of mind which enables you every now and then to throw off your load for a few hours and rest yourself. I fancy it must have been this which, when I

---

[1] "Life of Wilberforce," i, 78.　　　　[2] Pitt MSS., 189.

am with you, prevents my considering you as an object of compassion,
tho' Prime Minister of England; for now, when I am at a distance, out
of hearing of your foyning, and your (illegible) other proofs of a light
heart, I cannot help representing you to myself as oppressed with cares
and troubles, and what I feel for you is more, I believe, than even
Pepper feels in the moments of his greatest anxiety; and what can I
say more? . . .

Pepper Arden, to whom Wilberforce here refers, scarcely
lived up to his name. His character and his countenance alike
lacked distinction. The latter suffered from the want of a nose,
or at least, of an effectively imposing feature. What must this
have meant in a generation which remembered the effect produced by Chatham's " terrifying beak," and was dominated by
the long and concave curve on which Pitt suspended the House
of Commons! Further, Pepper lacked dignity. His manner was
noisy and inelegant.[1] He pushed himself forward as a Cambridge friend of Pitt; and the House resented the painful efforts
of this flippant young man to run in harness by the side of the
genius. Members roared with laughter when Arden marched in,
at Christmastide of 1783, to announce that Pitt, as Prime Minister of the Crown, would offer himself for re-election. The
effrontery of the statement was heightened by the voice and
bearing of the speaker. Nevertheless, Pitt, as we have seen,
made him Attorney-General. No appointment called forth more
criticism. He entered the peerage as Lord Alvanley.

It is the characteristic of genius to attract and inspire the
young; and Pitt's influence on them was second only to that of
Chatham. As we shall see later on, Canning caught the first
glow of political enthusiasm from the kindling gaze of the young
Prime Minister. Patriotism so fervid, probity so spotless, eloquence so moving fired cooler natures than Canning's; and
among the most noteworthy of those who now came forward
was Henry Addington. His father, Anthony Addington, had
started life as a medical man in Reading, and afterwards in Bedford Row, London, where Henry was born in 1754. In days
when that profession held a lower place than at present, this
fact was to be thrown in the teeth of the son on becoming Prime
Minister. Chatham, however, always treated his family physician
(for such Addington became) with chivalrous courtesy. Largely

[1] Wraxall, iv, 151.

by the care of the doctor William Pitt was coaxed into maturity after his " wan " youth.[1] It was natural, then, that the sons should become acquainted, especially as young Addington, after passing through Winchester School and Brasenose College, Oxford, entered at Lincoln's Inn while Pitt was still keeping his terms there.

Considering the community of their studies and tastes, it is singular that few, if any, of their letters of this period survive. Such as have come down to us are the veriest scraps. Here, then, as elsewhere, some evil destiny (was it Bishop Tomline ?) must have intervened to blot out the glimpses of the social side of the statesman's life. It is clear, however, that Pitt must have begun to turn Addington's thoughts away from Chancery Lane to Westminster; for the latter in 1783 writes eagerly against "the offensive Coalition of Fox and North." At Christmas, when Pitt leaped to office as Prime Minister, he sought to bring Addington into the political arena, and held out the prospect of some subordinate post. Addington accordingly stood for Devizes, and was chosen by a unanimous vote at the hustings in April 1784. Nevertheless, his cool and circumspect nature rose slowly to the height of the situation at Westminster. Externals were all in his favour. His figure was tall and well proportioned; his features, faultlessly regular, were lit up by a benevolent smile; and his deferential manners gave token of success either as family physician or family attorney. In fine, a man who needed only the spur of ambition, or the stroke of calamity, to achieve a respectable success. It is said that Pitt early bade him fix his gaze on the Speaker's chair, to which, in fact, he helped him in 1789, after Grenville's retirement. But, for the present, nothing stirred Addington's nature from its exasperating calm. As worldly inducements failed, Pitt finally made trial of poetry. During a ride together to Pitt's seat at Holwood, the statesman sought in vain to appeal to his ambition; but Addington—five years his senior, be it remembered—pleaded the disqualifying effects of early habits and disposition. Thereupon Pitt burst out with the following passage from Waller's poem on Henrietta Maria:

> The lark that shuns on lofty boughs to build
> Her humble nest, lies silent in the field;

---

[1] Pellew, "Life of Lord Sidmouth," i, 4.

> But should the promise of a brighter day,
> Aurora smiling, bid her rise and play,
> Quickly she'll show 'twas not for want of voice,
> Or power to climb, she made so low a choice ;
> Singing she mounts ; her airy notes are stretch'd
> Towards heaven, as if from heaven alone her notes she fetch'd.

Then the statesman set spurs to his horse and left Addington far behind.[1] It is curious that when Addington's ambition was fully aroused, it proved to be an obstacle to Pitt and a danger to the country in the crisis of 1803-4.

Adverting now to certain details of Pitt's private life, we notice that he varied the time of his first residence on Putney Heath (August 1784-November 1785) by several visits to Brighthelmstone, perhaps in order to shake off the fatigue and disappointment attendant on his Irish and Reform policy. At that seaside resort he spent some weeks in the early autumn of 1785, enjoying the society of his old Cambridge friends, " Bob " Smith (afterwards Lord Carrington), Pratt (afterwards Lord Camden), and Steele. We can imagine them riding along the quaint little front, or on the downs, their interchange of thought and sallies of wit probably helping in no small degree the invigorating influences of sea air and exercise. If we may trust the sprightly but spiteful lines in one of the " Political Eclogues," it was at Brighton that Pitt at these times especially enjoyed the society of " Tom " Steele, whom he had made Secretary of the Treasury conjointly with George Rose. Unlike his colleague, whose visage always bore signs of the care and toil of his office, Steele was remarkable for the rotundity and joviality of his face and an inexhaustible fund of animal spirits.[2] Perhaps it was this which attracted Pitt to him in times of recreation. The lines above referred to occur in an effusion styled—" Rose, or the Complaint,"—where the hard working colleague is shown as bemoaning Pitt's preference for Steele:

> But vain his hope to shine in Billy's eyes,
> Vain all his votes, his speeches, and his lies.
> Steele's happier claims the boy's regard engage,
> Alike their studies, nor unlike their age :
> With Steele, companion of his vacant hours,
> Oft would he seek Brighthelmstone's sea-girt towers ;

---

[1] Pellew, " Life of Lord Sidmouth," i, 38.	[2] Wraxall, iii, *ad fin.*

For Steele relinquish Beauty's trifling talk,
With Steele each morning ride, each evening walk;
Or in full tea-cups drowning cares of state
On gentler topics urge the mock debate.

However much Pitt enjoyed Steele's company on occasions like these, he did not allow his feelings to influence him when a question of promotion arose. Steele's talents being only moderate, his rise was slow, but he finally became one of the Paymasters of the Forces. In that station his conduct was not wholly satisfactory; and Pitt's friendship towards him cooled, though it was renewed not long before the Prime Minister's death.

For George Rose, on the other hand, despite his lack of joviality, Pitt cherished an ever deepening regard proportioned to the thoroughness and tactfulness of his services at the Treasury. In view of the vast number of applications for places and pensions, of which, moreover, Burke's Economy Bill had lessened the supply, the need of firm control at the Treasury is obvious; and Pitt and the country owed much to the man who for sixteen years held the purse-strings tight.[1] On his part Rose felt unwavering enthusiasm for his chief from the time of their first interview in Paris in 1783 until the dark days that followed Austerlitz. Only on two subjects did he refuse to follow Pitt, namely, on Parliamentary Reform, from which he augured "the most direful consequences," and the Slavery Question. That he ventured twice to differ decidedly from Pitt (in spite of earnest private appeals) proves his independence of mind as well as the narrowness of his outlook. He even offered to resign his post at the Treasury owing to their difference on Reform, but Pitt negatived this proposal. We need not accept his complacent statement that Pitt later on came over decidedly to his opinion on that topic.[2]

The tastes of the two friends were very similar, especially in their love of the country; and it was in the same month (September 1785) that each bought a small estate. We find Pitt writing at that time to Wilberforce respecting his purchase of "Holwood Hill," near Bromley, Kent, and stating that Rose had just bought an estate in the New Forest, which he vowed

[1] I distrust the charges of corrupt dealing brought against Rose respecting the next election at Westminster.
[2] "Diaries of George Rose," i, 32-37.

was "just breakfasting distance from town." "We are all
turning country gentlemen very fast," added the statesman. A
harassing session like that of 1785 is certain to set up a centri-
fugal tendency; and we may be sure that the nearness of
Holwood to Hayes was a further attraction. Not that Pitt was
as yet fond of agriculture. He had neither the time nor the
money to spare for the high farming which was then yearly
adding to the wealth of the nation. But he inherited Chatham's
love of arranging an estate, and he was now to find the delight
of laying out grounds, planting trees and shrubs and watching
their growth. Holwood had many charms—" a most beautiful
spot, wanting nothing but a house fit to live in "—so he described it to Wilberforce.[1] He moved into his new abode on
5th November 1785, and during the rest of the vacation spent
most of his time there, residing at Downing Street only on
Wednesdays, Thursdays, and Fridays. Many affairs of State
were decided at parties at Holwood, or, later on, at Dundas's
villa at Wimbledon.

Pitt admitted to Wilberforce that the purchase of Holwood
was a piece of folly; and this was soon apparent to all Pitt's
friends who had old-fashioned notions of making both ends
meet. That desirable result had rarely, if ever, been attained by
the son of the magnificent Chatham. Sparing for the nation's
exchequer, Pitt was prodigal of his own. The aristocratic
hauteur, of which all but his friends complained, led him to
disregard the peccadilloes of servants and the overcharges of
tradesmen. A bachelor Prime Minister, whose nose is high in
air, is good sport for parasites; and even before the purchase of
Holwood, Pitt was in difficulties. During one of the visits to
Brighthelmstone, "Bob" Smith undertook to overhaul his
affairs, and found old and forgotten bills amounting to £7,914.
The discovery came as a shock; for Pitt, with his usual hopefulness, had told his Mentor that, as three-quarters of his official
salary were due, he would have enough for his current liabilities.
A further scrutiny showed that tradesmen, in default of any
present return, took care to ensure an abundant harvest in the
future. The butcher usually sent, or charged for, three or four
hundredweight of meat on a Saturday, probably because Pitt
was often away for the week-end. The meat bill for January

[1] "Corresp. of Wilberforce," i, 9.

1785, when Pitt generally dined out, was £96, which, reckoning the price at sixpence a pound, implied a delivery of 34 hundred-weight. Other bills for provisions (wrote Smith to Wilberforce) "exceed anything I could have imagined." Apparently they rose in proportion to Pitt's absence from home. His accounts were kept by a man named Wood, whose book-keeping seems to have been correct; but Smith begged Wilberforce to urge on Pitt the need of an immediate reform of his household affairs.[1] Whether it took place, we cannot tell; for this is one of the private subjects over which Bishop Tomline chose to draw the veil of propriety.

An economical householder would have found relief from the addition of £3,000 a year to his income. That was the net sum which accrued to him after August 1792, from the Lord Wardenship of the Cinque Ports.[2] That Pitt felt more easy in his mind is clear from his letter to Lady Chatham, dated Downing Street, 11th November 1793. She had been in temporary embarrassment. He therefore sent £300, and gently chid her for concealing her need so long. He continued as follows: "My accession of income has hitherto found so much employment in the discharge of former arrears as to leave no very large fund which I can with propriety dispose of. This, however, will mend every day, and at all events I trust you will never scruple to tell me when you have the slightest occasion for any aid that I can supply."[3]

Unfortunately, Pitt soon fell into difficulties, and partly from his own generosity as Colonel of the Walmer Volunteers. As we shall also see, he gave £2,000 to the Patriotic Fund started in January 1798. But carelessness continued to be his chief curse. In truth his lordly nature and his early training in the household of Chatham unfitted him for the practice of that bourgeois virtue, frugality. That he sought to practise it for the Commonwealth is a signal proof of his patriotism. We shall see that his embarrassments probably hindered him from a marriage, which might have crowned with joy his somewhat solitary life.

In the career of Pitt we find few incidents of the lighter kind,

---

[1] "Corresp. of Wilberforce," i, 21-4.

[2] The gross income was £4,100: see Mr. E. W. Hamilton's estimate of Pitt's income (the total being £10,532) in App. C of Lord Rosebery's "Pitt."

[3] Pretyman MSS.

which diversify the lives of most statesmen of that age. Two
such, however, connect him with the jovial society of Dundas.
It was their custom to outline over their cups the course of the
forthcoming debates; and on one occasion, when a motion was
to be brought forward by Mr. (afterwards Earl) Grey, Dundas
amused the company by making a burlesque oration on the
Whig side. Pitt was so charmed by the performance that he
declared that Dundas must make the official reply. The joke
sounded well over wine; but great was the Scotsman's astonishment to find himself saddled with the task in the House.
Members were equally taken aback; and the lobbies soon
rustled with eager conjectures as to the reason why Pitt had
surrendered his dearly cherished prerogative. It then transpired
that the Prime Minister had acted partly on a whim, and partly
on the conviction that a speaker who had so cleverly pleaded a
case must be able to answer it with equal effect.[1]

The other incident is likewise Bacchic, and is also uncertain
as to date. Pitt, Dundas, and Thurlow had been dining with
Jenkinson at Croydon; and during their rollicking career back
towards Wimbledon, they found a toll-bar gate between Streatham
and Tooting carelessly left open. Wine, darkness, and the frolic-
some spirit of youth prompted them to ride through and cheat
the keeper. He ran out, called to them in vain, and, taking them
for highwaymen, fired his blunderbuss at their retreating forms.[2]
The discharge was of course as harmless as that of firearms
usually was except at point-blank range; but the writers of the
" Rolliad " got wind of the affair, and satirised Pitt's lawlessness
in the following lines:

> Ah, think what danger on debauch attends!
> Let Pitt o'er wine preach temperance to his friends,
> How, as he wandered darkling o'er the plain,
> His reason drowned in Jenkinson's champagne,
> A rustic's hand, but righteous fate withstood,
> Had shed a premier's for a robber's blood.

Gaiety and grief often tread close on one another's heels; and
Pitt had his full share of the latter. The sudden death of his
sister Harriet, on 25th September 1786, was a severe blow. She
had married his Cambridge friend, Eliot, and expired shortly
after childbirth. She was his favourite sister, having entered
closely and fondly into his early life. He was prostrated with

---

[1] G. Croly, " Mems. of George IV," i, 105, 106.   [2] *Ibid.*, 107.

grief, and for some time could not attend even to the public business which was his second nature. Eliot, now destined to be more than ever a friend and brother, came to his house and for some time lived with him. It will be of interest to print here a new letter of George III to a Mr. Frazer who had informed him of the sad event.

WINDSOR,
Sept. 25, 1786. 9.15 p.m.[1]

I AM excessively hurt, as indeed all my family are, at the death of the amiable Lady Harriot Elliot (*sic*); but I do not the less approve Mr. Frazer's attention in acquainting me of this very melancholy event. I owne I dread the effect it may have on Mr. Pitt's health: I think it best not at this early period to trouble him with my very sincere condolence; but I know I can trust to the prudence of Mr. Frazer, and therefore desire he will take the most proper method of letting Mr. Pitt know what I feel for him, and that I think it kindest at present to be silent.

G. R.

The King further evinced his tactful sympathy by suggesting that Pitt should for a time visit his mother at Burton Pynsent. In other respects his private life was uneventfully happy. The conclusion of the commercial treaty with France, the buoyancy of the national revenue, and the satisfactory issue of the Dutch troubles must have eased his anxieties in the years 1786-87; and after the serious crisis last named, his position was truly enviable, until the acute situation arising from the mental malady of George III overclouded his prospects at the close of the year 1788.

Certainly Pitt was little troubled by his constituents. Almost the only proof of his parliamentary connection with the University of Cambridge (apart from warnings from friends at election times how so and so is to "be got at") is in a letter which I have discovered in the Hardwicke Papers. It refers to a Cambridge Debt Bill about to be introduced by Charles Yorke in April 1787, to which the University had requested Pitt to move certain amendments in its interest. It will be seen that Pitt proposed to treat the request rather lightly:

DEAR YORKE,
    I am rather inclined to wish the Cambridge [Debt] Bill should pass without any alteration, unless you think there are material reasons

[1] Chevening MSS.

for it.—The impanelling the jury does not seem to be a point of much consequence, but seems most naturally to be the province of the mayor. —With regard to the appeal, I think we agreed to strike it out entirely. —As the Commission are a mixed body from the town, the county, and the University, there seems to be an impropriety in appealing either to the town sessions or the County Sessions, either of which may be considered as only one out of three parties interested. The decision of the Commission appears therefore the most satisfactory, and if I recollect right, it is final as the bill now stands.

Yours most sincerely,
W. PITT.[1]

In the whole of Pitt's correspondence I have found only one episode which lights up the recesses of his mind. As a rule, his letters are disappointingly business-like and formal. He wrote as a Prime Minister to supporters, rarely as a friend to a friend. And those who search the hundreds of packets of the Pitt Papers in order to find the real man will be tempted to liken him to that elusive creature which, when pursued, shoots away among the rocks under a protective cloud of ink. At one point, however, we catch a glimpse of his inmost beliefs. Wilberforce, having come under deep religious convictions in the autumn of 1785, resolved to retire for a time from all kinds of activity in order to take his bearings anew. Then he wrote to Pitt a full description of his changed views of life, stating also his conviction that he must give up some forms of work and amusement, and that he could never be so much of a party man as he had hitherto been. Pitt's reply, of 2nd December 1785, has recently seen the light. After stating that any essential opposition between them would cause him grief but must leave his affection quite untouched, he continued as follows:

Forgive me if I cannot help expressing my fear that you are nevertheless deluding yourself into principles which have but too much tendency to counteract your own object and to render your virtues and

---

[1] B.M. Add. MSS., 35684. In May 1790, Pitt drafted a letter to the members of the Senate of the University of Cambridge, asking for the support to his intended candidature for the office of High Steward, then vacant owing to the death of Lord Hardwicke. He expressed the hope that the crisis in public affairs would be deemed a sufficient excuse for not making the application in person. He was elected. The draft of the letter is in the Library of Pembroke College, Cambridge.

your talents useless both to yourself and to mankind. I am not, however, without hopes that my anxiety paints this too strongly. For you
confess that the character of religion is not a gloomy one, and that it is
not that of an enthusiast. But why then this preparation of solitude,
which can hardly avoid tincturing the mind either with melancholy or
superstition? If a Christian may act in the several relations of life,
must he seclude himself from them all to become so? Surely the principles as well as the practice of Christianity are simple, and lead not to
meditation only but to action. I will not, however, enlarge upon these
subjects now. What I ask of you, as a mark both of your friendship
and of the candour which belongs to your mind, is to open yourself
fully and without reserve to one, who, believe me, does not know how
to separate his happiness from your own.[1]

On the morrow, a Saturday, he called on Wilberforce at
Wimbledon, and the friends for two hours unburdened their
hearts to one another. We know little of that moving converse.
The two men had ideals so different that unison was out of the
question. The statesman, so we learn, had never reflected much
on religion, that is, in the keenly introspective sense in which
Wilberforce now used the word. To Pitt, as to most Englishmen, religion meant the acceptance of certain doctrines laid
down by the State Church, and we may describe it as largely
political and conventional, buttressing the existing order, but
by no means transforming life or character. One glance alone
we gain into the sanctuary of his thoughts; he told Wilberforce
that Bishop Butler's "Analogy" raised in his mind more doubts
than it answered—a proof (perhaps the only proof that survives)
of his cherishing under that correct exterior a critical and questioning spirit.

To Wilberforce, thenceforth, all doubts were visitations of the
devil. Indeed, the microscopic watch which he kept on his
thoughts and moods seemed likely to stunt his activities. From
this he was perhaps saved by his friendship with Pitt. True,
they could no longer tread the same path. Pitt obeyed that call
to action on behalf of his country which from his boyhood
had deadened all other sounds. Wilberforce for a long time
held aloof from politics as debateable ground beset with snares
to the soul. And yet, though the two men diverged, the
promptings of affection kept them ever within hail. No gulf

[1] "Private Papers of Wilberforce," 13, 14.

ever opened out such as Coleridge finely pictured as yawning
between two parted friends:

> They stood aloof, the scars remaining,
> Like cliffs which had been rent asunder;
> A dreary sea now flows between.

Indeed, Wilberforce found with some surprise that on most
questions they agreed as before[1]—a proof that there was no
desertion of principle on Pitt's part after the session of 1785.
We may go further, and assert that in their changed relations
the two friends exerted upon each other a mutually beneficent
influence. The new convictions of Wilberforce tended to refine
the activities of his friend; and Pitt's practical good sense
helped to launch the philanthropist on that career of usefulness
in which he could both glorify God and uplift myriads of
negroes.

A sharp difference of opinion respecting the war with France
overclouded their lives in the year 1793. Wilberforce fully
recognized the sincerity of the Cabinet's efforts to avoid a rupture, and admitted that Ministers had not pursued a "war
system." But shortly before the outbreak of hostilities, when
he was about to speak in favour of conciliation, Pitt took
the strange step of sending Bankes to him, earnestly begging
him not to speak, as it might do irreparable mischief, and promising him an opportunity for the statement of his views. That
opportunity did not come; and Wilberforce evidently resented
this attempt to make political capital out of their friendship.[2]
The breach between them did not widen until late in the
year 1794, when Wilberforce deemed it his duty to move an
amendment in favour of peace. Bankes and Duncombe supported it; but it was easily defeated. In the following year the
relations between Pitt and Wilberforce on this question became
so strained as to cause both of them deep distress. Indeed Pitt,
who generally enjoyed profound slumbers, for a time suffered
from insomnia. The only other occasions when sleep fled from
him were the sudden resignation of Earl Temple late in 1783,
the mutiny at the Nore, and the arrival of the news of
Trafalgar.

The old feelings began to reassert themselves, when Pitt

---

[1] "Life of Wilberforce," i, 113.   [2] *Ibid.*, ii, 10-13.

spoke strongly in favour of the Abolition of the Slave Trade
(26th February 1795); but the friends did not meet for nearly
a month, and then with some little embarrassment on both sides.
All shadows, however, vanished in a few months' time, when
Wilberforce came to see that his friend longed for peace so soon
as it was compatible with security. Thereafter their old friendship revived, though tinged with the sadness attending disappointed hopes.

Pitt did not so readily forget the independence now and
again displayed by Bankes, for instance, in opposing Parliamentary Reform, the Westminster Scrutiny, and the continuance
of the war. Though they were friendly at Cambridge, and
afterwards at Goostree's Club and in the House, Pitt never
warmed to Bankes, whose nature indeed was too precise, cold,
and prudent ever to call forth affection. Respected by all for
his sound but stolid speeches, he for forty years sat at Westminster as member for Corfe Castle. No one seems ever to have
thought of making Bankes either a Minister or a peer. At a
later time the circle of Pitt's friends included Canning and
Wellesley, who will receive notice in later chapters.

On the whole, Pitt seems to have been somewhat exacting in
his friendships. One of his early comrades complained that all
suggestions to the Prime Minister must, under pain of his resentment, go forth to the world as emanations of his wisdom.
This is to sacrifice friendliness and candour to egotism and parliamentary punctilio. True, no statesman can afford to neglect
prudential considerations; and we may freely grant that the
cautious calculations of Pitt rarely obsessed his whole being, as
that of Napoleon was dominated by his egotism. We do not
find Pitt acting, still less speaking, in the sense which prompted
the remark of Napoleon about an over scrupulous servant: " He
is not devoted to me; he does not want to get on."

It must be confessed that there is something wanting about
Pitt. He lacked geniality and glow alike in his treatment of
men, and in his attitude towards the aspirations of the age then
dawning. Probably this defect sprang from a physical basis. It
must be remembered that Chatham was nearly all his life a
martyr to gout. He bequeathed this weakness to his second son,
a fact which may account for the coldness of Pitt's nature. Just
as creatures with a torpid circulation love to bask in the sun, so
his chilliness may have prompted the cravings for the Bacchic

society of Dundas and Steele. In this respect he suffers by comparison with Fox, the full-blooded man, the impetuous foe, the open-handed, forgiving friend, whose character somewhat resembles that of Antony, deified by Cleopatra:

> For his bounty,
> There was no winter in 't; an autumn 'twas
> That grew the more by reaping; his delights
> Were dolphin-like; they showed his back above
> The element they lived in.[1]

[1] "Antony and Cleopatra," v, sc. 2.

CHAPTER XIII

ISOLATION

(1784, 1785)

The situation of Europe appears never to have been so critical at any epoch since the breaking out of the Thirty Years' War as it is at the present moment.—SIR JAMES HARRIS, 2nd *February* 1785.

THE American War of Independence left Great Britain in a critical situation both internally and in relation to other Powers. She had been at war with France, Spain, the Dutch Netherlands, and the United States, while the Baltic Powers threatened her with hostilities owing to her insistence on an exacting maritime code. As she refused to come to a compromise on these questions, the period of peace which followed after the Treaty of Versailles (September 1783) did not lead to a resumption of friendly relations with the States above named. She was in part hated, in part despised.

The prevalent feeling found striking expression in an intercepted letter of Frederick the Great, which our able ambassador, Sir James Harris, saw at St. Petersburg. The crabbed monarch therein described Great Britain as a land ruined by an unfortunate war, and unable ever again to become a formidable rival to France. Here the wish was father to the thought. "Old sourmug," as the Berliners dubbed him, had not forgiven his desertion by England at the close of the Seven Years' War, and never missed an opportunity of affronting George III and damaging his interests. It was he who, in the years 1778 and 1779, thwarted Harris's plan of effecting an Anglo-Russian alliance, which might have nullified the efforts of France in the American War; and now, at the end of that struggle, the resentful old King did his best to perpetuate the isolation of the Island Power. In name, he was our ally, the treaty of 1756 never

having been broken; but in reality he was the wiliest of
opponents, his fleeting fits of complaisance being designed to
make bad blood between England and the Emperor Joseph II.[1]

The ceaseless rivalry of Austria and Prussia would generally
have enabled Great Britain to count on the support of one of
those Powers. But while Frederick flouted us from senile
spleen, Joseph held aloof from motives of policy. Not only did
he hold England cheap, but he saw in her an obstacle to
one of his many schemes. As he was then one of the most
active of European rulers, we may well begin our survey of
foreign affairs by a short account of him and of his aims.

Joseph II (1780-1790) held the extensive lands of the House
of Hapsburg-Lorraine, ranging from the Milanese to Cracow,
and from the Carpathians to the Breisgau on the Upper Rhine;
but these States, especially those in Italy and Swabia, lacked
the strength that comes from continuity. His position as
" Emperor " (that is, elective head of the Holy Roman Empire)
implied little; for the confederate princes of that moribund
organism had almost complete sovereign powers in the component States. To breathe new life into "the Empire" was
almost hopeless; but he set himself to solidify and extend his
hereditary dominions by a series of attractively perilous projects.
He also sought to centralize at Vienna the governing powers of
his very diverse domains, and to carry out reforms, social,
agrarian, and religious, which aroused widespread opposition.
Many of his schemes were generous and enlightened, but they
stirred the resentment of landowners, priests, and Nationalists,
especially in Hungary and in his Belgic Provinces. In order to
carry out these programmes, he sought or maintained alliances
with the most powerful States, namely, Russia and France.

Here we are concerned chiefly with his connection with the
latter Power. Despite temporary causes of friction, the Franco-
Austrian alliance of 1756 still subsisted; and it had gained new
vitality by the marriage of Louis XVI (then Dauphin) with
Marie Antoinette, a daughter of Maria Theresa and sister of
Joseph II, whose efforts on behalf of Viennese policy were to

---

[1] "Malmesbury Diaries," ii, 24-26, 49, 55. The character and career of
Sir James Harris (the future Earl of Malmesbury) will concern us later.
Herr F. K. Wittichen, " Preussen und England in der Europäischen Politik—
1785-1788," *ad init.*, condemns the resentment of Frederick the Great as a
mistake, fatal to the interests both of Prussia and England.

effect something for that Court, at the expense of her popularity at Paris. Thus, early in the year 1785, when Joseph II revived a scheme, which had been thwarted in 1778, for the exchange of his discontented Belgic lands for the Electorate of Bavaria, all Europe saw in it the hand of Marie Antoinette. The absorption of Bavaria would have made the Hapsburgs absolutely supreme in Central Europe, while the transfer of the Bavarian Electoral House to Brussels would have broken down the Barrier arrangements which British statecraft had ever sought to build up on the North of France. The Treaty of Utrecht (1713) had assigned the then Spanish Netherlands to the House of Austria in order to set limits to the expansion of France; and the transfer could not be made without the consent of the signatory Powers, the chief being England.

In other respects, too, Joseph's Belgian policy ran counter to British interests. He had ordered the Dutch troops out of the fortresses (Mons, Namur, etc.), which, by the Barrier Treaty of 1715, they had the right to occupy at [the expense of those districts; and he further set at naught well-established rights of the Dutch, first by furbishing up certain musty claims to their frontier stronghold, Maestricht; and secondly, by declaring the navigation of the estuary of the Scheldt, below Antwerp, free from Dutch control. In the latter demand he undoubtedly had "natural law" on his side, while the law of nations was as clearly for the Dutch, the Treaty of Münster (1648) having empowered them to close that estuary to all commerce but their own. As a result the once flourishing trade of Antwerp was wellnigh strangled, and it was reasonable for Joseph II to seek to end this state of things. Nevertheless, his conduct in setting aside that treaty-right without consulting other Powers, was no less indefensible than the same action of the French Revolutionists in the autumn of 1792, which largely brought about the Great War. In fact, the conduct of Joseph II towards his own subjects and neighbouring States fitly earned him the designation, the "crowned revolutionist"; and, had his power of carrying out schemes equalled his facility in weaving them, he might have figured in history as a Teutonic Napoleon.

Equally disturbing and more incisive was the influence of Catharine II of Russia. It is needless to describe here the strange career of that daughter of a poor German prince who ultimately became Czarina. She was justly suspected of having connived at the murder of her consort Peter III; and her relations with her son, the future Paul I, were severely strained by her numerous amours. But no indulgences dulled the vision or the ambition of Catharine. Her freshness of mind and facility of expression dazzled her philosophic visitors, Diderot and Grimm; and these varied powers were held in leash by a virile will which made her one of the greatest political forces of the age. Her resolve to aggrandize Russia centred in two great enterprises, the partition of Poland and the overthrow of the Turkish Power. In the first partition of Poland (1772) she had the concurrence of Frederick the Great and the reluctant consent of Maria Theresa; but the death of the latter, in November 1780, removed all checks on Joseph II, who for fifteen years had been associated with her in the government of the Austrian States.

The two most daring rulers in Europe in the year 1781 came to an understanding which foreboded a general upheaval. Their arrangement did not take the form of a treaty, for Joseph, as Emperor, claimed precedence in all titles, which Catharine, proud of the comparatively new Imperial title of the Czars of Muscovy, refused to recognize. Accordingly, in May 1781, the punctilious sovereigns exchanged letters, binding themselves to mutual support; Joseph undertaking to assist the Czarina in her designs against the Turks, while she guaranteed to Joseph the integrity of his dominions, thus enabling him to adopt the forward policy whose developments in the Netherlands we have noticed.

In vain did Frederick the Great and England seek, though by widely diverse means, to dissolve this alliance. Capricious and violent in private life and in her likes and dislikes, Catharine showed statesmanlike firmness and caution in public affairs. Her firmness appeared in her refusal to take the tempting bait of Minorca which our ambassador Harris skilfully held out to her in 1780, if she would mediate in favour of England in the American War. She rightly saw more profit in heading the Armed Neutrality League; and Harris used all his arts in vain.[1] Her caution shines in her charming repartee to Diderot after the French philosopher had vivaciously sketched his plan of reno-

---

[1] " Malmesbury Diaries," i, 374, 402, 532. He thought her hasty, and swayed by passion or caprice; but events proved that she did not lack foresight or firmness.

vating Russia. "M. Diderot, you forget in all your plans of reform the difference in our positions; you only work on paper, which endures all things; it opposes no obstacle either to your imagination or to your pen. But I, poor Empress that I am, work on a sensitive and irritable medium, the human skin." In these phrases lies the secret of the success of Catharine and of the ultimate failure of Joseph. He forgot that the sentient skin is not parchment: she never forgot it.

For the present, their alliance promised to make them the arbiters of Europe, Catharine in the East, and her ally in the centre and the Netherlands. It was therefore desirable for Great Britain to gain their alliance, or at least their friendship. But our overtures were repulsed at both Courts. In vain did Sir Murray Keith, our respected envoy at Vienna, seek to undermine the unnatural alliance between France and Austria, and suggest a return to the traditional connection between the Courts of St. James and Vienna; the Francophile policy of the Austrian Chancellor, Kaunitz, was still in the ascendant.

In vain also did Alleyne Fitzherbert, now the British Ambassador at St. Petersburg, remind Catharine II of the many interests, trading and political, we had in common, and of the help we had given to the infant navy of Russia in officers and men, and in granting facilities for its repair at Portsmouth and Port Mahon.[1] With her, past services weighed but lightly as against present expediency. The assurances of the previous decade as to the natural links between England and Russia were ridiculed, probably because her keen eyes discerned, sooner than those of any British statesman, the eventual opposition of England to her scheme of seizing Constantinople. As a prelude to this enterprise she annexed the Crimea in the year 1783; and, as we shall see later, she thenceforth bent all her energies to the task of enthroning at Constantinople her grandson, Constantine. The alliance of Austria being essential, and the union of the Hapsburgs with France being but little impaired by Joseph's Belgic plans (at least up to the end of 1784), she courted Paris and slighted London. A proposal which Fitzherbert made at St. Petersburg in April 1784, for an alliance with Russia, Sweden, and Denmark, fell to the ground.[2]

Thus, the trend of European politics in the East, in Ger-

---

[1] Mahan, "Influence of Sea Power," i, 11.   [2] Martens, iii, 327.

many, and in the Netherlands told heavily against England, and increased the natural reluctance of any Power to seek the friendship of a beaten nation. It is at such times that the artificiality of the idea of the Balance of Power is seen. No State took the slightest interest in restoring the islanders to their rightful position in the world. For this they had to trust to themselves and to their young leader.

In point of fact, Pitt and his Foreign Secretary, the Marquis of Carmarthen, at first desired little more than to be left alone. Peace is always the greatest of British interests, and it was so pre-eminently at that time, when the interest on the National Debt absorbed three-fourths of the nation's revenue. Foreign Affairs interested the Cabinet but little, so we gather from the memoranda of the Marquis of Carmarthen (afterwards Duke of Leeds); but he there states that Pitt applied himself closely to the correspondence with ambassadors, and that, in a conversation which they had together at Wimbledon in May 1784, he found that they agreed as to the desirability of severing the connection of Austria with France, and of forming some alliance which would counterbalance the power of the French and Spanish Houses of Bourbon; but at the same time Pitt was strongly convinced of the need of avoiding any engagements which might lead to war.[1] That George III had lost his bellicose temper appears from the closing sentence of his letter of 6th July 1784 to Carmarthen: "Till I see this country in a situation more respectable as to Army, Navy, and Finances, I cannot think anything that may draw us into troubled waters either safe or rational."[2]

This sensible pronouncement was called forth by the proposal of Pitt and Carmarthen to make another overture to the Empress Catharine. An opportunity occurred owing to a recent compact between France and Sweden, according to the former a naval depôt and other special privileges at the port of Gothenburg. As this might enable French warships to control the mouth of the Baltic, it threatened the interests of England, Denmark, and Russia; and the British Cabinet, always intent on regaining the favour of the Czarina, began to sound the situation at St. Petersburg and Copenhagen. Carmarthen sought

---

[1] " Leeds Memoranda " (edited by Mr. Oscar Browning), 101.

[2] B.M. Add. MSS., 27914. This letter and other documents of interest will appear in my volume " Pitt and Napoleon Miscellanies."

the advice of Sir James Harris, and received the following witty reply:

Cuffnalls, Oct. 6, 1784.[1]

Should the Northern Lights be really enlightened, and a spark of common sense be added to Kitty's bright understanding I hope my friend Fitz[herbert] will accomplish the point we have all failed in. I cannot but suppose that the Ch[ancellor] and Lord C. will defer to your opinion, and that your next messenger will carry positive and particular instructions both to Hamlet and Semiramis.

"Semiramis" (Catharine) proved to be no less obdurate to Fitzherbert than to Harris, though the instructions issued to the former had been drawn up in a masterly manner by Pitt himself. It is clear that the young statesman took a keen interest in the overture to Russia; for when Carmarthen sent him a draft of his "Instructions for Mr. Fitzherbert," he sent the hitherto unpublished replies, which throw an interesting light on his relations to that Minister, and his views on foreign policy:

BRIGHTHELMSTONE, Wed^y night. *Oct.* 13, 1784.[2]

MY DEAR LORD,

I return you with many thanks the draft of the Instructions to Mr. Fitzherbert. I trouble you at the same time, as you permitted me, with the sketch of the Ideas which had occurred to me on the same subject. I have the satisfaction to perceive, as I flattered myself must be the case, that our Ideas do not seem to differ in any respect. I hardly need give you the trouble of reading my scrawl. I leave it however to your consideration, tho' hardly thinking anything in it will repay the time of perusing it. You will, I am sure, excuse a proof at least of my solicitude on a subject on which we feel equally interested.

That Carmarthen set a high value on the "scrawl," appears from the fact that it bears the pencil-mark, "sent to Russia the 15th." As it was probably the first diplomatic note ever penned by Pitt, it deserves to be quoted in full, especially as it proves that he was no advocate of isolation. He saw too well the dangers of it. Further, those who take pleasure in contrasting his orderly and forcible statement of ideas with a loose and feeble

---

[1] B.M. Add. MSS., 28060. "Lord C." may be Lord Clarendon, who had previously given advice to Lord Carmarthen.

[2] *Ibid.*

statement may consult the draft of Carmarthen, which that
Minister had the good sense to replace by Pitt's: [1]

It is His Majesty's earnest desire to regulate his conduct on the occasion of the late Treaty between France and Sweden, in the strictest
concert with the Court of Petersburg. And therefore, altho' it would
have been a great satisfaction to have known first what line appeared
to the Empress most proper to be pursued, we have no difficulty in
stating without reserve what the situation appears to us to call for. We
wish at the same time to know whether any other specifick measures
have been thought of by the Empress, and we are ready in every respect
to enter into the fullest and most confidential communication.

We are not aware of any treaty or of any other ground, which gives a
direct and absolute right to object to any arrangement which the King
of Sweden may have thought proper to make in this instance with
regard to a Port of his own dominions; altho' the possibility of its
being carried to the extent which there is reason to suspect is ultimately
intended cannot but occasion great jealousy, and altho' even in a commercial light, it may possibly not be a matter of indifference. The
difficulty of making a direct opposition in the first instance seems, by
Mr. Fitzherbert's report, to have struck the Ministers of the Empress in
the same manner. On this supposition, the only immediate step which
it appears natural to take is to desire from the Court of Stockholm an
explanation to what extent the privileges granted to the French are *bonâ
fide* intended to be carried. A representation to this purpose should,
we think, be made jointly in the names of the Courts of London,
Petersburg, and Copenhagen, if the latter Court should be disposed (as
we trust will be the case) to co-operate on this occasion. This may
produce such an explanation from Sweden as may furnish a strong
additional ground for interference hereafter to prevent the dangerous
designs of France, if she should be inclined to avail herself of the
privileges she has now acquired to carry them into execution. If the
answer should not be explicit and satisfactory, further measures should
be concerted to guard against the effects to be apprehended. Indeed,
whatever colour may be given to the transaction, it would not seem
wise to trust implicitly to assurances and explanations. In every light,
therefore, the only substantial security would be in an establishment of
that permanent and solid connection between this country and Russia

---

[1] B.M. Add. MSS., 28060. It is endorsed, in Pitt's hand: "Oct. 12, 1784,
Mem[m] for Instructions to Mr. Fitzherbert." Carmarthen's draft is almost
certainly that which is printed by Mr. Oscar Browning in the "Leeds
Memoranda," p. 103 *n.*; but the evidence here given shows that that draft
cannot be Pitt's, as Mr. Browning at that time (1884) naturally inferred.

and Denmark, which their common interests render on all accounts most desireable. Without such a system, [the] consequences of this attempt cannot be effectually obviated, direct opposition to it seeming hardly practicable; and desultory and unconnected efforts which terminate in one single and separate point (even if the occasion admitted of their being exerted to the utmost) promising comparatively but little effect. Explanations and assurances, however explicit, unless such measures are taken to enforce an adherence to them, will be but a feeble and precarious barrier against the encroaching spirit which has dictated this project. Even if this particular measure should be defeated, the same spirit (unless effectual and systematic steps are taken to counteract it) will show itself in other shapes and on innumerable occasions. This object therefore of an alliance between the three Courts seems to be the only measure, under the present circumstances, which promises effectual support to their common interests and to the general tranquillity of Europe. And there seems no reason to imagine that there can be any obstacle in the way of its completion, which a cordial and mutual inclination, and a free and open discussion will not easily remove.

All was in vain. There was more method in Catharine II's waywardness than Harris understood. Her aim being the preparation of a great fleet at Sevastopol with a view to the conquest of Turkey, she needed, as we have seen, the co-operation of Austria; but that implied friendship with France, and therefore coolness to England.[1] These motives long continued to govern the policy of the Empress, and prevented the formation of any good understanding with her.

As for the Emperor, Joseph II, there was small hope of an alliance with him. The emergence, early in 1785, of his pet scheme of a Belgic-Bavarian exchange was a palpable threat to the old Germanic System, of which George III, as Elector of Hanover, was a pillar; and he knew right well that the Court of St. James would steadfastly oppose the weakening of the Barrier in Flanders which must ensue from so violent a change. Sir James Harris summed up the opinion of our statesmen when he said that that Barrier against the encroachments of France had " ever been deemed essential to the interests of Europe in general

---

[1] This is well set forth in the despatches of Lord Dalrymple, British Ambassador at Berlin, to Carmarthen. The latter wrote to Harris on 24th February 1786, that Vorontzoff would try to persuade Catharine II to restore the " good system," and to induce Joseph II to help in the work; but nothing came of it (B.M. Add. MSS., 28061).

and to those of England in particular; but it is destroyed the
moment the Low Countries either belong to France directly, or
are governed by a sovereign devoted to her influence." [1]

We here touch upon a question which, after being the fruitful
cause of wars from the time of the Plantagenets, was soon to involve Great Britain in the struggle with Revolutionary France,
and yet again with Napoleon. The effort to prevent France acquiring complete control over the Netherlands was to be the
chief work of William Pitt—a career far other than that which
he had marked out for himself, and into which, as we shall see,
he was drawn most reluctantly. The struggle presents three well-
marked phases: the first concerns chiefly the disputes between
the Stadholder of the United Provinces and the Patriots, abetted
by France, which finally resulted in a complete triumph for the
former, thanks to the action of Prussia and England and the
formation of the Triple Alliance of 1788. In the second period
Revolutionary France, with the help of the Patriots, over-
ran those provinces, and set up the Batavian or Dutch Republic. The uneasy Peace of Amiens ended in 1803, largely
because Bonaparte insisted on treating that Republic as a
dependency of France; and Pitt's life closed in the midst of
the world-strife that ensued. But the Treaties of Vienna carried
out (what Napoleon never would have agreed to [2]) the erection
of a seemingly solid Barrier against France, the Kingdom of the
United Netherlands.

These mighty convulsions arose very largely from a contention as to the fate of the Netherlands. The importance of
States depends not so much on their size as on their situation;
and the Dutch and Belgic Netherlands, forming the fringes
of the French and Teutonic peoples, derive great importance
from that circumstance, or perhaps even more from their oc-
cupying the coast-line beside the mouths of the Rhine, Meuse,
and Scheldt, which contains fine harbours and is peopled by
an enterprising and industrious folk. The conduct of a British
Government with respect to those lands is, so to speak, a
barometric test of its skill and energy. None but the weakest

---

[1] "Malmesbury Diaries," ii, 104. Memorandum of 2nd February 1785.
[2] Even after the disasters of 1813 Napoleon wrote: "Holland is a French
country and will remain so for ever" ("Lettres inédites," 6th November
1813).

I   X

and most craven of Administrations has ever allowed a great hostile Power to dominate the mouths of those rivers. It was no idle boast of Napoleon that at his great naval port of Antwerp he held a pistol at the head of England. Doubly true would that vaunt be of a Great Power which held Rotterdam and Amsterdam. In a description of the struggle with France in 1785-7 for supremacy in the Dutch Netherlands, we are concerned with the prelude of what was to be a mighty trilogy of war.

The fatuity of Lord North's Administration was nowhere more glaringly shown than in the high-handed proceedings at sea which embroiled us with the United Provinces, but it should be remembered that three provinces out of the seven strongly objected to go to war. Accordingly, that ill-knit confederacy conducted the war without vigour; and, after Dutch commerce had suffered severely, it concluded peace with Great Britain in 1783, ceding the station of Negapatam in India. Resentment against England was blended with indignation against the Anglophile Stadholder, William V, who was accused of having paralysed the efforts of his country. He was even reported by the Patriots or democrats to have expressed the hope, after the Dutch success at the Dogger Bank, that the English fleet had not suffered much. These and other silly tales acquired some credibility from the fact that he was the son of the Princess Anne, daughter of George II, who had imbued him with a love of her country. As his guardian and instructor in statecraft was Duke Lewis of Brunswick, whose intermeddling finally hastened his departure from the country, the popular movement for the lessening of the Stadholder's powers acquired strength from the hatred of foreigners and foreign ways always so strong in that home-loving folk. These, then, were the circumstances which brought the disputes between the Patriots and the Orange party to a crisis in the years 1785-7, and threatened to plunge Europe into a great war. The immediate causes were petty and local. The possible results were of world-wide importance.

The functions of the hereditary Stadholder had undergone several changes according to the exigencies of the times. In the long struggle with Spain, as later with Louis XIV, the Dutch had wisely entrusted to the Princes of Orange the chief executive powers, only to go back to strictly republican and federal customs when the crisis was past. The same expedient held good during the invasion of the Maréchal de Saxe in 1746-7, and with a similar sequel. Thus, to the House of Orange the Dutch looked for a Cincinnatus in times of stress, but expected him afterwards to go back to his tulips. The advantage of such an arrangement is obvious, provided that the populace is fully agreed as to the time of summoning Cincinnatus and the time of dismissal; also that that illustrious House could ever furnish a supply of men doughty in war and submissive in peace.

But here lay the difficulty: that the Princes and their supporters objected to arrangements which implied phenomenal powers of activity and hibernation. A demand arose that the Republic should so far centralize its governing powers as to be ready against emergencies; and in 1747 the United Provinces adopted a constitution whereby the Stadholderate became a perpetual office, hereditary in the House of Orange. It was confirmed by all the provinces in 1766; and until recently no one had disputed the right of the Prince to command the armed forces, both military and naval, and to exercise a large amount of control over the executive functions of the provinces. He shared these last with the States General, representing all the provinces, and with the States of the several provinces. Nevertheless, these bodies, together with their Grand Pensionaries, Greffiers, and the Regents (or chief magistrates) of towns, looked jealously on his prerogatives and sharply resented any change tending to unify and centralize the forces of the nation.[1]

In truth, the task of holding together the United Provinces was like that of grasping oiled billiard balls. They were, in effect, independent States, having power to decide on peace and war, make treaties and raise loans. Differing in their constitutions, they also stood in different relations to the Stadholderate. The duties of the States General were to uphold the Union framed at Utrecht in 1579, and, as far as possible, to supervise foreign policy and national defence, the executive side of these functions falling to the Stadholder and a Council of State. But ratifica-

---

[1] See Colenbrander, "De Patriottentijd," i, 415, for the Prince's difficulty in forming (February 1784) a permanent force of 8,000 sailors subject to the Council of War and not to the provincial Estates; also "A View of the Policy . . . of the United Provinces" (Dublin, 1787). As Grenville wrote to Pitt from The Hague on 31st July 1787, that the Dutch understood their Constitution very imperfectly ("Dropmore P.," iii, 410), I may be pardoned for not seeking to unravel it here.

tion by the States of the several provinces, or at least by a majority of them, was needful to give validity to all such decisions and actions. When we further learn that the Regencies of the chief towns had the right of ratifying the decisions of the States of their provinces, we can understand the magnitude of the task which confronted the Stadholders and Marlborough in defending those clannish communities.

The alleged treachery of the Stadholder during the late war with England, together with resentment at his centralizing efforts, had now roused these local instincts to a state of fury, which William V seemed unable either to quell or to calm. In truth, that hapless ruler was irresolution personified. His *rôle* was always one of passivity. Rarely did he show a spark of spirit or turn the tables on his opponents, though he might easily have thrown on them the responsibility for the misfortunes of the war, of which they, not he, were the cause.[1] Compared with him, that other political nullity, Louis XVI, seemed a man of firmness and energy. Strange to say, the lottery of marriage had given to each of them an active and capable consort. In her smaller sphere, Wilhelmina, Princess of Orange, played a part not unlike that of Marie Antoinette. She was niece of Frederick the Great and shared in the strong qualities that are rarely eclipsed in the House of Hohenzollern; but for the present she was doomed idly to chafe at the humiliating restrictions of her lot. The lynx eyes of Sir James Harris soon detected her real feelings for her husband, which, though curbed by wifely duty, now and again broke forth. In the as yet unpublished letters of Harris to the Marquis of Carmarthen are sharp comments on the dullness and torpor of the Prince. These piquant words describe the relations of that ill-matched pair: " He is so jealous of her sense and power that he would not even go to Paradise by her influence; and she has so mean an opinion of his capacity, and, in general, that kind of contempt a high-spirited woman feels for an inferior male being, that I see no hopes of bringing them to that degree of cohesion so highly necessary for the completion of my future plans." [2]

The man who wrote these words had already seen much of

---

[1] " Malmesbury Diaries," ii, 92-4, 222-4.

[2] B.M. Add. MSS., 28060, Letter of 23rd August 1785. These " private " letters are often more interesting and important than those printed in the " Malmesbury Diaries," which form but a small portion of the whole.

men and affairs. Born at Salisbury in 1746, Harris was educated at Oxford, where his acquaintance with Fox instilled into him Whig principles. After completing his studies at Leyden, he entered the diplomatic service, served with distinction at Madrid and Berlin, and acted as ambassador at Petersburg in the years 1777-82, spending there, so it is said, £20,000 of his private fortune, in his country's service. Returning to England, he entered Parliament as member for Christchurch, and warmly supported Fox. His handsome presence and lively conversation won him high favour at Carlton House, and afterwards, probably at the suggestion of Pitt, he gave good advice to the Prince of Wales. A leader in society, as in the diplomatic world, the brilliant Harris was courted on all sides; but popularity did not dull his love for his wife; and the strong expressions of friendship which occur in the correspondence between him and Carmarthen show that these versatile and witty men (the latter wrote a comedy which earned the praise of Warton) had a deep fund of staunchness and fidelity. Their affection had some political results. The first article in the political creed of Sir James Harris was hatred of France; and the intervention of Pitt in the affairs of the Foreign Office may be ascribed to his perception of the Gallophobe bias which the vehement and persuasive Harris imparted to the policy of Carmarthen.

Such was the envoy who at the close of the year 1784 proceeded to The Hague, to uphold the cause of the Stadholder and England against the Patriots and France. The outlook seemed of the gloomiest. "There is not, I fear" (so he wrote on 7th December), "the most distant prospect of reclaiming this country." And again, on 11th March 1785: "We have nothing to expect from this country. Passive, tame, and void of every public virtue, they [the Orange party] will submit to everything. The Prince now talks of going away, of selling his demesnes in these provinces and retiring to Germany—a resolution which, if ever he carries it into execution, will compleat his character."[1] As for the refusal of Frederick the Great to help his niece Wilhelmina, it cut the chivalrous Harris to the quick. His private letters to Carmarthen breathe hatred against France, but contempt of Prussia. When Frederick coolly advised her to disarm the Patriots by coming to terms with France, the impetuous Harris

---

[1] B.M. Add. MSS., 28060.

burst forth: "The knot must be cut, not untied, and the King of Prussia's half measures rejected."[1] Admiration for that unfortunate princess added vehemence to his language. He found her far more frank and genuine than Catharine of Russia, needing very little of the flattery which he vainly lavished on "Semiramis." He succeeded in persuading the Princess to trust England rather than Prussia; and it is clear that he worked for a compact between Great Britain, Austria, and the Netherlands, with the inclusion of Russia and Denmark if possible. But at times, in hearing of the indignities that she daily had to bear at The Hague, he forgot mere questions of policy. "Now and then" (he wrote on 9th September 1785) "my thoughts get worldly, and I think of flesh and blood when I see a pair of fine eyes with the tears starting from them, but I soon suppress this idea."[2] Perhaps it was well that the Prince and Princess left The Hague and went to reside at Nymeguen, in faithful Guelderland, near the Prussian Duchy of Cleves.

As Pitt looked away from the turmoil at Westminster (it was the year of the Reform Bill and the Irish Propositions) he might well feel dismay at the almost indescribable welter on the Continent. On all sides the old order was breaking up. Two mighty Empires took the lead in disruptive schemes which menaced the smaller States with ruin. Intellectual keenness and military force helped on the coming cataclysm. Catharine and Joseph were by far the ablest rulers of their age. Frederick, a prey to moroseness, was content to wait for favours from Versailles which were never forthcoming. France as yet showed few signs of that weakness which was soon to overtake her. True, Louis XVI was a nonentity; but in Marie Antoinette the Austro-French alliance had its corner stone. Moreover, the French Foreign Minister, Vergennes, was a man of outstanding talents. His hostility to England had been notorious; and even now he was reviving the French East India Company, and was pressing the Sultan for trading facilities in Egypt and the Red Sea, which threatened our ascendancy in India.[3] To complete this brief survey, we may note that England had disputes with Spain concerning the rights of British merchants on the Mosquito Coast

---

[1] B.M. Add. MSS., 28060.   [2] *Ibid.*
[3] See the conversation of Joseph II with Sir R. M. Keith at Vienna in December 1785, on French designs on Egypt, as given in chap. xxi, *ad init.*

of Central America; [1] and the ill humour of the Court of Madrid lent some credit to persistent rumours of the formation of a Quadruple Alliance between Russia, Austria, France, and Spain, for the overthrow of England.

Having gained some knowledge of the chief players in the great game that was now opening, and of the vast issues at stake, we return to notice its varying fortunes, especially as they concerned Pitt. It should be remembered that, while the Marquis of Carmarthen wrote the despatches, the spirit which informed them was that of the Prime Minister. Carmarthen had ability, but it trickled off towards lampoons and plays. In *la haute politique* he never had very deep interest; but it is clear that Pitt soon found in it the fascination which has enthralled many a master mind.

As we have already seen, Joseph II early in 1785 led the way in two very threatening moves, namely, the proposal for the Belgic-Bavarian Exchange and the demand that the Dutch should cede to him Maestricht and throw open the navigation of the Scheldt estuary below Antwerp. It was characteristic of him that he should press both these disturbing claims in the same year, a fact which reveals his confidence in his alliances with Russia and France, and his contempt for the isolated Powers, Prussia, Holland, and Great Britain. In these two matters he used his allies as passive tools for the furtherance of his own ends; and this explains the concluding sentences of Harris's letter to Carmarthen quoted in part above: "The Emperor dupes Russia: France makes a fool of Prussia. In two words this seems to be the state of Europe. I wish England could take advantage of this singular position of affairs." [2]

Pitt and his colleagues were by no means so absorbed in managing the House of Commons as Harris hinted in his letter of four days later to Joseph Ewart at Berlin. The despatches of this able official, Secretary of the British Legation at the Prussian capital, had already warned them of their danger, and pointed to an alliance with Prussia as the only way of escape. The once Prussophobe Harris admitted to Ewart the force of these arguments; [3] and, as Hertzberg, one of the Prussian Secretaries of State for Foreign Affairs, favoured an English connec-

---

[1] Salomon, "Pitt," 309, 310; also Martens, iv, 133-9, for the treaty closing this dispute.

[2] B.M. Add. MSS., 28060.   [3] "Malmesbury Mems.," ii, 113-21.

tion, there was some hope that the long feud between Frederick the Great and George III would die a natural death. During a visit to London in May, Harris drew up convincing arguments in favour of a Prussian alliance, and the King suggested that he should go to Berlin to arrange matters.[1]

Unfortunately the martinet of Sans Souci was as unbending as ever. He would not hear of entering into a general alliance with England, either because he still hankered after a union with France,[2] or feared that an *entente* with the islanders would drive France into close union with Russia and Austria. His resolve was the more remarkable because the Duke of York had been at Berlin to arrange the accession of Hanover to the League of German Princes which Frederick was then forming as a counterstroke to Joseph's assault on the Germanic System.[3] That the Prussian monarch should have neglected to strengthen that inherently weak union by the support of England, is one of the puzzles of his reign. Had he done so, the League would have taken a long stride forward towards the unification of Germany. Frederick chose otherwise. He welcomed Hanover and repulsed Great Britain. The League therefore lacked the support that it might have had. England and Prussia went their own ways, and therefore yielded to France the first place in the affairs of Western Europe, particularly in Holland. Moreover the Imperial Courts hotly resented the inclusion of Hanover in the League, as will presently appear.

George III very rarely, if ever, consulted Pitt concerning Hanoverian affairs, the control of which he shared solely with the Regency at Hanover.[4] But the accession of the Electorate to the *Fürstenbund*, which took definite shape in August 1785, was not the purely Germanic affair which George III strove to represent it. The incident gave deep umbrage to Joseph and Catharine; and their anger fell scarcely less on Frederick than on the Elector of Hanover. Vorontzoff, the Russian ambassador at London, on 5th August handed in a sharp protest, which Pitt at once forwarded to Windsor. It hinted that if George III did not annul his treaty with Prussia and Saxony, Russia would form alliances disagreeable to England. As appears in the

---

[1] "Leeds Mem.," 111-13.

[2] Wittichen, *op. cit.*, 8, 25 *et seq.*, and 173, 174; "Malmesbury Mems.," 131.

[3] *Ibid.*, 118.   [4] Tomline, ii, 108; "Leeds Mem.," 116.

King's reply to Pitt, George scorned the threat, which proved to be harmless.

The natural outcome of this should have been an Anglo-Prussian *entente*. As Frederick and George had given deep offence to the Imperial Courts, it would have been reasonable for them to bury the hatchet and come to a secret compact for mutual defence. Hanover, which had so long been the cause of alienation, should now have brought them to a close union. For this consummation Ewart had long been working. He it was who first caught a glimpse of the brilliant prospects which an Anglo-Prussian alliance would open up; and with his perfervid Scottish nature (he was born at a manse near Kirkcudbright in 1759, the year of Pitt's birth) he set himself to win the confidence of the Prussian Minister, Count Hertzberg, and the respect of his chiefs at London. Possessing lively manners, a frank and pleasing address, natural shrewdness, perseverance, and zeal tempered with tact, he gradually won the confidence of Hertzberg, and saw him at least once, and often twice, every day. Thus he paved the way for a second proposal of a general alliance between England and Prussia. "*M. Ewart me tourmente beaucoup du plan,*" wrote Hertzberg on 5th July to the Princess of Orange.[1] For the present he toiled in vain; but it is clear that the first conception of the Triple Alliance of England, Prussia, and Holland, originated neither with Pitt nor Carmarthen, nor Harris, nor Hertzberg, but with Ewart. His chief at Berlin, Lord Dalrymple, was in the main a figure-head of the British Embassy, and did not favour an Anglo-Prussian compact. But Ewart plodded on at the basis of the fabric, which Pitt and Harris were destined to complete. The services of this lonely and pertinacious Scot have not received due recognition.[2]

The threats of the Czarina, however much they might be spurned at Windsor and Whitehall, furnished another reason why Pitt and Carmarthen should seek to come to some understanding with Prussia; but, having failed in the month of May,

---

[1] Colenbrander, iii, 16, quoted by Wittichen, 173.

[2] Joseph Ewart had been secretary to Sir John Stepney, then was Secretary of the Berlin Embassy in 1785-7. In 1788-91 he was ambassador. For Anglo-Prussian relations and Ewart's work, see Dr. Luckwaldt's excellent monograph, " Die englisch-preussische Allianz von 1788," 51 *et seq.* (Leipzig, 1902). By the kindness of General Sir Spencer Ewart, I was able to transcribe several of the letters of his forefather, Joseph Ewart. Some of them are published in an article in the " Edinburgh Review " for July 1909.

they were now warily on their guard. The feeling prevalent in diplomatic circles is piquantly expressed in Harris's letter of 23rd August to Carmarthen: " As for the King of Prussia if he is sincere, he will die; if not, he will of course deceive us; in both cases he should be used only as a tool, and, by being forced to speak out himself, compel others [*i.e.* Austria and Russia] to declare themselves."[1]

This passage probably explains why the Pitt Ministry, in sending Earl Cornwallis on an informal mission to Berlin, tied his hands by instructions of a stringent kind. Carmarthen on 2nd September cautioned the Earl not to commit this country in the slightest degree; and to hear much, but speak little to that " artful " monarch.

When such suspicions beset the interview, no good could result. On his side Frederick appears never to have taken the proposal seriously. He assured Cornwallis of his friendship for England, but remarked on the threatening state of things in Europe; France, Spain, Austria, and Russia were in alliance (which was false); Holland was in the power of France; Prussia and England were isolated, and, if united, were no match for the vast display of power opposed to them. The union between France and Austria was indissoluble (a very questionable statement in view of their opposing interests in the Netherlands); but it might be possible to arouse the jealousy of Catharine against Austria over the suggested partition of Turkey. As for France, she was seeking to make trouble for England everywhere, especially in India and Ireland. But he ended his jeremiad with praises of Pitt for his care of British finances. This tirade was evidently intended to discourage Pitt and to bring him as a suppliant for the alliance of Prussia. For if the Quadruple Alliance were a fact, what was to be gained by the two States remaining in isolation, especially as each of them had annoyed its neighbours? Frederick's real opinion appeared in the sharp rebuke which he sent to Count Lusi, his envoy at London, for venturing to suggest the desirability of an interview.[2]

The incident left the Pitt Ministry in worse straits than ever by revealing to all the world the friendless state of England. A note of anxiety may be detected in the letter which Pitt wrote to Harris on 13th October 1785. After referring to the

---

[1] Luckwaldt, 52, 53.   [2] "Cornwallis Corresp.," i, 202-11.

growing prosperity of the country, as enhancing its prestige, he added that he would say nothing about Dutch or continental politics—"for they seem in truth still too mysterious to form any conjectures on the turn either of them may ultimately take."[1] The words deserve notice; for they refute the notion that Pitt had formed any definite system.[2] His only plan at this time was to wait until the horizon cleared. Much may be said for this cautious opportunism; but it had the disadvantage of leaving us isolated at a time of great danger. We had done enough to incur the displeasure of two most dangerous sovereigns, Catharine and Joseph, but not enough to avert its probable consequences.

For the present, Ministers sought to recover the good will of Catharine. In semblance it was easily procurable. Vorontzoff for a time dangled before Carmarthen the prize of a Russian alliance, and sought to persuade him that the Empress was on the point of proposing it when she heard of Hanover joining the German League. The Austrian envoy, Kazeneck, also assured him that friendship with Russia would be the best means of preventing war with France. Carmarthen seems to have taken these offers at their face value and wrote to Harris that the road from London to Paris lay through Petersburg.[3] Similar proposals came from these envoys for some time; and Carmarthen cheered himself with a truly pathetic belief in their honesty.[4] Harris also, despite his knowledge of Catharine's anti-British bias, persisted in hoping for a return of her favour. He even drew up a memorandum recounting the advantages of an Anglo-Russo-Austrian League, for which Carmarthen was already angling; and in particular he deprecated any offer of alliance to Frederick, "unless compelled by events."[5] It is strange that

---

[1] "Malmesbury Diaries," i, 157.

[2] I disagree with Herr Salomon ("Pitt") on this point. It seems to me that Pitt's policy was essentially tentative, and remained so up to the year 1788.

[3] B.M. Add. MSS., 28060. George III showed more sagacity than his Ministers, witness the phrase in his letter of 7th August to Pitt: "An experience of twenty years has taught me not to expect any return for the great assistance she [Catharine] has received from this country."

[4] As late as 5th February 1786 he wrote to Harris: "We are on more friendly terms with Russia than for a long time" (B.M. Add. MSS., 28061).

[5] I have published this Memorandum along with other documents bearing on the years 1785-7 in the "Eng. Hist. Rev." for 1909.

Pitt and Carmarthen did not see that the advances of the Imperial Courts were designed merely to keep England and Prussia apart. But, in truth, the fault lay mainly with Frederick the Great, whose spleen was incurable.

Meanwhile the course of events in the Netherlands should have brought Prussia and England to terms. They need not have been public, still less offensive in aim; for that would have brought about a close union of France with Russia as well as Austria, an event which Pitt no less than Frederick sought to avert. But why Pitt and Carmarthen should not have welcomed a secret defensive compact with Prussia it is hard to say. If the princes and counts of Germany did not hesitate to brave the wrath of Joseph by union with Prussia, why should Great Britain? Frederick's shiftiness may be granted. But at this crisis there was a motive which might be trusted to keep him staunch, namely, self-interest. Both England and Prussia sorely needed an ally; yet they held severely aloof.

In the early autumn of 1785, Joseph II brought severe pressure to bear upon the Dutch to cede Maestricht to him, and to throw open the navigation of the Scheldt below Antwerp. Hostilities were on the point of breaking out, when France skilfully intervened, offered her mediation, and prevailed on the disputants to accept the terms which she offered. By the Treaty of Fontainebleau (8 Nov. 1785) the Emperor agreed to waive his exorbitant claims in consideration of the payment of 15,000,000 florins, for the half of which sum the Court of Versailles became responsible. That so heavily burdened a State should add to its financial difficulties excited some surprise; but in the political sphere Vergennes gained a signal triumph. By becoming paymaster to Joseph, he kept that wayward ruler in French leading strings; and, by saving Maestricht and the Scheldt navigation to the Dutch, he ensured the supremacy of France in that land. This compact was followed two days later by a Franco-Dutch treaty of alliance whereby the Court of Versailles guaranteed the possessions of the United Provinces; and each of the two States undertook to furnish ships and men to the other in case of attack.[1]

Meanwhile Pitt awoke to a sense of the danger, and urged Harris to use his utmost endeavours (short of an open breach

---

[1] Garden, "Traités," v, 60-72.

with France) to prevent the ratification of the treaty by the United Provinces. All that the envoy could do was to present to the States General at The Hague a Memorial declaring the continued interest taken by England in the affairs of the Republic. But of what avail was this academic statement without a conditional and secret offer of armed support, which everybody knew France would give rather than forego her triumph? Again, early in December, Pitt warned Carmarthen that Harris should " redouble every possible effort " to prevent the Franco-Dutch alliance.[1] This was merely to bid him fight with his hands tied.

France now held a most commanding position in Europe. By the new compacts she influenced Hapsburg policy, she forced Frederick the Great into almost abject deference, she allured Catharine, and she controlled the Dutch Netherlands. This last triumph crowned the life-work of Vergennes. The recent treaties relieved him from the disagreeable alternative of choosing between Austria and the United Provinces in case of a rupture. They emphasized the isolation of England. Above all, they prepared the way for joint action of the French and Dutch East India Companies which might prove to be fatal to British ascendancy in India.[2]

The meagre correspondence of Pitt at this time contains scarcely a reference to this very serious crisis. His letters turn mainly on finance, Irish affairs, and domestic topics such as the purchase of Holwood. On the Dutch problem there is not a word except the curiously curt reference in his letter of October 6 to Grenville: " I have written to Lord Carmarthen on the Dutch business much as you seem to wish." [3] The phrase is interesting as marking the commencement of the influence which Grenville was soon to gain over Pitt in foreign affairs; but its nonchalance is astounding. In part, no doubt, the passivity of the Prime Minister resulted from the determination of George III to hold aloof as King of England from all complications, how-

---

[1] " Malmesbury Diaries," ii, 175.

[2] On 7th March 1786 Harris reported to Carmarthen joint actions of the Dutch and French in the East, and that eight Dutch warships were to sail thither with troops on board. (B.M. Add. MSS., 28061.) The possession of the Cape of Good Hope by the Dutch rendered our communications with India precarious.

[3] " Dropmore P.," i, 258.

ever much, as Elector of Hanover, he might irritate Austria and Russia. As we shall see in the next chapter, George was beginning to be alarmed at the growing expenses of his family, and viewed the Dutch crisis mainly as involving burdensome demands on the Civil List. Here, then, as at so many points in his career, Pitt was handicapped by the King.

But it is also probable that in the disappointing year 1785, marked by the failure of his Reform and Irish measures, he suppressed the concern which he must have felt at the deepening isolation of England. We must remember that he had formed a resolve to play a waiting game in foreign affairs. On August 8 he wrote to the Duke of Rutland that, if the commercial treaty with Ireland became law, and peace lasted for five years, England would be able to look any Power in Europe in the face.[1] That explains why he tied the hands of Harris at The Hague and sent to Berlin overtures so cautious as to be received with polite disdain. His great aim was to lessen the National Debt; and the year 1785, with all its disappointments, witnessed a most extraordinary rise in Consols, viz. from $54\frac{1}{4}$ to $73\frac{1}{2}$. There was the strength of England's position. If she reduced her debt, while all the Continental Powers were ruinously increasing theirs, she must have the advantage when turmoil ended in war.

Pitt therefore adopted a policy of delay. So long as he could strengthen the navy, maintain the army at the ordinary peace footing, and enhance the nation's credit, he was content to bide his time, leaving Harris to combat French influence in Holland as best he could.[2] Such a policy was very far from brilliant; and, had not France in the next two years entered on a period of rapid decline, he might be censured for tamely waiting on events. For it is possible that a bold initiative at Whitehall in October, while Vergennes' Dutch treaties were taking shape, might have gained active support either from Prussia or from Joseph II, who had been on very cool terms with France. Pitt, however, preferred to hold back, even though the Bourbons gained control of the United Provinces. By his passivity in face of that diplomatic disaster we may measure his devotion to the cause of peace. And just as Queen Elizabeth often reassured her people at the gravest crisis by displays of frivolity, so too Pitt's absorption in tree planting at Holwood

---

[1] "Pitt-Rutland Corresp.," 111.   [2] "Malmesbury Diaries," ii, 172.

may have been a device for hiding his anxiety, reassuring the public, and preventing a fall in the Funds.

Serene hopefulness in the future of his country is a strong feature in the character of this great man; and we shall find occasions when he displayed this quality to excess. Certain it is that he never lost hope or relaxed his energies, even now, when Ministers and envoys evinced signs of gloom or despair. A proof of the prevalence of these feelings appears in one of the closing passages of a Memorandum which the Duke of Richmond, Master of the Ordnance, on 30th December 1785, sent to his colleague, Carmarthen. It was written owing to a singular circumstance, which reveals the impulsiveness of Pitt. The Duke had almost casually suggested the desirability of recovering some foothold in the Dutch Netherlands by inducing them to propose to include England in their recent treaty with France. This hint, which the Duke threw out in conversation, was at once taken up by Pitt, who, without consulting the Cabinet, urged Carmarthen to take steps to carry it into effect, and suggested that one of the Patriots might be bribed to make the proposal of including England, as if it were to test the sincerity of her offers of friendship. Of course the matter came to nothing; but the surprise of the Duke at Pitt's speedy adoption of the hint led him to descant on our isolation, and to harp on the well-worn theme of an alliance with Austria:—

Goodwood, December 30, 1785.

. . . If the Emperor and France keep well together, Leghorn will be also an inimical port,[1] as may Algiers and Marocco if their treaties with Spain go on. Holland seems lost to us both in Europe and the East Indies; and should the Emperor and Russia unite with France, Sweden must follow, and Denmark dare not be our friend. Under such circumstances what are we to look for but utter ruin! If France is disengaged on the Continent and assisted by Spain, Holland and Russia (to say nothing of America), we must be attacked with greatly superior forces in the East and West Indies and perhaps in Canada; but, what is still worse, we shall undoubtedly have the war brought into Ireland, and I very much doubt whether we can by any means avoid that country being divided, and a large part acting against us. If any of these points of attack succeed, and above all, if our navy should meet with any disaster from superior forces, the next step will be to bring the war into

---

[1] The Grand-Duke of Tuscany was a Hapsburg prince.

this country, and the best issue of such an event must be attended with much distress. In short, the natural and political advantages of France are such that I very much fear the consequences. To divert her attention by stirring up some powerful enemy on the Continent has been long and universally considered as our only resource, and yet unfortunately we seem to be obstructing the only Power capable of creating that diversion, which is the Emperor. . . .[1]

It was amidst fears so intense and prejudices so deep-seated that Pitt undertook the negotiations for a friendly commercial treaty with France which is the chief event of the year 1786.

[1] Pitt MSS., 332.

CHAPTER XIV

L'ENTENTE CORDIALE

(1786)

Thy father's fame with thine fair Truth shall blend.
His vigour saved from foreign foes the land,
Thy prudence makes each foreign foe a friend.
REV. W. MASON TO PITT, 1786.

THE nation is but the family writ large; and, just as families after a ruinous quarrel sometimes win their way back towards prudence and friendliness, so too nations now and again feel the force of the sociable instincts. Such a time was now at hand for Great Britain and France. The eight years of the American War of Independence had increased the debt of the Island Power by £115,000,000;[1] and so wasteful had been the conduct of the war by France that in the years 1778-1783, she had exceeded the total of her already large peace expenditure by £66,000,000.[2] Further, as that struggle brought to her few results beyond the satisfaction of rending the British Empire in twain, she was scarcely the better for it. In truth, while defeat led patriotic Britons to tread the humble paths of retrenchment and reform, the triumph of France allured her politicians into the stately avenues ending in bankruptcy and Revolution.

During the period of war, philosophy, science, and industry had been waging their peaceful campaigns; and now in the exhaustion or quiescence which beset both peoples, the still small voice of reason was heard. The responsiveness of thought in England and France is one of the most remarkable facts in the eighteenth century. Though political rivalry had five times over embroiled those peoples in deadly strife, yet their thinkers had

---

[1] Dr. Cunningham, "Eng. Industry and Commerce" (pt. ii, 546).
[2] B.M. Add. MSS., 28063. Eden to Carmarthen, 10th January 1788.

I   Y

never ceased to feel the thrill of sympathetic ideas, originated by "the natural enemy," which proved to be no less potent than the divulsive forces of statecraft. The Marconigrams of thought pass through storms, whether atmospheric or political; and it may be that finally the nations will become sounding-boards responding more and more to progressive ideas, and less and less to the passions of mankind.

Certainly the mental sympathy of England and France in that century was strongly marked. As is well known, the philosophy of Locke supplied Voltaire and Rousseau with most of the weapons of their intellectual armoury. From the English constitution Montesquieu drew many of the contentions which lend significance to his *Esprit des Lois*. The ideas of naturalism and sensibility were wafted hither from the garner of Rousseau. Philanthropy became a force in both lands about the same time but in diverse ways. In France it was in the main anti-clerical, springing from the indignant protests of Voltaire against atrocities such as that inflicted by the Church on Calas. In this land it may be traced to the Wesleyan revival, the motive which impelled Howard, Clarkson, and Wilberforce being distinctly religious.

On a lower plane we notice the immense vogue of English fashions in France, and of French *modes* in England. *Grands seigneurs* sought to copy our field sports, swathed themselves in English *redingotes*, and rose in the stirrups *à l'Anglaise*. The Duc de Chartres (the future Philippe Egalité) set the rage for English ways and fabrics, so that French industries seriously suffered. In 1785 the French Minister complained to our envoy that French draperies could not be sold unless they looked like English stuffs.[1] Britons returned the compliment. They swarmed into France. We find our envoy complaining that English families were settling in every French town, so that it might be well to devise an absentee tax which would drive them homewards.[2]

But no influence helped on the new cosmopolitanism so much as the spread of ideas of Free Trade. Here the honours lie with French thinkers. It was by residence in France and contact with the *Economistes*, Quesnay and Turgot, that Adam Smith was able to formulate the ideas soon to be embodied in the

---

[1] "F. O.," France, 18. [2] *Ibid.*

"Wealth of Nations." Here we may note a curious paradox. The practical islanders supplied their neighbours with political ideas which, when barbed by Voltaire and Rousseau, did much to gall France into violent action. On the other hand, the more nimble-witted people gave to its trading rival the fiscal principles (neglected at home) which furthered the extension of its commerce. Venomous use might be made of this contrast by that fast diminishing band of Anglophobes who see in all British actions perfidious attempts to ruin France; but it must be remembered that everything depends on the men who introduce and apply the new ideas, and that, whereas France was unfortunate in the men who promulgated and worked the political principles learnt in England, the islanders on the contrary had the wisest of counsellors. Contrast Voltaire, Rousseau, and Robespierre with Adam Smith and Pitt, and the riddle is solved at once.

Amidst the exhaustion of war, both nations were now ready to listen to all that was most convincing in the arguments of the *Economistes* and of Adam Smith. These exponents of the nascent science of Economics rendered a memorable service to the cause of peace by urging nations, like sensible traders, to rejoice in the prosperity of their neighbours, not in their poverty. Propinquity, said they, should be an incentive to free intercourse, not to hatred. Adam Smith pointed out in his "Wealth of Nations" (1776) that France could offer us a market eight times as populous as that of our North American colonies, and twenty-four times as advantageous if the frequency of the returns were reckoned. The British market, he said, would be equally profitable to France. He laughed to scorn the notion that France would always drain Great Britain of her specie, and showed that the worship of the "balance of trade" was accountable for much folly and bloodshed.[1] It is difficult to say whether these views had much hold on the English people. If we may judge from the passions aroused by Pitt's Irish Resolutions, it was slight. On the other hand the absence of any vehement opposition to the commercial treaty with France a year later, shows either that public opinion here was moving forwards, or that the Opposition felt it impossible to bring to bear on the absolute government of Louis XVI those irritating arguments which had had so potent an influence on the Irish people.

---

[1] "Wealth of Nations," bk. iv, ch. iii.

The influence of the *Economistes* in France probably did not count for very much. But they had shown their power during the brief but beneficent ministry of Turgot; and even when Marie Antoinette procured the dismissal of that able but austere Minister, one of his disciples remained in office, and was now Minister of Foreign Affairs. This was Vergennes. Few men at that time did more for the cause of human brotherhood than this man, whom Carlyle described as "solid phlegmatic . . . like some dull punctual clerk." A man's importance depends, after all, not so much on external brilliance as on the worth of his achievements; a statesman who largely decided the Franco-American alliance, the terms of peace in 1783, and the resumption of friendly relations with England, need not fear the verdict of history. In a little known fragment written in April 1776, Vergennes thus outlines an intelligent policy:

Wise and happy will that nation be which will be the first to adapt its policy to the new circumstances of the age, and to consent to see in its colonies nothing more than allied provinces and no longer subject States of the mother-land. Wise and happy will that nation be which is the first to be convinced that commercial policy consists wholly in employing lands in the way most advantageous for the owners, also the arms of the people in the most useful way, that is, as self-interest will enjoin if there is no coercion; and that all the rest is only illusion and vanity. When the total separation of America [from Great Britain] has forced everybody to recognize this truth and weaned the European nations from commercial jealousy, it will remove one important cause of war, and it is difficult not to desire an event which ought to bring this boon to the human race.[1]

Two years later, when France drew the sword on behalf of the Americans, Britons naturally scoffed at these philanthropic pretensions. The conduct of her Court and nobles was certainly open to the charge of hypocrisy, especially when Louis XVI issued the ordinance of 1781 restricting the higher commissions in his army to those nobles who could show sixteen quarters of nobility. Singular, indeed, to battle for democracy in the new world and yet draw tighter the bands of privilege in France! Yet Vergennes, Necker, and other friends of reform were not responsible for this regal folly; and they were doubtless sincere

---

[1] "Politique de tous les Cabinets de l'Europe . . .," ii, 402-3. It contains some "Mémoires" of Vergennes.

in hoping that the downfall of England's colonial system would inaugurate a new era in the politics and commerce of the world.

A proof of the sincerity of Vergennes is to be found in the 18th Article of the Treaty of Versailles (1783), which stipulated that, immediately after the ratification of the treaty, commissioners should be appointed to prepare new commercial arrangements between the two nations "on the basis of reciprocity and mutual convenience, which arrangements are to be terminated and concluded within the space of two years from the 1st of January 1784." For this clause Lords Shelburne and Grantham on the British side were chiefly responsible; and it is certain that the former warmly approved it.[1] Pitt, as Chancellor of the Exchequer in that Ministry, doubtless also welcomed the proposal; but I have found no sign of his opinions on the subject. The credit for this enlightened proposal may probably be assigned to Vergennes, seeing that he dictated terms, while the British Cabinet accepted them. There is a ring of sincerity in his words written on 1st February 1783 to de Rayneval, then his diplomatic agent in London: "It is an old prejudice, which I do not share, that there is a natural incompatibility between these two peoples. . . . Every nation must strive for the utmost prosperity; but this cannot be based on exclusiveness, otherwise it would be a nullity. One does not get rich from very poor nations."[2] This seems to be an echo of Adam Smith's dictum: "A nation that would enrich itself by foreign trade is certainly most likely to do so when its neighbours are all rich, industrious, and commercial nations."[3]

Statesmen on this side of the Channel were slower than their rivals in seeking to realize these enlightened aims. The fall of Shelburne's Ministry and the triumph of the Fox-North Coalition led to no important change in the Treaty, which was signed at Versailles in September 1783; but the commercial treaty was shelved for the present. With all his enlightenment in matters political, Fox had a limited outlook in the commercial sphere. He held the old Whig views, which for well-nigh a century had been narrowly national and mercantilist. Further, he hotly contested the claim put forward by the French

---

[1] Fitzmaurice, "Shelburne," iii, 260.

[2] "Précis du Traité de Commerce de 1786," by Count His de Butenval (Paris, 1869), 25.

[3] "Wealth of Nations," bk iv, ch. iii.

Government to consider all trading arrangements at an end, including those of the Treaty of Utrecht, if no arrangement were formed before the end of the year 1785.[1]

Such was the state of things when Pitt and Carmarthen took office at the close of the year 1783. The events described in the previous chapter will have enabled the reader to understand the need of great caution on the part of Pitt. Though the language of Vergennes was redolent of human brotherhood, his actions were often shrewdly diplomatic. In the United Provinces, as we have seen, his policy wore a twofold aspect. While supporting the Patriots, he claimed to be supporting the cause of democracy, but he also dealt a blow at British influence. Though he maintained the Austrian alliance, he coquetted with Prussia; and, while dallying with the Czarina in order to keep out England, he made a profitable bargain with Russia's enemy, Sweden, respecting Gothenburg. Thus on all sides he advanced the cause of enlightenment and the interests of France.

It is not surprising that this dextrous union of philosophy and statecraft (which resembles that by which Napoleon utilized Rousseau's advocacy of natural boundaries) earned the hatred of nearly every Briton. Carmarthen and Harris were deeply imbued with these feelings; and it is certain that Pitt, while taking the outstretched hand of Vergennes, half expected a dagger-thrust. We find Grenville writing to Carmarthen on 25th February 1785 concerning a plan, which Pitt had formed, for provisionally buying over a Mr. D. S. M. at Paris to send confidential news, especially respecting the plans and movements of the French in the East Indies. He was to receive 60 guineas a month for news sent to Daniel Hailes, Secretary at the British Embassy, and 250 guineas at the end of three months if his information gave satisfaction.[2] Other items make it clear that Pitt viewed with concern the activity of France in the East. The formation of a French East India Company in March 1785 was a threatening sign;[3] and in the summer came a report from Sir Robert Ainslie, British ambassador at Constantinople, that France was intriguing to gain a foothold

---

[1] Butenval, 23.   [2] B.M. Add. MSS., 28060.

[3] "F. O.," France, 14, Dorset to Carmarthen, 31st March 1785. See, too, L. Pingaud Choiseul-Gouffier, "La France en Orient sous Louis XVI" (Paris, 1887).

in Egypt on the Red Sea. Part of his despatch of 23rd July 1785 is worth quoting:

... The Porte has varied in her general opposition to establishing a trade through Egypt, by opening the navigation of the Red Sea to the flag of Christian Powers. The present undertaking and the late French mission to Cairo was in consequence of a plan devised by the late French ambassador to ruin our East India Company by an illicit trade under the protection of France, in which it was thought the Company's servants would join most heartily. It is clear that France adopted this scheme, but I can pledge myself the Porte was not consulted and that she will never protect a project by far more dangerous to her own interests than even to ours. It seems Count Priest hoped to elude the Ottoman bad humour by employing the navigation of the flags of all Christian Powers indiscriminately and to secure his trade by the protection of the Beys of Egypt, who certainly have aimed at absolute independence ever since the time of Ali Bey.[1]

The correspondence of Sir James Harris with Carmarthen shows that our Ministry kept a watchful eye on any symptoms which portended a union of the Dutch East India Company with that of France. Indeed, as we shall see, the reasons which prompted the resolute action of Pitt at the crisis of 1787 in Holland were largely based on naval and colonial considerations. Matters in the East were in an uneasy state. Once again, in January 1786, Hailes reported that the unsettled state of Egypt was known to be attracting the notice of the French Foreign Office, probably with a view to conquest.[2] The efforts which France put forth in 1785-6 for the construction of a great naval fortress at Cherbourg also claimed attention; and Britons were not calmed by the philosophic reflections of some peace-loving Gauls that the completion of that mighty harbour would render it impossible for England to make war on France.

In view of the lowering political horizon, is it surprising that Pitt was very cautious in responding to the proposals of the French Cabinet for a friendly commercial treaty? It is incorrect to say, as Harris did in a rather peevish outburst, that Pitt was too occupied with Parliament to attend to foreign affairs.[3] We now know that he paid much attention to them,

---

[1] Pitt MSS., 337.
[2] *Ibid.*, 333. Hailes to Fraser, 26th January 1786.
[3] " Malmesbury Diaries," ii, 112.

though the pressing problems of finance, India, Ireland, and Reform perforce held the first place in his thoughts. But he must have desired to gain a clearer insight into a very complex situation before he committed his country to a commercial treaty with France.[1] To have done so prematurely might have prevented the formation of that closer political union with Russia and Austria which British statesmen long and vainly struggled to effect.

But another motive probably weighed even more with Pitt in favour of delay. We have seen how fondly and tenaciously he clung to the hope of a commercial union between Great Britain and Ireland through the session of 1785. Surely it was of prime importance to complete the fiscal system of the British Islands before he entered into negotiations with a foreign Power. To have hurried on the French commercial treaty before that with Ireland was concluded would have been a grave tactical error. As a firm economic unit, Great Britain and Ireland could hope for far better terms from France than as separate entities; and this consideration almost certainly supplies the reason for Pitt's extreme anxiety to assure the industrial unity of these islands before he began to bargain with France; while it may also explain the desire of Vergennes to press on the negotiation before the British Islands had acquired fiscal solidarity. In fine, everything conspired to impose on Pitt a passive attitude. Vergennes, as the victor, could propose terms; Pitt, representing the beaten Power, could only await them. Such was the situation in 1784-5. An autocracy founded on privilege seemed to be threatening our political existence, and yet made commercial proposals which might have come from Adam Smith himself.

The British Government responded to them very slowly. In the spring of 1784 it appointed George Craufurd to act as our commissioner at Versailles for the drafting of a commercial arrangement, as was required by the treaty of 1783; but he did not receive his instructions until September. Rayneval, who had the full confidence of Vergennes, was the French commissioner; and at their first interview he asked that the principle of reciprocity should form the basis of the negotiations. To this the British Court demurred, and the affair remained in suspense for some months. On 3rd March 1785 Craufurd wrote to Car-

---

[1] "Malmesbury Diaries," ii, 157.

marthen that he was still waiting for replies to his notes of 30th September and 25th November, and that Vergennes had repeatedly expressed to the Duke of Dorset, the British ambassador, his annoyance at the loss of time. His resentment had recently taken a tangible form; he had issued an ordinance (*arrêt*) imposing a tax of sixty per cent. on all carriages imported from the United Kingdom. This action led Carmarthen to break his long silence on commercial matters and to protest against the tax as tending to " prevent that spirit of conciliation or friendly liberality so necessary at this time to produce any good effect for those commercial arrangements now in contemplation." [1] He also hinted that Great Britain might with perfect justice retaliate. Further, he repudiated the French claim, once again raised, that all commercial arrangements would lapse by the end of 1785, and maintained that the Treaty of Utrecht would afterwards equally be in force. After further delays Rayneval demanded that there should be absolute reciprocity in their commercial dealings, the basis of the most favoured nation being adopted where it did not infringe existing treaties. To this Carmarthen sent the following reply on 5th August:

Mutual benefits and reciprocal advantages are indisputably the objects we are inclined to pursue in the adjustment of this business; but to say at once that the two nations shall be entitled to those privileges which are alone allowed to the most favoured nations, by way of a basis to the negotiation and without weighing the nature and consequence of such privileges is totally impossible; and of this I think M. de Rayneval must be convinced when he recollects that it was a stipulation of this sort contained in the 8th and 9th articles of the Treaty of Commerce of Utrecht in 1713 that prevented those articles from ever being carried into effect. [2]

Considering that reciprocity and the most favoured nation treatment had been urged by Rayneval at his first interview with Craufurd in September 1784, it is difficult to see why Carmarthen felt flurried by the present proposal.

Meanwhile Vergennes had struck another heavy blow. He issued an *arrêt* forbidding foreigners to share in the French trade to the Barbary States, and on 10th July he prohibited the import

[1] " F. O.," France, 16.
[2] *Ibid.* The British Parliament in 1716 abrogated these clauses in favour of earlier and less liberal arrangements. Louis XIV consented to this.

of foreign cottons, muslins, gauzes, and linens into France. At once there arose a cry of distress and rage throughout Great Britain; and Carmarthen sent an energetic remonstrance against this further proof of the ill-humour of the French Government. Hailes at once informed him that the two *arrêts* had "been suspended with more forbearance than could reasonably have been expected, considering the detriment French manufactures have sustained, and the great advantage we have derived from the balance of trade being so much and so long in our favour. People in general think that this strong measure will hasten the conclusion of an arrangement between us."[1] Vergennes soon assured Hailes of his desire for a friendly arrangement, but he added that meanwhile the French Government had to look to its own needs and stop the enormous influx of British goods, for which the French public clamoured. Commerce and finance were then the chief care of the French Government. On 25th August Hailes reported the pains secretly taken by the French to attract skilled English workmen. On 22nd September Craufurd stated that further disagreeable events would happen unless some progress were made with the commercial treaty; Rayneval observed that, if we objected to reciprocity and the most favoured nation basis, it was for us to make a proposal. On 21st October Vergennes issued another unfriendly *arrêt* prohibiting the import of iron, steel, and cutlery; but Hailes continued to assure Carmarthen that Vergennes and Rayneval were anxious for a final settlement and that the *arrêts* were "meant to stimulate us to a conclusion of the commercial treaty as soon as possible."[2]

Pitt now began to bestir himself on this matter. In order to have at Paris a commissioner abler, or more acceptable, than Craufurd seems to have been, he made overtures to William Eden (the future Lord Auckland) with a view to his acting as special commissioner in his place. In the Auckland Papers at the British Museum there is an unpublished letter of Pitt to Eden, dated Brighthelmstone, 16th October 1785, in answer to one in which Eden had hinted that he would prefer the Speakership of the House of Commons, as Cornwall

---

[1] "F. O.," France, 16. Hailes to Carmarthen, 4th August 1785.

[2] *Ibid.*, Hailes to Carmarthen, 1st December 1785. The Chambers of Commerce at Paris, Versailles, and Montpellier protested against the *arrêts*. See Butenval, *op. cit.*, 36.

"obviously suffered while in the chair."[1] Pitt's reply is as follows:

It gives me great satisfaction to find that there remains no obstacle to your acceptance of either of the situations mentioned in my letter to Mr. Beresford, and that nothing seems left to settle but the mode of carrying such an arrangement into effect. I confess I am not aware of any means which could properly be taken to induce the Speaker to retire at present; and therefore in the interval I should very much wish to accelerate the execution of the other idea.[2]

Pitt then refers to some difficulties which make it desirable to defer the actual appointment until the session had begun. He suggests conferences, especially as in a fortnight he would be nearer to Eden. All this bespeaks a degree of nonchalance quite remarkable considering the importance of the questions at stake. Everything tends to show that Pitt felt far less interest in this negotiation than in that with Ireland, to which he had very properly given the first place. The effort to free trade between the two islands having now failed, there was no reason for further postponing the discussions with France.

Such seems to me the reasonable way of explaining his procedure. The contention of the French historian of this treaty, that Pitt was opposed to the commercial arrangement with France, and was only forced into it by the hostile *arrêts*, is untenable.[3] He maintains that it was the last *arrêt*, that of 21st October, which brought Pitt to his senses—"Mr. Pitt, who did not *then* wish for war, surrendered." This phrase reveals the prejudice of the writer, who, publishing his work at the time of Cobden's negotiations with Napoleon III, obviously set himself to prove that Free Trade was French both in the origin of the idea and in the carrying out in practice by statesmen. Passing over these claims, we should remember that Pitt had made his first overtures to Eden in the first week in October, some ten days before the appearance of the *arrêt*, which, in Butenval's version, compelled him to "surrender."

Pitt acted with much circumspection. He urged Eden to collect information on trade matters; but it seems that not until December did the new Council of Trade set on foot any official

---

[1] Pitt MSS., 110. Eden to Pitt, 12th October 1785. See, too, "Carlisle Papers," 644.

[2] B.M. Add. MSS., 34420.   [3] Butenval, 39

inquiries.[1] Perhaps the Irish negotiation, which was hurried on too fast, had given him pause. Meanwhile, however, France had gained another success by imposing her mediation on the Emperor Joseph II and the Dutch Government and settling the disputes between them. As appeared in the previous chapter, this treaty led to the conclusion of an alliance (10th November 1785) both political and commercial, with the United Provinces, which emphasized the isolation of England and secured the Dutch markets for France. Thus the delay in meeting the advances of Vergennes had been doubly prejudicial to British interests, and it must be confessed that Pitt's *début* in European diplomacy was far from brilliant.

If, however, we look into details, we find that Carmarthen hampered the negotiations at the outset by refusing to accept the " most favoured nation " basis of negotiation, and by throwing on France the responsibility for not proposing some " practicable" scheme. On 14th October 1785 he wrote to Hailes that Great Britain very much desired a commercial treaty with France, and was waiting for " specific proposals " from her; and again, on 4th November, that matters seemed hopeless, owing to Rayneval's obstinate adherence to his original scheme.[2] This pedantic conduct was fast enclosing the whole affair in a vicious circle. Meanwhile the sands of time were running out: and it seemed that England would be left friendless and at the mercy of any commercial arrangement which France chose to enforce after the close of the year. It is strange that Pitt did not insist on the furtherance of a matter which he judged to be "of great national importance." [3] But his only step for the present was to write a letter, signed by Carmarthen, asking for an extension of time beyond the end of that year. In reply Vergennes expressed the satisfaction of Louis XVI that Great Britain was seriously desirous of framing a commercial treaty and granted six months' extension of time.[4] A year was finally granted.

Notwithstanding this further proof of Vergennes' good will, the negotiation began under conditions so unfavourable to Great Britain as to call for a skilled negotiator; but the career of

---

[1] Carmarthen to Eden, 9th December 1785 (B.M. Add. MSS., 34420).
[2] Pitt MSS., 333.
[3] Pitt to Eden, 4th December 1785, in " Auckland Journals," i, 87.
[4] Vergennes to Carmarthen, 14th December 1785, in Pitt MSS., 333.

William Eden warranted the hope that he would bear the burden of responsibility triumphantly. Born in 1744, and educated at Eton and Christchurch, he early showed marked abilities, which were sharpened by practice at the Bar. He also devoted his attention to social and economic questions; and when, in 1780, he became Chief Secretary for Ireland under the Earl of Carlisle, he did much to promote the prosperity of that land, especially by helping to found the Bank of Ireland. He took keen interest in the treatment of prisoners, and proposed to substitute hard labour for transportation. The reform of the penal laws also engaged his attention. He had long been attached to Lord North's party, though his views were more progressive than theirs. By his marriage with the sister of Sir Gilbert Elliot he came into touch with the Whigs; and, though his petulant conduct in 1782 with regard to the resignation of the lord-lieutenancy by Carlisle caused general annoyance, he was largely instrumental in bringing about the Fox-North Coalition. Consistency sat lightly upon Eden; and when, in 1785, he hotly opposed Pitt's Irish proposals, similar in effect to his own of some years earlier, he was roundly abused by one of his friends for his factiousness.[1] The same correspondent soon had cause to upbraid him still further for his conduct in the autumn of 1785, when, leaving the Opposition, he went over to the Government side in order to act as special commissioner at Paris. The Duke of Portland coldly commended him for placing country above party; but the many saw in the move only enlightened self-interest and felt no confidence in him. Wraxall expressed the prevalent opinion when he said that there "existed in Eden's physiognomy, even in his manner and deportment, something which did not convey the impression of plain dealing or inspire confidence."[2]

Undoubtedly Eden was the ablest negotiator whom Pitt could have chosen for a difficult commercial bargain; Wedgwood at once wrote to say that he would have been his choice; and the remarks as to Pitt filching away a prominent member of the Opposition are clearly prompted by spite. After hearing much evidence on commercial matters at the Committee of Council, Eden set out for Paris at the end of March 1786, and was welcomed by Vergennes as a kindred soul. The Duke of Dorset

---

[1] B.M. Add. MSS., 34420. Letter of John Lees, 1st April 1785.
[2] "Auckland Journals," i, 89; Wraxall, iv, 229.

was somewhat offended at his coming, and held aloof. Fortunately he found it desirable to take a long holiday in England, during which time the affairs of the embassy were ably carried on by Eden and Hailes. A popular song of the day referred to this in the lines:

> For Dorset at cricket can play
> And leave Billy Eden in France, sir.

Dorset's services were, in fact, mainly social. He was liked by Marie Antoinette; and his *thés dansants* were frequented by the leading nobles.[1]

On Eden, then, and Pitt (for Carmarthen felt no trust in the French) lay the chief burden of the negotiations. It is clear that Pitt now took a keen interest in the affair; and as Vergennes, Rayneval, and Calonne (Minister of Finance) showed a marked desire to come to a fair compromise, the matter was soon in good train. The chief difficulties arose from the suspicions of Carmarthen and the desire of Jenkinson, head of the Council of Trade, to drive a hard bargain with France. Pitt could not be indifferent to the opinions of his colleagues; and his experience of British manufacturers was such as to make him press for the best possible terms. That he still felt some distrust of the Court of Versailles is clear from his letter of 19th April 1786 to Eden that their financial embarrassments were such as "to secure, at east for a time, a sincere disposition to peace."[2] By that time, too, he must have received Eden's letter of 13th April marked Private and confidential," which referred in glowing terms to the prospects of the negotiation:

It is a circumstance which I shall think a just subject of pride to us both in the present age and of merit with posterity if the result should be what at this moment seems probable. . . . France shows a disposition to encourage our trade if we remove the senseless and peevish distinctions which fill so many lines in our Book of Rates; and a decided resolution to obstruct it as much as possible if those distinctions are suffered to remain. In the same time all the speculations and exertions of our trade with this Kingdom are suspended, and the manufactures, the navigation and the revenue are suffering. Besides, all the trading

---

[1] J. Flammermont, "Correspondances des Agents diplomatiques étrangers avant la Révolution," 508.

[2] "Auckland Journals," i, 106.

and manufacturing parts of England are at this hour disposed to go much greater lengths than are now suggested. . . . It is even highly possible that this treaty may form a new epoch in history.[1]

Over against the enthusiasm of Eden we may set the distrust of Carmarthen, as evinced in his statement to that envoy on 29th April, that if France could ever be sincere, Eden would doubtless bring the bargain to a successful issue.[2] Far less complimentary were his references to Eden in private letters to Dorset and Harris. From the former he inquired: " How is our paragon of perfection relished in France? "[3] In a letter to Harris, who constantly maintained that Eden was playing the game for Versailles, not for London, Carmarthen referred to " the absurd and officious letter of our great commercial negotiator."[4] It is well to remember these jealousies; for, as Harris was the bosom friend of Carmarthen, he succeeded in persuading him that the whole negotiation with France was a trick of our arch-enemy. The letter of Harris, which called forth Carmarthen's ironical reply, ended with the statement that France sought " to depress us everywhere, to keep us in an isolated and unconnected state, till such time as they think they can cripple us irrecoverably by an open hostile attack."[5] These suspicions must have been passed on to Pitt after due sifting; and it speaks much for the evenness and serenity of his mind that he persevered with the negotiation in spite of the prejudices of his Foreign Minister. Naturally, also, he kept the affair in his own hands.

In truth, Pitt occupied a position intermediate between that of the incurably suspicious Carmarthen and of the pleased and rather self-conscious Eden. When the latter very speedily arrived at a preliminary agreement, or Projet, with Rayneval, and begged that it should be adopted as speedily, and with as few alterations as possible, Pitt subjected it to friendly but close scrutiny. His reply of 10th May has been printed among the Auckland Journals; but his criticisms were even more practical in a long letter of 26th May, which is among the Pitt Papers. The following sentences are of special interest:

---

[1] Pitt MSS., 110. I quote fully only from those letters which have not been published.

[2] "Auckland Journals," i, 112.

[3] B.M. Add. MSS., 28061. Letter of 19th May 1786.

[4] *Ibid.* Letter of 12th December 1786.   [5] *Ibid.*

The Principles on which the Projet is founded are undoubtedly those on which it is to be wished that this business may be finally concluded, both as they tend to the mutual advantage of the two Countries in their commercial intercourse, and as they include the abolition of useless and injurious distinctions. But on the fullest consideration it has not appeared to His Majesty's servants that it would be proper to advise the immediate conclusion of a treaty on the footing of that Projet without some additions to it which may tend to give a more certain and permanent effect to these principles . . . In addition to this, the Projet, as it now stands affords no security that general prohibitions or prohibitory duties may not at any time take place in either Country to the exclusion of whatever may happen to be the chief articles of trade from the other. It is true that the same motives which should guide both parties in the present negotiation might for a long time prevent their adopting a conduct so contrary to the spirit of the proposed agreement. But it cannot be the wish of either Court to trust to this security only. We ought by all the means in our power to remove even the possibility of future jealousy on these subjects. And it appears from the observations of the French Government on the first sketch of this Projet that they felt the force of this remark. There can therefore be no doubt of their readiness to concur in anything which can give it a greater degree of stability and certainty. And we shall probably arrive sooner at the great object—a solid and comprehensive settlement of the commercial intercourse between the two countries than by beginning with a Preliminary Treaty, unexceptionable indeed in its principles, but which would necessarily reserve some very important points for separate discussion, and would in the meantime leave the whole system incomplete and precarious.[1]

Pitt then pointed out to Eden that the discussion of a compact of a temporary nature would tend to unsettle the minds of traders and perhaps even to discredit the whole undertaking. Accordingly he enclosed a Declaration, which comprised the substance of the French Projet, but gave it a more permanent form and set limits to the duties which might thereafter be levied. The letter shows that he had got over his first suspicions and was now working for a more thorough and permanent settlement than that sketched by Rayneval. The draft of the British Declaration is in Pitt's writing—a proof that he had taken this matter largely into his own hands. The replies of Eden to him are both long and frequent; but most of those preserved in the British Museum are too faded to be legible. In that of 6th June he warned Pitt

[1] Pitt MSS., 333.

that France was ready to settle matters on friendly terms, but, as there were many intrigues against the treaty, Pitt should conclude it promptly. More favourable terms might possibly be gained for British cottons and steel; but it would be best not to press the Versailles Cabinet too hard.[1]

Pitt, however, refused to hurry matters. Indeed, the only part of this long effusion which he heeded, seems to have been that respecting steel and cottons. He further distressed Eden by his action with regard to silks. Under pressure from the London silk-workers, he found it necessary to continue to exclude all foreign silk-goods,[2] which caused Eden to remark on 17th June: "With what face I am to propose the admission of English cottons and the exclusion of French silks I do not well foresee."[3]

Most of the official letters between Pitt and Eden will be found in Lord Auckland's Journals. We will therefore glance only at some of their letters which have not been published. They show that Pitt sought by all possible means to lessen the duties on British cottons and hardware imported into France, and that he demurred to the abrogation of the Methuen Treaty with Portugal (1703) which had accorded to her wines exceptionally favourable treatment. Discussions on these and other topics were retarded by the long debates at Westminster concerning the Sinking Fund and Warren Hastings: so that on 13th July Eden ironically informed Pitt that all his letters to him since 10th June had miscarried. The close of the session (11th July) left Pitt freer for diplomatic affairs; he threw himself into the bargaining with much zest, and Eden more than once hinted that a great outcry would arise in France if their Ministers gave way to our demands.

Nevertheless, Pitt struggled hard to obtain the best possible terms not only for Great Britain but also for Ireland. Despite Eden's repeated appeals for urgency, he asked the Duke of Rutland, Lord Lieutenant of Ireland, to induce the Irish Chancellor of the Exchequer, the Speaker, and Beresford to come to London for the purpose of advising him on several matters that con-

---

[1] This letter of 6th June has no date of the year, and it has been bound up in vol. 28064 of the Add. MSS. in the British Museum for the year 1789 of the Auckland MSS. Internal evidence shows that the year should be 1786.

[2] Their memorial, dated 22nd February 1786, is from the London silk trade (B.M. Add. MSS., 34420). It states that "no alteration or modification whatsoever, short of the present prohibition of all foreign wrought silks, can ensure the silk trade to this country."

[3] Pitt MSS., 110.

I   Z

cerned Ireland, especially as to the admission or exclusion of French linens. This further delay wrung Eden's heart, and he wrote on 31st August: "Your political courage goes beyond mine, for I suppose that you look without anxiety on this fortnight's delay, which we are giving. In truth, if it is given in politeness to Ireland, it is a great compliment; for it is impossible to do more for Ireland than we have done."[1] He then made the noteworthy prophecy that, as the treaty could not possibly adjust all the topics relating to the trade of Britain and Ireland, it would lead up to a right settlement between the two islands. Certainly Eden equalled Pitt in foresight, however much he fell short of him in coolness, determination, and bargaining power.

These qualities appear very forcibly in the Anglo-French negotiation. It is probable that Pitt bargained too closely; but the reason is apparent if one looks at the scores of petitions that reached him from alarmed manufacturers. Lancashire was well to the front in its demands for favourable terms; and we therefore find Pitt holding out for only a 5 per cent. duty in France on British cottons. To this Rayneval retorted by claiming at least 20 per cent.—" M. de Vergennes was of opinion," wrote Eden, " for 15 per cent., and M. de Calonne, after much dispute, and by the aid of a paper in which I had urged for 5 per cent., split the difference and carried it for 10 (but with great doubts)."[2] Calonne, the cheerful and prodigal Controller of Finances, now began to take a closer interest in the treaty; he inveighed against Pitt for prohibiting French silks while expecting the almost free entry of British cottons, and said that there were 60,000 workers at Lyons who would curse him for this treaty. This explains why the French negotiators once again held out for 15 per cent., and, when that was rejected by Pitt, finally fixed it at 12 per cent.

Pitt also struggled to gain easier terms for Irish linens in France, and suggested that if this were conceded, the Dublin Parliament would probably accept the Anglo-French treaty *in toto*.[3] On the subject of hardware Pitt fought for the interests of Birmingham, as appears in the draft of a long despatch to Eden, of 4th September, with many corrections and additions in his

---

[1] " Pitt-Rutland Corresp.," 158; " Beaufort Papers " (Hist. MSS. Commission), 353.

[2] Pitt MSS., 110. Eden to Pitt, 23rd August.

[3] *Ibid.* Pitt to Eden, 12th September.

writing. Very significant is the last sentence, which is in his hand:

If you cannot obtain a reduction to 5 or $7\frac{1}{2}$ per cent. on iron, copper, or brass, you will endeavour to gain it on iron alone, that being a point which H. M.'s servants have most earnestly at heart, and in which the reasoning above stated seems conclusive in our favour. This is a point to be pressed to the utmost, but if you should find it *absolutely* impossible to carry it, it should not ultimately prevent your signing the treaty.[1]

The treaty, signed at Versailles on 26th September 1786, may be thus summarized: It granted complete freedom of navigation and trading rights between the two nations for their European dominions. The subjects of either kingdom were thenceforth free to enter the lands of the other without licence or passport, and free of any capitation tax—a privilege most unusual in those days—and to enjoy perfect religious liberty. In regard to the most important of French exports, namely, wine, Great Britain agreed to place her neighbour on the footing of the most favoured nation by lowering the duties to the level of those imposed on Portuguese wines. The duties on French vinegar and oil were also greatly reduced. The following articles nominally concerned both nations, but in practice applied almost entirely to British imports into France. Hardware, cutlery, and similar goods were not to pay more than 10 per cent.; cottons, woollens, muslins, lawns, cambrics, and most kinds of gauzes, not more than 12 per cent.; but silks, or articles partly silken, were prohibited as formerly. Linens were reciprocally to be charged at no higher rates than those levied on Dutch linens imported into Ireland, that is, at "the most favoured nation" rates. Sadlery, porcelain, pottery, and glass of all kinds, were to pay no more than 12 per cent. The highest impost retained was 30 per cent., levied on beer, perhaps because the interchange of that product was certain to be small. Countervailing duties might, however, be placed on certain articles. In the concluding forty articles of the treaty (one of the longest and most complex ever signed), the contracting Powers sought to lay down principles or regulations for the avoidance of disputes with respect to contraband and prohibited

---

[1] " F. O.," France, 20. For further details see my article in the "Eng. Hist. Rev." for October 1908.

goods, smuggling, privateering, the suppression of piracy, and other subjects. They also left themselves free to revise the treaty at the end of twelve years. It is noteworthy that each of the contracting Powers affirmed the principle of seizing and confiscating the goods of the other Power when found on an enemy's merchantman, provided that they were embarked after the declaration of war.[1]

The treaty disappointed the hopes of some enthusiasts, who hoped that it might include some proviso for arbitration. Among these was William Pulteney, who, on 14th September, wrote to Pitt in terms that deserve to be remembered. After pointing out the futility of prohibitive edicts, he continued:

It is to be considered whether this is not a good opportunity to ingraft upon this treaty some arrangement that may effectually tend to prevent future wars at least for a considerable time. Why may not two nations adopt, what individuals often adopt who have dealings that may lead to disputes, the measure of agreeing beforehand that in case any differences shall happen which they cannot settle amicably, the question shall be referred to arbitration. The matter in dispute is seldom of much real consequence, but the point of honour prevents either party from yielding, but if it is decided by third parties, each may be contented. The arbitrators should not be sovereign princes; but might not each nation name three judges, either of their own courts of law, or of any other country, out of whom the opposite nation should choose one, and these two hear the question and either determine it or name an umpire—the whole proceedings to be in writing? This would occasion the matter to be better discussed than is commonly done, and would give time for the parties to cool and most probably reconcile them to the decision, whatever it might be.

It has frequently occurred to my mind that, if France and England understood each other, the world might be kept in peace from one end of the globe to the other. And why may they not understand each other? I allow that France is the most intriguing nation upon earth; that they are restless and faithless; but is it impossible to show them that every object of their intrigue may be better assured by good faith and a proper intelligence with us, and might we not arrange everything together now so as completely to satisfy both? . . .[2]

Pitt, we may note, had sought to take a first step towards the

[1] "Parl. Hist.," xxvi, 233-54; "Auckland Corresp.," i, 495-515; Martens, "Traités," iv, 155-80.
[2] Pitt MSS., 169.

limitation of armaments, by suggesting that the two Powers should lessen their squadrons in the East Indies; but to this Vergennes, on 1st April 1786, refused his assent.[1] Seeing, too, that France was pressing on the works at Cherbourg, and forming an East India Company on a great scale, Pitt naturally restricted his aims to the establishment of friendly commercial relations. The progress made in this respect was immense. Powers recently at war had never before signed a treaty containing provisions of so wide a scope, and so intimate a character; and lovers of peace hailed it as inaugurating a new era of goodwill. "People in general," wrote the Duke of Dorset, from London, to Mr. Eden, "are very much pleased with your treaty: the principal merchants in the City don't choose to give an opinion about it; anything, if novel, is apt to stupify merchants. . . . I never saw the King in such spirits: they rise in proportion to the stocks, which are beyond the sanguine expectations of everybody."[2] The rise in Consols gave the verdict of the City in unmistakable terms, and it was generally endorsed. On 20th November the Marquis of Buckingham wrote: "My accounts are that all manufacturers are run wild in speculation. Our wool has felt it already."[3] A few cranks like Lord George Gordon declaimed against Pitt for selling his country to the French, but the majority of thinking men, even in the Chamber of Manufacturers, thankfully accepted the treaty. A Glasgow manufacturer wrote to Eden that Great Britain, having the best wool, the best iron, the best clays for pottery, the best coal, and by far the best machinery in the world, would soon beat the French in their own market.[4] This was the general opinion. Those who held it said nothing, but set to work to regain in France herself the market of which she had deprived us in America. The state of Great Britain and of France in the year 1789 showed which were the more durable, the triumphs of war or of peace.

Nevertheless, there was some opposition in the House of Commons. Early in the session of 1787, Fox brought forward the question of the treaty and pressed for delay, so that the feeling of the country might be ascertained. To this Pitt demurred, on the ground that members had had ample time to consider the

[1] "F. O.," France, 18.
[2] "Auckland Journals," i, 392, 6th October 1786.
[3] "Dropmore P.," i, 274.   [4] "Auckland Journals," i, 404.

questions at issue, and that trade would suffer from the continuance of the present uncertainty. The arts which had undermined Pitt's compact with Ireland were now once more practised. Burke twitted the Prime Minister with looking on the affairs of two great nations in a counting-house spirit; and the Chamber of Manufacturers, in which opinions were divided, sought to frighten members by a petition setting forth " the serious and awful importance of the treaty . . . comprehending a prodigious change in the commercial system of this country." [1] This stage thunder was speedily divested of its terrors by Pitt pointing out that four months had elapsed since the signing of the treaty, and yet the Chamber of Manufacturers had remained silent until that day (12th February). After showing that neither our old ally, Portugal, nor our manufacturers had cause for alarm, Pitt raised the question to a high level in a passage which furnished a dignified retort both to the gibe of Burke, and to those who denounced trade with our traditional enemy: " To suppose," he said, " that any nation can be unalterably the enemy of another is weak and childish. It has its foundation neither in the experience of nations nor in the history of man. It is a libel on the constitution of political societies, and supposes the existence of diabolical malice in the original frame of man." Then, coming once more to practical considerations, he affirmed that, though the treaty was advantageous to France, it would be more so to us. [2]

In reply, Fox made one of the worst speeches of his career. He asserted twice over that France was the natural enemy of this land, owing to her overweening pride and boundless ambition; and that by means of the present treaty she sought to tie our hands and prevent us engaging in any alliances with foreign powers. Portugal, he said, was now made a sacrifice and peace-offering to France. The House refused to follow the vagaries of the Whig leader by 258 votes to 118; and the provisions of the treaty were passed in Committee by substantial majorities within a fortnight. The treaty passed the Lords on 6th March by 74 votes to 24. [3] In due course the treaty was ratified, and

---

[1] "Auckland Journals," i, 404; "Parl. Hist.," xxvi, 342-78.

[2] Ibid., 392, 394.

[3] Ibid., 397, 398, 402, 424, 595. Mr. J. L. le B. Hammond in his able work, "Charles James Fox" (1903), defends his hero on the ground that monarchical France was the enemy of England.

the ports on both sides of the Channel were opened to free commercial intercourse on 10th May 1787.

Pitt undoubtedly erred in proclaiming his conviction that the treaty was more advantageous to Great Britain than to France. He clinched his triumph in Parliament, but he imperilled the treaty; and it is noteworthy that he made that statement after Eden had warned him not to do so.[1] It was a weakness of which he was rarely guilty. The French negotiators had often pointed out that they were running a great risk of inflicting much harm on their industries. This was sober truth. Indeed, their general acquiescence in Pitt's requests has always been a puzzle; for the belief of Vergennes in Free Trade was not shared by the other Ministers, except perhaps by Calonne; and it was certain that the manufacturers of Rouen, Amiens, and Lille would cry out against the sudden change from prohibition to a 12 per cent. duty on textiles.

Daniel Hailes set himself to solve the riddle for the satisfaction of the ever distrustful Carmarthen, who, on 29th September 1786, wrote to him privately: " our suspicions of the good faith and friendly professions of France in political matters ought to be in exact proportion to the facility she may have evinced upon matters purely commercial." He further suggested that her aim was perhaps to sever our good relations with States with which we had political and commercial ties.[2] Hailes, doubtless taking his cue from his chief, thereupon sought to find out the motives which had influenced the French Ministry, and summed up his conclusions in a long report. It gives an interesting but somewhat jaundiced account of affairs in that very critical year 1786—the year of the Diamond Necklace scandal and of the decision to convoke the Chamber of Notables for the rectification of abuses too deep-seated for Louis XVI to uproot. The report is too long to quote here except in its most important passage; but we may glance at its salient features. Hailes pointed out that France suffered nearly as much as England from the late war, which left her with a National Debt almost exactly equal to that of her rival; also that the hopes of Frenchmen to gain the trade of the United States had been blighted. The Court of Versailles had, moreover, not exercised " the wise management of venality and the

---

[1] Pitt MSS., 110. Eden to Pitt, 13th April 1786.
[2] " F. O.," France, 18.

œconomy of corruption and favor " which would have satisfied most of the privileged classes. Its partiality was as notorious as its extravagance; and the failure of the old commercial prohibitive system, as also of the recent prohibitive *arrêts*, was probably due to the corruption prevalent in Court and official circles; for, to quote Hailes's words:

> Every one having credit enough with the great, or the mistresses of the great, to procure an exemption, would not have failed to apply for it in favour of some dependent or other. It seems therefore probable that the French Government felt its own inability to give effect to its prohibitory laws against the importation of British manufactures, and in that respect, at all events, they may be said to have been gainers by the treaty.
>
> But I think I can take upon me to assure your Lordship that there exists another and no less principal cause of the eagerness of France to conclude the commercial arrangement. I mean that of the immediate relief of the *Trésor Royal* by the increase of the Revenue, an increase which, it may be presumed, will prove immense, from the sudden influx of all sorts of British merchandise paying the legal duties, as soon as the Treaty shall take effect. If this opinion should prove to be well grounded (and from the attention which I have paid to the late conduct of the Comptroller General [Calonne] I am much inclined to think it is) it will be a strong mark of the corruption of that Minister, who sacrifices to an immediate and temporary resource the dearest interests of his country.[1]

We need not lay much stress on the personal arguments here adduced; for Hailes may have been unduly influenced by the partisans of Necker or Breteuil, who were always at feud with Calonne. It is probable that Vergennes and Calonne were swayed by a deeper motive, namely, the desire to keep England quiet and friendly while they laid their schemes with a view to the ascendency of France in the Dutch affairs soon to be described, and thereafter to the combination of their efforts for the overthrow of British power in the East. Such an aim is consonant with the philosophic thoroughness of the character of Vergennes and the ambition of his showy colleague. Whether Pitt suspected some such design is uncertain; that Carmarthen did so can admit of no doubt.

[1] "F. O.," France, 18. Hailes to Carmarthen, 25th October 1786. The Duke of Dorset thought very little of Hailes, but Hailes's despatches show far more knowledge of France than the Duke's.

Much, however, may be said for Hailes's views. It is generally admitted that the prodigal Calonne sacrificed very much in
order to stand well with the Queen's party, and that his ardent
desire was to put a good face on things at the time of the
Assembly of the Notables early in 1787. There was every
reason for his concern. The future of France depended on the
docility of the Notables. If they were so far satisfied with the
state of affairs as to pass the reforms desired by the King and
Vergennes, the crisis which led up to the Revolution might
have ended peacefully. Unjust taxation, constant deficits, and
national bankruptcy were among the chief causes of the Revolution. Of course, Vergennes and Calonne could not foresee
events; but they knew that the future was gloomy in the
extreme unless the Notables induced the privileged classes to
take up their fair share of the financial burdens. If Ministers
were able to point to increased customs returns, the decline of
smuggling, and the cementing of friendly relations with England,
the Notables and the nobles at large might prove amenable to
reason (for Anglomania was still the fashion); and all might yet
go well. In these considerations probably lies the key to the
conduct of the French Ministry in the later stages of the
negotiation of 1786. With Vergennes the treaty was probably a
matter of principle; to Calonne it was a device adopted in the
course of that daring game of "neck or nothing," on which he
staked the destinies of France. Though he was the chief sinner,
Government and people alike behaved with incredible levity.
Alvensleben, reporting on the situation at Versailles in November
1787, said: "Everything here is a matter of ceremony, clothes,
varnish, phrases, national boasting, tinsel, intrigues; and everything is finally decided by forms."[1]

. This scathing report was written after France had lost her one
able statesman. Vergennes died shortly before the Notables
assembled; and they, having to deal with an irresolute King and
a political gamester, turned a deaf ear to counsels of Reform.
Probably, too, they were influenced by the outcry against the
commercial treaty, for it was general in all manufacturing centres,
and did not pass away, as was the case in Great Britain. The
Rouen Chamber of Commerce instituted an inquiry, the outcome
of which was a report affirming the marked superiority of

---

[1] Flammermont, *op. cit.*, 125.

British textile goods to those of France, and the impossibility of competing with them on the basis of the 12 per cent. duty. An able writer, Dupont de Nemours, gave an effective answer to the report; but, as generally happens in such cases, the defence attracted less attention than the attack.[1] We must further remember that merchants who lived under an oppressive system of taxation had every possible reason for " crying poor." Complaints against the commercial treaty were hurled at Arthur Young in every French manufacturing town which he visited in his tours of 1787 and 1788. Abbeville, Amiens, Lille, and Lyons declared against it in varying tones of anger or despair; the wine districts alone were loud in its praise.[2] Undoubtedly the French textile industries suffered severely for a time. The taste for English goods continued to depress home products, and that, too, despite the efforts of Marie Antoinette to set the fashion for the latter. In 1788 as many as 5,442 looms were idle in Lyons; but it is to be observed that this crisis was due either to the continued smuggling of English silk goods, to the preference for our fine cottons, or to the failure of the silk harvest in that year. The last cause was probably the most important.[3] The woollen and cotton trades alone could have been directly affected by the treaty. In them the conditions were undoubtedly bad in the years 1787, 1788. At Troyes 443 looms were not worked out of 2,600, and that proportion was usual throughout the east and north of France.

M. Levasseur, however, who has carefully investigated the causes of this crisis, attributes it largely to the utter prostration of public credit in France, and the issue of a coinage of doubtful value. The bad harvest of 1788, followed by a terribly cold winter, also intensified the distress. He concludes that, even so, the commercial treaty might ultimately have been advantageous to certain parts of the industrial economy of France; but it was applied suddenly in a time of political unsettlement and general distress.[4]

We must also remember that Calonne had for many months been squandering the resources of France. In accordance with

[1] See summaries of both in Butenval, *op. cit.*, chs. xv, xvi.
[2] Arthur Young's " Travels in France " (Bohn edit., 1889), 8, 9, 69, 107, 284.
[3] Levasseur, " Hist. des Classes ouvrières," ii, 776.
[4] This is the judgement of R. Stourm, " Les Finances de l'Ancien Régime et de la Révolution," 59.

his motto: " In order to establish public credit one must cultivate luxury," he had raised loan upon loan in time of peace, and
it has been estimated that in the forty-one months of his term
of office (1783-87) he borrowed 650,000,000 francs (£26,000,000).[1]
No fiscal experiment can have a fair chance under such conditions; and it is therefore a violation of the laws of evidence to
assert that the Commercial Treaty of 1786 was the chief cause
of the French Revolution.

Summing up the facts concerning this most interesting treaty,
we may conclude that the honour of originating it undoubtedly
belongs firstly to Vergennes, secondly to Shelburne, and only in
the third place to Pitt. It is clear that the French statesman
worked steadily for it during the negotiations of 1783, and used
all available means to bring it about even while Pitt showed no
responsive desire. As has been shown above, the young Prime
Minister had good reasons for not taking the matter up seriously
until the autumn of 1785. Indeed it would have been a tactical
mistake to press on the commercial compact with France until
he had put forth every effort to unite Ireland with Great Britain
by intimate trade relations. When those endeavours were frustrated by ignorance and faction, he turned towards France, but
slowly and suspiciously. Not until the negotiation was far advanced did he show much eagerness on the subject. But it is
the mark of a great Minister to keep a firm grasp upon colleagues
and subordinates at all important points; and Pitt saw the
futility of Carmarthen's prejudices no less than the possible
danger of Eden's Gallophile enthusiasm.

The hostile actions of the French agents in Holland, to which
we must soon recur, made him cautious on matters purely
political; and, while pushing on the commercial treaty, which
Carmarthen looked on as a trap, he took care to subject the
ardent fancies of Eden to cold douches like the following:
" Though in the commercial business I think there are reasons
for believing the French may be sincere, I cannot listen without
suspicion to their professions of political friendship." [2] As we
shall see in the next chapters, Pitt generally treated with wholesome scepticism the alarmist news sent by Harris from The
Hague. But the tidings from that quarter enabled Pitt to assess
at their due value the philanthropic professions of the *salons* of

" Cambridge Mod. Hist.," viii, 74.
[2] "Auckland Journals," i, 127. Pitt to Eden, 10th June 1786.

Paris. Not that he was indifferent to the golden hopes of that age. After the treaty was signed he gave expression to his hopes in words pulsating with a noble enthusiasm; but, while it was under discussion, he showed the balance of mind and keenness in bargaining which characterize a great statesman. We may also remark here that Pitt sought earnestly to bring about a favourable commercial treaty with Spain and Russia, but failed. The Czarina showed her hostility by granting to France a treaty on the basis of the most favoured nation.[1]

Finally, we may hazard the conjecture that, if the finances of France had received from the Court of Versailles and Calonne a tithe of the fostering care which Pitt bestowed on those of Great Britain, both countries would have profited equally from the free commercial and social intercourse inaugurated by this memorable compact. As it was, France slid fast down the slope that led to the chasm of Revolution; and in the midst of that catastrophe Robespierre and his followers, who represented the prejudices of the northern manufacturing towns, spread abroad the spiteful falsehood that Pitt's commercial policy had ever been aimed at the financial ruin of the French nation.

Martens, "Traites," iv, 196-223. For these negotiations with Spain and Russia, see Salomon's "Pitt," 237-44. A little later Pitt started commercial negotiations with Prussia and Holland, but nothing came of them. It is clear, however, that he sought to revise the whole of our commercial relations.

CHAPTER XV

THE DUTCH CRISIS

(1786, 1787)

If we lose the Netherlands, France will acquire what she has always considered as the climax of her power.—SIR JAMES HARRIS, 1st May, 1787.

His Majesty wishes only the preservation of the independence and true constitution of the [Dutch] Republic.—THE MARQUIS OF CARMARTHEN, 29th June, 1787 (B. M. Add. MSS., 35539).

WE have interrupted our survey of Pitt's foreign policy in order to present a connected account of that interesting episode, the commercial treaty with France. But this event took place in a year which witnessed the growth of a crisis so serious as to threaten ruin to that constructive effort. The crisis arose from the sharp conflict of interests between Great Britain and France in Dutch affairs, as described in Chapter XIII. As no adequate account has yet appeared in English on this question, I propose to treat it on a scale proportionate to its importance.

The reader will remember that the feuds between the Patriots, abetted by France and the Stadholder's party, had already aroused keen interest at London and Paris; that our able envoy, Harris, had bravely waged an unequal campaign for the Prince and Princess of Orange—unequal, because Pitt persistently forbade him to commit this country to the defence of their cause, though sentiment and policy linked it to that of England. Further, the general situation of the Powers then seemed irretrievably to doom the Prince's fortunes. Frederick the Great, in his desire to keep on good terms with France, refused to help his niece, Wilhelmina, Princess of Orange. Austria was allied with France, and Russia with Austria. Finally, neither Pitt nor the Marquis of Carmarthen deemed it possible to frame an alliance with Prussia; and all the advances which they made to the Czarina, Catharine II, and the Emperor Joseph II, were coldly

349

repelled. In fact, no Power cared for an alliance with England. The conclusion of the Franco-Dutch alliance of November 1785 seemed to close all doors against her. When the fortunes of a State have been on the decline, it is very hard to stop the downward movement. That was the position of Great Britain early in the year 1786.

The only sources of hope seemed to be in the imminence of the death of Frederick and in the outrageous actions of the Dutch Patriots. Their violent support of provincial rights and hatred of the Stadholder and his mildly centralizing policy were carried to strange lengths. The Estates of Holland decreed that no Orange songs were to be sung, and no Orange colours worn. Harris relates that a woman came near to be hanged for the latter offence. Even the vendor of carrots was suspect unless he left the roots in a protective coating of soil. To a home-loving people like the Dutch these pedantries became ever more hateful. The bovine character of the Stadholder was to some extent a safeguard; for who could reasonably claim that his colossal powers of inaction would ever be a danger to the Republic? It is fairly certain that he had the allegiance of the rural population everywhere, even in the Province of Holland; but the populace of the large towns was overwhelmingly on the side of the Patriots; and the Estates of Holland (a province which contained more than half the population, and more than half the wealth, of the whole Union) decidedly opposed him.[1] Of the smaller provinces, Guelderland, Zealand, and Friesland supported the Stadholder. Utrecht was torn with schism on this subject, the rural districts cleaving to him, while the city of Utrecht broke away, and defied his authority. As Pitt forbade Harris to take any step which would commit England to the defence of the Stadholder, that envoy continued to play an apparently hopeless game. But his skill, resource, his commanding personality, and occasional bribes, enabled him to continue the struggle, even in democratic Holland. His great difficulty was that France in April 1786 had let it be known that she would allow no other Power to interfere in Dutch affairs, and would forcibly oppose any such attempt. To strive against the Patriots while

[1] The contributions of the Provinces to the needs of the Union show their respective resources. Out of every 100 florins of federal revenue, Holland contributed 57¾, Friesland 11½, Zealand 9, Groningen 5¾, Utrecht 5¾, Guelderland 5½, Overyssel 3½, Drent 1.

they had a ground of confidence utterly denied to their opponents, was to condemn Harris to struggle against great odds, and
never has an unequal fight been more gallantly fought. The
worst symptom was the rise of bodies of armed burghers, styled
Free Corps, which soon attained considerable strength. Encouraged by success, the Patriots sought to depose William V outright, and proclaimed the Princess Regent during the minority
of her son. She rejected this scheme with indignation. Failing
here, they struck at the authority of the Prince by procuring
from the Estates of Holland his deposition from the command
of the regular troops of that province. This blow could not be
parried; and it dealt consternation among the loyalists.

There was no hope of help from Frederick the Great. For the
reasons previously stated he had hardened his heart against all
the appeals that came from the Princess of Orange; and she
finally rejected with scorn his advice that she should come to
terms with the Patriots and France. On 16th May 1786 Harris
summed up the relations of Prussia to France and Holland
in this sprightly way:

" Prussia says to France ' Do what you please in Holland, but
leave at least the appearance of a Stadholderian Government.'—
France replies—' We shall lose the confidence and support of the
Patriots and with it our whole influence in the Republic if we
mention the word " Stadholder "; take from us the odium of the
measure by declaring you cannot see him deposed. We then
may, without displeasing our friends, espouse his cause to a certain degree, and we shall both be satisfied.' " [1]

While the welter was ever increasing in this once prosperous
land, there came a gleam of hope from the East. On 17th
August 1786 Frederick the Great was gathered to his fathers,
and his nephew Frederick William II reigned in his stead. As
Prince Royal he had spoken warmly of his resolve to right the
wrongs of his sister, the Princess of Orange; but as King he
disappointed her hopes. His character was despicable. Extravagance and dissipation were accountable for private debts amounting to one million sterling at the time of his accession and soon

---

[1] For details see Luckwaldt, *op. cit.* On a similar plan, Harris had written
to Carmarthen on 3rd January 1786 that the idea of France keeping the
Stadholder in his position and England then aiding him is so monstrous
that Frederick " must think us mere novices in politicks " (B.M. Add. MSS.,
28061).

after to three-quarters of a million more.[1] But his irresolution was of more serious consequence. A vicious man may excel as a ruler; an unstable man, never. Frederick William had scarcely a feature in common with the masterful race of the Hohenzollerns. The contrast between him and his uncle was startling. In place of that silent, cynical, and dogged ruler, Berlin and Sans-Souci rejoiced in a handsome, affable monarch, who seemed made to win the hearts of all at first sight and to lose them on closer acquaintance. For it was found that with him work and policy depended on whims and moods. Swaying to and fro between energy and sloth, violence and timidity, he disconcerted his Ministers, until they came to see that the King's resolves were as fleeting as his feelings. After the first flush of activity wore away, languor pervaded every bureau of that centralized autocracy. On 6th January 1787 Lord Dalrymple, our ambassador at Berlin, wrote of the King: "in general he appears very indifferent about what is passing"; and he further reported that he urgently desired to "get rid of so irksome an affair" as his sister's troubles, and looked on the Prince of Orange as the chief cause of the dissensions in the Dutch Netherlands.[2] Another of our envoys, with more wit than is usually found in semi-official letters, summed up the difference between Frederick the Great and Frederick William II by saying that the former had the wisdom of Solomon, but the latter resembled that potentate only in respect of his overflowing harem. Mirabeau's opinion on the imminent downfall of the Prussian State is too well known to need quoting here.

Yet the nonchalance of Frederick William in foreign affairs is not wholly indefensible. Confronted by the alliance of those scheming and unscrupulous rulers, Catharine II and Joseph II, he could effect little until he had the friendship of one at least of the Great Powers; but France was pledged to Austria, and England was still averse from a Prussian alliance. On 20th October 1786 Dalrymple thus summed up his arguments against a compact with the Court of Berlin: "We might indeed form a temporary co-operation with Prussia for some particular purposes, as at present in the case of Holland, where little or no opposition is to be expected from the two Imperial Courts; but

---

[1] B.M. Add. MSS., 28061 and 28062. Dalrymple to Carmarthen, 20th October 1786, 23rd January 1787.

[2] "F. O.," Prussia, 11. So Luckwaldt, *op. cit.*, 52-7.

to enter into a general and permanent system with Prussia alone, without the concurrence of other Powers, would be a measure, in my apprehension, perfectly frantic, and only to be justified by a combination similar to that in 1756 being formed against us." Four days later, after an interview with Hertzberg, Dalrymple wrote that a Northern League between us and the Baltic Powers was out of the question during the lifetime of the Czarina, seeing that Turkish schemes stood first in her thoughts, and these implied alliance with Joseph.[1] As will shortly appear, the knowledge which the Turks had of these schemes was to lead to the Eastern War of 1787, which ended the suspense besetting Prussia and England.

For the present the isolation of these States left them in a most precarious position. The utmost they could hope for was to struggle on, waiting for a turn of Fortune's wheel in their favour. The first aim of the Court of Berlin was to thwart the Austrian scheme for exchanging the Belgic provinces for Bavaria. Joseph II still pursued this phantom, though he had his hands full in Brabant, where philosophism had again stirred up revolt, and his alliance with Catharine portended war with the resentful Turks. Frederick William believed, and perhaps rightly, that so long as the Austro-Russian alliance held good, Prussia could take no step Rhinewards. He therefore saw in the entreaties of his sister only a scheme to draw him into fatal courses; and when the entreaties became reproaches his answers became few and cold.[2]

Unfortunately, too, the influence of the veteran diplomatist, Hertzberg, was waning, because of an austere and somewhat superior manner which the young King resented. That Minister favoured a close understanding with England with a view to joint action at The Hague; but there was associated with him at the Foreign Ministry a colleague, Count Finckenstein, who strongly inclined towards France, thwarted Hertzberg's efforts, and prejudiced the King against an English alliance.[3] To add

---

[1] B.M. Add. MSS., 28061. See, too, "Malmesbury Diaries," ii, 212, for Carmarthen's view. "I never desire a connexion with Prussia unless Russia, and of course, Denmark, are included."

[2] All the despatches of this time serve to refute the statement of Lecky (v, 80) that the accession of Frederick William "greatly changed the situation" for the Princess of Orange.

[3] Wittichen, *op. cit.*, 63-5.

I   A A

to the perplexities of the time, Thulemeyer, the Prussian envoy at The Hague, supported France; and Harris suspected him, perhaps rightly, of having been bought over by the Patriots and their paymasters. He certainly thwarted the efforts of Görtz, a special envoy sent from Berlin to The Hague; and finally the Princess of Orange begged her brother, seeing that he would not help her, at least not to allow Thulemeyer to act in concert with De Verac, the French envoy at The Hague.[1] Early in May she sent a request for a loan of Prussian cannon in order to withstand the growing forces of the Patriots, but met with a refusal.

Matters, however, now took a turn for the better for that unfortunate Princess. Latterly the Court of Berlin had sought to arrange with that of Versailles a plan of joint intervention so as to end the strifes in the United Provinces in a way not too derogatory to the Prince of Orange. But this proposal was accompanied by conditions which were at once very tartly rejected by the Court of Versailles. This refusal of a friendly overture was to have far-reaching results, for the irritation of the Prussian monarch now led him to favour the idea of intervention in Holland.

This brief survey will have enabled us to understand the gradual development of Pitt's policy from strict neutrality to tentative and cautious activity. The change of attitude will be found to correspond closely with a change in Continental affairs which enabled him with little risk to raise his country once more to her rightful position.

It is the mark of a great statesman to keep his gaze on all the chief matters of public interest, to weigh their importance, and to make his policy the resultant, as it were, of the leading forces and best tendencies of his age. No one who has not a clear vision and ripe judgement can give such an assessment and act on it with tact and firmness. Small minds are certain to be diverted towards side issues and hastily to take up questions which are unripe for solution. From these faults Pitt's singular maturity of mind and steadiness of purpose kept him free. He saw that the greatest of British interests was peace; and, despite the pressing claims of Harris at The Hague, he refused to be drawn blindfold into the irritating and obscure questions there

[1] "F. O.," Prussia, 11. Dalrymple to Carmarthen, 21st April 1787.

at stake. True, it was important to keep the United Provinces from becoming dependent on France; but he believed that the efforts of the Patriots in that direction might be curbed by means of diplomacy. No statesman prefers a warlike to a peaceful solution unless all the resources of his own craft have been exhausted, least of all could the champion of economy, who naturally discounted the clamorous appeals of Harris for help.

There were reasons why our envoy should urge Pitt to adopt a more forward policy. In the autumn of 1786 the fortunes of the Stadholder steadily declined, and the raids of the Patriots on his prerogatives became more daring and successful. In September, as we saw, he was deprived of the command of the regular forces in the Province of Holland. His opponents, the Patriots, next strengthened their Free Corps, drew a cordon of troops along the frontiers of Holland, and overthrew his authority in the hitherto loyal provinces, Overyssel and Groningen. The city of Utrecht also defied him and elected Estates, while those of the still loyal Province of Utrecht assembled at Amersfoort. Other towns, even in the loyal provinces, seemed likely to follow the example of Utrecht. In face of these facts the appeals of Harris for help became more urgent than ever. On 24th October he wrote privately to Carmarthen: " As we are afraid to threaten, we must either bribe or give up the game." [1] But, realizing more and more that the obstacle to his forward policy lay in the peaceful resolves of Pitt, he wrote directly to him on 28th November, pointing out that France was making amazing strides everywhere at our expense, that she was on the point of gaining complete control over the United Provinces, and he hinted that that accession to her naval strength and to her resources in the East Indies would enable her soon to attack England in overwhelming strength.

Much could be said in favour of this view. The activity of France in the East, as we saw in the last chapter, had been very threatening, and it is clear that the schemes of St. Priest and other French agents in Egypt pointed out the path on which Bonaparte set forth with heroic stride thirteen years later. Dreams of a French Empire in the East haunted many minds at Paris in 1786. On 7th September, shortly before the signature of the Anglo-French commercial treaty, Hailes, Secretary of

[1] B.M. Add. MSS , 28060.

Legation at Paris, reported that the French Government seemed to be preparing for "the entire subversion" of British power in India; and he cynically added that when the time for action came, "then, as formerly, the rights of mankind will be held out as the pretext."[1] Even Eden sent word that there was talk of a design that France should gain control over all the Dutch ports in the East Indies.[2] When we remember that the Cape of Good Hope was a Dutch possession, and that the British lands in India were scattered and weak, we can appreciate the gravity of the crisis.

The surmises of Hailes and Eden were correct. There was a powerful party at the French Court which worked in alliance with the Dutch Patriots for the control of the East Indies. They saw their opportunity in the bankruptcy then threatening the Dutch East India Company; and in the winter of 1786 the Patriot leader, the Rhinegrave of Salm, sent to the Cabinet of Versailles a plan of a Franco-Dutch alliance with a view to the overthrow of the British power in India. Thanks to the pacific views of Louis XVI and Vergennes, nothing came of the scheme; but the Patriots then changed front and offered to hand over to France the important naval station, Trincomalee, in the north-east of Ceylon, to serve as a place of arms for France in case of war. This plan had a favourable reception at Versailles, some of the Ministers urging that 18,000 troops should be sent out under the command of General de Bouillé. This soldier (the hero of Carlyle's stirring account of the Mutiny of Nancy in 1790) states in his Memoirs[3] that he remained some time at Paris in hopes of receiving the order for the conquest of the British settlements in India; but he remained in vain; for the French Cabinet *found no opportunity for going to war*. The events now to be described will explain the sorry ending to these golden hopes; and the reader will bear in mind that the struggle of the rival Powers for ascendancy in Holland concerned the fate of Britain's Indian Empire no less than her position in Europe.[4]

---

[1] "F. O.," France, 18.   [2] Pitt MSS., 110.   [3] Bouillé, "Mems.," ch. i.

[4] Grenville during his mission to The Hague in August 1787 got an inkling of the wider scheme described above, as appears in his phrase "One's mind at once runs to Trincomale." So late as August 1788 Pitt was nervous about the fate of that port. See his letter to Grenville as to the rumour of 800 French troops sailing thither ("Dropmore P.," ii, 280, 353).

All the more astonishing, then, is the calmness of Pitt's reply to Harris of 5th December 1786. In it he directed him to do all in his power to keep together the Orange party, so that it might " act with advantage, both for their own country and for us, on some future day, if it should arrive." For the present, however, that party must " lie by," and avoid pushing things to an extremity which would commit both themselves and England.[1]

This cautious policy was perhaps in some measure due to the King, who strongly opposed a forward policy in the Netherlands. His chief preoccupation in the years 1786, 1787, was the extra-vagance of the Prince of Wales and the rapidly increasing ex-pense of his own family, to which he refers in pathetic terms. The news of the activity of Sir James Harris at The Hague "much affected" him; and when, on 7th January 1787, Lord Carmarthen wrote to Windsor in order to suggest a more ener-getic policy in the Netherlands, a sharp retort came, bidding that Minister remember "the disgraceful conduct" of England in the late war, and asserting that he (George III) refused to act as the *Draw-can-sir* of Europe.[2]

From the tenour of the King's letter to Pitt on 8th January we may infer that Carmarthen had kept his overture to Windsor secret; and Pitt, on hearing of it from the King, must have felt piqued at his colleague's action. Already they were on strained terms owing to Pitt having insisted on Carmarthen's presence at Court, despite indisposition, in order to present the Portuguese envoy; and a chief who demanded so strict an observance of etiquette was certain to resent any private attempt of his Foreign Minister to influence the King's opinions on a far weightier question. There is an apologetic tone in Carmarthen's hitherto unpublished letter of 8th January to Pitt. The first sentences refer to his ill health, and are omitted:

Hendon, Jan. 8, 1787.
My dear Sir,
I wish to lay before you *in confidence* my letter to the King of yesterday, together with His Majesty's answer of this morning's date, which I am free to confess to you has occasioned me a considerable degree of uneasiness. . . . You will, I am sure, do me the justice to remark the manner in which I have stated my opinion to the King and I have always understood your sentiments to be precisely the same in

[1] "Dropmore P.," ii, 251-5.
[2] *Ibid.*, 267, 268; "Leeds Memoranda," 117.

regard to the *object*, though perhaps more cautious (from prudential and well founded motives) in the means to be employed. I am free to own that, eager as I am for preventing France acquiring the absolute command of Holland, I have always thought we might succeed by means of private negotiation and intrigue. The experiment of trying to combat her with her own weapons would have some merit; and, convinced as I am that she has reckoned all along upon England not interfering, I think the present moment must not be passed by without our endeavouring to make the most we can of the Provinces which are opposed to Holland, and of the present firmness of the Prince and Princess of Orange. *L'Assemblée des Notables* is I think some security for the pacific disposition of France, or rather for her inability of indulging any of a contrary nature at present. I should hope we might have a meeting on Thursday for the Dutch business.[1]

The differences between Pitt and Carmarthen were greater than are here represented; and the joint influence of the King and Pitt prevented the adoption of the more spirited measures towards which he inclined. This was gall and wormwood to Harris. That able envoy, looking on helplessly at the brilliant diplomatic successes of France, failed to see the canker which was eating at her heart. The Assembly of the Notables was " the beginning of the end." It implied the inability of the absolute monarchy to carry the urgently needed reforms or to meet the ordinary expenses of the State. Pitt saw this. Further, while Harris admitted that he regarded France as " a natural enemy," Pitt looked on her as a possible friend. On the Dutch Question alone was there keen rivalry between the two States; and, in view of the growing financial difficulties of France, delay was more than ever advisable; for her efforts abroad must slacken as her vitality lessened under the load of debt that Calonne was gaily heaping up. In the meantime, until the Prussian monarch had the will, and England had the power, to intervene, Harris must continue his Sisyphus toil, and the Prince and Princess must suffer further indignities. Such was Pitt's policy. To our envoy it seemed unbearably mean; but it won in the end, and all the more surely for the delay. A Minister at the centre can often see things in truer perspective than an ambassador who is, after all, only at one point on the circumference.

Harris continued stoutly to roll the stone uphill. He helped

[1] Pitt MSS., 151.

to form an Association of the Provinces, towns and persons opposed to any change in the constitution; and, as the Stadholder in the early part of 1787 showed far more spirit and tact, the Patriots found it by no means easy to push the stone backwards. Harris declared on 20th April 1787 that the popular indignation ran strongly against the Patriots, who had not one-twentieth of the people on their side. This is incredible; but it is quite certain that his activity and the less determined policy of Montmorin, the successor of Vergennes at Versailles, put new heart into the Stadholder's party. Nevertheless, the Patriots carried the day at Amsterdam by sheer audacity, and compelled the Regents, or magistrates, to dismiss nine of their number. This act of violence, together with the increasing activity of William V and the signs of wavering at Versailles, led Harris to request an interview with Ministers at Whitehall.[1] He also bore a letter of the Princess to George III, which met with no favourable response.

A Cabinet meeting was held on 23rd May 1787, at which Harris was present, and submitted his opinions to a full discussion. Ministers met at Thurlow's house for dinner; and he in due course launched forth on the troubled sea of Dutch politics, stating at great length the arguments against intervention, then tearing them to pieces, and declaring even for war with France, if the need arose. Richmond, Master of the Ordnance, called for maps, discussed the military situation, and urged the need of speedy preparations. Pitt then admitted the immense importance of preserving the independence of Holland, and of facing war as a possible, but not probable, alternative; then, turning to Harris, he pressed him to say which course involved the greater risk, that of opposing France at once before she entirely dominated the Dutch Netherlands, or that of awaiting the issue of her present efforts. He also asked what kind of help the Orange party most needed. In reply to this and to similar questions from Thurlow, Harris urged that money should be supplied, especially to the Province of Guelderland; he declared that the supporters of the constitution would probably be overborne if they were not helped by England; that France was not in such a condition as to go to war in order to conquer Holland, but that when she

---

[1] "Malmesbury Diaries," ii, 299. "I am certain if we begin to roar, France will shrink before us" (Harris to Carmarthen, 5th May). See, too, Wittichen, 67.

had the upper hand there she probably would throw down the gauntlet. Stafford then declared in favour of intervention. Nevertheless, Pitt held firmly to his conviction, that no case was yet made out for a course of conduct which might possibly lead to war and so blight the budding prosperity of Great Britain. Carmarthen and Sydney did not speak. We may plausibly conjecture that the silence of the Foreign Minister betokened his disapproval of Pitt's views and his inability to controvert them.

So far as we can judge, Pitt alone was for complete neutrality. Nevertheless, his view prevailed. An interview which Harris had with him on the morrow did not change his sentiments; but, on 26th May, the Cabinet agreed to allow our envoy the sum of £20,000 so as to enable the loyal provinces to take into their pay the troops which had been disbanded by, or had deserted from, the forces of the Province of Holland.[1] On 10th June the further sum of £70,000 was advanced.[2]

Pitt's resolve was doubtless based on the difficulty of gaining an ally, for, as we have seen, the King of Prussia had recently refused the request of his sister for a loan of cannon and was proposing to concert plans with France for a joint mediation in Dutch affairs.[3] How was it possible for England alone to interfere for the Prince and Princess of Orange while their natural protector was making advances to their enemy? So little hope was there at present of aid from Prussia that on 12th June Carmarthen expressed to Harris his belief that the Orange party would get more help from the Emperor Joseph than from Frederick William. The torpor of that party was another depressing symptom. Time after time Carmarthen informed Harris that if the Prince's supporters desired help, they must bestir themselves: they had as yet the majority of the regular army and of the States-General on their side; and a fit use of this strength would save the situation.

Despite the efforts of Harris, the Patriots continued to gain ground. At the end of May their partisans wrecked the houses of the Prince's friends at Amsterdam, and crushed the reaction in his favour which had gathered head.[4] On 15th June the States-General decided, on the casting vote of the President,

---

[1] "Malmesbury Diaries," ii, 303-6.   [2] "F. O.," Holland, 14.
[3] "F. O.," Prussia, 11. Ewart to Carmarthen, 19th and 22nd May 1787.
[4] "F. O.," Holland, 14. Harris to Carmarthen, 1st June.

to admit the deputies sent by the illegal Estates of the city of Utrecht. This gave a bare majority to the Patriots, who then proceeded to deprive the Stadholder of the right to order the march of troops or the distribution of stores in the provinces outside Holland. Four days later, however, Harris was able to procure the rejection of this decree as illegal; and it was further decided that the Estates of Utrecht meeting at Amersfoort were the legal Estates of that province and could alone send deputies. Of course this change of front has been ascribed to English gold, and certainly it was due to Harris. This rebuff to the Patriots and the coyness of the French Court to their urgent demands for help may have led to the formation of a resolve which was to end the balancings of statesmen and the even pulls of parties. The solution of the Dutch problem was, in the first instance, due to a woman's wit.

About the middle of the month of June 1787, the Princess of Orange framed a plan for leaving her city of refuge, Nymeguen, and proceeding to The Hague with the aim of inspiring her crestfallen partisans. Hitherto the Orange party had shown the torpor which is the outcome of poor leadership. Of the Prince of Orange it might have been said, as it was said of Louis XVI, that he cooled his friends and heated his foes; but his consort had the fire and energy which he lacked. Harris once confessed that her frank, blue eyes could be " dangerous "; and in many ways her presence promised to breathe new life into her party.

As the journey to The Hague would involve some risk of insult from the Free Corps which formed a cordon on the frontier of the Province of Holland, she proceeded first to Amersfoort, where her consort was holding together his partisans in the Province of Utrecht, in order to gain his consent to this daring step. Thereafter she warned Harris and her chief friends at The Hague of her resolve, and asked their sanction, adding that the magnitude of the object at stake impelled her to run some measure of personal risk in order to compass it. Harris saw objections to the plan, but yielded to the representations of the Dutchmen. He, however, stated to Carmarthen his doubts whether she could make her way through the bodies of armed burghers, and asked his chief for instructions as to his course of action in case any violence were offered to Her Royal Highness.[1]

[1] " Malmesbury Diaries," ii, 322.

His apprehensions were in part to be realized. The princess set out from Nymeguen on 28th June with the ordinary retinue. While seeking to enter the Province of Holland near Schoon-hoven, she was stopped by a lieutenant commanding a body of Free Corps, who refused to allow her to proceed; his action was endorsed by the authorities; and she was obliged, though without much personal indignity, to put up at the nearest house where the lieutenant kept her and her ladies-in-waiting under close and embarrassing surveillance, until she consented that the question of her journey should be decided by the Estates of Holland. Then she was allowed to return to Schoonhoven, where she indited letters to the Grand Pensionary and others, declaring that her sole aim was to promote a reconciliation. The Estates of Holland refused to allow her to proceed, and she had finally to return to Nymeguen. This insult to royalty sent a thrill of indignation through every Court but that of Versailles.

Before describing the political results of the incident, we may pause to ask whether the plan of the Princess's journey was the outcome of the fertile brain of Harris. That was the insinuation of the French Foreign Minister, Montmorin, and it has often been repeated.[1] The charge has never been proven; and the following reasons may be urged against it. Harris certainly hoped to profit by her presence at The Hague, but obviously he doubted the possibility of her entering the province. Further, on 29th June, when he heard of her detention, he wrote to Car-marthen: "The event which has happened oversets our whole plan. Check to the queen, and in a move or two checkmate is, I fear, the state of our game." Not yet did he see that the check might be worth a Prussian army to the Orange party. All he saw was the present discouragement of that party, and the timidity of the States-General of the United Provinces, who now refused to censure the outrage. Carmarthen saw more clearly. "Don't be so disheartened by a check to the queen," he replied. "Cover her by the knight and all's safe. . . . If the King, her brother, is not the dirtiest and shabbiest of Kings, he must resent it." [2]

But had the Princess throughout laid her plans with a view to such an event? In this connection it is significant that Frederick

[1] "Auckland Journals," i, 521; Oscar Browning, "The Flight to Varennes and other Essays," 163.
[2] "Malmesbury Diaries," ii, 329.

William of Prussia had latterly shown great irritation against
the Court of Versailles owing to its summary rejection of his
offer of a joint mediation in the Dutch troubles. Montmorin
curtly declined every one of the preliminary terms which Hertzberg had succeeded in appending to that proposal. He also blamed
the Stadholder for all the ferment, and stated that, if the Prussian
monarch intervened in favour of the Orange party, he would
"only compromise himself to his entire loss."[1] This nagging
reply to a friendly overture cut the sensitive monarch to the
quick; he sent a spirited remonstrance, declaimed against the
bad faith of the French Government, and stated that he meant
now to complete his own plans in Holland, that he hoped to
have the support of England, and might draw the sword sooner
than was expected.[2] Ewart expected little result from all this;
but he was mistaken. Frederick William was a man of sentiment; and the appeal which now came from Holland was one
that stirred his being to its depths.

The Princess, on hearing of his resentment against France,
seems to have devised a course of action which would be likely
to make this mood lasting. Harris reported on 22nd June that
on the day before, "in consequence of a courier from Berlin, the
Princess of Orange, a few hours after he arrived, left Nymeguen
and set out for Amersfoort. She had time to write to nobody,
and the cause of this sudden departure is not to be guessed at."[3]
The short journey to Amersfoort was for the purpose described
above. That the Princess was acting in close concert with her
brother, and that Harris knew nothing as to the motives of her
conduct further appear in statements which (strange to say) are
omitted from his despatch of 25th June, printed in the
"Diaries." He informed Carmarthen that she was sending
a courier to Berlin, and that the present plan "completely does
away all the ideas which have been very prevalent here for these
three or four days, that His Prussian Majesty was so irritated at
the late answer from France as to be decided to assist the
Prince of Orange with men and money." Obviously the guile of
Sir James Harris was of the diplomatic, not of the feminine,
kind. Further, the fact that the Princess travelled with a retinue

---

[1] "F. O.," Prussia, 11. Ewart to Carmarthen, 6th June 1787. Ewart was
now *chargé d'affaires* at Berlin, Dalrymple having gone home on furlough.
He did not return, and Ewart became ambassador in August 1788.

[2] *Ibid.* Ewart's note of 30th June.   [3] "F. O.," Holland, 15.

made it almost certain that she would be stopped by the cordon of Free Corps on the frontier of Holland. If her chief aim had been to arrive at The Hague, she would have gone in disguise; for only so could she hope to pass through the troops. Her chief aim surely was to be stopped; and the more contumeliously, the better for her purpose.

Her letters written after the incident show that she desired to reap the full advantage from it. On 6th July Harris reported her expectation that, if England proposed to Prussia a plan for rescuing the Republic from France, it would be well received at Berlin; and that she grounded her confidence in the reports of those who knew the King of Prussia well. Ewart also on 10th July stated that she had written to Berlin in terms implying that the honour of the King was at stake fully as much as her own.[1] With these proofs of the discouragement of Harris, and of the keen insight of the Princess before us, may we not infer that she deliberately chose to submit herself to an insult from the Patriots in order to clinch a resolve which she knew to be forming in her brother's mind? His anger against France might then be fanned to a flame of resentment fed by injured family pride.

Fortunately for her purpose, the Estates of Holland waived aside the demand of the King of Prussia for immediate and complete satisfaction for the insult; and Frederick William vowed that he would exact vengeance at the sword's point. Hertzberg now saw within his reach the great aims which Ewart and he had so long pursued, an Anglo-Prussian compact which might ripen into alliance. But it was a task of much difficulty to stiffen that monarch's wavering impulses. Hertzberg rightly saw that English influence should not at first be pushed;[2] and only when the King's resentment at the insult began to cool, were the wider questions of the future discreetly opened to his gaze. Here again the situation was complicated; for Finckenstein worked on his fears of an attack from Austria, if he intervened in Holland; and Thulemeyer, the Prussian envoy at The Hague, darkened the royal counsels by sending an official warning that Prussia must expect no help from England, even if France struck at the Prussian expeditionary corps. Ewart, however, was able to show that this report closely resembled an earlier one from the same source. The only result, then, was to discredit Thulemeyer and

[1] "F. O.," Holland, 15; "F. O.," Prussia, 11.
[2] Luckwaldt, *op. cit.*, 66, 67.

pave the way for his disgrace. When further friendly assurances came from the Pitt Ministry, Frederick William gave orders for the mustering of 25,000 troops at his fortress of Wesel on the lower Rhine. Even now he was afflicted by the irresolution which for so many years was to paralyze the power of his kingdom; and it is doubtful whether he would have acted at all but for the initiative now taken by the Prime Minister of England.[1]

Pitt's change of attitude at this time is the decisive event of the situation. At once, on hearing the news of the insult to the Princess of Orange, he saw that the time for action had come. In a personal interview with Count Lusi, Prussian ambassador at London, he pointed out that this was a matter which solely concerned the Prussian monarch, and in which France had no right to interfere.[2] George III spoke in the same terms to Lusi at a *levée*. Further, on the receipt of Ewart's despatch of 7th July, reporting that Pitt had declared against any intervention whatever by Great Britain, Carmarthen sent a sharp denial, and stated that diplomatic support would have been offered earlier to Prussia in Dutch affairs, but for the strange conduct of Thulemeyer at The Hague. If that conduct did not represent the wishes of the Prussian Government, His Majesty " will be extremely ready to enter into a most confidential communication with His Prussian Majesty" on the means of preserving the independence of the Dutch Republic and the rights of the Stadholder. Carmarthen added the important information that Montmorin had declared that France would not thwart the Prussian monarch's resolve to gain reparation for the insult. That question he declared to be totally distinct from an interference in the domestic affairs of the Republic, which might be settled amicably by a joint mediation of the Powers most concerned in them, namely, the Emperor, Great Britain, Prussia, and France. The draft of this important despatch closed with this sentence, in Pitt's handwriting: " Could such a good understanding be agreed on, there can be little doubt that the affairs of Holland would be settled in an amicable way, to the satisfaction of all those who are interested in the welfare of the Republic." [3]

---

[1] Wittichen (78, 79) holds that Frederick William's hesitation came from concern about the Fürstenbund or the hope that France would join in a peaceful mediation in Holland.

[2] Lusi's report of 17th July 1787. Luckwaldt, *op. cit.*, 68.

[3] " F. O.," Prussia, 11. Carmarthen to Ewart, 17th July. There is nothing in

It is clear, then, that Pitt meant to encourage Prussia to energetic action, in case the Estates of Holland did not grant full reparation for the insult; but he looked on that step merely as preliminary to the others which would solve the whole question by a peaceful mediation of the four Powers above named. On learning that the Emperor had expressed his friendly interest in the Prince of Orange and his approval of Prussia's conduct, the Foreign Office sent off a despatch to Keith, British Ambassador at Vienna, bidding him to urge his active co-operation "and to make it, if possible, the means of establishing a cordial and confidential correspondence with that Court in future." [1] Joseph II did not respond to this friendly proposal, probably because of troubles lowering in the East. But the incident proves the reluctance of our Foreign Office to act with Prussia alone, and also its hopes of a peaceful mediation in Dutch affairs. According to news received from Paris, France did not seem likely to oppose Prussia's action, and even favoured the scheme of a joint mediation of the three Powers, which were then on cordial terms. [2]

In spite of the friendly assurances that came from London, and the manly advice of Hertzberg, Frederick William continued to vacillate in his usual manner. As we have seen, he had recently coquetted with the notion of a mediation conjointly with France alone; but, despite its curt rejection by the Court of Versailles, he now recurred to a similar scheme. [3] If France had played her cards well, she might even then have won the day at Berlin.

The conduct of the French Government at this crisis is hard to fathom. Its swift and unaccountable changes may perhaps be explained by the alternate triumph of peaceful and warlike counsels in the Ministry, which in the month of August under-

this despatch which warrants the statement of the editor of the "Malmesbury Diaries" (ii, 339 n.) that we then offered Prussia armed support if France attacked her, and promised to make a demonstration with forty ships of the line. That was not proposed until the middle of September, in reply to French threats.

[1] "F. O.," Austria, 14. Keith on 3rd August stated that the Emperor was friendly to us, but he was the ally of France, though he would not act with her in the Dutch Question.

[2] "F. O.," Prussia, 11. Carmarthen to Ewart, 27th July.

[3] Wittichen, 81, shows that Wilhelmina herself worked hard to dissuade her brother from a mediation conjointly with France.

went some alterations. Towards Great Britain the tone was at first quite reassuring, a fact which may be ascribed to the friendly relations between Montmorin and Eden. Our envoy had visited London in July, and therefore, on his return to Paris at the end of the month, fully knew the intentions of his chiefs. Their pacific nature appeared in a proposal, which he was charged to make to Montmorin, for the discontinuance of warlike preparations on both sides until such time as notice might be given for their renewal. On 4th August the French Minister cordially received this proposal,[1] and it was acted on with sincerity until the crisis of the middle of September. But Eden soon found that the French Court intended forcibly to intervene if the Prussian troops entered the United Provinces, and that Montmorin had rejected the recent proposal from Berlin for a Franco-Prussian intervention.[2] Here, surely, the French Minister committed a surprising blunder. The traditional friendship between their Courts should have led him to welcome a proposal which would have kept England entirely out of the question. Probably he counted on procuring better terms from the ever complaisant Court of Berlin. If so, he erred egregiously. By repelling the advances of Prussia, he threw that Power into the arms of Great Britain; and Pitt was shrewd enough to accord a hearty welcome.

[1] " F. O.," France, 25. Eden to Carmarthen, 4th August 1787.
[2] *Ibid.*, 8th August.

CHAPTER XVI

THE TRIPLE ALLIANCE

This treaty produced an effect throughout the whole of Europe by its mere existence, without military preparations or force of arms.—VON SYBEL.

Pitt has already astonished all Europe by the alacrity of the late armament, and his name as a War Minister is now as high as that of his father ever was.—THE EARL OF MORNINGTON TO THE DUKE OF RUTLAND, 17th October 1787.

THE events described in the last chapter had brought England and Prussia to a crisis at which, despite their strong mutual suspicion, common action was imperiously needed in order to save the Dutch Netherlands from French domination. As we have seen, no British statesman had ever acquiesced in the supremacy of France in that country; and it is clear from the British archives that Pitt now took a keen interest in thwarting her designs. The draft of the official answer to Eden's despatch of 4th August 1787 is entirely in Pitt's writing, and it was sent without alteration or addition by the Foreign Minister, Lord Carmarthen—an unusual circumstance, which shows the masterful grip of the chief over matters of high import. In this despatch, of 10th August, he welcomed the assurance of Montmorin that warlike preparations would be stopped until further notice. Great Britain would, however, renew them after due notice if France assembled a force at Givet, on the Belgian border. He then referred pointedly to rumours that French transports had sailed for Amsterdam—a measure which would prejudice "the great work of conciliation which it is so much the object of the two Courts to forward and promote." French ships were also reported as laying in stores of food in British ports, a proceeding which would have been stopped but for the friendly assurances now received. He then referred to the invitation of the loyal provinces of Friesland and Zealand, that

Great Britain would mediate on their behalf, and hinted that this might be done. The despatch closed with the following dignified remonstrance on the subject of the outrages of the Free Corps in Holland:

I am here also under the painful necessity of adding that the conduct held in the Province of Holland, apparently instigated by those who have all along appeared the instruments of France, seems to increase, instead of diminishing in violence. I enclose a copy of an address presented by the Free Corps of that Province, which it is intended that you should show to M. de M[ontmorin]. It cannot escape that Minister how little such a step is calculated to promote an accommodation or a suspension of hostilities, which his language so strongly recommends.[1]

Meanwhile Pitt had sent his cousin, William Wyndham Grenville, to collect information at The Hague. As we saw in Chapter XII, the attainments of that young statesman, then Paymaster of the Forces, were eminently sound. His hard and practical nature stood in contrast to the sensitive and imaginative Harris, about whom George III trenchantly wrote to Pitt, that he was so easily discouraged that it was well he held no military command. Probably Pitt held the same opinion about Harris, whose forward policy he had long held in check. That there was some widespread distrust of him is clear from the observation of the Duke of Dorset, that "he was playing the devil at The Hague."[2] In any case, it was well to have independent advice, and the selection of so young a man as Grenville is a tribute to his prudence and ability.

He reached The Hague on 30th July, and during his stay of about three weeks succeeded in clearing up many points preliminary to the mediation. The letters which passed between him and Pitt bespeak a resolve on both sides to settle matters peaceably if possible. The following sentence in Pitt's letter of 1st August is noteworthy: "It is very material that our friends should not lose the superiority of force within the Republic, while we are labouring to protect it from interference from without." Six days later he wrote that the prospect was still favourable,

---

[1] "F. O.," France, 25.

[2] "Auckland Journals," i, 520. Lord Loughborough, in a letter of 13th October 1787 to Lord Carlisle stated that Grenville's mission was not due to distrust of Harris ("Carlisle P.," 652). But this seems to me very doubtful in view of the letters between Pitt and Grenville.

but that, if French troops were to assemble at Givet, it might be needful to resume naval preparations, so as to reassure Prussia.[1] Equally hopeful in tone is his letter of 2nd August to Earl Cornwallis, Governor-General of India. After pointing out that Great Britain could not allow France to become mistress of the Dutch Netherlands, and thereby add enormously to her naval strength and her power of aggression in India, he expressed the hope that the mediation of the three Powers would take place; but, failing an apology from the Estates of Holland, the King of Prussia would order his troops into that province, and take steps for "maintaining the just rights of the Stadholder and the constitution and independence of the Republic." If war broke out, Cornwallis was at once to strike at the Dutch settlement of Trincomalee, in Ceylon; while a force from England would be sent to reduce the Cape of Good Hope—the first sign in Pitt's letters of the importance which he attached to that post.[2]

Despite suspicious signs to the contrary, the French Cabinet at that time probably wished for a peaceful mediation; but the Courts of London and Versailles differed sharply as to the way of action. Pitt and Carmarthen held that reparation to the King of Prussia for the insult to his sister was a purely personal affair, distinct from the political issues. France now denied this; she belittled the affront to the Princess, and induced the Estates of Holland to frame an apology which was in the main a justification of their conduct. If Montmorin had pressed that body to make an adequate apology, it would certainly have been forthcoming. The stiff-neckedness of the Estates of Holland was due to their expectation of armed support from France if matters came to the sword; and the action of the Marquis de Vérac, the French envoy, justified their confidence.

In truth, French policy wore different aspects at Paris and at The Hague. Montmorin assumed an air of injured innocence when Eden transmitted to him Pitt's remonstrances. On 15th August he indignantly denied the truth of the rumours about French transports sailing to Holland and of the food supplies drawn from England. He also complained of the harshness of Pitt's reference to the assembling of troops at Givet, an action

---

[1] "Dropmore P.," iii, 408-15. For the missions of Grenville to The Hague and Paris, see my article in the "Eng. Hist. Rev." for April 1909.

[2] Pitt MSS., 102.

which was a natural retort to the muster of Prussians at their fortress of Wesel on the Rhine; and he merely laughed at the address of the Free Corps.[1] A week later Eden reported that Montmorin was anxious to settle the Dutch troubles peacefully and speedily, and would therefore recall the over-zealous Vérac from The Hague. Pitt, however, refused to allow that Prussia was exceeding her just rights in claiming satisfaction for the insult. The fit way of ending the matter, he argued, would be for the Estates of Holland to apologize frankly and fully, whereupon the three Powers must insist on the dispersal and disarming of the Free Corps as a needful preliminary to the joint mediation.[2] On 28th August Eden heard that the French Government would not form the camp at Givet, it being understood that the Prussian monarch would limit his claims to the gaining of personal satisfaction, which France promised to procure from the Estates of Holland. This welcome news led Pitt to express the hope that an agreement would at once be framed for stopping the excesses of the Free Corps. Thus, so far as our dealings with Montmorin ran, there seemed, even at the end of August 1787, the likelihood of a peaceful settlement. A signal proof of Pitt's hopefulness is afforded by his letter of 28th August to Cornwallis at Calcutta. In this he speaks of the need of settling the personal question between the King of Prussia and the Estates of Holland as preliminary to the general settlement of the dispute. Even of that he cherished hopes, but he deemed caution and preparation so eminently necessary as to order the despatch of another regiment to Bombay.[3]

In truth, the central knot of the whole tangle was at The Hague. In order to understand the position there we must remember that the States-General, representing the Union, had not called on France for aid, in case of hostilities. Thanks to the skill and private influence of Harris, a majority of that body still upheld the claims of the Stadholder, deprecated any appeal to the Court of Versailles, and sought to procure from the Estates of Holland an apology to the King of Prussia. The Estates, however, stoutly refused to give anything more than a complacent explanation of the incident. The spirit which animated that assembly appears in the comment of one of the leading Patriots

[1] " F. O.," France, 25. Eden to Carmarthen, 16th August 1787.
[2] *Ibid.* Carmarthen to Eden, 24th August.
[3] Pitt MSS., 102; and " Cornwallis Corresp.," i, 333-7.

on the Prussian ultimatum: "A sovereign body can never apologize to the wife of its first servant."[1] The Memoirs of Count de Portes, a Swiss officer who espoused the cause of the Dutch Patriots and helped to raise a regiment for them, show the cause of their confidence. He wrote on 14th September: "Though the Prussians are at our gates, they seem to me still at the sport of politics, and I can scarcely believe that they will put themselves between our waters and *our French*. At the worst we will open our sluices and drown ourselves."[2]

There was the strength of the Patriots. In a legal sense their case was weak; but their audacious energy even now promised to snatch victory from the inert Orange party. The Free Corps in the months of July and August became more numerous and insolent than ever, and it was a notorious fact that hundreds of French officers and soldiers had passed into their ranks.[3] Thus strengthened, they marched about the country, taking some places by force, and in several cases deposing the Regents, or chief magistrates appointed by the Stadholder. On all sides they despoiled the property of opponents, and carried confusion to the gates of The Hague. On 1st August Harris thus summed up his hopes and wishes to Carmarthen: "If I am de-Witted, don't let me be outwitted, but revenge me."[4] Count Bentinck also wrote: "the majority of Holland have made themselves masters of our lives and property; . . . they are masters of the purse, and of the sword, and of the Courts of Justice."[5] That arch-intriguer, Vérac, on 31st August, the very day of his recall, assured the Patriots that France would never desert them. This boast was consonant with the whole policy of France respecting the Free Corps. She had rejected the Prussian proposal for their suppression, which accompanied the plan of a Franco-Prussian mediation. On 29th August Montmorin stated to Eden that it was impossible to disarm the Free Corps, and on 11th September when stiff remonstrances came from London on this subject, he airily declared that France could no more control those troops than the waves of the sea.[6]

---

[1] "Malmesbury Diaries," ii, 371.
[2] "Méms. du Comte de Portes" (1904), 92.
[3] "Auckland Journals," i, 234, 259.   [4] B.M. Add. MSS., 28061.
[5] "Dropmore P.," iii, 418.
[6] "F. O.," France, 25, 26. Eden to Carmarthen, 29th August and 11th September.

Is it surprising that the Pitt Ministry came to the conclusion that the real aim of the French Government was to amuse England and Prussia with fair words, until its partisans gained a complete mastery in the United Provinces and forced the States-General to send to Paris a formal demand for help, with which the Court of Versailles could not but comply? Whether Montmorin was playing a double game, or whether his hand was forced by other members of his Cabinet, is far from clear.[1] Certainly the contrast between his fair professions and French intrigues in Holland inspired increasing distrust, and served to bring about the *dénouement* which shattered the prestige of the French monarchy.

It was long before the crisis came. Only by slow degrees did Pitt, Carmarthen, and Harris shake off distrust of Prussia. The length of time attending the transit of despatches between London and Berlin (eleven days on the average even in summer) clogged the negotiations. At Paris the Prussian envoy, Görtz, intrigued against the Anglo-Prussian understanding, and represented Eden as minimizing the insult to the Princess of Orange. At once Pitt sent to Eden a courteous but firm request for an explanation of his words, which had caused a sensation at Berlin. Of course Eden was able to explain them entirely to Pitt's satisfaction.[2] But it is clear that the mutual dislike at London

---

[1] The feuds in his Ministry, and his consistently peaceful attitude, seem to absolve him from the charge of duplicity. French troops, disguised as Free Corps, were afterwards captured in Holland and had on them orders and instructions written by de Ségur, the French War Minister, who resigned in August 1787 ("Auckland Journals," i, 259). It seems probable therefore that some Ministers egged on the French agents and the Patriots, while Montmorin strove to hold them in check. Louis XVI also used his influence to prevent a war with Prussia, which he disliked (see Garden, "Traités," v, 85 *n*.). The appointment of Loménie de Brienne to a kind of dictatorship seems also to have made for peace; it coincides with the resolve, formed about 20th August (see Barral de Montferrat, *op. cit.*, 214), to recall Vérac from The Hague; and on 31st August Montmorin signed with Eden a convention for ending irritating disputes in East Indian affairs. I have no space to go into that question; but it had been reported (*e.g.*, by Eden on 9th November 1786, Pitt MSS., 110) that the French were about to gain control over Dutch East India ports. Rumours to that effect had embittered the contest in Holland, and they were laid to rest by that convention.

[2] See the MSS. of P. V. Smith in the "Beaufort P." (Hist. MSS. Commission) 357, for the parts of Pitt's letter of 8th September, omitted, very strangely, by the editor of the "Auckland Journals" (i, 191-2), also *ibid.*, i, 198.

and Berlin could have been ended only by the fears aroused by the action of France.

In order to remove the distrust prevalent at Berlin, Pitt and Carmarthen sent to that Court full copies of their correspondence with France, which convinced Frederick William of their good faith and the duplicity of Versailles.[1] He saw that France was dragging on the affair so that the approach of autumn might hinder the effective action of his troops. Suspicion of this helped to bring England and Prussia to accord. But the tidings which spurred on Pitt and Carmarthen to more decisive action came from The Hague. On 20th August Harris reported that a body of Free Corps was approaching that town, that he was preparing to leave it in haste, and had sent all important papers away. On hearing this news and perhaps that brought back by Grenville on 23rd August, the Cabinet resolved to send General Fawcett to Cassel to hire 5,000 Hessians for the help of the loyal Dutch provinces, and others for the British service—that detestable expedient which parsimony made inevitable at every alarm of war. Harris was also empowered to order up a British ship lying at Harwich, laden with gunpowder and stores for the help of the Stadholder's forces.[2] On the same day Carmarthen instructed Ewart to warn the Prussian Court that, though we had agreed with France to suspend warlike preparations, yet we were ready to send out at least as large a fleet as France could possibly equip.[3] Ewart, in his reply of 4th September, stated that but for this encouraging news Frederick William might once more have wavered, owing to the insidious intrigues of the French party, and the discouraging reports which came from the Duke of Brunswick. The nerves of that veteran were unstrung by visions of the spectral camp at Givet, and he mourned over the unpreparedness of his own force at Wesel, which, he declared, could not march before 7th September.[4] These tidings had once more depressed the royal thermometer at Berlin; but the news from London came just in time to send the mercury up again. On 3rd September, then, Frederick William drew up an ultimatum to the

[1] Luckwaldt, 71.   [2] "F. O.," Holland, 17.

[3] "F. O.," Prussia, 11. Carmarthen to Ewart, 24th August.

[4] Luckwaldt, 80 n., here corrects one of many mis-statements in P. de Witt's "Une Invasion prussienne en Hollande," 285, that the Prussians were ready to march by 20th July.

Estates of Holland, and bade Hertzberg come to a close understanding with England. On 7th September he resolved to recall Thulemeyer, and urged the British Government to declare
what forces it would set in motion if France attacked the Prussian army in Holland.[1]

Late on that day there arrived at Berlin news which ended
the last hesitations of Frederick William. The Porte, long
fretting under the yoke imposed by the Treaty of Kainardji,
and irritated by the proceedings of the Czarina, had declared war
on Russia. This came almost as a bolt from the blue. No one
had believed the Sultan capable of so much energy as to attack
the Muscovites; and rumours spread at Vienna and Petersburg
that this was due to British gold. The insinuation was probably
false. As will appear in Chapter XXI, the Turks had been
goaded into war, and relied on help from Sweden, perhaps
also from Prussia. Undoubtedly their action greatly embarrassed
Joseph II, who was bound by compacts with Russia, the enemy
of Turkey, and with France, her friend. Late on 7th September
Finckenstein pointed this out to Ewart, and added that Prussia
and England ought at once to frame an agreement, and intervene effectively without fear of France.[2] This time the decision
was final. Ewart reported that the news of Turkey's challenge
to Russia caused all the more joy at Berlin as the party of
Marie Antoinette had gained an ascendancy at Versailles, which
implied the strengthening of the Franco-Austrian alliance and
a proportionate loosening of the ties linking Joseph II to Russia.[3]
The reasoning was not sound; for it was probable that France,
acting in close concert with the two Empires, would partition
Turkey with a view to the seizure of Egypt and other commanding posts in the East.

Nevertheless, Prussia looked on the war in the East as
giving her a free hand in the West; and on 7th September
she decided to act in the Netherlands. Four days later a French
envoy, Groschlag, arrived in Berlin with offers, partly enticing,

---

[1] Hertzberg, "Recueil des Traités," ii, 428-30; "F. O.," Prussia, 12. Ewart
to Carmarthen, 4th and 8th September.

[2] *Ibid.* 8th September.

[3] "The prevailing opinion of this Court is the Emperor will . . . sacrifice
his alliance with Russia to that of 1756 [with France]" (Ewart to Keith,
11th September 1787. B.M. Add. MSS., 35539).

partly threatening, which might once more have drawn the
wavering impulses of the King towards Paris.[1] But now, after
many months of uphill fight, all the omens favoured the Anglo-
Prussian cause.

On 13th September, before the refusal of the Prussian ultimatum by the Estates of Holland had been received, the Duke of
Brunswick crossed the Dutch frontier. In Guelderland and
parts of Utrecht the Prussians were hailed as deliverers; even
the city of Utrecht opened its gates, owing to the cowardice of
the Rhinegrave of Salm, who soon abandoned the cause for
which he had blustered so long. Nowhere did the Free Corps
make any firm stand. Even in Holland their excesses had
turned public opinion strongly against them. It is said that the
weather prevented the opening of the sluices; but the half-
heartedness of the defence, and the eagerness of the Orange
party for deliverance, probably explain the *débâcle*. When the
Dutch have been united and determined, their defence of their
land has always been stubborn. Now it was not even creditable;
and this fact may be cited as damning to the Patriots' claim
that they stood for the nation. On 20th September the Prince
of Orange made his entry into The Hague amidst boundless
enthusiasm. Sir James Harris also received a striking ovation,
which rewarded him for the long months of struggle.

Now, while the Patriots were in consternation at their overthrow, our envoy clinched his triumph by persuading the Estates
of Holland to reverse their previous acts against the Stadholder's authority, and to rescind a resolution which they had
passed on 9th September appealing for armed aid from France.
The cancelling of this appeal on 21st September was a matter
of great importance, as it deprived France of a pretext for
armed intervention. The receipt of this news at Versailles
helped to cool the warlike ardour of the French Court.

There the temper of the Ministry had fluctuated alarmingly.
The recall of Vérac seemed to assure a peaceful settlement.
But on 4th September Montmorin sent to Eden a despatch which
ran directly counter to the British and Prussian proposals. It
stated that the Dutch towns, where the Free Corps had forcibly
changed the magistrates, " *ont déjà consommé la réforme; ... c'est
une affaire terminée.*" As for the Prince of Orange, he would do

---

[1] Wittichen, 92-4; also *ibid.*, 97, for the Anglo-Prussian Convention of
2nd October.

well to abdicate in favour of his son.[1] Pitt of course indignantly rejected both proposals; and his temper is seen in the phrase of his letter of 14th September to Eden, that if France was determined to keep her predominance in the United Provinces, she must fight for it.[2]

An acute crisis now set in. While Carmarthen warned Montmorin that England would not remain a quiet spectator of French intervention, that Minister on 16th September issued a Declaration that France could not refuse the appeal for help which had come from the Estates of Holland. He charged England with having plotted the whole affair with Prussia, and asserted that, inconvenient though the time was now that the fate of the Turkish Empire stood at hazard, France must in honour draw the sword.[3]

This Declaration drew from Pitt an equally stiff retort. In a circular despatch intended for all our ambassadors, which he himself drew up, he declared that England could not admit the right of France, owing to its treaty with the Dutch Republic, " to support a party in one of the Provinces in a measure expressly disavowed by a majority of the States-General; and His Majesty has repeatedly declared the impossibility of his being indifferent to any armed interference of France in the affairs of the Republic, which, if unopposed, must necessarily tend to consequences dangerous to the constitutional independence of those Provinces, and affecting in many respects the interests and security of his dominions. His Majesty has therefore found himself under the necessity of taking measures for equipping a considerable naval armament and for augmenting his land forces." Nevertheless he still desired " an amicable settlement of the points in dispute."[4] As many as forty sail of the line were immediately prepared for sea; and here we may notice that Pitt's care for the navy ensured a preponderance which virtually decided the dispute.

In order to see whether war might be averted, George III suggested, on 16th September, that someone should be sent to Paris who could deal with the French Ministers better than Eden

---

[1] "Auckland Journals," i, 192.   [2] *Ibid.*, 195.
[3] "F. O.," France, 26. Eden to Carmarthen, 11th and 13th September
[4] The original, in Pitt's handwriting, is in " F. O.," Russia, 15, dated 21st September, and inscribed " To all the King's Ministers abroad except Paris and The Hague."

did. Pitt therefore decided, on 19th September, to despatch Grenville, charging him distinctly to declare that Great Britain approved the action of the King of Prussia, and would resist an armed intervention by France; also that the settlement in the United Provinces must be such as to restore to the Stadholder his constitutional powers, and prevent the ascendency of the party hostile to Britain. A secondary aim of Grenville's mission was the forming of a friendly understanding with France for the cessation of warlike preparations on both sides of the Channel—a proof of Pitt's watchful care over the exchequer.[1]

Montmorin received Grenville coldly on 28th September at Versailles; but his reserve was merely a cloak to hide his discomfiture. Nine days before he had assured Eden, in the confidence which followed on a private dinner, that " if the Estates of Holland should prove so defenceless, or so intimidated as to give way to whatever might be forced under the present attack, he would advise His Most Christian Majesty not to engage in war." If matters went more favourably he would advise him to draw the sword; but, as for his own feelings, he was weary of the Dutch Question, and only sought the means for getting rid of it creditably, so that France might turn her attention to another quarter, obviously the East.[2] Grenville, after hearing all this from Eden, and receiving the good news from The Hague, of course put the right interpretation on Montmorin's *non possumus*, and sought to facilitate his stately retreat. He was at once waved back. Montmorin would make no promise as to her course of action so long as the Prussians were in Holland. Even on the question of disarmament by the two Powers—a matter of the utmost moment to France—he would make no pledge, though Grenville strongly urged him to do so. Two more interviews passed with the same frigid negations; and on 3rd October Grenville returned to London, harbouring a shrewd suspicion that the actions of the Court of Versailles would on this occasion tally with Montmorin's words.

Such proved to be the case. France did nothing, to the unbounded disgust of her partisans in Holland. Amsterdam shut its gates and endured a short siege from the Prussians in the belief that help must come from Paris. Our diplomatic agent,

---

[1] "Dropmore P.," iii, 426-36; E. D. Adams, *op. cit.*, 6, 7; "Buckingham P.," i, 326-31.

[2] *Ibid.* Eden to Carmarthen, 20th September.

W. A. Miles, writing from Liège on 1st October, reported that the burgomasters of Utrecht and Gorcum had passed through that city on their way to Paris in the conviction that "France would never leave them in the lurch, and that her troops would certainly march to the relief of Amsterdam."[1] Their consternation must have been great on reaching Givet to find that there was no camp there.[2] The truth then flashed upon them that the French agents had relied on bluster and the Free Corps. Disappointment at the inaction of the French Court probably hastened the surrender of Amsterdam, which opened its gates on 10th October. The capture by the Prussians of many French soldiers, who declared that they were acting for that Government, revealed the sinister conduct of some, at least, of the French Ministers, and of Vérac.[3] A letter of Grenville to Eden on 26th October 1787 shows the surprise and disgust of our Ministers at this flagrant bad faith. He says he is "mortified" at finding that Ségur, Minister for War, had sent signed orders for parties of French artillerymen to march north to the frontier, and put themselves under the command of an adventurer named Esterhazy. "His (Ségur's) orders again expressly direct the march into Holland in disguise, and point out the places where the men are to be equipped with *habits de paysan* for this purpose."[4]

The surrender of Amsterdam gave the last blow to the war party at Versailles. Up to 14th October Pitt felt the utmost concern, as appears in his letter of that date to Eden; but the reply of that envoy three days later showed that Ségur and his colleagues now bowed to the inevitable. Their peaceful mood was doubtless confirmed by the evasive and discouraging answer sent by Austria to the appeal for help.[5] The Emperor had a large force in Belgium, but none too large to hold down that people. Moreover, the prospect of war with Turkey imposed caution at Vienna.

The chief danger now was that France would join Russia and

---

[1] "Dropmore P.," iii, 435; "Méms. de Dedem de Gelder," 7.

[2] *Ibid.*, iii, 435.

[3] "F. O.," Holland, 19. Carmarthen to Harris, 12th October; "Auckland Journals," i, 234.

[4] B.M. Add. MSS., 29475.

[5] "F. O.," Austria, 14. Keith to Carmarthen, 24th October 1787. On 14th November Joseph II informed Keith that he thoroughly approved of the Dutch settlement.

Austria in the dismemberment of Turkey. Fear of such a step
haunted Pitt, who always surveyed the Dutch Question from the
standpoint of India. Thus we find him on 8th October charging
Eden to watch most carefully the attitude of France to the
events in the East. The replies of that envoy were, as usual, reassuring. France, according to Eden, only desired peace, and the
scheme of seizing Egypt was "wholly wild."[1] Pitt therefore
decided to press forward, and to persuade France to give an
unequivocal assurance of her pacific intentions, as a prelude to
disarmament on both sides. His letter of 14th October to Eden
on this topic shows a grip of essentials, together with a surprising
finesse. While anxious to induce France to disarm at the earliest
possible moment, he advised Eden to humour Alvensleben, the
special Prussian envoy at Paris, and to convince him that we
were giving Prussia firm support and were not disposed to patch
up a premature settlement.[2] Evidently Pitt's interest in diplomacy, though belated, was keen.

After long correspondence with Berlin, and much demurring
at Versailles, a Declaration and Counter-Declaration were drafted
and signed by the British envoys and Montmorin on 27th October. The French document averred that, as it had never been the
intention of the King of France to intervene in Dutch affairs, he
now retained no hostile views in any quarter respecting them,
and therefore consented to disarm.[3] This public denial of what
had notoriously been the aim of his Government, and this
promise to renounce all ideas of revenge on Prussia, sent a thrill
of astonishment through the diplomatic world. Never had France
so openly abandoned her partisans or so publicly proclaimed
her impotence. If Pitt (as French historians have asserted) had
persistently sought to humiliate the Court of Versailles, he could
not have succeeded more completely. But this Counter-Declaration was merely the climax of a diplomatic game which had
taken a threatening turn only since the beginning of September.
The fact is that the French Ministers, and still more their agents
in Holland, had precipitated the crisis by the actions of the Free
Corps at the very time which proved to be most unfavourable
for them. By their conduct they courted failure; but it was the
outbreak of war in the East which made that failure complete
and crushing.

[1] "Auckland Journals," i, 217, 221.   [2] *Ibid.*, 227, 228.
[3] *Ibid.*, 255-8; "Ann. Reg." (1787), 283.

On the other hand, the conduct of the friends of the House of Orange, after long delays and blunders, was singularly astute when the crisis came. The conduct of the Princess deserves the highest praise. The diplomacy of Harris and Ewart was a marvel of skill. As for Eden, he had little more to do than to obey orders, though he sometimes toned down the harsh phrases of Pitt and Carmarthen.[1] The action of the Prussians was trenchant, but it could not have been so but for their confidence in the promised support of the Sea Power. Pitt's fostering care of the national resources, and his rehabilitation of the navy had made it virtually impossible for the semi-bankrupt French State to enter single-handed on a war with Great Britain and Prussia. This was the determining factor in the problem; and every statesman at Paris, London, and Berlin knew it.

But something more than sound finance is needed in a complex and critical situation. There the qualities of foresight, tact, and determination are of priceless worth; and on all sides it was admitted that Pitt displayed them to a high degree. The restraint which kept Harris strictly within bounds until the fit moment arrived is not more remarkable than the boldness which reaped all possible advantages from the daring *coup* of the Princess of Orange. Eden wrote on 1st November, that he had *shuddered* at the courage of Pitt in braving the chances of a war with France.[2] But the young statesman knew how far he could go with safety; he discerned the essential fact that France could not fight, and that Montmorin adopted his negative attitude in order to hide that important secret. If Montmorin chose to justify her disarmament by assertions which were equally false and humiliating, that was a matter for him, not for the statesmen of Great Britain.

Pitt's conduct of this, his first great diplomatic campaign, shines all the more brightly by contrast with the vacillations of Frederick William and the stupendous blunders of the French Government. Adverting briefly to these last, we may note that France had little ground for interference so long as a majority of the States-General deprecated such action; and, thanks to Harris, that majority, except for a few days, held firm. The French Government therefore founded its hopes on the majority in the Province of Holland, and on the high-handed proceed-

---

[1] "Auckland Journals," i, 264.   [2] *Ibid.,* 263.

ings of the Free Corps, which it secretly abetted. Montmorin repulsed two overtures from Berlin because of the insistence of Prussia that those corps should be suppressed. This action it was, more perhaps than the resentment of Frederick William at the insult to his sister, which helped to bring Prussia and Great Britain into line. France also finally denied the right of Frederick William to gain reparation for that insult, though she at first recognized the justice of his claim. Further, when he sent forward his troops, she made ready for war, and then adopted the attitude of sullen resentment, which rendered a joint mediation by the three Powers impossible. This conduct in its turn implied the lapse of the Franco-Dutch treaty of 1785, and the triumph of British and Prussian influence in the United Provinces. Frenchmen also saw in this event another proof of the uselessness of the Austrian alliance on which Marie Antoinette had staked her popularity; and the *débâcle* in Holland was a deadly blow at the influence of that unfortunate Queen. Finally France admitted her defeat in terms at which friends and foes alike scoffed. Not without reason, then, did Napoleon afterwards assert that the French Revolution was due to three causes, the Battle of Rossbach, the Diamond Necklace scandal, and the ousting of French influence from the United Provinces in 1787. The judgement is curiously superficial in that it passes over the fiscal and agrarian evils which potently conduced to the great upheaval; but it reflected the opinion of that generation, which looked on deficits, dearths, and bread-riots as dispensations of Providence, of trifling import when compared with the decay in prestige of an ancient monarchy. Something may be said for this view of things in the case of France. For years that monarchy had lived on prestige. The surrender of October 1787 now proclaimed to the world its decrepitude.

With the events attending the restoration of the Stadholder's power and the constitution of the year 1747 we are not here concerned. Pitt had rightly refused to interfere until the efforts of the Patriots to establish French influence had become a positive danger to England. His interest in those troubles was largely grounded on naval and colonial considerations. If the United Provinces became an annexe of France, their fleet, their valuable colonies, and their once prosperous East India Company, would be cast into the balance against us. Now that this danger was past, he sought to remove all chance of its recurrence by suggesting the formation of a treaty of alliance with the Republic. On 5th October the first proposal to this effect was framed at Whitehall on condition that the two States should assist one another in case of attack, and guarantee the possession of their territories; but from the outset the Foreign Office set its face sternly against any concession such as " Free Ships, Free Goods," on which the Dutch were likely to insist.

There was, however, another stumbling stone in the way. The Dutch felt keenly the surrender of Negapatam to Great Britain, and they urged that, as that sacrifice had been forced on them in 1784 for the greater security of our settlements in the Carnatic, its retrocession was a natural consequence and a pledge of the friendship now happily restored. The Pitt Ministry, however, viewed the matter in the cold light of self-interest, and rejected the demand, in spite of the reiterated assurances of the Prince of Orange, the new Grand Pensionary, Van der Spiegel, and other friends of England, that they could not otherwise accept the proffered treaty. Even Harris finally confessed his inability to bend their will, and he advised Pitt and Carmarthen not to imperil the alliance on this single detail. Prussia, he said, had given way at some points in her negotiations with the Dutch; and it was impolitic for us to be too stiff.[1]

Pitt, however, would not give way. Probably he considered that the Stadholder's party, now in power, needed our support more than we needed his; or he may have grounded his decision on the need of preventing the rise of any Power other than that of England in South India, where Tippoo Sahib was always a danger. He refused to do more than offer to negotiate on this question within the space of six months after the signature of the treaty. The negotiation was never even begun; and thus the treaty signed at The Hague on 15th April 1788 was always viewed with disfavour by the Dutch. The guarantee of the restored Stadholderate by Great Britain, and the promise of each State to assist in the defence of the possessions of the other, were in themselves quite satisfactory; but the compact lacked the solidity which comes only from entire confidence and goodwill.[2]

[1] B.M. Add. MSS., 28063. Harris to Pitt, 22nd February 1788.
[2] Martens, iv, 372-7; Garden, v, 89-92.

The formation of an alliance with Prussia in the same year also came about in a manner more brilliant than sound. Of course, in all such affairs each Power tries to bring the other over to its own standpoint; and much tugging must needs take place between a military and a naval State. Frederick William and his chief statesman, Hertzberg, had just achieved the first success of their careers, and largely owing to the firmness of Pitt. Assured of their supremacy in Germany and Holland, they now sought to guard against the dangers threatening them from the East. The news which came in the month of November 1787, that Austria would join Russia in her war with Turkey, caused the gravest concern at Berlin, and therefore enhanced the value of a British alliance. The growing weakness of France and the power of Pitt to handle a crisis firmly therefore put a new face on Prussian policy. Instead of waiting on Paris, the Berlin Cabinet looked more and more expectantly towards London.

Already Frederick William had signified his desire for a union with the Dutch " in order to pave the way to a Triple Alliance between England, Prussia, and Holland as soon as it may be possible to accomplish it." [1] But the Pitt Ministry, distrustful of an alliance with Prussia unless Russia also came in, treated this overture very coyly. From a letter which the first Earl Camden wrote to Pitt on 18th October, we gather that the Earl was far more inclined to such an alliance than Pitt had shown himself to be at a recent meeting of the Cabinet. Camden favoured the plan as tending to consolidate our influence in Holland—a matter of the utmost moment. "We have escaped miraculously," he writes, " from the most perilous situation we ever experienced, and shall be mad if we slip the opportunity of rooting out the French interest in that country for ever . . . and that will be compleatly effected by a Prussian alliance." It would also free Prussia from slavish dependence upon France. As for the fear that it would drive France to a close compact with Russia and Austria, the Earl treated that danger as remote. [2]

Carmarthen, and probably Pitt also, looked on the danger as real enough to give them pause. Not till 2nd December did Carmarthen return any specific answer; and then he expressed the doubt whether it was desirable to form a Triple Aliance then,

[1] "F. O.," Prussia, 12. Ewart to Carmarthen, 27th September 1787.
[2] Pitt MSS., 119.

as there were rumours of a projected union between these three Powers, which might become a reality if England, Prussia, and Holland coalesced.[1] If that hostile league were formed, it would then be desirable to come to terms, and even to include Denmark, Sweden, and the lesser German States. It is curious that he did not name Poland; but here we find the first definite sign of that league of the smaller States with Prussia and Great Britain which afterwards played so important a part in Pitt's foreign policy.

The caution of Pitt was justified. In a few days' time Sweden came knocking at our door, asking for admittance along with Denmark. The adventurous character of Gustavus III will appear in the sequel. Here we may note that Carmarthen politely waved aside this offer of alliance from a suspicion that he was planning a blow at Russia.[2] The blow did not fall until the middle of July 1788; but then the sudden summons of the Swedish King to the Empress Catharine to hand back part of Russian Finland, and to accept his mediation in the Russo-Turkish War, showed the meaning of his proposal at Christmas 1787.

Only by slow degrees did the eastern horizon clear. But when France showed her resentment at the participation of Austria in the Turkish War, the spectre of a hostile Triple Alliance was laid; and then, but not till then, Pitt showed more favour to the Prussian proposals. Yet here again there was need of caution. The Eastern Question touched Prussia far more closely than England. If Joseph II gained his heart's desire—Moldavia and Wallachia—and Catharine extended her boundary to the River Dniester, the greatness and even the safety of Prussia and of Poland would be hopelessly compromised.[3] Accordingly Prussia sought by all means short of drawing the sword to help the Turks in their unequal struggle. She cantonned large forces near the Austrian border, hinted that she would be glad to offer her mediation for the purpose of securing a reasonable peace, and sent an official disguised as a merchant by way of Venice to Constantinople in order to encourage the

---

[1] Pitt MSS., 119. Carmarthen to Ewart, 2nd December 1787. Fraser, our envoy at St. Petersburg, reported on 1st November that Austria was proposing there a Triple Alliance, but it was coolly received (" F. O.," Russia, 15).

[2] *Ibid.* Carmarthen to Ewart, 26th December.

[3] See Ewart's masterly Memorandum in "Dropmore P.," ii, 44-9.

I   CC

Sultan to a vigorous prosecution of the war.[1] Hertzberg also urged the formation of a league between Prussia, England, and the smaller States with a view to the guarantee of the Turkish possessions in Europe.[2]

To this proposal the British Government gave no encouragement. So far as appears from the despatches of this year, the fate of Turkey was not a matter of much concern to Pitt and Carmarthen. Indeed, not until 2nd April did they vouchsafe an answer to the Prussian proposal of alliance; and then they based their acceptance on the need of safeguarding the situation in Holland. Other States, it was added, might be invited to join the Triple Alliance in order effectively to counterbalance the jealous efforts to which it might give rise; but Great Britain declined to bind herself to any guarantee of the Sultan's dominions. If he were in sore straits, Great Britain would support Prussia in gaining reasonable terms for him, but she would not favour any active intervention on his behalf. Still less would she support the notion (outlined by Hertzberg) that Prussia should acquire an indemnity for any gains that Austria might make in the present war.[3] The key-note of British policy was firmly struck in this sentence: " The great object which we have in view is the continuance of peace, as far as that is not inconsistent with our essential interests. It is with that view that the alliance of Holland has been thought so material, as rendering any attack upon us less probable. With the same view we are desirous of cultivating the closest connections with the Court of Berlin." [4] That is to say, the proposed Triple Alliance was to be a purely defensive league for the safeguarding of the three States and their colonies.

At Berlin, however, now that Catharine had finally waved aside the friendly offers of British and Prussian mediation, the Eastern crisis eclipsed all other topics. By degrees Hertzberg

---

[1] Luckwaldt, 100 *et seq.* Ewart found out the secret instructions issued to Dietz, and forwarded them to London on 8th April. They show that Prussia sought by all means to encourage the Turks, but laid her plans so as to get an indemnity in land in case Austria gained land in the south-east.

[2] " F. O.," Prussia, 13. Ewart to Carmarthen, 15th March 1788.

[3] *Ibid.* Ewart to Carmarthen, 15th January 1788. Lecky (v, 232) assigns the first rumours of Prussian indemnities in land to January 1789; but Ewart reported the beginnings of Hertzberg's plan in January 1788.

[4] *Ibid.* Carmarthen to Ewart, 2nd April.

laid his plans for the aggrandizement of Prussia, whatever might befall the Turks.[1] As will appear more fully in a later chapter, he expected that Joseph II would gain the whole, or large parts, of Moldavia and Wallachia. The armed mediation of Prussia was to lessen these acquisitions; and as a set-off to them Austria must cede Galicia to the Poles; while their gratitude for the recovery of that great province, torn from them in 1772, was to show itself in the cession to Prussia of the important fortresses and districts, Danzig and Thorn, so necessary for the rounding off of her ragged borders on the East. Such was the scheme which took shape in Hertzberg's fertile brain, and dominated Prussian policy down to the summer of the year 1791.

The watchful Ewart forwarded to Whitehall details of this gigantic "deal" (if we may use the Americanism); and as the scheme came to light it aroused deep distrust at Whitehall. At once the Prussian proposal wore a new aspect; and the draft of a treaty drawn up in this sense in the middle of April left little hope of a settlement between the two Powers. In reply to its proposals Pitt and Carmarthen pointed out the vagueness of the Prussian suggestions respecting Turkey, but hinted that an opportunity might come for befriending the Sultan if he were too hard pressed. Further, while promising to help Prussia if she were attacked, they again demanded the like succour from her if any of our colonies were assailed. They also desired to bring into the league Sweden, Denmark, and Portugal. For the present, however, they sought to limit the Anglo-Prussian under-standing to the Dutch guarantee, though a closer compact was to be discussed during the visit of the Prussian monarch to his sister at Loo.[2]

This last suggestion was for Ewart himself. The others he was to pass on to Hertzberg. That Minister chafed at this further rebuff to his plans, which now comprised the offer of the armed mediation of Prussia, England, and Holland to Catharine and Joseph. The fondness of Frederick William for France once more appeared; and the French party at Berlin venomously raised its head. England, they avowed, would gain everything from this one-sided compact; for her colonies were to be found in every sea. Why should the troops of the great Frederick be

---

[1] See his letter of 24th November 1787 to Dietz at Constantinople in Häusser, "Deutsche Geschichte," i, 225-6.

[2] "F. O.," Prussia, 13. Carmarthen to Ewart, 14th May 1788.

set in motion to help the islanders every time that one of their colonial governors lost his temper? Finally the King declared that he would not send his troops beyond the bounds of Germany and Holland.[1]

There seemed little chance of an agreement between the two Courts, until Frederick William set out for his visit to the Prince and Princess of Orange at Loo, and let fall the remark that he hoped to see Sir James Harris there. Already that envoy had asked permission to come to London; and, with the zeal of a convert to the Prussian alliance, he convinced Ministers of its desirability, even if they gave way on certain points. The Instructions drawn up for him on 6th June set forth the need of an Anglo-Prussian alliance in order "to contribute to the general tranquillity." He was also to sound the Prussian monarch as to the inclusion of other Powers, especially Sweden and Denmark; but discussions on this matter were not to stand in the way of the signature of the treaty.[2] George III, now a firm supporter of peace principles, favoured the scheme, as appears from his letter of the same date to the Princess of Orange. He there stated that he approved of an alliance with Prussia, though there might not be time to gain the adhesion of other States; and he expressed the hope that this compact would lead Austria and France to desire the continuance of peace, and thereby conduce to the termination of war in the East.[3]

Fortified by these opinions of the King and Cabinet, Harris prepared to play the game boldly. His handsome person, grand air, and consciousness of former victories gave him an advantage in the discussions with Frederick William, who, thanks to the tact of the Princess, laid aside his earlier prepossessions against the "dictator," and entered into his views. In order to keep the impressionable monarch free from disturbing influences, Harris paid the sum of 200 ducats to a chamberlain if he would ensure the exclusion of a noted partisan of France, Colonel Stein, from the royal chamber during a critical stage in the healing process. The climax came during a ball on 12-13th June. After midnight the King sought out Harris, invited him to walk in the garden, admitted the force of his arguments in favour of an immediate signature of the proposed treaty, and allowed him to speak to his Minister, Alvensleben. While fireworks blazed

[1] *Ibid.* Ewart to Carmarthen, 27th and 31st May 1788; Wittichen, ch. xx.
[2] B.M. Add. MSS., 28063.   [3] "Malmesbury Diaries," ii, 421.

and courtiers danced, the two Ministers drew up a provisional treaty, to which the King assented on the following morning, 13th June 1788.

The news of the signature of the Provisional Treaty of Loo was received at Berlin with an outburst of rage, when it appeared that nearly all the aims and safeguards striven for by Ministers and Francophiles had disappeared. Further negotiations ensued at Berlin; but they brought no material change to the Loo compact. The treaty signed at Berlin by Hertzberg and Ewart on 13th August 1788 was defensive in character. Each State promised to help the other, in case of attack, by a force of 20,000 men; but Great Britain was not to use such a force of Prussians outside Europe or even at Gibraltar. That contingent might be increased if need arose; or it might be replaced by a money equivalent. As was stipulated at Loo, the two Powers pledged themselves to uphold the integrity of the United Provinces and of their present constitution, and to defend that State by all possible means, in case of attack, the Dutch also affording armed help to either ally, if it were attacked. Two secret articles were added to the Berlin Treaty, the one stipulating that no military aid should be given to the party attacked unless the latter had on foot at least 44,000 men; the second provided that a British fleet should assist Prussia if the latter applied for it.[1]

Thus was formed an imposing league. The splendid army of Prussia, backed by the fleets and resources of Great Britain and the Dutch Republic, constituted a force which during three years was to maintain peace and assure the future of the smaller States. If we remember the state of woeful isolation of England up to the summer of 1787, the contrast in her position a year later is startling. It came about owing to the caution of Pitt in a time when precipitate action would have marred everything. His wise delay in the early stages of the Dutch crisis, and his diplomatic coyness in the bargaining with Prussia are alike admirable.[2] The British envoys, Ewart and Harris (Keith at Vienna deserves also to be named) were men of unusual

---

[1] The secret articles are in Ranke's "Fürstenbund," ii, 358; for the published treaties of 13th June and 13th August see Martens, iv, 382-5, 390-3; for the negotiations, Luckwaldt, 114-16, Salomon, "Pitt," 344-51. The accounts of these important events given by Tomline, Stanhope, and Lecky are brief and unsatisfactory.

[2] So Wittichen, 148.

capacity and courage; but then as now success depended mainly on the chief; and it has been shown that the guiding hand at Whitehall was that of Pitt.

His diplomatic triumphs recorded in this chapter were to have a marked influence on the future of Europe. It is not generally known how acute was the danger arising from the schemes of Catharine II and Joseph II. In popular imagination the premonitory rumblings of the French Revolution rivet the attention of the world to the exclusion of all else; but a perusal of the letters of statesmen shows that nine-tenths of their time were given to thwarting the plans of the imperial revolutionists. In truth French democracy could not have gained its rapid and easy triumphs had not the monarchies of Central and Eastern Europe shaken the old order of things to its base, so that even the intelligent conservatism of Pitt failed to uphold the historic fabric from the attacks that came from the East and the West. Well was it for Great Britain that her diplomatic position was fully assured by the autumn of the year 1788. For at that time lunacy beset her monarch, paralyzed her executive government, and threatened to place her fortunes at the mercy of a dissolute prince.

CHAPTER XVII

THE PRINCE OF WALES

Our Ministers like gladiators live;
'Tis half their business blows to ward or give.
The good their virtue would effect, or sense,
Dies between exigents and self-defence.
POPE.

He [the Prince of Wales] has so effeminate a mind as to counteract his
own good qualities, by having no control over his weaknesses.
THE EARL OF MALMESBURY, *Diaries*, iv, 33.

A PRIME Minister of Great Britain needs to be an intellectual
Proteus. Besides determining the lines of foreign and
domestic policy, he must regulate the movements of a complex
parliamentary machine, ever taking into account personal prejudices which not seldom baffle the most careful forecast. It is
not surprising, therefore, to find statesmen at Westminster often
slow and hesitating even when there is need of prompt decision.
The onlooker may see only the public questions at issue. The
man in the thick of the maze may all the time be holding the
personal clue which alone can bring him to the open. How
often has the fate of Europe turned on the foibles or favouritism
of Queen Elizabeth, Louis XIV, Queen Anne, Charles XII,
Catharine II. In the present age this factor counts for less than
of yore. Hence it comes about that many modern critics assess
the career of Pitt as if he were in the position of a Gladstone.
In point of fact he was more under royal control than Walpole
or Godolphin. He had to do with a Sovereign who in the last
resort gave the law to his Ministers, and occasionally treated
them like head clerks.

True, George III interfered with Pitt less than with his predecessors. That masterful will had been somewhat tamed during
the "bondage" to the Coalition, and almost perforce accepted the
guidance of his deliverer. The King even allowed Pitt to go

his own way respecting Reform, Warren Hastings, and the Irish Commercial Treaty. Family scandals and family debts for a time overshadowed all other considerations, a fact which goes far to explain the bourgeois domesticity of his outlook on Dutch affairs. In these years, then, he acquiesced in the lead of the heaven-sent Minister who maintained the national credit and the national honour. But in the last resort George III not only reigned but governed. Thus, apart from the Eastern War, which we shall consider later, everything portended a time of calm in the year 1788, when suddenly the personal element obtruded itself. There fell upon the monarch a strange malady which threatened to bring confusion in place of order, and to enthrone a Prince who was the embodiment of faction and extravagance.

The career of the Prince of Wales illustrates the connection often subsisting between the extremes of virtue and vice. Not seldom the latter may be traced to the excess of the former in some primly uninteresting home; and certainly the Prince, who saw the light on 12th August 1762, might serve to point the moral against pedantic anxiety on the part of the unco' guid. His upbringing by the strictest of fathers in the most methodized of households early helped to call out and strengthen the tendencies to opposition which seemed ingrained in the heirs-apparent of that stubborn stock. In the dull life at Kew or Windsor, bristling with rules and rebukes, may we not see the working in miniature of those untoward influences—fussy control and austere domination—which wearied out the patience of Ministers and the loyalty of colonists?

Moreover this royal precisian was not blessed with a gracious consort. Queen Charlotte's youthful experiences at the ducal Court of Mecklenburg predisposed her to strict control and unsparing parsimony. Many were the jests as to her stamping with her signet the butter left over at meals. It was even affirmed that apple charlottes owed their name to her custom of using up the spare crusts of every day. These slanders (for the latter story fails before the touchstone of the term *Charlotte Russe*) owed their popularity largely to her ugliness. One of her well-wishers, Colonel Disbrowe, once expressed to Croker the hope that the bloom of her ugliness was going off.[1] This sin revealed

[1] "Records of Stirring Times," 58, by the authoress of "Old Days in Diplomacy."

a multitude of others; and it is fairly certain that Queen Charlotte has been hardly judged. Some there were who accused
her of callousness towards the King during his insanity; and
the charge seems in part proven for the year 1804.[1] Others,
again, charged her with unmotherly treatment of the Prince of
Wales. Who can suffice for these things? Aristophanes coined
a happy phrase to denote lovers of the trivial in politics. He
calls them "buzzers-in-corners." Those who essay to write the
life of a great statesman must avoid those nooks.

One thing is certain. The Prince of Wales grew to dislike
both his father and mother. His temperament was far gayer
and more romantic than theirs. Some imaginative persons have
ventured to assert that a more generous and sympathetic training would have moulded him to a fine type of manhood. Undoubtedly his education was of the narrow kind which had
stunted the nature of George III; and when the King, with
ingrained obstinacy, continued to keep the trammels on the
high-spirited youth of eighteen, he burst them asunder. At that
age the Prince had his first amour (was it his first?), namely,
with the actress, "Perdita" Robinson.[2] The gilded youth of
London, long weary of the primness of Windsor, cheered him
on to further excesses, and Carlton House set the tone of the
age. In vain did the King seek to regain the confidence and
affection of his son.[3] His efforts were repulsed; and the debasing influence of Henry Frederick, Duke of Cumberland, inured
the Prince to every kind of debauchery.

As if this were not enough, the heir to the throne made a
bosom friend of the man whom his father most detested, Charles
James Fox. Through that charming libertine the Prince became
an *habitué* of the Whig Club, Brooks's;[4] and, as we have seen,
he helped to defeat the King's eager electioneering in the great
fight of 1784 at Westminster. Thenceforth the feud between
father and son was bitter and persistent. The Prince had all his
father's wilfulness, and far more than his stock of selfishness.

---

[1] Certain letters of the Earl of Liverpool recently sold in London show
that there was an open breach between King and Queen in 1804, and that
Pitt helped to patch it up.

[2] Huish, "Mems. of George IV," i, 60-2.

[3] H. Walpole's "Last Journals," ii, 480-1.

[4] Fox does not seem to have *introduced* the prince into bad company.
See Jesse, ii, 367-9, and Huish, i, 122-4.

So far as is known, he showed no sign of repentance, but argued himself into the belief that the King had always hated him from his seventh year onward.[1] There is nothing that corroborates this petulant assertion. The King had been a kind and even doting father, his chief fault being that of guiding too long and too closely this wayward nature.

By the summer of 1783 the quarrel had waxed warm on the subject of the immorality and extravagance of the Prince. At that time the Coalition Ministry startled the King by proposing to grant the sum of £100,000 a year to the Prince of Wales, exclusive of the revenues of the Duchy of Cornwall, which amounted to about £13,000 a year.[2] The King, having formerly received far less than that amount, considered it exorbitant. As we saw in Chapter VI, the Ministry would probably have fallen had not the Prince required his favourite to waive the proposal. Parliament then voted £30,000 to pay his debts, £30,000 to start his new establishment (Carlton House) and £50,000 a year out of the Civil List.

By the autumn of the next year the Prince defiantly proposed to travel abroad in order to ease his finances by evading his creditors. This the King forbade, and requested him to send in a detailed list of his expenses and debts. The result was a statement clear enough in most items, but leaving a sum of £25,000 unaccounted for. The King required an explanation of this, which the Prince as firmly refused to give, though he assured Sir James Harris it was a debt of honour. As the King refused to pass this sum, the whole matter dragged on, until in April 1785 the debts reached the total of £160,000. To escape the discomforts of his position, the Prince proposed to his friend, Harris, who was then in London, a term of residence at The Hague. The true reason for this proposal lies in the fact that the Prince had for some time been desperately in love with a fair young widow, Mrs. Fitzherbert, who was a Roman Catholic. In vain had he wounded himself as a sign of his undying passion for her: in vain had four of his friends sought to inveigle her into a mock marriage. In order to escape his importunities she had fled to the Continent; and the King refused him permission to pursue her.

Here, in truth, was the crux of the relations between father

---

[1] " Malmesbury Diaries," ii, 125.   [2] Pitt MSS., 228.

and son. King George saw no hope for the youth but in marriage with a Protestant princess. Prince George as firmly declared that he would not marry "some German frow," and racked his brains with designs to secure the Roman Catholic of his choice. Mrs. Fitzherbert's religion, her position as a commoner, and the anomaly of a morganatic marriage in these islands, rendered any connection with her odious in the eyes of the King. Besides, the Royal Marriage Act of 1772 forbade the marriage of any prince or princess of the blood under the age of twenty-six without the consent of the King. On all sides, then, the King had the Prince in his toils.

The Prince, realizing this fact, seems to have behaved as recklessly as possible in the hope of compelling the King to allow him to live abroad and marry Mrs. Fitzherbert. Such at least is the most charitable explanation of his early prodigalities. The debts, surely, were a means of forcing the hand of his father. But George was not to be gulled in this way. He, too, held firmly to his views, and the result was a hopeless deadlock. Pitt and Carmarthen sought to end it in May 1785. They threw out hints to Harris that the income of the Prince might be increased by Parliament if he would become reconciled to the King, cease to be a party man, and set about the discharge of his debts. Accordingly Harris waited on the Prince at Carlton House on 23rd May 1785, and suggested that on these conditions the Ministry would double his income, provided also that he set apart £50,000 a year for the discharge of his debts. To this the Prince demurred, on the ground that he could not desert Fox, and that the King's unfatherly hatred would be an obstacle to any such proposal. In support of the latter statement he requested Harris to read the King's letters to him, which were couched in severe terms, reprobating his extravagance and dissipation.

We cannot censure this severity. The gluttonous orgies of Carlton House were a public scandal, especially in hard times, when Parliament withheld the money necessary for the protection of Portsmouth and Plymouth. Both as a patriot and a father, George was justified in condemning his son's conduct; and it is clear that the hatred of the Prince for his father led him to put the worst possible construction on the advice from Windsor. At the close of his interview with Harris he declared vehemently that he never would marry, and that he had settled with his brother Frederick, Duke of York, for the Crown to devolve on his heirs.[1]

As illustrating the relations of father and son, I may quote an unpublished letter from Hugh Elliot to Pitt, dated Bright-helmstone, 17th October 1785, and endorsed by Pitt—"Shewn to the King."[2] In it Elliot states that he went to Brighton merely for bathing, but was soon honoured by the Prince's company and confidence. He had combated several of his pre-judices, and this had not offended him; but the Prince asked him to discuss matters with the King's Ministers, who would then report to the King. He then adds:

There is so much difficulty in putting upon paper the secret circum-stances I have learnt, or in detailing the imminent danger to which H.R.H. is exposed from a manner of life that can be thoroughly under-stood only by those who are eye-witnesses of it, that, out of respect to the Prince, I shall be justified in not dwelling upon so distressing a subject, but that I may be allowed to advance, that in my opinion H.R.H. risks being lost to himself, his family and his country if a total and sudden change does not take place. I will even venture to add that the Prince is at this moment not insensible that such a change is neces-sary and that it is one of the motives which make him desirous of visiting the Continent under such restrictions as the King may think proper to advise.

Elliot adds that the Prince would travel only with Colonels Lee and Slaughter and himself, if the King and Pitt approved of his going with him. The Prince hoped to economize and so win back the good opinion of the King and country. He (Elliot) would rejoice if he could further this course.

The desire of the Prince for foreign travel ended with the return of Mrs. Fitzherbert from her secret tour. The Prince's pursuit of her now became more eager than ever, and he suc-ceeded in inspiring her with feelings of love. Consequently, on 15th December 1785, he secretly married her, having four days previously assured his bosom friend, Fox, that there was no "ground for these reports which of late have been so malevolently circulated." It is now proved beyond possibility of doubt that the marriage was legal (except in the political sense above noticed), and that the Prince did his wife grievous

---

[1] "Malmesbury Diaries," ii, 129-31.   [2] Pitt MSS., 105.

wrong in persistently denying the fact.[1] She, with all the proofs in her possession, refrained from compromising him, and therefore had to endure endless slights. Many persons had the good sense to place her dignified silence far above his unblushing denials, and Society was rent in twain by the great question—"Was he married or not?" In view of these facts, is it desirable to present a full-length portrait of His Royal Highness? The wonder is that even in his Perdita days his name could ever be compared with the tenderest and most faithful of Shakespeare's lovers, Prince Florizel. That he allowed himself to be painted in that guise argues singular assurance. Was not Cloten more nearly his prototype?

It would be interesting to know whether the King and Queen were aware of the secret marriage. The Queen in a private interview pressed him to tell the truth; but he probably equivocated. Their action bespeaks perplexity. In private they treated Mrs. Fitzherbert kindly, but never received her at Court.[2] That Pitt was not ill-informed on the subject appears from the following hitherto unpublished letter from his brother, the Earl of Chatham. It is undated, but probably belongs to the month of December 1785:

Hanley, Wednesday.[3]

MY DEAR BROTHER,

I have had a good deal of conversation with Sir C—— on the subject you wished some information upon. The result of which leaves no doubt on my mind of the P[rince] having not only offered to marry Mrs. F., but taken measures towards its accomplishment. Many circumstances confirm this opinion, but this much is, I think, certain information, which is that the letters from the P. offering it were shown by himself to Mrs. S—— L——, the mother, from whom Sir Carnaby has it immediately, and the letter from Mrs. F. to her mother, in which she informs her of her consent. Sir C—— has seen an extract of, and is promised a copy of [it], which I shall see. It must, however, I think, still remain very doubtful, till the step is absolutely taken, whether it ever will, or whether it is more than a last effort to gain her without; but

---

[1] W. H. Wilkins, "Mrs. Fitzherbert and George IV," i, 81-105.

[2] *Ibid.*, i, 135-7; Langdale, "Mems. of Mrs. Fitzherbert," 127-8, 141, 142; Jesse, ii, 512, 513.

[3] Pitt MSS., 122. Sir Carnaby is Sir Carnaby Haggerston, who married Frances, the youngest sister of Mrs. Fitzherbert (*née* Smythe). Her mother was a daughter of John Errington of the Northumberland family of that name. His brother was the *confidante* of the Prince, as described above.

Sir C. and all her family seem perfectly convinced that he seriously and at all events intends it. They are averse to it; but the person in the P'ˢ confidence upon it and most employed in it is Mr. Errington, husband of Lady Broughton. He is supposed to be the person who is to go over as her relation to be present at the ceremony. I have endeavoured to learn what I cou'd as to the point of whether she wou'd change her religion or not. She at present says she will not; but Sir C—— seems to think that she might be brought to that whenever the marriage was declared. The present intention seems to be that it should be kept secret, but that, her conscience thus satisfied, she is to appear, and be received as, his mistress; and I believe it is pretty certain that he has a promise from a certain duchess to visit her and go about with her when she comes. . . .

Clearly the Earl of Chatham came very near the truth. Sir Carnaby Haggerston knew the secret, and chose to reveal a good deal of it. Mr. Errington was the bride's uncle, and gave her away at the secret ceremony at her house in Park Lane on 15th December.[1] The Duchess of Devonshire early recognized Mrs. Fitzherbert, and frequently entertained her along with the Prince.

The *liaison* with Mrs. Fitzherbert (for it was ostensibly nothing more) of course did not lessen expenses at Carlton House. The Prince insisted on her moving to a larger residence and entertaining on a lavish scale. As for Carlton House, it " exhibited a perpetual scene of excess, unrestrained by any wise superintendence." [2] It was therefore natural that the Prince's friends should ply Parliament with requests for larger funds in the spring of 1786. The matter came up, not inappropriately, during debates on the deficiency in the Civil List. That most brilliant of wits and most genial of boon companions, Richard Brinsley Sheridan, had now espoused the Prince's cause. With his customary charm he dragged in the subject of the monetary woes of his patron, pointing out that the dignity of the Crown demanded an ampler provision and the payment of the existing debts. Pitt replied that this matter was not before the House, and added that, as he had received no instructions on the subject, he would not be so presumptuous as to offer any private opinion on it.

Undeterred by this freezing rebuke to Sheridan, Fox on the

---

[1] W. H. Wilkins, *op. cit.*, i, 97.   [2] Wraxall, iv, 306.

next day raised the same question, maintaining that it was a national advantage for the Heir-Apparent to be able to live not merely in ease but in splendour. This patriotic appeal fell on deaf ears. The country gentlemen who on the score of expense had lately decided to leave Portsmouth and Plymouth open to attack, were not likely to vote away on the orgies of Carlton House an extra sum of £50,000 a year, which in fourteen years would have made the two great dockyard towns impregnable. Fox wisely refrained from pressing his demand, and vouchsafed no explanation as to how the nation would benefit from the encouragement of extravagance in Pall Mall.[1] Clearly the Prince's friends were in a hopeless minority. Accordingly he began more stoutly than ever to deny his marriage with Mrs. Fitzherbert; but in such a case character counts for more than oaths and asseverations.

So the miserable affair dragged on. The King refused every request for help for the Prince, doubtless in the hope that debt would compel him to give up his mistress. The debts therefore grew apace, until in the summer of 1786 Carlton House was in danger of being seized by the brokers. It is clear that Pitt sided with the King. George III frequently commended him for his wise advice; but unfortunately nearly all the letters from Pitt to his sovereign, especially on this topic, long ago disappeared from the Library at Windsor, a highly suspicious circumstance. We know, however, that, as early as March and April 1785, the King approved the messages drawn up by Pitt from the Sovereign to the Prince. In general they seem to have been drafted by the Minister; and the following draft, in Pitt's writing, but dated by the King and with one slight correction, remains as proof that Pitt was the mouthpiece for the royal rebukes. It is endorsed " Draft of Letter from the King to the Prince of Wales":

WINDSOR, *July* 8, 1786.[2]

After so often repeating to the Prince of Wales the same sentiments on the subject of his applications, and with so little effect, I should add nothing further at present. But I must express my surprise at receiving a letter from him in which he states himself to be convinced that he has no reason to expect either at present or in future the smallest assistance

---

[1] " Parl. Hist.," xxv, 1348-56; Wraxall, iv, 304-6.
[2] Pitt MSS., 103. For other references see the King's letters to Pitt in " Pitt and Napoleon Miscellanies."

from me. A reference to my last letter [1] and to the former correspondence might shew him what it was I expected before I could enter further on the consideration of the business. If he chooses to interpret what has passed into a refusal on my part to take measures in any case for his assistance, the consequence of his doing so can be imputed only to his own determination. [2]

That the details of the expenditure at Carlton House were laid before Pitt is clear from the evidence contained in the Pitt Papers. The packet entitled "Prince of Wales's Debts," affords piquant reading. For, be it remembered, at the very time when Pitt was straining every nerve to lessen the National Debt, to rebuild the navy, and to enable England to look her enemies once more in the face, the Prince was squandering money on rare wines, on gilding, ormolu, and on jewellery for Mrs. Fitzherbert, £54,000 being considered a "not unreasonable bill" by her latest biographer. [3] An official estimate fixes the total expenditure of the Prince for the years 1784-86 at £369,977 (or at the rate of £123,000 a year) and yet there were "arrears not yet to hand." Parliament had voted £30,000 for the furnishing of Carlton House; but in 1787 the Prince consulted the welfare of the nation by accepting an estimate of £49,700 for extensions and decorations ; and late in 1789 he sought still further to strengthen the monarchy by spending £110,500 on further splendours. They included "a new throne and State bed, furniture trimmed with rich gold lace, also new decorations in the Great Hall, a Chinese Drawing-Room, etc." The Pitt Papers contain no reference to the sums spent on the Pavilion at Brighton in the years 1785, 1786; but, even in its pre-oriental form, it afforded singular proof of the desire of the Prince for quiet and economy at that watering-place.

Much has been made of the retrenchments of July 1786, when the works on Carlton House were suspended, and the half of that palatial residence was closed. Whatever were the motives that prompted that new development, it soon ceased, as the foregoing figures have shown. The Prince's necessities being as great as ever, he found means to bring his case before Parliament in the debates of 20th, 24th, and 27th April 1787. Thereupon Pitt clearly hinted that the inquiry, if made at all, must be made

---

[1] The King altered this to "written message."   [2] Pitt MSS., 105.
[3] W. H. Wilkins, *op. cit.*, i, 161.

thoroughly, and that he would in that case b most reluctantly driven " to the disclosure of circumstances which he should otherwise think it his duty to conceal." The House quivered with excitement at the untactful utterance—one of Pitt's few mistakes in Parliament. Sheridan, with his usual skill and daring, took up the challenge and virtually defied Pitt to do his worst. Pitt thereupon declared that he referred solely to pecuniary matters.

Everyone, however, knew that the Fitzherbert question was really at stake; and the general dislike to any discussion, even on the debts, was voiced by the heavy Devonshire squire, who was to find immortality in the " Rolliad." Rolle asserted on 27th April that any such debate would affect the constitution both in Church and State. Undaunted by Sheridan's salvos of wit, he stuck to his guns, with the result that on the 30th Fox fired off a seemingly crushing discharge. As Sheridan had declared that the Prince in no wise shrank from the fullest inquiry, the Whig chieftain now solemnly assured the House that the reported marriage with Mrs. Fitzherbert was a low and malicious calumny. When the tenacious Devonian plied him with the final inquiry whether he spoke from direct authority, Fox replied with the utmost emphasis that he did.

We now know that Fox had been cruelly deceived by the Prince. But in that age the assertion of Fox was considered as almost final, save by those who marked the lofty scorn poured by Mrs. Fitzherbert on her unwitting traducer. In Parliament the victory lay with the Prince; but even there Rolle firmly refused to comply with Sheridan's challenging request and declare himself satisfied. To the outside world it was clear that either the heir to the throne or Fox had lied.

The letters of George III to Pitt in May 1787 and Pitt's suggestions for a settlement of the dispute, show that the perturbed monarch placed absolute confidence in his Minister. Very noteworthy is the King's assertion that there could be no reconciliation until his son consented to marry and to retrench his expenditure. His letter of 20th May 1787 to Pitt further proves that the proposal to add £10,000 to the Prince's income emanated from Pitt, and was acquiesced in somewhat reluctantly by the King.[1]

[1] This letter refutes the statement of Huish (*op. cit.*, i, 169) that Pitt was as pertinacious as the King in refusing to help the Prince.

This expedient brought about a partial reconciliation between father and son. On the strong recommendation of Pitt, Parliament allowed the extra £10,000 a year, besides granting £20,000 on behalf of the new works at Carlton House, and paying £161,000 towards the extinction of the Prince's debts, on his express assurance that he would not exceed his income in the future. The vote was unanimous. Thereupon the King waived the question of the Prince's marriage; so at least we may infer from the fact that they had a long interview on 25th May 1787 at the Queen's House (Buckingham House), at the close of which the Prince proceeded to greet his mother and sisters. The parents had few happier days than that; and their joy was crowned a little later by the return of Frederick, Duke of York, after a long residence in Germany. Fanny Burney describes the radiant gladness of the King and Queen as they paced along the terrace at Windsor with their soldier son; and the inhabitants of the royal city crowded to witness the pleasing scene. It speaks well for the Prince of Wales, that he posted off from Brighton on the news of his brother's home-coming, in order to double the pleasure of his parents. For a time, too, the Prince thought more kindly of Pitt; so we may infer from the statement of St. Leger to the Marquis of Buckingham that his feelings towards him had altered since the negotiation on the subject of his debts.[1] But these sentiments of gratitude soon vanished along with the virtuous and economical mood of which they were the outcome. Those who break their word naturally hate the man to whom they had pledged it.

In the winter of 1787-8 the two Princes again abandoned themselves to drinking and gambling. The dead set made against Pitt over the Warren Hastings trial and Indian affairs so far weakened his position that the Princes counted on his fall and hoped for the advent to power of the Fox-Sheridan clique. Certain it is that they drank and played very deep. General Grant, writing to Cornwallis, 6th April 1788, says:

The Prince [of Wales] has taught the Duke [of York] to *drink* in the most liberal and copious way; and the Duke in return has been equally successful in teaching his brother to lose his money at all sorts of play— *Quinze*, Hazard, &c—to the amount, as we are told, of very large sums

---

[1] " Dropmore P.," i, 362.

in favour of India General Smith [1] and Admiral Pigot who both wanted it very much. These play parties have chiefly taken place at a new club formed this winter by the Prince of Wales in opposition to Brooks's, because Tarleton and Jack Payne, proposed by H.R.H., were black-balled. [2]

At this new club, called the Dover House or Welzie's club, the Prince often won or lost £2,000 or £3,000 at a sitting. In other ways Frederick sought to better his brother's example, so that his company was thought *mauvais ton* by young nobles. [3]

Compared with these buffooneries, political opposition was a small matter. But the King deeply resented the nagging tactics of his son at any time of crisis. Such a time came in March 1788, when a sharp dispute arose between Pitt and the East India Company. It originated in the Dutch troubles of the previous summer. The prospect of war with France was so acute that the India Board sent out four regiments in order to strengthen the British garrisons in India. At the time the Directors of the Company fully approved of this step; but when

[1] Major-General Smith, M.P., was twice unseated for bribery. His nickname was " Hyder Ali."

[2] "Cornwallis Corresp.," i, 374, 375. Payne was a confidential friend of the Prince, who made him Comptroller of his Household and Lord Warden of the Stanneries in Cornwall.

[3] "Buckingham P.," i, 363, 364.
In the Pitt MSS., 228, is a Memorandum, endorsed January 1794, entitled "Heads of a Plan for a new Arrangement of the Prince of Wales's Affairs." It states that his debts then amounted to £412,511 5s. 8d; he owed £60,000 to Mr. Coutts the banker (Pitt's banker); and he might at any time be called on to pay as much as £170,000. It would be difficult to induce Parliament to pay any part of these debts. Moreover, such a demand "would afford a fresh topic of declamation to those who already use the expenses of Royalty as an engine to operate upon weak minds in order to effectuate their ultimate purpose, the overthrow of everything dignified, everything sacred, everything valuable and respectable in social life." The anonymous compiler therefore suggests the raising of a loan at 3½ per cent., so as to cover the "urgent" debts amounting to £349,511. Creditors would probably consent to the "defalcation" of 20 per cent. from what was owed them and be content with 3½ per cent. interest on the remainder.
A Mr. W. Fitzwilliam, of 45, Sloane Street, in May 1795 suggested a lottery for raising £2,100,000, of which £650,000 should go to the discharge of the Prince's debts, £1,000,000 to the archbishops for the forming of a fund for raising the stipend of every clergyman to £100 a year; £100,000 to be reserved as prizes in the lottery; and £50,000 to be set apart for expenses.

the war-cloud blew over, they objected to pay the bill. Pitt insisted that the India Act of 1784 made them liable for the transport of troops when the Board judged it necessary; and in February 1788 he brought in a Declaratory Bill to that effect.

At once the Company flung to the winds all sense of gratitude to its saviour, and made use of the men who four years previously had sought its destruction. Fox and Erskine figured as its champions, and the Prince of Wales primed the latter well with brandy before he went in to attack Pitt. The result was a lamentable display of Billingsgate, of which Pitt took no notice, and the Ministry triumphed by 242 against 118 (3rd March).

But the clamour raised against the measure had more effect two nights later, when Fox dared Pitt to try the case in a court of law. Instead of replying, Pitt feebly remarked that he desired to postpone his answer to a later stage of the debates. This amazing torpor was ascribed to a temporary indisposition; but only the few were aware that the Prime Minister had drunk deeply the previous night at the Marquis of Buckingham's house in Pall Mall in the company of Dundas and the Duchess of Gordon—that spirited lady whose charms are immortalized in the song, "Jenny o' Menteith."[1] Wit and joviality were now replaced by a heaviness that boded ill for the Ministry, whose majority sank to fifty-seven. Two days later, however, Pitt pulled himself and his party together, accepted certain amendments relating to patronage, but crushed his opponents on the main issue. To the annoyance of the Prince of Wales and Fox, the Government emerged triumphant from what had seemed to be certain disaster. Wraxall never wrote a truer word than when he ascribed Pitt's final triumph to his character. Even in his temporary retreat he had commanded respect, so that Burke, who hurried up exultingly from the Warren Hastings trial, was fain to say that the Prime Minister scattered his ashes with dignity and wore his sackcloth like a robe of purple.

The prestige of the Ministry shone once more with full radiance on the Budget night (5th May 1788). Pitt pointed out that the past year had been a time of exceptional strain. The Dutch crisis and the imminence of war with France had entailed preparations which cost nearly £1,200,000. The relief of the Prince of Wales absorbed in all £181,000. The sum of £7,000,000

---

[1] "Buckingham P.," i, 361; Wraxall, iv, 458; v, 77-9.

had been expended in the last four years on improvements in the naval service. He had raised no loan and imposed no new taxes. Nevertheless, the sum of £2,500,000 had been written off from the National Debt, and even so, there was a slight surplus of £17,000. The condition of the finances of France supplied the Minister with a telling contrast. It was well known that, despite many retrenchments, the deficit amounted to £2,300,000. In these financial statements we may discern the cause of the French Revolution and of the orderly development of England.

In vain did Fox and Sheridan seek to dissipate the hopes aroused by the Chancellor of the Exchequer. So experienced a financier as Pulteney justified his statement, and the country at large felt assured of the advent of a time of abounding prosperity. As for France, the inability of her statesmen, even of Necker, to avert the crisis caused by reckless borrowing and stupid taxation, seemed to be the best possible guarantee for peace. Pitt's concern at the re-appointment of Necker in August 1788 appears in a letter to Grenville in which he describes it as almost the worst event that could happen—a curious remark which shows how closely he connected the power of a State with its financial prosperity.[1] Thus the year 1788 wore on, with deepening gloom for France, and with every appearance of calm and happiness for the Island Power, until a mysterious malady struck down the King and involved everything in confusion.

[1] "Dropmore P.," i, 353. Grenville replied on 1st September that he thought the frequent changes in France would undermine her power and so check "that sort of intrigue and restlessness which keeps us in hot water even while we are most confident of the impossibility of any serious effect from their schemes." He then suggests an agreement as to the forces to be kept by the two Powers in the East (Pitt MSS., 140).

CHAPTER XVIII

THE REGENCY CRISIS

Dost thou so hunger for mine empty chair
That thou wilt needs invest thee with mine honours
Before the hour be ripe?
SHAKESPEARE, *Henry IV, Part II.*

The line which bounded the royal prerogative, though in general sufficiently clear, had not everywhere been drawn with accuracy and distinctness.—MACAULAY.

THE causes of insanity are generally obscure. In the case of George III the disease cannot be traced to a progenitor, nor did it descend to his issue, unless the moral perversity of his sons be regarded as a form of mental obliquity. It is highly probable that the conduct of the Prince of Wales and the Duke of York produced in their father a state of nervous tension conducive to, if not the actual cause of, madness. No proof of this is possible; but having regard to the King's despotic temper, his love of plain living, and his horror of gambling and debauchery, we may plausibly refer to a private cause the sudden breakdown of a strong constitution at a time when public affairs had become singularly calm.

Throughout the summer of 1788 he became steadily weaker. A stay at Cheltenham was of no avail. Indeed, an enemy of that place tried to assign the King's malady solely to its waters. The King had to forego the long walks and rides which had formerly tired out all his suite; and in October he returned to Kew much aged and broken. Nevertheless the indomitable will asserted itself in one curious detail. He always remained standing during interviews with his Ministers; and he is stated by George Rose to have kept on his feet for three hours and forty minutes during a portentous interview with Pitt, which must have strained his strength to the breaking point.[1] At the levee of 24th October at St. James's, he made a praiseworthy effort to appear well in order "to stop further lies and any fall of the stocks." But the effort was too great, as Pitt perceived afterwards during a private interview.

Nevertheless, on the following day the King removed to Windsor. There the decline in health continued, so that, after attending a hunt, he exclaimed to Lady Effingham: "My dear Effy, you see me all at once an old man."[2] Even so he continued his correspondence with Pitt much as usual, until on 5th November there came a sudden collapse.

Again we have to confess ignorance as to the final cause. Mrs. Papendiek, wife of the royal barber, ascribes it to the King's annoyance at the endeavour of the Duke of York to introduce Turkish military instruments into the band of the Guards. Rose mentions a discussion with the Duke at dinner on the 5th, relative to a murder. All, however, are agreed that the merest trifles had long sufficed to make the King flurried and angry, as had frequently appeared during the drives with the princesses. This peculiarity now suddenly rose to the point where madness begins. It is even said that at that dinner he without provocation suddenly rushed at the Prince of Wales, pinned him to the wall, and dared him to contradict the King of England. The Prince burst into tears, the Queen became hysterical, and it was with some difficulty that the King was induced to retire to his room. During that evening and night he raved incessantly, and the chief physician, Sir George Baker, feared for his life. A curious incident is mentioned by Mrs. Papendiek. She avers that on the following night the King arose, took a candle, and went to look at the Queen as she slept. She awoke in an agony of terror, whereupon he soothed her and seemed to take comfort himself. We may doubt the authenticity of the incident, as also the correctness of Mrs. Papendiek's narrative when she describes the offensive air of authority which the Prince of Wales at once assumed, his demand of an interview with the Queen, even on

---

[1] G. Rose, "Diaries," i, 86. The date of this interview is probably between 10th and 24th October 1788.

[2] "Fanny Burney's Diary," iv, 122. In a rare pamphlet, "A History of the Royal Malady," by a Page of the Presence (1789), it is stated that the King, while driving in Windsor Park, alighted and shook hands with a branch of an oak tree, asserting it to be the King of Prussia, and was with difficulty persuaded to remount.

political affairs, and his striking the floor with his stick to express displeasure.[1]

It is certain, however, that the behaviour of the Prince was far from seemly. He took the direction of affairs in the palace with an abruptness which caused the Queen much pain. "Nothing was done but by his orders," wrote Miss Burney; "the Queen interfered not in anything. She lived entirely in her two new rooms, and spent the whole day in patient sorrow and retirement with her daughters." Worst of his acts, perhaps, was the taking possession of the King's papers, a proceeding which his apologists pass over in discreet silence. Among those documents, we may note, were several which proved that Pitt had not seldom drafted the royal rebukes. In other respects the exultation of the Prince at least wore the veil of decency, therein comparing favourably with the joy coarsely expressed by his followers at Brooks's Club.[2]

Secret intrigues for assuring the triumph of the Whigs began at once. It is significant that that veteran schemer, the Lord Chancellor, Thurlow, proceeded to Windsor on 6th November, at the Prince's command, and dined and supped with him. The ostensible object of their meeting was to consider the mode of treating His Majesty, who had been violent during the night.[3] But the design of the Prince was to detach from Pitt the highest legal authority in the land. To this he was instigated by Captain Payne, Comptroller of his Household, who wrote to Sheridan that Thurlow would probably take this opportunity of breaking with his colleagues, if they proposed to restrict the powers of the Regent.[4] Payne augured correctly. Thurlow had his scruples as to such a betrayal; but they vanished at the suggestion that he should continue in his high office under the forthcoming Whig Ministry.

This bargain implied the shelving of Lord Loughborough, who for five years had attached himself to the Whigs in the hope of gaining the woolsack. Had Fox been in England, it is unlikely that he would have sanctioned this betrayal of a friend in order

---

[1] "Court and Private Life in the Time of Queen Charlotte," by Mrs. Papendiek. 2 vols. (1887); vol. ii, *ad init.*

[2] "Buckingham P.," i, 342.   [3] G. Rose, "Diaries," i, 87.

[4] T. Moore, "Life of Sheridan," ii, 27, where Payne also suggests that Sheridan should question Pitt about the public amusements, as it would embarrass him "either way."

to gain over an enemy. But, with Sheridan as go-between, and the Prince as sole arbiter, the bargain was soon settled. Light has been thrown on these events by the publication of the Duchess of Devonshire's Diary. In it she says: " He [Sheridan] cannot resist playing a sly game: he cannot resist the pleasure of acting alone; and this, added to his natural want of judgment and dislike of consultation frequently has made him commit his friends and himself." [1] Perhaps it was some sense of the untrustworthiness of Sheridan which led Fox, in the midst of a Continental tour with Mrs. Armstead, to return from Bologna at a speed which proved to be detrimental to his health. After a journey of only nine days, he arrived in London on the 24th. It was too late to stop the bargain with Thurlow, and he at once informed Sheridan that he had swallowed the bitter pill and felt the utmost possible uneasiness about the whole matter. [2]

The Whigs now had a spy in the enemy's citadel. At first Pitt was not aware of the fact. The holding of several Cabinet meetings at Windsor, for the purpose of sifting the medical evidence, enabled Thurlow to hear everything and secretly to carry the news to the Prince. Moreover, his grief on seeing the King—at a time when the Prince's friends knew him to be at his worst[3]—was so heartrending that some beholders were reminded of the description of the player in " Hamlet ":

> Tears in his eyes, distraction in his aspect,
> A broken voice, and his whole function suiting
> With forms to his conceit.

Such at least was the judgement of the discerning few, who, with Fanny Burney, saw more real grief in the dignified composure of Pitt after that inevitably painful interview. Authority to " inspect " the royal patient was entrusted to Thurlow, who thus stood at the fountain head of knowledge. Yet these astute balancings and bargainings were marred by the most trivial of accidents. After one of the Cabinet Councils at Windsor, Ministers were about to return to town, when Thurlow's hat could not be found. Search was made for it in vain in the council chamber, when at last a page came up to the assembled

---

[1] W. Sichel, " Sheridan," ii, 400.
[2] T. Moore, " Life of Sheridan," ii, 31-5; Campbell, " Lives of the Lord Chancellors," vii, 248, 239 (edit. of 1857).
[3] T. Moore, *op. cit.*, p. 29.

Ministers and exclaimed with boyish frankness: "My Lord, I found it in the cabinet of His Royal Highness." The flush which spread over the Chancellor's wrinkled visage doubled the effect of the boy's unconscious home-thrust.[1]

The question of the Regency has often been discussed on abstract constitutional grounds. Precedents were at once hunted up, namely, those of the years, 1326, 1377, 1422, and 1455, the last being considered on a par with the present case. But of course the whole question turned primarily on the probability of the King's recovery. Here it should be noted that George III had been afflicted by a mental malady for a few weeks in the year 1765, and that a Regency Bill was drafted but the need for it vanished.[2] This fact was not widely known, but it must have come to the knowledge of the Prince of Wales. In view of the sound constitution and regular life of the King, there were good grounds for hoping that he would a second time recover.

Nevertheless, the reports of Sir George Baker, on behalf of Dr. Warren and the other physicians, as sent to Pitt, were at first discouraging. As they have not before been published it will be well to cite them here almost *in extenso* from the Pitt Papers, No. 228. They are dated from the Queen's Lodge, Windsor:

Nov. 6. 9 o'clock:—Sir George Baker presents his comp[ts] to Mr. Pitt. He is very sorry to inform Mr. Pitt that the King's delirium has continued through the whole day. There seems to be no prospect at present of a change either for the better or worse. H.M. is now rather in a quiet state. *Nov.* 8, 1788. 8 o'clock:—The dose of James's powder which the King had taken before Mr. Pitt left Windsor produced a gentle perspiration but no diminution of the delirium; a second dose taken six hours after the first, is now operating in the same manner but with as little effect upon the delirium. *Nov.* 10, 1788. 8 p.m.:—H.M. has but little fever, is very incoherent, but without vehemence or bodily efforts, though his strength appears to be very little impaired. *Nov.* 12, 1788:—H.M. talked in a quiet but incoherent way the whole night and is this morning just as he was yesterday. He has eaten a very good breakfast. *Nov.* 15, 1788. 10 p.m.:—H.M. has been deranged the whole day, in a quiet and apparently happy way to himself. *Nov.* 16.

---

[1] Campbell, *op. cit.*, p. 251, who had the story from Thomas Grenville. See, too, Wilberforce, i, 386, 387.

[2] Dr. W. Hunt, "Political Hist. of England," x, 64-5.

10 a.m.:—This morning his discourse was consistent, but the principle upon which it went for the most part founded in error. *Nov.* 18, 10 a.m.:—H.M. had a good night, but the disorder remains unabated. *Nov.* 21:—H.M. has been . . . more than once under the influence of considerable irritation. *Nov.* 22. 10 a.m.:—H.M. is entirely deranged this morning in a quiet good humoured way. *Nov.* 22:—H.M. shewed many marks of a deluded imagination in the course of the day. In the evening he was more consistent.

[A letter follows from the Queen, that she consents to the calling in Dr. Addington.]

Nov. 24, 1788:—His Majesty passed the whole day in a perfectly maniacal state.[1] *Nov.* 25, 1788:—His Majesty was not enraged nor surprised at the strict regimen under which he was put at 5 o'clock this evening, but grew quieter and went to bed at 9 o'clock, and is now asleep.

From the outset Pitt viewed the case with grave concern, but by no means hopelessly. This will appear from the following new letters of Pitt, the former to Bishop Pretyman (Tomline), the latter to the Marquis of Buckingham:

Sunday, *Nov.* 10, [1788].[2]

MY DEAR BISHOP,

You will have heard enough already of the King's illness to make you very uneasy. The fact is that it has hitherto found little relief from medicine, and, what is worst of all, it is attended with a delirium the cause of which the physicians cannot clearly ascertain. On the whole there is some room to apprehend the disorder may produce danger to his life, but there is no immediate symptom of danger at present. The effect more to be dreaded is on the understanding. If this lasts beyond a certain time it will produce the most difficult and delicate crisis imaginable in making provision for the Government to go on. It must, however, be yet some weeks before that can require decision, but the interval will be a truly anxious one. . . .

[Private.]

Downing Street, *Nov.* 15, 1788.[3]

MY DEAR LORD,

I have not half time [*sic*] to thank you sufficiently for your very kind and affectionate letter, and for the communication thro'

---

[1] This letter fixes the date of Pitt's letter to Grenville, headed merely "Tuesday morning," in "Dropmore P." (i, 361). Pitt quotes the phrase "perfectly maniacal," and adds "I begin to fear the physicians have been more in the right than we thought."

[2] Pretyman MSS.   [3] Chevening MSS.

Grenville. You will learn from him that our last accounts begin to wear rather a more favourable aspect, tho' there is not yet ground for very confident hope. There is certainly now no danger to his life, but the other alternative, which there was some danger to apprehend, was, if possible, more distressing. It seems now possible that a total recovery may take place, but even on the best supposition there must still be a considerable interval of anxiety. . . .

Grenville, a man of singularly calm and equable temperament (which procured for him the Speakership of the House of Commons on the decease of Cornwall early in the next year) waxed indignant as he described to his brother the tactics of the Opposition. On 20th November he declared: "The Opposition have been taking inconceivable pains to spread the idea that his [the King's] disorder is incurable. Nothing can exceed Warren's indiscretion on this subject." [1] The conviction gained ground that the Royal physicians were in league with the Prince; and so high did feeling run that shouts were flung at them—" So much the worse for you if he does not recover." This exasperation of spirit waxed apace as the jubilation of the Prince's friends became insolently patent. Indeed more terrible than the lunacy itself was the spectacle of the intrigues to which it gave rise.

As the reports privately sent to Pitt by the physicians were far from hopeless, he determined to await developments as long as possible before taking any decided step. On 12th November he proposed to the Prince of Wales that Parliament, instead of meeting in the following week, should be adjourned for a fortnight, to which there came a ready assent.[2] On the 17th he asked leave to inform the Prince of what he proposed to do on the meeting of Parliament, but an interview was not accorded. Eight days later the Prince inquired whether he had any proposal to make, but was answered by a polite negative. The uneasy truce between them evidently neared its end.

In his resolve to sift to the bottom the nature of the disease and the probability of a cure, Pitt advised the calling in of his father's doctor, Addington, and he carried his point. On the 28th and 29th the Prime Minister himself saw the Monarch, who was pleased to see him, referred to questions discussed at their last interview, and showed incoherence chiefly in wander-

---

[1] "Buckingham P.," ii, 9.   [2] G. Rose, "Diaries," i, 87.

ing incessantly from one topic to another,[1] a characteristic of the converse of polite Society, which, if judged severely, would warrant the consignment to Bedlam of half of its most cherished talkers.

All observers are agreed that the King conversed quite rationally at times, as was also the case in the attack of 1804.[2] Pitt therefore resolved to do nothing which would distress the King in the event of his recovery. This it was which led him to decline all idea of a coalition with the Whigs, and to insist on restricting the authority of the Regent in regard to personal matters on which the King laid stress. The removal of the monarch to Kew House seems to have been the wish of the Prince as well as of the Cabinet; and it took place without mishap on 29th November.

Six days later Parliament re-assembled, and rarely has it had to face problems so novel and delicate. In contrast with other nations, England had been singularly free from the perplexities attendant on a Regency; but now she had to face them in an acute form. The monarch was not unpopular, and his heir was distrusted. Yet it was indisputable that, as Regent, he could choose his own Ministers; and his hatred of Pitt implied the dismissal of that Minister and the triumph of Sheridan, Fox, and the roystering set at Brooks's. Pitt felt little doubt on this point and calmly prepared to resume his practice at the Bar. The sequel must have been a sharp conflict between the Prince's friends and the nation; so that the fateful year 1789 would have seen the growth of a political crisis, less complex than that of France, it is true, but fully as serious as that from which the nation was saved by his timely decease in the summer of the year 1830. All this was at stake, and much more. For who shall measure the worth to the nation of the frugal and virtuous life of George III, and who can count up the moral losses inflicted on the national life by his son in his brief ascendancy?

The King's physicians having been examined by the Privy Council on 3rd December, their evidence was laid before Parliament on the following day. While differing at many points, they agreed that recovery was possible or even probable, but they could not assign a limit of time. Adopting a suggestion of Fox,

---

[1] G. Rose, " Diaries," i, 90.
[2] Ibid., 94; " Buckingham P.," i, 446; " Quarterly Rev.," cv, 490.

Pitt moved for the appointment of a Committee of the House for the examination of the physicians. It comprised twenty-one members selected from two lists suggested by the Ministry and the Opposition. The reading out of the final list led to a singular scene. Not much comment was made on the twenty names, but before reading out the last name, Pitt paused for a moment. At once the Opposition raised cries of " Burke." Still Pitt remained silent. The cries were renewed more loudly. He then very quietly proposed Lord Gower. Burke threw himself back in his seat, crossed his arms violently, and kicked his heels with evident discomposure.[1] The annoyance of the great Irishman was natural, as Pitt had evidently prepared to inflict the slight. The Upper House appointed a similar committee.

The report based on this inquiry was presented by Pitt to the House of Commons on the 10th. It comprised the evidence, not only of the royal physicians, but also of an outsider, the Rev. Dr. Francis Willis who, during twenty-eight years had supervised some 900 cases of lunacy at his residence near Boston. Everyone admitted his success in this trying work, which may be ascribed to the influence of a commanding personality, and the firm and judicious treatment which he substituted for the frequently violent methods then in vogue. He at once pronounced the case far from hopeless; and, if we may trust the stories told of the King and his new physician, there was even at the outset very much of method in the madness. Thus, on being informed that Willis was a clergyman, the patient remarked that he could not approve of his taking to the practice of medicine. This drew from Willis the remark that Christ went about healing the sick, whereupon the retort at once followed—" Yes; but I never heard that he had £700 a year for doing so." The acuteness of the King's faculties also appears in his remark that a letter which he had written to the Queen would not reach her, as his recent missive to the Duke of York had not been answered. Thereupon Willis offered to take it himself, and caused great joy to the sufferer by bringing back an affectionate letter in reply.

Yet the King soon felt the domination of his will. This appeared when the royal patient refused to go to bed. As the King petulantly resisted, Willis raised his voice in commanding tones which ensured complete submission. The trust which

[1] " Bland Burges Papers," 118.

Willis reposed in the King led him to lengths that were sharply censured. When the sufferer expressed a desire to shave himself and complained that a razor and even a knife had been withheld from him, Willis at once replied that he was sure His Majesty had too strong a sense of what he owed to God and man to make an improper use of it. He therefore brought a razor, and kept the monarch under his eye until the growth of five weeks was removed. This tactful treatment speedily wrought a marked change. Willis was far more sanguine than the other attendants.[1] In his evidence before the Committee on 9th December, he stated that the irritation was already subsiding, and that nine-tenths of his patients who had been similarly afflicted recovered, generally within three months from their first seizure.[2]

Willis's words aroused the liveliest hopes. In vain did the Prince's party and the physicians scoff at the assurance of the "quack" or "interloper." The Queen and the nation believed in Willis; and his report greatly strengthened Pitt's hands in dealing with the Regency. The more we know of the motives that influenced votes in Parliament the more we see that they turned on the opinions of the doctors. The desertion of the Duke of Queensberry to the Prince's party was due to a long conversation which he had at Windsor with the pessimistic Dr. Warren.[3]

The conduct of the Prime Minister was cautious and tentative. On 10th December, after presenting the medical evidence, he moved the appointment of a committee to investigate precedents. At once Fox started to his feet and poured forth a vehement remonstrance. What need was there for such an inquiry? It was merely a pretext for delay. The heir-apparent was of mature age and capacity. He had as clear a right to take the reins of government and to exercise the sovereign power during the King's illness as he would have in case of death. Parliament had only to determine when he had the right to exercise it; and as short a time as possible should elapse before the Prince assumed the sovereignty.

Here, as so often, Fox marred his case by his impetuosity. Pitt watched him narrowly, and remarked exultantly to his

[1] See his private reports to Pitt in "Pitt and Napoleon Miscellanies."

[2] "Parl. Hist.," xxvii, 697, gives the period as three months; "Buckingham P.," ii, 47, gives it (erroneously, I think) as five months.

[3] Wraxall, v, 243.

neighbour: " I'll *un-Whig* the gentleman for the rest of his life."
With eyes flashing defiance, he denounced his assertions of the
right of the Prince to assume the Regency as a breach of the
constitution, implying as they did that the House could not
even deliberate on the question. They must therefore in the first
place assert their own rights.

Fox at once rose, not to soften, but to emphasize his previous
statements. He questioned whether Parliament had the power
of legislating at all until the royal power were made good. Now
that the King had been admitted to be incapable, their assembly
was a Convention, not a Parliament. He next asserted that the
Regency belonged of right to the Prince of Wales during the
civil death of the King; and " that it could not be more legally
his by the ordinary and natural demise of the Crown." This was
tantamount to saying that English law recognized lunacy as
death, in which case an heir could at once possess the property
of a lunatic father, and a wife be divorced from an insane husband. Of course this is not so.[1] Fox concluded by asserting
that, if Parliament arrogated to itself the power of nominating
the Regent, it would act " contrary to the spirit of the constitution and would be guilty of treason."

Pitt, on the contrary, affirmed that the Prince had no such
claim to the Regency as would supersede the right of either
House to deliberate on the subject. He even ventured on the
startling assertion that apart from the decision of Parliament
" the Prince of Wales had no more right (speaking of strict
right) to assume the government than any other individual subject of the country."[2] This phrase is generally quoted without
the qualifying clause, which materially alters it. Pitt surely did
not mean to deny the priority of the claim of the Prince, but
rather to affirm the supreme authority of Parliament; the statement, however was undeniably over-strained. In the main he
carried the House with him. In vain did Burke declaim against
Pitt, styling him a self-constituted competitor with the Prince.
" Burke is Folly personified," wrote Sir William Young on 22nd
December, " but shaking his cap and bells under the laurel of
genius."[3] The sense of the House was clearly with the Prime
Minister, and the committee of inquiry was appointed.

At the outset, then, Fox and his friends strained their con-

---

[1] May, " Constitutional Hist.," i, 148.   [2] " Parl. Hist.," xxvii, 709.
[3] " Buckingham P.," ii, 71.

tentions to breaking-point. In a technical sense their arguments could be justified by reference to the dead past; but they were out of touch with the living present. Fox himself had admitted that no precedent could be found for this problem. A practical statesman would therefore have sought to adapt the English constitution (which is a growing organism, not a body of rigid rules) to the needs of the present crisis. By his eager declarations he left this course open for Pitt to take; and that great parliamentarian took it with masterly power. He resolved to base his case on the decisions arrived at in the Revolution of a century earlier which had affirmed the ascendancy of Parliament in all questions relating to a vacancy in the Crown or a disputed succession. Men said that he was becoming a Republican, and Fox a Tory.[1] Fortunately he had to do with singularly indiscreet opponents. After Fox had prejudiced the Prince's cause, Sheridan rushed in to mar its prospects still further. In the debate of 12th December he ventured to remind Pitt of the danger of provoking the assertion of the Prince's claim to the Regency. Never did Sheridan's hatred of Pitt betray him into a more disastrous blunder.[2] His adversary at once turned it to account:

I have now [he said] an additional reason for asserting the authority of the House and defining the boundaries of "Right," when the deliberative faculties of Parliament are invaded and an indecent menace is thrown out to awe and influence our proceedings. In the discussion of the question I trust the House will do its duty in spite of any threat that may be thrown out. Men who feel their native freedom will not submit to a threat, however high the authority from which it may come.[3]

We must here pause in order to notice the allegations of Mr. Lecky against Pitt. That distinguished historian asserted that the conduct of the Prime Minister towards the Prince "was from the first as haughty and unconciliatory as possible"; he claims that the plan of a Regency should have been submitted to the Prince before it was laid before Parliament; further,

---

[1] Sichel, "Sheridan," ii, 415.

[2] So thought the Duchess of Devonshire's friends. Sichel, "Sheridan," ii, 416.

[3] T. Moore, "Life of Sheridan," ii, 42, 43; "Parl. Hist.," xxvii, 730, 731.

I   E E

that, in defiance of the expressed wish of the Prince, " Pitt insisted on bringing the question of the Prince's right to a formal
issue and obtaining a vote denying it." [1] It is difficult to see on
what grounds this indictment rests. Surely it was the duty of
the Privy Council and Parliament first to hear the medical
evidence and to decide whether the need for the Regency
existed. That was the purport of the debate of 10th December,
the details of which prove conclusively that it was Fox who first,
and in a most defiant way, brought up the question of the
Prince's right to assume the Regency. Pitt, in a temperate and
non-committal speech, had moved for a " Committee of Inquiry,"
whereupon the Whig leader flung down the gauntlet for the
Prince; and two days later Sheridan uttered his threat.[2] Their
auditors must have inferred that they acted with the sanction of
Carlton House. In any case, the Prince's friends, not Pitt, provoked the conflict. When the glove was twice cast down, the
Prime Minister could do nothing else but take it up and insist
on having that question disposed of; otherwise Parliament might
as well have dissolved outright. We may admit, however, that
the intemperate conduct of Fox and Sheridan led Pitt to assert
the authority of Parliament with somewhat more stringency than
the case warranted.

To the contention, that the Prince ought first to have
been consulted on the proposed measure, I may reply that
such a course would have implied his right to dictate his terms
to Parliament; and that was the very question which Pitt wished
to probe by the Committee of Inquiry. Further, the historian's
assertion, that Pitt laid the Regency plan before Parliament
before submitting it to the Prince, is disproved by the contents
of Pitt's letter of 15th December, published in full by Bishop
Tomline.[3] In it the Prime Minister expressed his regret that his
words and intentions had been misrepresented to His Royal
Highness; for on several occasions he had offered to wait on him
but had received an answer that he (the Prince) had no instructions for him. He denied the accuracy of the report that he was
about on the morrow to submit to Parliament his plan for the
Regency. His motion merely affirmed the right of Parliament
to deliberate on the present emergency; but the course of the

---

[1] Lecky, v, 148.   [2] " Parl. Hist.," xxvii, 705-13.
[3] Tomline, " Life of Pitt," ii, 388-92. There is a copy of this in the Pretyman archives at Orwell Park.

recent debate had compelled him to outline his ideas. They were
these: that the Regency should be vested in the Prince, with
the power of freely choosing his Ministers, unrestrained by
any Council. He had declined, and begged still to decline, to
detail the other powers, because the House might reject his
opinions as to its right to deliberate on the present crisis. If he
gained its approval, he would be honoured by the Prince's permission to state to him the opinions which, after due inquiry,
Ministers were able to form on the further proposals that might
be submitted to Parliament.

Was this language " arrogant " and " unconciliatory "? Could
a Minister show more tact in seeking to harmonize the functions
of the monarchy and of Parliament? Far from bringing his
scheme cut and dried before Parliament and then foisting it
upon the Prince, Pitt was compelled by the attack of Fox to
outline his plan in Parliament, but he stated his views to the
Prince courteously, and at the earliest opportunity. The only
other possible alternative was to allow the Prince to take the
matter into his own hands and override the powers of Parliament. It is also noteworthy that not until the next day (16th
December) did Pitt move three Resolutions on the subject,
and these were of a preliminary character, affirming the right
and duty of Parliament to take steps for meeting the present
emergency.[1]

It should further be noted that the declaration of the Prince
of Wales of his wish not to press his right was not made until
the debate of 15th December in the House of Lords. The
Duke of York, in a very tactful speech, said that his brother
" understood too well the sacred principles which seated the
House of Brunswick on the throne of Great Britain ever to
assume or exercise any power, be his claim what it might, not
derived from the will of the people, expressed by their representatives and their Lordships in Parliament assembled." [2] If
Fox and Sheridan had treated the question in this way, there
would have been no dispute. On the other hand the Prince does
not seem to have sent a reply to the Prime Minister's missive;
and his discourtesy probably led to the discontinuance of further

---

[1] " Parl. Hist.," xxvii, 732-47. The date is given wrongly as 1st December;
it should be 16th December. So, too, on p. 778, are the numbers in the division, which should be: for Government, 268, Opposition, 204.

[2] *Ibid.*, 678.

communications from Pitt until that of 30th December, soon to be noticed.

The debates in the House of Lords were generally of small interest. But that of 15th December was memorable, not only for the tactful speech of the Duke of York noticed above, but also for the astute balancings of Thurlow. By the middle of December that political Blondin had seen the need of retracing his steps. As has already appeared, Fox strongly disapproved of shelving Loughborough in order to win Thurlow; and the clamour of the Whig peer, added to the arguments of Fox, led the Prince of Wales to retract his promise to the Chancellor. Even this, perhaps, would not have turned him had he not come to believe that Warren was wrong and Willis was right. Discerning a balance of gain in favour of fidelity to the King, he played that part with an emotion peculiarly affecting in so rugged a nature. His shaggy eyebrows rose and fell with great solemnity, as he deprecated these discussions on the " right " of this or that member of the constitution. They should await the inquiry into the precedents of the case. Meanwhile their duty was to preserve the dignities of the monarch intact until he should recover. Feelings of loyalty and gratitude imposed that duty, and particularly on himself, the recipient of so many benefits, " which whenever I forget, may God forget me."[1] Two men who listened to that climax expressed their feelings with diverse emphasis. Pitt, who knew all but the latest develop-ments of the Thurlow-Sheridan intrigue, exclaimed, " Oh! the rascal." In Wilkes a sense of humour, unclouded by disgust, prompted the witticism: " Forget you! He'll see you damned first."

On 30th December, that is, seven days before the preliminary proposals for a Regency came before the House of Commons, Pitt drafted his suggestions in a most deferential letter to the Prince of Wales. In brief they were as follows. Ministers desired that the Prince should be empowered to exercise the royal authority, the care of the King and the control of his household being, however, vested in the Queen. The Regent, also, could not assign the King's property, grant any office beyond His Majesty's pleasure, or bestow any peerage except on the King's

---

[1] " Parl. Hist.," xxvii, 680. That Thurlow or his friends expected his dis-missal, even late in the year 1789, appears from a letter of Pitt to George Rose contradicting a rumour to that effect (G. Rose, " Diaries," i, 98, 99).

children after attaining their majority—restrictions which merely
registered the belief that the King's illness was only temporary.
At this time (the dawn of 1789) there were clear signs to this
effect; and Willis drew up a report laying stress on his partial
recovery; but, on his pressing Warren to sign it, the Whig
practitioner refused.

Thus opened the most fateful of all years of modern history.
The Whigs, the erstwhile guardians of popular freedom and the
rights of Parliament, were straining every nerve to prove the
King hopelessly insane, to foist upon the English people a hated
Prince with unrestrained powers, as if Parliament had no voice
in the matter, and to discredit the Prime Minister by representing his conduct as unconstitutional, and his letter to the Prince
as insolent.

The best brains of the party were also concentrated on the
task of inventing for the Prince a telling and dignified rejoinder.
Political philosophy, law, and wit, came to his aid in the form of
Burke, Loughborough, and Sheridan. Or, rather, the first two
drafted the reply, which Sheridan then touched up. The
brilliant Irishman pronounced the effusion of his sager com-
patriot "all fire and tow," and that of the jurist "all ice and
snow." Fox, it seems, was to have revised the result; but the
charms of Devonshire House on New Year's Day detained
"Sherry" far into the night; and the document, hastily copied
by Mrs. Sheridan, was hurried off to Carlton House without the
promised recension at Holland House or Brooks's Club. Fox
was furious at this neglect, and called his friend names which
the latter preferred not to repeat to the Duchess.[1]

Such was this famous concoction. Connoisseurs, unaware of
the facts, have confidently pronounced it the mellow vintage of
Burke. Indeed, it is probable that the body of it may be his,
while the bouquet may be Sheridan's and the dregs Loughborough's; but, the personal ingredients being unknown, it is
useless to attempt a qualitative analysis. One thing alone is
certain, that the Prince wrote not a word of it, but merely signed
the fair copy when made out by Mrs. Sheridan. Thereupon the

---

[1] W. Sichel, "Sheridan," ii, 421-3. I cannot agree with Mr. Sichel (*ibid.*,
ii, 192) that the letter was Sheridan's. The Duchess's diary shows it to have
been a joint production. For the so-called Prince's letter see "Parl. Hist.,"
xxvii, 909-912, or "Ann. Reg." (1789), 298-302. For Pitt's reply see Stanhope,
ii, 18-20.

expectant Junto planned its public tapping, as an appetizing foretaste of the political wisdom of the new *régime*, Pitt meanwhile being dubbed a Republican and an insidious weakener of the executive power.

In more ways than one the situation was piquant. The *volte face* of parties was odd enough. Pitt seemed about to impair the strength of the hereditary principle and to exalt the power of Parliament; while the Whigs, who vehemently assailed the kingly prerogative in 1784, now as ardently belauded it in the person of the Prince. This contradiction extended even to details. Amidst all his appeals to precedents respecting a Regency, Pitt must in reality have resolved to discard them; and all research into the customs of the then almost absolute monarchy must have strengthened the case of those who scolded him for resorting to this device. But, in truth, all these inconsistencies vanish when we remember that the questions at issue were primarily medical and personal. Pitt's whole policy was therefore one of delay.

Owing to the death of the Speaker, Cornwall, and the subsequent election of William Grenville as his successor, the debates on the Regency were not resumed until 6th January; and ten more days elapsed before other preliminary questions were disposed of and the ministerial proposals were laid before the House. They were in substance the same as those submitted to the Prince on 30th December, except that a Council was now suggested for the purpose of assisting the Queen in the guardianship of the King and the regulation of the royal household.[1] It would be tedious to follow the course of the very lengthy debates which ensued. Ministers carried the Resolutions in both Houses; and the Prince somewhat grudgingly consented to act as Regent on the terms now proposed.

At the end of January Ministers proposed to legalize the proceedings of Parliament by the issue of letters patent under the Great Seal. A Commission was also appointed for the purpose of giving the royal assent and affixing the Seal to measures passed by the two Houses.[2] In spite of a vehement protest by

---

[1] "Parl. Hist.," xxvii, 946-7. Able speeches on the Government side were made by the Speaker (Grenville) and the Solicitor-General, Sir John Scott, the future Lord Eldon. See Twiss, "Life of Lord Eldon," i, ch. ix.

[2] See May, "Constitutional Hist.," i, 155, 156, for the arguments for and against this proposal.

Burke, that he worshipped the gods of our glorious constitution, but would never bow down to Priapus (Thurlow), these proposals were carried. Not until 5th February were preliminaries disposed of; and Pitt then produced his Regency Bill. As it happened, the Opposition marred its own prospects by these dilatory tactics; for in a fortnight's time it was known that the need for the Bill had vanished.

The importance of these debates centres in the treatment of a very complex question by the two great rivals, Pitt and Fox. The conduct of the former has been sufficiently outlined. It remains to say a few words on that of Fox. Few of his speeches are more ingenious than those on the Regency. As a forcible handling of a weak case they have few equals. But the House of Commons is rarely won over by a dazzling display of " tongue-fencing." It demands to see the applicability of arguments to the needs of the time. This has been its peculiar excellence Its deliberations are rarely lit up with the radiance of immortal truths; but they are suffused with the comforting glow of the domestic hearth. Fox forgot this. In contrast with the accepted Whig doctrine, he put forth claims which, if pressed to their natural conclusion, would have implied the restoration of monarchy of the pre-Revolution type. If it was true that the Prince of Wales could demand the Regency as a right, or even as a " legal claim," free from all restrictions, how much more could the King govern independently of Parliament? A Regent is to a King what the moon is to the sun—a merely borrowed and temporary splendour. Apart, then, from an inconsistency of conduct highly damaging to a statesman, Fox committed the mistake of pledging himself to a scheme of government which was not only obsolete but unworkable.

Those who plod through the wearisome debates on the Regency must be conscious of an air of unreality. The references on both sides of the House to the cases of Edward VI or Henry VI were, after all, illusory; for in those times the powers of Parliament were ill defined. The nearest parallel to the present case was supplied by the events of 1688; and though pedants might appeal to certain forms observed by the Convention of that year, the significance of those events undoubtedly lay in the assertion of the supremacy of Parliament in all cases of a temporary lapse of the royal power. The argument for the supremacy of Parliament in all doubtful cases acquired redoubled strength from the Act of Settlement of 1701, which set aside hereditary right in favour of the House of Brunswick.

The arguments of Fox as to the inherent right of the Prince of Wales to the Regency must therefore be pronounced archaically interesting but inconclusive for any member of the reigning dynasty. The fact that they were adopted by the Irish Parliament adds nothing to their force; for that body was known to act more from corrupt motives or from opposition to George III and his Lord-Lieutenant, the Marquis of Buckingham, than from monarchical zeal.[1]

The divisions in the Parliament at Westminster were also much influenced by similar considerations. The numbers of those who went over to the Prince's side were surprisingly large. Among the Peers, the cases of the Marquis of Lothian and the Duke of Queensberry attracted especial notice, as they had received many benefits from the King. Of those helped on by Pitt, Lord Malmesbury and Gerald Hamilton (commonly known as " Single-Speech " Hamilton) were the worst defaulters. The former, after calling on Pitt to assure him of his devotion, suddenly " ratted " to the Prince and sent a very lame letter of excuse. To this Pitt replied that he had certainly misunderstood every expression in their late interview, and begged his Lordship to act in any way he thought fit without troubling to send an apology.[2] Malmesbury sought to appease his friend Carmarthen by offering to call and discuss things in the old way; but, if he had lost his esteem, he would prefer to retire and feed goats on a mountain " out of the reach of d—d Kings and d—d Regents." [3] What Carmarthen thought of the defaulters appeared in his witty reply to someone who asked how it came about that Fox had let the cat out of the bag so soon—" To catch the rats, I suppose."

The pamphlet literature that sprang up at this crisis is highly interesting. The hacks employed by the Opposition persistently accused Pitt of aiming at dictatorial power—a theme on which

[1] For the intrigues and corruption at Dublin see " Dropmore P.," i, 385, 389, 395, et seq. The majority at Dublin dwindled away as soon as the King's recovery was known (ibid., i, 417-25), a fact which damages Lecky's case.
[2] " Bland Burges P.," 116, 117; Wraxall, v, 242, 243.
[3] B.M. Add. MSS., 28064.

they richly embroidered, despite the well-known fact that he was preparing to resume his position as a barrister. It is somewhat significant that, while the nation warmly supported Pitt, he was bitterly assailed by Grub Street and Soho. Anonymous writers confidently foretold his ascendancy and the ruin of England. " A few years, perhaps, and our boasted commonwealth may be numbered among the governments that cover the earth —the awful ruins of edifices once consecrated to the rights and happiness of the human kind."[1] A " Private Citizen " urged the drawing up of an address to the Prince begging him to take the full regal power as a " simple and obvious mode of restoring the constitutional government to its full vigour."[2] A flurried patriot declared that he knew of "but one alarming Regency, which is that of ambitious Ministers voting themselves in power."[3] Another citizen, surely of Jacobite tendencies, proved that no power in the universe could appoint a Regent; for he assumed that office solely by hereditary right. As for " Regent Ministers," they would every day prostitute the dignity of the Crown in the animosities of debate, and the state of England would soon be worse than that of Poland.[4] Similar in tone is an " Address to those Citizens who had resisted the Claim of the late House of Commons to nominate the Ministers of the Crown." The writer asserts that only sophistry can deny that the sole question now is whether Pitt and his colleagues shall be invested with the regal authority with unlimited powers and for an indefinite period.[5] These insinuations harmonize with those which Buckingham found in circulation at Dublin; that the King had long been insane, but Pitt had concealed the fact in order to govern without control; and that the plan of a restricted Regency was the outcome of the same lust for power.[6]

The falsity of these charges is obvious. Whether the Regency were a right or a trust, the Prince of Wales in the middle of February was about to become Regent; and if he chose to risk

---

[1] " Reflections on the Formation of a Regency " (Debrett, 1788), 17.

[2] "Thoughts on the present Proceedings of the House of Commons " (Debrett, 1788), 18.

[3] "Answer to the Considerations on . . . a Regency " (Debrett, 1788), 21.

[4] " A short View of the present Great Question " (Debrett, 1788), 11-15.

[5] *Op. cit.*, p. 6. Huish, " Mems. of George IV," i, 209, repeats some of these slanders against Pitt.

[6] " Dropmore P.," i, 377.

a conflict with Parliament he might at once dismiss Pitt and summon Fox to his counsels. On this all-important question there were no restrictions whatsoever. The restrictions solely concerned the relations between the Regent and the King, with two exceptions. These were the entrusting the Great Seal to a Commission, and the forbidding the Regent to create Peers except among the royal family; and here the aim obviously was to prevent the Prince obstructing legislation and swamping the House of Lords with his own nominees.

That the Prince did not dismiss Pitt was due, not to the lack of legal power to do so, but to the opportune recovery of the King. As appears by the reports of Dr. Willis, his health steadily improved throughout February. It is clear that Fox, who was drinking the waters at Bath, disbelieved the official bulletins on this subject and looked forward to a lease of power; for he wrote to Fitzpatrick on 17th February in terms of jubilation at the decision of the Irish Parliament, and added: "I hope by this time all idea of the Prince or any of us taking action in consequence of the good reports of the King are at an end: if they are not, do all you can to crush them. . . . I rather think, as you do, that Warren has been frightened. I am sure, if what I hear is true, that he has not behaved well. . . . Let me know by the return of the post on what day the Regency is like to commence."[1] From this it is obvious that the pessimism of Dr. Warren was not uninfluenced by political considerations.

The Prince was either better informed or more cautious than his favourite. On that same day a bulletin appeared announcing the King's convalescence. The signatories included Dr. Warren, who speedily fell into disgrace with the Prince's friends. On the 19th, at the request of the King, Thurlow had an interview with him and informed him of what had happened during his illness. We may be sure that the Chancellor's narrative illustrated that power of language to conceal thought which Talleyrand held to be its choicest function. Thurlow, on his return to town, moved the adjournment of the debate on the Regency Bill, which proved to be the beginning of the end of that measure.

A still severer test of the King's powers was afforded by his interview four days later with the Prince of Wales and the Duke of York. The Queen was present the whole time, and political

---

[1] "Memorials of Fox," ii, 302.

topics were of course avoided. Grenville asserts that after that interview the Princes drove straight to Mrs. Armstead's house in Park Street in hopes of finding Fox there and informing him of the King's condition. Certain it is that, according to Willis's report to Pitt, "the Princes expressed great astonishment and satisfaction to Colonel Digby after their interview with the King, remarking only one or two trifling circumstances in which they thought His Majesty was not perfectly right. The King has been perfectly composed since, and his anxiety to see Mr. Pitt increases to that degree that probably Mr. Pitt will receive a message to that purport to-morrow morning."[1] Accordingly Pitt saw his sovereign on the 24th, and found him calm and dignified, without the slightest sign of flurry or disorder of mind. He spoke of his illness as a thing entirely past, and with tears in his eyes thanked all those who had stood by him. Even his emotion did not derange his faculties or mar his equanimity.[2]

Meanwhile at Westminster the Opposition sought to vie with their rivals in expressions of loyal joy at the King's recovery. Viscount Stormont and other deserters to the Prince's side hastened to avow their satisfaction; and the Duke of York displayed some skill in depicting the heartfelt joy which filled his heart and that of his royal brother—sentiments which they further proceeded to illustrate by plunging into a round of orgies.[3] In the Commons Fox sought decently to draw a veil over the disappointment of his partisans.

The Providence which watches over the affairs of mortals sometimes wills that the _dénouement_ of a problem shall come with dramatic effect. It was so now. The recovery of the King occurred in the very week to which the Prince's friends were eagerly looking forward as the time of entry into his enchanted palace.[4] Their chagrin, at the very moment when the paeans of triumph were on their lips, recalls the thrilling scene in " Paradise Lost," where the fiends are about to acclaim Satan at the end of the recital of his triumph over mankind,

---

[1] Pitt MSS., 228. This is the last of Willis's reports to Pitt. It is undated, but must be of 23rd February. Willis ceased to attend the King on 11th March; but was at Windsor a short time in April and May.
[2] " Buckingham P.," ii, 125.
[3] " Parl. Hist.," xxvii, 1293-5; " Buckingham P.," ii, 122, 123.
[4] " Auckland Journals," ii, 288, 289.

and raise their throats for the shout of victory, when, lo, the sound dies away in

A dismal universal hiss

issuing from thousands of forms suddenly become serpentine.[1]

Such (if we may compare small things with great) was the swift change from exultation to disgust which came over the Prince's friends. Shortly before the critical day, the 19th, they had declared that, were the Regent in power only for twelve hours, he would make a clean sweep of all official appointments. Indeed, from the outset, he and his followers had let it be known that no mercy would be shown to the Pitt Administration and its officials.[2] There is a manifest absurdity in the assertion of Sir Gilbert Elliot, that Ministers and their adherents looked on the Prince's following "as a prey to be hunted down and destroyed without mercy."[3] Up to the 19th of February this phrase aptly described the aim of their rivals. So early as 13th December 1788 Sheridan informed the Marquis of Buckingham that the Prince intended to dissolve Parliament both at Westminster and Dublin; for the Opposition "could not go on with the old one in England; and the choice of a new one in Ireland would give them a lasting advantage, *which is true.*"[4] The large powers of patronage entrusted to the Regent would have influenced very many votes at the General Election, just as the prospect of princely rewards caused many place-hunters to change sides in the two Houses.

The lavishness of this form of bribery appears in a letter written by Sydney to Cornwallis about 20th February, wherein he asserts that the following promotions in the army were all but officially announced. Four Field-Marshals, thirty-one Generals, twenty Lieutenant-Generals, twelve Major-Generals, besides many Colonels and lower grades; also ten new Aides-de-camp—almost all for political reasons. It was further known that Portland would be Prime Minister; Stormont and Fox, Secretaries of State; Loughborough, Chancellor; Sandwich or Fitzwilliam, First Lord of the Admiralty;[5] Spencer, Lord-

---

[1] "Paradise Lost," x, 504-17.   [2] "Cornwallis Corresp.," i, 419.
[3] "Life of Sir G. Elliot," i, 272.   [4] "Dropmore P.," i, 386.
[5] The Prince promised this post to Sandwich; but on the remonstrance of the Duke of Portland and Fox, waived the point (W. Sichel, "Sheridan," ii, 415, 416).

Lieutenant of Ireland; Northumberland, Master-General of the Ordnance; Fitzpatrick, Secretary at War; Sheridan, President of the Board of Control.[1] We may note here that Northumberland and Lord Rawdon (afterwards the Earl of Moira) with some followers had formed a group standing somewhat apart, but acting with the Prince's friends on consideration of gaining office. They were called the Armed Neutrality; and their proceedings bore no small resemblance to a political auction, in which the Prince of Wales knocked down offices at discretion.[2]

The abrupt ending to these intrigues and bargains brought intense relief to every patriot. Independent observers, like Cartwright and Wyvill, had felt deep concern at the prospect of the rule of the Prince and Fox. " I very much fear," wrote the former to Wilberforce, " that the King's present derangement is likely to produce other derangements not for the public benefit. I hope we are not to be sold to the Coalition faction." Wyvill also wrote to Wilberforce: " Cabal I doubt not is labouring under his [Fox's] direction to overturn the present Government, while you and the other firm friends of Mr. Pitt are making equal exertions to prevent a change of men and measures. I think the general opinion is that the Prince has acted like a rash young man, that he is capable of being led into dangerous measures, and that men whom the nation greatly distrusts have all his confidence and esteem." [3]

Public opinion was, however, influenced by something more definite than distrust of the Prince and his favourites. By this time the nation confided entirely in the good sense and disinterestedness of Pitt. The Marquis of Buckingham expressed the general opinion when he called Pitt " the honestest Minister he ever saw." [4] Those qualities never shone more brightly than during the perplexing problem of the Regency. If he trammelled the Prince, it was in order to assert the supremacy of

---

[1] " Cornwallis Corresp.," i, 419. Another and more probable version was that Earl Fitzwilliam would be Lord Lieutenant of Ireland. Burke had striven hard to obtain the India Board of Control, "for the services and adherence of thirty years." So wrote James Macpherson to John Robinson. He adds: " If they agree, all the fat will be in the fire. A hint to the Prince would prevent it, for I plainly see his object is to carry on business as smoothly as he can" (" Abergavenny P.," 70).

[2] " Cornwallis Corresp.," i, 422.   [3] " Life of Wilberforce," i, 190, 191.

[4] " Dropmore P.," i, 363.

Parliament, and to prevent personal changes at Windsor which would probably have brought about a return of the King's malady. For himself, he prepared quietly and with dignity to resume his practice at the Bar. Had the recovery of George III been delayed another week, the Minister would have been found once more at Lincoln's Inn, looking on with his wonted serenity at the wholesale changes in the official world brought about by the vindictiveness of his rivals. So near was England then to the verge of a political crisis which would have embattled the nation against a Government foisted upon it by an unscrupulous Prince and a greedy faction.

Fortunately the crisis was averted; and, thanks to the wise measures taken by Pitt, the recovery of the royal patient was not interrupted by the sight of new faces around him at Kew and Windsor. Long and laboured explanations were afterwards offered to the King by the Prince of Wales, in which he had the effrontery to refer to the pain caused him when he " saw Her Majesty set up by designing men as the head of a system " which was " a device of private ambition." [1] After this he never was trusted or fully forgiven either by the King or Queen. Their confidence and that of the nation was heartily accorded to the Minister whose conduct had been as loyal and consistent as that of Laurentius in Pitt's early dramatic effort. Friends pointed to his simple and earnest regard for the public welfare throughout the whole dispute. By those qualities he peacefully solved a tangled problem and bound together the King and the people in a union of hearts such as had not been known since the accession of the House of Brunswick. On the evening of the day when George III resumed his regal functions, London was ablaze with illuminations which extended from Hampstead to Clapham and Tooting.[2] The joy of all classes of the people brimmed over once more at the Thanksgiving Service held at St. Paul's Cathedral on 23rd April, when the demonstrations of loyalty were such as to move the King to an outburst of emotion. The part played by Pitt was not forgotten. With difficulty he escaped from the importunities of his admirers, who had to content themselves with dragging his carriage back to his residence in Downing Street. Outwardly, this day marks the zenith of his career. True, he was to win one more diplo-

---

[1] " Memorials of Fox," ii, 329.   [2] Wraxall, v, 336.

matic triumph over the House of Bourbon, the importance of which has been strangely under-rated. But already there was arising on the horizon a cloud, albeit small as a man's hand, which was destined to overcloud the sky and deluge the earth. Only ten days after the Thanksgiving Service at St. Paul's there assembled at Versailles the States-General of France, whose actions, helped on by the folly of the French princes, led to the subversion of that august monarchy. By so short an interval did the constitutional crisis in Great Britain precede a convulsion which was destined to overturn nearly every Government in the civilized world.

CHAPTER XIX

AUSTRALIA AND CANADA

The outcasts of an old Society cannot form the foundation of a new one.—
Parl. Report of 28*th July* 1785.

The more enormous of our offenders might be sent to Tunis, Algiers, and
other Mahometan ports, for the redemption of Christian slaves; others might
be compelled to dangerous expeditions, or be sent to establish new colonies,
factories, and settlements on the coast of Africa and on small islands for the
benefit of navigation.—W. EDEN, *A Discourse on Banishment.*

THE first settlement of the white man on a Continent
where all was strange might seem to be a topic more
engaging, as well as more important, than the escapades of a
selfish young prince and the insanity of his father. But the piles
of printed paper respecting the affairs of Carlton House and the
Regency attest the perennial preference of mankind for personal
topics; and its disregard of wide issues that affect the destinies
of nations is seen in the mere scraps of information concerning
the early colonization of Australia. The statement of the late
Sir John Seeley that the British people founded an Empire in a
fit of absence of mind is nowhere more true than of the events of
the years 1787, 1788, which marked the beginning of a new epoch
of expansive energy.

There is a curious periodicity about the colonizing efforts of
the British race. At one time the islanders send forth swarms
of adventurers and make wide conquests. At another time the
colonies languish for lack of settlers; so that one is tempted to
compare these movements, albeit slow and irregular, with those
of the blood in the human organism. They have had beneficial
results. The contracting impulse has prevented that untimely
diffusion of the nation's energies which leads to atrophy of the
essential organs. But when these are once more in full vigour
they can do naught else but send forth their vitalizing streams.

By this systole and diastole the nation recovers strength and makes use of that strength. The variation of effort is doubly beneficent. It prevents the too great effusion of life-blood which enfeebled Portugal in the sixteenth century; and the recurrence of the colonizing instinct has saved England from the undue absorption in domestic affairs which until recently narrowed the life of France.

The terrible drain of the American War naturally concentrated the attention of Britons for some time on home affairs. The most imperious need of the body politic was rest; and, as we have seen, Pitt used all his tact and energy to bestow and prolong that boon. Fortunately, the loss of life had been slight. Lack of money rather than of men put a stop to colonizing efforts and induced the belief that they weakened the State. But the life-blood was there in abundance, ready to flow forth as soon as confidence returned and the will was quickened.

Meanwhile, for want of a firm and intelligent lead, the experiment began slowly and awkwardly. As is well known, it was excess of population, of a particular type, which led the authorities to take action. The savage penal code of that age hanged or immured in gaol numbers who would now escape with a small fine. As many as 160 offences were punishable with death, and this gives the measure of the code, in its less Draconian enactments. Indeed, but for sleepy Dogberries, and reluctant jurymen, a tenth part of the population might have lodged in the filthy gaols which formed the fruitful seed-bed of crime. Goldsmith in his " Vicar of Wakefield " asks whether the licentiousness of our people or the stupid severity of our laws was responsible for the numbers of our convicts doubling those of continental lands. The question impelled John Howard and Romilly to their life-long efforts.

Meanwhile the State continued to avert the need of building more gaols by extending its time-honoured methods, hanging and transportation.[1] During the years 1714-65 those two cures for overcrowding enjoyed increasing favour. Under the first George any one found guilty of larceny, either "grand" or "petit," might be transported to America for seven years. The same penalty was inflicted in the next reign on poachers who were caught, with arms in their hands, in the act of chasing or

---

[1] For some good results of transportation see Lecky, vi, 253.

taking deer in unenclosed forests; or, again, it fell to be the lot of those who assaulted magistrates or officers engaged in salving wrecks, and likewise on all who were married without banns or licence. It was reserved for the law makers of George III to allot seven years of transportation to all who stole or took fish " in any water within a park, paddock, orchard or yard, and the receivers, aiders and abettors." Sir William Eden, in his " Discourse on Banishment," cites these offences as about the average of the crimes punishable by transportation; but he hints that many less heinous offences led to the same dreary goal. That philanthropist apparently did not think it an ingenious means of torture to send some of these convicts to Algiers to rescue from life-long slavery the Christians caught by the Barbary rovers.

Meanwhile, the United States having closed their doors against poachers, thieves, and those who married in too great haste, a paternal Government found it necessary either to relax the penal code, to build more prisons, to commission more hulks, or to found new penal settlements. Georgian legislators, being practical men, turned their thoughts to the last alternative. The subject was brought up in the House of Commons by Burke on 16th March 1785. He asserted that as many as 100,000 convicts were then liable to transportation; and protested against the rigour, cruelty, and expense attending that mode of punishment. Lord Beauchamp again called the attention of the House to that topic on 11th April, when Pitt admitted the importance of finding a new penal settlement. The Gambia River in West Africa had been used for that purpose; and Burke now rose to protest against the inhumanity of sending convicts to any part of that deadly coast. He was interrupted by the Prime Minister, who assured him that such a plan was not in contemplation, and that a Report would soon be issued.[1]

Parliamentary Papers on this subject appeared on 9th May and 28th July. The latter is remarkable for the statesmanlike utterance, quoted as a motto at the head of this chapter, which shows that at least some of our politicians looked on a new settlement as something more than a chapel-of-ease of our prisons. In other respects the Report is somewhat puerile. It recommended the need of strict discipline in the new settle-

---

[1] " Parl. Hist.," xxv, 430-2.

ment, and pointed out the district of the River das Voltas as desirable. If this were the same as the River Volta of the Gold Coast, the Committee evidently regarded fever as the most effective of governors.

It is curious to speculate on the results that might have attended these weak and stumbling moves. Probably the strenuous opposition of Burke vetoed the Gambia and Gold Coast schemes; but the Government, still intent upon the Atlantic coast of Africa, sent a sloop, H.M.S. "Nautilus," to survey the south-west coast between 15° 50′ and 33°. Very fortunately for the future of the British people the whole coast was found to be inhospitable. If the *hinterland* of Walfisch Bay or Angra Pequeña had been less barren it is almost certain that the new penal colony would have been formed at one of those spots. Ministers also turned their attention to the coasts adjacent to Cape Town; for we find Pitt writing to Grenville on 2nd October 1785: "I have desired Devagnes also to send you some papers relative to a scheme of a settlement on the Caffre coast, to answer in some respects the purposes of the Cape, and to serve also as a receptacle for convicts, which I hope you will have time to look at." [1]

This points to a plan for settling some point of the coast of Caffraria, possibly Algoa Bay or what is now East London. There were special reasons for gaining a foothold in that quarter, seeing that the Dutch Republic was falling more and more under the control of France, and the union of those two Powers in the East would have threatened the existence of our Indian Empire. A British stronghold on the South African coast was therefore highly desirable; but perhaps matters were too strained in the years 1786 and 1787 for this menacing step to be taken.

Whatever may have been the cause, Pitt and his colleagues failed to find a point on the African coast suitable for their purpose, which was to found a penal settlement furnishing relief alike to the prison system and to British ships midway on the voyage to India. Had they discovered such a place the course of history might have been very different. The English-speaking race would early have taken so firm a hold of South Africa as to press on a solution of the Anglo-Dutch question. But in the

---

[1] "Dropmore P.," i, 257.

meantime the Pacific coast of Australia would have gone to France. The one study in which Louis XVI shone, and in which Pitt was most deficient, was geography. The lord of Versailles found his chief mental recreation in maps and books of travel. Already he had sent out expeditions to rival that of Captain Cook; and, as we shall see, only by the infinitesimal margin of six days did Britons secure a foothold in Australia in advance of their rivals.

The honour of turning the attention of Ministers to the Pacific coast of "New Holland" belongs to Sir Joseph Banks, James Matra, and Admiral Sir George Young. In his description of the voyage of Captain Cook along the coast of New South Wales, Banks had spoken of the rich soil and wealth of vegetation around Botany Bay, a description which undoubtedly led Matra and Young to take up the matter. Sir Joseph Banks did not pursue the theme. At least in his letters and papers in the British Museum there is no hint that he induced Pitt or Lord Sydney to people that terrestrial paradise. Perhaps the work of the Royal Society, of which he was President, engaged all his attention.

James Maria Matra, a Corsican who had long been in the British service and had accompanied Banks in the memorable voyage of Captain Cook,[1] was the first to formulate a definite scheme for the colonization of Botany Bay. In a long letter, dated 23rd August 1783, he pointed out to the Coalition Cabinet the great extent of the land, the fertility of the soil, and the paucity of the natives as marking it out for settlement, especially by the American Loyalists, whose dire distress then aroused deep sympathy. He also declared that the nearness of New South Wales to the Spice Islands, India, China, and Japan, was favourable for commerce; that the growth of New Zealand flax would provide endless supplies of cordage for shipping; and that, in case of war, the harbours of New South Wales would furnish a useful base of naval operations against the Dutch and Spanish settlements in the East. In his original scheme Matra did not mention settlement by convicts. He desired to found a colony either by means of United Empire Loyalists, or " marines accustomed to husbandry,"[2] a suggestion which re-

---

[1] Evan Nepean in a Report to Pitt sketched the career of Matra. He was afterwards Consul for Morocco (Pitt MSS., 163).

[2] "New South Wales Despatches," vol. i, pt. ii, 1-5.

calls, not very felicitously, the Roman plan of planting veteran soldiers on the outposts of the realm.

The discredit of making the first suggestion in favour of a convict settlement at Botany Bay probably belongs to Lord Sydney, Secretary of State for Home Affairs in the Pitt Cabinet. Matra had a conversation with him on 6th April 1784, in which the Minister hinted at the desirability of relieving the congestion in the prisons, which was giving trouble to the authorities. The details of the conversation are not known; but apparently it led Matra to add a postscript to his scheme, in which he referred to the interview and remarked on the frightful mortality among the convicts sent to the West Coast of Africa. Out of 746 sent there in 1775-6, 334 died, 271 deserted, and nothing was known of the remainder. Obviously in a distant and healthy climate like Botany Bay, men must either work or starve; certainly they could not return.[1] Nothing definite seems to have come of Matra's conversation with Sydney or his plan, even as now modified.

Scarcely more successful were the efforts of Admiral Sir George Young to interest Ministers in the subject. His scheme was sent by the Attorney-General, Sir Richard Pepper Arden, to Sydney on 13th January 1785. The admiral called attention to the facilities which New South Wales would enjoy for a lucrative trade with New Spain, China, and the East Indies. He laid stress on the fertility of the soil and the variety of climates in the new possession, which would ensure the growth of all tropical and sub-tropical products. New Zealand flax would by itself furnish several requisites for ship-building and repairing, thereby freeing us from dependence on Russia. Metals would probably be found; and thus at a small expense (about £2,000) an important commercial mart might be founded. Sir George Young deprecated any plan of emigration from Great Britain as weakening to her; but he suggested that the distressed American Loyalists should be transferred to New South Wales, and that labourers might be collected from the Society Islands and China. "All the people required from England are only a few that are possessed of the useful arts, and those comprised among the crews of the ships that may be sent on that service." He, however, added that convict settlements might

---

[1] "New South Wales Despatches," 6, 7; E. Jenks, "Hist. of the Australasian Colonies," 25.

most suitably be planted there. Finally, he claimed that the whole scheme would further the cause of religion and humanity, and redound to the prosperity and glory of King George III.[1]

The ideas and the phraseology of the Memorandum are so similar to those used by Matra as to suggest that Sir George Young founded his plan on that of the Corsican; and the Admiral at the end of his Plan introduced three sentences on the suitability of parts of New South Wales for convicts. Possibly this was inserted in order to attract Ministers. Nevertheless they took no action on the matter; and possibly, but for the pressure exerted by Lord Beauchamp and Burke on 11th April 1785, this vitally important question would have remained in abeyance. Pitt, however, then promised that Government would take it up. The "Nautilus" was accordingly sent to the African coast, with the result that we have seen; and the humiliating truth must be confessed that the Ministry showed no sign of interest, if we except the single sentence in Pitt's letter of 2nd October 1785, quoted above, respecting a settlement in Caffraria.

Not until 18th August 1786 do we find any sign that the Government sought to redeem its promise to Parliament. The Pitt Papers, however, afford proof that Ministers had before them at least one other scheme for the disposing of convicts elsewhere than in New Holland. On 14th September 1786 William Pulteney wrote to Pitt an important letter (quoted in part in Chapter XIV), which concluded as follows: "I mentioned to Mr. Dundas that a much better plan had been proposed to Lord Sidney [sic] for disposing of our felons than that which I see is advertised, that of sending them to Botany Bay; but his Lordship had, too hastily I think, rejected it; if you wish to know the particulars, Mr. Dundas can in great measure explain them, and I can get the whole in writing."[2]

Pitt gave no encouragement to his correspondent, and the official plan, already drafted, ran its course. On 18th August 1786, Sydney sent to the Lords of the Treasury a statement that, considering the crowded state of the prisons and the impossibility of finding a suitable site for a settlement in Africa, the King had fixed on Botany Bay, owing to the accounts given by those who had sailed with Captain Cook. As many as 750

---

[1] "New South Wales Despatches," 11-13. A copy of this "Plan" is in Pitt MSS., 342.

[2] Pitt MSS., 169.

convicts would therefore be sent out, along with 180 marines, provisions for two years, seeds, tools, and other necessaries for the founding of a settlement. The importance of growing New Zealand flax was named,—a sign that Ministers had consulted the reports of Matra and Sir George Young, and saw the need of having a naval station in the Pacific. A fortnight later Sydney sent a similar letter to the Lords of the Admiralty.[1]

In this halting and prosaic way did Ministers set their hands to one of the most fruitful undertakings of all time. We do not know which member took the initiative. Probably it was Sydney, as Minister for Home Affairs; but Pitt certainly gave his approval, and there are two letters which show that he took interest in details. One is his letter to Evan Nepean, Under Secretary for Home Affairs, requesting him to obtain from the Secretary of the Admiralty, Sir Charles Middleton, an estimate of the expenses of the expedition.[2] The second is a letter from the Lord Chief Justice, Earl Camden, to Pitt, who must have consulted him about the legal questions involved in the formation of the colony:

Hill St., Jany. 29, 1787.[3]

DEAR PITT,

. . . I have looked over the draught of the Bill for establishing a summary Jurisdiction in Botany Bay. I believe such a jurisdiction in the present state of that embryo (for I can't call it either settlement or colony) is necessary, as the component parts of it are not of the proper stuff to make jurys [*sic*] in capital cases especially. However, as this is a novelty in our constitution, would it not be right to require the Court to send over to England every year a report of all the capital convictions, that we may be able to see in what manner this jurisdiction has been exercised? For I presume it is not meant to be a lasting jurisdiction; for if the colony thrives and the number of inhabitants increase, one sh^d wish to grant them trial by jury as soon as it can be done with propriety.

Clearly, then, Pitt had a distinct share in the drafting of the Bill for establishing the settlement. The general plan had been decided at a Council held at St. James's Palace on 6th December 1786.[4] The Letters Patent forming the Courts of Law were

---

[1] " New South Wales Despatches," 14-23.   [2] *Ibid.*, 32.
[3] Pitt MSS., 119.
[4] " New South Wales Despatches," i, pt. ii, 30. See later (pp. 67-70) for the details of the Act of Parliament.

issued on 2nd April 1787; but it was not until 12th May that H.M.S. "Sirius" and "Supply," escorting the transports "Alexander," "Charlotte," "Scarborough," "Prince of Wales," "Friendship," and "Lady Penrhyn," set sail from Spithead on their dreary voyage of eight months. On 20th January 1788 Governor Phillip landed at Botany Bay, and a few days later he transferred his strange company to the land-locked and beautiful Port Jackson, on an inlet of which he founded the infant settlement of Sydney. He was just in time to anticipate the French expedition under La Pérouse, which sailed into the harbour only six days after Phillip landed at Botany Bay. Thus, by extraordinary good luck, despite all the delays at Westminster, the British narrowly forestalled their rivals in the occupation of that magnificent coast. Captain Cook, it is true, had claimed it for the British Crown; but in international law effective occupation is a necessary sequel to so vague and sweeping a declaration. The choice of the name "Sydney" for the infant settlement attests the conviction of Governor Phillip that the whole plan owed very much to the initiative of that nobleman. It is, however, strange that the name of Pitt was not given to some town or river of the colony; for he certainly played an important part in the undertaking.

Nevertheless, the whole question reflects no great credit either on Pitt or Sydney. Neither of them had shown much insight or eagerness in the matter. Especially may they and their colleagues be blamed for not having resolved, though at slightly increased cost, to found the colony worthily by means of the American Loyalists who had suffered so much for their devotion to King and Fatherland.

The question of the American Loyalists will be referred to later in this chapter; and it is not here suggested that those Loyalists who had migrated to the lands soon to be known as New Brunswick and Ontario should have been sent to the Southern Seas. There were many others, who had set sail with the British garrisons leaving New York and other towns, now available for that experiment. They were living in England in penury and with hope deferred, while the question of the indemnity in honour due to them from the United States slowly petered out. The British Parliament was investigating their claims and finally acknowledged its obligations to them; but in the meantime they were in want. Would not the Ministry have

consulted their interests and the welfare of the Empire by offering to them to commute their pecuniary claims for grants of
land and expenses of settlement in New South Wales? The
possible objection, that their claims had not been entirely investigated by the year 1787, is trifling. The offer might surely
have been made to those whose cases and characters were well
known, and who were suited to a life of hardship and adventure.
There must have been very many who would have preferred a
free and active life to one of wretchedness in London; and when
we reflect on the great accession of strength brought by the
Loyalists to Canada and New Brunswick, it will ever remain a
matter of regret that Ministers acted on the motive which appealed so forcibly to Lord Sydney, that of easing the pressure
on prisons.

For the time, it is true, their experiment was highly economical, the cost of the expedition and settlement at Sydney from
October 1786 to October 1789 being only £8,632, or one-
eighteenth part of the sum which in the year 1787 Parliament
unanimously voted for the discharge of the debts of a spendthrift
prince.[1] It is scarcely fair to read the ideas of our age into one
from which we have moved very far away, or to censure Pitt
for his complaisance to the future George IV, while he pared
down the expenses of the greatest colonial experiment of his
generation. No one could foresee the splendid future of the
" Isle of Continent." Even Matra and Sir George Young, who
gazed far ahead, believed that the work of the settlement must
be done mainly by Chinese and South Sea Islanders.

Nevertheless, seeing that the advantage of utilizing the energies
of American Loyalists was clearly laid before Ministers, it is
astonishing that they paid no heed to a plan which might ultimately have proved to be more economical even than the export
of convicts. Certainly it would have furnished the new land with
the best of colonists. The kith and kin of the men who built up
Ontario and New Brunswick would have laid broad and deep
the foundations of New South Wales. The greatest good fortune
of North America was the advent of Puritan leaders as founders
of a State; and the transfer to the Southern Continent of their
descendants, who rivalled them in the staunchness of their fidelity
to principle, would have been an Imperial asset of priceless

[1] J. Bonwick, "The First Twenty Years of Australia," 6.

worth. There are times when the foresight and imagination of a statesman mean infinitely much to the future of the race; and no action is more fruitful in results than the settlement of a new Continent. The Greeks did well to solemnize the sending forth of colonists by the honours of the State and the sanction of religion. And what they did for the founding of one more Greek city, Great Britain ought to have done for the occupation of a coast-line known to possess vast possibilities of growth.

The painful truth must be faced that in this matter Pitt lacked the Imperial imagination. Despite vague assertions to the contrary by professed panegyrists, I cannot find a word in his speeches or letters which evinced any interest in the Botany Bay experiment. Thus, in the debate of 9th February 1791, on the condition of the young settlements and the question of stopping the transportation of 1,850 more convicts, Pitt spoke of that experiment as if it were an improved and economical prison. His speech did not rise to the level of that of Sir Charles Bunbury and Mr. Jekyll, the mover and seconder of the motion for an inquiry into the whole subject of transportation. They both pleaded for more rational methods of punishment, wherein the depraved would cease to contaminate the less guilty. Bunbury commented on the alarming increase of crime of late years, the number of sentences of death having been doubled, while convictions for felony had quadrupled. Both he and Jekyll pressed for the construction of penitentiaries where the system of "that good and useful citizen, Mr. Howard," might be better enforced; and they mentioned the report that the settlements in New South Wales were ill-suited to this purpose, owing to the sterility of the soil.

To this last charge Pitt made no effective answer. So far as we can judge from the semi-official reports, he sought refuge in the miserable reply that "in point of expense no cheaper mode of disposing of the convicts could be found," and that, as the chief cost of starting that settlement had been already incurred—how paltry the cost we have seen—it would be foolish to seek for some other place where those expenses must again be met! He expressed his approval of penitentiaries, said nothing about that fruitful mother of crime, the penal code, and declined to take any steps for stopping the transport of the 1,850 convicts. It was something that, amidst these frigid negations, he did not oppose the motion for an inquiry into the condition of Botany

Bay. Curiously enough, he did not once name the only considerable settlement, Sydney,[1] so limited was his outlook on social
and colonial problems. Wide as were his views on most questions,
it must be admitted that here was his blind side; and he must
be held partly responsible for spreading over new lands a social
taint which long blighted their progress.

That taint was to vanish; and its disappearance in a few
generations is a signal proof that, under fit conditions, the
human race does not degenerate but wins its way to higher
levels. Nevertheless, in view of the power of historic ideas and
traditions, we must ever regret that Pitt and his colleagues did
not resolve to make the new settlement a living proof of Britain's
care for the staunchest and truest of her children.

By a transition which, however abrupt in a geographical
sense, is slight in the sphere of politics, we pass from the settlement of New South Wales to the adjustment of affairs in
Canada. Both questions resulted from the American War. The
refugees from the old American colonies, who now huddled
with their families in the purlieus of Soho, formed the tough
nucleus of what had been a very large and influential band of
men in the States. Writers of the school of Bancroft used to
treat the Loyalists as traitors who richly deserved the hanging
or shooting in cold blood which not seldom befell them at the
hands of righteous patriots. Those, however, who regard history,
not as a means of enforcing certain opinions, but of reflecting the
life of the time, are generally agreed that the Loyalists acted
from sincere conviction, which led them deliberately to face
cruel and prolonged persecution. At the outset of the war they
numbered about one third of the population of the States; and,
at least 20,000 of them joined the British forces.[2] By the end of
the war about 60,000 Loyalists were compelled to leave the
States, of whom nearly one half settled in the future province of
New Brunswick; some 10,000 went to found the British population in Upper Canada (Ontario); but many sailed with the
retiring garrisons to Great Britain.[3]

---

[1] "Parl. Hist.," xxviii, 1221-5. For an account of the new settlement see
"The History of New Holland, 1616-1787."
[2] Sabine, "The American Loyalists," 51 et seq.
[3] Sir C. P. Lucas, "Hist. Geography of the Brit. Colonies," v (Canada),
73.

It is with these last that we are here at first concerned. Their number was given as 428 in the official inquiry of 1782-3,[1] but that list was probably incomplete. Their condition soon became pitiable. By the Treaty of Versailles (September 1783) the American Congress pledged itself to recommend the States of the Union to restore the property confiscated from the Loyalists. The States ignored the recommendation. Pitt has sometimes been blamed for not doing more to press the fulfilment of this treaty obligation, which was carried out only by South Carolina. But he seems to have taken the only means possible, namely, of refusing to surrender certain of the western forts of the States, until satisfaction was accorded on this head.[2] John Adams, who arrived in London as ambassador from the United States in 1786, received that answer to his protest, a fact which suffices to disprove the statement that the clause of the treaty relating to the Loyalists was inserted merely for effect.[3]

Pitt further sought to carry out the stipulations for the collection of debts due to the Loyalists before the beginning of the war. He sent out a Mr. Anstey to deal with these thorny and almost hopeless claims. The matter dragged on; and a letter forwarded to the Prime Minister on 30th January 1787 refers to the inquiry as still incomplete.[4] In 1785 Pitt offered to grant due compensation to the American Loyalists; but long and most discreditable delays ensued. Several petitions forwarded to Pitt show that payments were either inadequate or were often deferred, and that the petitioners were in much distress.[5] The letter above referred to states that from £60,000 to £80,000 a year had been granted in pensions; but that in 1787, owing to deaths and other causes, the amount fell to £50,000. Even this

---

[1] Kingsford, " Hist. of Canada," vii, 216.
[2] I cannot agree with Professor E. Channing (" The United States, 1765-1865," 118) that the action of the States towards the Loyalists "was not an infraction of the treaty." The terms bound the United States to do their utmost to induce the component States to compensate the Loyalists. But they took only the slightest and most perfunctory steps in that direction. Pitt, as we saw in Chapter VI, distinctly enjoined it as a debt of honour on the United States, and cannot surely be held responsible for its evasion.
[3] Kingsford, " Hist. of Canada," vii, 215; Sir C. P. Lucas, " Hist. of Canada, 1763-1812," 214.
[4] Pitt MSS., 344.
[5] Ibid. The cases of Samuel Gale, Sir John Johnson, F. J. D. Smyth, and R. F. Pitt seem especially hard.

exceeds the average of the official amount by some £7,000.[1] The writer goes on to assert that the utmost possible had been done to relieve the distress, and shows the unreasonableness of the claim of some Loyalists for compensation for the loss of their professions. Finally the whole matter was cleared up by the proposal of Pitt to the House of Commons on 6th June 1788 to vote the sum of £1,228,239 to the Loyalists in proportion to the merits of their cases, and £113,952 to the claimants from West Florida. To this the House agreed, Burke commending the proposal as "a new: and noble instance of national bounty and generosity."[2]

Pitt evidently considered the question as settled by the distribution of this sum and of certain grants of land in Canada; for in the year 1792, when other claims were forwarded to him through the medium of Sir Henry Clinton, he replied as follows in a letter of 29th May 1792:

On the fullest consideration of the subject, I have not thought myself justified in proposing to open the Commission again for inquiry into those cases which were not brought forward within any of the periods before limited; and under these circumstances it seems impossible to give any compensation for particular losses. The plan has therefore been adopted of giving some provision by grants of land in Canada, to such persons of this description as may be willing to accept it; and of advancing them certain sums of money (according to the classes in which they have been distributed) for the purpose of assisting them in removing and in settling themselves. With respect to the three persons whom you particularly mention of the name of Plater, Harding and Williams, the granting to them the sums recommended by Col. Delancy was delayed from its appearing that they had formerly had an advance for the purpose of enabling them to go to America; but notwithstanding this circumstance it has been determined from the nature of their cases

---

[1] See J. E. Wilmott, "Hist. View of the Commission . . . of the American Loyalists" (London, 1815).

[2] "Parl. Hist.," xxvii, 610-19. The total expenses incurred on behalf of the American Loyalists as shown in the Budgets of the years 1784 to 1789 are as follows: £82,750; £190,019; £315,873; £132,856; £82,346; £362,922; or a total of £1,084,016. These sums are distinct from the special votes of £1,228,239 and £113,952 above referred to; which raise the total for those six years to £2,426,207. I take these figures from the Budgets as given in the Annual Registers. It is impossible to harmonize them with Wilmott's figures. He gives £3,112,455 as the total up to and including the year 1790.

and your strong testimony in their favour, to comply with this recommendation, which will be immediately carried into effect.[1]

The settlement of the Loyalists in Canada and Nova Scotia produced far-reaching results. About 28,000 settled in Nova Scotia, the larger portion of them selecting the banks of the River St. John. Besides being far removed from Halifax, the seat of government, they found themselves absolutely without influence in the administration, as the Governor refused to enlarge the Legislative Council by admitting one of their number. They therefore petitioned the Home Government for separation from Nova Scotia—a request which was at once granted (1784). Pitt thus showed his complete confidence in the Loyalists and in the policy of according full liberty in local affairs to a community which obviously needed such a boon.

Not very dissimilar were the results of the influx of the Loyalists into Canada Proper. About 10,000 of them crossed Lake Ontario or the Niagara River, and formed a thin fringe of settlements along the Upper St. Lawrence and Lakes Ontario and Erie. In 1784 Governor Haldimand granted to them large tracts of land, generally in proportion to the services rendered during the war.[2] In many cases, the settlement was of a semimilitary character; and everywhere the colonists took a pride in adding to their names "U.E.," to denote the United Empire for which they had fought and suffered. The lot of many of them was hard in the extreme; but it seems that even those who had been reared in luxury preferred the rigours of the Canadian winter in a log-hut to the persecutions which would have been their lot in the United States.

A settlement of a very different kind was that of de Puisaye and some fifty French royalists in the autumn of 1798. Puisaye was a man of fine physique and perseverance, as appeared

---

[1] Pitt MSS., 102. Colonel Delancey named by Pitt was probably Lieutenant-Colonel Stephen Delancey (1740-98), who helped to raise a loyal battalion at New York and finally became Governor of Tobago. His son, Sir William Delancey, was Wellington's Quarter-Master-General at Waterloo, where he was killed.

[2] Greswell ("Hist. of the Dominion of Canada," 144) states that £4,000,000 was then allotted to the settlers in Upper Canada. I can nowhere find any confirmation of this. Kingsford, "Hist. of Canada," mentions only grants of land and small sums of money; but states (vii, 217) that in all the sum of £3,886,087 was granted to the Loyalists in Great Britain.

in his continuance of the Breton revolt long after the unmanly
departure of the Comte d'Artois from the Ile d'Yeu in 1795
(see Chapter XXXVI). But by the year 1798 he wearied of
that fell work, and proposed with other adventurous spirits to
settle in Canada. The Duke of Portland and Windham favoured
the scheme; and a district named Windham was allotted to
them between York (Toronto) and Lake Simcoe. But the ill-
fortune of the French noblesse dogged them in the New World.
They arrived too late. Probably they knew nothing of the work
required of them. Even more probably they quarrelled, intrigued, and formed factions. Puisaye left the place and settled
for a time near the Niagara River, until at the Peace of Amiens
he went back to England. The Windham settlement went to
pieces, thus once more revealing the incompetence of that product
of the *ancien régime*, the French *seigneur*.[1]

The arrival of the United Empire Loyalists altered the
political situation in Canada in two ways: it provided for the
first time a relatively large body of English-speaking settlers,
and it brought to the front the question of representative institutions. Hitherto the French *habitans*, scattered sparsely along
the Lower St. Lawrence and the Richelieu Rivers, had shown
little or no desire in that direction ; but questions arising out
of the war caused some stir in those primitive communities. A
time of much unrest followed. The British merchants and
traders at Quebec and Montreal also had their grievances
against the Government and the French majority; so that in
1784 a Committee comprising men of those towns petitioned the
Governor for an elective House of Assembly.

In order to understand the meaning of this request, we must
remember that election had no place in the Canadian Government. By the Quebec Act of 1774, which regulated public
affairs for the colony, the administration of affairs rested with a
Governor representing the King, an Executive Council consisting of members selected by him, and a Legislative Council
formed on the same basis. The framers of that measure had also
frankly recognized the fact that the population of the colony was
overwhelmingly French. They therefore provided for the continuance of French law and French customs, both religious and

[1] Sir C. P. Lucas, " Hist. of Canada " (1763-1812), 230-2.

agrarian—a well-meant measure which, while ensuring the loyalty of the Canadians during the American War of Independence, aroused the anger of British settlers and merchants. The United Empire Loyalists in Upper Canada found these French customs insufferable. They had not left the United States in order to merge themselves in a community modelled on the France of Louis XIV.

Moreover, in other respects, the Quebec Act failed to meet the needs of the colonists; so that Fox described Canada as having no settled government.[1] Here he erred. The bane of that land was too much government. The settlers were beset by too many decrees, several of which were inapplicable to the needs of the growing mercantile communities at Quebec and Montreal, who found themselves hampered by the French laws and were in constant friction with the "ancient" colonists. They therefore sent the petition of 1784, requesting the bestowal of representative institutions and of British law, both mercantile and criminal; but they admitted the need of retaining French laws for agriculture, property, religion, and social life. Such an admission was repugnant to settlers in the upper districts, who in 1785 petitioned for entire exemption from French laws and customs.[2]

As was but natural, Pitt and his colleagues seem to have been perplexed by the difficulty of this problem, which certainly was one of infinite complexity. It soon appeared, as the outcome of official inquiries, that, taking Canada as a whole, there was only one English-speaking colonist to fifteen French. The small British population was centred almost entirely in Quebec and Montreal (even there it was only a third of the population), or else straggled along the Upper St. Lawrence into the almost unknown wilds between Lakes Ontario and Huron. How was it possible, at the bidding of so insignificant a minority, to repeal the French laws and enrage the majority? Would not France and the States be certain to intervene and thus fill to the full the cup of disaster?

For the present the Pitt Cabinet limited its efforts to the strengthening of the executive powers at Quebec by enlarging the powers of the new Governor-General, Lord Dorchester (1786) so that they extended over the upper districts, and also over

---

[1] "Parl. Hist.," xxviii, 505 (debate of 8th March 1790).
[2] Kingsford, op. cit., vii, 234-236.

New Brunswick and Nova Scotia. Meanwhile Pitt and Sydney awaited the results of the inquiries set on foot in Canada; and, though the resulting delay was irritating at the time, it proved to be beneficial; for before the Ministry at home could frame its Bill, the outbreak of the French Revolution had minimized the danger of intervention from France.

Mishaps to the despatches, the substitution of Grenville for Sydney as Home Secretary, in June 1789, and the General Election of 1790, further retarded legislation on this subject. Twice in the year 1790 Grenville had to apologize to the House for delays due to the terrible weather of the winter of 1789-90.[1] On the latter occasion he described his endeavours to get at the truth of the situation in Canada, his conferences with his colleagues, and his assiduity in drafting the Bill which he promised to place before them as soon as he received Dorchester's replies to certain questions. This declaration is interesting as showing that the famous Act of 1791 was really drafted by Grenville, and that he considered it his own. In view, however, of his very recent appointment to the Home Office, and of his intimate relations to Pitt, we may be sure that the spirit informing the measure was that of the Prime Minister. We now know, however, that Grenville was responsible for the proposal to confer hereditary titles on the members of the Governor's Legislative Council;[2] and it is significant that, while Pitt acquiesced in it, no such creation of a colonial nobility ever took place.

Grenville having been raised to the peerage in November 1790, Pitt moved for leave to bring in the Canada Bill to the Lower House (4th March 1791). In an explanatory speech, he stated the aim of the measure to be "to promote the happiness and internal policy [progress?] of the province and to put an end to the differences of opinion and growing competition that had for some years existed in Canada between the ancient inhabitants and the new settlers from England and America [*sic*] on several important points, and to bring the government of the province, as near as the nature and situation of it would admit, to the British Constitution." He therefore proposed to divide Canada into an Upper and a Lower Province, "the former for the English and American settlers, the lower for the Canadians."

---

[1] "Parl. Hist.," xxviii, 503, 627.
[2] "Dropmore P.," i, 507 (Grenville to Thurlow, 12th September 1789).

I   G G

The inconveniences that might result to the minority in the latter province would, he hoped, be averted by the election of a House of Assembly, which would propose measures, acting therein conjointly with a Legislative Council, of members nominated for life. As it has been stated that Pitt avowed his intention to create two provinces whose mutual jealousies would prevent rebellion, it is desirable to notice that in this first speech he insisted that separation would be the only means of ending the existing strifes and of according to each of them the blessings of the English Constitution.[1] We may also remark that Pitt seems to have paid no heed to the suggestion that the Lower Province might be governed autocratically, while Upper Canada had representative institutions. This would become impossible when the French *habitans* gained political consciousness; and Pitt was surely right in rejecting that makeshift.

His policy was, however, to be sharply criticized, especially by the British minority in Lower Canada. In a petition dated London, 15th March 1791 (which is printed in full in "Pitt and Napoleon Miscellanies"), seven firms engaged in the Canada trade pointed out the defects of the measure; and it is highly significant that some of their objections foreshadowed those which were to be so ably set forth in Lord Durham's Report on Canada (1839). The petition was drafted by Lymburner, a Quebec merchant who had drawn up that of 1784. The Memorialists declared that the Bill before Parliament would perpetuate many of the worst evils of the Quebec Act, which sprang from the attempt to impose one code of laws on two peoples differing widely in their manner of life, customs, and needs. They asserted that the only means of soothing the strifes was to apply English law to the English population and French law to the French; that any division of the colony would be artificial and would debar Upper Canada from maritime trade. The petition concluded with the statesmanlike suggestion that the only cure for the ills of Canada was to merge her two peoples in a self-governing community.

Already Dorchester had offered objections to the proposed division of Canada; but Grenville in his despatch of 20th October 1789 set aside his arguments on the ground that, while weighty as against the present non-representative system, they did not apply to that which was about to be proposed.

[1] "Parl. Hist.," xxviii, 1377-79.

When (he wrote) the resolution was taken of establishing a Provincial Legislature, . . . to be chosen in part by the people, every consideration of policy seemed to render it desirable that the great preponderance possessed in the Upper Districts by the King's antient subjects, and in the lower by the French Canadians, should have this effect and operation in separate Legislatures, rather than that these two bodies of people should be blended together in the first formation of the new Constitution, and before sufficient time has been allowed for the removal of antient prejudices, by the habit of obedience to the same Government and by the sense of a common interest.[1]

These words imply not so much distrust of the colonists as a sense of the need of proceeding tentatively with what was a novel departure. It is clear that Ministers looked on the proposed arrangements as more or less provisional, and in the last phrases we seem to catch a glimpse of a more peaceful future when reunion would be the natural step. For the present, Grenville continued, it would be well to strengthen the Governor's Legislative Council by according to its members some title of honour (a baronetage was first hinted at) which would attach them to the new institutions. Another desirable step was the reservation of Crown Lands in the new districts, in order to provide the Government with a fixed and improving revenue. Grenville even suggested that, had this been done in the original thirteen colonies, a cause of friction and revolt would have been removed.

Ministers must have had a deep sense of the advantages of their proposal when they disregarded the advice of the Governor-General and the firm opposition of the British settlers in Lower Canada and of their connections in London. The measure was pushed on, despite a long speech against it by Lymburner at the bar of the House, in which he asserted that the division of the provinces, when once accomplished, could never be reversed —an assertion falsified by facts in 1841. The debates on the subject were rendered memorable by an incident which will be described later (Chapter XXIV). Burke had persisted in dragging the French Revolution into the discussion, and, when interrupted by Fox, passionately declared that the friendship between them was at an end. As for the question before the House, Fox opposed, while Burke defended, the proposed divi-

---

[1] "Report on Canadian Archives," by D. Brymer (Ottawa, 1891).

sion of Canada. The Whig leader further objected to the proposal to make a legislative councillorship an hereditary honour; and he urged Ministers to increase the size of the Houses of Assembly. Pitt carried his proposal that they should number sixteen for the Upper Province and fifty for the Lower. Finally the House agreed to leave open the question of the hereditary tenure of councillorships; and it is noteworthy that no hereditary title was conferred. The Bill became law on 14th May 1791.

To discuss the suitability of this measure to Canada would involve a recital of events in that colony down to the time of Lord Durham's famous Report of 1839. All that concerns us here is the question of Pitt's attitude towards those complex problems. His conduct cannot be pronounced hasty or doctrinaire. Not until official evidence and advice were forthcoming did he and his colleagues sketch the first outlines of the scheme. But when he had made up his mind, he held on his way with resolute purpose. This will appear if we remember that three Ministers were successively responsible for the Bill. Sydney drafted it. Grenville revised the evidence and recast the Bill;[1] but it fell to Henry Dundas to amend it and carry it into execution. As the Bill was but little changed, we may infer that one mind was at all times paramount.

Canadian historians have generally allowed that the motives of Pitt were enlightened; and, the assertion sometimes made, that they were based on a resolve to make use of the hostility of French and British settlers so as to prevent revolt, is contradicted by all that is known of his manly and hopeful nature. His speeches ring with a feeling of confidence in the healing effect of representative institutions; and it should be remembered that, if in 1837 they were found inadequate to the needs of the progressive Upper Province, they yet nursed that little community into youth. This is all that can be expected from a measure which was necessarily tentative.[2] The chief objections against his division of the provinces were that it tended to weaken the British community in the Lower Province, while it also cut off the Upper Province from the sea and placed it at the mercy of the Customs' laws framed at Quebec.

To this it may be replied that, even if the infant settlements of the Upper St. Lawrence had remained bound up with the

[1] " Dropmore P.," i, 496, 497.
[2] See some good remarks on this by Sir C. P. Lucas, *op. cit.*, 268-70.

French districts, the English-speaking population would still have been in a decided minority, and that it was better to allow the United Empire Loyalists to carve out their own destiny, as they were doing in New Brunswick, in the hope that time would bring about an equipoise between the two peoples. The erection of a new Customs' barrier was truly a serious matter; but it resulted from geographical and racial conditions which were irreversible, save by the Act of Union, which, under happier auspices, came exactly half a century later. In the period 1791-1841 Upper Canada grew from a population of about 10,000 to 465,000; and in that fact may be found the best justification for Pitt's Canadian policy. When looked at from the point of view of 1791, it seems to deserve higher praise than has generally been its meed.

CHAPTER XX

THE SLAVE TRADE

Slaves cannot breathe in England; if their lungs
Receive our air, that moment they are free;
They touch our country, and their shackles fall;
That's noble, and bespeaks a nation proud
And jealous of the blessing. Spread it then,
And let it circulate through every vein
Of all your Empire—that where Britain's power
Is felt, mankind may feel her mercy too.
                                        COWPER.

GREAT movements are too often connected with the names
of one or two prominent men, to the neglect of others
whose services are highly meritorious. Laziness rather than
unfairness may be assigned as the cause of this mistake. The
popular consciousness, unable to hold together names, according
to gradation of merit, settles on one or two as convenient pegs
for the memory, and discards the remainder. Hence it comes
about that commanders acquire undying fame which may be due
to their chiefs of staff; and statesmen are reputed the authors of
measures which they accepted doubtfully from their permanent
officials.

It is by some such process of hasty labelling that the name of
Wilberforce is often affixed alone to the movement for the
liberation of the slaves. True, he deserves to hold a very high
place in the roll-call of the champions of philanthropy. But the
following short summary will suffice to suggest that many other
names, now wellnigh forgotten, deserve to be held in equal
honour. Of those who helped to arouse public opinion on this
question George Fox and William Edmundson come first in
point of time. They lifted up their voice in and after the year
1671 against the cruelties inflicted on negro slaves in Barbadoes
and elsewhere; but we do not find that their views on slavery

affected a large number of their co-religionists until the year 1727, when the Society of Friends in their annual meeting at London passed a resolution condemning both the slave trade and the owning of slaves.[1] This conviction spread to the Quakers of Pennsylvania (the " Quaker State") where worthy members of the Society succeeded in arousing public opinion even against the institution of slavery.

Reverting to England, with which alone we are concerned, we find the Quakers striving to stop the worst abuses of the Slave Trade. The Treaty of Utrecht (1713) had handed over to England a great part of that traffic; and Chatham himself boasted that his conquests in Africa during the Seven Years' War had placed almost the whole of it in British hands. When a man of his elevation of thought held this language, we can imagine that the many looked on the trade as a pillar of the Empire, and derided its few opponents as lunatics.

Not that public opinion was wholly blind to its evils. In the year 1750 Parliament had passed an Act forbidding the kidnapping of negroes; but it proved wholly ineffective; and, as the horrors connected with the Slave Trade became better known, the Society of Friends warned all its members to abstain from any connection whatever with so unholy a traffic (1758). Three years later it resolved to disown any who should disregard this warning.[2] Thus, to the religious zeal and consistency of the Friends we are indebted for the first attempts to abolish this traffic. No small community has ever rendered a greater service to the cause of religion and humanity.

It should be noted in passing that their action and that of later abolitionists helped to link together these two ideals in a manner which was to be infinitely fruitful. In this connection Granville Sharp, John Wesley, Clarkson, Paley, Wilberforce, Buxton, Zachary Macaulay, and many others may be named as proving the close union that subsisted between religious conviction and the philanthropic movement. The power of religion to impel to good works shone forth in all of them. Wilberforce gave scarcely a thought to the slaves until the work of grace began in his own heart. In 1774 Wesley published his work,

[1] Clarkson, " Hist. of the Abolition of the Slave Trade," i, 110-113. See p. 259 for a chart showing the names of those who had protested against the Trade from the times of Charles V, Ximenes, and G. Fox.

[2] *Ibid.*, 114, 115.

"Thoughts upon Slavery," which greatly furthered the cause. Indeed, it should be noticed as one of the influences marking off the philanthropic movement in England from that of France that here for the most part it was an offshoot of the Evangelical Revival, whereas in France the efforts of Voltaire and the Encyclopaedists imparted to similar efforts a strongly anti-Catholic bias. These facts were destined to mould the future of religion and politics in the two lands. Here philanthropists and statesmen were the mainstay of religion. There the slow cessation of persecution and the reluctant abandonment of privileges by the Roman Church ranged social reformers against her, with results that were to appear in the Revolution.

Fortunately, in England law reinforced the efforts of philanthropists. In 1772, Chief Justice Mansfield gave a decision that a slave who landed on English soil became a free man. The case arose out of the conduct of a West India merchant settled in London, who by sheer brutality had rendered a slave useless for work, had turned him adrift, but again claimed him when healed by a kind-hearted physician. Granville Sharp thenceforth made it the business of his life to see justice done to the negro race, and was chiefly instrumental in bringing the whole question to a practical issue by founding in 1787 the first Abolitionist Society.

Before adverting to its labours, with which Pitt so deeply sympathized, we may notice a few facts connected with the traffic in human flesh. The evidence of Robert Norris, of Liverpool, before a Parliamentary Commission in the year 1775 showed that of the 74,000 negroes believed to be taken annually from Africa to the New World, British ships carried about 38,000; French, 20,000; Portuguese, 10,000; Dutch, 4,000; Danish, 2,000. The greater part came from Bonny, New Calabar, the Gold Coast, and Loango. Gambia is credited with exporting only 700, a suspiciously low estimate. The same witness asserted that only one slave in twenty-seven died on the voyage, while one seaman in sixteen succumbed.[1] Estimates, however, varied very greatly. Macpherson gave 97,000 as the number of slaves imported into the New World from Africa in the year 1768.[2] Efforts were made by merchants to depict the passage on the ocean as pleasant, amusements being provided on the way.

[1] B.M. Add. MSS., 18272 (on the Slave Trade).
[2] Macpherson, "Annals of Commerce," iii, 484.

But it soon transpired that the chief amusement was compulsory singing, while the "dancing" proved to be jumping in chains at the sound of the lash. It was also known that very many negroes died soon after landing during the process known as seasoning to the climate and work; that the whip was freely used in the plantations; and that the mortality among the slaves was extremely heavy. In this connection the name of Burke deserves to be held in honour; for he proposed that the Attorney-General in each colony should be empowered to act as Protector of the negroes.

Thus, even before the Abolitionist Society began its labours, public opinion was beginning to brand the traffic with infamy. The year 1783 saw efforts made in Parliament to repress some of its worst abuses; and the Society of Friends then sent up the first petition for the total abrogation of the traffic in British vessels.[1] The year 1785 witnessed the publication of Clarkson's Latin essay on the subject; and a twelvemonth later it came out in English. In 1783 also the efforts of the Rev. James Ramsay, Rector of Teston, Kent, who had seen the evils of slavery during his residence at St. Kitt's, brought the subject home to the mind of his neighbour, Lady Middleton; and she in her turn impressed it as a Christian duty on Wilberforce to bring forward a motion in Parliament. As this appeal harmonized with the strong religious convictions now swaying the nature of the young member for Yorkshire, he felt strongly moved to take up the cause of the negroes. In the year 1786 he made many inquiries among African and West India merchants, and found much error in their information. After probing the matter, he resolved to consult Pitt as to his making this question the chief object of his life.

The conversation took place under an old oak-tree in Pitt's grounds at Holwood, above the steep descent into Keston vale. The opinions of the two friends, as we have seen, had somewhat diverged. Pitt did not sympathize with the pietism which now dominated the life of Wilberforce; but his religion was of a working type, and he may have welcomed the growth of convictions of a more practical kind, which would wean his friend from excessive introspection. Certain it is that he urged him to take up the cause of the slaves as one well suited to his character and talents. Wilberforce therefore resolved to give notice of his in-

[1] "Parl. Hist.," xxiii, 1026.

tention to bring the subject before Parliament. Would that we knew the details of that conversation illustrative of the character of two of the most interesting men of the age. Even so, the resolve there formed renders illustrious the tree under which it was formed, fitly called "Wilberforce's oak."[1]

The three strands of effort which we have traced from their feeble beginnings, viz., those originating with the Quakers, Granville Sharp, and Ramsay, were now to combine. In 1787, as we have seen, Granville Sharp, in connection with London Friends, formed a "Committee for procuring Evidence on the Slave Trade," which was to become the famous Abolitionist Society. At the first meeting on 22nd May 1787, only ten were present. Their names deserve to be recorded. Granville Sharp (Chairman), J. Barton, Thomas Clarkson, W. Dillwyn, S. Hoare (junr.), J. Hooper, J. Lloyd, R. Phillips, P. Sanson, J. Woods. All but two were Quakers, and the minutes and letters abound in "thous" and "thees." One of the aims of the Committee was to distribute Clarkson's and other pamphlets on the subject. In October 1787 the Committee received a letter from Brissot and Clavière, the future leaders of the French Girondins, expressing the wish to promote their views in France, where, as is well known, the abolitionists achieved a speedy but illusory triumph in 1790.

As there has been some controversy respecting the initiation of this movement, it is well to note that not until 30th October 1787 did the Committee receive a letter from Wilberforce. He then asked for information as speedily as possible. The Minutes of the Committee show that he was not a member until the year 1794, and it is an exaggeration to say that "he directed their endeavours."[2] Their aim was to stir up the great towns to petition to Parliament. In this they achieved a marked success. Indeed, it was rather the formation of a strong public opinion by the labours of the Committee, than the many motions in Parliament, which at last brought triumph to the cause. Manchester and Birmingham soon displayed great interest in the subject. A kindred society was formed at the latter town. That at London grew in importance, and funds came in rapidly.

[1] "Life of Wilberforce," i, 151; for a photograph of the tree see "Private Papers of W. Wilberforce," 17.

[2] "Life of Wilberforce," i, 152. The Minute Books of the Committee are in the B.M. Add. MSS., 21254, 21255.

William Wilberforce
from an unfinished painting by Sir T. Lawrence

Wilberforce wrote to Eden on 18th January 1788: "The fire is kindled in various parts of the Kingdom and the flame spreads wider and wider."[1] One of the petitions resulting from the labours of the parent committee deserves mention here. It came from 769 freemen cutlers of Sheffield, was dated 24th April 1789, and stated that, though the exports of petitioners to the African coast might fall off if the Slave Trade were abolished, yet they were so convinced of its inhumanity that they begged Parliament to sweep it away.[2]

Petitions of the same tenour had long been coming in, and Pitt therefore instituted an inquiry by the Privy Council respecting the whole question, including the condition of the slaves in the colonies.[3] One of the replies, that from Bermuda, of 10th June 1788, is typically optimistic. Governor Browne affirmed that the slaves in those islands were exceedingly well treated. Out of 4,900 slaves not more than five a year deserted. During the late war many had served on privateers and, when captured and taken to the United States, nearly all managed to make their way back to their masters. This report is a specimen of the arguments which compelled Ministers to some measure of caution.[4]

There is, however, abundant proof that Pitt, though a recent recruit to the movement, espoused it with enthusiasm. During the difficult negotiations with France in the autumn of 1787, we find Wilberforce informing Eden, our envoy at Paris, of Pitt's interest in the endeavour to stop the Slave Trade, a matter which would be greatly facilitated if France would agree to take the same step.[5] On 2nd November Pitt followed up his friend's letter by another appeal to Eden to induce the French Government "to discontinue the villainous traffic now carried on in Africa."[6] The following letter, hitherto unpublished, from Pitt to Eden, further shows his hope that Eden, who was soon to take the embassy at Madrid, would be able to influence that Court also:

Downing Street, *Dec.* 7, 1787.[7]

Mr. Wilberforce has communicated to me your last letter respecting the African business. The more I reflect upon it, the more anxious and

---

[1] "Auckland Journals," i, 307.
[2] Pitt MSS., 310.
[3] "Life of Wilberforce," i, 166.
[4] *Ibid.*
[5] "Auckland Journals," i, 240.
[6] *Ibid.*, i, 267.
[7] Pitt MSS., 102. For Eden's reply, see "Auckland Journals," i, 285.

impatient I am that the business should be brought as speedily as possible to a point; that, if the real difficulties of it can be overcome, it may not suffer from the prejudices and interested objections which will multiply during the discussion. Of course it cannot yet be ripe for any official communication; and when you transmit the memorandum, which I see you were to draw up, I hope it will be quite secret for the present. If you see any chance of success in France, I hope you will lay your ground as soon as possible with a view to Spain also. I am considering what to do in Holland, but the course of business there makes the secrecy, which is necessary at least for a time, more difficult.

The reply of the French Government in January 1788 was discouraging. Montmorin and his colleagues avowed their sympathy with the cause, but, fearing that it would not succeed in England, refused to commit themselves.[1] The advent of Necker to power in August aroused Pitt's hopes;[2] but he too temporized, thereby prejudicing the success of the cause in these islands. Spain refused to stir in the matter.

Meanwhile Wilberforce had given notice of a motion on the subject, but a severe illness in February and March 1788 left him in a state of weakness which precluded the least effort. Before leaving for Bath, he begged Pitt to bring forward the motion for him. The Prime Minister consented, says Wilberforce, " with a warmth of principle and friendship that have made me love him better than I ever did before." Nevertheless he acted with caution. Up to the beginning of the year 1788, at least, he had not brought the matter before the Cabinet, probably because he knew that most of its members would oppose him. In the country also a formidable opposition was arising, and, as usually happens in such cases, enthusiasts clamoured at delay as treason to the cause.[3] Perhaps it was this which led him to request a conference with Sharp. It took place on 21st April, and is thus reported in the Minutes of the Committee:

He [Granville Sharp] had a full opportunity of explaining that the desire of the Committee went to a full abolition of the Slave Trade. Mr. Pitt assured him that his heart was with us, and that he considered himself pledged to Mr. Wilberforce that the cause should not sustain any injury from his indisposition; but at the same time that the subject

---

[1] " Auckland Journals," i, 307. [2] " Dropmore P.," i, 353.
[3] " Auckland Journals," i, 304; " Life of Wilberforce," i, 170. See Pitt's etter of consent of 8th April 1788, in " Private Papers of W. Wilberforce," 17-19.

was of great political importance, and it was requisite to proceed in the business with temper and prudence. He did not apprehend, as the examination before the Privy Council would yet take up some time, that the subject could be fully investigated in the present session of Parliament, but said he would consider whether the forms of the House would admit of any measures that would be obligatory on them to take it up early in the ensuing session.[1]

On 9th May Pitt brought his motion before the House, but pending the conclusion of the official inquiry, he offered no opinion on the subject, for which he was sharply twitted by Fox and Burke. His conduct was far from pleasing to the more ardent spirits. One of them, the venerable Sir William Dolben, member for the University of Oxford, after inspecting a slave-ship in the Thames, determined to lose no time in alleviating the misery of the many living cargoes that crossed the ocean. He therefore brought in a Bill for temporarily regulating the transport of slaves in British ships. In the course of the discussions Pitt declared that, even though the proposed regulations involved the trade in ruin, as was maintained, he would nevertheless vote for them; and if the trade could not be regulated, he would vote for its abolition as "shocking to humanity, abominable to be carried on by any country, and which reflected the greatest dishonour on the British Senate and the British nation." He further startled the House by proposing that the regulations should become operative from that day—10th June. The hold which he had on members was shown by the division, fifty-six voting for the measure and only five against it. In the Upper House no minister save the Duke of Richmond ventured to defend this unusual enactment; and the Chancellor, Thurlow, spoke strongly against it. Sydney also opposed it, though with moderation (25th June). Pitt's feelings when he heard of their action are shown in a phrase of his letter to Grenville, dated Cambridge, 29th June, that if the Bill failed he and the opposers would not remain members of the same Cabinet. This declaration does honour to his heart and his judgement. It proves the warmth of his feelings on the subject and his sense of the need of discipline in the Cabinet. Had the measure failed to pass the Lords, a Cabinet crisis of the gravest kind would have arisen. As it was, however, the great efforts put forth by Pitt among his

---

[1] B.M. Add. MSS., 21255.

friends sufficed to carry the day against Thurlow by a majority
of two. We catch a glimpse of what an average man thought
of this incident in the pages of Wraxall. After adverting to the
nobility of Pitt's motives and the strength of Thurlow's arguments against the retrospective action of the Bill, the chronicler
thus passes judgement: "Thurlow argued as a statesman, Pitt
acted as a moralist." We also have the warrant of Wraxall for
stating that, not until George III gave his assent to the measure,
did Pitt "allow" him to prorogue Parliament.[1]

Ship-owners and slave-owners had, however, been driven only
from the first outwork of their citadel, and had time to strengthen
their defences before the matter came up again in 1789. After
a delay, caused by the King's malady and by the length of the
inquiry into the Slave Trade by a committee of the Privy
Council, Wilberforce brought the question before the House on
12th May in one of the ablest and most eloquent speeches of
that age. For three and a half hours he held the attention of
the House as he recounted the horrors which slave-hunting
spread through Africa, and the hell of suffering of the middle
passage. He showed how legitimate trade would increase with
the growth of confidence between man and man in that Continent,
and he asserted that the sympathies of King Louis XVI, Necker,
and the French nation would probably lead that country to follow our example in abolishing a traffic degrading to all concerned
in it. He then proved from official information concerning the
slaves in our West India islands, that wise treatment of them
and suppression of vice would ensure a sufficient increase of
population to meet the needs of the planters. He concluded by
moving twelve resolutions setting forth the facts of the case as
detailed in the Report of the Privy Council. This mode of
procedure earned general approval. Burke bestowed his blessing on the proposal (for such it was in effect) to abolish so
hateful a traffic. Pitt gave the measure his warm approval, but
stated that he was prepared to give a hearing to all objections.
One such he noticed, namely, that foreign nations would step in
and secretly supply our West India islands with slaves. He
declared that Great Britain was strong enough to prevent so
insidious a device; but he hoped, rather, that other peoples
would desire to share in the honour of abolishing the trade; and

[1] "Parl. Hist.," xxvii, 495-506, 598; "Dropmore P.," i, 342; Wraxall, v,
146, 149.

we might confidently negotiate with them to that end, or wait for the effect which our example would produce. Fox followed in the same strain, and prophesied that France would soon "catch a spark from our fire and run a race with us in promoting the ends of humanity." [1]

But these unanswerable arguments were of no avail against shippers, slave-owners, and colonial traders. In vain did Wilberforce point out that the prosperity of Liverpool did not depend upon the Slave Trade; for the tonnage of the slave-ships was only one-fifteenth of that of the whole port. Liverpool saw nothing but ruin ahead; and it must be admitted that that class of traffic was then by far the most lucrative to the growing city on the Mersey. It has been computed that in the decade 1783-93, Liverpool slave-ships made 878 "round voyages" (*i.e.* from Liverpool to the Guinea Coast, thence to the West Indies, and back to the Mersey), carried 303,737 slaves and sold them for £15,186,850. [2] It is not surprising, then, that Clarkson was mobbed when he went there to collect evidence as to the terrible mortality of our seamen engaged in the trade, [3] and was known to be purchasing "mouth-openers," those ingenious devices by which slavers forced open the mouths of those of their victims who sought release by voluntary starvation. Bristol, though it had only eighteen ships in the trade, was also up in arms; for it depended largely on the refining of sugar and the manufacture of rum. Even the veteran reformer, Alderman Sawbridge, foresaw ruin for his constituency, the City of London, if the trade were further interfered with. Persons of a rhetorical turn depicted in lurid colours the decay of Britain's mercantile marine, the decline of her wealth, and the miseries of a sugar famine. Others sought to frighten the timid by declaring that, as shippers and planters had embarked large sums of money in the trade in reliance on Parliament, they were entitled to absolutely full compensation for the heavy losses which must result from its abolition or further curtailment. [4] In short, all the menaces,

---

[1] "Parl. Hist.," xxviii, 41-75.

[2] Prof. Ramsay Muir, "Hist. of Liverpool," 193.

[3] *Ibid.*, 56. Out of 3,170 men who sailed in the slavers from Liverpool in 1787, 642 died and 1,100 were got rid of or deserted in the West Indies.

[4] See a curious letter in "Woodfall's Register" for 12th June 1789, in answer to authentic accounts of the horrors of the Slave Trade lately given in that paper by C. D. Wadstrom.

based on assumed legal rights, were set forth with vehemence and pertinacity.

The result was seen in the increasing acrimony of the opponents of abolition in Parliament. They poured scorn on the evidence adduced before the Privy Council in a way which brought from Pitt a sharp retort, but they insisted, and with success, on the hearing of evidence at the bar of the House. These dilatory tactics protracted the discussion until it was necessary to postpone it to the next year.

Before the end of the session of 1789 an important change came about in the Cabinet. Sydney had long disagreed with Pitt respecting the Slave Trade, and therefore, early in June, offered his resignation. There could be but one opinion as to his successor. William Wyndham Grenville had long shown high capacity both in diplomatic affairs and more recently in his conduct of the Speakership of the House. His speech on the trade marked him out as a strong supporter of Pitt; and on 5th June he became Secretary of State for Home Affairs with a seat in the Cabinet. His accession was a gain for the Administration and a further source of strength for Pitt, who had long felt great confidence in his judgement and tact.[1] Henry Addington, son of the physician who long attended the first Earl of Chatham, was chosen Speaker of the House of Commons by a large majority over the Whig nominee, Sir Gilbert Elliot.

One other change ought to have taken place. The language used by Lord Thurlow against Pitt had long been petulant, and his irritation against the abolitionists led him to strange lengths in the summer of 1789.[2] Their differences caused an almost complete rupture. But, for the present, Pitt could not insist on his resignation. On the question now at issue George III agreed with Thurlow.[3] He also seems to have been quite unaware of the shifty course adopted by the Chancellor at the beginning of his late malady and believed him to be thoroughly devoted to his person. It argues no small amount of self-restraint and honourable reticence in Pitt that he should have taken no steps to inform the King of the meditated defection of Thurlow. George III therefore continued to believe in the whole hearted devotion of the Lord Chancellor; and on two occasions during the year 1789 he wrote to Pitt expressing his desire that the

[1] "Dropmore P.," i, 278.   [2] *Ibid.*, i, 487.
[3] "Auckland Journals," i, 221; Wraxall, v, 139.

two Ministers should endeavour to work together cordially for the good of the realm.[1] It is consonant with what we know of Thurlow's character that he presumed on the King's partiality towards him, and played the part of the one necessary man in a way highly exasperating to Pitt. But the precarious state of the King's health and his known dislike of dismissing old servants availed to postpone the inevitable rupture until the year 1792. The retention of Thurlow may be considered one of the causes of the failure of the abolitionists at this time.

In the spring of the year 1790 the champions of the Slave Trade believed that they saw signs of waning enthusiasm on the part of the public, and on 23rd April sought to stop the further examination of witnesses at the bar of the House. Wilberforce, Fox, and Pitt protested against these tactics, but Pitt intimated that he did not consider the question one which Ministers were pledged to support. The case for a free and full inquiry was overwhelming, and it was continued. That Pitt acted in close connection with Fox on this whole question appears by his letter to Wilberforce on 22nd April, which further shows that he also considered the evidence so voluminous and important as to afford little hope of the question being disposed of in that session.[2]

This was most unfortunate. The friends of abolition never had a better opportunity than in the early part of 1790. Later on in that year the risk of war with Spain (see Chapter XXIV) and the prospect of a revolt of the slaves in the French West Indies began to turn Britons against a measure which, they were told, would weaken the mercantile marine and lead to the loss of the West Indies. In this case, as in many others, the influence of the French Revolution militated against the cause of steady reform in England. The National Assembly had early declared the principle of freedom of the slaves in the French colonies; but owing to the violent opposition of the planters and merchants, the decree remained a dead letter. In the spring of 1790 the question came up once more; but again the majority sought to shelve the question. Lord Robert Stephen Fitzgerald, the British envoy at Paris, commended the prudence and self-restraint of the Assembly "in not agitating the two great ques-

---

[1] Stanhope, ii, App., ix, xi.
[2] "Parl. Hist.," xxviii, 711-14; "Life of Wilberforce," i, 266, 267. The evidence ran to 1400 folio pages (ibid., i, 281).

I   H H

tions concerning the emancipation of the negroes and the abolition of the Slave Trade, which had at the first setting out raised
so violent a spirit of party." [1] The planters and West India
merchants still threatened that the Colonial Assemblies (established in the year 1787) would declare their independence if
those decrees were passed, on the ground that they were not
bound by the acts of the French Assembly. Mirabeau, along
with all practical statesmen, forebore from pressing the point;
and it is highly probable that the politic caution of the French
reformers, despite their sensibility and enthusiasm, told upon
public opinion in England.

Such were the discouraging conditions amidst which a General
Election was held in the summer of 1790. It increased Pitt's
hold on the House of Commons; but, as he had refrained from
making the Slave Trade a ministerial question, the result did
not imply the victory of abolition. In the month of November
he took a step which furthered the prospects of the cause. He
recommended Grenville for the peerage as Baron Grenville,
partly in recognition of his services, but mainly because he
needed a trusty friend and capable debater in the Upper House
as a check on Thurlow. He assured Wilberforce that distrust
of the Lord Chancellor was the true reason that prompted the
transfer of Grenville to the Lords. [2] We find Pitt writing on
24th November 1790 to his mother in high spirits. He hoped
for great things from Grenville in the Upper House. As for
"prophets of schisms," they would be refuted. The opening of
the new Parliament would find the Ministry in "more strength
than has belonged to us since the beginning of the Government." [3]

The question came before Parliament on 18th and 19th April
1791, when Wilberforce in a masterly way summarized the
official evidence and moved for leave to bring in a Bill abolishing the Slave Trade. Some of the arguments on the other
side were curious. Grosvenor admitted that the trade was an
"unamiable" one, but he declined to "gratify his humanity at
the expense of the interests of his country, and thought we
should not too curiously inquire into the unpleasant circumstances with which it was perhaps attended." Less finnikin was
the objection raised by Lord John Russell and others, that, if
we suppressed the trade, France, Spain, and Holland would step

[1] "F. O.," France, 34. Fitzgerald to Leeds, 2nd April 1790.
[2] "Life of Wilberforce," i, 284.   [3] Pitt MSS., 12.

in to take it up. This and the question of vested interests formed the only reply to Wilberforce, Fox, and Pitt. The Prime Minister declared that he had never been more interested in the fate of any proposal than the present one. He brushed aside the pleas of opponents, as wholly untenable, " unless gentlemen will in the first place prove to me that there are no laws of morality binding upon nations, and that it is no duty of a Legislature to restrain its subjects from invading the happiness of other countries and from violating the fundamental principles of justice." He then proved from the statistics then available that the numbers of the slaves in the West Indies would under proper treatment increase in such a degree as to supply the labour needed for the plantations, without bringing ruin upon Africa. But argument and reasoning were useless. Mammon carried the day by 163 to 88.[1]

The events of the year 1791 further depressed the hopes of philanthropists. After much wobbling on the subject the National Assembly of France passed a decree liberating the slaves in French colonies, and granting to them the full rights of citizenship (15th May). The results were disastrous. Already there had been serious trouble in the French West Indies, owing to the progress of democratic ideas among the mulattos and slaves; and the news that they were thenceforth politically the equals of planters and merchants, who had ever resisted their claims, led to terrible risings of the slaves, especially in the west of St. Domingo, where plantations and cities felt the blind fury of their revenge. By the end of the year the most flourishing colony of France was a wreck.[2]

The heedless haste of French reformers worked ruin far and wide. Extremes are fatal to the happy mean; for the populace rarely takes the trouble to distinguish between reckless innovation and the healing of a palpable grievance. Among the unfortunate results of the French Revolution not the least was the tendency to extremes of feeling produced by it in France and all neighbouring peoples. Those who approved its doctrines generally became giddy with enthusiasm; those who disapproved turned livid with hatred. Burke in his " Reflections on the French Revolution " had lately set the example of treat-

---

[1] " Parl. Hist.," xxix, 250-359.
[2] " Hist. de la Rév. à Saint Domingue," by A. M. Delmas. 2 vols. Paris, 1814; " Hist. Survey of . . . San Domingo," by Bryan Edwards. 1797.

ing the whole subject in a crusading spirit. The flood of senti-
mentality, unloosed by that attractive work, was now near high-
water mark; and for a space the age of chivalry seemed about
to return.

The news of the horrors at St. Domingo came opportunely
to double the force of his prophecies. The cause of the slaves
suffered untold harm.[1] Any change in existing customs was
dubbed treason to the Commonwealth. Men did not stop to
contrast the rash methods of the *Amis des Noirs* with those
advocated by Pitt. Still less did they ask how the stoppage of the
importation of infuriated negroes into the West Indian colonies,
and the more humane treatment of those who were there, could
lead to a servile revolt. Wilberforce was fain to exclaim that nothing was so cruel as sensibility. His campaign against the Slave
Trade made little or no progress in the early part of 1792. "People
here," he wrote, " are all panic-struck with the transactions in
St. Domingo and the apprehension, or pretended apprehension,
of the like in Jamaica." Many friends advised him to postpone
all further action for a year until the panic was over. Among
these was Pitt, so we may judge from the curt reference of
Wilberforce to what went on at an informal committee meeting
on the subject: " Pitt threw out against Slave motion, on St.
Domingo account." He also speaks of a slackening of their
cordiality.

The folly of Clarkson in advocating Jacobinical ideas at a
meeting held at the Crown and Anchor in the Strand further
damaged the cause. Nevertheless, detestation of the Slave
Trade was still very keen. Friends of the slaves began to for-
swear sugar and take to honey. Petitions against the traffic in
human flesh poured in at St. Stephen's; and those who spoke of
delay were held to be backsliders. This is the sense which we
must attach to a phrase in a letter sent to Wilberforce: " From
London to Inverness Mr. Pitt's sincerity is questioned, and
unless he can convince the nation of his cordiality in our cause,
his popularity must suffer greatly."[2] The questioning was needless. Pitt considered the time inopportune for bringing the
motion before a Parliament which had already rejected it.
When, however, Wilberforce persisted, he gave him his enthusiastic support.

[1] " Life of Wilberforce," i, 295-6, 340, 342.   [2] *Ibid.*, i, 344.

The debate of 2nd April 1792 was remarkable in more ways than one. The opponents of the measure now began to shift their ground. Colonel Tarleton, member for Liverpool, continued to harp on the ruin that must befall his town; but others, notably Dundas, and the Speaker (Addington) admitted the evils of the trade, and the probability that in a few years the needs of the planters might be met from the negro population already in the islands. Dundas therefore moved an amendment in favour of a " moderate " reform, or a "gradual " reform. Fox manfully castigated this proposal, which assumed that there might be moderation in murder. Nevertheless Jenkinson (the future Earl of Liverpool) made a trimming speech in favour of regulating, not abolishing, the trade.

Pitt then arose. The rays of dawn were already lighting up the windows on the east when he began his memorable speech. First, he expressed his satisfaction that members were generally agreed as to the abolition of the traffic being only a question of time. Mankind would therefore before long be delivered " from the severest and most extensive calamity recorded in the history of the world." Grappling with the arguments of Jenkinson and Dundas, he proceeded to show that the immediate abolition of the Slave Trade would in many ways be an advantage to the West Indies, as it would restrict the often excessive outlay of the planters and deliver our colonies from the fear of servile insurrections like that of St. Domingo. Planters must rely upon the natural increase of the black population which would accelerate under good treatment. If, said he, that population decreases, it can be only from ill treatment. If it is increasing, there is no need for a trade which involves a frightful loss of life both on sea and in the process of " seasoning " the human freitage in the West Indies.

Adverting to the Act of 1750, which was claimed as authorizing the trade, Pitt proved from its wording that the supply of negroes for our colonies was then deemed to be essential, and that a clause of it, which was continually violated, expressly forbade the use of fraud or violence in the procuring of the cargo. But, even if that law rendered the trade legal, had any Legislature a right to sanction fraud and violence? As well might a man think himself bound by a promise to commit murder. He next scouted the argument that, if we gave up the trade, other peoples would rush in and take our place. Would France, now that she had abolished slavery? Would Denmark, seeing that she had resolved gradually to abolish the trade? As to other lands, it was more probable that they would follow the example soon to be set by this land.

Having traversed the statements of opponents, Pitt raised the whole question to a higher level by reminding the House of the export of slaves from Britain to Rome, and by reconstructing with mordant irony the arguments of Roman senators on its behalf, as a legitimate and useful device for using the surplus population of a hopelessly barbarous people. Warming to his theme, he thrilled his hearers by contrasting the state of these islands, had they continued to supply the Roman slave-mart, with the freedom, happiness, and civilization that now were their lot. He besought members, as they valued these blessings, to see to it that they were extended to Africa; and, catching inspiration from the rays of the sun which now lit up the Hall, he pictured the natives of Africa in some not distant future "engaged in the calm occupations of industry, in the pursuits of a just and legitimate commerce. We may behold the beams of science and philosophy breaking in upon their land, which, at some happy period in still later times may blaze with full lustre; and, joining their influence to that of pure religion, may illuminate and invigorate the most distant extremities of that immense Continent. Then may we hope that even Africa, though last of all the quarters of the globe, shall enjoy at length in the evening of her days, those blessings which have descended so plentifully upon us in a much earlier period of the world. Then also will Europe, participating in her improvement and prosperity, receive an ample recompense for the tardy kindness (if kindness it can be called) of no longer hindering that Continent from extricating herself out of the darkness, which, in other more fortunate regions, has been so much more speedily dispelled:

> Nos . . . primus equis Oriens afflavit anhelis,
> Illic sera rubens accendit lumina Vesper." [1]

Continuing in this lofty strain, in which enthusiasm and learning, reason and art, voice and gestures, enforced the pleadings of a noble nature, he avowed his faith in the cause of immediate abolition of the Slave Trade. The House thought otherwise. By

---

[1] Virg. " Georg.," i, 250: " On us the rising sun first breathed with panting steeds, there ruddy Vesper full late kindles his fires."

192 votes to 125 it accepted Dundas's amendment in favour of gradual abolition.[1] So far do the dictates of self-interest outweigh with many men those of righteousness and mercy, even when these are reinforced by the most moving appeals. Fox, Grey, and Windham agreed that Pitt's speech was one of the most extraordinary displays of eloquence ever heard. If such was the opinion of opponents, we may imagine the impression produced on friends. Wilberforce declared that the speaker was as if inspired when he spoke of the hope of civilizing Africa —a topic which he (Wilberforce) had suggested to him on the previous morning.[2]

The outcome was not wholly disappointing. Three weeks later Dundas brought forward his resolutions for a gradual abolition of the trade. Wilberforce and Pitt failed to induce the House to fix 1st January 1795; but they carried it with them for 1st January 1796, though Dundas proposed a date four years later. The House of Lords, however, in deference to the speeches of the Duke of Clarence, and Lords Hawkesbury and Thurlow, proceeded to involve the whole question in uncertainty by deciding to hear the evidence on it at their own bar (8th May, 1792). Some votes were decided by Thurlow's asseveration that this would not involve delay. The Archbishop of Canterbury soon came to see his mistake; and after a sleepless night he wrote on 9th May to Pitt that he was tortured by doubts as to the outcome of the affair. " My vote was given under a strong impression from the Chancellor's solemn statement that an examination before a committee of the whole House would not be a cause of delay. . . . My conviction of the necessity of the abolition of the horrid trade is firm and unshaken." He adds that he will explain his vote on the first possible occasion, and hopes that Pitt will show this letter to Grenville and Wilberforce.[3]

The Archbishop ought to have known that, with Thurlow,

---

[1] "Parl. Hist.," xxix, 1133-58.

[2] "Life of Wilberforce," i, 346. Lord Auckland (who, as Mr. Eden, had been a philanthropist) referred sarcastically to Pitt's speech: "Mr. Pitt has raised his imagination to the belief that the trade ought, at all events and risks, to be instantly discontinued. . . . Some people are urging this business upon a mischievous principle" ("Auckland Journals," ii, 400).

[3] Chevening MSS.

solemnity was often the cloak of maliciousness. It was so now. The examination of witnesses proceeded very slowly. On 5th June, after hearing only five of them, the Lords decided to postpone the hearing of others until the following year.[1] The dismissal of Thurlow, which (as we see in a later chapter) followed on 15th June 1792, was due in the last instance to his pert censures of Pitt's finance; but it may be ascribed also to his acrimonious opposition to Pitt on the question of abolition, and to his underhand means of defeating him in the House of Lords.

Other events also seemed to tell against the philanthropists. The connection of some of them with the Radical clubs, and their use of addresses and petitions to overbear the opposition in Parliament clearly made a bad impression on Pitt. After issuing the royal proclamation against seditious writings in May 1792 he showed his disapproval of their methods; and during the subsequent negotiations for a union with the moderate Whigs, in order to form a truly national administration, he confessed to Loughborough that he must make some concession to the Whig Houses on the question of abolition.[2] This is the first clear sign of his intention to shelve the measure until the return of more settled times.

They were not to come for wellnigh a decade. The declaration of war by the French Republic on 1st February 1793 turned men's minds away from philanthropy to destruction. The results were soon visible. A measure proposed by Wilberforce, to prohibit the supply to foreigners of slaves in British ships, failed to pass the Commons, despite the able speeches of Pitt, Fox, and Francis in its favour (5th June 1793). In the Lords meanwhile the Duke of Clarence (the future William IV) spoke against the original proposal with great bitterness, denouncing the abolitionists as fanatics and hypocrites, and expressly naming Wilberforce among them. This insolence was far from meeting with the chastisement that it deserved; but his words were taken as a sign that the royal family was pledged to the support of the odious traffic.

It may be well to notice here a remarkable effort of the chief abolitionists, and to add a few words about the men themselves. Early in the year 1791 some of them sought to show that under favourable conditions negroes were capable of self-government.

---

[1] Clarkson, *op. cit.*, ii, 460.   [2] " Malmesbury Diaries," ii, 464.

Accordingly they formed a Sierra Leone Committee for the purpose of settling liberated slaves on that part of the coast of West
Africa. In the Pitt Papers is a letter of 18th April 1791,
from the first overseer, Falconbridge, to Granville Sharp, which
the latter forwarded to Pitt, giving a heartrending account of
the state of the thirty-six men and twenty women who formed
the settlement. Fevers and ulcers were rife. Outrages by white
men had made the tribes defiant, and a native chief hard by was
far from friendly. Falconbridge adds : " That lump of deformity,
the Slave Trade, has so debauched the minds of the natives
that they are lost to every principle of honor and honesty.
The scenes of iniquity and murder I daily hear of, occasioned
by this damnable traffic, make my nature revolt." He had
named the bay and village Granville Bay and Town; but, as the
latter was already overgrown with bushes, he was planting another at Fora Bay. He concludes—" For God's sake send me a
ship of force (warship)."[1] Such were the feeble beginnings of a
colony of which Zachary Macaulay was to be the first Governor.

Here, as in other parts of this philanthropic movement, Pitt
displayed little or no initiative. To the cause of abolition he
gave the support of his eloquence and his influence in Parliament; but he gave no decided lead in these and cognate efforts, a
fact which somewhat detracts from his greatness as a statesman
in this formative period. The merit of starting the movement
and of utilizing new openings belongs to the Quakers, to Granville Sharp, Clarkson, Wilberforce and his friends. The member
for Yorkshire had grouped around him at his abode, Broomfield,
Clapham Common, or at his town house in Palace Yard, Westminster, a number of zealous workers, among whom Henry
Thornton, James Stephen (his brother-in-law), Thomas Babing-
ton, and Zachary Macaulay were prominent. His chief correspondents were Dr. Milner (Dean of Carlisle), Lord Muncaster,
Sir Charles Middleton, Rev. John Newton, and Hannah More.
With these and other members of the Abolitionist Society he
was in constant touch; and their zeal for social reform and for
the evangelical creed (which led to his Clapham circle being
styled the " Clapham Sect") led to great results. In the religious
sphere Wilberforce and his friends were largely instrumental in
founding the Church Missionary Society (1798) and the Bible

---

[1] Pitt MSS., 310. See " Life of Wilberforce," i, 305, 307, 323.

Society (1803). Their efforts on behalf of the poor and the mitigation of the barbarous penal code (a matter ever associated with the name of Romilly) were also to bear good fruit. For the present all their efforts against the Slave Trade seemed to be in vain. It was pressed on feverishly in the year 1792. Between 5th January and 4th May of that year there sailed from London 8 slave ships, from Bristol 11, from Liverpool 39. The total tonnage was 11,195 tons. Another official return among the Pitt Papers (No. 310) gives the following numbers of slaves taken in British ships from West Africa to the West Indies in the years 1789 to 1795 (the figures for 1790 are wanting):

YEAR.	SLAVES TAKEN.	DIED ON THE VOYAGE.
1789	11,014	1,053
1791	15,108	1,397
1792	26,971	2,468
1793	11,720	869
1794	14,611	394
1795	7,157	224
Total	86,581	6,405

These figures suggest a reason for the falling off of interest in the question after 1792. The trade seemed to be falling off; and the mortality at sea declined as the cargo was less closely packed. This, however, was but a poor argument for not abolishing a trade which was inherently cruel and might revive with the return of peace. In 1794 the Commons seemed friendly to abolition. Pitt, Fox, Whitbread, and other friends of the cause pleaded successfully on behalf of Wilberforce's Bill of the previous year. Once more, however, the influence of the Duke of Clarence, Thurlow, and Lord Abingdon availed to defeat the proposal. Grenville also voted against it as being premature. The Lords proceeded to illustrate the sincerity of their desire for further information on the topic by shelving the whole inquiry.

A sense of despair now began to creep over many friends of the movement. If abolitionist motions could only just pass the Commons, to be at once rejected by the Lords, what hope was there for the slaves? Their cause was further overclouded by the sharp disagreement of Wilberforce and Pitt respecting the war with France. As we shall see in a later chapter, Pitt and the majority of his supporters, together with the Old Whigs, belived that the war must go on until a solid peace could be obtained. Wilberforce and many of the abolitionists thought otherwise. During the latter part of the year 1794 and the first weeks of 1795 the two friends were scarcely on speaking terms; but even during that sad time Pitt wrote to Wilberforce (26th December 1794): "Nothing has happened to add either to my hopes or fears respecting the Slave Question with a view to the issue of it in the next session, but I think the turn things take in France may be favourable to the ultimate abolition." Pitt spoke powerfully against Dundas's amendment in favour of gradual abolition at some time after the conclusion of the war; but these procrastinating tactics carried the day by 78 to 61 (26th February 1795).

In the following year matters at first seemed more hopeful. Twice did Pitt and Wilberforce beat the supporters of the trade by fair majorities; but on the third reading of the Abolition Bill it was lost by four votes. Wilberforce noted indignantly that enough of its supporters were at the Opera to have turned the scale. The same apathy characterized the session of 1797, when the mutinies in the fleet and the sharp financial crisis told heavily against a measure certain to entail some losses in shipping and colonial circles.. At this time Pitt seems to have lost heart in the matter. This appeared in his attitude towards a plausible but insidious proposal, that the Governors of Colonies should be directed to recommend the local Assemblies to adopt measures which would improve the lot of the negroes and thus prepare the way for the abolition of the Slave Trade. Than this nothing could be more futile ; for the Governors and Assemblies were known to desire the continuance of the trade. Yet Pitt urged Wilberforce to accept the motion if it were modified; but, on Wilberforce refusing, he "stood stiffly by him." They were beaten by a majority of thirty-six—a proof that the House wished to postpone abolition to the distant future.[1]

The negotiations for peace with France, which went on at Lille during the summer of that year, offered an opportunity for

----

[1] "Life of Wilberforce," ii, 196; Clarkson, op. cit., ii, 475.

including a mutual guarantee of the two Powers that they would abolish the Slave Trade. Pitt seems to have disapproved of introducing this question into the discussions, either from a fear of complicating them, or from a belief that it would be treated better after the conclusion of peace.[1] His reluctance was misconstrued by Wilberforce, who sent him the following letter:

Hull, August 1, 1797.[2]

. . . I am afraid the negotiation is not in such a state as to render the idea I started of negotiating unconditionally for the abolition of the Slave Trade a practical question very necessary to be just now discussed. But if the negotiation should wear a more promising aspect, let me beg you seriously to weigh the matter. Dundas is friendly to the notion, as indeed I must do him, and myself too, the justice to say that I believe he would. Grenville ought to be so, and all the rest except Lord Liverpool are either neutral or friendly. I must honestly say, I never was so much hurt since I knew you as at your not receiving and encouraging this proposal, which even Lord Liverpool himself ought to have approved on the ground on which he used to oppose.[3] Do, my dear Pitt, I entreat you reconsider the matter. I am persuaded of your zeal in this cause, when, amidst the multitude of matters which force themselves on you more pressingly, it can obtain a hearing; but I regret that you have so been drawn off from it. Indeed regret is a very poor term to express what I feel on this subject. Excuse this, from the fulness of my heart, which I have often kept down with difficulty and grief.

My dear Pitt let me intreat you, as I see another bishop is dead, to consider well whom you appoint. I am persuaded that if the clergy could be brought to know and to do their duty, both the religious and civil state of this country would receive a principle of life.

The rupture of the Lille negotiation by the French falsified these hopes and served to justify Pitt for not weighting it with a contentious proposal. But for the present at least, he had lost hope in the cause. It is true that he always spoke strongly on its behalf during the ensuing efforts put forth by Wilberforce.[4] But the buoyancy of his belief was gone, and some even of his friends accused him of apathy.[5] This is probably unjust. A

---

[1] See "Life of Wilberforce" (ii, 224) for an accusation against Pitt and the Government in this matter.

[2] Pitt MSS., 189.

[3] Lord Liverpool (as Mr. Jenkinson) had opposed on the ground that France, etc., would take up the trade if we let it fall.

[4] Clarkson, *op. cit.*, ii, 485.

[5] Letter of James Stephen (June 1797) in "Life of Wilberforce," ii, 225.

man may believe firmly in a measure, and yet be convinced that it cannot pass under present conditions. In that case he will do his best, but his efforts will be those of an overburdened horse unable to master the load.

More than once he annoyed Wilberforce by preventing a useless discussion of the question.[1] Insinuations of insincerity were therefore hurled at Pitt. Indeed they seem to have gained wide credence. We find his young admirer, Canning, writing at Brooksby, near Leicester, on 15th December 1799, that very many friends doubted whether he now desired to carry abolition, while some even commended his prudence in doing less than he professed in the matter. Canning found it far from easy to eradicate this notion from the minds of his hosts, the Ellises, by informing them of the object of a secret mission to the West Indies then undertaken by Smith.[2]

It may be well to postpone to a later chapter the question of Pitt's attitude towards abolition in his second Ministry, that of 1804-6. But we may notice here certain criticisms which apply mainly, of course, to the years 1788-1800. He has been censured for not making abolition a Cabinet question.[3] But how could he do so when the majority of Ministers opposed it? For a short time only the Duke of Richmond and he favoured abolition. The substitution of Grenville for Sydney strengthened his hands; but even then he was in a minority in the Cabinet on this question. Further, the House of Lords consistently, and by increasing majorities, scouted the measure; and the House of Commons, even under the spell of Pitt's eloquence, refused to decree immediate abolition, and that, too, before the shadow of the great war shrouded the whole subject in disastrous eclipse. After the last year of peace of Pitt's ministerial career, other considerations came uppermost. The need of keeping up the mercantile marine, both as a source of wealth and as a nursery for the royal navy, cooled the zeal of many friends of the movement. Windham opposed it in a manner that earned him the title of Macchiavelli. Others also fell away; and even the eloquence of young Canning on its behalf did not make up for defections. The better class of West India planters and mer-

---

[1] As in June 1798. See "Life of Wilberforce," ii, 286.
[2] For this letter see "Pitt and Napoleon Miscellanies."
[3] Lecky, v, 64-6; J. L. le B. Hammond, "Fox," 60.

chants tacitly agreed to the limitation of the Slave Trade; and
with this prospect in view many friends of the cause relaxed
their efforts.

Further, when the King, a decided majority both in the Cabinet
and in the House of Lords, and a wavering majority in the Commons, were unchangeably opposed to immediate abolition, what
could a Minister do? The ordinary course of conduct, resignation, would have availed nothing. As nearly all the Ministerial
bench disliked the proposal, no coherent Cabinet could have
been formed. True, a Ministry composed of Pitt, Grenville,
Fox, Burke, Sheridan, and Wilberforce might perhaps have
forced the measure through the Commons (to see it fail in the
Lords); but so monstrous a coalition could scarcely have seen
the light; certainly it could not have lived amid the storms of
the war. Besides, the first duty of a Minister after 1792 was to
secure for his country the boon of a solid peace. As we shall
see, that was ever Pitt's aim; and grief at seeing it constantly
elude his grasp finally cost him his life. Further, the assumption that he could have coerced the members of his Cabinet
because they differed from him on this question is untenable.
He was able to secure the retirement of Sydney because he was
not highly efficient, and of Thurlow on the ground of con-
tumacy. But to compel useful and almost necessary Ministers
like Dundas or Camden to retire, when the majority in both
Houses agreed with them, would have set at defiance all the
traditions of parliamentary life.

The criticisms noticed above are based on the assumption
that Pitt was all-powerful and could bend the Cabinet and Parliament to his will. This is an exaggeration. Where, as in the
case of pocket boroughs and the Slave Trade, members felt their
interests at stake, they somnolently resisted the charms of his
oratory and trooped into the opposite lobby. The British people
is slow to realize its responsibilities, but in the end it responds
to them; and in these years of defeat at Westminster the efforts
of Clarkson, Granville Sharp, and others spread abroad convictions which were to assure an ultimate triumph.

The failure of Pitt to carry the abolition of the Slave Trade
or materially to improve the condition of the negroes was to
have a sinister influence on our position in the West Indies.
While the slave owners and shippers and their friends at Westminster refused to budge an inch, the French Jacobins eagerly

rushed forward and proclaimed the equality of all mankind. Therefore early in the course of the Great War the slaves rallied to the tricolour; and Toussaint l'Ouverture, the ablest of negro leaders, enthusiastically marshalled their levies in Hayti for the overthrow of British rule. In a later chapter we shall trace the disastrous sequel. Colonel (afterwards Sir John) Moore noted in his Diary that the negroes were for the most part fanatical for liberty; and, after committing deeds of desperation in its name, died defiantly with the cry *Vive la République* on their lips.[1] Here we touch on one of the chief causes for the frightful waste of British troops in the West Indies. With discontent rife in our own colonies, the struggle against the blacks, especially in Hayti, placed on our men a strain unendurable in that pestilential climate. The Hon. J. W. Fortescue, the historian of the British Army, estimates its total losses in the West Indies during the war of 1793-1802 as not far short of 100,000 men. Whatever the total may be, it is certain that at least half of that woeful sacrifice resulted from the crass stupidity and brutal selfishness displayed by mercantile and colonial circles on this question.

In the last four chapters we have taken a survey of questions of great interest in British and colonial history, and have therefore interrupted the story of Pitt's dealings with continental affairs. It is time now to recur to events of world-wide import, namely, the ambitious schemes of the Sovereigns of the East and the great popular upheaval in France.

[1] " Diary of Sir John Moore," i, 234.

CHAPTER XXI

THE SCHEMES OF CATHARINE II

I came to Russia poor; but I will not die in debt to the Empire; for I shall leave her the Crimea and Poland as my portion.—CATHARINE II.

IN the spring of the year 1787 the ablest potentate in Europe set out on a State progress to the newly annexed provinces in the South of her Empire. It was carried out with an energy and splendour which illustrated the union of the forethought of the West with the barbaric splendour of the East. A great flotilla of galleys bore the Sovereign, her chief courtiers, the ambassadors of Great Britain, Austria, and France, and numerous attendants down the course of the Dnieper to the city of Kherson near its mouth. By day the banks were fringed with throngs of the peasants of Little Russia, brought up to order, while ever and anon the shouts of Cossacks, Calmucks, and Circassians impressed the beholders with a sense of the boundless resources of that realm. By night the welkin flared with illuminations; and the extent of the resting-places, which had arisen like exhalations at the bidding of her favourite, Prince Potemkin, promised the speedy inroad of civilization into the lands over which the Turk still held sway. In truth, far more impressive to the mind's eye was the imperious will of which these marvels were the manifestation, the will of Catharine II.[1]

At her invitation there joined her near Potemkin's creation, the city of Ekaterinoslav, another monarch of romantic and adventurous character. Joseph II of Austria, head of the Holy

[1] It has been said that the journey was undertaken partly with the view of seeing whether Potemkin had honestly used the money given him for the warlike preparations in the South; and that he hastily did his utmost to impress the Czarina favourably. This last is of course highly probable; but, as we shall see presently, the journey had been projected in 1785. Moreover, Potemkin, while improvising crowds of peasants, could not improvise the warships launched at Kherson.

Roman Empire, now reluctantly turned towards the eastern conquests to which she had long beckoned him. Together they proceeded on the progress southwards to Kherson, which they entered under a triumphal arch bearing the inscription in Greek, "The way to Byzantium." A still more impressive proof of the activity of her masterful favourite awaited them. Potemkin had pushed on the work of the new dockyard at Kherson; and as a result they witnessed the launch of three warships. The largest, of 80 guns, was christened by Catharine herself, "Joseph II."[1]

Thence the imperial procession wended its way to the muchprized acquisition, the Crimea. In that Tartar Khanate the fertile brain and forceful personality of Potemkin had wrought wonders. It was but four years since the Empress, in her joy at the annexation of that vantage-ground, had pointed on the map to the little township of Akhtiar, re-named it Sevastopol, and ordered the construction of a dockyard and navy. Now, in June 1787, as the allied sovereigns topped the hills which command that port, the Hapsburg ruler uttered a cry of surprise and admiration. For there below lay a squadron of warships, ready, as it seemed, to set sail and plant the cross on the dome of St. Sophia at Constantinople.

Hitherto Joseph II had not shown the amount of zeal befitting an ally and an admirer. True, he had not openly belied the terms of the compact of the year 1781, which had been his sheet-anchor amid the storms of his reign. But that alliance had been the prelude to vast schemes productive at once of longing and distrust. They aimed at nothing less than the partition of the Ottoman Empire in Europe. The glorious days of Prince Eugène were to be recalled, and, on the expulsion of the Tartar horde over the Bosphorus, Austria was to acquire the Turkish lands which that warrior had gained for her by the Peace of Passarowitz (1718), namely, the Banat of Temesvar, the northern half of Servia, and the districts of Wallachia as far as the River Aluta. The only direct gain to Catharine was to be the Tartar territory north of the Black Sea as far as the Dniester. As for Moldavia and Wallachia, they were to form an independent kingdom under a Christian Prince (a plan finally realized in 1858); and the remainder of the Balkan Pen-

---

[1] "F. O.," Russia, 15. Fitzherbert to Carmarthen, 3rd May 1787. Fitzherbert accompanied the Empress throughout this tour. His letters are of high interest.

I   I I

insula was to be ruled by the favourite grandson of the Empress, Prince Constantine.

Outwardly this partition seemed to offer a fair share to Austria. But it was soon clear that the grasping genius of Muscovy would transform the nominally independent kingdoms of Constantinople and Roumania into feudatories and bar to Austria the way to the Lower Danube, the Aegean, and the Lower Adriatic. Not yet were the lessons of the first partition of Poland forgotten at Vienna.[1] Then, too, the Austro-Russian compact had but slightly advanced the interests of Joseph II in Germany. Catharine had done little to further his pet scheme of the Belgic-Bavarian Exchange; and, apart from feminine fumings, she had not seriously counteracted the formation of the League of German Princes whereby Frederick the Great had thwarted that almost revolutionary proposal (1785). Probably this accounts for the reluctance of Joseph to give rein to the southward impulses of the Czarina in that year. At its close Sir Robert Murray Keith, British Ambassador at Vienna, reported that the Czarina's tour to Kherson was postponed, and four days later he recorded a remarkable conversation in the course of which the Emperor revealed his dislike of the dangerous schemes then mooted for the partition of the Turkish Empire. " I can tell you for certain," he said, " *que si jamais tous les coquins se rompent avec l'Empire Ottoman*, France is firmly determined to strike a bold stroke by making herself mistress of Egypt. This I know with certainty from more quarters than one; and M. Tott himself told me at Paris that he had travelled through all Egypt by order of his Court to explore that country in a military light and to lay down a plan for the conquest of it." [2]

In these words we have probably the reason for the deferring of the Russian schemes against Turkey. They are also noteworthy, as they must have tended to deepen the distrust which Pitt and Carmarthen felt for France. Her chief Minister, Vergennes, figured as the protector of Turkey against Russia, recalling thereby the policy of Louis XV's reign, which in 1739 availed to tear away from Austria the conquests of Prince Eugène and restore them to the Sublime Porte. But under this show of championship there seems to have lain an alternative policy, that of furthering the partition of Turkey, provided that

[1] See Sorel, " La Question d'Orient," 300 *et seq.*

[2] " F. O.," Austria, 11. Keith to Carmarthen, 3rd and 7th December 1785.

France acquired Egypt, and some other vantage posts in the Levant. As we have already seen, France was busy in Egypt and the Orient with schemes which probably would have startled the world had she rivetted her hold on the Dutch Netherlands in the year 1787.

The accession of the facile and dissolute Frederick William to the Prussian throne in 1786, and the preoccupation of England and France in the Dutch crisis which followed, now left Joseph free to comply with the request of the Czarina that he would join her in the journey to the Crimea. After long hesitations he reluctantly gave his assent. His aged Chancellor, Prince Kaunitz, the champion of the connection with Russia and France, advised him to direct the imperial conferences towards the Bavarian Exchange and the dissolution of the Fürstenbund. Catharine willed otherwise. Under her influence the views of Joseph underwent a notable orientation. He came back to Vienna virtually pledged to a war for the partition of Turkey.

The change in Joseph's policy was a tribute to the potency of the Czarina's will. In her personality, as we have already seen, there were singular powers of fascination and command. Her vivacity and charm, varied by moods of petulance or fury, made up a character feminine in its impulsiveness and of masculine strength. The erstwhile Princess of Anhalt-Zerbst, who by a series of audacious intrigues, and probably by the murder of her consort Peter III, had become the greatest autocrat of the century, still retained the intellectual freshness of youth. Her character and career present a series of bizarre contrasts. The poverty of her upbringing, the dissolute adventures of her early life, and the outrageous crimes of her womanhood would have utterly tainted a personality less remarkable and attractive. But in the loose society of St. Petersburg it had long been customary to gloze over lapses of virtue by easy descriptions, like that which the stately rhetoric of Burke applied to the chivalry of Versailles, that "vice itself lost half its evil by losing all its grossness."

Certainly the intellectual keenness and social witcheries of the sorceress threw a charm over her rout. French and German philosophers praised her learning and wit, but innate shrewdness kept her from more than a passing dalliance with the unsettling theories which were to work havoc in France. Here as in her amours she observed some measure of worldly prudence;

so that no favourite could count on a long reign of pillage. Thus, whether by whim or by design, she kept devotion and hope ever on the stretch; and one might almost apply to her, even at the age of fifty-nine, Shakespeare's description of Cleopatra:

> Age cannot wither her, nor custom stale
> Her infinite variety; other women cloy
> The appetites they feed; but she makes hungry
> Where most she satisfies.

Like the " serpent of old Nile," Catharine had many weaknesses; and they might have worked her ruin in the more strenuous age which followed; but fortune brought her to the front at a time when Frederick the Great desired the friendship of Russia, and when Hapsburg policy vacillated between the conservatism of Maria Theresa and the viewiness of her son Joseph. Thus the Czarina could work her will on the decaying Powers, Turkey and Poland, and raised the prestige of her Empire to unimagined heights.

A few shrewd observers were not dazzled by this splendour. Sir James Harris, who went as British envoy to Russia in 1778 to cultivate the friendship, and if possible the alliance, of Catharine, rightly probed the inner weakness of her position. It lay in the suddenness of her rise, the barbarousness of her people, the unblushing peculations of Ministers and officials, and the shiftiness of Muscovite policy. This last defect he traced to the peculiarities of the Empress herself, which he thus summed up: " She has a masculine force of mind, obstinacy in adhering to a plan, and intrepidity in the execution of it; but she wants the more manly virtues of deliberation, forbearance in prosperity, and accuracy of judgment, while she possesses in a high degree the weaknesses vulgarly attributed to her sex—love of flattery and its inseparable companion, vanity; [and] an inattention to unpleasant but salutary advice." Six years later he sharpened his criticism and described her as led by her passions, not by reason and argument; her prejudices, though easily formed, were immovable; her good opinion was liable to constant fluctuations and whims; and her resolves might carry her to any lengths.[1] Such, too, was the opinion of the Comte de Ségur, the French ambassador, who wrote about the Turkish schemes renewed in 1787: " We are so accustomed to see Russia throw herself offhand into

---

[1] " Malmesbury Diaries," i, 204, 534.

the most risky affairs, and Fortune has so persistently helped her, that there is no accounting for the actions of this Power on the rules of a scientific policy." [1]

This peculiarity was far from repelling Joseph II. While pluming himself on the application of reason to politics, that crowned philosopher forgot to take counsel of her twin-sister, prudence. On his polyglot Empire, which already felt the first stirrings of the principle of nationality, he imposed central-izing laws, agrarian, social, and religious, which speedily aroused the hostility of those whom he meant to uplift. Along with all this he pushed on schemes which unsettled Germany, Belgium, and Poland; and now, as if all this were not enough, he was drawn into the vortex of the Turkish enterprises of Catharine.

It is a mistake to assume that Joseph had no practical aims in view. He hoped to acquire from Turkey territories which would open up trade on the Adriatic and the Lower Danube, and he counted on strengthening the Russian alliance to which he trusted for the furtherance of his aims in Germany and Belgium. Yet rarely has a monarch formed a resolution more fraught with peril. In truth it resulted from the mastery gained by an abler and more determined nature over one that was generous but ill-compacted, daring but unsteady. Had the Emperor surveyed the situation with care, he must have seen that it favoured Catharine rather than himself. She was beset by no troubles at home; while his lands, especially the *Pays Bas*, heaved with disloyal excitement. She had appeased the Turcophile feelings of France by granting a favourable com-mercial treaty; and Montmorin, the successor of Vergennes, was weaker in himself and less able to support the Sultan. In short, Catharine had her hands free, while Joseph had them full. [2]

The alliance between Russia and Poland at this time acquired new vitality. During her triumphal tour Catharine received the homage of her former lover, Stanislaus, King of Poland, and received from him the promise of the help of 100,000 Polish troops for the Turkish war, and "likewise for any other contest" —a phrase aimed against Prussia, if she dared to intervene. The value of the promise soon became open to doubt. The monarch

[1] Wazilewski, "Le Roman d'une Impératrice," 418.

[2] Keith reported on 30th August 1787 ("F. O.," Austria, 14) that the Emperor "saw this storm coming with deep regret," and that the ferment in his Belgian lands would prevent his taking action against Turkey.

in Poland had long been a figure-head, while the real power lay
with the powerful and ambitious nobility, which, under the lead
of the Czartoryski and Potocki families, ever chafed at Muscovite
ascendancy, and now declined to help Catharine in humbling
their natural ally, the Sultan. In 1790 their views were to prevail; but, for the present, the resources of Poland seemed at her
beck and call.

The prospects of Catharine therefore were brilliant in the
extreme. But for once Fortune played her false. After the
departure of the Emperor from the Crimea, and while she still
fondly surveyed the warlike preparations at its new dockyard,
there came news of the alarming prospects for the harvest in
Russia. "The Empress," wrote Fitzherbert on 24th July, "almost
immediately after leaving the Crimea fell under a great and
visible depression of spirits, accompanied at times with violent
gusts of ill humour; and in this state remained with very little
intermission till our arrival here [Czarko-zelo]." He ascribed
these moody humours to the failure of the corn crop, which
necessitated the immediate purchase of 5,000,000 roubles' worth
of foreign grain, and the distribution of Potemkin's army in
widespread cantonments.

To wage a great campaign while bread stood at famine prices
was impossible. In this predicament the Empress decided to
hide her retirement by a parade of diplomatic bluster. She despatched to Constantinople a special envoy, Bulgakoff, to lay
claim to the Principality of Georgia, and to submit this and
other matters in dispute to the mediation of France and Austria. The move was dexterous; but in such a case the success
of a game of bluff depends on the adversary not perceiving the
weakness of which it is the screen. Now, the Sublime Porte,
though usually inert, divined the secret, and resolved to withstand these endless affronts. During thirteen years orthodox
Moslems had writhed under the humiliations of the Treaty of
Kainardji (1774), which acknowledged the complete independence of the Tartar Khans of the Crimea and the Kuban valley,
and in vague terms admitted the Czarina to be the protectress
of the Christian subjects of the Porte. In 1783, thanks to
Austrian support, Catharine seized the Crimea; and now she
laid claim to Georgia. The cup of humiliation was full; and the
pride of Moslems scorned to drink it.

The despatches of Sir Robert Ainslie, British ambassador at

Constantinople, show clearly enough the motives that prompted that Government to strike an unexpected blow. On 25th June 1787 he reported to Carmarthen that the Porte looked on the journey of the Czarina and her warlike preparations as designed to wear out the patience and the resources of the Turks, who aleady were said to have 240,000 men ready near the Danube, and others in Asia. If, he added, she did not explain her present conduct, "I am afraid they will commence hostilities," and "strike a home blow in the Crimea." On 10th July he stated that there could be no solid peace so long as Russia held the Crimea in defiance of the Treaty of Kainardji. "The honour of the Sultan, the security of this Empire, the interest of the Mahometan religion, and those [sic] of justice all require that . . . the independence of the Crimea should be re-established. It is true, the Porte agreed to the cession; but that act, torn from her weakness, was involuntary and unjust. In short, it can only be binding until a good opportunity offers to cancel its effect. This, my Lord, seems the opinion of the Cabinet and the motive of their extensive preparations, but they are diffident of success and afraid to attack unless Russia herself furnishes pretext." He adds that the Turkish Ministers believed Bulga-koff's mission to be designed to "spin out the summer"; but that the Turkish levies could scarcely be kept together.[1]

As for the temporizing offers of mediation from France and Austria, the Porte would have none of them, and refused to accept any in which Great Britain had no share. The Grand Vizier cherished the hope that Austria and Russia were not really united by treaty, and seemed to desire, rather than to avoid, a rupture. On 30th July the Reis Effendi asked our ambassador what England would do in case of a Russo-Turkish War. Ainslie replied that she would "keep strict neutrality," and strongly urged the need of peace. "Never will we purchase peace on the dishonourable terms held out by Russia," replied the Turkish Minister, and he added with oriental subtlety that, unless she gave way, war must come "before many months are elapsed." Ainslie thought that this portended war in the spring of 1788.[2]

But on 16th August the Sultan struck swiftly and hard. Doubtless he had heard news of the famine in Russia and the

---

[1] "F. O.," Turkey, 8.
[2] Ibid. Ainslie to Carmarthen, 9th August 1787.

dispersion of Potemkin's forces. It was clear that for a time the
would-be aggressor was reduced to the defensive. Was it not
well, then, to deliver the blow rather than wait for it to fall in the
next year, and perhaps from both Austria and Russia? True,
the Turks were not ready—they never were so. But their recent
successes over the Mameluke Beys in Egypt and the rebellious
Mahmoud Pacha in Albania emboldened them to take a step
which completely surprised all the Cabinets of Europe. On
16th August, after a long conference with the Grand Vizier,
Bulgakoff and five members of his suite were apprehended and
marched off to the Seven Towers, there to be kept in close
custody. This was the Turkish way of declaring war to the
knife. The Porte defended it on the ground of outrages to its
flag at Kinburn and Sevastopol;[1] but the incident added rancour to the hatred of Catharine, and she swore to glut her revenge
upon the insolent infidels. Her rage was all the greater because
for once she was outwitted. Fitzherbert, on hearing of the novel
declaration of war by the Turks, stated to Carmarthen[2] that it
must have upset all her calculations, for he knew that the
blustering language used by Bulgakoff " was in fact intended to
produce the contrary effect." [3]

These events were destined potently to influence the career of
Pitt. In one respect they affect his reputation; for Catharine in
her fury accused him of inciting the Turks to attack her.[4] The
charge was not unnatural. She had long shown her spleen
against England in bitter words and hostile deeds. More than
once she thrust aside Pitt's overtures for an alliance; and she
rejected his proposals for a commercial treaty while she granted
that boon to France (January 1787). Further, the outbreak of
war in the East came very opportunely for Great Britain and
Prussia at the crisis of the Dutch embroglio and enabled the
Court of Berlin confidently to launch its troops against the

[1] " F. O.," Turkey, 8. Ainslie to Carmarthen, 17th August 1787.
[2] " F. O.," Russia, 15. Despatch of 22nd September. Fitzherbert was
then coming home ill. His place was filled by Fraser.
[3] In view of these facts I cannot agree with the statement of Prof. Lodge
(" Camb. Mod. Hist.," viii, 316) that the action of the Turks "was dictated
by passion rather than by policy." It seems to me a skilful move, especially
as they already had reason to hope for help from Prussia and Sweden.
Häusser (i, 225) wrongly terms it a " desperate resolve."
[4] " F. O.," Russia, 15. Fraser to Carmarthen, 5th October 1787.

Patriots in Holland. The tilt given from Constantinople to the delicately poised kaleidoscope of diplomacy had startling results. The mobile Powers—Russia, Austria, and France—were fixed fast, while the hitherto stationary States, Prussia and England, were set free for swift action.

Nevertheless it is untrue that the tilt came from Pitt and Carmarthen. They still clung to the traditional British policy of befriending Russia, which Fox had enthusiastically supported. Our Government instructed Fraser at St. Petersburg to express regret at the outbreak of war and to offer, conjointly with Prussia, our good services for the restoration of peace. Pitt also informed Vorontzoff, Russian ambassador in London, of his desire for a good understanding with Russia, and stated that he would not oppose acquisitions of Turkish territory. All the evidence tends to prove that he strove to prevent hostilities, which must upset the existing order in the East and probably end in a general war. As the concern of Prussia was equally great (it being certain by the end of 1787 that Austria would join in the war) the two Protestant Powers drew together for joint action though not, as yet, for actual alliance.[1]

In fact, we find here the reason of the coyness of Pitt in framing that compact. He still preferred to have Russia, rather than Prussia, as an ally. But his advances to Catharine ended with the impossible retort that he must recall Ainslie from Constantinople. Nevertheless it was not till the middle of March 1788 that Pitt took a step displeasing to her by forbidding her agents to hire Russian transports in England.[2] The Empress showed her annoyance at these stricts notions of neutrality by publicly receiving the famous American privateer, Paul Jones.[3]

Pitt's attitude towards Austria was at first equally friendly. On 14th September 1787 Carmarthen sent to Vienna assurances that the Russo-Turkish War would make no difference to the friendship of George III for Austria, and that we should main-

---

[1] See Ewart's Memorandum to Pitt in "Dropmore P.," ii, 44-9 for an admirable survey of events; also Wittichen, 130-5, and Häusser, i, 223-5.

The surprise of Prussian statesmen at the outbreak of war seems quite sincere; and evidence is strongly against the statement of Sorel ("L'Europe et la Rév. franç.," i, p. 524) that Hertzberg egged on the Turks, and later on Sweden, to war.

[2] "F. O.," Russia, 15. Carmarthen to Fraser, 18th March 1788.

[3] *Ibid.* Fraser to Carmarthen, 9th May.

tain " the determined system of this country to contribute as far as possible to the continuance of the public tranquillity, or to its speedy restoration if unhappily it should be interrupted." By these and other proposals Pitt and Carmarthen vainly sought to detach Austria from Russia, and also to conjure away the spectre of a Triple Alliance between France, Russia, and Austria, which long haunted the courts of Whitehall. Early in 1788, that ghost was laid by the Austrian attack upon the Turks, which France had striven to avert, and Pitt felt free to accept the proffered alliance of Prussia which, as we saw in Chapter XVI, finally came about in August 1788.[1]

The campaign of that year is devoid of interest. Scarcity of bread on the Russian side and the usual unpreparedness of the Turks clogged the operations, which led to a sharp conflict only at one point. The fortress of Kinburn, recently acquired by the Russians, commanded the estuary formed by the converging Rivers Dnieper and Bug. It stood opposite the Turkish fortress, Oczakoff, which was deemed the chief bulwark of the Ottomans in the East. Early in October 1788 they made an attempt to seize Kinburn as a prelude to the hoped-for conquest of the Crimea. But in that fortress was a wizened little veteran, who ate bread with the soldiers, startled them at dawn by his cock crows, and summarized his ideas on tactics by the inspiriting words: " At them with the cold steel." The personality of Suvóroff was worth an army corps, for it was bound up with triumph. He now waited within the walls of Kinburn until the Turkish fleet landed 5,000 choice Janissaries below the town. Then by a furious sally, flanked by a charge of ten squadrons of horse on the wings, he broke up that fanatical band and drove it into the sea. Only 700 Turks survived. The affair was not of the first importance, but it heartened the Russians for the greater enterprises of the next year.

Meanwhile Catharine, fuming at the sorry beginning of her war of conquest, upbraided her ally with his tardiness in coming to her help. But Joseph was in a difficult situation. The ferment in the Netherlands and Hungary was increasing. The close union of England and Prussia in Dutch affairs caused him much concern; and, as we have seen in Chapter XIV, the French

---

[1] " F. O.," Austria, 14. On 23rd September Ewart reported that Spain had " positively declined the pressing overtures of France to enter into a Quadruple Alliance with her and the two Imperial Courts" (" F. O.," Prussia, 14).

Ministry was fain to huddle up the disputes in Holland, partly in order to be free to support the Sultan. Montmorin resolved to thwart the partition of the Turkish Empire and brought pressure to bear upon Kaunitz, who ever looked askance on oriental adventures.[1] Nevertheless, by the month of November Joseph had decided on war. The Austrians made a discreditable attempt to surprise Belgrade; and in February 1788 war was declared.

The ensuing campaign was fertile in surprises. As often happens, the Allies waited for one another to start the campaign, and thus lost the early part of the summer. The Russians, owing to the armament of the Swedes and the incapacity of Potemkin, did far less than was expected; and the brunt of the Ottoman onset finally fell upon the Austrians. Joseph was compelled to fall back towards Temesvar on the night of 20th September; and a panic seized the Imperialists. That motley host, mistaking the shouts of its diverse races for the war cry of the Turks, fired wildly upon the supposed pursuers; and the Ottomans, hearing the babel din, finally pressed on the rout and captured 4,000 men and a large part of the artillery and stores. Pestilence completed the work begun by the Moslems; and thus it came about that the efforts of 200,000 Austrians effected nothing more than the surrender of Chotzim and three other frontier strongholds of the second rank. The disgrace dimmed the lustre of their arms, undermined the health of the Emperor, and gave new heart to Hertzberg and the numerous enemies of the Hapsburg realm.

The chief cause of this ignominious failure is ultimately traceable to an influence that had long been at work far away, namely, the restless ambition of Gustavus III of Sweden. In the summer of the year 1788 that monarch suddenly drew the sword against Catharine, and from the vantage ground of his Finnish province marched towards St. Petersburg. This threatening move compelled the Empress to recall part of her forces, condemned the rest of them to the defensive, and thus exposed the Austrians to the spirited attack above described.

[1] "F. O.," Austria, 14. Keith to Carmarthen, 6th October 1787. On 10th October he reported that France would acquiesce in Joseph's eastern policy if he would help her against England and Prussia in the Dutch dispute. On 24th October he stated that Austria refused to do so. On 14th November Joseph II informed him privately that he must make war on Turkey.

Seeing that Pitt was held to be ultimately responsible for these events, we must pause here to sketch the character and career of Gustavus III. Of the three monarchs dealt with in this chapter he is not the least interesting. Rivalling Catharine in intellectual keenness and moody waywardness, he excelled her in generosity, virtue, and chivalry. There is in him the strain of romance which refines the schemes, and adds pathos to the failures, of Joseph II; but the Swede excelled the Hapsburg alike in grit, fighting power, charm, and versatility. He was a bundle of startling opposites. Slight of figure, naturally delicate and pensive, he threw himself eagerly into feats of daring and hardihood. By turns poet and humourist, playwright and warrior, devout but an incorrigible intriguer, he lured, enthralled, browbeat, or outwitted the Swedish people as no one had done since the days of Charles XII. In truth he seemed a re-incarnation of that ill-starred ruler, especially in his power of calling forth the utmost from his people, and leading them on to feats beyond their strength. From the midsummer day of 1771 on which the young King opened his Estates with a speech from the throne, it was clear that his iron will and captivating address might regain for the Crown the power torn from it some years before by the Caps, the faction of the opposing nobles and burghers. Fourteen months later Gustavus struck his blow. Despite the Russian gold poured in for the support of the Caps, the King gained the people and the army to his side, locked the recalcitrant Senate in their Chamber, overthrew the usurped authority of the Riksdag, and thenceforth governed in the interests of his people. It was characteristic of him that he prefaced his *coup d'état* by the first performance of a Swedish opera, the libretto of which he had himself revised.[1]

Thenceforth " the royal charmer" governed at will, and Sweden regained much of her old prestige. The traditional alliance with France was renewed; and for a time the jealous Catharine seemed to acquiesce in the new order of things at Stockholm. In reality she never ceased to intrigue there, as also at Warsaw, seeking to recall the days of schism and weakness. The extravagance of Gustavus played into her hands. Little by little the factions regained lost ground; the Riksdag of 1786 threw out all but one of the royal measures; and the King was fain to govern more absolutely.

---

[1] Nisbet Bain, "Gustavus III and his Contemporaries," ch. ix.

The Russo-Turkish War now gave him the chance for which his restless spirit longed, namely, to attempt to recover part at least of the trans-Baltic lands ceded to Russia, and to dissolve a secret Russo-Danish alliance which aimed at the overthrow of the present *régime* in Sweden. He therefore allied himself with the Sultan on condition of receiving a yearly subsidy of 1,000,000 piastres. He further sounded the Courts of Berlin, Warsaw, and Paris, but received no encouragement. At London, as we have seen, his overtures at Christmas 1787 were set aside. They were renewed in the spring of 1788, and received more attention, it being then the aim of Pitt to bring some of the secondary States into the projected Triple Alliance. But the ardent spirit of Gustavus far outleaped the mark. His demands for money were suspiciously large. "Sweden," so Carmarthen wrote to Harris on 20th June 1788, "has a most voracious appetite for subsidies, but from the enormous extravagance of her demand has put it out of our power to proceed further at present on that head." [1]

This was fortunate; for Gustavus was then preparing to throw down the gauntlet to Russia. Early in July he set sail for Helsingfors, and launched at Catharine a furious ultimatum, bidding her cede Carelia and Livonia to the Swedes, and restore the Crimea to the Sultan. On the receipt of that astonishing missive the imperial virago raged, wept, and swore by turns. The crisis was indeed serious. In and near St. Petersburg were only 6,000 troops.

Nevertheless she acted with her wonted vigour. She called up the Militia; and her fleet, commanded by Admiral Greig and officered largely by Britons, prepared to dispute with Gustavus the mastery of the Gulf of Finland. [2] In this it succeeded. It dealt the smaller naval force of the Swedes a severe check, and soon cooped it up in Sveaborg. Meanwhile the advance of the Swedes from their Finnish province on the Russian capital was stopped by a mutiny of the officers, which soon spread to the rank and file. The causes of this event are still obscure. The admirers of Gustavus ascribed it to the factiousness of nobles and the bribes of Catharine. The Swedish Opposition, and also Charles Keene, British envoy at Stockholm, explained it as the natural outcome of

---

[1] B.M. Add. MSS., 28063.
[2] Greig and the other Britons had long been in the Russian service. I cannot find that they were recalled.

the extravagance and ambition of the monarch who, not content with violating the constitution and ruining the finances of his realm, wantonly plunged it into a struggle for which he had not prepared. Consequently, when his ill-clad and ill-fed militia found that the Russian raids into Finland were a myth, and that the only enemies were royal ambition and famine, they at once thwarted the former by constituting the army as a " confederation," and declaring their resolve for peace. If there must be war with Russia, let it be declared legally by a freely elected Diet at Stockholm.[1] The Swedish crews at Sveaborg, where food and warlike munitions were alike wanting, partly joined in the movement; and the universality of the discontent, which compelled Gustavus to return helplessly to Stockholm, is perhaps sufficient proof that influences were at work more widespread than party spirit and more potent than foreign gold.

However the fact may be explained, it is certain that the Swedes, when almost within striking distance of the Russian capital, halted, sent offers of an armistice, and then retreated into Finland. Catharine was saved; but after the capture of Oczakoff from the Turks she vented her spleen in one of her icily brilliant *mots*: " As Mr. Pitt wishes to chase me from St. Petersburg, I hope he will allow me to take refuge at Constantinople."

It was natural for the Empress to suspect England and Prussia of complicity in the Swedish enterprise; for she herself in a similar case would have egged on Gustavus. But the evidence in the British archives proves that neither George III nor Frederick William, Pitt nor Hertzberg, had a hand in the matter. George III and Pitt loved peace because it was economical. Through the spring and summer they were trying to effect a pacification. On 16th May 1788 the Foreign Office sent off a despatch to Ainslie urging him to co-operate with Dietz, the Prussian Minister at the Porte, in order, if possible, to pave the way for a joint mediation of England and Prussia with a

---

[1] " F. O.," Sweden, 7. Keene on 26th August 1788 reported to Carmarthen the facts so far as he knew them, and also in a later "Account." His bias against the King is obvious, and leads me to discount his assertions, *e.g.*, that of 9th September, that the war with Russia was at an end, owing to the offer of peace to Catharine by the Swedish officers, and had become merely "a domestic quarrel between the King and nation." Doubtless it was for this and similar statements that Keene was recalled in December 1788, Liston taking his place.

view to a pacification in the East; but he was to beware of entering into other plans that the Court of Berlin might have in view, a hint against the ambitious scheme of exchanges now forming in Hertzberg's brain. On Swedish affairs the despatch continued thus: "The Swedish armament causes much speculation both in Russia and elsewhere: the avowed purpose is the necessity of having a respectable force in that Kingdom while Russia is fitting out so formidable a fleet."[1] From this and other signs it is clear that Pitt and Carmarthen, far from expecting war in the Baltic, were intent on plans for stopping it on the Danube and Black Sea.

As for Frederick William, he did not desire war in the North, because it must curtail his pleasures; and Hertzberg, because peace would leave him free to weave his plans more systematically. Ewart, our active and zealous envoy at Berlin, who knew Hertzberg thoroughly, informed Carmarthen on 19th June that Prussia was very cautious as to forming any connection' with Sweden.[2] Nine days later he reported that Gustavus had made an alliance with Turkey, but probably would not attack Catharine unless she sent a fleet from Cronstadt round to the Mediterranean. On 25th July, after referring to the Swedish declaration of war against Russia, he added that the Court of Stockholm hoped for the support of Prussia only so far as to keep Denmark quiet. As for himself, he had rebuked the Swedish envoy.[3]

In truth the action of Gustavus annoyed both England and Prussia. They expressed to him their disapproval of his conduct in strong terms. On 29th August Carmarthen wrote to Ewart censuring the action of Gustavus, but adding that the Allies must intervene to stop the war in the Baltic.[4] Pitt also, on hearing of the Danish armament, resolved to save Gustavus from utter ruin. On 1st September he wrote as follows to Grenville (not, be it noted, to Carmarthen): "We had before written to Berlin with power to Ewart to send an offer of our joint mediation if the King of Prussia agreed, and this seems now the more necessary. Our intervention may prevent his

---

[1] " F. O.," Turkey, 9. So, too, Lecky, v, 231.
[2] See, too, Frederick William's words on this topic in Dembinski, " Documents relatifs à l'histoire . . . de la Pologne (1788-91)," i, 21.
[3] " F. O.," Prussia, 13. See, too, " Dropmore P.," ii, 47.
[4] " F. O.," Prussia, 14.

[Gustavus] becoming totally insignificant, or dependent upon Russia, and it seems to me an essential point."[1] Eight days later Carmarthen assured the Prussian Court of his satisfaction that it would join in the proposed mediation.[2]

The crisis was indeed most urgent. Catharine was thinking far less of flitting to Constantinople than of ousting Gustavus from Stockholm. Her treaty with Denmark contained secret clauses which bound that Court to alliance with her in case of a Russo-Swedish war; and the young Prince Royal of Denmark, though by marriage a nephew to Gustavus, was only too eager for a campaign which promised to lead to the partition of the Swedish kingdom. The excellent navy of the Danes, and their possession of Norway, gave them great facilities for the invasion of the open country near the important city of Gothenburg; and, that once taken, they could easily master the South, and leave the factions at Stockholm to complete their work.

Fortunately there was at Copenhagen one of the ablest of British envoys. Hugh Elliot, brother of Sir Gilbert Elliot, was a man of spirit and resource. His demeanour and habits of mind were as much those of a soldier as of a diplomatist; and nature had endowed him with the stately air and melodramatic arts which avail much at a crisis.[3] For some time past he had suspected the ambitious views of the Prince Royal of Denmark, who despite his minority, ruled the land through the all-powerful Minister, Count Bernstorff. Their conduct was now sinister. Ostensibly they regretted that their treaty with Russia compelled them to attack Sweden, and welcomed Elliot's suggestion of British mediation as a means of preventing such a calamity.[4] Possibly this was Bernstorff's real conviction; for Elliot found out later that the Russian party had sworn to ruin him unless he favoured a warlike policy.

Certain it is that Bernstorff had instructed Schönborn, the Danish envoy in London, to use honeyed words to Carmarthen, which virtually invited England's friendly mediation. In reply Carmarthen "told him that the King lamented extremely the rupture which had taken place between Russia and Sweden, and assured him of His Majesty's earnest desire to contribute as far as possible to the restoration of the tranquillity of the North."

[1] "Dropmore P.," i, 353.   [2] "F. O.," Prussia," 14.
[3] "Memoir of Hugh Elliot" by the Countess of Minto.
[4] "F. O.," Denmark, 10. Elliot to Carmarthen, 2nd, 6th August 1788.

Carmarthen sent off a special messenger to Elliot to enable him
to propose immediately the mediation of England, Prussia, and
Holland between Denmark and Sweden.[1] Bernstorff received
this offer on 25th August in the friendliest manner, and promised to check the warlike ardour of the Prince Royal. Four
days later Elliot had an interview with the Prince in the hope
of refuting the persistent rumours that England had incited
both the Sultan and the King of Sweden to attack Russia. The
Prince accepted his denials, but assured him that the Danes
must fulfil their treaty obligations to Russia.

This serious news led Pitt once again directly to intervene in
diplomatic affairs, and to draft the despatch of 9th September to
Elliot. He there stated that the instructions already sent off to
him, and to Ewart at Berlin, manifested the earnest desire of
the British Government for the ending of hostilities in the
Baltic, "which might be injurious to the balance of power in that
part of the world." He deplored the aggressive intentions of
the Danish Court, as being alike opposed to its real interests
and certain " to extend the mischiefs of the present war in a
manner which cannot fail to excite the most serious attention,
and to have a great effect on the conduct, of all those Courts who
are interested in the relative situation of the different Powers of
the Baltic."[2]

Pitt, then, deeply regretted the outbreak of war in the North,
but none the less resolved to prevent the threatened dismemberment of Sweden. The Prussian Court held even stronger views
on the subject, and expressed its indignation at the Danish
inroad into Sweden " after the repeated assurances given by the
Danish Minister of pacific and moderate dispositions."[3] So keen
was the annoyance at Berlin that Frederick William resolved to
draw up a Declaration that, if Denmark attacked Gustavus,
16,000 Prussians would forthwith invade the Danish Duchy of
Holstein. Ewart at once informed Elliot of the entire concurrence of Prussia with England, and thus enabled him to
play a daring game. On the evening of 17th September, acting
on the advice of Ewart, he resolved to take boat for the Swedish
shore, and proceed to the headquarters of Gustavus. The news

---

[1] " F. O.," Denmark, 10. Carmarthen to Elliot, 15th August.

[2] *Ibid.* This draft, in Pitt's handwriting, was copied and sent off without
alteration.

[3] " F. O.," Prussia, 14. Ewart to Carmarthen, 16th September 1788.

I

which finally prompted this decision was that the Swedish monarch had decided to accept the proffered mediation not of the Allies, but of France.[1] Elliot hoped to reverse this decision and to secure the triumph of British and Prussian influence at the Swedish Court. He had not, it appears, received Pitt's despatch cited above, or even the special Instructions sent a little earlier; but he knew enough to warrant his speaking in lofty tones, which were destined to dash the hopes of Catharine and the Prince Royal of Denmark.

We left Gustavus at Stockholm. There he did his best to quell the discontent of the burghers; but it is probable that a Revolution would have broken out but for the threat of a Danish invasion and the impending loss of Gothenburg. The national danger tended to still the strife of parties; and the King, commending his queen and children to his people, rode away to Dalecarlia in order to arouse the loyal miners and peasants of that region against the invaders. Though he harangued them on the spot where Gustavus Vasa made his memorable appeals, their response was doubtful; but, having raised a small band, he proceeded towards the threatened city.[2]

On his way he met the British envoy at the town of Carlstadt. For eleven days Elliot had searched for the King, and now found him without troops, without attendants, and with a small following of ill-armed peasants (29th September, 1788). Bitterly the monarch exclaimed that, like James II, he must leave his kingdom, a victim to the ambition of Russia, the treachery of Denmark, the factious treason of his nobles, and his own mistakes. Thereupon Elliot replied: "Sire, give me your Crown; I will return it to you with added lustre." He then told him of the offer of mediation by England and Prussia on his behalf. At first, mindful of his engagements to France, Gustavus hesitated to accept it. Had he known that Elliot was acting without official instructions he might have slighted the

[1] "F. O.," Prussia, 14. Elliot to Carmarthen, 17th September. He states that Ewart had strongly urged him to go and see the King of Sweden in person. So, once again, we note the daring and initiative of Ewart. For a sharp critique on Ewart's excess of zeal see Luckwaldt, "Zur Vorgeschichte der Konvention von Reichenbach" (Berlin, G. Stilke, 1908), 237-9.

[2] The statements of Keene ("F. O.," Sweden, 7) imply that the King was at the end of his resources at Stockholm, and had but a limited success among the dalesmen. They rebut the statements in the "Memoir of Hugh Elliot," 304.

offer. In truth, Elliot was acting only on the general direction, that he was "to prevent by every means any change in the relative situation of the Northern nations." If this formula was vague, it was wide; and it sufficed, along with the more definite support from Berlin, to decide the fate of Sweden. Gustavus at once resolved to place himself wholly in Elliot's hands. The latter therefore made his way to the Danish headquarters; while the King proceeded to Gothenburg.[1] At that fortress the spirit of the defenders was as scanty as the means of defence. But affairs took on a new aspect when, at nightfall of 3rd October, a drenched and weary horseman sought admittance at their gate. A tumult of joy arose in the town when it was known that Gustavus was in their midst, the precursor of succouring bands. Now there was no thought of surrender.

Nevertheless, things would have gone hard with the burghers had the Danes pushed their attack home. This they seemed about to do. Elliot in his interview at their headquarters made little impression on the Prince Royal and the Commander-in-Chief, the Prince of Hesse. Their kinship to Gustavus seemed but to embitter their hostility; and they undoubtedly hoped, after the reduction of Gothenburg, to dismember the Swedish realm, and aggrandise the closely related houses of Russia and Denmark. They pressed on to Gothenburg and made ready for an assault. But in the meantime Gustavus, receiving help from seamen on British vessels in the harbour, encouraged the citizens to make ready and man the guns. So firm a front did the defenders present that the Danes on 9th October assented to Elliot's offer of an armistice of eight days. Within that time the Prussian Declaration reached their headquarters, and lust of conquest now gave way to fear of a Prussian invasion of Jutland. Again therefore Elliot succeeded in prolonging the armistice, which finally was extended to six months (13th November— 13th May 1789).

It is clear, then, that the initiative boldly taken by Ewart and Elliot, backed by the threats from Berlin, saved Sweden from a position of acute danger. The King of Sweden himself con-

---

[1] Keene on 26th September wrote that the Allies' offer of mediation had made a great impression at Stockholm. Count Düben, the Minister, thanked him for it, but said it would perplex the King, as he did not wish to disoblige France. A truce of eight months was necessary; but the King would not make peace with Russia unless Russian Finland were restored to him.

fessed in a letter to Armfelt that Elliot's *grand coup* in effecting an armistice had saved his kingdom, had restored the balance of Europe, and covered England with glory. Erskine, British Consul at Gothenburg, also declared that but for " the spirited and unremitted exertions of Mr. Elliot, there is not a doubt but this city and province would have fallen into the hands of the enemy on their first advancing." [1] Elliot also described his achievements in flamboyant terms, which were called forth by an unmerited rebuke of our Foreign Office, that his instructions were to restore peace, not to threaten the Danes with war. [2] His reply of 15th November ran as follows: " The success of my efforts has been almost miraculous. . . . Had I arrived at Carlstadt twenty-four hours later than I did; had I negotiated with less *energy* or success at Gothenburg than what has drawn upon me the resentment of Russia and the abettors of the boundless ambition of that Court, the *Revolution* in Sweden was compleated, and a combination formed in the North equally hostile to England and Prussia." He then charged Bernstorff with duplicity in expressing a desire for peace, " while the Danes were marching on an almost defenceless town, the capture of which decided irrevocably the fate of Sweden and the Baltic." . . . " Six weeks after my arrival in Sweden a victorious army of 12,000 men, animated by the presence of their Prince, in sight of a most brilliant conquest, were checked in their progress by my single efforts; were induced to evacuate the Swedish territories, and consented to a truce of six months. . . . Perhaps in the annals of history there is not to be found a more striking testimony of deference paid by a foreign prince to a King of England than what the Prince Royal of Denmark manifested upon this trying occasion." He then stated that the efforts of the Prussian envoy were of no avail owing to the dislike in which he was held; and that only his [Elliot's] influence availed to undo the harm caused by a violent action of Gustavus III in the middle of October.

It would be interesting to know what Pitt thought of this bombast; but on 5th December Carmarthen guardedly com-

[1] " F. O.," Sweden, 7.

[2] The rebuke may have been due to Elliot's silence; for in a P.S. to a letter of 16th October to Ewart, Elliot said: " Write everything about me to London; I have never written myself, having acted hitherto without instructions " (" F. O.," Prussia, 14). As we have seen, he had acted largely on the advice of Ewart; and Liston, on finding this out, suggested to Carmarthen the need of cautioning Ewart not to go too fast (Luckwaldt, *op. cit.*, 238).

mended the magniloquent envoy, and urged him to gain over Denmark to the Triple Alliance; for, as Catharine had now declined the mediation of the Allies, while Gustavus had accepted it, Denmark could justly refuse her demands for help in the next campaign. Ostensibly Denmark refused; but, owing to the profuse expenditure of the Russian Embassy at Copenhagen (estimated by our *chargé d'affaires*, Johnstone, at £500 a day[1]), Catharine gained permission to have fifteen warships from the White Sea repaired in that dockyard.

Gustavus III no sooner found himself safe than he laid his plans for humbling his enemies both at home and abroad. He summoned a Diet, and proceeded to educate the electors in their duties by drawing up a list of the ten deputies whom the men of Stockholm should choose. They held other opinions, and sent up six declared opponents of the King.[2] On the whole, however, the Estates were with him, and he imposed a constitution on the recalcitrant Order of the Nobles, whereby he gained absolute control of foreign policy. This triumph for autocracy took place at the end of April 1789, only a week before the assembly of the States-General at Versailles, which sounded the knell of the House of Bourbon. Gustavus informed Elliot of his resolve to keep at peace with Denmark, because a war with her "would turn me from my great aim—the safety of the Ottomans and the abasement of Russia." He therefore begged Elliot to assure the prolongation of the Danish armistice for six months. That envoy had now come to see that the chief danger of Sweden lay in "the romantic projects of glory and aggrandisement formed by the Sovereign himself"; and he pointed out the need for the Allies to prescribe the terms of peace before he succumbed to the superior forces of Russia.[3] Already Catharine had announced her resolve in the words— "When Gustavus has had his say to his Diet, I will have my say to him."

With Elliot's view of things Pitt and the Duke of Leeds (formerly Marquis of Carmarthen) were in complete accord. On

---

[1] "F. O.," Denmark, 10. Despatches of 30th November, 5th and 27th December. On 10th April 1789 Carmarthen assured Elliot of the desire of H. M. for a Danish alliance. He also commended him less coldly than before ("F. O.," Denmark, 11).

[2] "F. O.," Sweden, 7. Keene to Carmarthen, 30th December, 1788.

[3] "F. O.," Denmark, 11. Elliot to the Duke of Leeds, 30th May 1789.

24th June they informed him that Gustavus must not expect
the Allies to make peace for him on his own terms, but only on
that of the *status quo ante bellum*. In this effort England would
cordially join in order to keep the balance of power in the Baltic.
" I cannot," continued Leeds, " too often repeat the earnest desire
of this Government to conciliate the Court of Denmark in the
first instance; nor do we lose sight of another material object—
I mean, a cordial and permanent connection with Russia." Above
all, England would not go to war unless the balance of the
Baltic Powers were seriously endangered, to the detriment of
the commercial States.[1]

Here, then, we have another proof of the peaceful and cautious
character of Pitt's policy. He distrusted the crowned Don
Quixote of the North, was resolved to save him only on England's terms, viz., the *status quo*, and hoped that the pacification
might lead up to an alliance with Denmark and finally with
Russia. In fact, he kept in view the Northern System which had
guided British statesmen of the earlier generation. His aims
were frustrated by the shifty policy of Denmark and the vindictiveness of Catharine. " Hamlet" and " Semiramis," as Harris
once termed them, thought lightly of England and longed for
the partition of Sweden. Accordingly the Danish fleet convoyed
the fifteen Russian men-of-war, long refitting at Copenhagen,
into the Baltic, until they joined the Cronstadt squadron of
twenty-six ships near Bornholm, and thereby secured for it a
superiority in that sea. The Duke of Leeds sent a sharp protest
to Copenhagen, with the hint that furthur actions of this kind
might entail disagreeable consequences for Denmark.[2] Even
with this unfair help accorded to Russia, the Swedes sustained
no serious reverse either by land or sea. Gustavus summed up
the results of the campaign in the words: " After fighting like
madmen about every other day for two months, here we are at
the same point at which we started." Nevertheless he had
clogged the efforts of Catharine against the Turks, and thus
enabled his allies to prolong the unequal struggle against two
great empires. Neither the loss of Oczakoff, nor the accession
of the less capable Sultan, Selim III, daunted the resolve of the
Ottomans to continue a war which was for them an affair of
religious zeal and national honour.

[1] " F. O.," Denmark, 11. Leeds to Elliot, 24th June.
[2] *Ibid.*, Leeds to Elliot, 21st August 1789.

CHAPTER XXII

PARTITION OR PACIFICATION?

He who gains nothing, loses.—CATHARINE II.

We cannot be considered as in any degree bound to support a system of
an offensive nature, the great end of which appears to be aggrandisement
rather than security.—PITT and the DUKE OF LEEDS, 24th June 1789.

THE excess of an evil tends to produce its own cure. The
resources of two great Empires were being used for a
partition of the Turkish dominions, in a way which must have
led to a succession of wars without benefiting the Christians of
the East. But the prospect of the aggrandisement of Russia
speedily led the hardy Gustavus to strike a blow at her northern
capital; and when Catharine incited the Danes to deal a counterstroke at his unguarded rear, Great Britain and Prussia intervened to prevent the overthrow of Sweden and of the balance of
power in the Baltic. Thus, forces which pressed on towards
Constantinople produced a sharp reaction in widening circles
and prompted States to attack or arm against their neighbours
—Sweden against Russia, Denmark against Sweden, and England and Prussia against Denmark. Consequently Gustavus III
might claim to have saved the Turkish Empire; for his action
brought into the arena England and, to some extent, the Dutch
Republic.

Less obvious but more potent was the influence of Prussia.
Her forces, cantoned along the Austrian and Russian borders,
halved the efforts of those Empires against the Turks and
encouraged the Polish nationalists to resist Russian predominance at Warsaw. Thus, by the year 1789, instead of moving the
forces of two Empires and of Poland against the Turks,
Catharine found her energies clogged, her resources strained,
and only one important conquest achieved, that of Oczakoff.
Over against this triumph she had to set the menacing attitude

of the Triple Alliance lately framed by Great Britain, Prussia, and the Dutch Republic.

For a time the Czarina cherished the hope that the insanity of George III, and the accession of the Regent, would lead to the downfall of Pitt and the reversal of British policy. On $\frac{8}{19}$ December 1788 she wrote to her ambassador at London, Count Vorontzoff (Woronzow), charging him to make overtures to Fox and the Dukes of Portland and Devonshire for the renewal of the Anglo-Russian alliance, which for the last five years she had spurned. With a vehemence of style, in which feelings figured as facts, she inveighed against Pitt for slighting her many offers of friendship, for allowing Ainslie and Elliot to incite Turkey and Sweden to attack her, and for entangling himself in the dangerous and visionary schemes of Hertzberg. All this, however, would be changed when the Prince of Wales and Fox came to power.

On $\frac{19}{30}$ January Vorontzoff replied that he had seen Fox, who accorded him a hearty welcome, and said that in a fortnight the Regency would be established. He (Fox) would then be Foreign Secretary, and would be able to speak of England's treaty obligations to Prussia. The language of Fox showed some measure of caution, and partly palliated the gross imprudence of according an interview at all. A little later (perhaps before receiving Vorontzoff's answer) the Empress expressed her admiration of the reply sent by the Prince of Wales (it was really Burke's and Sheridan's) to Pitt, as it argued distinguished talents. The Prince and Fox, she said, would certainly prevent their people being dragged at the heel of Prussia. As for herself, she declared her wish to grant them a commercial treaty, which she had refused two years before. The correspondence throws a curious light on the feline diplomacy of Catharine and on the singular folly of Fox.[1] It also prepares us for the unpatriotic part which he played in the Anglo-Russian dispute of the year 1791. The recovery of George III, about the time when Catharine indited the latter epistle, pricked the bubble, and left Pitt in a position of greater power than ever.

Thus, in the spring of 1789, the general position was somewhat as follows. England, Prussia, and Holland, acting in close concert, were resolved to prevent any revolutionary

[1] " Vorontzoff Archives," xvi, 258-67.

changes in the Baltic. This implied that Denmark could not attack Sweden, and that Gustavus might war against Catharine until she chose to accept the mediation of the Allies for the re-establishment of the *status quo ante bellum*. As for the other Powers, France was almost a nullity owing to the internal troubles which were leading up to the Revolution. Spain was friendly to the Allies and favoured the cause of Sweden and Turkey.[1] Moreover the Poles, acting on hints from Berlin, were beginning to shake off Russian tutelage and to feel their way towards a drastic reform of their chaotic polity. Early in 1789 the Prussian Court sought for a close political and commercial union with Poland. The ensuing compact freed the Poles from the obligations contracted by King Stanislaus with his former mistress, Catharine II; it further promised to bind their realm to England and Holland; above all, it opened up vast possibilities for the regeneration of that hapless people.

As for the concert of the two Empires, discords were already heard. Joseph II, alarmed at the turmoil in Hungary and Belgium, as well as disgusted at the results of his first Turkish campaign, talked of waging merely a defensive war, and of offering easy terms to the Ottomans. Potemkin, puffed up by the capture of Oczakoff, announced his resolve that Moldavia and Wallachia should never fall to the Hapsburgs—an aim that had been distinctly formulated at Vienna. Russia herself, a prey to the greedy gang who fawned on the Empress and drained her treasury, seemed unable to bear for long the strain of war on two frontiers, and of precautionary measures against Prussia. The Court of Berlin, as Mirabeau had pointed out, was honeycombed by intrigues and favouritism; but it was sound at the core compared with Russia. The French author of the " Secret Memoirs of the Court of St. Petersburg " states that in the declining years of Catharine the Russian finances were exploited in a way more disgraceful than even France had seen; that none were so little as the great; and that officers notoriously lived on the funds of their regiments. Catharine herself once jauntily remarked about a colonel—" Well! If he be poor, it is his own fault; for he has long had a regiment." It speaks volumes for the patriotism and stupidity of the troops that they still had enough of the old Muscovite staunchness to carry them to victory over the Turks.

---

[1] " F. O.," Prussia, 15. Ewart to Carmarthen, 17th January 1789.

But such was the case. In the campaigns of 1789 the army of
Suvóroff gained several successes, and the troops of Joseph II,
once more urged onwards by that ruler, also had their meed of
triumph.

This was partly due to the death of Abdul Hamid I, which
brought to the Ottoman throne a feebler successor, Selim III
(April 1789). The Grand Vizier, the soul of the war party, was
soon overthrown, and the next commander-in-chief, the Pacha of
Widdin, impaired by his slothfulness the fighting power of the
Ottomans.[1] Belgrade and Semendria were lost. But even more
serious, perhaps, than these reverses was the emergence of plans
at Berlin which portended gain to Prussia at the expense of
Turkey. We are concerned here with European affairs only so
far as they affected British policy, and must therefore concentrate
our attention on the statecraft of the years 1789 and 1790, which
threatened sweeping changes on the Continent and brought into
play the cautious conservatism of Pitt. The French Revolution
and its immense consequences will engage our attention later.

As we saw in Chapter XVI, the Prussian statesman, Hertzberg,
had long been maturing an ingenious scheme for the aggrandisement of Prussia, by a general shuffling together of boundaries
in the East of Europe.[2] On 13th May 1789 he presented it in
its complete form to Frederick William, who, after long balancings on this question, now accorded his consent. The Prussian
monarch thereby pledged himself, at a favourable occasion, to
offer his armed mediation to Russian, Austria, and Turkey. If
the two Empires overcame the Sultan, as seemed probable,
Prussia was to threaten their frontiers with masses of troops and,
under threat of war, compel them to accept her terms. If, however, victory inclined to the crescent, Dietz, the Prussian envoy
at Constantinople, was to remind the Sublime Porte that the
triumph was largely due to Prussia's action in enabling Sweden
to continue the war against Russia, and in thwarting Catharine's
plan of an invasion of Turkey by the Poles. Dietz was also to hint

---

[1] On 22nd May Ainslie reported the slothful preparations for war. He
had stated earlier that Russian money was at work at Constantinople to
bring about a mediation by the Bourbon Courts in favour of peace (" F. O.,"
Turkey, 10).

[2] See Häusser, i, 225-37, for its earlier developments; also for the more
warlike plans at Berlin of a general alliance with Poland, England, Sweden,
and Denmark for the humbling of Russia and Austria.

" in a delicate and not threatening manner," that if Prussia threw her weight into the scales against the Turks, the new Coalition must speedily overwhelm her. " Therefore the Porte will do well not to balance on that point," but will accept Prussia's terms.[1] There was a third alternative, that the war would drag on indecisively, in which case the exhaustion of the belligerents must enable Prussia to work her will the more readily.

Accordingly Hertzberg hoped that, however the fortunes of war inclined, he would gain his ends. They were as follows. The Turks, if victorious, must sacrifice their gains (the Crimea, etc.) at the demand of Prussia, and thus enable her to compel Austria to restore to the Poles the great province of Galicia, torn from them in the partition of 1772. The Poles in their turn were to reward Frederick William by ceding to him the fortresses of Danzig and Thorn, along with part of Great Poland, which so inconveniently divided Prussia's eastern lands.

The same general result was to follow in the event of Russia and Austria driving back the Turks to their last natural barrier, the Balkans. Prussia was then to draw the sword on behalf of Turkey and Sweden, restore the balance in the South-East, and give the law to all parties. In that case, it appeared (though Hertzberg wavered on this point), Austria might acquire Moldavia and Wallachia from Turkey, and thereby close against Russia the door leading to the Balkans. At times Hertzberg stated that Austria must in any case gain those commanding provinces, which would sever her friendship with Russia.[2] As for Catharine, she might retain the Crimea, and gain land perhaps as far as the Dniester. On the whole, however, Hertzberg hoped that Prussia need not go to war, but that the Turks would make a good enough stand at the Danube to enable the mere appearance of the splendid army of Prussia on the frontiers of the two Empires to enforce his demands.

Much has been written for and against this scheme. Among the many projects of that time it holds a noteworthy place. Certainly it would greatly have simplified the boundaries of Eastern Europe. The recovery by Poland of her natural frontier

---

[1] I quote from the instructions drawn up by Hertzberg on 26th May, for Dietz, which he imparted to Ewart, who sent them on to Whitehall on 28th May —a step which earned him the distrust of Hertzberg (" F. O.," Prussia, 15). The Pitt Ministry knew of them earlier than other Courts.

[2] Dembinski, i, 240.

on the south-west, the Carpathians, would strengthen that State, and enable her, with the help of her Prussian ally, to defy the wrath of the two Imperial Courts. Hertzberg believed that the Poles would gladly accept the offer. For was not the great province of Galicia worth the smaller, though commercially valuable, districts on the lower Vistula which would go to Frederick William? Further, would not a good commercial treaty between the Allies (in which England, it was hinted, might have her share) make up for the loss of the prosperous city of Danzig? In truth, the proposal reminds one of the schemes for scientific frontiers which Rousseau outlined and Napoleon reduced to profitable practice.

It might have succeeded had nations been mere amoebae, divisible at will. Traders and philosophers might acclaim Hertzberg as the Adam Smith of Prussia and Poland. In truth, his plan was defensible, even on its Machiavellian side—the aggrandisement of Prussia, ultimately at the expense of the Turks. For it might be argued that the ultimate triumph of the crescent was impossible, and that only the action of Sweden, Prussia, and to a less extent England, could avert disaster. Hertzberg also claimed that Prussia and her Allies should guarantee to Turkey the security of her remaining possessions, and deemed this a set-off to the disappointments brought by his other proposals.

Nevertheless the balance of argument was heavily against the scheme. As the Pitt Cabinet pointed out in a weighty pronouncement on 24th June, Hertzberg proposed to use Turkey as a medium for the attainment of his ends, which were the depression of Austria and the aggrandisement of Prussia. However well and successfully the Turks fought, the gain was to accrue to Frederick William, not to the Swedes, who were fighting desperately for the Ottoman cause. True, Prussia promised in the last resort to help the Sultan to recover some of his lost provinces; but even then, the acquisitions of the two Empires at the end of costly campaigns were scarcely to balance those of Prussia and Poland. Well might the British Cabinet say of the Turks: " It seems very doubtful whether either their power or their inclination would answer the expectations of the Court of Berlin."

After this ironical touch the verdict of the Pitt Ministry was given to Ewart as follows:

You will not fail to assure the Ministers at Berlin of the satisfaction with which the King will see any real and solid advantages derived to His Prussian Majesty by such arrangements as may be obtained by way of negotiation and without the danger of extending those hostilities [which] it is so much the interest of all Europe to put an end to. We cannot but acknowledge the friendly attention manifested by His Prussian Majesty towards his Allies in taking care not to commit them in the event of the Porte acceding to the proposed plan of co-operation, the operations of which go so much beyond the spirit of our treaty of Alliance, which is purely of a defensive nature, and by which we cannot of course be considered as in any degree bound to support a system of an offensive nature, the great end of which appears to be aggrandisement rather than security, and which from its very nature is liable to provoke fresh hostilities instead of contributing to the restoration of general tranquillity.

In discussing these points, and indeed upon every other occasion, I must beg of you, Sir, to remember that it is by no means the idea of His Majesty, or of his confidential servants, to risk the engaging this country in a war on account of Turkey, either directly or indirectly; and I am to desire you would be particularly careful in your language, to prevent any intention of that nature being imputed to us. I think it necessary to mention this distinctly, as I observe in one of your dispatches, you state the continuance of the Northern War *as in some degree advantageous*, as it would be a powerful *diversion in case the Allies should take part in the Turkish War.* This I must again observe to you is an object by no means in our view.

With respect to any future guarantee of the Ottoman Empire it is impossible for us to commit ourselves at present. The consideration will naturally arise how far such a guarantee is either necessary or beneficial when the terms of peace come under discussion. The effect which a guarantee of the Turkish possessions might create in Russia likewise deserves some consideration; and I cannot but observe that the whole tenor of these Instructions [those sent to Dietz] seems likely to throw at a greater distance the chance of detaching Russia from Austria and connecting it with us; whereas hitherto it has been our object, and, as it appeared to us, that of Prussia, while we made Russia feel the disadvantage of being upon distant terms with us, and avoided doing anything which looked like courting her friendship, still to avoid pushing things to an extremity or precluding a future connection.[1]

At several points this pronouncement challenges attention. Firstly, it does not once refer to the feelings and prejudices of the

[1] " F. O.," Prussia, 15. Leeds to Ewart, 24th June 1789.

peoples who were to be bartered about. Only four days previously the Commons of France had sworn by the Tennis Court Oath that they would frame a constitution for their land—a declaration which rang trumpet-tongued through England; but not the faintest echo of it appears in the official language of Pitt and the Duke of Leeds. Their arguments are wholly those of the old school, but of the old school at its best. For, secondly, they deprecate changes of territory forced by a mediating Power on the people it ostensibly befriends, which tend to their detriment and its own benefit. They question whether Prussia can press through these complex partitions without provoking a general war—the very evil which the Triple Alliance has sought to avoid. Certainly England will never go to war to bring them about; neither will she draw the sword on behalf of Turkey. On the contrary, she hopes finally to regain the friendship of Russia. Most noteworthy of all is the central criticism, that the aim of Hertzberg is "aggrandisement rather than security." We shall have occasion to observe how often Pitt used this last word to denote the end for which he struggled against Revolutionary France and Napoleon; and its presence in this despatch bespeaks the mind of the Prime Minister acting through the pen of the Duke of Leeds.

The defensive character of Pitt's policy further appears in a despatch to Ewart, also of 24th June, cautioning that very zealous envoy that all possible means are being taken to win over Denmark peacefully to the Triple Alliance, in order that it may "command the keys of the Baltic." Gustavus is to be warned that the Allies cannot help him unless he agrees to forego his hopes of gain at the expense of Russia, and "to act merely upon the defensive." The *status quo ante bellum* would be the fairest basis of peace in the Baltic, and it would prove "that the real object of our interference was calculated for general views of public utility, and not founded upon any motives of partiality for one Power or resentment to another."

For a time events seemed to work against the pacific policy of Pitt and in favour of the schemes of Hertzberg. The summer witnessed not only the advance of the Russians and Austrians into the Danubian Provinces, but also the wrigglings to and fro of the Danish Court, which enabled the Russian squadron at Copenhagen to join the Cronstadt fleet and command the Baltic. Nevertheless, Prussia felt that she had the game

in her own hands, however much her Allies might hold aloof;
for the Austrian Government was distracted by news of the
seething discontent of the Hungarians, of the Poles in Galicia,
and, above all, of the Brabanters and Flemings. Joseph II, too,
was obviously sinking under these worries, which seemed to
presage the break up of his Empire.[1] The Prussian Court therefore resolved to concentrate its efforts on wresting Galicia and
the Belgic Provinces from the Hapsburg Power, especially as
the Porte, despite its recent defeats, refused to listen to Dietz
when he mentioned the cession of Moldavia and Wallachia to
the infidels.[2] Until the Moslems had learnt the lessons of
destiny, it was obviously desirable to set about robbing Austria
by more straightforward means.

The folly of Joseph II favoured this scheme of robbery.
His reforms in the Belgic Provinces had long brought that
naturally conservative people to the brink of revolt, so that in
the spring of the year 1789 plans were laid not only at Brussels
but also at Berlin for securing their independence. Hertzberg
sought to work upon the fears of Pitt by hinting that Austria
might call in the French troops to stamp out the discontent—a
contingency far from unlikely, were it not that France was
rapidly sliding into the abyss of bankruptcy and revolution. By
a curious coincidence the repressive authority of Joseph II was
exerted on 18th June, the day after the Third Estate of France
defiantly styled itself the National Assembly. While Paris was
jubilant at the news of this triumph, the mandates of the
Emperor swept away the Estates and ancient privileges of
Brabant. As this action involved the suppression of the ancient
charter of privileges, quaintly termed *La Joyeuse Entrée*, the
Brabanters put into practice its final clause, that the citizens

---

[1] " F. O.," Prussia, 15. Ewart to Leeds, 12th July. In it he pointed out that
the alternative Prussian plan, that of forcing Turkey to give up Moldavia
and Wallachia to Austria, she giving up Galicia to the Poles, and they
Danzig and Thorn to Prussia, was most objectionable; but Hertzberg felt
able to force even that through. Leeds commended Ewart for opposing
those extreme proposals.

[2] *Ibid.* Ewart to Leeds, 10th and 11th August, 3rd September. It is not
surprising to find from Ainslie's letter of 22nd October to Ewart that the
Porte distrusted all the Christian Powers (France and Spain were still offering their mediation) but England least (" F. O.," Turkey, 10). Dietz held
scornfully aloof from Ainslie, and played his own game.

might use force against the sovereign who infringed its provisions. "Act here as in Paris" ran the placards in Brussels and other cities. The capture of the Bastille added fuel to the fire in Belgium; and the nationalist victory was completed by a rising of the men of Liége against the selfish and deadening rule of their Prince Bishop.[1]

The likeness between the Belgian and French Revolutions is wholly superficial. Despite the effort of Camille Desmoulins to link the two movements in sympathy—witness the title of his newspaper "Les Révolutions de France et de Brabant"—no thinking man could confound the democratic movement in France with the narrowly national and clerical aims of the majority in Brabant and Flanders. True, an attempt was made by a few progressives, under the lead of Francis Vonck, to inculcate the ideas of Voltaire and Rousseau; but the influence of the Roman Church, always paramount in Flanders, availed to crush this effort. Van der Noot and the clericals gained the upper hand, and finally compelled the Vonckists to flee over the southern border.

In the month of July Van der Noot declared in favour of a Belgian Republic under the guarantee and protection of England, Prussia, and Holland. He set on foot overtures to this end which met with a friendly response at Berlin and The Hague.[2] The Prussian Court sent General Schliessen to discuss the matter with the British Government; but Pitt and Leeds behaved very guardedly on a question involving a recognition of the Belgian revolt and the end of the Barrier System on which we had long laid so much stress. Their despatch of 14th September to Ewart emphasized the difficulties attending Van der Noot's proposal, even if his statements were correct. At the same time Ministers asserted that the Allies must at all costs prevent the Belgians becoming dependent on France, a noteworthy statement which foreshadows Pitt's later policy of resisting the annexation of those rich provinces to the French Republic or Empire. For the present, he strongly advised Prussia and Holland to await the course of events and do nothing "to threaten the interruption of that tranquillity it is so much their interest, and, I trust, their intention, to preserve." Above all, it would be well to wait for the death of Joseph II, already announced as imminent, seeing

---

[1] "Corresp. of W. A. Miles," ii, 142.

[2] Letter of the Grand Pensionary of 1st August, in Ewart's despatch of 10th August ("F. O.," Prussia, 16).

that his successor might grant to the Belgians the needed concessions.[1]

The Belgians seem to have trusted the Pitt Cabinet far more
than Hertzberg, whose restless policy aroused general distrust.
They made two overtures to the British Court. The former of
these, strange to say, came through a French nobleman, the
Comte de Charrot, who called on Lord Robert Fitzgerald, our
envoy at Paris, on or about 21st October, and confided to him
his resentment against France, his warm sympathies with the
Belgians (he was a descendant of the old Counts of Flanders),
and his fear that France would dominate that land after the
downfall of Austrian authority. He besought Fitzgerald to forward to the Duke of Leeds a letter warning the Cabinet of the
efforts of the National Assembly to form a party among the
Brabanters and Flemings, who, however, were resolved not to
accept the rule of a foreign prince, but to form a Republic under
the protection of Great Britain. To this end they were willing
to place in her hands the city of Ostend as a pledge of their
fidelity to the British connection. A German prince, he added,
would never be tolerated, save in the eastern provinces, Limburg
and Luxemburg. His letter, dated Antwerp, 15th October, to
the Duke of Leeds, is couched in the same terms.[2]

The proposal opens up a vista of the possibilities of that
strange situation. By planting the British flag at Ostend, and
by allowing Prussia to dominate the eastern Netherlands, Pitt
could have built up once more a barrier on the north-east of
France. All this was possible, provided that Charrot's proposals were genuine and represented the real feelings of the
Belgians. Evidently Pitt and Leeds distrusted the offer, which
seems to have been left unanswered.

Early in November, when the plans of the Belgian patriots
for ousting the Austrians were nearing completion, they sent as
spokesman Count de Roode to appeal for the protection of
George III. Pitt laid the request before the King; and the
result will be seen in Pitt's letter to the Count:

Downing St. Nov. 13, 1789.

I have received the letter which you honoured me with, informing
me that you were employed on the part of the people of Brabant to

---

[1] "F. O.," Prussia, 15. Leeds to Ewart, 14th September 1789.
[2] "F. O.," France, 33. Fitzgerald to Leeds, 22nd October 1789.

solicit the King's protection, and desiring to see me for the purpose of delivering a letter to me on that subject. I thought it my duty to lay these circumstances before His Majesty, who has not been pleased to authorize me to enter into any discussion in consequence of an application which does not appear to be made by any regular or acknowledged authority. I must therefore, Sir, beg you to excuse me, if, on that account, I am under the necessity of declining seeing you for the purpose which you propose.[1]

Somewhat earlier the Duke of Orleans had come on a mission to London, ostensibly on the Belgian Question, but really for a term of forced absence from Paris. It will therefore be well to describe his visit in a later chapter.

Cold as were Pitt's replies to de Roode, he certainly kept a watchful eye on Belgian affairs. For, on the one hand, if Joseph II succeeded in establishing despotic power at Brussels, he would gain complete control over the finances and armed forces of that flourishing land, with results threatening to the Dutch and even to Prussia. If, however, the Brabanters succeeded as the Flemings had done, French democracy might rush in as a flood and gallicize the whole of that land to the detriment of England. Pitt therefore approved of the Prussian proposal to send troops to occupy the Bishopric of Liége, seeing that the deposed bishop had appealed to Austria for armed aid. With the prestige gained by the military occupation of Liége, Hertzberg hoped to dominate the situation both in the Low Countries and in the East. Most pressingly did he urge the need of instantly recognizing the independence of the Belgian provinces; but after long arguments Ewart convinced him that it might be better, even for Prussia, to press for the restoration of their old constitution, with all its limitations to the power of the Emperor, under the guarantee of the three Allies. If Ewart succeeded with Hertzberg, he failed with Frederick William, who on that and other occasions showed himself "very elated" and determined to tear from Austria that valuable possession, as well as Galicia.[2] Hertzberg did his utmost to persuade England to combine the two questions so as the more to embarrass Austria; but he met with steady refusals.

---

[1] Pitt MSS., 102. The Count renewed his proposal early in 1790, but received a similar rebuff on 1st February 1790.

[2] "F. O.," Prussia, 16. Ewart to Leeds, 28th November and 8th December 1789.

On 30th November Pitt took the sense of the Cabinet. It was clearly in favour of non-intervention and the restoration as far as possible of the previous state of things. Nevertheless, the men of Brabant, in case of defeat by the Imperialists, were encouraged to hope that the Allies would declare for the restoration of the old constitution. On the other hand, in case of victory, they were to be induced "to take steps for preventing the prevalence of democratical principles."[1] Obviously, then, Pitt desired to keep out both Prussian and French influence, and to leave the Belgians free to come to terms with the successor of Joseph II after the imminent demise of that monarch. Events favoured this solution. In December Brussels and all parts of Brabant shook off the yoke of the Imperialists, who retired to Luxemburg. Early in the year 1790 deputies from the nine Belgic provinces met at Brussels, declared the deposition of Joseph, and formed a Federal Congress for mutual protection. The clerical and conservative party, headed by Van der Noot, sent to Paris an appeal for support, which found no favour either with Louis or the National Assembly, the King desiring not to offend Austria, and the French deputies distrusting the aims of the majority at Brussels.

Pitt and his colleagues were equally cautious. On the news of the successful revolt of Brussels, they seemed for a time to incline to the Prussian plan of recognizing the independence of Belgium,[2] and on 9th January 1790 they framed a compact with Prussia and Holland with a view to taking common action in this affair. But the most urgent demands from Berlin in favour of immediate action failed to push Pitt on to this last irrevocable step. It does not appear that the King controlled his action; for at that time he was so far absorbed in the escapades of his sons (those of Prince Edward were an added trouble) as to be a cipher in all but domestic concerns. Pitt and Leeds therefore had a free hand. They were influenced probably by the news that Joseph, despite the progress of his mortal disease, had resolved to subdue the Netherlands. The tidings opened up two alternatives—war between Austria and Prussia, or the possibility of a peaceful compromise after the death of Joseph and the accession of his far more tractable brother, Leopold. These seem to have been the motives underlying the decision

[1] "Leeds Memoranda," 147.
[2] "F. O.," Prussia, 16. Leeds to Ewart, 13th December 1789.

of the Pitt Cabinet, early in 1790, to defer any decisive action by the Allies. The Duke of Leeds pointed out to Ewart on 9th February that the feuds between the Belgic provinces made them useless as allies; that any immediate recognition of their independence would have "mischievous effects"; and that a reconciliation between them and their future ruler seemed highly probable. They should, therefore, not be encouraged to hope for recognition by the Allies. Leeds closed by very pertinently asking the Court of Berlin "how far this new Republic, once established, could be (and by whom) prevented from becoming indirectly, if not directly, totally dependent upon France." The argument derived added force from the fact that a "French emissary" was then at Brussels offering the recognition by France of the proposed Belgian Republic, with the help of 20,000 troops against any who should oppose it.[1] This offer was not official; but as the moods of the National Assembly varied day by day, it might at any time become so. Certainly the chance of French invervention added a sting to the reproaches soon to be levelled at Pitt from Berlin.

They were called forth by the missive above referred to, and by a "secret and confidential" despatch of the same date. In the latter Pitt and Leeds warned Ewart that the proposed armed mediation of Prussia against Catharine and Joseph was outside the scope of the Triple Alliance. The British Government wished Prussia the success which might be expected from the power of her army, the flourishing state of her revenue, and the present doubtful condition both of Russia and Austria; but it could not participate in "measures adopted without the previous concurrence of the Allies."[2]

A storm of obloquy broke upon Ewart when he announced these decisions. The Court of Berlin insisted on the need of immediately recognizing Belgian independence, adding a threat that otherwise those provinces would do well to throw themselves upon France. Our ambassador partly succeeded in stilling the storm,

---

[1] "F. O.," Prussia, 17. Ewart to Leeds, 18th February 1790. I can find neither in our archives nor in the Pitt MSS. any confirmation of the statement of Father Delplace ("Joseph II et la Rév. Brabançonne," 148) that Pitt suggested to the "ambassador" of the Belgian Estates their election of the Duke of Mecklenburg-Strelitz, and that the ambassador demurred, because he was a Protestant. Pitt never recognized any Belgian envoy as having official powers, and took no step that implied Belgian independence.

[2] "F. O.," Prussia, 17.

especially when news came of tumults at Brussels and the uncertainty of the outlook throughout Brabant. Frederick William then
recognized the wisdom of waiting until affairs were more settled,
but he declared that he " was abandoned by his Allies," and that,
unless Galicia could be detached from Austria, he would prefer
to see the Netherlands go to France.[1] This piece of royal pettish-
ness served at least to show that his friendship for England depended on her serving his designs against Austria.

Here was the weakness of the Triple Alliance. The Allies
had almost nothing in common, except that the British and
Dutch both wished to live in peace and develop their trade.
Prussia, on the contrary, saw in this time of turmoil the opportunity of consolidating her scattered Eastern lands by a scheme
not unlike the Belgic-Bavarian Exchange. On the score of
morality we may censure such plans; but vigorous and growing
States will push them on while their rivals are abased, and
will discard Allies who oppose them. In this contrariety of
interests lay the secret of the weakness of the Anglo-Prussian
alliance during the upheavals of the near future. It also happened that the House of Hohenzollern matured these plans
at the very time when the fortunes of the House of Hapsburg,
after touching their nadir, began once more to rise; and the
revival of Austria under Leopold II helped Pitt to maintain
the existing order of things in Central Europe against all the
schemings of Hertzberg. The success of Pitt in this work of
statesmanlike conservation marks the climax of his diplomatic
career; and, as it has never received due attention, I make no
apology for treating it somewhat fully in the following chapter.

[1] " F. O.," Prussia, 17.   Ewart to Leeds, 22nd February 1790.

CHAPTER XXIII

PARTITION OR PACIFICATION (Continued)

I want the trumpet of an angel to proclaim to the ears of sovereigns that it is become their universal interest as well as their moral duty to have a period of peace.—Lord Auckland to Sir Robert Murray Keith, 7th May 1790.

PROBABLY at no time in the history of Europe have all the leading States been so bent on plans of mutual spoliation as in the closing weeks of the life of Joseph II of Austria. The failure of his schemes and the probability of a break up of the Hapsburg dominions whetted the appetites of all his neighbours and brought Europe to the verge of a general war. In these circumstances it was providential that one Great Power stood for international morality, and that its counsels were swayed by a master-mind. The future of Europe depended on the intelligent conservatism of Pitt and the duration of the life of his political opposite, Joseph II. That life had long been wearing rapidly away; and on 20th February 1790 he died, full of pain, disappointment, and regret that crowned the tragedy of his career.

His death brought new life and hopes to the Hapsburg peoples. The new sovereign, Leopold II, his brother, soon proved to be one of the astutest rulers of that race. He has been termed the only ruler of that age who correctly read the signs of the times.[1] If Joseph was called the crowned philosopher, Leopold may be styled the crowned diplomatist. Where the former gave the rein to the impulses of Voltairian philosophy and romantic idealism, his successor surveyed affairs with a calculating prudence which resulted, perhaps, from the patriarchal size of his family—he had twelve children—and from his long rule in the Grand Duchy of Tuscany.[2] Certainly he

---

[1] Lord Acton, " Lects. on Mod. Hist.," 304.   [2] Keith's " Mems.," ii, 257.

knew how impossible it was to thrust advanced Liberal ideas and central institutions on the tough and unenlightened peoples of the Hapsburg realm. Above all he discerned the folly of aggressive foreign policy while all was turmoil at home. He therefore prepared to pacify his subjects before the war cloud hanging over the Riesengebirge burst upon Bohemia.

His caution and pliability opened up a new future for Central Europe. Had the headstrong and pertinacious Joseph lived much longer (though some gleams of prudence lighted on him in his last months) revolts could scarcely have been staved off in Hungary and the Low Countries, where even his belated concessions inspired distrust. Above all, he could never have coped with the forceful policy of Prussia. There is little room for doubt that the continuance of his life would have involved the loss of the Belgic provinces, Galicia, and, perhaps, even Bohemia. The Hohenzollerns would have leaped to heights of power that would always challenge to conflict; and Europe, a prey to Revolution in the West, must have been torn at the heart by deadly strifes, both dynastic and racial.

In closing the sluices against the currents about to be let loose at Berlin, Pitt had latterly counted on the well-known prudence of Leopold of Tuscany. On 26th February, before the decease of Joseph was known in London, the British Government stiffly opposed the Prussian plan of acknowledging the independence of the Austrian Netherlands. Great Britain—so ran the despatch to Ewart, our envoy to Berlin—had covenanted merely to prevent the Emperor making " an unrestrained use of the wealth and population " of those provinces, and to obviate the possibility of their going to swell the power of France. England (added Pitt in a side note of his own) must counteract French intrigues in Brabant; but they were unofficial, and would probably fail.[1] He therefore deprecated any action which must lead to a war with Austria; but he offered to help Prussia in restoring the former state of things in the Low Countries. Stress was then laid on " the necessity of enabling Sweden to defend herself by another campaign against Russia "; England would

---

[1] On 19th March Fitzgerald reported to Leeds (" F. O.," France, 34): " M. Van der Noote has made a second application to His Most Christian Majesty and the National Assembly, which has met with a similar reception with [sic] the former, the letters having been returned unopened." Lafayette moved an amendment, but it was shelved.

pay her part of the sum needed for the support of Gustavus, and would also secure the neutrality of Denmark; but war against Russia and Austria was denounced as altogether foreign to our cardinal principle of restoring the former condition of things. Pitt and Leeds closed their despatch with the following noteworthy words:

The commencement of hostilities against the Imperial Courts, either indirectly by an immediate recognition of the Belgic Independence, or directly by our joining in the measures of offensive operations which Prussia may feel it her interest to adopt, would go beyond the line which this country has uniformly laid down, and from which it does not appear that the present circumstances should induce her to depart. If either the joint representations of the Allies, or the subsequent measures such as they have been here stated, should be successful in bringing about a peace on the terms of the *status quo*, this country would then be willing to include Turkey, Poland, and Sweden in the alliance and to guarantee to them the terms of that pacification.[1]

In order to understand the importance of this pronouncement, we must remember that at this time the chances of success attending the dismembering schemes of the two Empires and those of Prussia were curiously equal. In bulk Russia and Austria had the advantage. Their armies also seemed likely to drive the Turks over the Balkans in the next campaign, unless potent diversions in the rear impaired their striking power. But these diversions were imminent. The fate of the Hapsburg dominions still hovered in the balance. Catharine was face to face with another Swedish campaign which her exhausted exchequer could scarcely meet. How then could these two Empires withstand the shock of 200,000 trained Prussians, with the prospect that an Anglo-Dutch fleet would sweep the Russian warships from the sea? And this was not all. Hertzberg had already detached Poland from the Russian alliance and was on the point of adding the resources of that kingdom to his own;[2] and the prospect of consolidating Poland, both politically and geographically, opened up hopeful vistas for that interesting people and the whole European polity. Above all it promised to strengthen Prussia on her weakest flank.

[1] "F. O.," Prussia, 17. Leeds to Ewart, 26th February. Several sentences of the draft of this despatch are in Pitt's writing.
[2] Dembinski, i, 62-73, 274-8.

It is not surprising, then, that the ambitious and enterprising Dietz exceeded his instructions by signing a treaty with the Porte on 31st January 1790. He thereby pledged Prussia to make war on Russia and Austria in the spring, and not to lay down her arms until she secured for the Sultan an " honourable and stable peace," which assured safety for Constantinople against an attack by sea. If the Turks were victorious, Prussia promised to secure the Crimea for them. The Sultan, on his side, promised to compel Austria to restore Galicia to the Poles, who were, if possible, to be brought into the Triple Alliance. Finally Prussia, England, Holland, Sweden, and Poland were to guarantee the Turkish possessions as then defined.

These grandiose designs were furthered by the Prusso-Polish treaty, signed at Warsaw on 29th March. By it Frederick William, in case of hostilities, would send 18,000 men to assist the Republic, which would send 8,000 horsemen and half that number of footmen, or an equivalent in money or corn.[1] In case of great need the numbers of troops might be raised to 30,000 and 20,000 respectively. More important than this material succour was the advantage of marching through Polish Vol-hynia down the valley of the Dniester to cut the communica-tions of the Russian army on the lower Danube. Meanwhile the Poles would overrun Galicia, and the Prussians invade Bohemia and Moravia for the purpose of inciting the Czechs and Hun-garians to open revolt. On the whole the chances of war favoured Frederick William and his Allies, especially when the British Government agreed to join with Prussia in subsidizing Sweden for the campaign of 1790. The valour of the Swedes and their nearness to the Russian capital compelled Catharine to concentrate her efforts largely against them, and the prospect of a Prusso-Polish alliance aroused grave fears at Petersburg. "Everyone here wears a look of consternation," wrote the Prussian

---

[1] Hertzberg, " Recueil," iii, 1-8. Ewart reported on 4th January 1790 that Hertzberg was holding over the Polish treaty, and that it would be wholly "vague and ostensible." Clearly Ewart thought that Hertzberg would leave the door open to coerce Poland into giving up Danzig and Thorn (" F. O.," Prussia, 17). Article 2 of the treaty made this still possible. See, too, Frederick William's letter of 11th April 1790 to the King of Poland, and the projected treaty of commerce, in Martens, iv, 126-35.

The statement of the "Ann. Reg." of 1791 (p. 12), that the Triple Alliance became "a species of Sextuple Alliance," by the inclusion of Poland, the Porte, and Sweden, is incorrect.

envoy to his Court on 5th February. Probably this explains the passing flirtation of Catharine with England, which Pitt seems to have taken at its true value, in view of the exorbitant terms previously offered by her to Gustavus.[1]

In fact, the air was charged with insincerity and intrigue. The Prussian alliance with the Poles, which might have brought salvation to that distracted people, was accompanied with extremely hard conditions. Hertzberg saw in it the opportunity of once more forcing on his scheme of gaining Danzig and Thorn in return for the halving of the Prussian duties on Polish trade down the Vistula. His Shylock-like insistence on these terms deprived the compact of all worth from the outset; for the Poles claimed, and with reason, that the cession of those valuable districts should be bought, not by the halving of certain customs dues, but by the recovery of the whole of Galicia from Austria. In these demands the Court of Berlin seemed to concur; but ultimately, as we shall see, it allowed them to be frittered away under pressure from Vienna. As a result, the Poles felt no less distrust of Prussia than of the two Empires; and our envoy at Warsaw, Daniel Hailes, found that British policy alone inspired a feeling of confidence, and that a keen desire prevailed for a close alliance with England.[2]

Pitt also, guided by our naval experts, who wished England to be freed from dependence on Russia for naval stores, saw the advantage of a compact with Poland, provided her trade were freed from Prussian shackles. But his hands were so far tied by his alliance with Prussia, that he supported her demand for Danzig (not Thorn), if it were accompanied by an enlightened commercial treaty in which England might have a share. Events soon proved that greed rather than enlightenment prevailed at Berlin. That Court clung to its demand for Danzig and Thorn, and its envoy at Warsaw, the subtle, scheming, and masterful Lucchesini, more than once showed a disposition to hark back to the policy of Frederick the Great, and to choke the disputes with Austria and Russia by a partition of Poland.[3]

[1] Dembinski, i, 281, 283, 285.

[2] "F. O.," Poland, 4. Hailes to Leeds, 6th and 7th January, 27th February, 29th March 1790.

[3] *Ibid.* On 14th August Hailes reported a remark of Lucchesini, that Prussia could easily seize Danzig and Thorn at the next war. Lucchesini was replaced by the young and inexperienced von Goltz in October. For a sketch of Lucchesini see Keith's " Mems.," ii, 360.

For a time this seemed to be the natural upshot of an *entente* which unexpectedly came about between Berlin and Vienna. Not long after his accession Leopold wrote to his brother of Prussia in the terms of sensibility then in vogue. Frederick William answered in equally effusive strains; and but for the austere domination of the old Chancellor, Kaunitz, at Vienna, and the "turbulent genius" of Hertzberg at Berlin, there seemed a faint hope of a reconciliation.[1] But Kaunitz knew well how to keep up the bitterness against the upstart Protestant State; and Hertzberg had resolved to keep his master up to the high level of his own ambitions. Ingeniously he sowed the seeds of discord between the Imperial Courts by suggesting that Catharine should accept the mediation of the Allies with a view to a peace with the Porte.[2] This would leave Austria at the mercy of Prussia, and involve the loss of Galicia and the Netherlands. This last topic lay near to the heart of his Sovereign. Lord Auckland wrote thus on 19th March from his new Embassy at The Hague: "I have the fullest evidence that nothing less than absolute and inevitable necessity will induce him [Frederick William II] to contribute by word or deed to replacing the Netherlands under their old Government." And three weeks later he expressed his astonishment that, in view of the widespread anarchy, Prussia and all Governments should not feel it their prime duty to restore those ideas of order and just subordination to legal authority which the world so urgently needed. Otherwise the European fabric would be sapped by French theories and succumb to a new series of barbarian invasions.[3]

These were the views of Pitt, though he expressed them with less nervous vehemence. His aim, and that of his colleagues, was to bring Austria first, and afterwards Russia, to a pacification. They reminded the Court of Berlin that Leopold had "neither the same predilection for Russia, the same jealousy of Prussia, [n]or dislike to the mediation of England" as Joseph had displayed, and that the *status quo* might now find favour at Vienna. Leopold, they added, could not possibly accept the last proposal of Hertzberg, of ceding Galicia to the Poles on con-

[1] "F. O.," Austria, 20. Keith to Leeds, 3rd, 7th, and 14th April.
[2] "F. O.," Prussia, 17. Ewart to Leeds, 18th March.
[3] B.M. Add. MSS., 35542. Auckland to Keith, 19th March and 6th April 1790.

dition of being allowed to regain the Netherlands.[1] The British Cabinet also, on 30th March, charged Keith to press for an immediate armistice between Austria and Turkey, with a view to summoning a Congress of the Powers for a general pacification, which Great Britain earnestly desired. But, they added, with a touch of guile, as it would take much longer to communicate with St. Petersburg, they hoped that Austria would act alone, and immediately grant an armistice to the Turks. If Austria would further pledge herself to admit the restoration of the old constitution in the Netherlands, Keith might accept this as satisfactory, and send off a courier to Constantinople to warn Ainslie to bring the Porte to reason.[2]

The aim of saving Austria from many dangers is here so obvious that one learns with astonishment that Kaunitz received these offers most haughtily. The belated concessions granted by Joseph on his death-bed to his malcontent subjects had met with his approval, but only, as it seems, in order to press on the war with Turkey *à outrance*, as if that, and that alone, would impose on the Court of Berlin. With senile obstinacy and old-world *hauteur*, he repulsed Keith, who thereupon executed a skilful flanking move by appealing to the Vice-Chancellor, Count Cobenzl. This astute diplomat saw the gain that might accrue from the British proposals, and assured Keith that his Sovereign had received them with "very great satisfaction." Seeing his advantage, the British envoy warned Cobenzl against the extravagant claims of Potemkin, and urged him to work hard for a separate armistice with Turkey, now that "the most upright Court in Europe" offered its good services for that purpose. He further hinted that the recent treaties of Prussia with Turkey and Poland were a serious menace to Austria, and that the British proposal now made to her was "pointed and peremptory." Finally they agreed that Kaunitz should so far be humoured as to draft the official reply, but that Cobenzl should be its interpreter on behalf of Leopold II. With this odd arrangement Keith had to put up for some weeks; and in that time the desire for peace grew apace at Vienna.[3]

---

[1] B.M. Add. MSS., 35542. Leeds to Ewart, 19th and 30th March.

[2] "F. O.," Austria, 19. Leeds to Keith, 30th March; Ranke, "Fürstenbund," ii, 375; Kaunitz to Leopold, 16th March.

[3] *Ibid.* Keith to Leeds, 24th April, 1st and 15th May; Keith's "Mems.," ii, 261.

Any other way of looking at things was sheer madness. The ablest of Austrian Generals, Marshal Laudon, warned Leopold of the terrible risks of a war against both Prussia and Turkey. The Aulic Council also knew full well that the almost un- bounded influence of Prince Potemkin over the Czarina was ever used against Hapsburg interests, that pampered favourite having sworn vengeance against all who promoted the erection of Moldavia and Wallachia, which he coveted for himself,[1] into an independent principality. This scheme, so fatal to Haps- burg hopes, played no small part in sundering the two Empires. While, therefore, Leopold armed, as if for war with Prussia, he was secretly disposed to treat for a separate peace with the Turks if they would cede to him the limits of the Peace of Passarowitz, namely, North Servia and Wallachia as far east as the River Aluta. On the other hand he was resolved (so he told Keith on 9th May) to fight rather than lose the Netherlands, and in that case intended to gain the alliance of France by a few cessions of Belgian land. Still he hoped for a peaceful settle- ment through " the wise and kind intervention of England."[2]

The position was now somewhat as follows: Leopold had staved off a general revolt in his dominions by soothing con- cessions or promises, but he insisted on the continuance of hostilities against Turkey in order, as he said, to predispose her to peace. To the Brabanters and Flemings he granted an armistice, but seemed about to send forces thither as if for the restoration of unlimited power. Meanwhile Sweden and Turkey continued the unequal fight against Russia, and the Triple Alliance imposed prudence on Denmark. In this uneasy equi- poise England offered her mediation, not only to the belligerents —Russia, Austria, Turkey, and Sweden—but also to Prussia, with a view to a general armistice for the discussion of a settlement.[3]

Nowhere did this proposal meet with a cooler reception than at Berlin. Accordingly, on 21st May, Pitt and Leeds justified their conduct in a despatch to Ewart, in which the hand of the Prime Minister is plainly visible. He declared his earnest desire for the joint intervention of the three Allies, but explained that it was possible only by adhering to " that system of moderation to which he [His Majesty] has uniformly endeavoured to adhere."

---

[1] Dembinski, i, 279.   [2] " F. O.," Austria, 19. Keith to Leeds, 10th May.
[3] Hertzberg, " Recueil," iii, 58.

England desired to see the power of Sweden and Turkey maintained, and would secretly advance a subsidy to Gustavus, but did not feel justified in going to war with the two Empires. If Prussia drew the sword, England would not only keep France and Denmark quiet, but would also prevent the march of Austrian troops to the Netherlands during the armistice there. The earnest hope was expressed that Prussia would give up the Galician project, and limit her gains to the restoration of the former boundaries, with a few reasonable changes. Nothing was further from the wish of England than to sacrifice the interests of Prussia to those of Austria.[1]

It soon appeared that Pitt and Leeds were prepared to meet the Court of Berlin half way. On receiving the curt refusal of Catharine to the British offer of mediation, they admitted that the Prussian plan of exchanges of territory was not objectionable in itself, if Austria agreed to it—a large assumption. The arrangement might be that Russia should retain the Crimea and all her present conquests up to the Dniester, that is, inclusive of Oczakoff. In that case she must restore to Sweden the wider Finnish limits of the Peace of Nystadt. As for Austria, she should gain North Servia and West Wallachia as far as the River Aluta—the Passarowitz limits; and she ought to retain the whole of Galicia except the districts about Brody, Belez, and Cracow. As a reward for these services to Poland, Prussia would gain her heart's desire—Danzig, Thorn, and the Wartha territory. These would be " not sacrifices, but exchanges of territory." [2]

The British Cabinet would clearly have preferred the *status quo*; but in this alternative scheme it sketched arrangements highly favourable to Prussia, Austria, Russia, and Sweden, less so to Poland, but wholly unfavourable to the Turks. Certainly

---

[1] " F. O.," Prussia, 17. Leeds to Ewart, 21st May. Gustavus had pressed Prussia to advance to him 8,000,000 Swedish crowns, and 7,000,000 more next year if the war continued. He urged her to attack Russia at once. Sweden must obtain the wider boundaries of the Peace of Nystadt (Ewart to Leeds, 10th May). Early in June Prussia advanced 100,000 as a subsidy to Sweden, and as many more on behalf of England, on condition that *Gustavus would not make a separate peace with Russia* (Ewart to Leeds, 4th June).

[2] " F. O.," Austria, 20. Leeds to Keith, 23rd May (" Secret and Confidential "). Frederick William's plan of exchanges drawn up on 12th May was curiously similar (see Dembinski, i, 303, 305).

it corresponded more nearly to the actual or probable fortune of war, the prospects of the Moslems being at this time gloomy, those of the Swedes doubtful, but those of Prussia brilliant. The Sultan, it was hinted, might be soothed by the guarantee of his possessions and the hope of admission to the Triple Alliance along with Sweden and Poland.[1] This curious despatch shows that Pitt and Leeds cared little about Turkey, and that their adhesion to the *status quo* was conditioned by a politic opportunism.

A sudden and perplexing change now came over Hapsburg policy. Possibly Leopold relied on the wheedling assurances of support received from Catharine. Certain it is that in the middle of June he demanded " indemnities " for the proposed gains to Poland and Prussia; and his haughty tone was not lowered by the news of a sharp defeat inflicted by the Turkish garrison of Giurgevo on the Austrian besiegers. Bared to the waist, and armed with sword and dagger, they suddenly burst from the gates in three uncontrollable torrents, which swept the Imperialists out of trenches and camp, and far on to the plain. In vain also did Keith warn Cobenzl not to rely on Russia. The Hapsburgs now seemed bent on dismembering Turkey and defying their northern neighbours.[2] At the end of June Leopold declared his resolve not to treat with the rebels in the Netherlands, and to denounce the armistice with them. Probably this threatening tone was a screen to hide the weakness of Austria's position. On all sides her enemies held her fast. The Hungarians and Flemings firmly demanded their ancient rights; and persistence in the game of bluff must have led to the break up of her dominions.

Another curious change also came over the scene on the arrival of news at Berlin that Potemkin had offered to restore to the Porte all the Russian conquests of the present war, on condition of peace. This sudden adoption of the *rôle* of peacemaker by that ambitious and masterful favourite has never been fully explained.[3] It may have been due either to Turkish bribes or

---

[1] " F. O.," Austria, 20. Leeds to Keith, 8th June.

[2] *Ibid.* Keith to Leeds, 16th, 19th, 20th, and 30th June.

In face of these facts I reject the account given by Kaunitz on 24th July 1790 (in Vivenot, " Kaiserpolitik Oesterreich's ") that Austria had consistently sought to treat at Reichenbach on the English basis of the *status quo.*

[3] Pitt and Leeds thought it a device to evade England's offer of mediation (Leeds to Ewart, 25th June).

to a crafty resolve to checkmate Hertzberg's scheme of making
Turkey pay for Prussia's gains. For how could the professed
friend and ally impose on the Porte sacrifices far greater than
those demanded by the enemy? The report that Leopold was
disposed to accept the *status quo*, finding it far less objectionable
than Hertzberg's plan of exchanges, also gave food for thought.
Accordingly, Frederick William, before opening negotiations
with Austria, decided that this should form the general basis,
but with certain modifications. The Turks were to be warned
that, as Prussia's armaments had saved them from destruction,
they would now do well to conclude an armistice with Austria
and hope for admission to the Triple Alliance. They should
also humour their preserver by giving up Western Wallachia to
Austria, so that she in her turn might cede the outer districts of
Galicia to the Poles, who of course would yield to Prussia her
reward for these troublesome bargainings. As for Great Britain,
she was expected to favour these scientific readjustments because
the trade of the Vistula would then be freed from obstacles, and
be opened to her by favourable commercial treaties. Such was
Hertzberg's final plan for the preservation of the *status quo*.[1]
In order to secure the acquiescence of the Turks, he had long
kept the Porte on tenter-hooks by delaying the ratification of
Dietz's treaty, and by ordering the recall of that masterful envoy.
On the other hand, the Turks were left with a glimmer of hope
of eventual assistance from Berlin.

Accordingly, Prussian policy seemed about to win a brilliant
triumph at the proposed Conference of Reichenbach, where the
Triple Alliance and Austria (Russia having refused Britain's
mediation) were to thrash out these questions; and nothing is
more curious than to watch the collapse of Hertzberg's ingenious
web. In order at the outset to settle matters separately with the
Austrian envoy, Spielmann, the King of Prussia held Ewart
aloof because the British Ambassador consistently warned
Hertzberg against the complicated exchanges projected by him.
Thereupon Ewart drew up a Memorial insisting that England
must be a principal party, and that, as both Austria and Prussia
had promised to admit the *status quo* as the basis of negotiation,
the latter could not make war on the former if she consented to

---

[1] " F. O.," Prussia, 18. Ewart to Leeds, 11th June. He encloses a copy of
the Prussian despatch of 5th May from Constantinople, sent by Knobelsdorff.
(See also Hertzberg's " Recueil," iii, 76-8.)

it. In that case, or even if he (Ewart) were excluded from the Conference, Great Britain must cancel her engagements to Prussia. He further declared his conviction that Austria would retract her extreme claims and listen to reason.[1]

This sharp protest had some effect on Hertzberg; but the chief difficulty was now with Frederick William. At the head of his splendid army, he seemed to court war. He sent a courier to the Porte to ratify Dietz's treaty; and he cut off all communications with Austria as though hostilities had begun. At the first three sessions of the Conference (27th-29th June) the Austrian and Prussian envoys indulged in eager but vague wrangling; but the arrival of news from Constantinople that the Turks would never concede the Prussian demands sufficed to depress the bellicose ardour of the monarch. As there was a serious risk of the Porte coming to terms with Russia and Austria, he now harked back towards the *status quo*. This move, which the Duke of Brunswick and Möllendorf heartily supported, gathered strength when it appeared that Poland would accept none of Hertzberg's benefits. The arrival of the British note of 2nd July to the same general effect ended the last efforts of Frederick William for Danzig and Thorn.[2] He now gave Hertzberg written orders to abandon at once the whole scheme of exchanges " since it could only serve to commit him with Great Britain as well as with the Porte and Poland." Whence it appears that Hertzberg's scientific and philanthropic plans fell through simply because all the States concerned utterly repudiated them.

The renunciation, however, was made not unskilfully. The Prussian and British Ministers were careful to keep secret Hertzberg's change of front and thus prepared a surprise for Spielmann. That envoy having put forward some equally untenable schemes of aggrandisement, Ewart rose and read out a Memorial, drawn up in concert with his Prussian and Dutch colleagues, demanding an exact restitution of the old boundaries. In vain did the Hapsburg Minister seek to wriggle out of the dilemma by betraying Prussia into glaring inconsistency. Prussia stood firm; and finally he reduced his demands to Orsova and district. Even this cold comfort was denied him.

[1] " F. O.," Prussia, 18. Ewart to Leeds, 27th June.
[2] Ranke, "Fürstenbund," ii, 376-85; Dembinski, 82-4, 314; "Bland Burges P." 142-4.

The Triple Alliance was inexorable. Thereupon he demanded the dissolution of Prussia's compacts with Turkey and Sweden, only to meet with the reply that the Austro-Russian alliance must first be annulled.[1] Thus Hertzberg, even in the hour of personal defeat, brought down the Hapsburg schemes in utter collapse; and the result of the discussions at Reichenbach was the recurrence to the *status quo*—the very same arrangement which Pitt and Leeds had throughout declared to be the best of all solutions.

Hertzberg's annoyance at the destruction of his pet plans must have diminished when he heard from Vienna that Austria had secretly empowered Potemkin to make her peace with the Turks on that same basis. If this be true, each of the rivals was playing a game of bluff at Reichenbach; and the sight of the two Ancient Pistols eating the leek in turn must have filled Ewart with a joy such as falls to few diplomatists. Even as regards the Belgians, the British suggestion held good. They were to regain their ancient constitution together with an amnesty for past offences, and a guarantee by the three Allied Powers.[2] Frederick William, in complimenting Hertzberg on the end of the negotiations at Reichenbach, added that they must now assure themselves, through Ewart, of England's support in imposing the *status quo* on Russia.[3] A new chapter in the relations of the Powers and in the career of Pitt lay enfolded in this suggestion.

Shortly after this happy ending to the disputes in Central Europe came the news of a settlement of the war in the Baltic. Once again Gustavus III startled the world. After his sudden and furious attack on Catharine, and her no less fierce counter stroke, it seemed that the struggle must be mortal. But many circumstances occurred to allay their hatred. The aims of the Czarina had always trended southwards; and the war in Finland was ultimately regarded chiefly as an annoying diversion from the crusade against the Turks. Moreover the valour of the Swedes, who closed the doubtful campaign of 1790 with a decided success at sea, added to the difficulties of campaigning

---

[1] " F. O.," Prussia, 18. Ewart to Leeds, 16th July. See too Vivenot, 5.

[2] For the protest of the Belgian Congress against the Reichenbach compromise, which dashed their hopes of independence, see Van der Spiegel, " Négociations . . . des Pays Bas autrichiens," 303-6.

[3] Ranke, " Fürstenbund," ii, 387.

in Finland, left little hope of conquest in that quarter so long as the Triple Alliance kept the Danes quiet and subsidized Gustavus. Catharine was in fact fighting against the forces of nature and the resources of England, Prussia, and Holland. Gustavus, too, even in the year 1789 felt the sobering influences of poverty. In 1790 they threatened him with bankruptcy, and at that same time the outlook was far from bright in Finland. Fortunately, the Russians were not in a position to press Gustavus hard. But nothing could stave off the advent of bankruptcy unless the Allies promptly advanced a considerable sum. This they were not prepared to do, for his unceasing importunities had wearied them out. The Dutch declined to help in a matter which concerned them but little, and after long negotiations at Stockholm Great Britain and Prussia agreed on 31st July to advance £200,000, or only two-thirds of the minimum named by the King. By the month of August 1790 the treasury at Stockholm was absolutely empty, so our envoy, Liston, reported.

While Gustavus was chafing at the restraints of poverty, Catharine held out to him alluring hopes. So soon as she heard of the turn which affairs were taking at Reichenbach she resolved to end her quarrel with him in order the better to browbeat Prussia and England. Leopold had early informed her of his resolve to conclude the Turkish war, in accordance with the demands of the Allies; and he also warned her of their intention to deprive Russia of her chief conquest. With a quickness of insight and a magnanimous resolve instinct with the highest statesmanship, she resolved to end the war in the Baltic by offers which would appeal irresistibly to a knight-errant struggling with debts and worries. She therefore despatched a courier to him in Finland, holding out virtually the same terms which the Allies had guaranteed to him.

Gustavus did not long hesitate. It is true that he had the promise of seventeen British battleships, which were in the Downs ready to sail to his succour; Prussia also had already sent one half of the subsidy which he demanded; and he had pledged his troth to the Allies not to make a separate peace with Russia. That step, however, he now decided to take; and the impression afterwards prevailed at London and Berlin, that Russian money had some influence on his decision.[1] However

---

[1] On 7th September Bland Burges wrote to Lord Auckland that Russia had paid heavily for the Swedish peace (B.M. Add. MSS., 34433).

that may be, he sent Baron Armfelt to treat for peace. Where both sides were bent on a speedy settlement, difficulties vanished; and thus on 14th August 1790, the Peace of Werela was signed. It restored the few gains of territory which the belligerents had made, and gave permission to the Swedes to buy grain in Russian ports. The treaty was remarkable chiefly for its omissions. No mention was made of previous Russo-Swedish treaties, which gave the Empire some right to interfere in Swedish affairs. As Liston pointed out, the absence of any such claim was a personal victory for Gustavus; for it increased his authority and depressed that of the Russophile nobles. The King at once asserted his prerogative by condemning to death, despite the entreaties of Liston, the ringleader of the mutiny in Finland and by incarcerating two others for life.[1] Events were to show that the faction was cowed but not wholly crushed. The bullet of Ankerstrom repaid the debt of vengeance stored up in September 1790.

Equally strange was the abandonment of the Turks by their headstrong ally. Gustavus had gone to war ostensibly in order to prevent their overthrow, and now he left them at the mercy of Catharine. It is true that the signature of the Reichenbach Convention three weeks earlier ended their conflict with Austria; but the indignation of the Sultan, the wrath of the King of Prussia, and the quiet contempt of Pitt manifested the general feeling of the time.[2] Gustavus had salved his conscience by requiring Catharine to accord lenient treatment to the Moslems. The Czarina was quite ready to make any promises to this effect, if they formed no part of the treaty with Sweden. She assured Gustavus of her desire to renew the Treaty of Kainardji rather than continue the war; and Gustavus decided, so he informed Liston, " to trust to the elevated and honourable character of the Empress" on this point. Liston had his doubts. He ventured to express his surprise at the generosity of the imperial promises, which implied the restoration of the Crimea to Turkey, and he remarked that the combined pressure of Great Britain and Prussia had not availed to extort so great a boon. Gustavus, however, persisted in his estimate of the character of Catharine, doubtless because she humoured his latest plan, a crusade to Paris on

---

[1] " F. O.," Sweden, 11. Liston to Leeds, 17th and 24th August, 3rd, 7th, and 10th September.

[2] *Ibid.* Liston to Leeds, 23rd November; Dembinski, i, 84.

behalf of the French monarchy, while she further promised him
the sum of 2,000,000 roubles for his immediate needs.[1] She, too,
sang loudly the praises of the man whom she had sworn to
ruin. The cause of this new-born enthusiasm will appear in
due course.

From the Swedish point of view much might be said for
the action of Gustavus. He had rid himself and his land from
the irksome tutelage of Russia: he came out of the war with
no loss of territory, the first Russo-Swedish war of the century
of which this can be said; his martial energy had inspirited
his people; and he had overthrown a corrupt and unpatriotic
aristocracy. But, from the standpoint which he took up at the
outset of the war, his conduct had proved him a shifty ally, who
merited the suspicion of his former comrades. Nevertheless he
had played no small part in checking the subversive schemes
of Catharine and Joseph. Thanks to him the Moslems maintained a struggle which gave time for the army of Prussia and
the diplomacy of Pitt to exert themselves with effect. Had he
stood by his promises, the Triple Alliance would probably have
brought Russia to terms favourable to the interests both of
Turkey and of Poland.

Even as matters stood at the end of that year of turmoil, 1790,
Pitt might reflect with something of pride that his efforts had
decisively made for peace and stability. He it was who had been
mainly instrumental in saving Sweden from ruin, the Hapsburg
States from partition, and Prussia from Hertzberg's policy of
exchange and adventure. Moreover, at that same time British
policy won another success at a point which has always been
deemed essential to the maintenance of equilibrium in Europe.

The recovery of his authority in the Belgic provinces lay
near the heart of Leopold II. His letters and those of Kaunitz
show that he consented to patch matters up at Reichenbach
largely in order that he might be free to subdue Brabant
and Flanders. True, he admitted the mediation of the Triple
Alliance in those affairs; but his missive to Catharine shows
that he acquiesced in that convention only in order to prevent
the disruption of his dominions, and that he hoped to evade
some at least of its provisions by means of an " eternal alliance "
with Russia. As will appear in a later chapter, fidelity to

---

[1] " F. O.," Sweden, 11. Liston to Leeds, 23rd November 1790.

Russia involved a policy of procrastination and trickery towards
Turkey, Prussia, England, and the Belgians. The conduct of
Austria in the Eastern Question helped to checkmate Pitt and
secure a diplomatic triumph for Catharine in the year 1791.

Here we may notice that Leopold and Kaunitz, so soon as
the threat of war from the Prussian side passed away, and their
own troops in Luxemburg were reinforced, took a stern tone
with the men of Brabant and Flanders. At the Conference held
at The Hague for the settlement of those affairs, the Austrian
envoy, Count Mercy, refused to extend the time of the armistice
in those provinces, and warned the three mediating Powers that
their services would no longer be recognized by the Viennese
Court. Austrian troops also began to march towards Brussels.
Thereupon Lord Auckland hotly protested against this high-
handed proceeding; and the British Cabinet threatened to send
a large fleet to co-operate with the Prussians and Dutch in preventing the re-conquest of Belgic lands by Leopold.[1] This threat,
formidable in view of the large armament kept up by England,
even after the end of the Spanish dispute, emanated largely from
Pitt himself. For Ewart, who was then in London on furlough,
wrote to Auckland on 28th November 1790 concerning the
opinions of Ministers:

Some difference of opinion existed; but I trust Mr. Pitt will write to
your lordship himself in a satisfactory manner; and you know better
than I do of what consequence the opinions of others are. I confess I
am very uneasy about the explosion this affair must have produced at
Berlin; but I trust the explanations sent from hence will have given
satisfaction both there and with you on the great principle of making
the Emperor adhere—*bon gré, mal gré*—to his engagements for re-establishing the [Belgic] Constitution: and it appears impossible he should
venture in his present situation to risk the consequences of a refusal.[2]

Pitt's firmness won the day. Leopold shrank from a contest
with the Allies, and consented to a convention which was signed
on 10th December at The Hague. The ancient customs and
privileges of the Pays Bas were to be restored (including those
of the University of Louvain and the Catholic seminaries), and
an amnesty granted to all concerned in the recent revolt.
Leopold promised never to apply the conscription to his Belgian

[1] Vivenot, 9, 10, 39-52; Hertzberg, "Recueil," iii, 175-83; also 111-74 for
correspondence on the Bishopric of Liége.
[2] B.M. Add. MSS., 34435.

subjects, and he recognized the guarantee of Great Britain, Prussia, and Holland for the present arrangements.

The satisfaction of Pitt at this turn of affairs appeared in the order to place the British navy on a peace footing—a measure which we can now see to have been premature, in that it encouraged Catharine to reject the demands of the Allies, and Leopold to display the duplicity which often marred his actions. The failure of Pitt to coerce the Czarina will engage our attention later; but we may note here that, on various pretexts, Leopold refused to ratify the Hague Convention, and left Belgian affairs in a state which earned the hatred of that people and the suspicion of British statesmen.[1]

For the present, as the shiftiness of Leopold and the defiance of Catharine could not be surmised, there seemed to be scarcely a cloud on the political horizon. By the end of the year 1790, the policy of Pitt, cautious at the beginning of a crisis, firm during its growth, and drastic at the climax, had raised Great Britain to a state of prosperity and power which contrasted sharply with the unending turmoil in France, the helplessness of Spain, the confusion in the Hapsburg States, and the sharp financial strain in Russia. In truth, the end of the year 1790 marks the zenith of Pitt's career. In seven years, crowded with complex questions, he had won his way to an eminence whence he could look down on rivals, both internal and external, groping their way doubtfully and deviously.

Of these triumphs, those gained over foreign Powers were by far the most important, except in the eyes of those who look at British history from the point of view of party strife. To them the events of this fascinating period will be merely a confused background to the duel between Pitt and Fox. Those, however, who love to probe the very heart of events, and to pry into the hidden springs of great movements, which uplift one nation and depress another, will not soon tire even of the dry details of diplomacy, when they are seen to be the gauge of human wisdom and folly, of national greatness and decline.

[1] On 26th July 1791 Grenville, then Foreign Minister, wrote to Ewart that he hoped the sad straits of the Royal Family at Paris would induce Leopold to ratify the Hague Convention, and that the Allies must settle the Belgian constitution in such a way as to satisfy the rights of the sovereign and the just demands of that people (B.M. Add. MSS., 34438). See, too, Sybel, bk. ii, ch. vi.

In the seven years now under survey, England emerged from defeat, isolation, and discredit which bordered on bankruptcy, until she soared aloft to a position of prestige in the diplomatic and mercantile spheres which earned the envy of her formerly triumphant rivals. Strong in herself, and strengthened by the alliance of Prussia and Holland, she had to all appearance assured the future of the Continent in a way that made for peace and quietness. Pitt had helped to compose the strifes resulting from the reckless innovations of Joseph II, strifes which, had Hertzberg succeeded, must have led to a general war. The importance of this work of pacification has escaped notice amidst the dramatic incidents of the Revolution and Napoleonic Era. For in the panorama of history, as in its daily diorama, it is the destructive and sensational which rivets attention, too often to the exclusion of the healing and upbuilding efforts on which the future of the race depends. A more searching inquiry, a more faithful description, will reveal the truth, that a statesman attains a higher success when he averts war than when he wages a triumphant war.

CHAPTER XXIV

THE FRENCH REVOLUTION

A disposition to preserve, and an ability to improve, taken together, would be my standard of a statesman. Everything else is vulgar in the conception, perilous in the execution.—BURKE, *Reflections on the French Revolution.*

Ideas rule the world and its events. A Revolution is the passage of an idea from theory to practice.—MAZZINI, *The French Revolution of* 1789.

THAT the career of Pitt is divided into two very diverse portions by the French Revolution is almost a commonplace. Macaulay in artful antitheses has pointed the contrast between the earlier and the later Pitt; poets, who lacked his art but abounded in gall, descanted on the perversion of the friend of liberty into the reactionary tyrant; and Jacobins hissed out his name as that of " the enemy of the human race."

If we carefully study the attitude of Pitt towards the French Revolution, we shall find it to be far from inflexible. It changed with changing events. It was not that of a doctrinaire but of a practical statesman, who judges things by their outcome. He has often been blamed for looking at this great movement too much from the standpoint of a financier; and the charge is perhaps tenable as regards the years of the Jacobin ascendancy, when the flame kindled by Rousseau shrivelled up the old order of things. But the ideas prevalent in 1793 differed utterly from those of 1789, which aimed at reforms of a markedly practical character.

There was urgent need of them. As is well known, the unprivileged classes of France were entangled in a network of abuses, social, fiscal, and agrarian, from which the nobles had refused to set them free. Despite the goodwill of Louis XVI, the well-meant efforts of his chief minister, Necker, and the benevolent attempts of many of the clergy and some nobles, the meshes of Feudalism and the absolute monarchy lay heavily on the land up to the time of the Assembly of the States-

General at Versailles in May 1789. It is of course a gross error to assume that the French peasants were more oppressed than those of other continental lands. Their lot was more favoured than that of the peasantry of Spain, South Italy, Prussia, and most parts of Germany, to say nothing of the brutish condition of the serfs of Poland and Russia.[1] Those of France were more prosperous than Arthur Young believed them to be. They kept on buying up plot after plot in ways that illustrate the ceaseless land-hunger of the Celt and his elusive stubbornness.

But he would be a shallow reasoner who argued that, because the poverty of the French peasants was less grinding than it appeared, therefore the old agrarian and fiscal customs were tolerable. The most brilliant display of what Carlyle called "tongue-fencing" cannot justify a system which compels millions of men to live behind a perpetual screen of misery. To notice the case of that worthy peasant whose hospitality was sought by Rousseau during his first weary tramp to Paris. The man gave him only the coarsest food until he felt sure of his being a friend of the people and no spy. Then wine, ham, and an omelette were forthcoming, and Jacques Bonhomme opened his heart. " He gave me to understand," said Rousseau, " that he hid his wine on account of the duties, and his bread on account of the tax; and that he would be a lost man if he did not lead people to suppose that he was dying of hunger. All that he told me about this subject—of which previously I had not had the slightest idea—made an impression upon me which will never be effaced. There was the germ of that inextinguishable hatred

---

[1] It is too large a topic to discuss here why the Revolution did not break out in those lands; but I may hazard these suggestions: (1) Feudalism was there still a reality. The lords mostly lived on their estates, spent their money there, and performed the duties which the French nobles delegated to bailiffs, while they themselves squandered the proceeds at Paris or Versailles. Hence (2) a perilous concentration of wealth at those centres, which attracted thither the miserable, especially in times of distress like the severe winter of 1787-8. (3) In the other lands named above, the barriers of princely and feudal rule kept the people isolated in small States or domains and prevented common action. (4) Political and social speculations were brought home to the French as to no other people by the return of the French troops serving in the United States. (5) The mistakes of Louis XVI and Necker in May—June 1789, and the precipitation of the reformers at Versailles caused a rupture which was by no means inevitable, and which few if any had expected.

which developed later in my heart against the vexations endured by the poor, and against their oppressors." [1] Multiply the case of that hospitable peasant a million times over, and the outbreak of the Revolution becomes a foregone conclusion. The only surprising thing is that the *débâcle* did not come far earlier.

But the old order rarely breaks up until the vernal impulses of hope begin potently to work. These forces were set in motion, firstly, by the speculations of philosophers, the criticisms of economists and the social millennium glowingly sketched by Rousseau. Ideas which might have been confined to the study, were spread to the street by the French soldiers who had fought side by side with the soldiers of Washington, and became on their return the most telling pleaders for reform. Thus, by a fatal ricochet, the bolt launched by the Bourbons at England's Colonial Empire, glanced off and wrecked their own fabric.

The results, however, came slowly. It is often assumed that the destructive teachings of the Encyclopaedists, the blighting raillery of Voltaire, and the alluring Utopia of Rousseau would by themselves have been the ruin of that outworn social order. But it is certain that no one in France or England, up to the eve of the Revolution, anticipated a general overturn. Ultimately, no doubt, ideas rule the world; but their advent to power is gradual, unless the champions of the old order allow decay to spread. Furthermore, constructors of ingenious theories about the French Revolution generally forget that nearly all the ideas given to the world by Voltaire, Montesquieu, and Rousseau, were derived from the works of Hobbes, Locke, and Bolingbroke. The sage of Ferney drew his arrows from the quiver of English philosophy, and merely added the barbs of his own satire; Montesquieu pleaded on behalf of a balance of political powers like that of England; and all that was most effective in the " Social Contract" of the Genevese thinker came from Hobbes and Locke. The *verve* of Frenchmen gave to these ideas an application far wider than that which they had gained in their island home. Here the teachings of Locke formed a prim parterre around the palace of the King, the heir to the glorious Revolution of 1688. When transferred to that political forcing-bed, France, they shot up in baleful harvests.

It is the seed-bed which counts as well as the seed. The

---

[1] Rousseau, " Confessions," bk. iv.

harmlessness of philosophic speculation in England and its destructive activity in France may be explained ultimately by the condition of the two lands. In the Island State able Ministers succeeded in popularizing an alien dynasty and promoting the well-being of the people. Retrenchment and Reform were not merely topics of conversation in *salons*; they were carried out in many parts of the administration. This was specially the case after the peace of 1783, which left France victorious and England prostrate. There the fruits of victory were not garnered; and the political fabric, strained by the war, was not underpinned. Thinking men talked of repair, but, thanks to the weakness of the King and the favouritism of the Queen, nothing was done. Here the ablest constructive statesman since the time of Cromwell set about the needed repairs; and his work, be it remembered, coincided with the joyous experiments of the Court of Versailles to maintain credit by a display of luxury. The steady recovery of England and the swift decline of France may be ascribed in large measure to Pitt and Calonne.

It was against definite and curable ills in the body politic that the French reformers at first directed their efforts. In May—June 1789 the ideals of Rousseau remained wholly in the background. The Nobles and Clergy (as appears in their *cahiers*, or instructions) were, with few exceptions, ready to give up the immunities from taxation to which they had too long clung. Those of the Tiers Etat, or Commons, laid stress on fair taxation, on the abolition of the cramping customs of Feudalism, whether social, agrarian, or judicial, on the mitigation of service in the militia, while some even demanded better lighting of the streets. The Nobles and Clergy asked for a limitation of the powers of the Crown; and the Commons desired a constitution; but it was to resemble that of England, save that larger powers were left to the King, the Ministers being responsible to him alone. Few of the *cahiers* of the Commons asked for a fusion of the three Orders in one Assembly; and not one breathed the thought of a Republic.[1] Their bugbear was the game laws, not the monarchy; the *taille à miséricorde* and the *corvées*, not the Nobles; the burdensome tithes, not the Church.

As at Paris and Versailles, so among the peasants. At first,

---

[1] Prof. Aulard ("La Rév. Franç.," chs. iv-vi) has proved that there was no republican party in France until December 1790, and that it had no importance until the flight of the King to Varennes at Midsummer 1791.

even in troublous Franche Comté, their thoughts did not soar beyond taxes and feudal burdens. Arthur Young calmed a demonstration against himself by telling excited patriots near Besançon of the differences between taxes in England and France:

Gentlemen [he said] we have a great number of taxes in England which you know nothing of in France; but the *tiers état*, the poor, do not pay them, they are laid on the rich; every window in a man's house pays; but if he has no more than six windows, he pays nothing; a Seigneur, with a great estate, pays the *vingtièmes* and *taille*, but the little proprietor of a garden pays nothing; the rich, for their horses, their carriages, their servants, and even for liberty to kill their own partridges; but the poor farmer nothing of all this; and what is more, we have in England a tax paid by the rich for the relief of the poor.[1]

Who would not sympathize with these people! They were staggering under burdens piled up by a monarchy absolute in name, but powerless in all that made for reform and retrenchment. Where Louis XVI by his weakness, and the Queen by her caprice, had failed to right the wrong, the nation was bent in succeeding; and it is highly probable that, if the King had shown more tact in dealing with the Commons, and they a little more patience, the popular movement might have progressed peacefully for a decade, with wholly beneficent results. We, who know how one event led on to another, find it difficult to escape from the attractive but fallacious conclusion that the sequence was inevitable. The mind loves to forge connecting links, and then to conclude that the chain could not have been made otherwise—a quite gratuitous assumption. At several points it was the exceptional which happened. A perusal of the letters of intelligent onlookers shows that they foresaw, and most naturally, a wholly different outcome of events. They looked to see a few drastic reforms, a time of unrest, and then the remodelling of the monarchy *à l'Anglaise*.

As for Pitt, he waited to see whither all this would tend. His attitude towards France in the early part of 1789 was distinctly friendly. He assured the French ambassador, M. de Luzerne, that France and England had the same principles, namely, not to aggrandize themselves and to oppose aggrandizement in others, and he added that he hoped for the assistance of France

[1] A. Young, "Travels in France," 213 [Bohn edit.].

to assist Sweden and Turkey against the powerful Empires that were seeking their overthrow.

This declaration bespoke his fixed resolve to save Europe from the ambitious schemes of the other monarchs; and, now that France accepted Anglo-Prussian ascendancy in Holland and abandoned her forward policy in the Orient, she might serve to redress the balance of power. Such views were consonant with Pitt's lofty aim of winning over " the natural enemy." In truth, they were the outcome of common sense, even of self-interest. The suspicion and dislike were all on the side of the Court of Versailles. Montmorin and Luzerne were haunted by the fear that Pitt meant to pour oil on the smouldering discontent in France, and shrivel up the Bourbon power. There is not a shred of evidence that he ever entertained these notions. That they were harboured at Versailles merely showed that a Power which has rent another in twain cannot believe in the goodwill of the injured nation; and this suspicion was one of the many causes begetting irritation and alarm in Paris. On the other hand it must be remembered, as one of Pitt's greatest services, that his protests against the American War and his subsequent efforts for an *entente cordiale* with France, had so far effaced resentment on this side of the Channel, that the strivings of Frenchmen after political freedom and social equality aroused the deepest interest. The majority of our people sympathized with Fox, when, on hearing of the fall of the Bastille, he exclaimed: " How much is this the greatest and best event that has happened in the world." [1]

Official prudence or natural reserve kept Pitt silent on these affairs, and on the horrors of the ensuing Jacquerie, which speedily cooled the first transports of Britons. We know, however, that he must have viewed the financial collapse of France with secret satisfaction; for in August—September 1788 he wrote to Grenville in terms which implied that the recovery of the credit of France, then expected under the fostering care of Necker, would be a very serious blow, implying as it did the resumption of her aggressive schemes in the East.[2] Now, however, the disorders in France aroused his pity; and on 14th July, before he can have heard of the fall of the Bastille, he wrote to his mother that France was fast becoming " an object of compassion even to

---

[1] " Mems. of Fox," ii, 361.   [2] " Dropmore P.," i, 353-5.

a rival."[1] There is no sign that he feared the spread of demo-cratic opinions into England. The monarchy had never been so popular as since the mental malady of the King. On the whole, then, Pitt surveyed the first events of the Revolution from the standpoint of a diplomatist and financier. France seemed to him doomed to a time of chastening and weakness which might upset the uneasy equilibrium of Europe.

Already he had come into touch with the French people at a very sensitive point, and in a way which illustrated their eager expectancy and his cool and calculating character. On 25th June Necker sent to him an urgent appeal begging that he would sanction the export of flour from Great Britain to France in order to make good the scarcity which there prevailed. If the request must come before Parliament, he trusted that the boon would speedily be granted by a generous nation, and by a statesman "whose rare virtues, sublime talents, and superb renown have long rivetted my admiration and that of all Europe."[2]

In sharp contrast to this personal and effusive request was the cold and correct demeanour of Pitt. He sent the following formal reply, not to Necker, but to the French ambassador, the Marquis de Luzerne:

Downing Street, 3rd July, 1789.[3]

Mr. Pitt presents his compliments to the Marquis de Luzerne. He has felt the strongest desire to be able to recommend sending the supply of flour desir'd by Monsʳ Necker and had hopes from the information at first given him by Mr. Wilson that it would be practicable; but, having afterwards received some contrary information, he thought it necessary that the subject should be examined by the Committee of Council for the Affairs of Trade, whose enquiry was not clos'd till this morning. Mr. Pitt has now the mortification to find that, according to the accounts of the persons most conversant with the corn trade, the present supply in this country compar'd with the demand, and the pre-carious prospect of the harvest render it impossible to propose to Par-liament to authorize any exportation.

Three days later Pulteney brought the matter before the House of Commons and deprecated the export of 20,000 sacks of flour to France which had been talked of. Pitt thereupon stated that skilled advice was being taken as to the advisability

---

[1] Stanhope, ii, 38.   [2] Pitt MSS., 163.   [3] *Ibid.* 102.

of allowing such an export, in view of the shortness at home, and the gloomy prospects for the harvest. Wilberforce, Dempster, and Major Scott urged the more generous course towards our suffering neighbours; but others pointed out that, as the price of home wheat was rising (it rose seven shillings the bushel on that very day), any such proposal would enhance that perilous tendency at home without materially benefiting the French. Even at the present figures export was forbidden under the existing Corn Law; but Pitt mentioned that a curious attempt was on foot at Shoreham to depress the price from forty-eight shillings to forty-four in order to procure the export of 8,000 sacks of flour to Havre. As the transaction was clearly fictitious, he had directed the Customs officers to stop the export. On 13th July Grenville, in the absence of Pitt, asked leave to introduce a Bill for the better ascertaining and regulating the export of corn; and the House at once agreed.[1]

Such, then, was the beginning of Pitt's relations to French democracy. They are certainly to be regretted. His reply to Necker's request is icily correct and patriotically insular; and his whole attitude was a warning to the French not to expect from him any deviation from the rules of Political Economy. Of course it is unfair to tax him with blindness in not recognizing the momentous character of the crisis. No one could foresee the banishment of Necker, the surrender of the Bastille, on the very day after Grenville's motion, still less the stories of the *pacte de famine*, and their hideous finale, the march of the *dames des halles* to Versailles, ostensibly to get food. Nevertheless, the highest statesmanship transcends mere reason. The greatest of leaders knows instinctively when economic laws and the needs of his own nation may be set aside for the welfare of humanity. The gift of 20,000 sacks of flour outright would have been the best bargain of Pitt's career. It would have spoken straight to the heart of France, and brought about a genuine *entente cordiale*. His conduct was absolutely justified by law. The Commercial Treaty of 1786 with France had not included the trade in corn or flour, which had long been subject to strict regulations, and therefore remained so. Moreover, the Dublin Government did not allow the export of wheat to Great Britain until home wheat sold at more than thirty shillings the barrel;

---

[1] "Parl. Hist.," xxviii, 226-31. For the tricks used in order to get corn exported to France, see "Auckland Journals," ii, 367.

and in that year of scarcity, 1789, when the harvest was extremely late, and the yield uncertain even at the beginning of December, the fiat went forth from Dublin Castle that no wheat must for the present cross the Irish Sea to relieve the scarcity in England.[1] If that was the case between the sister kingdoms, Pitt certainly acted correctly in forbidding the export of flour to France.

Meanwhile, Anglo-French relations were decidedly cool. The Duke of Dorset, our ambassador at Paris, reported that it was not desirable for English visitors to appear in the streets amid the excitements that followed on the fall of the Bastille; and an agent, named Hippisley, employed by him, reported that "the prejudices against the English were very general— the pretext taken being our refusal to aid the French with grain, and our reception of M. Calonne, which, they contended, was in deference to the Polignacs."[2] The Duke of Dorset also referred to the prevalence of wild rumours as to our efforts to destroy the French ships and dockyard at Brest, and to foment disorders in France.[3]

Certainly we were not fortunate in our ambassador. In the year 1786 the Duke of Dorset had often shown petty touchiness in his relations with William Eden, besides jealously curbing the superior abilities of his own subordinate, Daniel Hailes. Now that they were gone, his despatches were thin and lacking in balance. After the fall of the Bastille, he wrote to the Duke of Leeds that "the greatest Revolution that we know of has been effected with, comparatively speaking, . . . the loss of very few lives. From this moment we may consider France as a free country, the King as a very limited monarch, and the nobility as reduced to a level with the rest of the nation." He described the tactful visit of Louis XVI to Paris on 17th July as the most humiliating step he could possibly take. "He was actually led in triumph like a tame bear by the deputies and the city militia." He added, with an unusual flash of insight, that the people had not been led by any man or party, "but merely by the general diffusion of reason and philosophy."

---

[1] "Dropmore P.," i, 549, 550; "Corresp. of W. A. Miles," i, 739.

[2] "F. O.," France, 32. Mem. by Hippisley, 31st July 1789. Calonne for some time resided at Wimbledon House. He was received, though very coolly, at Court.

[3] They were set forth in much detail in Paris newspapers of 25th July.

I   N N

Nevertheless, though the King's youngest brother, the Comte d'Artois, and his reactionary followers were scattered to the four winds, Dorset had the imprudence to write to congratulate him on his escape. The letter was intercepted, and the populace at once raised a hue and cry against the British embassy, it being well known that the Duke was on the most familiar terms with the highest aristocracy. Dorset thereupon wrote to the Duke of Leeds urging the need of stating officially the good will of England for France; and that Minister at once expressed " the earnest desire of His Majesty and his Ministers to cultivate and promote that friendship and harmony, which so happily subsists between the two countries." Dorset communicated this to the National Assembly on 3rd August; but that was his last official act. He forthwith returned to England, presumably because of the indiscretion related above.

During the next months the duties of the embassy devolved upon Lord Robert Stephen Fitzgerald (brother of the more famous Lord Edward), who was charged to do all in his power to cultivate friendly relations with the French Government, and, for the present at least, to discourage the visits of English tourists.[1] The new envoy certainly showed more tact than Dorset; but his despatches give the impression that he longed for the political reaction which he more than once predicted as imminent. We may notice here that the Pitt Cabinet showed no sign of uneasiness as to the safety of its archives at the Paris embassy until 5th March, when orders were issued to send back to London all the ciphers and deciphers. The attitude of Pitt towards French affairs was one of cautious observation.

In the meantime affairs at Paris went rapidly from bad to worse. The scarcity of ready money, the dearness of bread, and the wild stories of the so-called *pacte de famine*, for starving the populace into obedience, whetted class-hatreds, and rendered possible the extraordinary scenes of 5th and 6th October. As is well known, the tactlessness of the Queen and courtiers on the one side, and on the other the intrigues of the Duke of Orleans and his agents, led up to the weird march of the market-women

---

[1] "F. O.," France, 33. Leeds to Fitzgerald, 31st July. In B.M. Add. MSS., 28063, is a letter of the Duke of Richmond to the Marquis of Carmarthen of 21st September 1788, thanking him for sending to the Paris embassy his nephew, Lord R. Fitzgerald, in place of Daniel Hailes.

and rabble of Paris upon Versailles, which brought the Royal Family captive into the capital.

The absence of the Duke of Orleans being highly desirable, he was sent to London, ostensibly on a diplomatic mission, but really in order to get rid of him until affairs should have settled down.[1] The pretext was found in the troubles in the Austrian Netherlands. As we saw in the previous chapters, nothing could be more unlike the growingly democratic movement in France than the revolt of the Flemings and Brabanters against the antinational reforms of Joseph II of Austria. Men so diverse as Burke and Dumouriez discerned that truth. The great Irishman in a letter to Rivarol termed the Belgian rising a resistance to innovation;[2] while to the French free-thinker it was *une révolution théocratique*. Nevertheless, as many Frenchmen cherished the hope of giving a prince to the Pays Bas, it was thought well to put forth a feeler London-wards; and Philippe Egalité in fancy saw himself enthroned at Brussels.

Such a solution would have been highly displeasing both at Westminster and at Windsor; and there is no proof that the Duke even mentioned it at Whitehall. In point of fact his mission was never taken seriously. George III, with characteristic acuteness in all matters relating to intrigue, had divined the secret motive of his journey and expressed it in the following hitherto unpublished letter to the Duke of Leeds:

WINDSOR, *Oct.* 19, 1789. 9.55 a.m.[3]

The language held by the Marquis de Luzerne to the Duke of Leeds on the proposed journey of the Duke of Orleans does not entirely coincide with the intelligence from Lord Robert Fitzgerald of the Duke's message to the States General [*sic*] announcing his absence as the consequence of a negotiation with which he is to be employed at this Court. I confess I attribute it to his finding his views not likely to succeed or some personal uneasiness for his own safety. . . .

The King argued correctly; and doubtless his suspicions ensured for the Duke a chilly reception at the Foreign Office. On 22nd or 23rd October Leeds saw him at his residence in London, but could get from him no more than polite professions of regard for England. Leeds thereupon urged Fitzgerald

---

[1] See the threats of Lafayette to the Duke of Orleans in Huber's letter of 15th October 1789 to Lord Auckland ("Auckland Journals," ii, 365).

[2] Burke, "Corresp.," iii, 211.   [3] B.M. Add. MSS., 27914.

to find out whether the Duke's "mission" was a plausible pretext for securing his absence from Paris; to which our envoy replied that everyone at Paris spoke of him with indifference or contempt, and that Lafayette had discovered proofs of his complicity in the outrages of 5th to 6th October, and therefore had him sent away. On 6th November Fitzgerald added that Louis XVI had given the Duke no instructions whatever. Leeds had already come to much the same conclusion. On 30th October he saw Orleans, who merely suggested a close understanding between England and France, especially if the Emperor should march an army into his Belgic provinces. Leeds coolly replied that the desire of Joseph II to crush the revolt was most natural, and that France would do well to restore order at home rather than look with apprehension on events beyond her borders. As he accompanied these remarks with expressions of sincere commiseration for Louis XVI, Orleans must have seen that the secret of his involuntary mission was divined. This seems to be the only notice of it in the British archives. His sinister reputation and his association with loose company in London soon deprived him of all consequence.

Pitt's attitude towards the Belgian Question has been already described. He seems to have given more time and thought to it than to the French Revolution—a fact which is not strange if we remember that the future of the Belgic lands was of untold importance for Great Britain. To secure their independence from France she had many times poured out her blood and treasure; and Pitt was destined to spend his last energies in the greatest of those efforts. Moreover, as we have seen, the European polity was far more seriously menaced by the schemes of Catharine, Joseph, and Hertzberg than by French reformers; and no one expected that in a short time the shifting kaleidoscope of European States would be altogether shivered by blows dealt from Paris. We, who know the outcome of events, are apt to accuse Pitt of shortsightedness for not concentrating his attention on France; but the criticism rests on the cheapest of all kinds of wisdom—wisdom after the event. In Pitt's mind the advent of militant democracy aroused neither ecstasy nor loathing. His royalism had nothing in common with the crusading zeal of Gustavus III, and therefore did not impel him to rescue the Bourbons from the troubles which resulted so largely from their participation in the American War. Here, as everywhere, Pitt allowed cold reason to rule; and reason suggested that the Bourbons might atone for that stupendous blunder as best they could. Besides, the experience of nations, as of families, forbade the interference of an outsider in domestic quarrels. Apart from its bearing on Belgian affairs, the French Revolution is scarcely named in Pitt's correspondence of this time.

Still more curious is it that the letters of George III to his Minister contain not a single reference to the Revolution. This silence respecting events of untold import for all crowned heads is explicable if we remember that to most men they seemed but the natural outcome of mismanagement and deficient harvests, which statesmanship and mother Nature would ere long set right. The proneness of George to look at everything from his own limited point of view was also at this time emphasized by ill health and family troubles, which blotted out weightier topics. Thus, on 1st May 1789, he declared his annoyance at the sudden return of Prince William from the West Indies —a proof that his paternal commands would never be obeyed. The Prince, he says, must now have the same allowance as the Duke of York. " I have," he adds, " but too much reason to expect no great comfort but an additional member to the opposite faction in my own family." He concludes with the desire that some arrangement may be made for the Queen and the princesses in case of his death; for his whole nervous system has sustained a great shock in the late illness. On 9th June the King again expresses to Pitt his regret that Prince William declines to return to sea. His letters during the rest of that exciting year are devoid of interest if we except the effort to reconcile Pitt and Thurlow referred to in Chapter XX.

The King's domestic dronings are varied on 14th January 1790 by an excited declaration that a frigate must be provided at once in order to convey Prince Edward, afterwards Duke of Kent, to Gibraltar, as it was of urgent importance that he should at once leave London.[1] On 3rd March he records his heartfelt

---

[1] Pitt MSS., 102. No reason is assigned for this expatriation, which was probably due to the return of the prince from Geneva without permission. That the commander at Gibraltar, General O'Hara, received a hint to be strict with the young prince seems likely from his rebuke on a trifling occasion: "If you do not do your duty, I will make you do it" (" Napoleon and Sir Hudson Lowe," by R. C. Seaton, 32).

joy at the failure of Fox's attempt to procure the repeal of the
Corporation and Test Acts; and on the 28th of that month
occurs the first reference to the French Revolution which I have
found in the King's letters. He then expresses to Pitt regret
that the papers forwarded by the Comte d'Artois (younger
brother of Louis XVI) and his political agent, Calonne, contain
so little real information about the affairs of France. He continues thus: " Mr. Pitt's answer should be very civil, and may be
very explicit as to no money or other means having been used
to keep up the confusion in France; and M. de Calonne ought
to convey those assurances wherever he thinks they may be
of use."[1] Readers who have an eye for the ironies of history
may notice that the first of the myriad stories thrown off by the
perfervid Gallic imagination, as to the ubiquitous potency of
British money in creating famines, arming assassins, and trumping up Coalitions against France, originated with the royalist
exiles, who saw in the French Revolution the first manifestation
of the wonder-working power of " Pitt's gold."

That statesman's opinion concerning the Revolution was first
made known during the debates on the Army Estimates
(5th and 9th February 1790). Having inserted in the King's
Speech a reference to the friendly assurances which he received from all the Powers, and a guarded statement that
the internal troubles in certain states engaged the King's " most
serious attention," he was twitted by champions of economy
with a slight increase in the army. True, the total provided for
was only 17,448 officers and men; and part of the increase was
due to the drafting of 200 men to keep order in the infant colony
of New South Wales. But even these figures, which

> barely could defy
> The arithmetic of babes,

aroused the compunctions of Marsham, Fox, and Pulteney.
They complained that, though most of our Colonial Empire
had been lost, yet our army had been increased by thirteen
regiments since the disastrous peace of 1783. Marsham deemed
this increase " alarming," and wholly needless in view of the
paralysis of France. Fox did not repeat the stale platitude
that a standing army was a danger to liberty; for, as he pointed

---

[1] Pitt MSS., 102. I have not found Pitt's letter to Calonne, though there
are two others of 1795 to him.

out, the French soldiers had shown themselves to be good citizens; but he opposed the present vote on the ground of economy, and because it was urgently necessary to strengthen the public credit, which could be done only by reductions of expenditure. He repeated these arguments in the second debate, that of 9th February.

On both occasions Pitt defended the proposed vote for the army, on the ground that "a small saving now might prove the worst economy, by involving us in disputes which might be attended with greater additional burthens to the kingdom." In the latter debate he skilfully used the admission of Fox, that any one who three years before had foretold the present convulsions in France would have been deemed a lunatic, in order to enforce the need of preparedness, it being no excuse for responsible Ministers to exclaim in the midst of disasters—"Who would have thought of it?" Then, as was his wont, he opened up wider vistas in this noble but, alas, less prophetic strain:

The present convulsions of France must, sooner or later, terminate in general harmony and regular order; and though the fortunate arrangements of such a situation may make her more formidable, it may also render her less obnoxious as a neighbour. . . . Whenever the situation of France shall become restored, it will prove freedom rightly understood; freedom resulting from good order and good government; and thus circumstanced France will stand forward as one of the most brilliant Powers in Europe; she will enjoy just that kind of liberty which I venerate, and the valuable existence of which it is my duty, as an Englishman, peculiarly to cherish; nor can I, under this predicament, regard with envious eyes, an approximation in neighbouring States to those sentiments which are the characteristic features of every British subject. Easier, I will admit with the right hon. gentleman, is it to destroy than rebuild; and therefore I trust that this universally acknowledged position will convince gentlemen that they ought, on the present question, not to relax their exertions for the strength of the country, but endeavour to regain our former pinnacle of glory, and to improve, for our security, happiness and aggrandisement, those precious moments of peace and leisure which are before us.[1]

This statesmanlike utterance was not prompted by considerations of the mutability of human affars. The bent of Pitt's mind was too practical to be influenced by copy-book maxims.

[1] "Parl. Hist.," xxviii, 351.

Already, on 21st January, the first rumours had reached the
Foreign Office, which portended serious friction with Spain. To
this question we must devote the following chapter.

It will be well, however, to conclude this chapter by a few
remarks on the standpoints from which Pitt and Burke viewed
the French Revolution. They were in truth so different as
scarcely to admit of comparison. The judgements of Pitt were
those of a statesman of an objective order of mind, who weighed
events carefully, judged men critically, and was content to
change his policy as occasion required. In his view institutions
were made for men, not men for institutions. But his zeal for
Reform was tempered by respect for the verdicts of the past and
by the knowledge that the progress of mankind must be slow if
it is to be sure. He had lost much of his earlier zeal for Parliamentary Reform, but only because the people had seemed to
care little for it, and were sincerely attached to their time-worn
institutions. His attitude towards this great question during the
stormy years of the Jacobin ascendancy will concern us later;
and we need only notice here that, even at that time of political
ferment, he never declared that under no circumstances would he
bring in a Reform Bill, but always left open a door of hope in
that direction when quieter days should return. For the present
he repressed all movements which he considered seditious,
dangerous, or likely to cause divisions; and for that alone he
may be condemned by friends of progress.

From the other side he is censured for his lack of sympathy
with the woes of a distressed King and Queen. Certainly we
miss in his utterances any gush of genuine feeling on a subject
which touched the inmost springs of emotion in our people.
True, he had small ground for liking Louis XVI and his consort. The King of France had dealt the British Empire a
deadly blow in America; and Marie Antoinette was an inveterate
intriguer against England. Even up to the flight to Varennes
at midsummer 1791, she impelled her brother, Leopold II of
Austria, in his anti-English courses, which, as we shall see, cost
us so dear. What was worse, she even accused England of
having instigated all the disorders of which she was the victim.
Nevertheless, it would have been generous to attribute this
spitefulness to her narrow training and bitter sorrows. Pitt
would have been a more engaging figure if he had occasionally
shown a spark of that indignation which burnt so fiercely in

Burke. If he had any deep feelings on the subject, he chose to conceal them, perhaps from a conviction that the expression of them would do more harm than good.

Well would it have been for the cause of peace if the champion of French royalism in these islands had obeyed the dictates of reason which held Pitt tongue-tied. Unfortunately sentiment and emotion at this time reigned supreme in the great mind of Burke. Every student of history must admire the generous impulses which were incarnate in the great Irishman. They lent colour to the products of his imagination, and they lit up his actions with a glow which makes his blunders more brilliant than the dull successes of mediocre men. Where sentiment was a safe guide, there Burke led on with an energy that was not less conspicuous than his insight. Where critical acumen, mental balance, and self-restraint were needed, the excess of his qualities often led him far astray. The true function of such a man is to interpret the half-felt impulses of the many. If he seek to guide them to definite solutions, his ardent temperament is apt to overshoot the mark. Observers noted how Burke's vehement conduct of the Warren Hasting's affair injured his cause; and many more were soon to discern the same failing when, with Celtic ardour, he rushed into the complex mazes of the French Revolution.

Opinions will always differ as to the merits of his remarkable book on that subject. Its transcendent literary excellences at once ensured it an influence enjoyed by no other political work of that age; but we are here concerned with his " Reflections " not as literature, but as criticism on the French movement. Even in this respect he rightly gauged some of the weaknesses of Gallic democracy. He was the first of Britons to discern the peril to the cause of freedom when the brutal fury of the populace broke forth in the hour of its first triumph, the surrender of the Bastille, and still more in the Jacqueries that followed. He also gave eloquent and imperishable expression to the feeling of respect for all that is venerable, in which the French reformers were sadly deficient; and, while he bade them save all that could be saved of their richly-storied past, he truly foretold their future if they gave rein to their iconoclastic zeal. In my judgement the passage in which Burke foretells the advent of Bonaparte is grander even than that immortal rhapsody on the fate of Marie Antoinette and the passing away of the age of chivalry. The one is the warning of a prophet; the latter is the wail of a genius.

Equally profound are his warnings to the French enthusiasts of the danger of applying theories to the infinite complexities of an old society. To quote some sentences:

The science of constructing a commonwealth, or renovating it, or reforming it, is, like every other experimental science, not to be taught *a priori*. Nor is it a short experience that can instruct us in that practical science, because the real effects of moral causes are not always immediate. . . . The science of government being therefore so practical in itself, and intended for such practical purposes, a matter which requires experience, and even more experience than any person can gain in his whole life, however sagacious and observing he may be, it is with infinite caution that any man ought to venture upon pulling down an edifice, which has answered in any tolerable degree for ages the common purposes of society, or on building it up again, without having models and patterns of approved utility before his eyes. . . . The nature of man is intricate; the objects of society are of the greatest possible complexity; and therefore no simple disposition or direction of power can be suitable either to man's nature, or to the quality of his affairs. When I hear the simplicity of contrivance aimed at and boasted of in any new political constitutions, I am at no loss to decide that the artificers are grossly ignorant of their trade, or totally negligent of their duty. . . . The rights of men in governments are their advantages, and these are often in balances between differences of good, in compromises sometimes between good and evil, and sometimes between evil and evil. . . . I cannot conceive how any man can have brought himself to that pitch of presumption to consider his country as nothing but *carte blanche*, upon which he may scribble whatever he pleases.

We are here reminded of the saying of Dumont, the friend of Mirabeau, that the fear of being thought officious and interfering is as universal among the English as is the desire of the French of taking a prominent part and interfering in everything.[1] This home thrust by the able Swiss thinker goes far to explain the difference between the Revolution of 1688 in England and that of a century later in France. Vanity, love of the sensational, and, a mania for wholesale reconstruction on geometrical designs largely account for the failures of the French revolutionists; and Burke's warnings on these heads were treated with the petulant disdain characteristic of clever children.

[1] Dumont, "Souvenirs sur Mirabeau," ch. x.

for its keen insight into the causes that made for disruption or revolt in the European lands, not even excluding Great Britain.[1] In this one respect Burke excelled Pitt, just as nervous apprehension will detect dangers ahead that are hidden from the serene gaze of an optimist. Wilberforce judged Pitt to be somewhat deficient in foresight;[2] and we may ascribe this defect to his intense hopefulness and his lack of close acquaintance with men in this country and, still more, on the Continent. Burke found that both the Prime Minister and Grenville had not the slightest fear of the effect of revolutionary ideas in this Kingdom "either at present or at any time to come."[3] Here Burke was the truer prophet. But how could Pitt sift the wise from the unwise in the copious output of Burke's mind? They mingle so closely as to bewilder the closest observer even now, when the mists of passion enveloping those controversies have partly cleared away. Sentiment palpitated visibly in all Burke's utterances; and the teachings of the philosopher were lost amidst the diatribes of the partisan.

In fact, it was difficult for a practical statesman to take the orator seriously. In April 1791 he had furiously attacked Pitt's Russian policy; and, as we have seen, the differences between them were more than political, they were temperamental. No characteristic of Pitt is more remarkable than the balance of his faculties and the evenness of his disposition. No defect in Burke's nature is more patent than his lack of self-control, to which, rather than to his poverty, I am inclined to ascribe his exclusion from the Whig Cabinets. Irritability in small things had long been his bane; and now to the solution of the greatest problem in modern history he brought a fund of passion and prejudice equal to that of any of the French *émigrés* who were pestering the Courts of Europe to crush the new ideas by force.

Yet, however much Pitt mistrusted Burke the politician, he admired him as a writer; so at least we gather from a somewhat enigmatical reference in Wilberforce's diary. "22nd November (1790): Went to Wimbledon—Dundas, Lord Chatham, Pitt, Grenville, Ryder. Much talk about Burke's book. Lord Chatham, Pitt and I seemed to agree: *contra*, Grenville and Ryder."[4] If this entry be correct, Wilberforce and Grenville were destined

---

[1] Burke's "Works," iii, 347-93 (Bohn edit.).
[2] "Private Papers of Wilberforce," 71.
[3] Burke, "Corresp." iii, 344.   [4] "Life of Wilberforce," i, 284.

soon to change their opinions. It may be that Pitt and Wilberforce agreed with Burke owing to their dislike of the iconoclastic methods of the French democrats, and that Grenville's cold nature was repelled by the sentimentalism of the book.

In their judgements on the French Revolution Pitt and Burke stood not far apart. Pitt knew France no better than the great Irishman, and he distrusted theorizers and rash innovators fully as much, especially when their symmetrical notions were carried out by mobs. But the two men differed sharply as to the remedy. Burke came to believe more and more in armed intervention; Pitt saw in it ruin for French royalists and turmoil throughout the Continent. Here again the difference was in the main one of temperament. In Burke's nature the eagerness and impulsiveness of the Celt was degenerating into sheer fussiness, which drew him toward the camp of the *émigrés* who strutted and plotted at Turin and Coblentz. Pitt's coolness and reserve bade him distrust those loud-tongued fanatics, whose political rhapsodies awoke a sympathetic chord in no ruler save Gustavus of Sweden. True, Catharine of Russia shrilly bade them Godspeed; but, as we shall see, her distant blessings were the outcome of Muscovite diplomacy rather than of royalist zeal.

Pitt and Grenville, who saw other things in life besides the woes of Marie Antoinette and Jacobin outrages, were resolved not to lead the van of the monarchical crusade. They might approve Burke's sage production, the "Appeal from the New to the Old Whigs," which won the warm commendation of the King, as well as of Grenville, Camden, and Dundas, but they were bent on maintaining strict neutrality on the French Question. Pitt and his cousin met Burke more than once in the summer and autumn of 1791; but they kept their thoughts veiled, probably because Burke was working hard for the royalist league which the French Princes hoped to form. The general impression produced on Burke was that the Court of St. James would certainly not act against the champions of monarchy, but would preserve a benevolent neutrality. Other observers took a different view. The Russian ambassador, Vorontzoff, declared that Pitt was a democrat at heart, and kept up the naval armaments in order to intimidate the royalists, while he sent Hugh Elliot to Paris to concert measures along with Barnave.[1] These

[1] Burke, "Corresp.," iii, 238, 239, 255, 267, 274, 275, 278, 291, 302, 308, 336, 342.

stories are of value merely because they illustrate Pitt's power of holding back his trump cards and thereby rehabilitating the national prestige, which had recently suffered at the hands of the Czarina. At such a crisis silence is often a potent weapon. The Arab "Book of Wisdom" asserts that wisdom consists in nine parts of silence; while the tenth part is brevity of utterance. If Burke had realized this truth, his political career would not have ended in comparative failure. By acting on it, Pitt disconcerted his interviewers and exasperated his biographers; but he helped to keep peace on the Continent for nearly a year longer; and he assured that boon to his country for nearly two years. Had Burke been in power, the coalesced monarchs would have attacked France in the late summer of 1791.

CHAPTER XXV

THE DISPUTE WITH SPAIN

It is bad economy to tempt an attack, from a state of weakness, and thus by a miserable saving ultimately incur the hazard of a great expense.—PITT, *Speech of 9th February* 1790.

ON 21st January 1790 there arrived at Whitehall news of an outrage committed by a Spanish officer on the crew of a British vessel trading on the dimly known coast which was destined to be called Vancouver Island. The affair became infinitely more serious on 11th February when the Spanish ambassador in London, the Marquis del Campo, forwarded to our Foreign Minister, the Duke of Leeds, an official demand that the British Government should punish certain interlopers who had ventured to trade and settle at Nootka Sound on that coastline, which Spain then considered as part of her Californian domain and for ever closed to outsiders. This demand produced a state of tension between the two nations, and subsequent incidents threatened to involve us in war, not only with Spain, but with her ally, France. As the outcome of this Nootka Sound dispute was the acquisition by Great Britain of a coastline of infinite value to Canada and the Empire at large, it will be well briefly to describe its origin, its settlement, and its bearing on the French Revolution.

Nootka Sound, a fine natural harbour on the western coast of what is now called Vancouver Island, was explored and named by Captain Cook in the course of his memorable voyage of the year 1778. He stayed there one month, and bought from the Indians a number of furs which proved to be of great value in the eyes of the Chinese. In the following years British and Spanish ships touched at Nootka; but owing to the American War, or to the torpor of mercantile enterprise in those days, nothing definite came of the discovery until the year 1785.

Certain merchants of the British East India Company trading to China then resolved to open up trade between that country and the west coast of America. The commodities sought for the Chinese market were furs and ginseng, a plant used as a drug by the celestials. In the following year two small vessels, the "Sea Otter" and the "Nootka," sailed to the American coast, and though the former was wrecked, the latter carried back to China a valuable cargo. The owners replaced her by the "Felice" and "Iphigenia," which in 1788 sailed to the same coast. The senior captain, John Meares, a retired lieutenant of the royal navy, bought a piece of land at Nootka from the Indian chief, Maquilla, formed a small settlement, fortified it, and hoisted the British flag. His vessels then traded along the coast as far as 60° and 45° 30', that is, beyond the Columbia River on the south, and as far as Mount St. Elias, in what is now the United States territory of Alaska, but was then recognized as belonging to Russia's sphere of influence.[1]

At Nootka the adventurous pioneers built a sloop of 40 tons, the "North-West America," and bought from Indian chiefs the right of "free and exclusive" trade with their subjects. As autumn drew on Meares sailed away to China in the "Felice," and there persuaded other merchants to combine in order to form an Associated Company for developing this lucrative commerce. Accordingly, three more ships, the "Prince of Wales," "Princess Royal," and "Argonaut," set sail for Nootka in the spring of 1789 under the command of Captain Colnett, who was to reside at that settlement. It is curious to note thus early the emergence of the yellow question, for he carried with him seventy Chinamen who were to settle there under the protection of the Associated Company—a proof that the occupation of Nootka was to be permanent.

Strange to say, the Spanish Government, acting through its Viceroy of Mexico, was then bent on the acquisition of this very same district. By virtue of the Bull of Pope Alexander VI, and the treaty of Tordesillas (1494), which speedily followed, Spain claimed exclusive right over the Pacific Ocean and all the western coast of America as far north as latitude 60°, beyond which were the Russian settlements in Alaska. In the year

---

[1] The following narrative is founded mainly on documents in "F. O.," Spain, 17, 18, 19; but I have found a monograph by Dr. W. R. Manning, "The Nootka Sound Controversy" (Washington, 1905), most serviceable.

1774, that is, four years before Cook's enterprise, a Spanish captain, Perez, had sailed to Nootka and as far north as latitude 55°. But no account of his voyage, or of one made in the following year, had been given to the world. Neither had the Spaniards made any attempt to trade at Nootka, nor to form a settlement, until they heard of the efforts of the Russians and English to open up trade with the natives. Then, indeed, they took alarm; and the Viceroy of Mexico despatched two vessels, under the command of Captain Martinez, with orders to warn off intruders, and, in case of armed resistance, to use force in vindicating the claims of Spain. The Viceroy and Martinez knew nothing concerning the new developments at Nootka, and had in view the Russians rather than the British.

Long before the arrival of Colnett, and while the "Iphigenia" alone was at Nootka, there sailed in, on 5th May, a Spanish frigate, the "Princesa." Shortly after she was joined by a sloop. Meares had previously provided Douglas, the captain of the "Iphigenia," with papers proving that she was a Portuguese ship, hailing from Macao, the Portuguese settlement near Canton. In reality, however, she was a British ship with a British cargo. Despite the arguments of Douglas, Martinez soon divined the truth, and took possession of her as well as the infant settlement of Nootka.[1] A little later he seized the "North-West America"; and when the "Argonaut" arrived from China, she too fell into his hands by a treacherous ruse, so Colnett averred. The "Princess Royal" was the next victim. Fortune certainly favoured Martinez in having to deal with the British ships as they dropped in singly; and he played his game with skill and success.

The truth respecting the subsequent occurrences cannot be disentangled from the false or exaggerated accounts of the disputants. Meares, Colnett, and Douglas asserted on oath that they had been treacherously seized and barbarously treated. Martinez declared that his behaviour throughout was humane and considerate. His statements were backed by those of certain American traders who were there present; but, as they for a time made common cause with Martinez, their evidence is not convincing. The assertions of Meares and Colnett

---

[1] I cannot agree with Dr. Manning (p. 360) that there were no signs of a British occupation of Nootka when Martinez arrived. The reverse is antecedently probable, and is asserted in Meares' "Memorial."

on this point are antecedently credible, it being the habit of Spain to treat interlopers as little better than privateers. Martinez compelled his prisoners (so they asserted) to assist in building a stockade, and subsequently treated Colnett with so much indignity that he tried to commit suicide, and Hanson, one of his petty officers, actually did so. The Spanish commander then traded with the captured vessels, and finally collected skins estimated by Meares to be worth about 7,500 Spanish dollars. The British ships and crews were afterwards taken to the Spanish port of San Blas, where the governor treated them with more consideration, and, though regarding them virtually as privateers, released them and submitted the fate of their ships to an official inquiry. The whole truth of the Nootka incident will probably never be cleared up. What concerns us here is the impression produced on Pitt by the statements of Meares. They were set forth in a Memorial, dated London, 30th April 1790. Meares laid stress on the perfidy and cruelty of Martinez, and estimated his own losses at 500,000 Spanish dollars, apart from the ruin of the trade along the Nootka coast.[1]

Reports of these events filtered through to London very slowly. Merry, British _chargé d'affaires_ at Madrid, sent the first vague rumours of them in a despatch which, as we have seen, reached Whitehall on 21st January; but the situation became fraught with danger on 11th February, when the Spanish envoy in London handed in a despatch drawn up in terms no less haughty than misleading. After presenting a distorted view of the Nootka incident, del Campo asserted the right of Spain to absolute sovereignty in those districts "which have been occupied and frequented by the Spaniards for so many years." He further requested the British Government to punish such undertakings as those of Meares and Colnett, but closed with the statement that the British prisoners had been liberated through the consideration which the King of Spain had for His Britannic Majesty.

Compliance with this demand was, of course, out of the question, for it would have implied the closing of the north-west coast of America to every flag but the red and yellow ensign of Spain; and the request for the punishment of British sea-

---

[1] The "Memorial" is among the British archives in "F. O.," Spain, 17. For a critique of it see Manning.

men, whose ships had admittedly been seized, added insult to injury. Pitt and his colleagues as yet knew very little of the facts of the case. The dimness of the notions then entertained about that region appears in a phrase used by Robert Liston, our envoy at Stockholm, that the waters behind Nootka Sound may be the opening to the long-sought North-West Passage.[1] In any case the demands of Spain carried with them their own condemnation. Accordingly, on 26th February, the Duke of Leeds replied to del Campo that the act of violence committed by Martinez "makes it necessary henceforth to suspend all discussion of the pretensions set forth in that letter until a just and adequate satisfaction shall have been made for a proceeding so injurious to Great Britain." [2]

The writing here was that of Leeds, but the resolve was the resolve of Pitt. The original draft of this despatch is in the handwriting of the Prime Minister. As at so many crises, he took the conduct of affairs directly into his own hands; and Leeds, though he doubtless agreed with him, was only his mouthpiece. George III and Pitt were equally desirous of peace; but on this occasion their determination was immutable. Satisfaction must be given for the insult, or else war must ensue. In his despatch of the same date to Merry at Madrid, the Duke stoutly contested the right of Spain to the exclusive sovereignty, commerce, and navigation of the coasts north of California, and asserted the determination of the Court of St. James to protect its subjects trading in that part of the Pacific Ocean.[3]

When the facts stated on oath by Meares were known by Ministers, they realized the extreme gravity of the case. Their demand for satisfaction having been ignored by the Court of

---

[1] Liston to Auckland, 14th September 1790 (B.M. Add. MSS., 34433).

[2] "F. O.," Spain, 16.

[3] *Ibid.* That this resolve was that of the whole Cabinet appears in the following letter in the Pitt MSS. It is from Pitt to Leeds:

"Downing Street, Tuesday morning, *Feb.* 23, 1790.

"I cannot help begging to remind your Grace of the wish expressed that the answer to the Spanish ambassador should if possible be circulated before our meeting to-day. I am the more anxious about this, as no one would like to give a final opinion on the terms of a paper of so much delicacy and importance without having had an opportunity of considering them beforehand."

Madrid,[1] they determined, at a Cabinet Council held on the evening of 30th April, to demand "immediate and adequate satisfaction for the outrages committed by Mr. de Martinez," and to back up that demand by the equipment of several ships of the line. George III agreed with his Ministers, though with some reluctance; and the press-gang set to work on 4th May to man the new squadron. The affair came as a bolt from the blue. Most of the sailors in the Thames were seized; and the prospect of war caused Consols to drop three per cent. Ministers, however, were justified in taking this step. After the Spanish note of 20th April they saw that Spain would not renounce her exclusive right to the Pacific Coast of America save under pressure of force.[2] The question of peace or war turned on two things; the relative naval strength of the two Powers, and the ability of the Court of Madrid to gain an ally, presumably France.

Deferring for the present the question of the Franco-Spanish Alliance, we notice that on sea Great Britain had a decided superiority over Spain. Though the Spanish marine was far from weak it could not cope with the imposing force which the care and energy of Pitt had amassed at our dockyards. As has been pointed out in Chapter IX, he frequently inspected the details of construction, and held the Comptroller of the Navy personally responsible to him for the due progress of new ships and the efficiency of the fleet. Thanks to his close supervision, and the large sums voted for the navy, there were at this time no fewer than ninety-three sail of the line fit for active service.[3]

This gratifying result cannot be ascribed to the First Lord of the Admiralty. In July 1788, on the resignation of Lord Howe, Pitt raised his brother, Lord Chatham, to that responsible post, Lord Hood being added to the Admiralty Board. Chatham was personally popular but proved to be indolent as an administrator, his unpunctuality earning him the nickname of "the late Lord Chatham." That excellent administrator, Sir Charles Middleton (the future Lord Barham), refused to serve under him after the reforms recommended by a Commission of Inquiry were shelved, and in March 1790 resigned office, pointing out,

[1] See del Campo's note of 20th April, in Manning, 374, 375.
[2] "Dropmore P.," i, 579, 580; "F. O.," Spain, 17.
[3] "Journals of Sir T. Byam Martin" (Navy Records Soc.), iii, 381, 382.

however, that the Navy and dockyards were never better prepared for war.[1]

Despite the formidable strength of the British navy, Spain
might have entered on a contest with some chance of success.
We are apt to forget that her period of swift decline under
Charles IV had only just begun. His predecessor, Charles III,
who died in 1788, had raised the credit and power of that land
almost to the lofty heights of ancient days. He had helped to
humble the might of England in the American war, and his
army and navy were kept in a state of efficiency which enabled
Spain to rank as one of the Great Powers. On his death there
came an insidious change. In place of vigour and even-handed
justice there crept in all the evils linked with sloth and favouritism. The statesman Count Floridablanca, who had done much
to promote the prosperity of Spain, saw his influence sapped by
the intrigues of the minions of the Queen, who was to be the
evil genius of the realm. But in the year 1790 the dry-rot had
not appreciably affected that imposing fabric. Outwardly Spain
appeared to be almost a match for the Island Power. Towards
the end of July 1790, she had at sea thirty-four sail of the line
and sixteen smaller craft.[2]

The pride of two of the most susceptible nations having been
touched to the quick, war seemed inevitable. On 10th May Pitt
moved for a vote of credit of a million sterling for the necessary
armament; this was at once agreed to.[3] Parliament also supported
the Ministry by large majorities whenever the Opposition attempted to censure their action on points of detail. Several
pamphlets appeared inveighing against the monstrous claims of
Spain to the control of the Pacific. There was a weak point in
her armour, and at this Pitt aimed a deadly shaft. Already the
Spaniards of South and Central America were restive under the
galling yoke of their colonial system, which was so contrived
as to enrich officials and privileged merchants in Spain at the
expense of the new lands. The result was that at Quito a pound
of iron sold for 4s. 6d., and a pound of steel for 6s. 9d.[4] It is not
surprising that the stoutest spirits longed to break loose from
a Government by comparison with which that of England in
the United States had been mildness and wisdom personified.

---

[1] " The Barham P." (Navy Records Soc.), ii, 337-47.
[2] Manning, 408.　　　　　　　　　　[3] " Parl. Hist.," xxviii, 785.
[4] " Wealth of Nations," bk. iv, ch. vii, pt. 2.

The mouthpiece of the discontent of the land now called Venezuela was a man of strongly marked personality, Miranda by name. An exile from his native city of Caracas, he had spent several years wandering about Europe, until the events at Paris drew him to that focus of enthusiasm and effort. There he became acquainted with Brissot and others who were interested in the emancipation of subject peoples. But now the prospect of a war between England and Spain attracted him to London. Pitt invited him to a first interview on the evening of 9th May. The daring adventurer there unfolded his plan of revolutionizing Spanish America; and, in case of war, his commanding personality and intrepid spirit would have stirred up a serious ferment. Here was a formidable weapon against Spain; and Pitt in the course of several interviews with Miranda prepared to use it with effect. Hopes ran high in London that Spain would be crippled by the action of her own sons in the New World, a fitting return to her for assisting the revolt of the English colonists a decade before. Auckland, our envoy at The Hague, wrote on 29th June 1790: "It is believed there are serious troubles in South America; but that circumstance seems to afford the strongest reason for avoiding a quarrel with England. It is wonderful to a cool bystander to see with what infatuated alacrity several sovereigns are running towards the embarrassments which have brought Louis XVI and his dominions to the distracted and desperate state in which we now see them." [1]

Meanwhile Pitt and Leeds had nailed their colours to the mast in the despatch of 4th May, which dismissed the reply of the Spanish Court, dated 20th April, as wholly inadmissible. By way of retort to its claim of exclusive possession of the seas and coasts north of California up to latitude 60°, the British Government asserted for its subjects in those parts the "unquestioned right to a free and undisturbed

---

[1] B.M. Add. MSS., 35542. Miranda's relations with Pitt were renewed in 1804. On 13th June 1805 he sought to dispel some suspicions which Pitt had formed of him, and added: "Je n'ai jamais départi un instant des principes politiques et moraux qui formèrent notre première liaison politique en 1790." See, too, an interesting article on Miranda in the "Amer. Hist. Rev.," vol. vi, for proofs of the dealings of Pitt with Miranda at that time. On 12th September 1791 Pitt wrote to him stating that he could not grant him the pension he asked for, or the sum of £1,000: £500 must suffice for the expenses incurred during his stay in London (Pitt MSS., 102).

enjoyment of the benefits of commerce, navigation, and fishery, and also to the possession of such establishments as they may form, with the consent of the natives, in places unoccupied by other European nations."[1] In this declaration lies the charter of the future colony of British Columbia. Alleyne Fitzherbert, who had already had a creditable record in diplomacy, now proceeded on a special mission to Madrid to make good these claims, if possible by peaceable means. Among the twenty-two "Instructions" is one bidding him weaken the Family Compact of 1761, which bound together the Kings of France and Spain in close alliance, and point out to the Spanish Ministers the desirability of substituting for it a friendly understanding with Great Britain both in political and commercial affairs.

From the outset Pitt and his colleagues realized that the question of peace or war depended largely on France. Had that Power been in a condition to fight, the Bourbon States would certainly have contested England's claim, and in that case she might have been for ever excluded from the Pacific Coast of America. Fitzherbert therefore stayed a few days at Paris (an indisposition afforded a pretext for delay) in order to fathom those turbid waters. The foreign policy of France was still nominally in the hands of Montmorin; but that Minister, never strong, had been almost cowed by events. Fitzherbert found him most gracious, but he could not explain away the recent order for equipping fourteen sail of the line at Brest. The most threatening symptom, however, was the warlike attitude of the royalist side of the National Assembly, which on 20th May he thus described to the Duke of Leeds:

. . . I can plainly perceive that many other members of the aristocratical faction are anxious to avail themselves of the opportunity to bring on a war, in the hope that the general distress and confusion which must almost inevitably follow, might ultimately tend to the reestablishment of the royal authority upon its former footing. Many strong indications of this design have appeared in the insidious language which they have held of late, speaking of Great Britain both in the National Assembly and without doors. However, their opponents begin to be aware of their drift, and it seems to have been principally with a view of guarding against such designs that the latter have chosen the present time for carrying into execution their plan of transferring the power of making War and Peace from the Crown to the National

[1] "F. O.," Spain, 17.

Assembly. It also appears highly probable that, when this question shall be disposed of, it will be followed up by some motion tending to invalidate, if not entirely to annul, the Family Compact.

How curiously the wheels of human action act and interact! The outrage on British sailors on the dimly known coast of Vancouver Island furnished French democrats with a potent motive for driving another nail into the coffin of the old monarchy. In any case the right of Louis XVI to declare war and make peace would have been challenged—for how can Democracy allow a Sovereign wholly to control its policy at the most important of all crises—but now the need was overwhelming. If the old prerogative held good, the rusty link that bound together the fortunes of France and Spain would compel free Frenchmen to fight their English neighbours whenever a Spanish captain thought fit to clap in irons British voyagers to the Pacific.

The question aroused gusts of passion at Paris. Enormous crowds waited outside the Tuileries while the deputies hard by were debating this question (16th and 22nd May). To the surprise of the people the royal prerogative was upheld by Mirabeau. The great orator descanted forcibly on the need of energy and secrecy in the diplomacy of a great nation, and reminded those who ascribed all wars to the intrigues of Courts that popular assemblies had often declared war in a fit of passion. He remarked that members had all applauded a speaker who advocated war against England if she attacked Spain, and the expenditure of their last man and their last crown in reducing London.[1] Few of Mirabeau's speeches were more convincing. Nevertheless, on coming forth from the Chamber he was threatened with violence; and a pamphlet, " Great Treason of Count Mirabeau " was hawked about the streets. His reasoning, however, ensured the carrying of a compromise on 22nd May. The right of declaring war and making peace was vested in the King: and war was to be decided only by a decree of the Legislature, on "the formal and necessary proposition of the King, and afterwards sanctioned by him."[2] The position was thus left far from clear; and Camille Desmoulins, referring to the ups and

---

[1] " Travaux de Mirabeau" (1792), iii, 319.
[2] W. Legg, " Select Documents on the Fr. Rev.," i, 226 and F. Masson, " Département des Affaires étrangères," 79, 80.

downs of the debate, summarized it thus: "The question was decided, firstly, in favour of the nation, secondly, in favour of the King; thirdly, in favour of both." The royalists were highly displeased. Their best speaker, Cazalès, declared that nothing was now left to the monarchy—an exclamation which probably revealed his disgust at the passing away of the opportunity of a war with England.

Meanwhile Pitt had worked hard to array his allies, Prussia and Holland, against Spain. In this he succeeded. In particular, he offered to the Dutch a considerable subsidy for arming a squadron as if for war. To this topic he referred in a letter of 18th May 1790, to Auckland. After informing him that the teller-ship of the Exchequer would be reserved for him, or one of his sons, besides a pension of £2,000 a year on retirement, he continued thus:

I cannot help adding how much satisfaction I have felt in your account of everything at The Hague. You have done us a most essential service in bringing the States into a disposition to act at the present moment with a dispatch so unusual to them. This messenger carries instructions to you to engage for the expenses which you have stated to be likely to be incurred for fitting out ten sail-of-the-line. You will, I am sure, take care that the expense shall not be swelled beyond what is really necessary; but, if even a greater sum should be really wanting, we shall not scruple to give it; and, if you find that they can go on to prepare a still greater number of ships, it will be so much the better. I can hardly form at present a conjecture of the event of our prepara-tions, as I can hardly conceive either that the Spaniards will ultimately persist, or that they can have gone so far without a determination not to recede. I hope we shall be able to send an answer about the com-mercial treaty very soon.[1]

Pitt's economy is here seen to be far removed from the penny-wise and pound-foolish kind. If necessary, he was prepared to lavish subsidies on the Dutch, and on Prussia as well, in order to overawe Spain. The Duke of Leeds and he were of one mind as to the need of the most energetic measures. On 2nd June the Duke wrote to him that the Spanish proposals were quite inadmissible, and that Great Britain could not possibly accept "any measure short of a direct and unqualified satisfaction for the insult." Spain of course would refuse, and therefore war

[1] B.M. Add. MSS., 29475.

must follow: it could not be avoided without disgrace to one side or the other.[1] This rigid attitude prepares us for the part which the Duke played in the dispute with Russia nine months later.

In this case Pitt agreed with him, apparently because the point at issue concerned our interests and our honour far more nearly. Indeed the tone of the Spanish replies left small hope of peace. Count Floridablanca protested against the British demand that full reparation must be made to the victims of Captain Martinez, before the Spanish claims could be considered. "The Spanish Minister," wrote Merry from Madrid on 24th May, "is persuaded that we have at all events taken the resolution of breaking with this country.... Our tone of language to this Court he represents as insufferable, and while on his part he still wishes to preserve peace, he seems to think that Spain will unavoidably be driven to the necessity of defending herself." Spain, he adds, was arming twenty-five warships, and had already two squadrons at sea.[2]

Her pretensions appear in the despatch of the Spanish Governor of Mexico, dated Mexico, 11th May 1790. After stating that he had released the "Argonaut" and "Princess Royal" in order to maintain harmony with England, he remarked that Martinez had "acted agreeably to the laws and royal ordinances, which not only absolutely prohibit any kind of navigation, establishment, or commerce of foreigners on our South Sea Coasts of both Americas, but moreover strictly command they be looked upon as declared enemies, without considering such treatment a breach of national faith or contravention of the treaties of peace." Whence it followed that Martinez might with impunity have hanged Meares, Colnett, and their crews on his yardarms. These claims were thus endorsed in the Spanish circular note of 4th June, which based them on the Treaty of Utrecht (1713):

It also appears that, in spite of the attempts of some adventurers and pirates of various nations on the Spanish coasts of the said South Sea and the adjacent islands, Spain has continued her possession, recovering what has been endeavoured to be usurped from her, and performing for this purpose the necessary reconnoitres and voyages, by the means of which and of repeated acts she has preserved her dominion, of which she has always established and left signs, which reach to places the nearest to the Russian establishments in that part of the world.

---

[1] Pretyman MSS.   [2] "F. O.," Spain, 17.

The efforts which the Court of Madrid then put forth at St. Petersburg and Vienna showed its resolve to concert a league against England in which Denmark was to be included. This scheme, as visionary as the grandiose dreams of Alberoni, caused our Ministers some concern, until they found that their Allies, Prussia and Holland, were resolved to support them. On 20th May Hertzberg assured Ewart, that Prussia would fulfil her engagements, if Spain pushed matters to extremes.[1]

Nevertheless, for a time everything portended war. Fitzherbert, after reaching Aranjuez on 10th June, became convinced that Floridablanca, for all his peaceful assurances, intended to force a rupture at the first favourable opportunity. The Spanish Court absolutely refused to grant satisfaction for the injury done to Meares and Colnett, because that would imply the right of British subjects to be at Nootka.[2] For the very same reason the Pitt Cabinet pressed its preliminary demand. It also brushed aside the Spanish pretensions of sole sovereignty on the Nootka coasts, because British and other seamen had for some little time traded there—an assertion difficult to maintain.[3]

The deadlock was therefore complete; and, if Spain could have looked forward to help either from France, Russia, or Austria, war would inevitably have ensued. It is of interest to observe that, as the crisis became acute, Pitt adopted his usual habit of writing the drafts of the most important despatches; and they were sent off without alteration. He thus disposed of the suggestion of Floridablanca, that the whole matter in dispute should be settled by arbitration. " Your Excellency will not be surprised that they are such as cannot be adopted. The idea of

---

[1] "Dropmore P.," i, 585, 588. Auckland to Grenville, 15th May and 8th June 1790. On 22nd May Kaunitz, the Austrian Chancellor, assured Keith, our ambassador, that he heartily wished for the settlement of the Nootka Sound dispute. He blamed Floridablanca as rash ("F. O.," Austria, 20).

[2] "F. O.," Spain, 17. Fitzherbert to Leeds, 16th June 1790. Earl Camden, a valued member of the Cabinet, wrote on 29th June to Pitt expressing grave concern at this answer from the Spanish Court. He added these words: "War, as I always thought, was inevitable, and to temporize impossible. The jealousy of that Court gave the first provocation, and their pride refuses satisfaction. The consequence is evident. We have no choice, for the outrage at Nouska [sic] cannot be a subject of discussion. I trust in the spirit of the Kingdom and your own wisdom and good fortune, and have no doubt this will terminate to your honour" (Pitt MSS., 119).

[3] "F. O.," Spain, 18. Leeds to Fitzherbert, 5th July.

an arbitration upon a subject of this nature must be entirely out of the question; and a reservation such as that contained in the second proposal would render the satisfaction nugatory, as it would refer to subsequent discussion the very ground on which that satisfaction is demanded." [1]

The outlook was not brightened by the suggestion of Floridablanca, that Spain should keep the whole of the coast from California up to and including Nootka; that from that inlet northwards to 61°, British and Spaniards should have conjointly the right of trading and forming establishments; and that British sailors should enjoy certain fishery rights in the South Sea on uninhabited islands far removed from Spanish settlements. [2] These proposals seemed, as they doubtless were, a device to gain time until France, Austria, or Russia could step forth and help Spain; and Pitt refused to admit these "chimerical claims of exclusive sovereignty over the American Continent and the seas adjacent," which were to Spain herself "rather matter of useless pride than of actual advantage." [3] Towards the end of July more peaceful counsels prevailed at Madrid, probably because the weak and luxurious King, Charles IV, disliked war, and dreaded contact with Revolutionary France. Further it must have transpired that Russia and Austria, owing to their war with Turkey, were not likely to give more than good wishes to Spain. Either for these reasons, or because he hoped that delay would tell in favour of Spain, Floridablanca signed with Fitzherbert on 24th July a Declaration that Spain would give satisfaction for the seizure of British vessels and their cargoes at Nootka. On 5th August Grenville informed the King of this auspicious turn of affairs. [4]

But now, while the Court of Madrid abated its pretensions, French patriots began to rattle the sword in the scabbard. For reasons which are hard to fathom, the Spanish request for armed assistance, which reached Paris on 16th June, was not presented to the National Assembly until 2nd August. On that day Montmorin informed the deputies of the continuance of naval preparations

[1] "F. O.," Spain, 18. Despatch of 5th July to Fitzherbert. Of course, this does not imply that Pitt would never admit arbitration, but only that he judged it inadmissible in the present case.

[2] *Ibid.* Fitzherbert to Leeds, 12th July.

[3] *Ibid.* Leeds to Fitzherbert, 17th August.

[4] Manning, 405, 406; "Dropmore P.," i, 603, 606.

in England, and declared that, unless French aid were accorded to Spain, she would seek an ally elsewhere. The statement was well calculated to awaken jealousy of England; and members came to the conclusion that the islanders were seeking, in the temporary weakness of France, to bully the Court of Madrid out of its just rights. Consequently the whole matter was referred to the newly appointed Diplomatic Committee which supervised the work of the Foreign Office.[1] As this body now practically controlled French diplomacy, everything became uncertain; and it is not surprising that Pitt and Leeds declined to disarm now that the question of peace or war depended on an emotional Assembly and its delegates.

At the head of this new controlling body was Mirabeau. As Reporter of the Committee he held a commanding position, which was enhanced by his splendid eloquence, forceful personality, and knowledge of the shady by-paths of diplomacy. The Report which he presented to the Assembly on 25th August was, in effect, his. While minimizing the importance of the Nootka dispute, scoffing at the old diplomacy, and declaring that Europe would not need any diplomacy when there were neither despots nor slaves, he yet proposed that, pending the advent of that glorious age, France must not abrogate her treaties but continue to respect them until they had been subjected to revision. Further, in place of the Family Compact of the Kings of France and Spain, he proposed to substitute a National Compact, based on the needs of the two nations. On the following day he continued his speech and moved that France and Spain should form a national treaty in the interests of peace and conformable to "the principles of justice which will ever form the policy of the French." What was far more significant, he himself added a rider for the immediate armament of forty-five sail of the line and a proportionate number of smaller vessels. This was carried immediately.[2]

Seeing that the Assembly passed this vote at the very time

---

[1] "Despatches of Earl Gower (1790-1792)," 23, edited by Mr. Oscar Browning. Gower succeeded Dorset as ambassador at Paris on 20th June 1790.

[2] "Travaux de Mirabeau," iv, 24-49, which shows that this was not the work of the Assembly, but the proposal of Mirabeau. W. A. Miles reported ("Corresp.," i, 255), that Mirabeau received from the Spanish ambassador one thousand *louis d'or* for carrying this proposal.

when the terrible mutiny at Nancy was at its height, the feelings of the deputies must have been of the bellicose order which
Mirabeau had previously deprecated. Despite the pressing need
for peace, France seemed to be heading straight for war. On
ordinary grounds her conduct is inexplicable. Everywhere her
troops were clamouring for arrears of pay; her sailors could
scarcely be kept together; and the virtual bankruptcy of the
State was a week later to be quaintly revealed by the flight of
Necker to Switzerland. The King and his Ministers disapproved
the arming of so large a fleet; for Montmorin confessed to Gower
his surprise and regret, adding the comforting assurance that it
would be done as slowly as possible. The mystery deepens
when we know that Floridablanca continued to speak in peaceful
tones. On 19th August he admitted to Fitzherbert that he
desired help from Russia and Austria, but felt complete indifference as to what France might do. Aid from her, he said, would
lead to the introduction of democratic principles, which he was
determined to keep out, if need arose, by a cordon along the
frontier, as one would exclude the plague.[1]

Here probably we have the key to the enigma. The recent
action of Mirabeau (for the arming of the French naval force
was his proposal, not Montmorin's) rested on the assumption
that Spain did not mean to draw the sword. His agents at the
various Courts kept him well abreast of events, and doubtless
he foresaw that Charles IV's hatred of democracy would bar the
way to an alliance of the two peoples such as was now projected. Why, then, should Mirabeau have threatened England
with war? His reasons seem to have been partly of a patriotic,
partly of a private, nature. He desired to restore the prestige of the French monarchy by throwing its sword into the
wavering balances of diplomacy. As to the expense, it was
justifiable, if it tended to revive the national spirit and to quell
the mutinous feelings of the sailors. Work, especially if directed
against " the natural enemy," would be the best restorative of
order at the dockyards, and prevent the deterioration of the navy.
But apart from these motives Mirabeau may have been swayed
by others of a lower kind. His popularity had swiftly waned
during the previous debates. He might revive it by pandering
to the dislike of England now widely prevalent. Manufacturers

---

[1] " F. O.," Spain, 18. Fitzherbert to Leeds, 17th August.

who suffered by English competition and Chauvinists who dreaded her supremacy at sea were joining in a hue and cry against Pitt;[1] and Mirabeau gained credit by posing as the national champion. Further, by holding peace and war, as it were, in the folds of his toga, he enhanced his value in the diplomatic market. His corruptibility was notorious. Even the sums which he drew from the King were far from meeting the yawning gulf of his debts.

In the present case there was much to tempt him to political auctioneering. There were present in Paris two political agents to whom Pitt had confided the task of humouring the French democrats and dissolving the Family Compact. These were William Augustus Miles and Hugh Elliot. The former was a clever but opinionated man, half statesman, half busy-body, capable of doing good work when kept well in hand, but apt to take the bit into his teeth and bolt. He had already looked into the affairs of Brabant, Liége, and Frankfurt for Pitt; and as early as 4th March the Prime Minister summoned him to Downing Street for the purpose of sending him to Paris; but not till the middle of July did he finally entrust to him the task of inducing French deputies to annul the Family Compact. That this was to be done secretly appears from the order that he was to have no dealings whatever with the British Embassy.[2] Unfortunately the letters which passed between Pitt and Miles at this time have all been destroyed.[3] But we know from other sources that Miles was charged to prepare the way for an Anglo-French *entente*. He certainly made overtures to Talleyrand, Mirabeau, and Lafayette; he was also elected a member of the Jacobins Club, and worked hard to remove the prejudices against England. These he found exceedingly strong, all the

---

[1] "Gower's Despatches," 29; "Corresp. of W. A. Miles," i, 162, 163.

[2] *Ibid.*, i, 41-8, 150.

[3] In the Pitt MSS. there is a packet (No. 159) of Miles's letters to Pitt, beginning with 1785. On 13th May 1790 Miles wrote to Pitt that George Rose had informed him he could not see how Pitt could employ him. Miles begged Pitt for a pension as a literary man. There is no other letter to Pitt until 10th December 1790, dated Paris:—" My attachment to your interest and a sincere desire to give every possible support to your Administration induced me to engage without difficulty in the enterprise proposed by Mr. Rose, and to accept of a salary inadequate to the expenses of the most frugal establishment," viz., £400 a year. He adds that he has trenched on his private property, and concludes by asking for the consulate at Ostend.

troubles in the fleet being ascribed to her. By 11th October he had fulfilled his mission, and informed George Rose that Pitt might, if he chose, form a close working alliance with the French nation. About the same time he conceived for Mirabeau the greatest contempt, and asserted that it was "impossible to know him and not to despise him." [1]

Elliot was a man of far higher stamp than Miles. As we have seen, he had had a distinguished diplomatic career, and might be termed the saviour of Gustavus III in the acute crisis of 1788. He was brother of Sir Gilbert Elliot (first Earl of Minto), and of Lady Auckland. In the summer of 1790 he was home on furlough. On 7th August he wrote from Beckenham, Auckland's residence, congratulating Pitt on a favourable turn in the Spanish dispute. When the outlook once more darkened he requested leave to go to Paris in order to use his influence with his friend, Mirabeau, in the interests of peace. Pitt must have referred the proposal to the King, and received a very guarded reply, dated Windsor, 26th October. George enjoined great caution, as we had hitherto held entirely aloof from the French troubles, and must on no account be mixed up in them. Yet, for the sake of peace, he did not object to this attempt, so long as it was entirely unofficial; but he was "not sanguine that Mr. H. Elliot and his French friend" would succeed where so much caution and delicacy were necessary. [2]

As this affair is wrapped in mystery, and concerns not only the peace of the world, but also that most interesting personality, Mirabeau, the draft of an undated letter of Pitt to the King must be quoted in full:

Mr. P. takes the liberty of submitting to your Majesty's Perusal two private letters which he received to-day from Paris, one from Lord Gower, and the other from Mr. H. Elliot. The latter went thither a short time since, principally from curiosity, but previous to his departure, mentioned to Mr. P. that he had formerly happened to be in habits of much intimacy with M. de Mirabeau, and might probably have an opportunity of learning something from him respecting the views of the prevailing party in France on the subject of the discussions with Spain. Mr. P. recommends to him to be very cautious not to commit anybody by his conversation, but to endeavour to find out whether there was

---

[1] "Corresp. of W. A. Miles," i, 171, 172, 199.
[2] "Beaufort P.," etc. (Hist. MSS. Comm.), 368.

any chance of making them see in a just light the nature of our disputes with Spain, and of thereby preventing or delaying their taking a part in the war, if it should take place.

The suggestions in Mr. Elliot's letter seem to furnish matter for much consideration; possibly there may be found means of improving this opening to some advantage with a view to preserving or restoring peace, or to retarding the succours which France might furnish to Spain.[1]

This letter is undated. George III's missive of 26th October seems to be a reply to it or to one very like it. But Pitt's letter implies the receipt of Gower's and Elliot's despatches of 26th October. I have found no other despatch from Gower enclosing one from Elliot except of that date. Four days previously Gower had written to Pitt:

Mr. Elliot's communication with Mr. de Mirabeau has been more successful than I imagined it was likely to be: it has procured an easy means of maintaining a good understanding between His Majesty's Ministers and the prevailing party in the National Assembly, if such a correspondence should be found necessary.[2]

In the letter of 26th October Gower informed Pitt:

Mr. Elliot has brought the prevailing party in this country to act according to their true interest; and, if they meet with proper encouragement from you, they seem ready to go any lengths towards enforcing our claims with regard to Spain; and they are, I believe, sincere in their desire to promote a real and effectual good understanding between the two countries. I shall be extremely happy to co-operate with Mr. Elliot in a negotiation which appears to me so desirable.[3]

The words " proper encouragement " *donnent furieusement à penser*. Elliot in a long letter of 26th October, recounted his interview with a deputation from the Diplomatic Committee, and his success in winning it over to the British side. In the former of two paragraphs, which are omitted by Earl Stanhope,[4] Elliot describes the promise given him by the Committee, that, even if Spain went to war, and formally demanded the aid of France, such aid would not be forthcoming until the British case had been fully investigated. The second of the two passages deserves quotation in full. It occurs near the end of the letter:

[1] Pitt MSS., 335.
[2] *Ibid.*, 139. See, too, " Gower's Despatches," 38, 39, with note.
[3] Pitt MSS., 139.　　　　　　　　　　[4] Stanhope, ii, 60, 61.

What has taken place in my more intimate conversations with individuals cannot be committed to paper. But I have every reason to
believe that I am more master of the secret springs of action here than
anybody else could have been. Everything I have either said or done
has always been previously concerted and has ever answered my most
sanguine expectations. . . . I am inclined to believe that, after the
disturbances at Brest are known at Madrid, the Spaniards will make
peace rather than expose their fleets to any junction with French ships.[1]

The hints here given imply that Mirabeau, and probably other
patriots as well, accepted British money, but both our envoys
were discreet enough to give few details in writing. It is quite
probable that Mirabeau first accepted Spanish gold for procuring
the vote for the arming of forty-five French sail of the line, and
then accepted an equivalent sum from Miles or Elliot for the
decree which rendered that step innocuous. His control over the
Assembly was scarcely less than Montmorin's;[2] and that nervous
Minister would certainly welcome a course of action which enhanced the prestige of France, and yet averted all risk of war.
Nevertheless, Pitt did not set much store by the help of Mirabeau. He decided to bring the whole dispute to an immediate
issue, without waiting for the issue of the golden proposals of
Elliot and Miles. Possibly he heard from other sources that
France would do no more than rattle the sword in the scabbard;
or else he was emboldened by the marked success and zeal
attending the British naval preparations, the mutinies in the
French fleet, the readiness of our Allies to play their part, and
the unreadiness of Spain. A brief survey of these considerations
will reveal the grounds of his confidence.

The chance of hostilities with the two Bourbon Courts was
threatening enough to call forth all the energies of the race.
Through the months of August, September, and October naval
preparations went on with the utmost vigour. Officers and men
vied with one another in zeal to equip and man the ships with
all possible speed and thoroughness. Sir John Jervis afterwards
assured the House of Commons that he had seen captains pay-

---

[1] Pitt MSS., 139.
[2] F. Masson, " Département des Affaires étrangères," 86 *et seq.*

In the Pretyman MSS. is an undated letter of Elliot to Pitt (probably of
November 1790) referring to his interview with Pitt that morning, and explaining that his phrase to the Diplomatic Committee, " the glorious Revolution," was meant only for Frenchmen!

ing out their own money by hundreds of pounds in order to expedite the equipment; others sailed their ships down Channel with mere skeleton crews in order to hasten the rally at Plymouth; and by dint of drills from sunrise to sunset the crews were hardened to their work.[1] In truth, the dominant fact of the situation was England's overwhelming supremacy at sea over Spain, and possibly over Spain and France together.

The Triple Alliance also proved to be a reality. The prospect of a war with Spain was, of course, distasteful both at Berlin and The Hague; but our Allies admitted that Spain was the aggressor, and signified their readiness to support us. This should be noted, for it imposed on Pitt a debt of honour to support Prussia when her summons for help against the Czarina arrived at Whitehall in the month of March following.

Further, the ambitions of the Czarina already threatened the equilibrium of Europe; and in this fact we find the last, and perhaps the most cogent, of the reasons why Pitt and his colleague resolved to have done with the Spanish dispute before the Eastern Question came to a crisis. This appears very clearly in Leeds' despatch of 2nd October to our ambassador at Madrid, which was in effect an ultimatum to that Court. He warned Fitzherbert that the Spanish proposals were quite inadmissible, and that "neither the circumstances of the negotiation, nor the relative situation of the two countries and of other Powers in Europe can allow of any further delay"; he therefore pressed for the immediate acceptance of the British demands. An explanatory note accompanied the ultimatum, stating that Spain ought to desire the preservation of the existing system in Europe, which was threatened solely by the Empress Catharine, who spurned the counsels of moderation offered by the Allies.[2]

It appears, then, that the threatening aspect of affairs in the East in part accounts for Pitt's sudden and imperious demand. He resolved to finish with Spain so as to have his hands free for the Eastern Question. As appeared in an earlier chapter, the Czarina, Catharine II, had recently concluded peace with Sweden; and, despite the promised negotiations of the Viennese Court for peace with the Turks, she seemed determined to press them hard, and to wring from them a district then deemed necessary to the defence of the Ottoman Power. Her dalliance

---

[1] "Parl. Hist.," xxviii, 907.   [2] "F. O.," Spain, 19.

with Spain was far from serious; but she might, if allowed time, concert a formidable league against England. The voice of prudence, therefore, counselled the immediate coercion of Spain, while Russia was entangled in a still doubtful strife. Machiavelli shrewdly remarked that " the Romans never swallowed an injury to put off a war; for they knew that war was not avoided but only deferred thereby, and commonly with advantage to the enemy." [1]

But Pitt needed not to go to Machiavelli. Facts spoke more convincingly than words to a nature like his; and the news from Paris and Madrid called aloud for a display of energy. The insubordination at the French dockyards and the news from Paris had told on the nervous and pedantic King of Spain. On 16th September Fitzherbert wrote to the Duke of Leeds that that monarch had very decidedly expressed his resolve never to have an alliance with France on the basis of a National Compact as proposed by Mirabeau. It appears, then, that the great orator had a decisive effect in working on the fears and scruples of His Catholic Majesty, and thus assuring the isolation of Spain. If Mirabeau received British money from Miles and Elliot a month or so later, he might claim it as payment for valuable services already rendered. However that may be, it is certain that Pitt, on receiving the glad news from Fitzherbert on 27th September, decided to take vigorous action. Fitzherbert advised tact and patience in dealing with that proud Court; but Pitt and Leeds waived aside the advice and resolved to thrust their adversary into a corner. In view of the more complaisant attitude of the Spanish Government, their action was unchivalrous; but it was justified by the tidings which had arrived of cruelties perpetrated by a Spanish warship on the captain of a English merchantman in the Gulf of Florida, who was set in the bilboes in the blazing sun.[2] Public opinion would certainly have supported Pitt in case of a rupture with an enemy whose claims

---

[1] Machiavelli, "The Prince," ch. iii.

[2] McDonald's affidavit of 25th September 1790. On this case Bland Burges wrote to Auckland on 30th September (B.M. Add. MSS., 34433) that he was convinced of its authenticity, and that Spain was clearly seeking a quarrel with us. He referred to the signature of the Reichenbach Convention as strengthening our position. On 21st September he wrote to Auckland of the "intolerable suspense" of the Spanish affair, and hinted that Spanish gold had probably bought the recent peace between Sweden and Russia. The position of Bland Burges as permanent secretary at the Foreign Office gives weight to these remarks.

and customs were still those of the fifteenth century; and he was resolved to end the dominion of Spain in the North Pacific with as little ceremony as Cromwell had shown in his expedition against Jamaica in 1654.

Now there was little fear of war. The pride of Charles IV centred in trophies of the chase; and his weak and slothful nature revolted at the thought of an alliance with France on Mirabeau's terms. Moreover, Russia and Austria had paid little heed to the recent appeals of Floridablanca, and there was war with the Moors outside Tangier. Was not this enough? For a few days the Council of Ministers breathed threats of war. Floridablanca struggled hard against the relentless grip which had closed around him. But he was helpless, and he knew it. Therefore on Sunday, 24th October, the Spanish Minister, after much angry remonstrance, gave way, and agreed to the British terms.

Meanwhile, Pitt had allowed Fitzherbert to recede slightly on some of the conditions, and urged that Spain should be invited to frame an alliance with us, both political and commercial. As usual, in affairs of great moment, he himself wrote the draft of this despatch, which was sent off without alteration.[1] This skilful angling was of no avail. Spanish pride was too deeply wounded to admit of any possibility of alliance, whether political or commercial, for many years to come. In other respects Pitt gained his point; and the following letter to Bishop Pretyman (Tomline) shows his relief at the end to the long strain:

Thursday, *Nov.* 4, 1790.[2]

DEAR BISHOP,

The decisive answer arrived this morning and is perfectly satisfactory. The Spanish Minister at last agreed, on the 24th of October, to a *projet* of a Convention containing all we wish, and it was settled that it should be actually signed in three days from that time. The terms will be found to secure all that we could demand in justice, or had any reason to desire.

Accordingly, on 28th October 1790 (after four days, not

---

[1] "F. O.," Spain, 19. Despatch of 8th October. For details see Manning, *op. cit.*, chs. xi-xiii. I cannot, however, agree with Dr. Manning's assertion (p. 440) that it looks as if Pitt and Leeds desired war. The terms of Fitzherbert's despatch of 16th September, which Dr. Manning does not notice, surely convinced Pitt that Spain would on no account use the French alliance on Mirabeau's conditions.

[2] Pretyman MSS.

three), the Court of Madrid signed the Convention which opened up a new future for the North Pacific. By it Spain agreed to restore the buildings and lands at Nootka to the British subjects whom Martinez had dispossessed. Reparation was also to be made for any outrages committed by the subjects of either Power against those of the other since April 1789.[1] Britons and Spaniards were to have full liberty to trade in North-West America, that is, to the north of the Spanish settlements; but of course all the coasts to the south of them were to remain closed as heretofore. Spain, however, conceded entire freedom of navigation and fishery in the Pacific Ocean and the South Seas, except that, in order to preclude all intercourse with her colonies, British ships were forbidden to approach within a limit of ten maritime leagues.

The British public greeted this happy issue of events with characteristic reserve. As Spain stood for commercial monopoly and political reaction, the rebuff dealt to her ought to have pleased the Whigs. But party rancour increased in proportion to Pitt's success. Hope deferred made the hearts of his opponents sick; and to this cause we may attribute curiously acrid verdicts like that of Auckland's correspondent, Storer, who exclaimed on 22nd October, with the jauntiness of ignorance: " Here we are, going to war, and for what? A place, the name of which I can scarcely pronounce, never heard of till lately, and which did not exist till t'other day. Pitt is tired of peace. He bullied France so effectually three years ago that he is determined to try the same thing with Spain." Storer also says that our officers were in high spirits at the idea of a voyage to *Mexico*, and were buying Ulloa's " Voyage" so as to study the *South Sea* coasts.[2] Whence it would appear that geography was not a strong point with Storer, and that in his eyes wars were worth waging only on behalf of well-known names. How curiously parochial is this habit of mind. Yet Pitt was destined soon to find out its self-assertiveness and tenacity in the case of another un-euphonious and dimly-known place—Oczakoff.

The insular, matter-of-fact way in which the House of Com-

---

[1] " F. O.," Spain, 49 (Drafts of Lord Grenville), shows that the sum of £50,000 was finally demanded from Spain as compensation. For the Convention of 28th October 1790 see "Parl. Hist.," xxviii, 916-18, and Martens, iv, 492-9.

[2] "Auckland Journals," ii, 374.

mons viewed Pitt's diplomatic triumph received apt illustration in the debate of 14th December, when Duncombe and Alderman Watson moved and seconded a resolution of thanks to His Majesty for the Convention with Spain. They dwelt on the advantages of the peaceful settlement which it secured, and augured well for the increase of British trade to the South Seas. But Pulteney declared that we had won too much from Spain, and should ever feel her ill will. Besides, a Pacific whale was worth only £90, as against £170 for a Greenland whale. Alderman Curtis fell foul of these statements in a maiden speech "which possessed all the blunt characteristics of commercial oratory." He said that he himself was a fisherman, and gloried in the character. He rejoiced to state that more ships than ever before were now fitting out for whaling in the Pacific; and he himself had sold Pacific whale-oil for £50 a ton, while the Greenland oil fetched only £18 or £19 a ton. Mr. (afterwards Earl) Grey sought to raise the debate from these blubbery platitudes to the levels of diplomacy; and, differing from his friend Pulteney, censured the Convention because it gained us nothing; for it laid down no definite limits in those new lands, and it granted us access to them conjointly with the Spaniards. Consequently, where our traders settled on one hill, the Spaniards might build a fort on another close by. Windham then censured Ministers because they had secured neither adequate reparation to our outraged honour nor definite rights to our traders. Thereupon a General Smith opined that the Convention was of no advantage to us, because the people of Nootka Sound were "a species of cannibals." In other respects it was "disgraceful to the real interests of the country"—an assertion which Rolle and Ryder proceeded to refute, on the ground that the result had been well worth the three and a half millions spent on naval preparations. (In reality the sum was £2,821,000.)

Fox also wandered deviously until he caught at a possible clue, that offended honour was the only justifiable cause for war. In this case, he declared, Ministers had not gained for us due reparation. It fell infinitely short of what was obtained in the dispute about the Falkland Islands in 1771.[1] Further, we now gained no material advantage from Spain; for British ships had sailed into the South Seas despite the Spanish laws; and the receipts from that trade had grown in five years from £12,000 to £97,000. (He

---

[1] For this see Hertz, "British Imperialism in the XVIIIth Century."

omitted to state that previously that trade had been killed by the war with Spain.) He next asserted that we secured little or nothing in the North Pacific, because the limits of Spanish America were still left vague, and we gave up the right of settlement on the coasts of South America. In fact, the treaty was one of concessions, not of acquisitions. This, he added, was on a par with our foreign policy as a whole; for our new ally, Sweden, had come to terms with Russia behind our backs, thus lowering us in the eyes of the world; and we had failed to coerce Russia. "In our words was confidence: in our acts was fear."

Pitt in his reply had little difficulty in proving that the present case differed entirely from that of the Falkland Islands, and that the treaty secured for us trading rights which Spain had hitherto always contested. There was therefore every ground for hoping for a great increase of trade to the Pacific. The House agreed with him by 247 votes to 123. But in Pitt's speech, as in the whole debate, we find no wide outlook on events. The arguments are of the Little Peddlington type; and, after wandering through those teasing mazes, one feels a thrill of surprise that the British people ever came out into a large and wealthy place. The importance of Pitt's triumph has received scant notice at the hands of historians. Macaulay, in his brilliant sketch of Pitt's career, dismissed the affair in the clause—"England armed, and Spain receded." Lord Rosebery remarks that the settlement of the affair was honourable for England, and not dishonourable to Spain. Even Stanhope and Lecky on their far ampler canvases merely described the terms of the settlement without revealing its momentous results.[1]

Far different were the judgements of enlightened Spaniards. They saw in the treaty of 28th October the beginning of the end of their world-empire. The official Junta at Madrid protested vehemently against the surrender on the ground that it "conceded to England what has always been resisted and refused to all Powers since the discovery of the Indies." Herein lies the significance of the Spanish defeat. Their Empire rested on monopoly. It is little to the point to say that English traders occasionally ventured into the Pacific. They did so at their peril; and the recent revival of Spanish power threatened to rivet once more the chains of privilege on that vast domain.

[1] Stanhope, ii, 63; Lecky, v, 209; Lord Rosebery, "Pitt," 102; Mr. C. Whibley, "Pitt," 129.

Now that they were shattered, the whole cramped system was doomed to fall. Just as the irruption of Cromwell's fleet into the Spanish West Indies in 1654 sounded the knell of Spanish domination in those seas, so too the signing of this Convention presaged the end of their Empire in the Pacific. The advent of the Union Jack on equal terms with the red and yellow flag of Spain has always implied the retreat of the latter. In religion, commerce, and political life the two ensigns represent ideals so utterly at variance that they cannot wave in friendly neighbourhood. One or other must go: and the primacy of Pitt and Godoy sufficiently explains the advance of the one and the retreat of the other in the ensuing years. In one other respect the crisis was important. The British archives show that the Courts of Madrid and St. Petersburg were then making overtures which would probably have led to the complete appropriation of that coast-line; and the interlocking of those two rigid systems might have implied the exclusion for ever of the British flag from the Pacific coast. No one, not even Pitt himself, could foresee the rich harvest of results one day to be reaped from his action in that summer and autumn. The winning of a few log huts at Nootka Sound seemed a small thing then. But in this age of the triumphs of steam and electricity we can discern its importance in world politics. The infant settlement on Vancouver Island, and on the mainland opposite, inspired the pioneers of Canada with hope as they threaded their way through the passes of the Rockies and the Selkirks. Possibly one of them

> like stout Cortez, when with eagle eyes
> He stared at the Pacific,

caught a glimpse of a strange future, when Canada, the child of Richelieu, would enter into the northern heritage of old Spain, and become a Pacific Power.

All this lay enfolded in the winning of that inlet. Nay, more. We can now see that British Columbia holds in the West a strategic position not unlike that of Egypt in the Orient. Both are vital links in our chain of communication. Pitt, could he have known it, helped to fashion the keystone of the arch of Empire in the Occident. He played his part manfully in preparing for a day when Canada would stretch hands across the seas to India and Australia; when the vivifying forces of science and commerce would endow with a common life the conquests of Wolfe and Clive, and the lands discovered by Captain Cook.

CHAPTER XXVI

PITT AND CATHARINE II

Beware
Of entrance to a quarrel, but being in,
Bear't that the opposed may beware of thee.
SHAKESPEARE, *Hamlet.*

U P to the spring of the year 1791 Pitt had achieved a series
of remarkable triumphs in his foreign policy. After lifting
his country from the depths of penury and isolation, he seized
favourable opportunities for checkmating French influence in
Holland, and framing the Triple Alliance with that Republic
and the Kingdom of Prussia. During the years 1788-90 this
alliance gave the law to Europe. It rescued Gustavus III from
ruin; it prescribed terms to Austria at the Conference of
Reichenbach, and thereby saved the Turks from the gravest
danger; it served to restore the ancient liberties of the Brabanters and Flemings; it enabled England to overawe Spain
and win the coast of the present colony of British Columbia;
last, but not least, Pitt, by singular skill, thwarted the dangerous
schemes of the Prussian statesman Hertzberg at the expense of
Poland.

Successes like these are apt to beget feelings of jealousy or
fear; for gratitude rarely figures among the motives that determine the course of national policy. Certainly this is the case in
the story now before us, which tells of a rebuff dealt to Pitt, the
unweaving of his plans for the equitable pacification of Europe,
and the formation of new groupings which leave Great Britain
isolated and her statesmen discredited. The importance of the
crisis, and the light which it throws on the peace-loving character
of Pitt, warrant a closer examination of details than has yet been
given to the subject. We must remember that at every emergency the British Foreign Office was directed by Pitt, not by its

chief, the Duke of Leeds. This appears in a sentence of Ewart's letter of 28th November 1790 to Lord Auckland—"I trust Mr. Pitt will write to your lordship himself in a satisfactory manner; and you know better than I do of what consequence the opinions of others are." The imperious Minister was now to encounter a will as tough, and a pride as exacting, as his own. Catharine of Russia stood in his path, and defied him to apply to her his scheme of pacification, to which Leopold of Austria had yielded grudging assent.

There were several reasons why Pitt should expect from the Czarina a similar acquiescence. Her finances were utterly exhausted by four years of war. Her favourite, Prince Potemkin, had won victories; but he and his dependents had battened on the Treasury, and her triumph heralded the approach of bankruptcy. The plague was devastating her armies in the south; and even Russia seemed unable to endure the waste of another campaign. The Muscovites placed their hopes in a dash of their fleet on Constantinople; but how could that be effected if England sent a strong squadron into the Black Sea to help the Turks? And while she screened the Moslem capital, the presence of her warships in the Baltic must complete the ruin of the Baltic provinces. Two fifths of their exports by sea went to Great Britain; and they drew thence goods worth 7,308,000 roubles as against 2,278,000 from all other lands.[1] The internal state of Russia also gave cause for concern. The extravagance and licentiousness of the Court, flaunted in face of struggling traders and half-starved peasants, were a perpetual challenge to discontent; and the best informed observers believed that, if Prussia and England held firm, the Empress must humble her pride and accept their terms. They were by no means extravagant. Russia was to give up the conquests of the present war, particularly the lands east of the Pruth, which were virtually in her hands; but she might retain the Crimea—the object for which the Sultan had cast down the gauntlet.

At the very time when the British demands were nearing the banks of the Neva, victory crowned the efforts of the Russians on the Lower Danube. Ismail, the stronghold which commanded the only available entrance into Turkey, now that the Austro-Turkish armistice kept Wallachia neutral, fell before the prowess

---

[1] "F. O.," Russia, 20. Trade Report of the Baltic ports for 1790.

of the assailants (22nd December 1790). After some successes against the Turkish flotilla and the batteries fringing the river banks, Potemkin began the siege of the city itself; but its deep fosse, fed from the Danube, and its double line of ramparts defied all his efforts. Then he bent his pride and sent for Suvó-roff. The advent of "the little father" put new heart into the 31,000 besiegers.—"To-day for prayer: to-morrow for drill: the next day victory or a glorious death."—By these words, and by the contagion of his enthusiasm, he worked his men up to a pitch of fury. Skill came to reinforce their fanaticism. By night a strong flotilla dropped down stream to assail the town on that side, while on the other six columns advanced stealthily against the walls. A sharp frost favoured the enterprise; and under cover of a misty dawn the assailants rushed forward at all possible points. The defenders met fury with fury. A long day of carnage ensued, the Moslems, men and women alike, fighting desperately for creed, country, life, and honour. At last Suvó-roff's reserves gained a foothold and overwhelmed the exhausted garrison. Then ensued a night of slaughter, plunder, and outrage. Some 30,000 Turks perished. The consequences of this victory were great. The hold of the Sultan on the Danube was loosened, while the Russians prepared to deal a blow at the heart of the Ottoman dominions. Thus, once again, the personality of Suvóroff proved to be worth an army. Indeed, it changed the course of history. For now, when the proud Empress held the keys of the Danube, how could she consent to give back to the infidels Suvóroff's former conquest, Oczakoff? Diplomacy also furthered the aims of Catharine, and told against those of Pitt. Much depended on the good faith of Leopold II in keeping his promises to the Triple Alliance, pledged at the Conference of Reichenbach in July 1790. He had agreed to accept the *status quo ante bellum* as a basis of settlement for his disputes with the Belgians and for his war with Turkey. Now, nothing ought to have been simpler than the restoration of his conquests to the Porte, provided that the plenipotentiaries of the Powers, who met at Sistova late in 1790 to reduce them to treaty form, were inspired by good faith and pacific desires.

But distrust and intrigue soon enveloped in mystery phrases that were clear as day. The Turks opposed to the superior force of Austria all the chicanery of oriental delays. Their astrologers discovered that very many days were unsuitable for the conduct

of business; and their envoys often fell ill. Hopes ran high at
the Porte that England and Prussia would draw the sword
against the Czarina. The Emperor Leopold and his equally
wily Chancellor, Prince Kaunitz, also saw in delay an opportunity
of wriggling out from the engagements so reluctantly made at
Reichenbach.[1] Scarcely was the ink of that compact dry before
Kaunitz bemoaned to his envoy in London the lack of any conquests at the end of " a ruinously expensive war." This magnanimity he ascribed to his desire to be again on good terms
with England, despite her unjust treatment of a once valued
ally. After these crocodile tears there came the significant suggestion—Would not England instruct her envoy to deal leniently
with Austria in the ensuing negotiations with the Turks, and
allow her to gain a few little advantages?[2] Leopold also wrote to
his offended ally, Catharine, assuring her that he would never
really make peace with the Turks until she had secured from
them conquests proportionate to the successes of her troops.
Let Austria and Russia keep in close touch and form an eternal
compact.[3] Here, then, we probe one of the causes of the defiant
rejection by Catharine of Pitt's demand for the *status quo*. He
believed, and very naturally, that the Austro-Russian alliance
was wholly severed; while, in point of fact, Austria was secretly,
but effectively, playing the game of her late ally.[4]

But there was another cause of his failure. The Semiramis of
the North could at need abase her pride and clasp the hand of
a hated foe. As we have seen, she had grasped that of Gustavus III; but only for the most potent of reasons. She saw in
that vain and impulsive sovereign a convenient tool, who might
serve her well in case of a British naval demonstration against
Cronstadt. For some time the Swedish monarch held back his
hand. Auckland wrote early in November 1790 that Gustavus
either from vanity or from penury, might once more attack her;
but the price which he asked from the Allies was enormous:

---

[1] " Mems. of Sir R. M. Keith," ii, 355-74; Sybel, bk. ii, ch. vi. The Congress of Sistova was adjourned on 10th February for some weeks.

[2] Vivenot, 5.

[3] *Ibid.*, 9, 10; Beer, " Die orientalische Politik Oesterreichs," App. I.

[4] " F. O.," Russia, 20. " The Emperor still continues, notwithstanding his
professions, to flatter the Empress that he may yet enter the lists in her
favour" (Whitworth to Leeds, 18th January 1791). See Keith's letters from
Sistova, showing the resolve of Austria to evade the Reichenbach terms,
and wring Orsova from the Turks ("Mems. of Sir R. M. Keith," ii, 365 *et seq.*).

—" I am assured on good authority that he talks of 10,000,000 rix
dollars for the first campaign, and 7,000,000 for every succeeding
one." [1] Rumour, then, saw in Gustavus not merely a knight errant,
but a shrewd bargainer; and we now know that he had come to
some secret understanding with Catharine. By methods not very
unusual in that age, the British Embassy at Stockholm managed
to procure and decipher a letter of the Swedish monarch to his
envoy at London, Baron Nolcken, dated 7th December 1790.
In it he expressed regret and annoyance that England still
kept a large fleet ready for service in the Baltic, and urged
Nolcken to point out that the British ships would find great
difficulty in procuring provisions in that sea, as Sweden must
refuse them.[2] The experience of our sailors, especially in the
years 1810-11, has since corroborated that statement.

This was not all. Gustavus was then revolving a grandiose
project for the invasion of Normandy by Swedish and Russian
troops, in order to crush the French Revolution. Catharine
humoured the notion, more, it would seem, with the aim of pro-
tecting herself from British warships than of re-establishing
Louis XVI;[3] for, as was often to appear, her royalist heroics
never led to definite action. To the Tancred of the North, however, her friendship seemed all important; and it was therefore
possible that, in the interests of monarchy, he might add his
fleet to hers. Pitt had cause to fear such a hostile combination;
for on 11th February 1791 Ewart assured him that the Empress
of Russia was convinced, " since her peace with Sweden, that no
British fleet could operate in the Baltic with any success, and
that the [British] Minister would risk the loss of his popularity
by such an expedition." [4] Her surmise was to be justified by
events. Nevertheless, Pitt cherished the hope of browbeating
Russia; and, as the sequel will show, this would have given to
the hard-pressed Poles a precious time of reprieve. For it was
not so much Turkey as Poland whose fortunes were at stake.
The events of the years 1791, 1792, virtually decided the doom
of that interesting people, and opened to the Muscovites the
way into the heart of Europe.

As we saw in Chapter XXIII, the Prusso-Polish treaty of

[1] B.M. Add. MSS., 34435.   [2] " F. O.," Sweden, 11.
[3] R. Nisbet Bain, " Gustavus III," ii, 120-3. See, too, Geffroy, " Gus-
tave III et la Cour de France."
[4] Pitt MSS., 332.

I   Q Q

29th March 1790 spread dismay at Petersburg. But the lavish use of Russian gold among the ruck of the Polish nobles in the Diet at Warsaw soon strengthened the anti-Prussian prejudices of that impulsive and passionate body; and the insatiable land-hunger of Hertzberg ere long begot a feeling that the ally was the worst enemy. The feeling was not of recent growth. In the year 1775, that is, three years after the first partition of Poland, Prussia sought to strangle the export trade of that land by imposing heavy customs dues on all Polish products sent down the Vistula, a policy which caused an indignant patriot to declare their removal to be almost as vital as the recovery of Galicia to his country's welfare.[1] All the more did the Prussians persevere in their policy, which clearly involved the ruin of the trade of the free city of Danzig (a close ally of the Polish State) as a prelude to its annexation.[2] Along with it they hoped to secure the cession of the Polish fortress and district of Thorn.

The Diet at Warsaw hotly resented this conduct, declaring that the loss of those much prized districts could be compensated by nothing less than the whole of Galicia. Accordingly, when Prussia began to bargain with Austria for the cession to Poland of only part of Galicia, the rage of the Poles knew no bounds; and, as we saw, the Court of Berlin finally fell back on Pitt's policy of the *status quo*. Nevertheless, even after the settlement at Reichenbach, Frederick William and Hertzberg harked back to the former scheme, so that, at the end of the year 1790, the Poles decided to ask the British Government for advice and help. For this purpose they sent to London as special envoy Count Oginski, their Minister at The Hague. He had two interviews with Pitt, whom he describes as "very polite, speaking French with an English accent, but fluently enough and with marked precision." At first Pitt let his visitor discourse at length, refrained from committing himself, and then suggested a second meeting. By that time he had before him several maps and a memorial from London merchants against throwing open the navigation of the Vistula, as it would end their special privileges. On this he remarked that merchants thought about nothing but trade, and launched into an argument on behalf of the advantages of the Prussian scheme, as providing Poland with what she most needed, a good commercial treaty with Prussia.

[1] "F. O.," Poland, 4. Hailes to Leeds, 12th June 1790.
The Prussians forced the Danzig trade to Elbing. Dembinski, i, 101.

He also showed to Oginski a letter of the King of Prussia in favour of that proposal. Turning to wider topics, he urged the Count to press on his people the need of better agriculture, an extended system of canals, and other means of transport and export. England, he said, needed Polish corn, timber, flax, and hemp, as a counterpoise to the Russian trade in those articles; and, as the fortunes of Poland, both political and commercial, touched us closely, the Prusso-Polish settlement must not be such as to harm our interests. He then charged Oginski to declare this to his Government, and expressed his intention of giving similar instructions to Hailes at Warsaw.[1] That active and intelligent envoy had long been working, in consort with Ewart at Berlin, for the inclusion of Poland in the Anglo-Prussian compact, as a means of deadening the poison of Russian influence in the Republic; and in a pamphlet which he either wrote or inspired, he depicted in glowing colours the results attainable by "a grand federative chain (England, Holland, Prussia, Poland, and, perhaps, Sweden and Turkey) which would assure a long time of peace to our hemisphere."[2]

Similar thoughts, though of a more practical trend, were shaping themselves in the mind of Pitt. The interview with Oginski and the reports from Berlin and Warsaw convinced him of the need of a compact with Poland and the Scandinavian States as a safeguard against Russia. Consequently the Foreign Office on 8th January 1791 despatched to Francis Jackson at Berlin (then acting as *locum tenens* for Ewart) instructions of far-reaching import. They set forth the reasons why England and Prussia should prepare the way for joint alliances, not only with Poland, but also with Denmark and Sweden, if that were possible. The Court of Berlin, it was hoped, might rise to the height of the situation and render possible so desirable a consummation.

At that time the fortunes of Poland appeared radiant with promise. Late in the year 1790 the Court of Warsaw sought to free itself from Prussian dictation and Muscovite intrigue by a compact with the Sultan which would assure a free exit for Polish products down the River Dniester (then in Turkish territory) to the Black Sea. Selim III welcomed an offer which promised to strengthen both lands against their common enemy, Russia; and it seemed likely that Poland would

[1] "Mems. de Michel Oginski," i, 92-9.
[2] "F. O.," Poland, 5. Hailes's despatches of January 1791.

gain the right of navigation in the Black Sea for fifty of her ships. Had this come about, she would have lessened her dependence on Prussia in the Vistula valley, besides securing valuable markets in the Levant. But it was not to be. The Sultan, then in sore straits for the next campaign against Catharine, insisted that the Poles should declare war upon the Czarina whatever Frederick William might do, and thus ensured the failure of a compact which promised to range the two threatened States along with England and Prussia.[1] If the Poles had had timely support from Berlin and London, there is little doubt that they would have clogged the efforts of Catharine, besides escaping from the tutelage of St. Petersburg. In that case the league outlined by Hailes and, in part at least, approved by Pitt would have come within the bounds of possibility. Other requisites were the abatement of Prusso-Polish jealousies, and the adoption of a sound and steady policy by Gustavus III. Such were the difficulties in the way of Pitt. It will ever redound to his honour that at this time of intrigue and rapine he sought to assure the union and the preservation of the lesser States.

Among the warping influences of the time not the least was the policy of Hertzberg. After the success of the Triple Alliance in compelling Austria to come to terms with Turkey, he pressed England to help in compelling the Czarina to adopt the same course; and, as he had recently supported Pitt in coercing Spain, the latter felt in honour bound to respond. But Hertzberg had long been shifting his ground. He valued the alliance with England and Holland chiefly because it secured Prussia's western frontier and coast-line, thereby enabling her to play a bold game in the East, and to prepare to round off her then almost scattered domains in the valley of the Vistula. There the Polish districts around Danzig and Thorn ate into her lands and might even become a source of danger if that singular Republic once more passed under Muscovite control. We may freely admit that to a military State like Prussia the situation was annoying, and that Pitt himself, had he been in office in Berlin, would have sought to assure her eastern frontier by some plan of exchange. In truth, his despatches and his converse with Oginski show that he appreciated the difficulties of the Court of Berlin and tried to induce the Poles to cede Danzig (not Thorn) to Prussia in

[1] "F. O.," Poland, 4. Hailes to Leeds, 1st and 11th December 1790.

exchange for a good commercial treaty. It is therefore false to assert, as German writers have done, that he showed no regard for Prussian interests. Unfortunately his solution of the difficulty proved to be impracticable. Polish national sentiment was very susceptible on this point; and a special decree of the Warsaw Diet finally forbade any cession of the national territory, though (strictly speaking) Danzig was only allied to the Republic.

But long before the failure of Pitt's well-meant attempt at compromise Hertzberg had been seeking to compass his aims by secret help from the Power which ostensibly he was about to coerce. Seeing that Pitt had thwarted his earlier schemes by the pacification of Reichenbach, he made covert advances to Russia, and that, too, at the time when Frederick William had expressly charged him to drop the Danzig-Thorn proposals. Opening his heart to the Russian envoy, Alopeus, he said that, if the Empress limited her claims to such a trifle (*peu de chose*) as Oczakoff and the land up to the Dniester, the two Powers could easily come to a friendly understanding, provided that Russia did not thwart the scheme just named. He then suggested that, as he was forbidden by the King to make that proposal, it would be well that it should come from St. Petersburg; in which case he would give it his hearty support. Indeed, he would find no difficulty in proving that the support of Russia and the gains aforesaid were far more desirable than the friendship of England, from whom Prussia had received nothing in return for all the services she had rendered.[1] This is in germ the Second Partition of Poland. Betraying his own Sovereign and his allies, England and Poland, Hertzberg invited the Power which he was ostensibly threatening, to work her will on Turkey provided that she helped Prussia to secure the two coveted Polish districts. Even in that age of duplicity and violence conduct such as this bore the mark of infamy. It led to the fall of the schemer, but not until his treachery had sapped Pitt's policy at the base.

As chance would have it, this insidious offer was made known at St. Petersburg on the very day when the British and Prussian envoys presented their demand for the restitution by Russia of

---

[1] Dembinski, i, 103, 104. Alopeus to Ostermann, 6th December 1790 (N.S.). The British archives show that Hertzberg continued to smile on our efforts to coerce Russia, and encouraged the Turks to do their utmost against her. Jackson to Leeds, 4th January 1791 (" F. O.," Prussia, 20).

all her recent conquests. The result can readily be imagined. Catharine, knowing the Prussian threats to be mere stage thunder, resolved to defy both Powers.[1] To Whitworth the Russian Vice-Chancellor, Ostermann, behaved as much in sorrow as in anger. He complained of the unprecedentedly menacing tone adopted by the Allies. He declared that the Empress would never accept their terms, and would limit herself strictly to an acceptance of the good offices of England, "inasmuch as they may tend to procure for her the indemnity she requires—Oczakoff and its district." Rather than forego this, she would commit her fortunes into the hand of Providence, braving all perils rather than tarnish the glory of a long and splendid reign by a craven surrender. Whitworth saw in this declaration a threat of war, but he little knew who was the special Providence of the situation. In fact he flattered himself that, despite the news of the capture of Ismail by the Russians, the Empress must give way under the pressure of the Triple Alliance. His verdict was as follows:

Abandoned by her Allies [Austria and Denmark], destitute of internal as well as external resources, without confidence in the persons she is obliged to employ at the head of her fleet and army, both of which are incapable of acting against a formidable enemy; and, added to this, a strong spirit of discontent against the Government and its measures prevalent throughout the country—how can we suppose it possible that, under such circumstances, pride and obstinacy can maintain their ground? These, however, are the only motives which influence the Court of Petersburg.[2]

Whitworth's forecast deserves to be borne in mind; for he, together with Ewart or Jackson at Berlin, and Hailes at Warsaw, was best qualified to judge of Russia's power of resisting the British demands. Ewart, our able ambassador at Berlin, spent the winter of 1790-1 in England for the benefit of his health; and there are signs in his correspondence with Pitt that he fully explained to him and to other Ministers the importance of the issues at stake. He showed that, unless Turkey retained the Oczakoff district, both she and Poland would be liable to further encroachments from Russia. He declared that the British demand of a restitution of that district by Russia,

[1] Dembinski, i, 108-10. Ostermann to Alopeus, 1st January 1791 (N.S.).
[2] "F. O.," Russia, 20. Whitworth to Leeds, 8th January 1790.

sent off on 14th November, would be firmly supported at Berlin; and, he continued, "though the Empress of Russia may, and probably will, make some difficulties at first, there can be little doubt of her accepting the terms offered before the spring, since she never can venture to risk the consequences of a refusal." Ewart, then, was more positive than Whitworth that Catharine would not risk a war with the Allies; and Pitt, with his sanguine spirit, doubtless had the same expectation. Ewart also opened up wide vistas in the diplomatic sphere. He advised Pitt to bring not only Turkey but also Poland into the Triple Alliance; for this step would at once overthrow the influence of the Bourbon Courts at Constantinople and that of Russia at Warsaw.[1]

Despite Grenville's disapproval of the latter proposal, Pitt and Leeds decided to act on it; and, as we have seen, sent an offer of alliance to the Polish Court.[2] The matter was of urgent importance; for rumours of Hertzberg's underhand clutches at Danzig and Thorn had reached Warsaw and gave new strength to Muscovite intrigues. The prospect of an alliance with England was warmly welcomed by Polish patriots; and there is little doubt that, had Hertzberg loyally supported Pitt's resolve to check the advance of Russia, a completely different turn would have been given to national developments in the East of Europe.

At the outset, the British Cabinet had reasons for trusting Hertzberg. Through the year 1790 he insisted on the need of strenuous action against Russia. It was his policy rather than that of Pitt, who at first took it up somewhat doubtfully. There is not a sentence in the British despatches which has a warlike ring. In the month of December the fleet was placed on a peace footing once more—a grave tactical error, for it lessened the effect of the British "Declaration" at St. Petersburg; and in the missive of 8th January to Jackson, the hope is distinctly expressed that war may be avoided. There were good grounds for such an expectation. Spain appeared to favour the cause of the Allies; and Leopold, at the end of a fruitless strife, might be

---

[1] Pitt MSS., 332. Ewart to Pitt, 16th November 1790.
[2] "F. O.," Poland, 5. Leeds to Hailes, 8th January 1791. This evidence and the facts stated later on, in my judgement refute the statement of Lecky (v, 287) that the political security of Poland did not enter into the motives of Pitt's policy.

expected to oppose the aggrandisement of Russia. Pitt therefore refused to prepare for war until the intentions of the doubtful States—Austria, Spain, Denmark, and Sweden—were better
known.[1]

The horizon cleared but slowly. The Danish Court declared
its intention of not breaking with the Empress, who had guaranteed to it the Duchy of Holstein. Austria, while assuring the
Allies that she would not take up arms for Catharine, favoured
her claims at the Conference of Sistova. As for Gustavus III,
he seemed to be holding out for the highest bid for his alliance.
In the middle of February he assured Liston (it was between the
acts of the Opera) that he was not pledged to Russia, and might
join the Allies on consideration of a subsidy of £1,500,000 for
each campaign. Spain also balanced at times, as if her sole
object were to restore her waning prestige; but on the whole
she opposed the threatened entrance of Russia into Mediterranean
politics, as France would probably have done had she been less
torn by internal strifes.[2]

On the whole, then, the general situation favoured the Allies,
provided that they were true to one another. But here lay the
chief difficulty. The divergence of interests between the Maritime States and Prussia could be reconciled only by generous
forbearance and whole-hearted good faith. Britons and Dutchmen wanted peace, provided that their navies and their commerce would not suffer from the stride of Russia southwards.
The Court of Berlin cared less for commerce (except as a means
of coercing Poland), but longed for a better frontier on the
East. Unfortunately good faith was not then characteristic of
Prussian policy. Jackson suspected Hertzberg of duplicity, but
believed his power to be on the wane. Moreover, other counsellors, especially the latest favourite, Bischoffswerder, seemed
true to the British alliance. The King probably intended to
keep troth; but he either could not or did not prevent the
secret intrigues of Hertzberg from undermining the efforts of the

---

[1] " F. O.," Prussia, 20. Leeds to Jackson, 8th January 1791.
[2] *Ibid.* Jackson's despatches of 23rd January, 12th, 17th, 26th February,
1st March; "F. O.," Russia, 20. Whitworth's despatches of 14th, 18th,
25th January (on the "defection" of Spain from Russia); "F. O.," Sweden,
20, Liston to Leeds, 17th February. For the fears of Marie Antoinette
and the French Court that British armaments were aimed at France,
see Sorel, ii, 181, 182.

Allies both at Warsaw and St. Petersburg. One of the great mistakes of his reign was in not dismissing that statesman outright; but instead of that he merely ordered him once more to desist from his pet scheme, the acquisition of Danzig and Thorn.

The policy of the Court of Berlin now took one more turn underground. The King, weary of the haughty airs and restless ways of Hertzberg, and desirous of putting forth a feeler towards Vienna, sent Bischoffswerder on a secret mission to the Court of Vienna (February 1791). Hertzberg knew no more of its aims than did Frederick William of the intrigue of his Foreign Minister with the Russian Chancery. Thus Prussian policy was two-headed. The official head, while echoing the menacing tones of Pitt to Russia, secretly encouraged that Power to retain all its conquests, provided that Prussia acquired the two coveted towns on the Vistula; and Bischoffswerder sought to allure the Emperor. The King's favourite (a poor Saxon nobleman who had won his way at Court by chameleonic subservience to all the royal moods) was charged to confer direct with Leopold, and to propose that the two States should mutually guarantee their present possessions and aim at excluding Russian influence from Poland. He was also to suggest the peaceable acquisition by Prussia of Danzig and Thorn in exchange for commercial privileges granted to the Poles.[1] Leopold II smiled so graciously on these proposals as to elicit from the envoy the ecstatic description : " *Quelle bonté; quelle clarté: et quelle sérénité!*" This benignity enticed Bischoffswerder on to make the singular offer that, if the Emperor granted Prussia her heart's desire, she on her side would not persist in applying the strict *status quo* against Austria at Sistova.

Even this enticing proposal did not dissolve either the hatred of Kaunitz for Prussia or the determination of Leopold to favour Catharine. Both the Emperor and his Chancellor saw that Prussia was seeking to set them against Russia; and policy prompted them to work for a war between those two Powers.[2] No suspicion of these hidden motives ruffled the equanimity of the amateur diplomatist, who flattered himself that he had won over Leopold and assured the isolation of Russia. Full blown with pride he returned to Berlin, and advocated energetic

---

[1] Vivenot, *op. cit.*, 78, 79.

[2] *Ibid.*, 98 *et seq.* Cobenzl to Kaunitz, 4th March 1791; Beer, "Leopold II, Franz I, und Catharina," 39 *et seq.*

measures against Russia, the result of which will appear in due course.[1]

We must now return to London in order to sift somewhat closely the evidence which came in from various quarters. In a question of so much importance and complexity, which influenced the fate of the East as well as the career of Pitt, we cannot proceed too cautiously; and the inductive method here attempted seems to be the only means of avoiding hasty decisions, and of re-constructing the history of the crisis.

The Dutch, as might be expected, were far less eager than Prussia for the humbling of Catharine's pride, especially as they had recently lent her a considerable sum of money. Lord Auckland, our envoy at The Hague, entered into their views and set them forth with his usual ability. From the beginning of this question he opposed the energetic measures recommended by Ewart; and certain expressions in his letters smack of personal dislike to that ambassador.[2] His position at The Hague kept him in touch with the British couriers passing through to the northern and eastern capitals; and his very voluminous papers (a small part only of which has seen the light) yield proofs of his activity in urging Pitt and the Duke of Leeds to patch matters up with Russia. In a letter of 2nd February 1791, to Huber, he deprecates any attempt to coerce Russia, even though it may be crowned by success:

The state of our debt, of our revenue, of our trade, and the unsettled disposition of mankind in general, forms altogether a great object of importance in my ideas, far beyond that of taking a feather out of the cap of an old vixen or of preserving a desert tract of ground between two rivers to the Turks, whose political existence and safety will probably not be diminished if they are obliged to have their barrier upon the Dniester, or even on the Danube. Besides I see many symptoms . . . which irrefragably prove to me that our friends at Berlin are in general at least as much afraid of a Russian war as I am. . . .[3]

[1] I differ from Dr. Salomon ("Pitt," 514) as to the motives which impelled the Prussian King at this time.

[2] On 29th July 1791 Auckland wrote to Grenville about Ewart's "misconceived energy and violence" (B.M. Add. MSS., 34438). See, too, "Auckland Journals," ii, 392-3.

[3] B.M. Add. MSS., 34436. Ewart must somehow have seen this letter, for he quoted some of its phrases in his letter of 11th February to Pitt (Pitt MSS., 332). See, too, his letters of 8th February and 5th March to Lord Grenville in "Dropmore P.," ii, 31, 38.

In the following letter, dated The Hague, 7th March, he sought to win over Lord Grenville to his views:

It appears from these despatches that we have nothing to expect from the Danish Ministry, which is immoveably devoted to Russia; and that Sweden, unless previously purchased by the Empress, would possibly undertake one campaign against her upon payment of £1,500,000. [He names other expenses amounting to another £1,500,000.] . . . In plain truth, this phantom of Oczakow has appeared to me for some time to beckon us towards an abyss of new debts and endless difficulties at a moment of general fermentation in the world when it may be essential perhaps to the very existence of our Government and of many other civilized States that we should maintain our own internal peace and the uninterrupted course of our prosperity.[1]

Auckland's chief opponent, Ewart, now had the ear of the Cabinet. On 8th March he frankly informed Auckland that his health had so far recovered as to permit him to return to Berlin; but he believed his duty to lie in London where he frequently saw the chief Ministers. He added that the meeting of the Cabinet, which was to decide as to the means of coercing Russia, would take place very shortly; further, that Ministers "have admitted my statement of facts to be just; so that the whole can be reduced to a simple calculation. I can venture to assure your Lordship in the most positive manner that nothing is to be apprehended from the present state of the Prussian Cabinet; and I will answer for its being much better than ever it was, provided we go on."[2] Clearly, then, Ewart had some difficulty in convincing Pitt and his colleages that Russia would give way if the Allies showed a determined front.

Pitt himself was now beset by doubts whether the Oczakoff district was worth the risk of a war. As will shortly appear, Catharine had left the extent of her territorial demands discreetly vague, so that the Whigs were able to assert that Russia wanted merely the barren strip of land around Oczakoff. The town itself was held to be a valuable possession because it commanded the entrance to the large estuary called the Liman, which is formed by the Rivers Dnieper and Bug. Auckland, however, brought to judgement an able witness, a Dutch admiral, Kingsbergen, who, after serving in the Russian navy several

[1] B.M. Add. MSS., 34436.   [2] *Ibid.*

years in those waters, declared that Oczakoff was of little importance either to the Turks or the Russians. Pitt took up this
question with alacrity, and on 7th March wrote to Auckland for
definite answers to these inquiries. Whether the Turks, if they
resumed possession of Oczakoff, could hinder the junction of
Russian squadrons sailing from Kherson and Sevastopol, and
thereby hamper the preparations for an attack on Constantinople?
Whether the retention of Oczakoff by Russia would not enable
her to command the southern exit of Polish commerce, namely,
down the River Dniester to the Black Sea? Also, whether Oczakoff could not be so strengthened (rumour described it as in
part demolished) as once again to defy a Russian attack?[1]

To these searching questions Admiral Kingsbergen made the
following replies. Oczakoff did not command the entrance to
the Liman, as that was four cannon-shot wide, and the navig-
able channel was nearer to the Kinburn, or Russian, side than to
Oczakoff. Neither of these places was a port; and the value of
Kherson (the naval station on the Dnieper) was much overrated. Russia would do well to spend all her energies on
Sevastopol or Balaclava, to which places she could easily bring
all the naval stores from the Don or Dnieper district. Those
ports would be the best starting points for an attack on Constantinople, which the Turks, even if masters of Oczakoff, could
in no wise prevent. When he (Kingsbergen) in 1773 prepared a
plan for attacking Constantinople he took little thought of the
Turkish garrison at Oczakoff. Indeed that town must always be
isolated and a source of expense, even of danger, to the Porte. The
admiral felt unable to say whether the cession of Oczakoff and its
district to Russia would adversely affect the trade of Poland to
the Black Sea, and he opined that it would not much extend
the power and population of Russia in the south.[2]

In this last conjecture the admiral was wholly wrong. We
can now see that the acquisition by Russia of the valuable territory in question, on which now stands the port of Odessa, opened
up to her almost boundless possibilities of controlling the Balkan
Peninsula and of strangling Poland. On the naval matters
referred to by Pitt, Kingsbergen's answer bore the stamp of experience and authority. It proved that Oczakoff in itself was of

---

[1] "Auckland Journals," ii, 382.

[2] B.M. Add. MSS., 34436. Auckland to Leeds, 15th March 1791; also in
"F. O.," Holland, 34 (received on 19th March).

little worth; but it did not prove that the whole district up to
the Dniester was equally valueless.

We have proof of Pitt's anxiety to probe this question
thoroughly. In the Pitt MSS. is a long memorandum which aims
at showing that the growth of Russia's power and trade in
the Baltic was to our advantage, as she supplied us with much
needed naval stores, through a sea over which we could exercise
some measure of control. But her progress to the Black Sea and
the Mediterranean was greatly to be deprecated; for she would
then furnish those stores to our rivals, France and Spain, through
ports which were never blocked by ice. Further, if she gained
the Oczakoff district, she could shut out the trade of the Poles
from the Black Sea, while extending her own markets through
the Levant and the Mediterranean, to our detriment. The prospects of her gaining Constantinople are also dwelt upon; and the
conclusion of the anonymous writer is that we ought at all costs
to hinder her southward march, even while we hailed her as a
friend in the Baltic.[1] Doubts of various kinds also beset the
mind of the Duke of Leeds. On 11th March he wrote thus to
Auckland:

. . . The present situation of affairs is, I confess, by no means pleasant,
and perhaps, all things considered, the most perplexing point is to
extricate ourselves from the risk of a war, *salvo honore*. We are in my
opinion so far committed as to render this, however desirable, extremely
difficult, if not impracticable. [He then states that the successes of the
Russians make it difficult now to insist on the absolute *status quo*, of
which he had never wholly approved.] Yet in my mind [he continues]
it behoves us (considering the part we have so decidedly, tho' perhaps
not very wisely, taken,) more than ever to abide by our former determination, or the Empress's ambition will be gratified, not only at the
expense of the Turkish territory, but of the reputation of this Government. So much for the engagements (thanks to Prussia) we have entered
into. I will now beg to call your Lordship's attention to the extent of
the Russian conquests, which I think deserving the most serious attention on our part. Oczakow and its district, it seems is (or at least was)
all the Empress in her moderation will insist on keeping. This district
by the bye (according to Woronzow's language, as well as my own suspicion) includes the whole tract of country from the Bog [*sic*] to the
Dniester. However barren the soil may be, the command of the latter
river, its *embouchure* being at the mercy of Russia, will operate a con-

----

[1] Pitt MSS., 337.

siderable change in the influence of that Power in the Black Sea, whether with a view to hostile operations or to commercial engagements, and completely shut out Poland from her southern *débouché*.[1] . . .

Nothing is more singular in this letter than the confession of the Foreign Minister that he does not know exactly what extent of land the Empress demands—a matter infinitely favourable to the Opposition in Parliament. Certainly the Duke of Leeds and Whitworth had not manœuvred skilfully in leaving this all-important question in doubt.

To resume, then, we find that neither Pitt nor his colleague knew the extent of the Czarina's demands, which, at the request of Prussia, they were about to oppose; that Leeds secretly doubted the wisdom of this policy; that Pitt found out by 19th March the comparative unimportance of Oczakoff itself, however valuable the whole territory might be to Polish merchants; that the Dutch were most reluctant to take any part in the dispute; that Austria was playing a dilatory and threatening game at Sistova; and last, but not least, that Prussian policy began to show signs of weakness and wavering.[2]

Now, the crux of the whole question was at Berlin. Jackson had not fathomed the depths of Hertzberg's duplicity. He did not know of his having prompted Russia to suggest to Frederick William a secret bargain at the expense of Poland; but on 6th March he stated that Danzig and Thorn still held the first place in that statesman's thoughts, despite the express veto of his master. The Prussian Minister sought to justify his behaviour by assuring Jackson that, in case of a war with Russia, Leopold would step in and dictate his terms to Prussia as a revenge for her treatment of him at Reichenbach. Accordingly, Hertzberg refused to take comfort from Jackson's remark that the splendid army of Prussia (numbering 208,000 effectives) would be a match for the exhausted and badly led forces of the two Empires, distracted as they would be by the efforts of the Ottomans in the south. He also affected great concern lest England should play him false by sending only a small fleet into the Baltic. But Jackson saw, rightly enough, that the two phantoms, a triumphant Austria and a skeleton British fleet, were conjured up merely as an excuse for doubling back to the

---

[1] B.M. Add. MSS., 34436.
[2] "Mems. of Sir R. M. Keith," ii, 367-70, 379.

forbidden fruit—Danzig and Thorn. Hertzberg finally suggested the advisability of toning down the allied demands in order to mollify the Czarina.[1] Thus the first suggestion to this effect came, not from Pitt or Auckland, but from the man who had first advised the use of coercive measures against Russia. Is it surprising, then, that up to 20th March 1791 Pitt declined to take any vigorous steps against Catharine? The whole trend of events prescribed caution and delay until the policy of Prussia showed signs of consistency and firmness. But now the whole situation was suddenly to change owing to causes which must be set forth in the following chapter.

[1] "F. O.," Prussia, 20. Jackson to Leeds, 9th March. See Heidrich, "Preussen im Kampfe gegen die Franz. Revolution" (1908), ch. i, for the causes of the double face worn by Prussian policy at this time.

CHAPTER XXVII

THE TRIUMPH OF CATHARINE II

*A pretty piece of work Mr. Pitt has made of this Russian war. I think all the foxhounds will have a fine chase at him next session.—*LADY MALMESBURY TO SIR GILBERT ELLIOT, 24*th August* 1791.

THE success of Pitt in playing the part of Petruchio to Catharine depended mainly on the steadiness of the Prussian and British Governments, the honest neutrality of Leopold, the goodwill of Gustavus, and the conviction of the Czarina that she was hopelessly outmatched. We have already seen that the actions of the Austrian and Swedish sovereigns were ambiguous. It remains to consider the conduct of the Prussian monarch. On 11th March 1791 Frederick William wrote the following autograph letter to Count Redern, his Minister in London:

[*Translation.*]

Having a sure belief that Austria desires to draw closer to me and my Allies, and that the Emperor has declared to the Empress of Russia that he cannot assist her in a war that might result from her refusal to accept the *status quo*, I wish England to consider whether the best course of action would not be that of inducing Russia by means of superior forces, both naval and military, to follow the example of the Emperor. But, in case England cannot resolve on so vigorous a course of action, the cession of Oczakoff would be its natural outcome. It seems to me incontestable that Russia by the possession of that place gains over Turkey a superiority which may be very prejudicial to the interests even of England. As the decisive moment is drawing near, I await a definite declaration on this subject.

Here was a distinct challenge to our good faith as an ally of Prussia. The Duke of Leeds received it on 19th or 20th March. Jackson's covering despatch supplied a curious commentary on the royal missive. He had found out that Hertzberg's plan of aggrandisement at the expense of Poland was much more widely favoured at Berlin than he believed to be possible. General Möllendorf feared a war with Russia in view of the threatening attitude of Austria. Count Schulenberg thought the position very difficult, but hoped that the presence of a "large" British fleet in the Baltic might overawe Catharine and end the dispute. Even Bischoffswerder, who had returned from his mission to Vienna in the most buoyant spirits, expressed concern at the irresolute mood of Frederick William; but he promised to report progress after an interview which he was to have with him at a private dinner on that day. Late in the evening the favourite declared that he had convinced the monarch of the falseness of Hertzberg's information about Austria. In fact, the dinner and Bischoffswerder's conversation brought Frederick William to see the need of bold measures against Russia; and he drew up forthwith that inspiriting challenge to England. Bischoffswerder also assured our envoy that the anti-British intrigues were the work of Anglophobes like Prince Henry of Prussia, or of those who wished to maintain the influence of the reigning favourite, the Countess Dönhoff, and keep the King immersed in his pleasures.[1]

A more damning explanation of the King's action cannot be conceived; and we learn with some surprise that the royal appeal carried the day at the British Cabinet's meetings of 21st and 22nd March, when Ministers had before them the declaration of the Dutch admiral as to the comparative uselessness of Oczakoff. The final resolve was formed on 25th March, when the ultimatum to Russia was drawn up and sent to the King for his approval.[2] Evidently it was the arrival of Frederick William's letter that clinched the matter. On the 27th the Foreign Office sent off despatches to Berlin and St. Petersburg, warning Jackson and Whitworth of the definite demand of the Allies, that Catharine must restore to the Turks all her conquests exclusive of the Crimea. The Allies hoped to induce Gustavus by the joint offer of a sum of £200,000, or even £300,000, to grant the use of his ports to the British fleet destined for the Baltic.[3]

[1] "F. O.," Prussia, 20. Jackson to Leeds, 11th March 1791 (received 19th March).

[2] "Leeds Mem.," 150-2.

[3] Leeds to Jackson, 27th March 1791. Russia then was seeking to form an alliance with Sweden and Denmark with a view to declaring the Baltic a *mare clausum* (" F. O.," Russia, 20. Whitworth to Leeds, 25th March 1791).

I   R R

The British ultimatum to Russia took the form of a " representation," the original of which is in Pitt's handwriting. It pointed
out that, the *status quo* having been adopted as the basis of the
treaties concluded between Austria and the Porte and Russia
and Sweden, the Allies had hoped that the Empress of Russia
would accept the same reasonable terms for her peace with the
Sultan. But, as this was not the case, the two Courts now desired
to point out that any further accession of territory to Russia
was far from necessary to her, and must seriously weaken the
Turkish dominions. They therefore invited the Empress to
declare her readiness to offer reasonable terms to the Sultan.
The failure to give a favourable answer within ten days would
be regarded as a refusal.[1] Pitt also sought to infuse energy
into the Dutch Government. On the same day he directed
Auckland, our ambassador at The Hague, to request the equipment of a Dutch squadron with a view to a cruise to the Baltic
along with the British fleet, it being certain that Catharine would
give way before so great a superiority of force.[2]

It seemed, then, that Pitt and his colleagues had nailed their
colours to the mast; and their behaviour in Parliament betokened
no lack of resolve. On the day following (28th March) Pitt presented the King's message as to the need of further naval armaments. Fox, "with more than usual solemnity," demanded that
Parliament should know the reasons for the present request; but
Pitt declined to promise any more information than that contained in the brief official statement. Fox at once censured this
refusal as "a very new, violent and extraordinary step indeed."
Pitt here showed a want of tact. A more sympathetic nature
would have felt the pulse of the House and discerned feverish
symptoms. Already members had been alarmed by the outbreak
of war against Tippoo Sahib; and though Ministers had convicted that potentate of aggressions against our ally, the Rajah
of Travancore, yet the House evinced more than its usual
jealousy respecting foreign entanglements, and resented Pitt's
demand for warlike preparations. In refusing to explain the
grounds for his present action the Prime Minister behaved as a
correct diplomatist, but an indifferent parliamentarian.

On 29th March the Whig leaders in the Lords showed their
former fondness for the Russian alliance in a series of startling

[1] " F. O.," Russia, 20. Leeds to Whitworth, 27th March 1791.
[2] " F. O.," Holland, 34. Pitt to Auckland, 27th March.

assertions. Earl Fitzwilliam denied that the retention of Ocza- koff, or even Akerman, would in the slightest degree injure British interests. Lord Porchester reprobated the ambitious con- duct of the Prime Minister, which almost led him to hope that France might recover her strength, so as to check his career. The country, he added, was in the deepest distress,[1] and would be ruined by the hostilities now imminent. The Earl of Carlisle declared that Russia was naturally our friend, and that we ought to have formed alliances that were useful, not such as would drag us into a criminal war. The naval armament against Spain had served merely to "pillage the public and make a show between Portsmouth and the Isle of Wight." Lord Stormont then treated the House to a disquisition on Turkish history to prove that the Porte had always been the tool of France against the two Empires; and it was her game we now were asked to play. For the rest, it would be " extremely disagreeable " to send a fleet into the Baltic if Sweden, deserted by us, showed herself unfriendly. The Duke of Richmond damned the proposal with faint praise, and he was guardedly followed by the Lord Chancellor, Thurlow. Nevertheless, Ministers held their own by ninety-seven votes to thirty-four.

On the same day Pitt brought the matter before the Commons in a somewhat cold and ineffective manner. He showed that the interests of Europe demanded the restoration of the old bound- aries in the East; and that the weakening of Turkey would undermine the defensive system which we had formed with Prussia. From the meagre report of his speech it would appear that he did not refer to the importance of upholding Poland or of hindering the approach of Russia to the Mediterranean. Con- sequently all the life and glow of the debate was on the side of the Opposition. Coke of Norfolk, in a characteristically acrid speech, declared that he believed neither in the abilities nor the integrity of the Prime Minister, who now, as in the case of the Spanish dispute, bade them throw away the nation's money without showing a single reason why. Lambton followed in the same vein, asserting that a war with Russia would yield no prize in galleons and ingots, but merely in bear-skins. At what point, he asked, had Russia injured our interests or insulted our honour? Doubtless Ministers had promised the King of Prussia to go to

---

[1] Contrast with this the admission of Storer: " Our taxes have proved this year beyond example productive " ("Auckland Journals," ii, 389).

war with the Czarina. If so, they should state it clearly. Other members then demanded more information before they supported the administration. For the defence, Steele spoke weakly, urging that the House must trust the executive.

Fox, on the contrary, declared that Pitt had "enveloped himself in mystery and importance," and that his speech was "finely confused but very alarming." The Minister had not shown how the balance of power was endangered by the Czarina's policy. It would be time enough to go to war when she attacked Prussia, or sought to drive the Turks out of Europe—a scheme which the orator held up to ridicule. He then protested against our attacking Russia "for the recovery of a single town [sic]," and proceeded to indict Ministers because "they first stirred up the Turks to their own destruction to war upon Russia: they next raised the King of Sweden against the same Power, and afterwards they lost the benefit of his arms by shamefully abandoning him." Finally they had disarmed, after settling the dispute with Spain, and thus put the nation to the expense of this new armament. It is difficult to think that Fox was so ill informed as to believe these charges, the falseness of which has been proved in Chapters XXII and XXIII. In fact, these indictments merely showed him to be the trustful receptacle of the anti-British slanders started by foreign Chanceries. Nevertheless, being urged with his wonted power, they struck home; for it is ever the bent of a popular Assembly to ascribe the worst motives for actions which it dislikes.

Pitt replied with admirable temper. He showed that the recent advance of Russia southwards brought about a situation wholly different from that which existed when Fox was in power; he declared that Russia had several times rejected our proffered friendship, and that our alliances with Prussia and Holland were most advantageous. Prussia, however, would be seriously weakened if the Muscovites triumphed completely over the Sultan, and would in that case be unable to cover the Dutch Netherlands or maintain the independence of Poland. He then showed how closely this latter topic touched us; for, if we upheld Poland and cultivated trade with her, she would send us the naval stores for the supply of which we at present depended on Russia. Commercial and political motives, therefore, alike bade us set bounds to the boundless ambitions of Russia.

The effect of his statesmanlike speech (the first in which the

Eastern Question in its new phase received adequate treatment) was lessened by a vehement harangue from Burke, who was angry with Ministers for diverting attention from French affairs. At that time he and his son were striving to prepare the way for an armed intervention of the monarchs in the interests of Louis XVI; and he therefore upbraided the Cabinet for support-ing "a horde of barbarous Asiatics" against the Czarina, a declared champion of royalty.[1] "All that is holy in religion," he said, "all that is moral and humane, demands an abhorrence of everything which tends to extend the power of that cruel and wasteful Empire." "Any Christian Power is to be preferred to these destructive savages." . . . "Why are we to be alarmed at the Russians' capture of a town? The Empire of Turkey is not dismembered by that. We are in possession of Gibraltar, and yet Spain is not dismembered." This appeal to sentiment and this fine disregard of the facts of geography (for the district in ques-tion is about the size of Scotland) told with much effect; and it was with some difficulty that the Government mustered 228 votes as against 135 for the Opposition.[2]

The next debates, of 12th and 15th April, brought up Grey, Whitbread, and Sheridan in their most combative moods. The last taunted Ministers with being led at the heel of Prussia, whose only desire was to seize Danzig and Thorn, and to have the upper hand at Warsaw. While not calling the tune, we were to pay the piper. He (Sheridan) was sick of the parrot cry, "Confidence! Confidence!" Ministers did not deserve it. Their conduct in Holland in 1787 had been a blow to popular liberty. And now the son of Chatham was intriguing in all the Courts of Europe, and figuring as "the posture-master of the Balance of Power." Undismayed by this brilliant invective, Dundas once more appealed for a continuance of the confidence which Ministers had merited by their conduct; and the House accorded it by 253 votes to 173. On 15th April the figures were 254 to 162.[3]

It is clear, then, that Pitt kept his party well together, despite the fact that his hands were tied by official reserve, while the Opposition ramped at large in the unalloyed bliss of ignorance.

[1] See Burke's "Correspondence," iii, 268, where he calls Ewart "a little, busy, meddling man, little heard of till lately."
[2] "Parl. Hist.," xxix, 33-79.
[3] Earl Stanhope (ii, 115) does not give the last figures, which show that the Ministry regained ground on 15th April.

Storer might choose to tell Lord Auckland that "the country throughout have told Mr. Pitt that they will not go to war."[1] But, apart from an influential deputation from Manchester, there was no decided protest. Seven weeks later Pitt admitted to Ewart that it would have been difficult to keep his party together in the event of war, and if he had "to state, as would then be indispensable, the precise ground on which it arose."[2] But the news which arrived up to 27th March clearly warranted the hope that Russia would give way. Then, however, the diplomatic situation underwent a curious change.

On the 27th, then, that is, on the very day on which the Cabinet sent off the decisive despatches referred to above, most disconcerting news from Lord Auckland reached the Foreign Office. It was to this effect:

With respect to the good disposition of the Count of Vienna, which is made the groundwork of His Prussian Majesty's Instruction of the 11th inst. to M. de Redern, I think it material to mention to Your Grace that, in a subsequent letter of the 12th, *in cypher*, which is gone by this day's mail to M. de Redern (and which I have happened to see), His Prussian Majesty states in terms of the strongest uneasiness that the Emperor's conduct becomes more suspicious and that he evidently intends to defeat the whole Convention of Reichenbach; that he has given up his own opinion to that of Messrs. de Kaunitz and Cobenzl and, particularly, that he is collecting large magazines and preparations in the neighbourhood of Cologne, which M. de Redern is instructed to mention to Your Grace as a subject of just uneasiness.[3]

This sudden transition from a warlike resolve to timorous prudence in part resulted from the Prussian monarch's habit of listening to two sets of advisers. Hertzberg whispered peaceful advice into one ear, while the other took in the bellicose counsels of Bischoffswerder; and the royal mind sent forth to London both sets of impressions. Other proofs were soon at hand betokening a reaction towards pleasure and inertia. Hertzberg, so Jackson reported, sought to enforce the cession of Danzig and Thorn as a *sine quâ non* of Prussia's acting conjointly with England—a step which obviously aimed at hindering such action.

Still more important was the news that came from Copen-

---

[1] "Auckland Journals," ii, 388.
[2] Pitt to Ewart, 24th May 1791; Stanhope, ii, 116; Tomline, iii, 260.
[3] "F. O.," Holland, 34.

hagen. On 27th March there reached the Foreign Office a despatch from Francis Drake, our envoy at Copenhagen, who was destined one day to win unenviable notoriety as the dupe of Napoleon's secret police, and to figure in French caricatures as a ruffled mallard flying off with bottles of invisible ink. At present he merely forwarded a pacific proposal of Count Bernstorff. In the hope of averting strifes in which Denmark must inevitably suffer, that Minister had begged the Czarina to accept the terms of the Allies if they were modified in her favour. When Catharine smiled on the proposal, Bernstorff assured Drake of his desire to reconcile the Courts of St. Petersburg and London without compromising the dignity of George III. He declared that Catharine had eagerly welcomed the prospect of a peaceful arrangement, and hoped that the Allies would appreciate the force of her reasons for rejecting the strict *status quo ante*, seeing that she had been unjustly attacked by the Turks, and had won a brilliant triumph. While restoring to them a large part of her conquests, she was determined to retain " a single fortress and a desert region in order to gain a safer frontier." She therefore hoped that the Allies would show their moderation by substituting a limited *status quo* for their present demand. Bernstorff added the suggestion that she should have all the land up to the Dniester, on condition that the walls of Oczakoff were razed for all time, and that no military colonies should be founded in the ceded territory, which also should remain waste. He further hinted that Russia might be induced to grant England a favourable commercial treaty.[1]

This last was added as a bait especially tempting to Pitt, who had been much annoyed by the failure of his efforts in that direction in 1787, and now found the Dutch obdurate to some parts of his proposed commercial treaty with them. Is it too much to assume that, if the news which arrived on 27th March concerning the shifting of Prussian policy and the reasonableness of the Czarina had reached him two or three days earlier, he would have led the Cabinet to a far different decision? The

---

[1] " F. O.," Denmark, 13. Drake to Leeds, 12th March.

In B.M. Add. MSS., 34436, I have found proofs that Auckland on 19th March forwarded by special packet duplicates of the proposals described above, adding his own comments to them, of course in a favourable sense. They probably reached Whitehall about 24th March, but by that time the Cabinet's bellicose decision had gone to Windsor and received the King's assent.

speeches of Ministers in Parliament were now marked by coolness and caution, characteristics which came out even more strongly on 12th and 15th April.

The searchings of heart in the Cabinet on the anxious days 30th March—10th April are laid bare in the memoranda of the Duke of Leeds. The Duke of Richmond and Grenville were opposed to the use of coercion against Russia. Pitt, Leeds, Thurlow, Camden, and Chatham at first resolutely maintained their position. At the second meeting of the Cabinet, on 31st March, Stafford joined Grenville and Richmond. Pitt also heard of the defection of the Duke of Grafton and his sons. Camden seemed shaken by the news before them ; and Thurlow attained a prudent neutrality by diplomatic slumber. Pitt himself was now impressed with the need of circumspection; and, on the ground of the proposals from Denmark, advised the sending of a special messenger to Berlin, to request Jackson not to forward the ultimatum to Russia. Leeds objected to the Danish proposal being assigned as the reason for delay, and declared that if the despatch were sent in that form, Grenville must sign it, for he could not.[1] Pitt then agreed to tone down the despatch into a request for a few days' delay. This was his first decided disagreement with Leeds. He sought to end it by friendly conversation, but in vain; for the Duke believed the honour of the Cabinet to be tarnished by so unworthy a surrender.

Pitt took a more sanguine view of the situation, as appears in some hitherto unpublished letters that passed between him and Ewart. That over-wrought envoy had departed for Buxton in the belief that he had persuaded the Cabinet of the certainty of Catharine acquiescing in the demands of the Triple Alliance. What must have been his chagrin, then, to receive a letter from Pitt, of 6th April, begging him to return to town at once. " Events have taken a turn here," wrote Pitt, " which seem to leave little or no chance of pushing our Plan to its original extent, and that the best thing we shall have to —(?) it is some modification, which perhaps, however, may be so managed as to provide more fully than could have been expected for the general object."[2] This sounds the hopeful note which was rarely missing from Pitt's utterances. Evidently he wished that Ewart should return

[1] "Leeds Mem.," 157, 158; also despatch of 31st March to Jackson, in " F. O.," Prussia, 20.
[2] From Major-General Sir Spencer Ewart's MSS.

to Berlin to make the best of the situation. Ewart had an interview with him, on or about 10th April, which he described in a
letter of 14th April to Jackson, his *locum tenens* at Berlin. He
found Pitt as deeply impressed as ever with the importance of
the political and commercial objects at issue, which were

well worthy of every exertion. "But," continued Pitt, "all my efforts to
make a majority of the House of Commons understand the subject
have been fruitless; and I know for certain that, tho' they may support me at present, I should not be able to carry the vote of credit. In
short, Sir, you have seen that they can be embarked in a war from
motives of passion, but they cannot be made to comprehend a case in
which the most valuable interests of the country are at stake. What,
then, remains to be done? Certainly, to risk my own situation, which
my feelings and inclination would induce me to do without any hesitation; but there are unfortunately circumstances in the present state of
this country which make it certain that confusion and the worst of consequences might be expected, and it would be abandoning the King."
    After stating several facts in confirmation [Ewart says], and repeat-
ing, even with the tears in his eyes, that it was the greatest mortification he had ever experienced, he said he was determined not to knock
under but to keep up a good countenance : that the armaments should
therefore continue to be made with vigour, and the fleet to be made
ready for sailing; and that in the meantime he hoped means might be
found to manage matters so as not to have the appearance of giving up
the point, but modifying it so as to prevent any serious bad consequences
from ensuing, tho' he repeated that he was well aware that the difference between any such plan would always be very great and extremely
mortifying.[1]

This revelation of Pitt's feelings and intentions is of the
highest interest. Nowhere else do we hear of wounded pride
bringing tears to his eyes; and nowhere do we find a clearer
statement of his desire to resign, were it not that such a course
would abandon the King and the country to a factious Opposition. He therefore resolved on a compromise, the weakness of
which he clearly saw, because it would satisfy Parliament and
his opponents in the Cabinet without too much offending
Prussia or unduly exalting the horn of the Czarina. Ewart
decided to return to Berlin to help on his chief, to whom he
expressed unfaltering devotion. It is further noteworthy that Pitt
at this time desired to send the fleet to the Baltic; and we may

---

[1] From Major-General Sir Spencer Ewart's MSS.

reasonably infer that the subsequent reversal of that salutary resolve was the work of Grenville.

One other detail in Ewart's letter claims attention. Why did Pitt assign so great weight to the opposition in Parliament? Had he received private remonstrances? Rumour says that Dundas and others warned him to desist from his scheme. But, as we have seen, his majority held well together. On 12th April he beat Fox by eighty votes, and on the 15th by ninety-two. How is it possible to reconcile this increase with wavering or luke-warmness? I think it probable that Pitt chose now and at a later date to ascribe his change of front to parliamentary opposition (on which he could descant), while it really resulted from difficulties in the Cabinet, on which he had to keep silence. Further, he may have hoped that if Ewart, the soul of the forward policy, consented to return to Berlin, the Duke of Leeds would find it consonant with his own dignity to retain office.

If so, he was disappointed. Before the Cabinet meeting of 10th April he had convinced himself that the pacific overtures of Catharine sent through Bernstorff were genuine and sincere. He also pointed out to the Duke that the violent language of the Opposition would certainly encourage the Empress to reject the absolute *status quo*. The inference was irresistible, that England and Prussia must be content with securing rather less for Turkey. Pitt decided in favour of this course, and on 15th and 16th April, drew up the drafts of despatches to this effect, in the hope that Leeds would sign them. The Duke, however, declined to do so, and, by the King's leave, Grenville appended his signature.

This implied a ministerial change; and on 21st April Leeds returned the seals to the King after the Drawing Room at St. James's Palace. Thus disappeared from the forefront of history a personality whose sprightliness and charm earned him a high place among the wits and amateur playwrights of that age, and whose jealousy for the honour of England at this crisis won the regard even of those who differed from him. He was far from being a great Foreign Minister. At every crisis Pitt took the reins into his own hands, and at other times the business of the Foreign Office went on somewhat loosely, Keith complaining at Vienna that in the year 1788 he received only one reply to fifty-three despatches sent from that capital.[1] The Duke's tenure

---

[1] "Keith Mems.," ii, 219, 228.

of office was marked by two of the greatest triumphs ever won by peaceful means, namely, over France in 1787 and Spain in 1790; but these, as we have seen, were essentially the work of Pitt. There could be but one successor to Leeds. Grenville, though a far from attractive personality, possessed qualities of shrewdness, good sense, and untiring assiduity. He was strong where Leeds was weak, namely, in system, thoroughness, and equability; but he was weak where Leeds was strong, namely, in managing men. George III certainly approved of the accession of Grenville to power, and sent to him the seals on the same day. After some delay, arising from Pitt's desire that Cornwallis should succeed Grenville at the Home Office, Dundas took that appointment.[1]

On 20th April, then, Ewart was instructed to return to Berlin for the purpose of explaining to Frederick William that the difficulties arising from the trend of public opinion and the opportunity afforded by the Danish proposals induced the British Government to seek for a peaceful compromise with Russia. Pitt also urged the desirability of Austria joining the Triple Alliance. As to the new Russo-Turkish boundary, it should be fixed if possible East of the Dniester, namely, at Lake Telegul, the lands eastward up to the River Bug being also left a desert.[2]

Ewart arrived at Potsdam on 29th April (a remarkably quick journey), and found Frederick William in a gracious mood. The King agreed to Pitt's new proposals, and highly approved of the overtures to Austria. While expressing mortification at the change of front towards Russia, he assured Ewart of his belief in the good intentions of the British Ministry. It is easy to see that Frederick William felt some relief at the prospect of avoiding a war, of which nearly all his counsellors expressed disapproval. Hertzberg on 24th April assured Lucchesini that a war with Russia would probably be the tomb of the Prussian monarchy.[3] There was, indeed, every need for caution, owing to the doubtful attitude of Austria. Lord Elgin followed the Emperor Leopold to Florence for the purpose of urging him to join the Triple Alliance; but, while receiving the overture with Tuscan gracious-

---

[1] "Dropmore P.," ii, 54-6; Dr. Hunt, "Pol. Hist. of England," x, 328.
[2] "F. O.," Prussia, 21. Grenville to Ewart, 20th April 1791. The details given above refute Sorel's statement (ii, 208) that Pitt changed front *brusquement*, and charged Fawkener to say that he would give way about Oczakoff.
[3] Dembinski, i, 449.

ness, he in effect waived it aside. In vain did our envoy follow
the Emperor from city to city for some weeks, and urge him to
join the Allies. Leopold, with his usual penetration, saw that
the situation favoured the two Empires, provided that they held
together; and Pitt's offer appeared to him merely an ingenious
means of separating them. Further, Kaunitz detected the rift
in the Anglo-Prussian concert, and the hatred of England
which pervaded the letters of Marie Antoinette to the Emperor
may also have strengthened his resolve to dally with Pitt's proposals, even while he took the most effective means of thwarting
them. The Polish Revolution of 3rd May 1791, soon to be
described, also led Leopold to draw closer to Russia. Thus,
despite affable converse with Elgin in the towns of Lombardy,
he instructed his envoys at Sistova to raise their demands and
assume an arrogant tone. The Turks received this rebuff with
oriental composure, and, having the support of Keith and
Lucchesini, resisted this flagrant attempt of Austria to shuffle
out of the Reichenbach compact. Accordingly the early days
of June 1791 witnessed a break in the negotiations and a rapid
increase of warlike preparations on the Danube—a turn of
affairs highly favourable to Catharine.[1]

The indignation of Pitt and Grenville at the double-dealing of
Leopold finds expression in a note of the latter to Auckland
(6th July): " If the Emperor does break faith with us at last, he
does it in a manner so directly and personally disgraceful to
himself, that it is hard to suppose he can make up his mind to
hear all that he must hear in such a case."[2] In these words we
see the cause of the distrust of the Emperor which clogged all
attempts at an Anglo-Austrian compact directed against French
democracy. Events, therefore, told heavily against Pitt's efforts
to bring about an honourable compromise with Russia. Nothing,
however, is further from the truth than to represent his offers to
Catharine as a humiliating surrender. The instructions to

[1] Vivenot, i, 126-37, 172-6; Clapham "Causes of the War of 1792," ch. iv;
"Keith's Mems.," ii, 436-41, 448. So, too, Whitworth to Leeds, 22nd April
1791: "Count Cobenzl continues buoying them [the Russians] up with the
hopes of his Court taking a part in the war" (" F. O.," Russia, 20).

[2] B.M. Add. MSS., 34438. The despatches printed in Vivenot (i, 172-81)
show that the arrival of Bischoffswerder at Milan on 11th June helped to
thwart the efforts of Lord Elgin. Elgin suggested to Pitt on 15th June that,
if war broke out, he could convict the Emperor of hindering the pacification
(Pitt MSS., 132).

Fawkener, the special envoy to St. Petersburg, were as follows: Either the whole of the Oczakoff territory as far west as the River Dniester should be left neutral and uninhabited; or it should become Russian on condition of lying waste; or the Russian boundary should be drawn east of the Dniester, no fortress being constructed in the ceded territory.[1] It is worth noting that the Turkish envoy at Berlin thought these terms satisfactory. Fawkener was to agree to the third and least desirable alternative only in case Austria proved obdurate. But in this respect he was allowed a certain latitude, provided that Turkey retained adequate means of defence on that side. In order to avoid any appearance of menace, the British fleet was not to enter the Baltic or the Black Sea, a resolve much resented at Berlin and Warsaw.[2]

Frederick William received Fawkener most cordially at Sans Souci on 11th May. He showed some concern at the Manchester petition to Pitt, as it would stiffen the tone of the Czarina; he urged the sending of a British squadron to the Black Sea to ward off the threatened attack on Constantinople, and stated his preference for the third of the alternatives named by Grenville. Fawkener therefore felt bound to place it first in his proposals to the Czarina: and it is noteworthy that Prussian diplomacy once again favoured a concession to Catharine larger than Pitt was disposed to grant. Inward satisfaction at the course of events was, as usual, accompanied by many sneers at the weakness of British policy.[3] Gustavus of Sweden adopted a similar tone. He assured Liston of his readiness to receive the British fleet and to arm against Russia, provided that the Allies would grant him the needful subsidies. Liston, knowing his shiftiness, received these offers with polite incredulity. Certainly they had no effect at Whitehall.

Pitt's change of front ruined his influence in the North;[4] and in diplomacy prestige counts for so much that Catharine had

[1] "F. O.," Prussia, 21. Ewart to Grenville, 13th May.

[2] "F. O.," Russia, 21. Grenville to Fawkener, 6th May; "F. O.," Poland, 5. Hailes to Grenville, 19th May. Yet as late as 6th July Grenville informed Ewart that in the last resort England would fight on behalf of Prussia, though Ewart was to work hard to avert war (" Dropmore P.," ii, 124).

[3] "Dropmore P.," ii, 93, 94. Ewart to Grenville, 8th June. Hertzberg's influence was lessened by the addition of Schulenberg and Alvensleben to the Foreign Department at Berlin early in May.

[4] B.M. Add. MSS., 34437. Liston to Grenville, 27th May 1791.

virtually won her case by the end of May. Fawkener arrived at St. Petersburg on 24th May, and soon found himself involved in a series of gorgeous fêtes which proclaimed the wealth and power of the Empress and her entire indifference to all that England might do. For the irksome details of business he was referred to the Ministers and Prince Potemkin. The latter boasted in his lordly way of his resolve to seize Constantinople, wage eternal war on the miscreant Turks, and finally conquer Egypt. After a delay of three weeks the Empress received Fawkener graciously at a ball; she assured him of her admiration of Burke's "Reflections" on the French Revolution, and expressed her horror of that event as well as her regret at the sympathy of Fox with it. She petted her grandson, Alexander, and ostentatiously avoided all reference to the subject of Fawkener's mission, except that, when a dog chanced opportunely to bark, she said, "Dogs that bark do not always bite." So matters dragged on, it being the aim of Catharine to gain another success on the Danube, to win over Leopold definitely to her side (as Fawkener found to be the case by 21st June), and to sow discord among Britons.[1]

In this last she achieved a startling success. On 17th June there arrived at St. Petersburg Mr. (afterwards Sir) Robert Adair, who later on was to figure as a diplomatist under the Ministry of Fox and that of All the Talents. We may accept his solemn declaration, in a letter written in the year 1842, that Fox had no hand in sending him on this so-called "mission";[2] but we are able to correct Adair's version in several respects, from documents in the "Pitt Papers," which Bishop Tomline, when challenged by Adair, thought fit to withhold.[3]

Adair asserted in 1842 that his object in going to Russia was not to oppose Pitt's policy of recovering Oczakoff, because that Minister had already renounced it in obedience to the mandate of Parliament. This, as we have seen, is incorrect; for when

---

[1] "F. O.," Russia, 21. Fawkener and Whitworth to Grenville, 19th, 27th, 31st May, 18th and 21st June. So, too, Ewart wrote to Grenville, on 18th June (after receiving news from St. Petersburg): "No answer will be given (by the Russian Ministers) to the Allies till after the return of the last messenger to London, for the purpose of knowing if they might rely with certainty on the English Government being unable to take active measures in any case" ("F. O.," Prussia, 21).

[2] "Memorials of Fox," ii, 383-7.

[3] Pitt MSS., 337; Tomline, iii, 308-12.

Adair left England, in May 1791, warlike preparations were still going on.[1] He admits that Fox said to him before starting, "Well: if you are determined to go, send us all the news"; and that Fox provided him with a cipher so that that news might elude the prying eyes of British diplomatists. It may be, as Adair says, that he and he alone was accountable for this odd attempt to direct the foreign policy of his country. But it is highly probable that Vorontzoff (Woronzow), the Russian ambassador in London, abetted the scheme. On 2nd May Whitworth wrote that Vorontzoff's despatches had given great satisfaction at the Russian capital. "He assures his Court that Russia has many friends and partisans in England, and affirms pretty positively that His Majesty's Ministry will have no small difficulty in carrying through their measures contrary to the interest of the country."[2] Further, the account of Adair's "mission," given by William Lindsay, Whitworth's secretary, states that Adair came with strong letters of recommendation from Vorontzoff, while the Duchess of Devonshire commended him to Whitworth. He travelled viâ Vienna, where he stayed with the Russian ambassador. At St. Petersburg he at first received countenance from the British embassy, owing to the high recommendations which he brought with him, and he was presented at Court by Whitworth himself!

Thus Adair found his path everywhere strewn with flowers. Catharine smiled on him and plied him with important questions, ironically asking him whether the British fleet had set sail. Fawkener, on the other hand, she treated with marked coldness. The British embassy, however, had its revenge; for Lindsay opened the letters, which Adair trustfully asked him to take to London, and apparently was able to decipher the ciphered parts, which gave hints to Fox for an attack on Pitt. But Adair was more than a purveyor of hints for the Whig orators. It is clear that he stiffened the resistance of the Russian Government. "He shows," so Whitworth wrote privately to Grenville, on 21st July, "the most virulent opposition to His

---

[1] "Auckland Journals," ii, 388.
[2] "F. O.," Russia, 20. 2nd May. "I have long thought Woronzow decidedly and personally hostile to the present Government in England, and am persuaded that he suggested the idea of employing Mr. Adair as an envoy from Mr. Fox to the Empress." Grenville to Auckland, 1st August 1791. (B.M. Add. MSS., 34439.)

Majesty's measures, and takes great pains to counteract the negotiation."[1] In official documents Whitworth and Fawkener depict him as a vain, meddlesome, ignorant person, concerned with stockjobbing no less than with diplomacy. But it is certain that his presence at St. Petersburg, and the biassed information which he supplied, greatly harmed the cause of the Allies; and Pitt, after seeing copies of Adair's letters, was justified in hinting that his action had prejudiced the success of Britain's efforts at St. Petersburg. As for Fox, Catharine showed her regard for him by placing his bust between those of Demosthenes and Cicero in her palace; and Adair, on his departure, received from the hands of Potemkin a ring containing her miniature.[2]

Such is the story of this singular " mission." Even before its details were fully known at Whitehall, Ministers debated whether they should not take action against Adair. On 29th July Grenville wrote to Auckland, à propos also of a recent letter of Fox to Barnave: " Is not the idea of Ministers from Opposition to the different Courts of Europe a new one in this country? I never heard of it before, and should think that, if it can be proved, I mean legally proved, it would go very near to an impeachable misdemeanour."[3] Ministers, however, decided to treat Adair's " mission " with the silence of contempt. Probably their judgement was correct; for the finesse of Vorontzoff and Catharine, if fully revealed to the world, would have covered the Opposition with obloquy, but the Cabinet with ridicule; and in politics the latter alternative is more to be feared. Apart, therefore, from one scornfully vague reference by Pitt to the damage done to the nation's interests by a partisan intrigue at St. Petersburg, little was heard of the affair.

The reader who wades through the dreary debates on the Russian Question early in 1792 will probably conclude that Adair's tour belongs to the annals, not of diplomacy, but of electioneering.[4] Fox, Grey, Sheridan, and Whitbread proved to their own satisfaction, from Russian sources of information, that Pitt, besides wasting the public money on futile preparations for

---

[1] B.M. Add. MSS., 34438.

[2] " F. O.," Russia, 22. Whitworth to Grenville, 5th August.

[3] B.M. Add. MSS., 34438. Wraxall (i, 202; ii, 34) thought Fox deserved impeachment for sending Adair.

[4] " Parl. Hist.," xxix, 849-1000. Whitbread's motion was finally negatived by 244 to 116 (1st March 1792).

war, had been outwitted and publicly flouted by the Czarina. They did not prove that the occasion called for no effort to curb her ambition, or that Pitt was not justified in taking up the challenge which their factious conduct had emboldened her to fling down. In one sense it is unfortunate that the Foxites did make further diplomatic excursions; for the result might have been the addition of interesting gargoyles to the edifice of the party system in the form of Opposition embassies, worked by fallen Ministers, disappointed place-hunters, and discharged clerks.

Meanwhile other events were working against Pitt. The successes of the Russian arms had been crowned by the capture of Anapa, near the River Kuban, and their triumph seemed assured both in Asia and Europe. The Russian Black Sea fleet was preparing to deal a blow at Constantinople; and, for a time, as we have seen, the Turks were distracted by the prospect of the renewal of war with Austria.

Yet here again, by one of those sudden turns of fortune which have so often saved the Ottoman Empire, the designs of the Viennese Court were cut short. At Padua, during his Italian tour, the Emperor Leopold heard the news of the capture of the King and Queen of France by the rabble of Varennes. This ignominious ending of his schemes for a counter-revolution in France stirred the sluggish blood of the Emperor. On 6th July he wrote to his brother Maximilian that it was high time to save Marie Antoinette and stifle the French plague. A forward policy in the West implied moderation in the East, and even the Prussophobe Chancellor, Kaunitz, saw the need of a definite peace with the Sultan. Accordingly, Austria waived her demands for parts of Wallachia and Servia, and made peace with the Porte at Sistova on 4th August, on condition of receiving Old Orsova.[1] Thus the Varennes incident, which involved the royalist cause in ruin, brought salvation to the Moslems.

The desire of Leopold to crush the French Revolution was to have far-reaching consequences, which will concern us later. Here we may remark that the woes of Marie Antoinette and the *volte-face* of the Emperor produced a marked effect at St. Petersburg. Hitherto, all had been bluster and defiance. So late as 15th July Fawkener reported that the Empress had lately

---

[1] Vivenot, i, 547; Martens, v, 244-9.

seemed inclined to conquer and keep all that she could; but the
news from France impelled the Vice-Chancellor, Ostermann, to
declare that all animosities should now be laid aside and "that
every nation in Europe should unite [against France] whenever
any proper plan could be agreed on."[2] Thus, here again, the failure
of the royalist attempt in France helped to avert the utter break-
down of the Anglo-Prussian case. Even so, the Czarina won the
day at nearly every point. Little by little the Allies gave up all
the safeguards on which Pitt had at first insisted; and on 26th
July their envoys consented to the acquisition by Russia of all
the Turkish lands east of the Dniester, provided that the Czarina
agreed not to hinder the navigation of that river. On the whole,
the Porte sustained no very serious loss, considering the collapse
of its defence, the slight interest felt on its behalf both at London
and Berlin, and the marked dislike of Catharine for England
and Prussia. She hated Pitt, but she despised Frederick William.
How then could she, in the midst of her military triumphs, give
way to the demands of the Triple Alliance, whose inner weakness she had probed?

Nevertheless, the intervention of the Allies was not the failure
that has often been represented. It checked the soaring ambitions of Potemkin. The Roumans, Bulgars, and Greeks had to
thank the Allies for delivering them from this selfish adventurer.
Their day of liberation was deferred, but it came ultimately in
far better guise than as a gift from Catharine and her favourite.
Strange to say, he fell a victim to fever, and expired by the
roadside in Moldavia as he was proceeding to the front; and
this event, which wrung the heart of Catharine, had no small
share in facilitating the signature of the Russo-Turkish treaty
(on the terms required by the Allies) at Jassy early in the
following year.

Other influences were leading Catharine towards peace. In
the spring of the year 1791 Poland entered on a new lease of
life. That the Poles should alter their constitution without her
permission was a grievous affront, for which she inveighed
against them as rebels. Thenceforth Warsaw, rather than Constantinople, took the first place in her thoughts. Apart from
this, the prospects of the Poles were radiant with promise;
and the student who peruses the despatches of Hailes, British

envoy at Warsaw, cannot but picture the results that might have occurred had the Poles received adequate support from Prussia and England against the Muscovites. The confederated Diet at Warsaw then showed a reforming zeal equal to that of the French National Assembly. In the middle of April it struck off the shackles from the burghers and made them citizens. Early in May, when the political horizon darkened, fear cowed even the Russophiles, while a storm of patriotic fervour swayed the Diet, and burst through the two barriers which hemmed in the national life. There was no hubbub in this memorable sitting. No swords flashed forth, as had happened on many a petty pretext. Emotion held the Assembly spellbound, while the majority swept away those curses of the land, serfdom and the elective kingship. Thereupon one of the leading obstructives aroused general astonishment by proposing that members should swear to uphold the new order of things. King Stanislaus evinced his patriotic zeal by calling on the Bishop of Cracow to administer the oath, which deputies and visitors alike recorded with shouts of joy. The exulting throng of nationalists and their recent converts then sallied forth and took the oath once more at the foot of the high altar of the Cathedral; and the sullen dissidence of some thirty of Russia's henchmen served but to emphasize the overwhelming triumph of intelligence and patriotism.[1]

Such was the peaceful Revolution of 3rd May 1791 at Warsaw. It sent a thrill of exultation through France, and moved Burke to a splendid panegyric, which he crowned with the startling statement that the events at Warsaw were probably the purest good ever conferred upon mankind.[2] Even Grenville's cold and insular nature warmed and dilated at the news; and he bade Hailes express the interest of Great Britain in the new constitution, especially as it would benefit the cause of the Allies.[3]

But the ill fortune which dogged the steps of the Poles willed that in this time of their revival the Alliance, from which alone they could hope for safety, should go to pieces. The refusal of England to send a fleet either to the Baltic or the Black Sea

---

[1] "F. O.," Poland, 5. Hailes to Grenville, 5th May, along with a letter by a Polish deputy.

[2] Burke, "Appeal from the New to the Old Whigs." Burke did not see that by fighting Russia's battle in Parliament, he was helping to undermine the liberties of Poland.

[3] "F. O.," Poland, 5. Grenville to Hailes, 25th May.

depressed the influence of England at Berlin. " Oh! how my
blood boils, my dear Sir," wrote Ewart to Keith on 18th June.
" Our influence was all powerful so long as it was maintained
with the necessary vigour; and the moment we flinched, all the
Powers, as if by common consent, turned the tables upon us."[1]
This proved to be the case. The web of Ewart's diplomacy,
the toil of four years, which connected England with Prussia,
Sweden, Poland, and Turkey, was unravelled in as many weeks.
The general trend of events helped on the work of dissolution;
and among the sinister influences at Berlin, jealousy of the
reviving power of Poland played no small part. Hertzberg,
whose fortunes were now on the decline, sought to postpone his
fall (it came early in July) by exciting animosity against the
Courts of London and Warsaw. To his reckless charge against
Pitt, of seeking to ruin Prussia by a war against the Muscovites,
he now added a jeremiad against the Polish reformers of
Warsaw—" The Poles have just dealt the *coup de grace* to the
Prussian monarchy by making their kingdom hereditary and
adopting a constitution better than that of England."[2] Dislike
of its Allies was now the prevalent feeling at the Prussian Court,
and by the end of June Frederick William decided to have an
interview with Leopold for the purpose of coming to a friendly
understanding.[3]

This resolve, fraught with evil for Poland, was clinched by
the news of the capture of the King and Queen of France at
Varennes. Concern at their ignominious position now began to
influence the Central and Eastern Powers. The wrath of the
Czarina fell upon French democrats; for in the nature of this
extraordinary woman sentiment and passion always ran an even
race with foresight and reason. In her present mood the French
Revolution and all its abettors were anathema. The results
were curious. The bust of Voltaire was deposed from its place
of honour and huddled away amidst lumber. Within a short
space the bust of Fox, now that he had served her purpose,
shared the same fate. More important, perhaps, if less striking
to the imagination, is the fact that she now formed a close
alliance with Sweden. Early in October Gustavus III ended his

---

[1] " Keith Mems.," ii, 448, 449.
[2] Dembinski, i, 451. Hertzberg to Lucchesini, 7th May 1791.
[3] " F. O.," Prussia, 21. Ewart to Grenville, 25th June. For Bischoffswerder's second mission to Vienna see Sybel, bk. ii, ch. vi.

long balancings by espousing the side of Russia, with a view to
eventual action against France.[1] The decline or collapse of the
Anglo-Prussian Alliance followed as a matter of course so soon
as Frederick decided to clasp the hand of Leopold. It is curious
to find Pitt and Grenville, even at the end of August 1791,
seeking to include Austria in the Triple Alliance, when statesmen
at Berlin and Vienna were scoffing at England, and were adopting an offensive policy at variance with the pacific aims cherished
at Whitehall. Kaunitz and Bischoffswerder looked about for
a scape-goat, and found him in Joseph Ewart. Auckland had
also been making a dead set at this able ambassador; and
some hitch in the negotiations attending the marriage of the
Duke of York with the eldest daughter of the King of Prussia
served to increase his troubles at this time. But the following
hopeful letter which Pitt wrote to him on 2nd September must
have salved his mental wounds:

> . . . Many events have certainly concurred to disappoint the accom-
> plishment of very important objects, and to produce in some respects
> an unfavourable change both in Prussia and elsewhere. But the general
> state of Europe, taking in the whole, affords so favourable a prospect to
> this country that we have great reason to be contented. Any temporary
> fluctuation in the disposition at Berlin is therefore, at the moment, of
> less consequence. The connection between Prussia and Austria, what-
> ever right we have to complain of the steps which have led to it, cannot,
> I think, produce any permanent mischief to our system; and, at least, I
> am convinced that the best chance of preventing it is to mark no sus-
> picion on our part to preserve as much good humour and cordiality as
> possible. For the rest, in the singular and uncertain state of Europe,
> our chief business must be to watch events and keep ourselves quiet.
> I have been sincerely concerned not to have more favourable accounts
> of your health. . . .

The prospects, so far as concerned the freedom of Poland and
the peace of the West, were worse than Pitt anticipated. Ewart
foresaw the course of events more correctly. A little later he
obtained the recall for which he had some time been pressing;
but he had the mortification of seeing Morton Eden, the brother
of his rival, Lord Auckland, installed in his place. He retired to
Bath for treatment by his brother, a medical man; but an
internal disease of long standing developed very suddenly on

---

[1] Martens, v, 262-71.

25th January 1792, and ended his life two days later amidst delirium. The details, as set forth in the family papers, show that the delirium of his last hours was the outcome of acute internal troubles, which resembled appendicitis. They serve also to refute the wild rumours that Ewart went raving mad as a result of political disappointments, or that he was poisoned by some Russian agent.[1] The last letter which Pitt wrote to this brilliant but most unfortunate diplomatist shows a chivalrous desire to screen him from needless anxiety:

Downing Street, *Jan.* 20, 1792.[2]

Your letter having come at a time of very particular engagement, it was impossible for me to answer it sooner. Your recollection of what pass'd between the Duke of York and yourself is certainly different from the manner in which I am told that H.R.H. understands it; but no difficulty whatever will arise from this circumstance in settling the business; nor do I see any reason for your entertaining any apprehension of its producing any consequences disagreeable to yourself. I am very sorry that you should already have felt so much on the subject. The train in which the business now is will, I am in hopes, relieve you from any further anxiety or trouble respecting it, and makes it wholly unnecessary to dwell further upon it.

Worse than private misfortunes was the blow dealt to the Polish cause. The rebuff encountered by the Allies at St. Petersburg deeply depressed the reformers of Warsaw. On the return of Fawkener through the Polish capital, King Stanislaus expressed grave concern at the abandonment of all the safeguards for Turkey and Poland on which Pitt had at first insisted. The cession to Russia of all the land up to the Dniester seemed to him to presage ruin to the Poles—" Nor did my pointing out [added Hailes] the attention which had been paid to their interests by the preservation of the liberty of the Dniester produce any advantageous effect."[3]   In truth, Stanislaus knew Catharine well enough to see in her triumph the doom of

---

[1] I am indebted to Major-General Sir Spencer Ewart for these particulars and for permission to copy and publish these letters of Pitt. The poison story first became current in one of Fox's letters published in the "Mems. of Fox." For letters of Dr. Ewart at Bath on his brother's affairs see " Dropmore P.," ii, 181, 253, 256.

[2] Pitt MSS., 102.

[3] " F. O.," Poland, 5. Hailes to Grenville, 21st August 1791.

his kingdom.[1] Just as the ascendancy which she acquired over Turkey by the Treaty of Kainardji led naturally, perhaps inevitably, to the First Partition of Poland, so now the principle of the Balance of Power impelled Austria and Prussia to look about for lands that would compensate them for the expansion of Russia. Those lands could be found most easily in Poland, less easily in France. So it came about that the principle which Pitt invoked for the greater security of the smaller States, became in the hands of Catharine and her powerful neighbours a pretext for schemes of aggrandisement and pillage.

Thus fell to pieces the "federative system," whereby Pitt hoped to group the weaker States around England and Prussia. The scheme was due in the first instance to Ewart. Pitt adopted it when he believed the time to be ripe; but he postponed action too long. Had he pushed his plans forward in the autumn of 1790, as soon as the dispute with Spain was settled, and maintained the naval armaments at their full strength, he would probably have gained a peaceful triumph over Catharine. In that case the accession of Poland, Sweden, and Turkey to the Triple Alliance would naturally have followed. There would then have been no invasion of France by Austria and Prussia; still less would there have been any spoliation of Poland. The practical manner in which the Poles reformed their commonwealth opened up vast possibilities for the east of Europe; and the crushing of those hopes under the heel of a remorseless militarism is probably the severest loss which the national principle has sustained in modern times.

Nevertheless, though Pitt showed a lack of nerve at the crisis, yet, in view of the duplicity of Prussia, the doubtful attitude of Leopold and Gustavus, the marvellous resourcefulness of Catharine, and the factious opposition of the Whigs, he cannot be blamed. At times, new and subtle influences warp the efforts of statesmen. This was so in the year 1791. Pitt was striving to build on the basis of the Balance of Power. But that well-trodden ground now began to heave under the impact of forces mightier than those wielded by monarchs and chancellors. Democracy sent out its thrills from Paris as a centre, and the gaze of statesmen was turned from the East to the West. Thenceforth the instinct of self-preservation or of greed marshalled the

---

[1] Herrmann, "Geschichte Russlands," vi, 445.

continental chanceries against the two reforming States. The "Zeitgeist" breathed against the plans of Pitt, and they were not. In their place there came others of a far different kind, inspired by hopes of territorial gains in Poland and the overthrow of liberty in France.

INDEX

I T T

CHISWICK PRESS: CHARLES WHITTINGHAM AND CO.
TOOKS COURT, CHANCERY LANE, LONDON.